p. 5
p. 413

W9-BPL-493

Praise for Earlier Editions

"**A**n essential guide you'll want to read cover to cover."
—*Money*

"**U**nique! Offers sound advice ... easy to understand ... well done."
—*The Christian Science Monitor*

"**W**orthy ... helpful ... a sound introduction ... one of the better money manuals."
—*Working Woman*

"**M**ay well be the definitive volume on managing your money over the long haul ... impressive ... informative."
—*Dallas Morning News*

"**V**aluable ... for the neophyte and sophisticated financial planner."
—*The New York Times*

"**T**o the point, well-explained, up-to-date."
—*Inc.*

"**I**ntelligent advice."
—*Success*

The Author

Grace W. Weinstein is one of the nation's leading writers on personal money management. Her "Your Money" column appears in *Good Housekeeping* magazine each month, and her "Money Manager" (formerly "New Jersey Investor") section regularly appears in the Newark, New Jersey, *Star-Ledger.* She has been a syndicated columnist with Universal Press Syndicate and has published scores of articles in such leading consumer magazines as *Money, McCall's, Kiplinger's Personal Finance, Woman's Day,* and *Working Mother.* The author of eight other books and a frequent guest on radio and television programs, Weinstein is particularly interested in how our relationships are affected by money matters.

Currently a member of the Consumer Advisory Council of the Federal Reserve Board and a trustee of the Consumer Financial Education Foundation, Weinstein is a past two-term president of the American Society of Journalists and Authors. She was a founder and the first president of the Council of Writers Organizations. A graduate of Cornell University, Weinstein lives in New Jersey with her husband, an architect.

Also by the Author

Children and Money: A Parents' Guide
Men, Women and Money: New Roles, New Rules
The Bottom Line: Inside Accounting Today
Life Plans: Looking Forward to Retirement

And, for young people:

People Study People: The Story of Psychology
Money of Your Own

THE LIFETIME BOOK OF MONEY MANAGEMENT

Highlights

The Lifetime Book of Money Management offers easy-to-understand financial advice on how to make the most of your money now and at all the stages of life. It provides valuable guidance for the young and old, single and married, one-income breadwinner and two-income couple, worker and retiree.

Newly updated to reflect changing life-styles and economic conditions, *The Lifetime Book* presents workable money management strategies for young singles worried about the cost of living, couples buying a first home, mothers pondering the financial advantages and disadvantages of re-entering the work force, parents planning to pay for their children's college educations, the "sandwich generation" coping with both children and parents, and retirees deciding how to invest to fund a longer life span. It also includes such crucial information as how to confirm the stability of a bank or insurance company, create a personal benefits package, set the financial ground rules for a second marriage, allocate your assets, and refinance your mortgage.

The Lifetime Book is divided into 24 chapters over these 9 sections:

■ Where Are You Now and Where Are You Going?
■ Putting Your Money to Work: Cash Management
■ Putting Your Money to Work: Investments
■ Putting Your Money to Work: Credit
■ Spending Your Money: Housing
■ Spending Your Money: An Automobile
■ Spending Your Money: Higher Education
■ Protecting Yourself: Insurance
■ Looking Ahead

Each chapter concludes with a list of **Key Points** summing up the essential elements of that chapter. Ninety tables, 25 worksheets and figures, and more than 230 personalized questions and answers make financial planning a simpler process.

The Lifetime Book features an extensive **Suggested Reading** list, is thoroughly cross-referenced, and contains a detailed subject index to quickly point the user to much-needed information.

T H E LIFETIME MONEY BOOK OF

MANAGEMENT

ALL NEW · REVISED · Third Edition

Grace W. Weinstein

VISIBLE INK

DETROIT   WASHINGTON, D.C.   LONDON

THE LIFETIME BOOK OF MONEY MANAGEMENT

Grace W. Weinstein

Published by **Visible Ink Press** ™
a division of Gale Research Inc.
835 Penobscot
Detroit MI 48226-4094

Visible Ink Press™ is a trademark of Gale Research Inc.

While the author and publisher have made every effort to ensure the reliability of the information presented in this publication, Visible Ink Press does not guarantee the accuracy of the data contained herein.

This publication is a creative work fully protected by all applicable copyright laws, as well as by misappropriation, trade secret, unfair competition, and other applicable laws. The author and editors of this work have added value to the underlying factual material herein through one or more of the following: unique and original selection, coordination, expression, arrangement, and classification of the information.

All rights to this publication will be vigorously defended.

Copyright © 1983, 1987, 1993
Grace W. Weinstein

Designer: Mary Krzewinski
Technical Design Services Manager: Arthur Chartow
Art Director: Cynthia Baldwin

⊛ This book is printed on recycled paper that meets Environmental Protection Agency standards.

ISBN 0-8103-9444-8

Printed in the United States of America
Published simultaneously in the United Kingdom by
Gale Research International Limited
(an affiliated company of Visible Ink Press and Gale Research Inc.)

All rights reserved, including the reproduction in whole or in part in any form. No part of this book may be reproduced in any form without permission in writing from the publisher, except by a reviewer who wishes to quote brief passages in connection with a review written for inclusion in a magazine or newspaper.

10 9 8 7 6 5 4 3 2 1

Third Edition

**For my parents,
Esther and David Wohlner,
to whom I owe so much**

Contents

Introduction

"The world of personal finance changes, in large ways and small, even faster than seems possible."

These opening words to the second edition of *The Lifetime Book of Money Management* are as true today as they were in the 1980s. When the original edition was published in 1984, we were living through a period of the highest inflation this country had ever known. When the second edition saw the light of day in 1987, inflation and interest rates had subsided but Congress had just passed the Tax Reform Act of 1986, supposedly tax "simplification" and the tax act to end all tax acts.

Today the country may be edging out of severe recession, but large numbers of people are either out of work or fearful of losing their jobs. Tax "reform" has been all but dismantled, as tax rates inch upward and the system becomes more complex. The family home, for years the greatest source of wealth for middle-class Americans (one that could be tapped to send children through college or to fund retirement) can no longer be counted on to increase in value or even to hold steady and not lose ground. Our health insurance system is in disarray, ripe for reform that may (or may not) be imminent.

Many of the rules of the financial game have changed, turned upside down by an unpredictable economy, new attitudes toward spending and saving, and changing life-styles. On the economic front, inflation is down and interest rates have subsided, which is great if you want to buy a house (mortgage rates are at their lowest in 20 years) but not so great if you're living on a fixed income (interest on savings accounts and certificates of deposit are also low). In terms of changing attitudes, after the spend-as-we-may 1980s, we're more conscious—needfully—of getting value for our money. And if you look at the way we live, financial advice must now be geared to all kinds of living units: the "traditional" nuclear family as well as single-person, single-parent, live-together, and multi-generational households.

Today you need to know, and this book tells you:

■ How to cushion yourself and your family against job cutbacks

■ What kind of housing decisions are appropriate in an era when house values are, at best, holding steady

■ How to invest for maximum return, in a low interest-rate environment, without taking undue risks

■ How to help elderly parents while putting children through school and planning your own retirement

■ How to cope with a growing tax burden

■ How to prepare for dramatic change in the way we pay for health care.

In the topsy-turvy world in which we live, you may believe that successful money management is a myth. It's not. You *can* learn to make the most of what you have, to make your assets grow, and to achieve your goals. In order to do so, you don't have to be an economist, or even to understand how the economy works, although it probably won't hurt if you do. You do have to invest the time to learn as much as you possibly can about the practical ins and outs of personal finance. You have to learn enough to be willing to make decisions, to take action. And you have to know *how* to take action, and to apply this practical know-how to your own life, at the stage of life you're in right now, the stage you're approaching, and the stage on the most distant horizon.

Money management, in short, is not a quick fix. It's not a one-answer-fits-all solution. The answer you need to a particular financial problem has to be an answer tailored to you. It has to recognize both your temperament (do you gleefully take risks, or shudder at the thought?) and your position in the cycle of life (are you financially responsible for yourself alone, or for the well-being of a spouse, small children, and/or dependent parents?).

The Lifetime Book of Money Management will show you how to make the most of the money you have, at your current stage of life and at all the stages that lie ahead. It offers useful guidance whether you are single (living alone or with others) or part of a pair (in a traditional nuclear family or a contemporary one of any size or shape). It provides advice to you as city-dweller or suburbanite, as a single-income household or a multi-income unit. Whether you want to establish credit or keep your debt load manageable, find some money to invest or implement an asset allocation strategy, choose the best life insurance policy or finance a car or pay as little income tax as possible, this book will help.

You'll find an overview of the life cycle in Chapter 1, followed by chapters on specific topics from budgeting through retirement planning. Within each chapter practical information is linked to life stages, because the investments you make at 35, as just one example, are seldom the investments you will want to make at 65. Your needs across the board—in housing, life and health insurance, even the way you save for college—change with your age and with the configuration of your life at various ages. Within each chapter, too, you'll find nuts-and-bolts financial information buttressed by the experiences of real people and by questions and answers on specific points. Read Chapter 1 now, then the chapters of immediate concern in your financial planning; refer to other chapters as the need arises. Each chapter is part of the whole, yet each stands alone.

Details may change: Interest rates will go up or down, laws and tax codes will be amended, the regulations that govern financial institutions will be tightened or loosened according to the whims of government and the sometimes contradictory opinions of "experts." But the information set forth in *The Lifetime Book of Money Management,* tailored to your own individual situation, should serve you well for some time to come.

Grace W. Weinstein
July, 1993

Acknowledgments

Appreciative thanks go to a great many people and organizations, too many to list. I would like to single out the following, however, with special thanks for their special help:

- Thomas P. Ochsenschlager of Grant Thornton
- Ralph Engel of Rosen & Reade
- Harold Evensky, CFP, Evensky & Brown
- Peter Packer, Runzheimer International
- Janel Patterson, the Health Insurance Association of America and the American Council of Life Insurance
- Joseph M. Re, Octameron Associates
- Gerri Detweiler, BankCard Holders of America
- Don White, Group Health Association of America
- Kevin Barber and Mark Mandernack, Kemper National Insurance Companies
- Steve Norwitz of T.Rowe Price
- Jeanne Salvatore and Barbara Taylor Burkett, the Insurance Information Institute
- Burke Christiansen, American Society of CLUs and ChFCs
- Elizabeth Johnson, National Association of Realtors
- Elizabeth Christy, National Association of Home Builders
- John Clark, Social Security Administration

And a special word of thanks to Carol DeKane Nagel, a meticulous and caring editor.

Author's Note

This book is as up-to-date as possible. But laws change from time to time, and vary from state to state. You should seek the advice of a qualified financial adviser (accountant, lawyer, financial planner, stockbroker, insurance agent, etc.) when making your personal financial decisions.

Where Are You Now and Where Are You Going?

CHAPTER 1

Life Cycle Planning

- Ed is 22, a senior in college, and worried about what comes next. As a freshman, he saw recruiters flock to campus and graduating seniors choosing among multiple job offers. But times have changed. Many of last year's seniors are still unemployed, and Ed is thinking about graduate school or the Peace Corps as a temporary alternative. One problem, however, is the debt he took on to attend college in the first place; it will be postponed, but not forgiven, if he remains in school. But what then? Will jobs be any easier to find in a few years?

- Sherry, Ed's sister, is 28 and engaged to be married. Raised in a society shaped by affluence and molded by ever-present inflation, Sherry has everything figured out: She'll start married life in an apartment, but she'll have a home of her own, because that's what people do. She'll go into debt to buy that home, and to acquire other possessions as well, because that's also what people do. She'll keep working after children are born, so money will never be a problem. Her optimism is as intense as Ed's pessimism.

- Rob is their father. At 53, he is doing well with his own accounting firm. His early years were shaped by his parents' experience of the Depression, but his own youth was lived in the economic boom that followed World War II. He thinks his parents' frugality excessive, can't quite accept the free-spending ways of his daughter's generation, and is worried about what the future holds for both his children. Rob is, in fact, somewhat concerned about his own approaching retirement. He's afraid continually rising prices will make it increasingly difficult to live on a limited income.

- Fred is 82 and recently retired from the consulting work he took on after his first retirement at age 70. He married and became a father during the Great

Depression of the 1930s, at a time when he was grateful for a civil service desk job instead of the law school he had always wanted but could not afford. His whole life has been shaped by the memories of those years: of his father losing a prosperous business, of neighbors out of work, of his own struggles to make ends meet and raise a growing family. The children are long since grown, and Fred and his wife, Trudy, have been financially comfortable for quite a few years. But old memories are hard to shed. Fred is still reluctant to buy on credit, still scrupulous in keeping track of expenditures. He suspects it's simply too late to change.

■ Fred's older brother, Al, is facing a new set of problems. At 86, his health is failing and his wife has developed Alzheimer's disease. Al saved and scrimped all his life, but still isn't sure how he'll pay for the care his wife will need, first at home and then, probably, in a nursing home. And, if he depletes the family's savings on her care, what will happen to him?

Managing money well demands an understanding of the surrounding economic climate as well as of your own place in the life cycle. Each generation is shaped by different economic expectations, expectations which often (as in Ed's case) must give way to a new reality.

The traditional life sequence—school, job, marriage, child-rearing, back to being a couple as children leave the nest, back to being alone as one spouse dies—has its counterpart in monetary terms: Income typically rises gradually from young adulthood through the child-rearing years, remains relatively stable from the middle years until retirement, then stays fixed or actually declines after retirement and in widowhood. Outgo, in the same sequence, starts low, rises for the setting-up-housekeeping expenses of early marriage, declines briefly, rises sharply with the arrival of children and still more sharply with the college years, and falls off abruptly as children leave the nest. The ascending lines, if this pattern were to be graphed, would be roughly parallel—except that the peak of outgo, associated with the growing family, frequently occurs ten full years earlier than the peak of income, which is attained in the middle years.

But this neat sequence is no longer universal. Young adults marry later, or not at all. Married couples often defer parenthood; many do not have children at all. Half of all marriages dissolve long before widowhood. The divorced remarry, form new families, and face the expenses of those new families against the backdrop of continuing expense for the existing family. All of these demographic changes reshape the face of society. They also affect the financial planning of the people involved.

Wherever you are in the life cycle, whether you're following a traditional sequence or charting a new path, you can make your money work for you. Whatever your temperament, too, you can manage your money well. Look at the following sequence in terms of the financial tasks you face at different ages.

Financial Planning Throughout the Life Cycle

Ages 13-18

- Learn to budget through handling an allowance.
- Start to save toward future goals.
- Develop financial understanding by working for pay.
- Open a bank account.
- Begin to think about future career options.

Ages 19-24

- Begin to live independently.
- Identify long-range goals.
- Train for career.
- Attain financial independence.
- Build savings toward long-term goals.
- Establish a credit identity.
- Begin to invest.
- Protect belongings with insurance.
- Develop a financial record-keeping system.

Ages 25-40

- Provide for childbearing and child-rearing costs.
- Provide for expanding housing needs.
- Manage increased need for credit.
- Invest for capital growth.
- Expand career goals.
- Build an education fund.
- Add to property insurance to protect possessions.
- Purchase life insurance to provide for a growing family.
- Write a will; name guardian for children.
- Involve every member of the household in financial management.

Ages 41-54

- Continue career development, possibly consider a career change.
- Diversify investments.
- Provide greater income for growing needs.
- Continue to build education funds, provide education for children.
- Consider moving to a larger house, possibly buying a vacation home.
- Begin to develop estate plan.
- Explore retirement goals.
- Review and revise will as necessary.

Ages 55-64

- Evaluate and update retirement plans.
- Shift a portion of assets toward income-producing investments.

- Consider dropping life insurance if no longer needed.
- Think about providing for long-term health care through insurance or savings.
- Decide where to live in the first stage of retirement.
- Meet responsibilities for aging parents.
- Review estate plan.

Ages 65-74

- Reevaluate budget to meet retirement needs.
- Continue investing for growth as well as income.
- Investigate part-time employment and/or volunteer work for retirement.
- Be sure health insurance is in place to supplement Medicare.
- Review will.
- Write a letter of instructions to accompany will.

Ages 75 and over

- Shift most or all investments from growth to income.
- Consider a living will, a health care proxy, and a durable power of attorney for financial affairs.
- Think about ways to reduce taxable estate.
- Consider places to live for the remainder of retirement.
- Share financial management and household management tasks with spouse, tell trusted children about your affairs.

Look at the following life stages in terms of where you are now, where you expect to be, and where you hope to be. Then apply the money management techniques in this book, and you'll be able to take charge of your financial fortunes.

Financial Planning for Singles

The rise in the number of people who live alone is one of the major changes in living patterns of our era. In 1970, one-person households accounted for about 17 percent of all American households; by 1990 the percentage had risen to a startling 24.6 percent. More than half are young singles, concentrated in urban areas; the rest are widows and widowers over the age of 65, many of them aging in place in smaller towns and villages around the United States. And a growing number are middle-aged women, both divorced and never-married.

THE YOUNG ADULT

In part, this dramatic growth in the number of singles is due to fewer and later marriages. The 1990 census showed that more than 22 percent of Americans over the age of 18 had never married; the comparable figure in 1980 was 20 percent and in 1970 just 16 percent. More than half of never-married 25- to 29-year-olds live in households of their own, mostly as renters rather than owners. Many other young singles haven't yet made the transition to independent living.

Finding a first job in the recession-weary 1990s is not an easy task. Nearly one-third of the nation's entry-level jobs had evaporated by the time the college graduates of 1992 hit the job market. To make matters worse, new graduates found themselves competing with older workers, both skilled and experienced, who had lost their positions in layoffs and company cutbacks. For many young adults, this has meant continuing studies instead of bringing home a paycheck, living with Mom and Dad instead of on their own, and postponing financial self-sufficiency.

Nonetheless, these are the years to develop good financial habits for the future. When you do find a job, your income may be low compared with your anticipated income in the future, but your needs, as a single adult, should also be lower. This is the time, therefore, to build a cushion for the years ahead. It may be tempting to spend virtually your entire salary on self-indulgence, on travel and compact disks and entertainment (especially if you're living with your parents or sharing expenses with a roommate). But you'll do much better in the long run if you anticipate the spending needs you will face in the stages to come. If you build a savings plan by setting aside at least 10 percent of your take-home pay in the highest-yielding investments you can safely tackle (see Chapter 5 on risk vs. return), you'll be more than independent. You'll be free, free to leave one job and move on to another, free to live the way you want to live, and eventually, if not right now, free to live in a place of your own.

Q My daughter is fiercely independent, has been since high school days. Now that she's out of college, she won't take any help from us at all. Yet she lives in a neighborhood that makes me fear for her safety. Is there any way we can get her to accept help?

A Your daughter's fierce independence may be healthier than clinging dependence at this stage. While most young adults shed parental ties gradually, many find it very important to prove themselves by refusing all help. When this is the case, they usually become more flexible once they've made their point. You'll probably find that your daughter will welcome a smoothing of the way later on. Meanwhile, if you're actually concerned for her safety, see if you can make a business arrangement with her. She might accept a loan, complete with her written promise to repay and your assurances that you will accept repayment, in order to move to better quarters.

If you're a young adult who plans to remain single and childless, if only for a few years, you can plot the growth of rising income without charting against it the rising cost of family obligations. This can mean a significant difference in the way you save and how. Risk-bearing investments may suit your style, for example, while they might be totally out of the question for the parents of young children. At the same time, you'll have to ensure a secure future without relying on anyone else.

Part of ensuring a secure future is planning your own personal benefits package (see p. 49). Put money in a profit-sharing or 401(k) plan if your employer offers one, even if retirement seems a lifetime away. Be sure you have health insurance that will survive a job change or the loss of a job. You may not need life insurance, if you have no one dependent on your income, but you should consider disability income insurance to provide replacement income if you are unable to work because of an illness or accident.

THE MATURE SINGLE

If you're thrust into singlehood in your middle years, after fifteen or twenty or however many years of marriage, you will have to restructure your financial life as well as your emotional life. You'll be ahead of the game if you've paid attention to financial matters right from the start, if you've owned property, established credit, made independent investments.

If you are an older adult and have been alone for a lifetime, you've probably ordered your financial affairs to your liking; you've had decades of training. If you're alone in the later years because of divorce or widowhood, however, you may have a lot to learn about money management. You may have to look at fixed or diminishing income in a time of rising costs, and plan accordingly.

Financial Planning for Live-Togethers

Lots of people have roommates, of the same sex or the opposite, for reasons of companionship as well as economy but with no romantic implication. Others have romance in mind as well. In 1981, 1.8 million households (or 2 percent of all households) consisted, in Census Bureau jargon, of "unrelated couples of the opposite sex." By 1991 there were 3 million such households, 32 percent of which contained at least one live-in child.

If you are sharing a household with someone, you have to decide some basic questions: who owns what, who buys what, who pays for what, and who is left holding the bag when one of you decides to call it quits. These questions need answers if yours is a strictly platonic arrangement, if you are roommates for convenience. But they get very sticky indeed if your relationship is complicated by romance. Then what you have is all the economic and emotional realities of marriage, without the protection provided by law. This is when you must establish your own safeguards.

Some couples draw up a contract, a legal document that spells out the responsibilities and obligations of each partner. A contract can forestall legal battles should you come to an angry parting of the ways. The simplest agreement, if you want to waive all financial claims on each other, might state:

- that neither of you has an obligation to support the other,
- that neither of you has any intention to share earnings or property with the other,
- that any property acquired while you live together belongs to the purchaser thereof.

If you do intend to be mutually responsible, your contract should spell out that intent. If you want your partner to inherit your belongings should you meet a sudden mishap, write a will. Husbands and wives have some automatic rights of inheritance; live-togethers do not. (Be sure to write a will, whether or not your living arrangements are sanctified by law, if you have a dependent child.)

If you and your partner have different intentions and expectations as you start out together, it would be a good idea to reach an understanding of each other's position. But what if you're allergic to contracts? What if you're living together, instead of getting married, precisely because you don't want your relationship sullied by the law? Then, at the very least, be aware of what you're doing and talk through your financial arrangements.

OWNERSHIP

This should be your first consideration. To forestall confusion and distress if you do break up (the landlord may not let you back in to claim your stereo if your ex-partner changes the lock on the door), keep track of ownership as you go along. Specify, in writing, who owns what. Did you buy the stereo while your partner purchased the dining-room set? Write it down. Did you contribute jointly to the purchase of a car? Write it down. Did one of you buy the VCR, or the car, while the other took care of food and rent and utilities for a number of months? Write that down too.

KEEPING ACCOUNTS

This can be a murky area. Should you pool your incomes? keep joint bank accounts? buy property together? It depends, of course, on your relationship. But it also depends on some cold, hard financial facts of life.

With a joint account, either partner has full access to the total account. That's fine, as long as the relationship lasts. But you might want to consider trust accounts instead, in which each partner has limited access to the other's money. Or, to keep things simple, you might maintain a joint household account for your joint living expenses and separate accounts for your personal expenses. Unless your incomes are roughly the same, by the way, identical contributions to your joint account might not be appropriate. Consider, instead, contributing an equivalent proportion of your individual earnings.

That will leave each of you about the same proportion of your income for personal expenditures.

Whether you see living together as a permanent arrangement or as a temporary one, try to look ahead. Take advantage of reduced living costs (two don't live quite as cheaply as one, but they do live more cheaply together than alone), and establish a savings plan for the future. Organize your financial life for what might be as well as for what is, and you'll be able to take control of your life.

Financial Planning for the Newly Married

Jeff and Anne both come from traditional middle-class families. Both fathers were breadwinners; both mothers were homemakers. But Jeff's father turned over his weekly paycheck and his mother paid all the bills, balanced the accounts, and made many of the spending decisions. Anne's father, by contrast, doled out weekly allowances to both wife and children and made all the major family spending decisions himself. Jeff expects Anne to make her own decisions; she, instinctively, consults him before she buys more than groceries. He doesn't understand why she does, and she doesn't understand why he gets irritated.

Such differences may very well show up in your marriage. One of you may be hooked on saving even at the expense of comfort, while the other prefers to save what's left over after making life comfortable. One of you may believe that all income is joint income and should be put in a common pot, to be drawn on as needed; the other may insist on separate ownership and separate responsibility. One of you may be a scrupulous record-keeper, while the other is far more casual.

Most of these differences will probably be resolved over a period of time, some by adopting one partner's viewpoint and some by compromise. And, gradually, you should develop a team approach to most money matters. If you don't always agree, and you probably won't, you will still develop an acceptable set of procedures for day-to-day money management. (If you don't, your marriage is going to be in trouble.)

In developing these procedures, you'll come face to face with your expectations about spending. You probably expect to live well because both of you are earning. But if you live up to the level of those earnings—with frequent dinners out, expensive trips, a car or two—you may find that expectations outstrip reality. If you live up to the level of those earnings without a thought for the future, you're setting the stage for future conflict over money.

You'll also come face to face with your individual attitudes about the source of your income. Even among today's two-income couples, it's possible to find interesting variations on the theme of whose money is whose. It all comes down to the fact that the spouse who controls the purse strings (or is perceived to do so) is the spouse who rules the roost.

Money that you earn during the marriage is one thing. Money that you bring to the marriage, inherit, or are given is quite another. Even though *your* marriage will last forever, it can be wise to keep separate names on separate assets. Set up a separate savings or brokerage account, and don't add your spouse's name to that account. Keep meticulous records. And bear in mind: State law differs, but if you tap your separate account to buy a joint asset, such as a house, you've probably given up claim to at least half of the money in the account.

WHO MAKES THE DECISIONS?

When young couples earn roughly similar amounts and have similar career expectations, the game of whose money is whose is psychological more than strictly financial. But it is still real. Is his income supposed to cover the household budget, while hers goes for the "extras" that make life fun? Is she supposed to run the household out of her salary, while his goes for the big-ticket items like travel and recreation? Who, really, makes the spending decisions?

A lot may depend on who earns the larger paycheck. But more may depend on your attitudes toward that paycheck. Few of today's young couples hold what Caroline Bird in *The Two-Paycheck Marriage* (Rawson, Wade, 1979) called a "pin money" attitude, where the wife's earnings are played down by both husband and wife in the interests of traditional male supremacy.

But each couple sets its own rules. In my book, *Men, Women and Money: New Roles, New Rules* (NAL, 1986, 1988), I describe a range of techniques from totally separate accounts to pooling everything. My suggestion: Mingle enough money to cover household accounts, more if you like, but keep some money separate. This makes for ease of management, while permitting independent decision-making.

As you start out together, it will help your financial planning to understand where you and your spouse stand in attitudes and expectations. It will also help if you address practical matters right from the start. If you're both earning, how will you handle your respective salaries? What kind of bank account will you establish? Who will pay the bills and balance the checkbook? Whose health insurance coverage will pay for medical costs? Who will hold title to the property you acquire together? Read the chapters on banking, investments, and housing before you leap to joint ownership on all your possessions; it isn't always a good idea. And don't let a romantic glow prevent you from tackling these practical financial questions; tackling them now may preserve the romance later on.

MARRIAGE AS AN ECONOMIC PARTNERSHIP

Jane and Edward, a Wisconsin couple, agreed to use her income to support the household while they invested his for their future. They did so for fourteen years. Then they were divorced. Edward claimed that the house and all the investments belonged solely to him, since they had been purchased with his earnings and were held in his name. Jane was horrified. She would have saved some of her own earnings had she not thought they were working together. Moreover, as she told the court, he couldn't have made the investments at all without her assumption of his legal responsibility to support the family. The court was not impressed. It held that Jane and Edward's intention to save the money for both of them was not enough to give her a legal right to any of the money.

If Jane and Edward's case came before a Wisconsin court today, this could not happen. Many state laws with respect to marital ownership of property have changed, and more are changing. So far, however, most of the changes deal with the disposition of property after divorce (see p. 21). Most laws are silent with respect to property ownership during an ongoing marriage. You may view your marriage as an economic partnership, but the state may not. You'll find out only if your marriage ends. But be aware, as you start out together, that the state in which you live is a third party to your marriage. Keep the state in its proper role, that of inactive and invisible partner, by maintaining your financial affairs with care. Keep track of who earns what, and who buys what, and you'll have the documentation you may someday need.

As you start out together, too, keep your eye on the future. Right now, your living costs are probably on the low side. You don't need as much living space as a couple with children, for instance, so your housing budget may be minimal. You're young and, probably, healthy, so medical costs are few— although you should make sure that you have health insurance that will cover you into the future. You do have housekeeping setup costs, for furniture and such, but these purchases can be spread over time. With two incomes, your discretionary spending power may be at its highest point for the next twenty years. Enjoy that discretionary spending power—but use it, too, to invest in your future.

Standard advice used to call for a working wife to save all or most of her earnings, against the inevitable day when she became a full-time homemaker. That day is no longer inevitable. You may not intend to become a full-time homemaker, whether or not you ever intend to have children. You should, nonetheless, establish a savings plan with a significant portion of your combined income. Those savings can be drawn on to pay the heavy cost of child care if you do have a baby and then return to work. They can cushion the financial shock if you intend to return to work and then, as a growing number of young mothers are doing, decide to stay home for a while instead. They can even come in handy, without children at all, if one of you is laid off or simply wants a change of career. And those savings can help to maintain your standard of living against a rising cost of living and, invested wisely, secure your future.

The National Conference of Commissioners on Uniform State Laws, in its draft of a Uniform Marital Property Act, speaks of the need for defining "interspousal economic relationships" during marriage. Right now, the Conference points out, "a linear diagram of marriage would have a beginning, and end, and something in-between. For most of us, the in-between is the marriage. Yet the framers of laws have tended to be exclusively concerned with the beginning and the end."

The Committee on the Uniform Marital Property Act, with the belief that the end of marriage by either divorce or death will be far less traumatic if economic relationships during marriage are clearly delineated, recommends that states adopt legislation holding that:

■ Property acquired during marriage by a couple, by the personal effort of either, is property to be owned by both and defined as "ours," as "marital property."

■ Property brought into the marriage or acquired afterward by gift is not marital but individual property. Any appreciation in its value remains individual property (the house your father leaves you becomes more valuable and you sell it; the appreciated value is yours); any income from the property becomes marital property (you rent out the house, and the rental income belongs to both you and your spouse).

■ Either spouse can deal as an owner with most marital property—buying, selling, entering into contracts, and so on.

■ Spouses have the right to create their own "marital property agreement" and may contract to do so. Both must agree in writing to any such contract.

Many of these principles already apply in community property states (see p. 21). The drafters of the Uniform Marital Property Act suggest that economic rewards stemming from the personal efforts of each spouse during marriage should be owned in equal shares in every state. "It is seen as a system of elemental fairness and justice that those who share the work of establishing and maintaining a marriage should share equally in the acquisitions of that marriage." Wisconsin, so far, is the only state to adopt the Uniform Marital Property Act.

Financial Planning for Parents

A shrinking portion of the population, married couples with children were a majority of households in 1960 but occupied just one household in four by 1990. In part this drop reflects the growing number of older couples who no longer have children at home. But it also reflects the growing number of young couples who are choosing to defer parenthood or to forgo it altogether.

Parenthood today, in other words, is often a deliberate choice and not necessarily an automatic corollary of marriage. That choice is made on a number of grounds, the least of which is probably economic. Still, if you decide to have children, economic considerations soon gain importance. Children cost a lot, both to have and to raise. It's best to be prepared.

THE COSTS OF HAVING CHILDREN

Economists consider the costs of having children in terms of both direct maintenance costs and what they call "opportunity costs." The direct costs are all those out-of-pocket costs that mount up from the time a child is conceived until the day that child turns 18 (college costs are another kettle of fish). Direct costs are examined in some detail on p. 17. Opportunity costs are less tangible but no less real: They are losses of opportunities for economic betterment, opportunities lost because of the presence of children. These indirect costs are difficult to pin down, but some studies show that they often exceed direct costs.

Mothers who go right back to work after a maternity leave of several weeks may not suffer reduced income (although they will face higher direct outlays for child care), but mothers who drop out of the labor force for several years, or who work part-time or at less demanding jobs, forgo both income and career advancement. Missing out on an annual after-tax income of just $20,000 adds up to $100,000 in the five years until your child starts kindergarten (assuming the unlikely situation of no promotions and no raises).

The money spent on child-rearing, moreover, whether you forgo income or not, is not available for spending on an enhanced life-style or for investing to cushion your future. This can require both a psychological adjustment and a financial one. Two incomes may have enabled you to keep up with inflation while living the life you wanted to lead. When one of those incomes is curtailed or when a great deal of money is spent on a third member of the family, other expectations have to be reduced.

The sum of direct and opportunity costs varies by geographic region and by where you live within a region (it generally costs more to raise children in the Northeast than in the South, more in urban areas than in rural), by educational level (the better-educated mother usually earns more and therefore loses more if she steps out of the work force), and by economic level (the more you earn, the more you're likely to spend on your children). But you do effect some savings if you have more than one child; the per-child costs are reduced as your family increases.

In general, the direct out-of-pocket costs associated with raising a child from birth to age 18 in 1991, excluding college, ranged from just under $81,000 for two-parent families in rural areas to almost $180,000 in the urban Northeast. Single-parent families spend about 5 percent more. By now, depending on where you live and on your income level, total costs may be considerably higher. Let's see how the direct costs break down.

Table 1.1: Estimated Annual Expenditures on a Child by Husband-Wife Families, Overall United States, 1991[1]

Age of Child	Total	Housing	Food	Trans-portation	Clothing	Health Care	Education, Child Care, and Other
Income: Less than $31,200							
0-2	4,520[2]	1,830	690	610	330	250	810
3-5	4,820	1,770	770	660	360	230	1,030
6-8	4,810	1,770	990	710	390	250	700
9-11	4,660	1,640	1,120	640	400	260	600
12-14	5,350	1,580	1,200	970	650	260	690
15-17	5,700	1,550	1,360	1,220	610	280	680
Total	89,580	30,420	18,390	14,430	8,220	4,590	13,530
Income: $31,200 to $50,400							
0-2	6,400	2,420	850	1,020	420	320	1,370
3-5	6,800	2,360	990	1,080	450	300	1,620
6-8	6,760	2,370	1,250	1,160	490	320	1,170
9-11	6,570	2,230	1,410	1,080	500	330	1,020
12-14	7,320	2,170	1,490	1,410	820	330	1,100
15-17	7,780	2,150	1,660	1,670	780	350	1,170
Total	124,890	41,100	22,950	22,260	10,380	5,850	22,350
Income: More than $50,400							
0-2	9,160	3,630	1,040	1,400	520	400	2,170
3-5	9,640	3,570	1,250	1,450	560	370	2,440
6-8	9,500	3,570	1,500	1,570	590	400	1,870
9-11	9,310	3,440	1,690	1,500	610	410	1,660
12-14	10,160	3,380	1,850	1,820	970	410	1,730
15-17	10,690	3,350	1,950	2,080	930	430	1,950
Total	175,380	62,820	27,840	29,460	12,540	7,260	35,460

Source: Family Economics Research Group, U.S. Department of Agriculture.

Notes: [1]Estimates are for the younger child in a two-child family. [2]For each year of the age grouping.

Childbearing

Birth is the first budgetable expense. In 1989 (the most recent figures available) the Health Insurance Association of America came up with a national average of $4,334 for the physician and hospital costs associated with a normal pregnancy and delivery—$2,842 for the hospital stay and $1,492 for medical expenses. The total rises to $7,186 for the one in four having a cesarean delivery; the difference is due to a longer hospital stay and to surgeon's fees. Neither figure, of course, includes maternity clothing, a layette or baby furniture.

Your direct outlay will be lower, despite skyrocketing medical costs, if you're covered by hospital and medical insurance that includes maternity benefits. But your costs may be higher, possibly much higher, if you don't have maternity coverage, if you live in a region where hospital and medical care is more expensive, and if the birth is complicated. Your costs will also be higher if you want more variety in maternity clothes or indulge yourself in buying the baby's layette.

Table 1.2: Estimated Annual Expenditures on a Child by Single-Parent Families, Overall United States, 1991[1]

Age of Child	Total	Housing	Food	Transportation	Clothing	Health	Education, Child Care, and Other
Income: Less than $31,200							
0-2	3,930[2]	1,410	730	1,010	190	90	500
3-5	4,960	1,640	760	1,270	260	150	880
6-8	5,390	1,880	1,000	1,220	300	160	830
9-11	5,690	1,880	1,070	1,340	330	190	880
12-14	5,550	1,730	1,210	1,310	630	220	450
15-17	5,860	1,830	1,270	1,480	620	200	460
Total	94,140	31,110	18,120	22,890	6,990	3,030	12,000
Income: $31,200 or more							
0-2	8,150	3,110	1,090	1,770	280	240	1,660
3-5	9,500	3,340	1,190	2,120	370	340	2,140
6-8	9,840	3,580	1,470	2,000	410	360	2,020
9-11	10,240	3,580	1,670	2,150	450	410	1,980
12-14	10,020	3,430	1,780	2,110	820	460	1,420
15-17	10,410	3,530	1,840	2,330	810	430	1,470
Total	174,480	61,710	27,120	37,440	9,420	6,720	32,070

Source: Family Economics Research Group, U.S. Department of Agriculture.

Notes: [1]Estimates are for the younger child in a two-child family. [2]For each year of the age grouping.

Child-rearing

Although the cost of rearing your children from birth to age 18 depends in part on where you live (rural areas, predictably, are less expensive than urban areas), a look at national averages can be instructive. Direct costs in 1991 ranged from $89,580 for the 18 years for a family earning under $31,200 to $175,380 for a family earning over $50,400. The outlay covers housing, food, transportation, clothing, health care, and a catch-all category grouped as education/child care/other. See Tables 1.1 and 1.2 for a breakdown of costs—and bear in mind that inflation, even at a moderate 3 or 4 percent, raises these numbers year by year.

Table 1.3: Day Care Costs Nationwide

Ten Most Expensive Metro Areas Location	Cost Per Week
Boston, MA	$122
Minneapolis, MN	120
New York, NY	118
Philadelphia, PA	105
Manchester, NH	103
Washington, DC	101
Anchorage, AK	96
Hartford, CT	92
Chicago, IL	91
Buffalo, NY	91
Wilmington, DE	91
Standard City, USA	**80**

Ten Least Expensive Metro Areas Location	Cost Per Week
Jackson, MS	$46
Salt Lake City, UT	46
Casper, WY	47
Mobile, AL	49
Tucson, AZ	50
New Orleans, LA	55
Tampa, FL	57
Boise, ID	58
Little Rock, AR	58
Columbia, SC	59

Source: Runzheimer International.

Cost estimates of child-rearing, as these tables indicate, include a child's share of the family's overall costs for such things as housing and transportation as well as direct expenditures on behalf of the child. If you have a child, therefore, your out-of-pocket costs won't necessarily increase by these annual

Q I think our 10-year-old daughter should have regular spending money. My husband prefers to screen every request for money. Who is right?

A You are. Children need regular spending money so that they can learn to budget, to plan ahead, and to take responsibility for spending wisely. If you make all their decisions for them, children don't get the necessary practice in handling money. Let them make small mistakes now, with small sums, and they'll be less likely to make big mistakes later on, when they have money of their own. This allowance checklist may be helpful:

■ Be consistent. Children need to know what they are getting and when, or they can't make budgetary decisions.

■ Set the allowance amount in consultation with your child, and evaluate it regularly.

■ Be realistic in determining the amount; remember inflation. While you don't want your child to have too much money, too little means there will be nothing to buy and nothing (except frustration) to be learned.

■ Be sure that the allowance, whatever pre-allocated sums it includes (bus fare and the like), also includes some "bubble gum money," a discretionary sum that the child can spend without explanation; this is the real learning tool.

■ Keep the allowance separate from your child's responsibility to perform household chores or to do his or her best in school; don't use the allowance to punish misbehavior. Money has enough emotional links; using it this way within the family reinforces those links and undercuts objective lessons in money management.

■ Be flexible. Don't bail your child out regularly or you will undercut the purpose of the allowance, but don't be rigid either. If your child manages well most of the time, occasional extra help may be in order.

totals. And when a child leaves home you won't have this much money added to your discretionary spending power.

One important ingredient, child care, may be seriously underestimated in these cost breakdowns. An occasional baby-sitter can cost a few hundred dollars a year. But you can't go back to work with an occasional baby-sitter. The cost of full-time care ranges from $20 to $50 a week for family day care (a group of children tended in a care giver's home), from $45 to $125 a week for a child care center, from $100 to $300 a week or more, plus room and board, for a live-in care giver. (Some child-care costs, of course, are tax-deductible; see Chapter 20.)

Specific costs depend on where you live, but the arithmetic yields some staggering annual totals. A periodic survey by Runzheimer International (see Table 1.3) indicates an annual cost for a 3-year-old in a for-profit out-of-home day care center in 1992 ranging from $2,392 in low-cost Jackson, Mississippi, to $6,344 in high-cost Boston, Massachusetts. The national average, for what Runzheimer calls "Standard City, USA," runs to $4,160. These figures, by the way, reflect costs for day care centers in suburban communities outside the central city.

You'll also need more living space as your family grows, you'll start thinking about protecting your family through life insurance, and you'll run up sizable medical bills or (unless you have employer-paid group health insurance) sizable health insurance premiums. Even healthy children need regular checkups and inoculations—and you may find that your health insurance doesn't cover preventive and diagnostic care (see Chapter 19). Your children will need more and more clothes to fit rapidly growing bodies and will consume more and more food to make those bodies grow.

Child-rearing always costs more than parents anticipate, with more of the family income going to meet fixed costs than in any other stage of the life cycle. If you're prepared, it may be easier.

College Costs
The cost of higher education has exceeded the rate of inflation for a number of years. On average, according to the College Board, a student at a four-year private college paid $10,498 for tuition and fees in the 1992-93 school year, up 7 percent from the prior year, and $4,575 for room and board, up 5 percent. Some schools, notably the prestigious Ivy League institutions, cost considerably more. Others, including some outstanding state universities, cost a good deal less.

Wherever your child attends college, you'll be paying the bills with after-tax dollars, and you're bound to feel the pinch. Disposable personal income does, as a rule, rise along with inflation, but to many parents it never seems to rise fast enough. The pinch may be particularly tight if you're an older "triple-squeeze" parent, paying for college at the same time that you're helping elderly parents and planning for your own retirement.

You'll find detailed plans for projecting college costs and meeting them in Chapter 17, but you'll come out ahead if you count them in, from the beginning, as part of the cost of child-rearing.

Single Parents

If you're a single parent, for whatever reason, you're very familiar with the problems of solo child-rearing. And you have a lot of company. In 1960, just one of ten American children lived in single-parent households; by 1990, the figure was one in four.

One of your biggest problems may be collecting court-ordered child support from your ex-spouse. States have done a notoriously poor job of enforcing collection, with the result that uncollected child support may total $5 billion a year. But help may be at hand. On the federal level, one proposal which has bipartisan support would have the Internal Revenue Service collect child support through payroll deductions, much the way income taxes are collected. It would also guarantee minimum payments to families where the IRS failed to collect. Another proposal, which would require state-by-state approval, would do away with support claims bouncing from state to state by giving control to courts of the state where the child lived at the time of the divorce—even if the support-owing parent subsequently moved elsewhere.

Until federal or state lawmakers take action, here's a suggestion for custodial parents unable to secure payment of court-ordered child support through state agencies: Try one of the private collection agencies who have gotten into the act, with some success. Parents who have a court order in effect and who are not receiving Aid to Families with Dependent Children can call (800) 729-2445 for referral to a local agency; be prepared to pay an up-front fee of about $35 plus 20 to 25 percent of what's collected.

Financial Planning for Divorce

Marriages used to end primarily by death, only occasionally by divorce. Not today. Today the reverse is true, and more marriages end by legal dissolution than by death. Divorce may take place at any age or stage, from newly married to senior citizen. Whenever it happens, if it does, it has a significant impact on your current financial situation and on the planning you must do for the future. The legal fees for the divorce itself are just the first step.

DISTRIBUTION OF ASSETS

Be sure that you remember all your assets as you give thought to divorce, and make a list before you see your lawyer. Some commonly overlooked items:

■ The cash value of whole life insurance
■ Vested pension benefits
■ Prepaid taxes

Community Property States

If you've lived in one of the eight community property states (Arizona, California, Idaho, Louisiana, Nevada, New Mexico, Texas, and Washington) or in Wisconsin, there is a presumption that all property acquired during marriage is jointly held. This joint ownership does not include property that one of you inherited or that was acquired before the marriage. Even in these states, however, where everything appears to be clear-cut, there are often complications. If a down payment was made on a house by one partner, with money brought into the marriage by an inheritance, is the house community property? Or is just the appreciated value of the house, above the initial purchase price, considered community property? State law differs, even among community property states ("fault" is at issue in some jurisdictions, when it comes to divorce settlements), and judges have a fair amount of latitude in making decisions.

Equitable Distribution

"Common law" states, those without community property laws, traditionally adhered to the concept of title. Here, legal title to property is the deciding factor. If title to securities is in one spouse's name, for instance, it doesn't matter whose money was used to make the purchase; that spouse is presumed

Q My husband and I have agreed to an amicable divorce after twelve years of marriage. We've agreed about the way our property is to be divided. Do I have to use a lawyer? Or is it okay to fill out the forms in a "do-it-yourself" divorce kit that I've seen on sale?

A You don't have to use a lawyer, if you don't own much property and you agree on everything, but you might be wise to consult one before proceeding. You may agree on the distribution of assets, but have you thought about sorting out the value in life insurance policies? What about pension accumulations? What about the tax implications of your agreement? If you don't secure legal advice, you may be haunted in later years by a distribution you make now. If you have children, don't even consider a do-it-yourself divorce; conflicts over custody and child-support payments can develop far into the future. If you don't have children, a consultation with an able lawyer will tell you if your case is as simple as it seems.

to be the owner and will retain the asset at divorce. That's what happened to Jane in the example on page 11.

But this traditional respect for ownership has been superseded, almost everywhere, by divorce laws with equitable distribution provisions. Now, no matter whose name is on the title, marital property is (at least in theory) divided according to both its source and the need of both parties. If the divorce goes to trial, the judge may consider a number of factors: the length of the marriage, the contribution of each spouse to the building of assets (including the asset of one spouse's business or professional career), the employability of the respective spouses, who has custody of children, and so on.

"Equitable," when all these factors come into play, is not the same as "equal." Don't expect a fifty-fifty split. In many instances wives are receiving less than they would have under old laws. Accurate record-keeping is now more essential than ever so you can document, if necessary, a down payment on a house made through a gift from your parents or the fact that your spouse's professional career was made possible through your sacrifice of career options.

Equitable distribution, although it deals only with distribution of assets at the dissolution of a marriage, goes a long way toward converting marriage from a strictly social partnership to an economic partnership. But it also means that the previously absolute duty of a husband to support his wife and a father to support his children has been repealed. A wife in a state with equitable distribution laws, whether or not she has worked outside the home, is generally presumed to be capable of economic equality. She may receive temporary maintenance (today's version of alimony), but she will be expected to become self-supporting. Conversely, the wife may now owe maintenance payments to her husband.

The division of assets, in any case, is only the beginning.

STARTING OVER

Making a new start, once the property is divided and the decree is final, has financial ramifications, too. Two households now have to be supported on an income that previously may have had to stretch to meet the needs of one family. A nonearning partner must learn to become economically self-sufficient, a task easier for younger divorcees than for older ones. A single parent has extensive financial obligations with often meager financial resources. Credit must be obtained, insurance needs met, investments handled.

A SECOND MARRIAGE

Remarriage is not without its financial constraints. A man may still have to provide financial support for the children of a first marriage while bringing up the children of a second marriage. Either spouse may owe maintenance payments to a first partner, even after marriage to a second.

With serial marriages, and larger and larger extended families—one out of three Americans is now in a stepfamily relationship—there are sometimes extended financial obligations. If your children by your first marriage live with your ex-husband, whose health insurance pays their bills? If your second wife remained on good terms with the mother-in-law from her first marriage, and that mother-in-law is now ill and alone, will you support your wife's desire to help her out? If your husband grants a business loan that he can ill afford to a brother-in-law from his first marriage, will you feel that you and your children are unfairly deprived?

Talk about your attitudes and expectations. Before marrying again:

- Tell each other what you own and what you owe.
- Discuss your goals and objectives.
- Consult a tax adviser about the impact on your taxes.
- Review and rewrite your wills, making conscious decisions about how much to leave to the new spouse and how much to children from your prior marriage.
- Review your life insurance with an eye to protecting your new family.
- Consider changing beneficiary designations, not only on life insurance but on retirement plans as well.
- Balance your investments, while keeping them separate, so that you're properly diversified both individually and jointly.
- Consider a prenuptial agreement.

PRENUPTIAL AGREEMENTS

Some of the problems related to property settlement in divorce may be resolved in advance if you sign a prenuptial ("before marriage") contract (sometimes called an antenuptial contract or agreement), spelling out mutual rights and obligations. It's difficult, of course, to anticipate divorce while in a happy marriage. It's even more difficult to contemplate divorce as a possible stage of life before you marry at all. But in the overall scheme of financial life

---

Q My children from my first marriage live with me and my new husband, but they're covered under their biological father's health insurance at work. I pay the doctor bills, then have to wait and hope that he'll file the claims and reimburse me. Does it have to be this way?

A No. Some insurance companies are developing policies that prevent absentee parents from taking revenge on custodial parents by refusing to file claims or pass on reimbursement. Under these plans, the children's bills are paid first by the custodial parent's insurance plan. If you don't have your own health insurance, the stepparent's plan pays second. The last resort is the noncustodial parent's plan. Talk to the insurance companies involved and see if you can make this new arrangement.

planning, it's important to contemplate all the possible scenarios. If Act II turns out to contain a divorce, you'll be better prepared if you've thought ahead as you've acquired assets and established title to them.

Prenuptial agreements are particularly important in second marriages, when there are children to protect, and in situations where there is a significant disparity in wealth and income. If you are widowed or divorced and have substantial income or a sizable estate, for example, entering into a prenuptial agreement may be a good idea. Such an agreement can spell out what property will remain in your own name and which will be pooled, as well as how your estate will be divided in case of death or divorce.

Most states recognize properly drawn prenuptial agreements. To make sure yours is properly drawn, consult an attorney and follow these guidelines:

- The agreement should be in writing.
- It should be entered into freely, by both parties, and signed well in advance of the wedding date.
- Each of you should be represented by a separate attorney, one who is experienced in family law.
- Full disclosure of assets, liabilities, and obligations is essential; if the courts believe one of you is trying to put something over on the other, the agreement will not be upheld.

Financial Planning for the Empty Nest

You thought it would never happen, but it has: The last college tuition bill has been paid, the last child has moved out. Now you can look forward to years, perhaps decades, in an empty nest. That nest is probably pretty well feathered; with more women in their forties and fifties working outside the home and with the income of men at a lifetime peak, income per family member is higher than ever. This income peak comes, for most people, just as outgo is reduced. Costs related to child-rearing, by and large, are finished. The mortgage may also be paid up, and housing costs reduced. Major purchases, for appliances and the like, have long since been made and are now limited to replacement items and luxury items.

With higher income and reduced family obligations, now might be the time to alleviate any creeping midlife restlessness: to make a career change, to go back to school, to take a year off to recharge your batteries. With proper financial planning, it can be done.

But there are still some potential areas of financial strain in these middle years.

GROWN CHILDREN

Your children's continued demands, financial and/or emotional, may put a strain on your pocketbook and on your marriage. Some young adults continue to demand parental support; some, finding the going rough in the outside world, move back into the parental home. Others, of course, won't take help that you really want them to have. You have to take stock of your own family constellation. At the same time, however, you've earned your financial independence and should not be reluctant to say so. Think twice before you permit an adult child to expect regular support. Think twice, too, if you're hanging on and refusing to let go. Adult children need to grow up; you're not doing them any favors if you keep the apron strings tied.

Boomerang children, moving back into the parental home after the loss of a job or a failed marriage, pose special problems. You want to help, but you also want to see these young adults back on their financial and emotional feet. To help them get there: Set the ground rules, in advance, before grown-up children move back to the nest. Decide how much money your child can contribute to the household, and reach an agreement on how chores will be shared. Offer support, in other words, but don't make life so comfortable that the "children" never move out.

GRANDCHILDREN

Ready or not, here they come. You may be in the prime of life, fully preoccupied with your own career and nowhere near retirement age, yet find yourself a grandparent. Fifteen to 20 percent of today's grandparents are under age 50 and—with longer life expectancies—can expect to enjoy grandparent-grandchild relationships for a good three decades.

Those relationships need not entail any financial obligation, although you may want to help your children establish a college fund (see Chapter 17). You'll probably be thrilled to buy toys and clothing for your grandchildren, and you may want to provide them with life's "extras"—summer camp, for example, or a trip (with you).

The delayed marriages and child-bearing of recent years, however, may mean a drastic shift. People who become parents later in life also become grandparents later. In fact, if you're in this group, you may find yourself in a triple squeeze: coping with college costs, elderly parents, and your own retirement at one and the same time. If this scenario lies in wait for you, start planning now; save and invest as much as you can, using the guidelines in later chapters, so you'll enjoy the years to come.

AGED PARENTS

New obligations to parents frequently surface at about the time children are ready to stand alone. With lengthening life spans, in fact, you may also find yourself responsible for elderly grandparents. Here, too, there's a double bind. The elderly, like the young, are better off if they are independent. Don't encourage a parent to move in with you just because that parent has been widowed. Don't assume responsibility for decisions that parents can make for themselves.

But do recognize that abilities often (not always) diminish once people reach their late eighties or their nineties. You may find yourself needing to step in to help an aged parent manage financial affairs or to arrange housing or health care. Chapter 22 details the steps you may want to take in anticipating your own later years or helping your parents through theirs.

AN ADDED INCOME

When a wife returns to paid employment in the middle years, as often happens when women have stayed home during the child-rearing years, it can create financial strains even while it produces augmented family income. The biggest problem can stem from the increased tax bite. The second paycheck is piled on top of the existing one, says the New York State Society of Certified Public Accountants, and may be taxed at the higher rate on the combined income (see Chapter 20).

This is not an argument for women to forgo paid employment and stay at home. Far from it. But, if you or your spouse returns to work after a period of remaining at home, be sure to figure the net income after related costs. Look at commuting, clothing, and lunch expenditures, as well as the tax bite, before deciding what you'll do with all the "extra" money. It may take a couple of years before going back to work appears financially worthwhile.

Financial Planning for the Later Years

While inflation has put the squeeze on people with fixed incomes, the retirement years are seldom the problem many people anticipate. Some expenses—notably health care—go up. But many expenses do go down. In addition to reduced household expenses—your mortgage is probably paid up—you can probably count on reduced outlays for clothing, for transportation, and for incidentals. Just eliminate commuting, daily lunches out, office attire, and the occasional office gift or contribution, and you may be ahead several thousand dollars a year.

RETIREMENT

You may not retire for twenty or more years, but planning ahead, long before you actually retire, is the key to successful living in retirement. Whether you stay in the same job you've held these many years or make a midlife career switch, you'll want to give some thought to the lower income years ahead. You should divert as much current income as you can into high-yielding investments, and shelter some from taxes, if you're eligible, in an Individual Retirement Account or other tax-sheltered retirement plan. Then, shortly before you retire: Cut back on expenses to approximate retirement income. Make any necessary major purchase—buy a new winter coat, if you'll need one, or have the house reroofed—while income is still coming in.

Arrange for continuation of your health insurance coverage or buy supplemental insurance. Refer to Chapter 19 for details on health insurance and to Chapter 21 for information on estate planning. Retirement planning itself is covered in detail in Chapter 23.

WIDOWHOOD

If you're married, prepare your spouse to live alone as you approach retirement. One of you has probably paid the bills and kept the books and decided how much insurance to buy and where to invest, just as one of you has probably assumed the tasks of dealing with appliance repairmen and storing out-of-season clothes and changing a fuse when it needed changing. One of you probably knows where all the filed checks are, and the income tax records, and the safe deposit key.

Go through the house and go through your financial affairs, now, and give your partner a crash course in survival skills. It's bad enough to cope with the inevitable grief when one of you is left alone. It's intolerable to also have to cope with day-in, day-out details of living that you know nothing about.

KEY POINTS

- Your spending patterns are shaped by your temperament, your stage of life, and the economic climate in which you live as well as by the amount of money you have and the skill with which you manage that money.

- The stages of your life, from youth through old age, can be plotted in monetary terms.

- Anticipating life's stages enables you to plan ahead and to stay in charge of your financial affairs.

- You can do a great deal with the money you have. You can make your money work for you, no matter how much or how little you have, if you make financial plans and follow through.

CHAPTER 2

Budgets and Record-keeping

Before you develop an investment strategy, analyze your insurance needs, or even decide which banking services to use, you have to come to grips with how much money you have and how you use that money. Then you can look at how much money you expect to have and plan to use that money in the best possible way. That best possible way won't be according to some abstract principle; it will be the way that suits you best.

Taking charge of your finances so that your money will work for you entails both analysis and record-keeping, both long-term plans and here-and-now action. The first step is to identify your personal goals and objectives. Then you can ensure success by periodically monitoring your cash flow, assessing your net worth, and keeping systematic records—all in the interest of accumulating your assets and making them work for you.

Goals and Objectives

What do you want out of life? Other than keeping your head above water and a balance in your bank account, what do you want to be able to do? A lot of people never stop to look ahead, too caught up in day-to-day living to determine where they are going. You have to be farsighted to develop a workable financial plan.

Try setting up a three-part program, consisting of goals, objectives, and action:

Goals are an expression of your values, a long-range look ahead at what is most important to you. What is your financial destination? Enough money to open your own business? to buy a house? to send your children to college? to travel around the world? to quit working and play tennis? to endow a favorite charity? to ensure a comfortable retirement? Whatever your financial goal or goals, you have to identify each one clearly before you can take any action.

Objectives are a step-by-step path to your personal goals. Once you've clarified a long-term goal, a goal that may take many years to reach, you can break it down into specific attainable objectives.

Action, the hard core of your financial program, is the here-and-now day-to-day behavior that will make both objectives and goals possible.

For example: You are in your late forties. The nest is empty and the children are out of college and on their own. You've decided that your primary goal, right now, is to ensure a worry-free retirement. That's a worthy goal, but it's both vague and long-term. It needs to be reduced to manageable objectives. Your specific objectives might include the establishment of an adequate cash reserve, income-producing investments, and ventures for long-term capital gain. The action you take to meet those objectives and thereby meet your long-term goal might include setting up a budget to monitor spending, reduc-

Christopher Martin, a recent college graduate, is living with his parents to save money so that he can accumulate enough to rent and furnish his own apartment. But saving isn't easy. In addition to a college loan and an auto loan, Chris, like many young singles, spends a lot on entertainment and clothing. But Chris doesn't know how much he spends until he does a budget. This is what he finds:

Monthly Outgo:

Educational loan:	$ 80
Auto loan:	150
Auto maintenance:	120
Contribution to parents' household:	100
Lunches:	50
Clothing:	75
Personal care:	30
Entertainment:	75

Chris decides to cut back on clothing and entertainment in order to save more toward housing.

Source: *Coping With Change*, U.S. Department of Agriculture.

ing expenditures across the board to free funds for investment, and securing good financial advice.

Worksheet 2.1: A Personal Goals Statement

Rank the following financial goals from 1 to 10 in terms of their importance to you:

_____ Increase my standard of living
_____ Financial security at retirement
_____ Increase my net worth by ____%
_____ Reduce my tax burden
_____ Pay for a college education for my children
_____ Provide for my family in the event of my (or my spouse's) death
_____ Buy a house
_____ Minimize the cost of probate and estate taxes
_____ Control the distribution of assets to my heirs
_____ Plan for long-term or nursing home care

Other goals:

_____

_____

_____

_____

If you could change two things about your current financial situation, what would you change?

1) _____

2) _____

Source: *Financial Planning: A Common Sense Guide for the 1990s,* The Institute of Certified Financial Planners.

The same breakdown of goals, objectives, and action can help you to clarify all of your financial planning. But it can't be undertaken in a vacuum. You'll also want to look at decision-making and the art of communication.

MAKING DECISIONS

Decision-making should be purposeful. Sidestepping decisions doesn't work; it simply leads to decision-making by default. If you do nothing about finding a new job, you've made a decision, conscious or unconscious, to stick with the one you have. If you do nothing about seeking out a solid investment for some spare funds, you've made a decision, conscious or unconscious, to leave your funds where they are.

No decision has to be forever. Circumstances change, *you* change, and your decisions will change as well. That's the point of life cycle planning: to make the decisions appropriate at each stage of life.

If you're married or living in any sort of permanent relationship, however, don't do your financial planning alone. Two of you will have to live with the system you devise, and two of you had better be involved in devising it. Two of you will have to work together in setting both the goals and objectives and the course of action which both of you will have to follow. Think through your personal goals, and share them with your partner. Be sure that you share the same goals or, at least, that you understand each other.

Decisions in a partnership are made in a variety of ways: by mutual agreement, by accommodation (that is, agreeing to disagree), by compromise, or by concession.

Mutual agreement may be preferable, but it isn't always possible. You may agree on some things, disagree on others. Consensus is more likely, however, if you openly discuss your goals and objectives. Don't assume that your partner's goals are the same as yours, or allow your partner to make assumptions about you. Don't be like the couple shocked to find out that *he* had always assumed they would retire to a little cottage in snow-covered Vermont while *she* had always known they were retiring in the sunny South. Talk to each other.

The Brainstorming Technique

When you do talk to each other and reach an impasse, it's time for a new form of discussion. Brainstorming is a tried-and-true method in which you put forth all the possible solutions to a particular question, not just the two solutions you've both fixed on, in the quest for an answer that will suit you both. If you're at odds about where to live in retirement, torn between sun and snow, there is probably a third place you'd both enjoy; you don't have to limit your choice to one or the other.

If you're brainstorming about investment possibilities, for instance, because you're conservatively inclined and your spouse feels it's worth some risk for potential gain, run through every type of investment that comes to mind, from a savings account to an oil-and-gas-exploration deal. An even-tempered verbal free-for-all--don't interrupt each other, don't raise your voices, and don't discard any suggestion as too preposterous—will place a wide-ranging menu of alternatives up for consideration. Then, when your imaginations are exhausted and the list is complete, evaluate each item in terms of personal preference.

If one of you has strenuous objections to investing in diamonds, drop that thought right away. If one of you is violently opposed to putting money in oil exploration, don't do it. If one of you is absolutely certain that money in a savings account is money wasting away, drop this idea too. Measure the remaining alternatives in terms of how they will meet your previously determined joint goals and objectives. Look at the consequences of each alternative: Is there a reasonable chance of making a profit on this investment? Will money have to be tied up for a long time on that one, too long a time for comfort? What are the tax implications? What's the actual degree of risk? Will you still be speaking to each other if the investment doesn't pan out? Then, and only then, make your decision.

And bear in mind that many decisions don't have to be an either-or proposition. When it comes to investments, for example, your spouse may be risk-averse while you believe that you have to risk money to make money. Don't argue. Instead, invest separately as well as together. This way, you won't look over each other's shoulder all the time—and you'll have the individually-owned assets that every married couple should have.

The "Planning Board" Technique

When you have a few thousand dollars to invest, and suspect that you'll be making other investments later on, you can take turns suiting each other's wishes. But what if you're committing your lifetime savings and making a choice that will be difficult to reverse? What if you're at odds, for example, about where to live in retirement?

The Kidds, for instance, knew they wanted to move. They'd never liked the industrial town his business had brought them to thirty-two years ago. They'd made the best of it, but now their children lived elsewhere, their friends were retiring and pulling up stakes, and they were ready to move on as well. But where to? He had always loved their vacation cottage in Vermont, with its quiet fishing lakes and winter solitude. She detested winter and, moreover, was eager to live closer to the children.

One way the Kidds might clarify their own priorities and resolve differences of opinion is to make a planning board of all the options. In this procedure, suggested by Sidney Simon of the University of Massachusetts, you make out a slip of paper for each of your housing choices. The slips should include every possibility, not only housing types ("condominium" or "cottage" or "rental apartment") but location ("Florida" or "Vermont" or "the town where I grew up" or "a college town where I can take classes"). Write out the slips over a period of days or weeks or months, while you gather information about all your options, and collect them in an envelope. Then make a date to open the envelope and review the slips of paper. Place them in order of their importance to you. It sounds simple, but writing out the choices and physically arranging them before you actually does clarify their relative importance.

This can work for you, as an individual. It works best for a couple if you make duplicate slips of paper as you go along. Then, when the envelopes are opened, you each arrange the slips in the order of your personal preference. A comparison can then be made. If moving back to your hometown is on the bottom of both your lists, that choice is quickly dropped. If you can't find a good compromise and you're still at odds, try arguing each other's point of view. If you want Florida, try making the case for Vermont, and have your spouse step in your shoes. Sooner or later, you'll come to a meeting of the minds—even if the solution involves splitting the year in residence in two different locations.

While this book is about finances, and this chapter is about setting goals and implementing them, it's vitally important to make decisions via open communication before you try to develop a financial strategy.

Q We keep meaning to get our finances sorted out, but we never seem to get around to it. Would a financial planner help?

A Maybe. A good financial planner can help you reach your financial goals. But it's important to understand how the process works. Some planners make their money from commissions on the products (mutual funds, insurance, etc.) that they sell you; although there are good commission-based planners, this can be a conflict of interest. Other planners are "fee-only" planners, charging an hourly rate or a flat fee for preparing a financial plan; there's no conflict of interest here, but these planners can be expensive. A comprehensive plan can cost $3,000 or more, although many planners will prepare less costly plans to help you meet specific goals, such as saving for college. And some planners work on a combination of fee and commission, charging a flat fee for the financial plan itself and then earning commissions on products they sell.

Moreover, there are no regulations governing financial planners; anyone can hang out a shingle and go into business. Get recommendations from friends and other professional advisers such as your accountant or lawyer. Then interview several candidates and ask these questions:

■ What is your professional training? How do you stay up-to-date?
■ How do you get paid? Will you tell me exactly how much you earn on any specific product you sell me to implement my plan?
■ Do your clients earn an income similar to mine?
■ Can I see a sample of a written plan?
■ Will you give me names of long-term clients I can talk to?
■ What is your attitude toward risk?
■ Do you belong to any professional organizations?

Your Financial Plan

When their last child graduated from college and left the nest, the Links sold their suburban home and moved to Manhattan. With $295,000 in hand from the sale of the house plus $115,000 in joint annual income, the 58-year-old couple felt that the time had come for some well-deserved self-indulgence. But $2,800 in rent, $590 a month for garaging two cars, dinners out virtually every night of the week, and an impulse expenditure of $20,000 for a boat soon put both their bank account and their marriage in distress. The Links sought financial counseling. By preparing an income-outgo statement (which they had never done before), they discovered that they had annual expenditures of $16,000 over and above annual income. Analysis also showed the need to minimize taxes, along with the need to plan for retirement. The counselor made some specific suggestions—such as chartering the boat on occasional weekends to see if this would be an appealing post-retirement activity. But the key to saving both pocketbook and marriage was the simple process of sitting down and taking a good hard look, together, at their finances.

Your personal financial plan has to support what you (and your partner, if you have one) really want to do—not what someone else thinks is good for you. There are no hard-and-fast rules for what proportion of your income should go for what. But financial planner Scott Shires of Littleton, Colorado, has worked out some suggestions geared to help build savings. Table 2.1 indicates what percentage of your income, at various life stages and income levels, might go to savings and spending goals. (In his zeal to boost savings, in fact, Shires admits to underestimating the amounts actually spent on both housing

---

For information about and referrals of financial planners, contact:

Institute of Certified Financial Planners (800) 282-7526
    (Planners who have earned the CFP designation)

International Association for Financial Planning (800) 945-4237
    (Planners who qualify for IAFP's "Registry" program)

National Association of Personal Financial Advisors (800) 366-2732
    (Fee-only planners)

American Society of CLU and ChFC (800) 392-6900
    (Insurance agents and planners)

American Institute of Certified Public Accountants (800) 862-4272
    (CPAs who have specialized in personal financial planning)

and taxes; this is a model, therefore, not a portrait of fact. For information on what Americans are actually spending, see pages 36 and 39.)

────

Table 2.1: Scott Shires's Budget Suggestions, Designed to Boost Savings

	Single	Married/no kids	Married/2 kids	Retired
Earning:	$25,000-$35,000	$50,000-$75,000	$55,000-$80,000	$40,000-$50,000
Annual outgo				
Housing:	20-24%	17-22%	16-20%	13-16%
Taxes:	16-18%	19-20%	15-17%	17-19%
Transportation:	12-13%	5-7%	5-6%	5-6%
Debt payments:	4-5%	4-6%	3-4%	1-2%
Insurance:	3-4%	6-7%	7-8%	8-9%
Food:	9-10%	7-8%	8-9%	5-7%
Clothing/ personal care:	5-8%	4-6%	5-7%	4-6%
Child care/ education:	1-2%	1-2%	7-10%	1-2%
Entertainment/ hobbies/vacations:	6-9%	9-10%	8-10%	11-13%
Medical:	2-3%	3-4%	4-5%	10-12%
Contributions/ gifts/dues:	4-7%	5-7%	4-5%	8-10%
Miscellaneous:	1%	1%	1%	1%
Savings:	8-9%	9-10%	7-8%	6-7%

Source: Shires Financial Group, Littleton, Colorado.

You may not fit any one of the patterns shown in Tables 2.1 and 2.2. But you can put your financial house in order if you:

- Make a budget
- Assess your net worth
- Keep adequate records

Budgeting Without Pain

There are definite advantages to keeping a budget. You'll see exactly where you are, in terms of current income and outgo. You'll then be able to adjust your outgo to match your income, and trim any excess spending so that you can save for up-and-coming expenditures. You'll be able to stop the dribbling away of money in nonproductive and non-gratifying ways, the kind of dribbling away that inevitably occurs when you're not keeping track. You'll be able to zero in on your personal goals and objectives and make your dreams come true.

Table 2.2: The Consumer Expenditure Survey Household Budget Breakdown

The Consumer Expenditure Survey tracks what people spend (not including taxes, debt service, or savings) and shows a household budget breakdown as follows:

	All consumers	Consumers 65 and over
Food:	17%	18%
Housing:	31%	33%
Clothing/personal care:	7%	5%
Transportation:	18%	16%
Health care:	5%	12%
Entertainment:	5%	4%
Reading/education:	2%	1%
Insurance/pensions:	9%	4%
Cash contributions:	3%	6%
Miscellaneous:	2%	2%

Source: 1990 Consumer Expenditure Survey.

Note: Numbers do not add up to 100% because of rounding.

Despite the clear advantages of drawing up a budget—and you're probably nodding your head in agreement as you read—most people want nothing to do with the whole tedious process. But budgets, despite their reputation, need not be dull and forbidding. Simply remember: A budget is a tool to help you stay on top of your financial affairs. You can and you should develop and use a budget that you can live with, a budget that will serve you instead of the other way around. Here are some varieties to consider:

A LOOK OVER YOUR SHOULDER

One budget technique involves looking back, without looking ahead. This essentially short-term exercise allows you to see where your money is going. Then you can decide if where it's going is where you want it to go. If it is, fine; if not, you can mend your ways.

Case Study: A Young Family

Kyle and Janice Reading have been married about five years. This is the second marriage for both. They have two children living with them—three-year-old Justin and seven-year-old Rene, Janice's child from her first marriage. Kyle's son from his first marriage, ten-year-old Kevin, spends most weekends with the Readings.

The Readings, with a monthly net income of $1,678, are facing two important decisions: Can they afford to buy a house? Should Janice, who left her secretarial job when Justin was born, return to paid employment?

When they look into an appealing new town house development in their neighborhood, they find that buying into the development would unbalance their budget. In fact, with the new housing expenses, outgo would total $587 more than income.

Clearly, this is an incentive for Janice to return to the work force. But can she make enough money so that its worthwhile? When Janice finds a secretarial job with an after-tax income of $967 a month, the Readings sit down to do another budget. Here is how they figured that accepting the job would enable them to buy the house:

Monthly net salary: $967

Work-related expenses:	
Child care:	200
Bus fare:	40
Additional clothing:	20
Lunch and coffee breaks:	40
Added household expenses: (convenience foods, etc.)	20
Miscellaneous: (office collections, etc.)	10
Total work expenses:	330

Subtract Janice's work expenses of $330 from her net salary of $967, and the Readings have an additional $637 to spend. They buy the house.

Source: *Coping With Change*, U.S. Department of Agriculture.

Table 2.3: The Commerce Department's Consumer Expenditure Survey Tracks What People Spend.

Item	All Consumer Units	Under 25	25-34	35-44	45-54	55-64	65+	65-74	75+
Income before taxes:	$31,889	$14,089	$32,325	$41,208	$43,451	$35,309	$18,842	$21,501	$15,435
Percent homeowner:	62%	8	44	67	75	80	78	82	73
Average annual expenditures	$28,366	$16,518	$28,107	$35,579	$36,996	$29,244	$18,546	$20,895	$15,448
Food at home:	2,485	1,285	2,340	3,134	3,008	2,601	1,917	2,106	1,654
Food away from home:	1,811	1,476	1,760	2,246	2,482	1,830	1,009	1,199	752
Alcoholic beverages:	293	318	365	370	324	254	126	166	71
Housing:	8,886	4,845	9,349	11,354	10,719	8,610	6,130	6,591	5,527
Clothing:	1,617	1,034	1,571	2,310	2,165	1,557	768	972	489
Transportation:	5,122	3,498	5,415	6,082	7,051	5,298	2,884	3,466	2,132
Health care:	1,480	403	981	1,415	1,597	1,791	2,208	2,197	2,223
Entertainment:	1,422	833	1,471	1,837	1,966	1,507	700	914	423
Personal care:	364	212	315	447	478	412	268	305	218
Reading/education:	559	892	459	653	916	539	191	204	173
Tobacco products:	274	216	275	316	361	326	157	209	91
Cash contributions:	816	146	411	876	1,299	923	1,026	937	1,141
Insurance, pensions, and Social Security:	2,592	972	2,761	3,700	3,847	2,958	718	1,071	261
Miscellaneous:	645	388	634	837	784	658	442	558	292

Source: Consumer Expenditure Survey, 1990.

Note: Income taxes are not included in these tables yet, in some instances, expenditures exceed income. Income may be underreported, or people may go into debt.

This technique may prove effective if you constantly find yourself in the position of having $40 in your pocket on Monday and $6 on Tuesday, and no recollection of what happened in between. Simply record, faithfully and without exception, every single penny you spend. Carry a small notebook and write down every newspaper, bus fare, haircut, paperback book, and cup of coffee as well as every business lunch, bag of groceries, and item of clothing. Do this for a month and you'll have a clear picture of where the money goes. Then, without the need to continue the record-keeping indefinitely, you can cut back on the silly little expenditures that add up without giving you much pleasure.

THE SET-ASIDE BUDGET

This goal-oriented exercise is keyed to well-honed motivation. If you are determined to buy a new car or to vacation in the Orient, decide how much you'll need. If you'll need $3,200 for a down payment on the car you want to buy a year from now, you'll need to set aside $266 a month until then (actually less if you're going to put the money into an interest-earning vehicle, as you will, instead of in a cookie jar). If the car is super-important to you, you'll take that $266 off the top of your take-home pay each month and put it aside for the car. Don't let anything interfere with your goal; simply erase that $266 from your take-home pay, as if you took a cut in salary, and arrange the rest of your spending accordingly.

This budget can help you to reach a specific objective, but it does have some limitations. If you're operating close to the margin to begin with, it's not going to help you very much to cut back still further. It leaves no cushion for emergencies, unless you've already got a comfortable savings account. It won't help you keep pace with inflation. And it's essentially a limited venture, not the kind of tool that will help you control all your financial affairs.

ENVELOPES, JARS, AND PIGGY BANKS

In this slightly more all-inclusive version of the set-aside budget you'll allocate all your take-home pay according to category. If you convert a weekly paycheck to cash, for instance, you'll then put the needed dollars into an envelope (or whatever) designated according to need: rent, food, gasoline, lunches, savings, and so on. You may find yourself eating gasoline money from time to time, as you borrow from one envelope or another, but that's okay if it all comes out right in the end.

This kind of budget is essentially an operating tool, not a planning tool. It can help you to control your spending, but it may not help you with a key element of a good financial plan: accumulating resources for the future. To do this, you'll have to go to a bit more trouble.

A CASH FLOW FORECAST

The most useful budget is one that identifies current income and outgo and projected income and outgo. It takes some effort, but if you take a few hours to set up a detailed cash flow forecast, and then spend half an hour every month keeping it up to date, you'll get a firm grip on your financial affairs. This cash management approach, while it may seem complicated at first glance, can be approached in a simple step-by-step way. Use the sample Income-Outgo Worksheet on p. 41 as a guide.

Income

Start by identifying your current income. On a single sheet of paper, list all your definite sources of income: salary, interest, dividends, royalties, commissions, rents—anything you know you'll have in hand in the course of the year. Put down the annual totals. You can break them down to a monthly basis later on. Use after-tax, take-home income to work with, because it's spendable income that you're allocating.

On a separate sheet (or on the same sheet, in a parallel column), identify your projected income a year from now. Don't count uncertain income in either column. You may work regular overtime but, unless it's contractually guaranteed, it could stop. You may have been the happy recipient of a year-end bonus every year for the last six years, but this too could come to an unhappy end. You may have received an annual cash gift from your father, as he disposes of his estate during his lifetime, but he could find another use for his money. Such income, which you may or may not actually receive, should be designated for extra savings or allocated for luxuries. Enjoy it, in other words, but don't count on it.

Outgo

On another sheet of paper identify your current outgo, by category, on an annual basis. Pull together current figures from your checkbook and charge account records. Then identify anticipated expenditures in the same areas a year from now. Convert your annual figures to monthly ones, so that you can allocate funds ahead of time for an annual insurance premium or a semiannual tuition bill. Round all figures to the nearest $5, too, to make the task easier.

Set up your outgo categories in descending order, from fixed to variable. Start with those expenses that are both fixed and absolutely essential: housing (rent or mortgage payments), insurance, taxes (other than those withheld), savings (yes, savings are essential and should be a fixed off-the-top portion of your income). Then list the variable but essential categories: food (both at home and out), housing repair and maintenance, utilities, clothing, medical care, transportation. Don't forget pocket money for lunches, haircuts, bus fare, and the like. Next come not-so-essential items (in economic, not emotional, terms): entertainment, recreation, travel, contributions, gifts, hobbies. Rank these flexible expenditures in order of their importance to you, before you decide how much you'll spend in each category. A midwinter vacation may seem extravagant, an extra to be ruthlessly cut back in the interests of a balanced budget, but if that vacation is the only thing that will keep you sane you may choose to cut back in other areas instead.

Worksheet 2.2: Tracking Income and Outgo

	Monthly Income			Monthly Outgo	
	This year	**Next year**		**This year**	**Next year**
			FIXED EXPENSES		
Your own salary	___	___	Housing (mortgage or rent)	___	___
Your spouse's salary	___	___	Household insurance	___	___
Bonuses	___	___	Medical care, including health insurance	___	___
Commissions	___	___			
Tips	___	___	Other insurance	___	___
Interest	___	___	Taxes	___	___
Dividends	___	___	Installment purchases (auto and others)	___	___
Rental property	___	___	Savings	___	___
Royalties	___	___			
Social Security	___	___	**VARIABLE EXPENSES**		
Pension benefits	___	___	Food, at home and out	___	___
Profit-sharing	___	___	Home maintenance and repairs	___	___
Annuities	___	___			
Life insurance benefits	___	___	Utilities and fuel	___	___
Other	___	___	Telephone	___	___
TOTAL	___	___	Clothing	___	___
			Transportation	___	___
			Entertainment/recreation	___	___
			Travel and vacations	___	___
			Clubs and organizations	___	___
			Hobbies	___	___
			Gifts and contributions	___	___

OPTIONAL EXPENSES

	This year	Next year
Housing (a second home or a major home improvement)	___	___
Transportation (a second car)	___	___
Extended travel (two months in Europe?)	___	___
Other (a boat? a recreational vehicle?)	___	___
TOTAL	___	___

You can also look at outgo in terms of "definite," "maybe," and "wouldn't-it-be-nice." "Definite" expenditures, fixed and variable, include the essential items listed above. "Maybe" items include entertainment and recreation, travel and vacations, clubs and organizations, hobbies and sports, gifts and contributions. The "wouldn't-it-be-nice" category includes all your heart's desires, the things you'd do if only you had the money and the things you will be able to do if you make a budget and stick to it: a vacation home in the country, a trip around the world, a recreational vehicle, a boat, a complete redecoration of your home.

MONITORING YOUR CASH FLOW

If you take your cash flow forecast a step further and monitor your actual spending, you can see what changes you must make, on a month-to-

Q How can I possibly budget? I work in sales and on commission, and never quite know what the year's income will be or even a given month's. Yet I have to pay my rent on a regular basis. My income has gone up each year of the last five, but I'm not secure enough to believe that it will necessarily continue to rise; it could go down if I have a bad year or if I get sick. How can I allocate my money for current expenses and plan ahead for the future?

A You need an extra dose of self-discipline. Try to set aside some money from each check you receive, no matter how difficult it may be, to cover the times when there may be no checks at all. You have to build up a cushion of savings to tide you over the slow periods as well as to cover any personal crises or emergencies. Set up your personal budget, first, by charting your income over a period of six months to a year. Then build up your savings by spending an amount no more than midway between your lowest monthly income and your average monthly income. As your savings increase, along with your confidence that your earnings will stay about a certain predictable level, you'll be able to spend more.

But don't forget taxes. If income tax is not withheld, you'll have to file quarterly estimates and have enough cash on hand to pay these estimates. You can also make taxes work for you: If a large year-end fee will dramatically increase your taxes, consider splitting it between two calendar years. What's important for the salaried, moreover, is even more important for you: Keep accurate records of all your income and all your outgo, especially your business-related, tax-deductible outgo.

month basis, to stay on top. Worksheet 2.3 shows a cash flow chart developed by New York's Citibank. To make such a chart for yourself, list each allocation category across the top of a sheet of paper. Under each category, set up two columns: debit and credit. The debits will be the amount you actually spend in each category each month; the credits represent your annual forecast figure divided by twelve. The amounts won't come out even each month, but you'll carry over any accumulated surplus or deficit and start each month with the net amount then available.

Worksheet 2.3: Cash Flow Chart

UTILITIES/ HOUSING		REPAIRS		TAXES		INSURANCE	
Debit	Credit	Debit	Credit	Debit	Credit	Debit	Credit
——	——	——	——	——	——	——	——
——	——	——	——	——	——	——	——
——	——	——	——	——	——	——	——

LOAN PAYMENTS		TRANSPOR- TATION		SAVINGS		MEDICAL	
Debit	Credit	Debit	Credit	Debit	Credit	Debit	Credit
——	——	——	——	——	——	——	——
——	——	——	——	——	——	——	——
——	——	——	——	——	——	——	——

INVESTMENTS		EDUCATION		POCKET MONEY		FOOD/ LIQUOR	
Debit	Credit	Debit	Credit	Debit	Credit	Debit	Credit
——	——	——	——	——	——	——	——
——	——	——	——	——	——	——	——
——	——	——	——	——	——	——	——

HOME APPLIANCES/ FURNISHINGS		CLOTHES		VACATION/ RECREATION		GIFTS/ CONTRIBUTIONS	
Debit	Credit	Debit	Credit	Debit	Credit	Debit	Credit
——	——	——	——	——	——	——	——
——	——	——	——	——	——	——	——
——	——	——	——	——	——	——	——

If you spend a lot on clothing in April, for instance, as you build up your spring wardrobe, you'll probably exceed your monthly allocation for clothing.

But since you probably won't spend as much in May, once your wardrobe has been brought up to date, you can catch up then and come out even. In other categories, such as food and housing, your actual spending should come out close to your estimate. If it doesn't, over a period of several months, you've got to make some adjustments to avoid serious trouble.

Keeping track of expenses in this specific debit-credit way will show you where your budget is working and where it is not. You may have to raise your annual forecast in one category and cut back in another. A child might be sent to camp for two weeks instead of four, for instance, to free money for other family needs. Or you may decide to cut back on restaurant meals in order to send a child to camp.

You'll also change your spending patterns as you move into different stages of life; recognizing those changes and taking advantage of them is essential. Children outgrow camp and start to stay at home instead; perhaps they even find a summer job. What happens to the camp money then? Is it absorbed, unnoticed? Or do you make a deliberate decision about what to do with it? Life cycle planning enables you to look ahead, to anticipate freed money that can then be used for other purposes, and to anticipate and meet the costs associated with a new life stage. Those costs may be part of obligations to others (college for your children, support for your aged parents). They may also represent obligations to yourself (a new career direction which requires time out for training, a festive celebration of your twenty-fifth wedding anniversary). Cash flow forecasting combined with a monitoring system will give you the clearest financial portrait of all.

BUDGET TIPS

Whichever form of budget you decide is best for you:

■ Review it regularly to be sure it's up-to-date and serving your needs.
■ Plan for large once-a-year expenses by allocating one-twelfth of the necessary sum each month.
■ Include adequate provision for taxes. Unless you're on straight salary with no outside income, you'll probably owe some extra income tax. If you'll owe $500 or more in tax, over and above the amount withheld from your salary, you may have to pay an estimated quarterly tax. See Chapter 20 for details.
■ Put an inflation factor in your budget. Inflation is low right now, hovering at 3 to 4 percent a year. But it hasn't been many years since we had inflation of 10 percent, 12 percent, even more; those days could recur. If you bring home $40,000 in after-tax income, you'll need an additional $3,200 to compensate for an inflation rate of 8 percent. If you figured on 5 percent inflation for the year and designed your budget to absorb an increase of only $2,000, an 8 percent rise would leave you $1,200 in the hole—$1,200 that would have to come out of long-term savings or put you into debt. So, beyond your provisions for systematic savings, try to

calculate an inflation factor. The best bet is to use the inflation rate for the preceding year as you do your personal forecast (remembering, all the while, that an additional cushion may be a wise idea).

Net Worth

A budget will help you control your spending on a month-to-month or even year-to-year basis. But a budget shouldn't stand alone. The best way to measure your financial progress is through assessing your net worth and charting its changes over the years. Net worth represents the success with which you are converting income into assets. A net worth statement will signal your ability to handle more debt. And it will indicate whether or not you are keeping pace with inflation.

Your personal or family net worth, simply put, is the sum of all assets minus the sum of all liabilities. Put another way, it's what you would have if you sold everything you own and paid back everything you owe. Here is a sample Net Worth Worksheet to use as a guide:

Worksheet 2.4: Net Worth

Current Assets		Current Liabilities	
Checking accounts	_____	Mortgage (balance due)	_____
Savings accounts	_____	Taxes	_____
Certificates of deposit	_____	Debts (including installment loans)	_____
U.S. Savings Bonds (current value)	_____	Insurance premiums	_____
Life insurance (cash value)	_____	Charge account balances	_____
Securities (market value)	_____	Charitable pledges	_____
Annuities (surrender value)	_____	Other	_____
Pension (vested interest)	_____	TOTAL LIABILITIES _____	
Real estate (market value)	_____	Subtract total liabilities from total assets:	
Business interests (market value)	_____		
Residence (market value)	_____	Total assets: _____	
Furnishings, jewelry, auto, etc. (current market value)	_____	- Total liabilities: _____	
Other	_____		
TOTAL ASSETS _____		= TOTAL NET WORTH _____	

ASSETS

Start by listing your liquid assets: cash on hand, savings and checking accounts, deposits in money market funds, the cash value of life insurance policies, the market value of securities. Include the current value of certificates of deposit, savings bonds, money owed you by others—and don't forget the security deposit on your apartment, if you're a tenant. Then tally the current market value (not what you paid for the property, but what you could get if you sold it) of your home, car, jewelry, appliances, coin or art collections, etc.

LIABILITIES

Now add up everything you owe: mortgages, outstanding loans, charge account balances, insurance premiums, tuition payments, taxes due. Don't forget yet-to-be-paid medical bills or charitable pledges. Subtract your total liabilities from your total assets and you'll have your net worth.

If the liabilities add up to more than the assets, you've got a negative net worth—and some major changes to make in the way you manage your money. Make those changes by going back to your operating budget. See if you can eliminate some spending and build up your savings. If you can't manage to save at least 5 percent of your after-tax income (and that's a bare minimum) you'll have to take harsher measures. Cut out your use of credit, rearrange your style of living, and get down to basics.

If your net worth is positive, that's good. But is it working for you in the best way possible? Can you do better?

As you prepare your net worth statement, bear in mind that day-to-day activity doesn't always change the bottom line. In this example, Bill Smith has a positive net worth on May 15 of $4,830. He then goes out and spends $1,000 on a new stereo. On May 16, Bill still has a positive net worth of $4,830. But look at the difference:

ASSETS:	May 15	ASSETS:	May 16
Cash on hand:	$ 150	Cash on hand:	$ 150
Savings account:	1,700	Savings account:	1,700
Car:	9,400	Car:	9,400
Apt. Furnishings:	1,275	Apt. Furnishings:	2,275
Total assets:	$ 12,525	Total assets:	$ 13,525
LIABILITIES:		LIABILITIES:	
Car loan:	$ 7,130	Car loan:	$ 7,130
TV loan:	325	TV loan:	325
Credit card debt:	240	Credit card debt:	1,240
Total liabilities:	$ 7,695	Total liabilities:	$ 8,695
NET WORTH:	**$ 4,830**	**NET WORTH:**	**$ 4,830**

Source: *The Six Cups: How to Manage Your Money,* John T. Blankinship, Jr., and Charles E. Foster II.

ANALYZE YOUR NET WORTH

The net worth figure alone won't tell you very much. If you analyze the figure and compare it with succeeding years, however, you'll be using the information to improve your financial position. You might even set a target and measure your increased net worth against that target.

Your analysis, at least once a year, should include the kind of questions a corporation would ask itself. For example:

Is Your Net Worth Growing More Than the Annual Rate of Inflation?

The first time you perform this exercise, you'll have to estimate, but in the future you can be precise. Compare the year-to-year change in net worth; if the percentage increase is less than the rate of inflation in your area, you are falling behind in terms of purchasing power. You can find out the local inflation rate by calling the nearest office of the Bureau of Labor Statistics. Once you have the figure, multiply the total value of your assets by the inflation rate to find out the dollar rate of increase you need.

Your net worth may grow without deliberate action on your part. Staying on the job may increase your assets in the form of built-up pension benefits. Making monthly mortgage payments reduces your debt and increases your net worth by increasing the equity in your home. But this kind of accidental growth won't help you in the battle against inflation. Take deliberate action and you can make your net worth grow in significant ways.

You can consciously build your net worth by investing savings, reinvesting the income that your investments produce, and enjoying capital appreciation. To do this, first you have to save enough to invest, then you have to invest it wisely. (If Bill Smith had invested his $1,000 instead of buying a stereo, in the box on p. 46, he would have added to his net worth rather than

Q It seems as if the only way to make our savings grow, when interest rates are so low, is to take more risk with our money. Can you recommend an investment with little risk and a good return?

A The best investment you might make would be paying off debt. If you're carrying credit card or installment debt at 18 percent or 20 percent interest, while you're earning 3 percent or so on your savings, you'll secure a much better return by paying down the debt than you could on any investment. Just don't spend all your savings this way; you need to keep enough cash on hand (the equivalent of at least two to three months' income) to cope with any emergency that might arise.

keeping his net worth steady while increasing his credit card debt.) See Chapters 5 and 6 for details on investment strategy and investment vehicles.

You may also wind up with a reduction in net worth from one year to the next if assets produce little or no income or capital appreciation, if you allow yourself to be overburdened by expensive short-term liabilities, or if you simply spend too much and save too little for new investment.

The remaining steps in your net worth analysis will help you pin down the cause of increase or decrease in your net worth. They will help you change the mix of your assets and liabilities to achieve more growth.

What is the Ratio of Assets to Liabilities?

According to the Federal Reserve Board, the typical American has about $6 in assets for every $1 in debt, a ratio that has held steady for some years. Just what ratio is right for you, however, depends on your age and income potential. If you are still moving toward your peak earning years, you can assume greater liabilities because you know that you'll be in a position to pay them off. If you are nearing retirement, you should try to increase assets and reduce liabilities.

The right ratio for you also depends on your temperament. You can assume more debt in the expectation of potentially greater gain, as long as it won't lead to chronically sleepless nights.

What is the Ratio of Short-term Liabilities to Long-term Liabilities?

Although debt is no longer intrinsically "bad" in late-twentieth-century America, some kinds of debt are still better than other kinds. Long-term debt, used to finance the purchase of assets that will create more wealth, can be good; an outstanding example is long-term mortgage debt. Short-term interest-bearing debt, if it is used to finance day-to-day living costs, is bad because it produces no return; an example is the use of charge accounts and credit cards to purchase groceries.

Interest charges, moreover, are steep. Paying interest on everyday items (interest that isn't even tax-deductible) reduces the amount of money you have to save and to invest in productive assets.

What is the Ratio of Fixed to Liquid Assets?

Fixed assets, such as your house or a collection of antique silver, increase in value but are hard to tap; you have to find a willing buyer before you can turn such assets into cash. Even though housing values have come down in many parts of the country, you may still find that the inflated housing prices of the 1980s left you with as much as half of your net worth tied up in your equity in your home. Yet you need some funds readily available as operating expenses and for emergencies. Liquid assets are those that can be converted quickly to cash, such as bank accounts and securities.

The appropriate split between fixed and liquid assets, for you, depends on age, income, and personal preference. It also depends on the extent to which you are cushioned in other ways. If, for instance, you are adequately covered by medical insurance, disability income insurance, unemployment insurance, and a second income in the household, you may not need more than two to three months' income on hand in a savings account or money market fund. If you're single, between jobs, and/or without insurance coverage, you'll be safer with at least a six-month cushion.

However much cushion you decide you need, don't invade that amount to cover short-term debts or to splurge on a trip to Europe. The need for cash can be both urgent and unexpected. One man, for instance, recently started a management job with excellent fringe benefits. But he had not yet received his hospitalization insurance card when he was rushed to the hospital with bleeding ulcers. Without the proof of insurance, the hospital was firm: A check for $1,500 would precede admission.

YOUR PERSONAL BENEFITS PLAN

The manager in the above example is fortunate, despite both his illness and his temporary need for cash to cover expenses, he has health insurance. He also has an excellent benefits package, including long-term disability coverage and a pension.

Many of us, these days, aren't so lucky. Even if you currently work at a job with benefits, you can't count on remaining in that job. Even if you do, you can't count on the benefits package remaining intact. You would be wise, therefore, to put your own personal benefits plan in place. Buy individual health insurance (see Chapter 19) while you're healthy and insurable; you won't collect double benefits from a group and an individual plan, but you'll be very happy you have that individual plan in place should you lose your group coverage. Buy disability income coverage, too (see p. 552), to replace income lost from a long-term illness or an accident that leaves you unable to work at your usual occupation. And plan your own retirement (see Chapter 23), without counting on receiving a pension from your employer or tax-free Social Security retirement benefits from Uncle Sam.

WORKING WITH YOUR NET WORTH

Now that you've drawn up your net worth statement and analyzed it in terms of your own situation and your own goals, don't put it aside and forget it. Bring it up to date at regular intervals (as often as quarterly if inflation surges once again) to see if:

- Your investments are keeping up with inflation or ought to be replaced.
- Your insurance coverage is adequate.
- Your overall net worth is outpacing inflation for real growth.
- You are meeting your savings goals.

Between-Jobs Survival Skills

The money management skills outlined throughout this book will help you to survive a period of unemployment. But some are more important than others. If you're out of work, for any reason, here are the things you should do:

MARSHAL YOUR RESOURCES

Look to all possible sources of funds to get through the between-jobs period:

- Savings. Try to establish, *before* you're unemployed, a readily accessible savings "cushion" equivalent to at least six months' earnings.
- Severance pay. Keep it liquid, readily accessible, and resist stockbrokers and other salespeople who would have you buy profitable (for them) investment products.
- Investment income and, if necessary, sale of income-producing assets; this is the rainy day you've been saving for.
- Unemployment compensation. How much you'll get, and specific eligibility requirements, are determined by the state in which you live. But do apply; don't assume that you're not eligible because, for instance, you received some severance pay. (**Note:** Unemployment insurance is fully taxable.)
- Life insurance. A loan against the cash value in an older whole life insurance policy may be available for as little as 5 to 8 percent; newer policies carry a variable rate of interest. Life insurance loans do not have to be repaid (although the face amount of the policy will be reduced by the amount of any outstanding loan).
- Earnings of other family members. Now, if ever, is the time for you all to pull together.
- Your own earnings from temporary or part-time or free-lance work. Can you tutor students? take in typing? do research? set up as a consultant in any field? Assess your skills carefully, and see what you can do to bridge the employment gap.

Note: You may be tempted to take the funds in your 401(k) or profit-sharing plan and use the cash either for living expenses or to pay off a major obligation such as your mortgage. Don't. If you can possibly keep that money working toward your retirement, by leaving it in your current employer's plan or rolling it over into a tax-sheltered Individual Retirement Account, you should. If you can't, if you must tap the money, new rules permit you to take some out and roll the rest over. But bear in mind that you'll have to pay ordinary income tax on the proceeds (in fact, your employer will be required to withhold 20 percent of the distribution) and, if you're under age 59½, you'll face tax penalties as well. The combination could take 40 percent or more off the top, leaving you with a much smaller retirement nest egg than you anticipated.

CUT BACK ON SPENDING

Don't wait until unemployment is a fact; cut back on spending just as soon as you see unemployment as a possibility. Reduce day-to-day outlay: Brown-bag your lunch, set up a car pool, stop smoking. Defer major purchases: Put off buying a new car, or a new coat, until your income is stable. Swap services with friends: Trade upholstery for automobile repairs, baby-sitting for a haircut. Pool resources: Buy food cooperatively, set up a home repair tool center.

And take a good hard look at housing, probably your single largest budget item. Think about renting out a spare room in your house, or taking in a roommate in an apartment. Give up your own housing, as a last resort, and move in with relatives. Sublet your apartment, if your lease permits, or rent out your house, but try not to dispose of either permanently. You want to reduce expenses temporarily, not cut yourself adrift.

Note: Talk to your mortgage lender, without delay, if you'll have difficulty meeting monthly payments. Try to work out a repayment plan, acceptable to both you and the lender, under which your regular mortgage payments may be temporarily reduced or suspended, even if the payments must be extended over a longer period of time. Ask the lender, too, whether you are eligible for any government mortgage protection plan.

SET UP A SURVIVAL BUDGET

Match your reduced income against your reduced expenditures and do a six-month cash flow projection. If you can't last six months (you'll probably need more time than you think you will to land a new position), go back and cut outgo some more. Most budgets contain some fat; now is the time to pare that fat, and you'll have a healthier financial diet when you're back to work.

Remember: You don't have to match your usual gross pay. Federal income and Social Security taxes, the devilish duo that take the biggest chunk of your gross income, will be all but eliminated when you're between jobs. So all you have to come up with is your net income minus the discretionary spending you can eliminate.

SPEND MONEY WISELY

As you do your survival budget, be sure to allocate enough money for your job search. You'll probably need at least $200 to $300 a month to get your resume typed and printed, get to interviews, take people to lunch. You'll need more if you travel to another city in search of a job.

Some job-related expenses—including travel, placing classified ads, and the typing of resumes—are tax-deductible if you are seeking a new job in the same line of work (see pp. 574-576 for details). But you do have to spend the money first. And you do have to keep receipts.

This may also be a good time to invest money in retraining and self-improvement, to learn new skills and beef up old ones. But investigate services and prices first; a low-priced adult education course may provide the same training as a high-priced seminar.

KEEP IMPORTANT INSURANCE IN FORCE

Personal property insurance is important—now is not the time to replace your car or repair your home out of your own pocket—so keep up the premiums if you possibly can.

Health insurance, however, is even more important. With a semiprivate hospital room (*just* the room) costing an average of $297 a day in 1990, you can't afford to be unprotected. Here's what you can do:

- Sign up for your spouse's health insurance plan, if you're eligible.
- Continue your own group coverage, by paying the premiums yourself. Under federal law, any employer with more than 20 employees must allow you to do so for a period of 18 months.
- If you work for a smaller company, find out, before you leave your job, if you can convert your group health insurance to individual coverage. The premium will go up, and some benefits may be reduced, but there will be no lapse in coverage.
- Ask an insurance agent about interim health insurance, a full-coverage short-term policy usually written for a maximum of six months, sometimes renewable for another six months.
- Check into group insurance plans offered by professional and social organizations. Most are hospital indemnity plans, paying specified amounts per day if you are hospitalized, rather than comprehensive health insurance. They are better as supplementary coverage than as primary coverage, but they are clearly preferable to no coverage at all.

USE CREDIT WITH CARE

A line of credit may extend your financial resources, but using credit without a paycheck to pay the bills can be very dangerous. Don't use a credit card to take up the slack in your budget. You'll wind up with bills you can't pay at an interest rate you can't afford.

If you're having trouble meeting existing bills, talk to your creditors and work out a repayment plan. Don't ignore the bills, hoping they'll go away; you may do lasting damage to your credit rating. (See Chapter 8 for more information on handling credit, in good times and bad.)

If you really don't see a way to pay your bills, get help. You can get the address of the consumer credit counseling agency nearest you by writing to the National Foundation for Consumer Credit, 8701 Georgia Ave., Suite 601, Silver Spring, MD 20910.

Keeping Track

Now that you have drawn up budget sheets and net worth statements, what are you going to do with them? What do you usually do with bills, receipts, and financial records of all kinds? Are you the stash-them-in-a-shoe box type? Or do you have organized folders, by year and by category, so that you can find records when you need them?

Clearly, organization is better than chaos. But most of us shy away from organizing just as we shy away from budgets. The former, like the latter, need not be difficult. You simply have to decide what to keep and where.

You'll find some motivation for the task if you ask yourself these questions:

- What would happen if your home were burglarized or destroyed by fire? Would all your important records disappear along with your possessions?
- Who, besides you, knows where to find important information on family assets and obligations?
- How easy would it be for any other member of your family to figure out your record-keeping system?

WHAT TO KEEP

A rule of thumb: Keep the papers you will need to document facts for as long as those facts might be questioned.

Some things have to be kept virtually forever: records on a home purchase and home improvements, because they will substantiate a tax claim when the house is sold; buy and sell documents on securities, paintings, rare coins, and other assets whose sale may have tax consequences; old tax returns themselves so that you have a record of your affairs over the years. Insurance policies should be retained for several years after the expiration date, in case a delayed claim is filed. And you'll want to keep your budget sheets and net worth statements to chart your progress over the years.

Other records need to be kept for limited periods of time. Any papers that document a tax deduction (other than those related to capital gains or losses, detailed above) should be kept for a minimum of three years after the filing of that return; that's the usual audit period for federal income tax returns. (State laws on tax audits vary; check with local authorities to determine appropriate record-keeping periods. And remember: In cases of fraud, all bets are off. Both the Internal Revenue Service and local tax authorities can investigate suspected fraud years later.) Tax records to be kept for at least three years include bills for medical services, bills substantiating home office deductions or business travel, records of casualty or theft losses, and so on.

Other bits and pieces of the paper storm that drift through your life may be discarded almost immediately. Bills from gasoline companies and department stores, for instance, may be disposed of as soon as your payment is accurately credited. Credit card statements showing finance charges need no longer be kept; consumer interest is no longer a tax-deductible item. (But you may want to keep department store and credit card statements for a few months in case there's a problem with a purchase.)

WHERE TO KEEP IT

A rule of thumb: Keep irreplaceable papers in the safest possible location; keep current files where it's easy and convenient to work with them; keep back records out of the way but accessible.

Safekeeping for Irreplaceable Documents

A safe deposit box is the best place for papers that are either extremely valuable or difficult to replace, such as birth and marriage certificates, deeds, titles, and securities. But check with your bank before you place your will or your life insurance policies in safe deposit. In many states a box is sealed upon the death of the owner, and, while access may be obtained specifically for the purpose of locating a will, it may take time and add unnecessary trouble at a difficult moment. Suggestion: If you're married, one of you can rent the safe deposit box while the other can be your deputy, allowed to enter the box at will.

If you don't have a safe deposit box, a fireproof box is the second best location for these papers. Look for a metal box labeled as to its fire resistance, but don't expect it to be burglarproof as well.

Current Files

You might try an accordion file, with a pocket for each month of the year or for each category, for such items as bills to be paid and receipts for those recently paid, premium notices, bank statements, and your ongoing budget sheets. Other items to keep on hand: insurance policies, warranties, mortgage statements, credit card data, employment and health records, and a list of what's in your safe deposit box.

Q I've always filed my canceled checks, along with the bank statement, by month and year. Now I have several boxes of canceled checks to review before I can figure out which are the tax-related items to keep and which I can throw away. Is there a better way of doing this?

A As you reconcile each month's bank statement, sort your canceled checks by category. Then store them in files labeled by tax-related category: medical bills, home improvements, and so on. Keep the rest, filed by month, for a year or until you're sure you won't need to prove that you've paid a bill; then discard. This method has two advantages: You'll have all your tax records properly filed, and you'll reduce the avalanche of paper you would otherwise keep on hand.

Inactive Records

Anything over three years old, as a rule, belongs either with your permanent (but inactive) records or in the wastebasket. Your yearly net worth statements, tax returns for prior years, and the documentation for those returns can be tucked away in an attic or closet, out of the way yet accessible if you need them.

You can keep your papers wherever you like, but the key to organization is knowing where they are. So make up a list of exactly what you have. Key the list so that the location of every document will be clear. Whether it's in the upper-left-hand desk drawer in your bedroom, in the fireproof box in the basement, or in the safe deposit box at your local bank, you (or, when it comes to that, whoever is handling your affairs) will know exactly where everything is. You might end up with a list something like this:

Inventory of Valuables

Items	Key
Bank books: **D**	**D**: desk drawer
Safe deposit key: **D**	**A**: accordion file, bedroom
Tax records: **A**	**B**: bank vault
Insurance policies: *	**K**: drawer next to sink, in kitchen
Savings bonds: **B**	* fireproof box, bedroom closet
Appliance warranties: **K**	
Copy of will: *	

Make another list and itemize, by number, every insurance policy, credit card, and savings bond. Duplicate both lists; keep one copy at home and one in your safe deposit box.

 KEY POINTS

- Identify your goals and objectives, and plan a course of action to meet those goals and objectives, and you'll take the essential first step toward successful money management.

- Use a budget to help adjust outgo to income, to track your spending, and to ensure that you use your money in the ways that matter most to you.

- Prepare your own personal benefits plan so that you'll be protected no matter where you work, and even if you lose your job.

- Draw up a net worth statement each year to see if you're making progress toward your personal objectives.

- Organize your financial records.

Putting Your Money to Work: Cash Management

CHAPTER 3

Checking Accounts

■ You're single, just out of school, with a brand-new job. Where should you open your new checking account? And should that account be an interest-earning NOW account?

■ As a two-income couple you divide the responsibility for household expenses. Should you, then, pay those expenses out of a single joint checking account? Or should you maintain separate individual accounts?

■ With children approaching the teen years you're stepping up your college savings program, using certificates of deposit at your neighborhood savings and loan. Is this the best place for this money?

Your personal financial plan will change over time to meet your changing needs. Wherever you are in life, however, whether you're currently building a nest egg to buy your first house or, mortgage payments finished, are looking ahead to retirement, there are three building blocks to your personal financial plan: managing your cash on hand, investing for capital growth, and extending your resources through judicious use of credit. The line separating these three building blocks has blurred in recent years, as you can now handle your checking needs through a money market mutual fund, invest through banks, even secure credit through a brokerage firm. Moreover, savings that you might place in a certificate of deposit (CD) at one time could do better in EE bonds (U.S. Savings Bonds) or a short-term bond fund (holding corporate or municipal bonds) at another. So bear in mind, as you read, that Chapters 3 through 8, on cash management, investing and credit, overlap a great deal and should be read as a group.

In fact, it's best to take what might be called a "holistic" approach to your finances. Look at every piece of the puzzle—how to manage your cash flow, how much you spend on credit, how much you earn on investments—as part of a comprehensive effort to manage your money well.

Before you can invest or secure credit, however, you have to have cash on hand. So managing your cash comes first. The basic tools of cash management are checking and savings accounts. Both are available at a variety of traditional financial institutions: commercial banks, savings and loan associations, mutual savings banks, and credit unions. Both, in somewhat different form, are also becoming available at other institutions.

Commercial banks are sometimes called full-service banks because, originally established to serve business, they offer an entire range of financial services. If, for instance, you need to transfer cash overseas, you may have to go to a commercial bank. If you want a financial institution to manage a trust, you may turn to a commercial bank.

Savings and loan associations (S&Ls) and **mutual savings banks** (grouped with S&Ls as "thrifts"), by contrast, have traditionally provided personal financial services: home mortgages, home improvement loans, college loans, money orders, and so on. Both thrifts and banks had some turbulent times in the 1980s and many have merged with stronger institutions.

Credit unions are nonprofit cooperative institutions, organized by people who have a "common bond." That bond most often is a place of employment; it may also be a club or church or community group, even a residential area. Credit unions often pay more interest on deposits, charge less on loans, and have fewer fees than other institutions. Although credit unions are expanding their services—with credit cards and NOW accounts (savings accounts on which funds can be drawn) and Individual Retirement Accounts (IRAs)— many are small and may not have the funds to make home mortgages or other sizable loans.

These distinctions, particularly those between banks and thrifts, used to be sharp and clear. Banks were the only place to find checking accounts and credit cards and trust services. Thrifts were the place to go for home mortgages. Both offered savings accounts, but thrifts were permitted to pay slightly more in interest (in order to encourage the deposits that would then be available for home mortgages). Credit unions were a good place for an auto loan but were legally prohibited from making mortgage loans, offering revolving lines of credit, and paying interest on checking. Many of these restrictions have now been lifted and many of these distinctions, although not all, have been erased.

Nonbank banks are also getting into the act. Today you can write checks on a money market mutual fund, use a short-term bond fund instead of a savings account, secure credit through a brokerage firm or the telephone company.

Some observers forecast financial supermarkets, places where you'll be able to do just about anything and everything connected with money: make deposits and withdrawals, write checks, take a loan or get a credit card, buy insurance or securities or a house. In an effort to compete, banks and thrifts have been expanding their services, selling mutual funds and annuities; many also offer incentives to customers willing to consolidate accounts (see p. 62).

But will you want to bundle your financial transactions under one roof? There are disadvantages as well as advantages:

- Right now, if you take a loan in a bank where you do your checking and saving, that bank can tap your account if you are delinquent on the loan. The bank can't do it if your savings account is elsewhere. What will happen if all your financial transactions are in one centralized location?

- Right now, too, some people are concerned about a loss of privacy on financial transactions. If your entire financial profile—where you live, what you've borrowed, who you've paid—is centrally located, are you in danger of a real invasion of privacy?

As brokerage houses, mutual funds, credit card issuers, and large retail establishments start to offer competing financial services, traditional financial institutions will change still more. Today's revolution in financial services may dramatically affect the way in which you manage your cash.

While the deregulation that permits multiple players in the financial marketplace can spark competition among financial institutions, deregulation does not always work in favor of the consumer. As financial institutions have greater freedom to set their own rules, and their own fees, consumers need to be increasingly alert.

How to Decide Which Institution to Use

The key things to evaluate are services, cost, convenience, size, and stability.

Q My sister told me that her bank is now paying interest on only some of the money in her account. Are banks allowed to do this?

A No longer. Until the Truth in Savings Act took effect in June 1993, some banks (mostly in the Southeast) tried to reduce their costs by paying interest on only 88 percent of checking account balances, justifying the practice by citing the 12 percent they must put aside to meet Federal Reserve liquidity requirements. Under the 1993 legislation banks, thrifts and credit unions must pay interest on the entire balance in interest-earning accounts; they must also disclose how yields are calculated and provide complete information about rates and fees. If they change the rules to your disadvantage, you must be notified in writing 30 days before the change is made; this gives you time to find another bank.

SERVICE

Look, first, at the services offered. All institutions may be permitted to offer various services; not all institutions may choose to do so. What's the point of building your reputation as a good customer so that you can secure a college loan for your child if the place where you do your checking and saving doesn't choose to write college loans? Find out before you open your account what services are offered. The list will change from time to time, but the current list will give you a fairly good idea of where the institution stands in the competitive scheme of things.

COSTS

Costs count too. Financial institutions raised retail service fees dramatically in the early to mid-1980s; the pace of fee increases slowed in the late 1980s but began accelerating again in the 1990s. Banks call this realistic pricing, to meet the increasing costs of doing business. It isn't entirely the fault of individual institutions; the Federal Reserve Board is now charging banks and thrifts for services that used to be free. But the definition of "realistic" may vary; one institution may charge $10 to stop payment on a check, another may charge $20. Some may offer free use of automatic teller machines (ATMs), while others charge a per-use fee, even for making a deposit or checking your balance.

You can save several hundred dollars a year by using a bank that pays more in interest and charges less in fees. A study of New York City banking institutions by the city's Department of Consumer Affairs found that a customer with a balance averaging around $750 for the year could gain as much as $28.75 at one institution while *losing* $216.48 at another. Ask your bank for a schedule of charges. And remember: Under the Truth in Saving laws, you must be notified 30 days in advance of any change.

One way to keep costs down at many institutions, if you're willing to forgo diversification and do all or most of your banking in one place, is to take advantage of the "perks" that go along with consolidating accounts. For example: Chemical Bank, a pioneer in "relationship" banking, offers no-fee checking, preferential loan rates, higher interest on CDs and IRAs, and various

Q When I applied for a loan, the bank wanted me to authorize automatic deductions from my savings account to repay the loan. Must I do so?

A No. You may arrange for automatic deductions if you find this a convenient way to repay the loan, but you don't have to do so. If you default on the loan, however, the bank can take the money from your checking or savings account in that bank.

discounts to customers who maintain a minimum balance in a combination of checking, savings and other accounts. One big plus: a single monthly statement summarizing activity in all the accounts.

Another way to keep costs down is to become a "mature" adult. The definition of "mature" varies, ranging from age 50 to age 65, but many banks, savings associations, and credit unions have special packages of services for older people. Free checking is at the heart of every program. Additional perks often include free check printing, free traveler's and cashier's checks, free or discounted safe deposit boxes, and higher interest rates on deposits. Many institutions go beyond the purely financial to offer special travel packages, buying club memberships, credit card and key registries, and discount pharmacy and eye wear services.

CONVENIENCE

Convenience is also a factor, although too many people rate it first. The fact that the bank or thrift is located near your home or your workplace may not be as important as the speed and courtesy with which personnel respond to customers. Take a look, some lunchtime, at the length of lines and the way they are handled.

But accessibility is important. There may be little reason to stick with a bank after you've moved to another neighborhood. If you do, in fact, continue banking in the same place after it's no longer convenient to get there, you may find yourself holding on to checks longer than you should before depositing them. In this era of automatic teller machines, of course, you don't need access to the institution itself to do your basic deposits and withdrawals. A lot depends on your personal preferences, and how comfortable you are with banking by machine. But should you have a more complicated transaction, from buying travelers checks to taking an auto loan or applying for a mortgage, you'll value accessibility.

SIZE

The size of the institution may make a difference. Large institutions may be able to offer more services; smaller ones may be more responsive to you as an individual, more willing to grant a loan or to call you if a mistake is detected in your account rather than levying an automatic charge. But large banks can be human and small banks can offer extensive services. The only way to be sure is to ask.

Perhaps more important: Size may have a bearing on stability, although some of the biggest "money center" banks are the ones in the most trouble after periods of ill-chosen real estate investments and loan defaults by third-world governments. And bigger banks, according to a study of bank mergers by the New York City Department of Consumer Affairs, pay less on deposits and charge more for loans. Many large commercial banks, despite their ads for services tailored to the individual, would rather stick to business clients.

STABILITY

The stability of the institution, more difficult to judge, also matters. Both banks and thrifts have run into a great deal of difficulty in the last few years. For thrifts the problems began in the high-interest rate years of the early 1980s when institutions were locked into long-term low-interest mortgage loans on the incoming side and forced to pay then-current high yields on the outgoing side. The problem continued, for both banks and thrifts, with real estate investments that lost value in the recession of the 1990s. Management fraud compounded the problems for many institutions. For credit unions, problems can stem from inexperienced management (many smaller credit unions rely on volunteers) and from the economic difficulties inherent in being concentrated in a single company or industry.

Whatever the specific cause, many seemingly stable institutions have given way and had to be salvaged by merger with others. Many others are likely to do so within the next few years.

For the customer, the key point here is federal insurance. Deposits in federally insured institutions, whether banks or thrifts or credit unions, are insured up to $100,000. For safety's sake, don't keep more than that in one account under one name; when you open an account, start with no more than $90,000 so that interest won't bump you over the insured maximum too quickly. If no buyer is found for a failed bank, insurers (FDIC for banks and thrifts, National Credit Union Administration [NCUA] for credit unions) usu-

Q My salary is deposited directly into my checking account. I pay bills by check from this account. What happens to both the deposited checks and the outstanding checks I've written if the bank fails?

A Nine out of ten bank "failures" actually end in mergers with another, stronger institution. So you would see no difference in direct deposit or your checking account other than a change in the name of the bank or thrift. When a failed bank is not acquired, the Federal Deposit Insurance Corporation (FDIC) asks another institution to accept direct deposits; if you don't have an account at that institution, and don't choose to open one, it will issue a cashier's check to you for your money. You can then arrange to move direct deposit elsewhere. Also, if the failed bank is not merged or acquired, checks you've written that hadn't cleared prior to the bank's closing would be returned to you and you would have to pay the bills again—although you could probably avoid additional interest charges by explaining the reason for the delay.

ally pay all deposits in full, with interest to the day of closing, within a few days of the closing.

Table 3.1: Veribanc Evaluations of Banks, Thrifts, and Credit Unions

Ten years of evaluations by Veribanc, a rating agency, reveal a changing financial industry. There are fewer banks, thrifts, and credit unions today, and more are likely to fail, but in the long run the survivors may be stronger. The colors in the ratings match those on traffic lights: green for go (these institutions are OK), yellow for caution (be careful here), red for stop (steer clear of these).

	12/31/81	12/31/86	12/31/92
Banks:			
Green:	14,465	9,842	11,152
Yellow:	325	4,002	949
Red:	53	727	150
Thrifts:			
Green:	1,703	1,419	1,446
Yellow:	1,296	1,066	517
Red:	780	769	243
Credit Unions:			
Green:	16,809	8,336	10,147
Yellow:	2,690	5,308	2,813
Red:	1,824	1,078	645

Source: Veribanc, Inc.

Don't expect any early warning from federal regulators. While they monitor troubled banks and maintain lists of those likely to go under, they won't reveal this information, fearing a depositors' run on the bank that could accelerate failure. So, in this era of serious questions about the stability of financial institutions, you have to look out for yourself. A look at your bank's "statement of condition" or, if it is publicly owned, its annual report to stockholders is a good idea. These documents can be tough to interpret, however, so do this:

- Be alert. If your local newspaper carries a story about a management shakeup at your bank, or publicizes negative results from a regulatory exam, think about making a switch.
- If you want to look at the numbers, Warren Heller, research director of Veribanc, suggests you be sure that the institution's ratio of equity capital to assets is at least 5 percent and that the institution has been profitable for at least the last year and a half. (Regulators are closing banks with a ratio below 2 percent—it's a slightly different ratio, but

the difference is complex and not worth noting here—but you want the extra margin of safety offered by a 5 percent ratio.)

■ If the numbers won't make any sense to you, and you're worried about a particular institution (bank, savings and loan, or credit union), place a toll-free call to Veribanc at (800) 442-2657. This rating service codes banks in plain English, by color and by stars. Green, with three stars, is the highest (and safest) rating; fewer than 30 percent of all U.S. banks are in lower categories, but so are 99 percent of bank and S&L failures. Veribanc will give you an instant rating over the telephone at a cost (billed to your credit card) of $10 for the first institution and $5 for each additional one. The telephone report is backed up with a written confirmation. For $35 you can buy a "blue ribbon" report of the most stable banks in your region.

Evaluating a Credit Union

Most of the criteria that apply to banks and thrifts may also be applied to credit unions. Right now, credit unions are in better health than banks and thrifts. But there are some additional points to check before putting money into a particular credit union. The Credit Union National Association suggests:

■ Make sure that the credit union is insured. Almost all credit unions, whether state or federally chartered, carry federal deposit insurance from the National Credit Union Insurance Fund (the initials you'll see

---

Q I have several accounts in one bank: individual savings and checking, a Christmas Club, time deposits, and a retirement account. I also have a joint account with my wife and a trust account for my son. How much insurance do I have?

A All of your individual accounts are insured by the Federal Deposit Insurance Corporation for a total of $100,000 (except Individual Retirement Accounts, which are separately insured up to $100,000); if your accounts add up to more than this, you might think about moving some of them to another institution. Your joint account and your trust account are each separately insured, because of their different form of ownership, to $100,000. This insurance, by the way, applies only to the closing of the institution, not to loss sustained in any other way.

on the window sticker are NCUA). About 5 percent are privately or cooperatively insured. Federal insurance is safer.

- Ask members about the credit union's reputation. If you hear complaints about processing mistakes or bad service, the credit union may be inadequately managed. Small credit unions often save money by relying on volunteer labor; that labor may be more or less competent.
- Find out what proportion of the credit union's assets are in outstanding loans of longer than five years. Be wary if more than 15 percent of assets is committed to investments, including fixed-rate mortgage loans, with maturities of five years or more.
- Look at financial statements. The ratio of capital to assets will vary with the size of the credit union, but institutions at the national average of 7.5 percent can lose 7 percent of assets and still pay off all members' savings with remaining assets. The NCUA begins to monitor a credit union's capital-to-asset ratio when it drops to about 3 percent.

Choosing a Checking Account

Before you open a checking account, compare fees and services at two or three institutions:

Worksheet 3.1: Choosing a Checking Account

	A	B	C
Name of bank, thrift or credit union:			
What is the fee for:			
Monthly service			
Each deposit			
Each check			
Using an ATM at the institution			
Using an ATM elsewhere			
Stopping payment			
Bouncing a check			
Inquiring about a balance			
Help with balancing your checkbook			
What is the minimum balance required to avoid fees?			
For interest-earning accounts, what is the:			
Interest rate			
Compounding method			
Minimum balance to earn interest			

Does the institution offer:

Direct deposit	_____	_____	_____
Payroll deduction	_____	_____	_____
Overdraft protection	_____	_____	_____
Telephone transfers	_____	_____	_____
Telephone bill-paying	_____	_____	_____
Home equity loans	_____	_____	_____
College loans	_____	_____	_____

Types of Checking Accounts

Checking or transaction accounts are used to transfer funds. The money you should keep in your checking account, therefore, is money you plan to use in the very near future to make purchases or pay bills. Unless you have an interest-earning checking account (more on this in a moment) you'll be wasting money by keeping idle cash in a checking account. Any extra money, any money not immediately needed, should be earning interest.

There are several types of checking accounts:

- **Special accounts** are for people who don't write many checks. You can keep as little as you like in this type of account, but you'll pay monthly maintenance fees typically ranging from $2.50 to $2.75.

- **Regular accounts** may be free of charge, but they typically require that you maintain a minimum balance. The national average minimum balance required is $500, but some banks require considerably more. When the account balance falls below the minimum, monthly charges run an average of $4 to $5.

- **NOW accounts** are technically savings accounts on which funds can be drawn; the credit union equivalent is called a share draft account. Both actually function as interest-earning checking accounts. Although it's better to earn interest than to leave funds idle, NOW accounts are not necessarily the right answer for everyone—particularly now that high fees can easily outweigh low interest earned.

SHOULD YOU OPEN A NOW ACCOUNT?

Interest on checking, at first glance, sounds like a gift. But it's a gift with strings attached. NOW accounts are expensive to administer, and costs are passed on to the consumer. Before you open a NOW account, therefore, you owe it to yourself to ask some hard questions:

- What minimum balance will you have to maintain to forestall service charges? Minimum balance requirements have been inching up since the first heady days when every financial institution was competing for NOW account customers; the average, nationwide, is now $1,500. But it's still possible to find minimum balance requirements of $500 or less. (At some commercial banks, by contrast, the minimum balance requirement may be as much as $3,000—although some banks will count all of your accounts, including time deposits, toward that minimum.)

- Could you earn higher interest elsewhere on the minimum balance required? Money market mutual funds often pay a higher rate of interest with few if any fees. But money market mutual funds are not insured. See p. 133 for a fuller description.

- What charges will the bank impose if the balance falls below the required minimum? Maintenance fees, when this happens, typically run $7 to $8 a month, although some institutions assess a per-check charge of 20 cents or 25 cents instead. Some do both. And some also stop paying interest if the balance falls below a designated amount.

- What interest rate is the institution offering? Some pay higher interest on accounts with larger balances. And some have "stair-step" rates so that differing amounts of interest are earned on money within a single account.

Should you open a NOW account? If you customarily maintain a sizable balance in your checking account, the answer may be yes. If you don't keep much money in checking, you could wind up paying more in service charges than the interest your account will earn. Think about your own checking needs before you decide. And shop around, comparing both yields and fees.

Money Market Deposit Accounts were introduced by financial institutions in an effort to compete directly with the money market mutual funds offered by mutual fund families (see Chapter 6). Money market deposit accounts often earn a bit less in interest than money market mutual funds, but have the advantage of being insured by the FDIC. Deposit insurance is very attractive, particularly in an era when financial institutions fail with astonishing rapidity.

But money market deposit accounts and money market mutual funds are not the same animal. Before you transfer all your savings from a money market mutual fund into an insured money market deposit account, here are the things you should know:

- All your money in a money market mutual fund earns interest at the same rate. This is generally true even if your balance falls below the minimum required to open the account. Banks and thrifts, on the other hand, often have "tiered" or "stair-step" rates in which higher interest rates are paid on higher balances. Some banks and thrifts also charge fees for maintaining the accounts.

- Most money market mutual funds permit unlimited check-writing, although checks may have to be for $500 or more. Banks and savings institutions don't usually specify the size of an individual check drawn on a money market deposit account, but they are required to limit the number of third-party transactions per month to six, three of them by check. You can also withdraw cash from your account as many times as you like, without penalty.

■ Interest rates paid by funds change daily; those paid by banks and savings institutions may change daily or be guaranteed for as long as a month. Banks and thrifts may pay any interest rate they choose; some will pay more than others. If you're interested in this type of account, as always, it pays to shop around.

Reserve or overdraft checking is an extension of regular checking to include a permanent line of credit; you can't bounce a check if you have overdraft checking because you will be automatically incurring a loan instead. You'll also automatically become liable for interest on the loan, because this form of checking account is actually an extension of credit (see Chapter 7).

Joint Accounts

You and your spouse open a joint checking account so that you can pool your earnings and each write checks as necessary. You and your college stu-

Q I was glad I had overdraft protection when I accidentally overdrew my account. But I thought I paid off the overdraft right away, and it keeps showing up, with more interest due, on my bank statement. What's going on?

A Overdraft protection sometimes works in mysterious ways. Your bank appears to be among the group that require some specific action to end the overdraft even though you have deposited more than enough money in your account to cover it. Go talk to an officer at your bank and find out what you must do.

Overdraft protection is a useful thing to have, but it's a good idea to understand how it works before you activate it by writing a larger check than you can cover. Some institutions charge considerably more in interest than others, and some transfer money only in increments of $50 or $100 so that you can wind up owing interest on $100 when you've actually borrowed $10. Some trigger a home equity loan or an unsecured line of credit.

dent son or daughter have a joint checking account so that you can handle banking chores at home while the child handles them at school. You and your elderly parent have a joint checking account so that you can manage your parent's affairs. You are single and so is your brother; you open a checking account together so that the money will automatically belong to the one who survives the other.

Are any or all of these joint accounts a good idea?

Joint accounts do offer convenience. But they also have some disadvantages:

■ All the money in the account legally belongs to either one of the joint owners. Either one of you, therefore, can empty the account. Husbands and wives have done this to each other when a marriage turns sour. Children have done it to parents.

■ Even when the relationship remains both joyous and honest, joint ownership may not always run smoothly. During your lifetime, you must be sure to enter every check you write. After death, the surviving co-owner may be temporarily short of funds because some states (not all) require that an account be frozen for a time when one co-owner dies. You may be able to gain access, but it may be difficult.

■ Estate taxes pose the last hurdle. The Internal Revenue Service has always assumed that the total sum in a joint account belongs to the first to die. The total, accordingly, was counted in the valuation of the estate for estate tax purposes... *unless* the other co-owner could conclusively prove that the funds belonged to him or to her. This is no longer true with respect to joint accounts held by husband and wife, who are each

Q We have been married for four years and are both working. Should we pool our earnings in a single joint account? And what should we do when I stop working, as I plan to do next year, to have a baby?

A Many marriages run smoothly with every penny merged in joint accounts. But it's a good idea, both psychologically and financially, to maintain separate accounts as well. With an individual account you won't be stuck if your spouse leaves or dies. As important, assuming that you live happily ever after, you'll retain a sense of independence—and the ability to buy him a gift without his knowing what it cost. You may also want to take care of your own personal expenses without explanation. Put aside some of your own earnings now, in a separate account. And keep that separate account alive in the years to come.

assumed to own half of any joint asset. But the old rules still hold for joint accounts with other people. If you have a joint account with a brother or a niece because you want that relative to have the money after your death without any estate taxes, it won't work. Keep the account to yourself and leave the money to your relative in your will.

Using a Checking Account

Whichever type of checking account you decide is right for you, there are some things you should know:

WRITING CHECKS

Checks are the equivalent of cash. Unless they are written carefully and endorsed properly, they may be cashed for the wrong amount or by the wrong person.

When you write a check, use a pen (and not the variety with erasable ink). Start as far to the left as possible in writing the amount in words, and fill in any unused space with a line. Start right next to the $ sign in filling in the amount in numbers, and don't leave excessive space between numbers or someone could fill in some extra digits. Make a record of each check—its amount, date, and purpose—just as soon as you write it. (If you're in the habit of carrying loose checks, with no stub on which to make an entry, record the check on some piece of paper and then transfer the entry to your checkbook as soon as you return home.) If you make a mistake while writing a check, don't cross it out. Tear up the check. And be sure to write "VOID" across that space in your check register.

Keep your checks, canceled checks, and checkbook in a safe place and notify your bank if they are missing. A dishonest person could make good use of your account number and samples of your signature.

Note: If you borrow a deposit slip to make a deposit, *cut out* any account number other than your own. You can't simply cross it out because the magnetic characters will be read by a computer and your money may be deposited to someone else's account.

ENDORSING CHECKS

An endorsement transfers ownership of the funds represented by the check. If you simply sign your name on the back of a check made out to you, anyone may cash it. If you place a restriction on the endorsement, however, the bank must honor the restriction. You might write "For deposit only" followed by your account number and signature (and should do so if you are depositing checks by mail); with this endorsement the check must be deposited to your account. Or, if you want to transfer the funds to someone else, you may write "Pay to the order of" and the person's name, followed by your own signature. That person may then, in turn, make the check payable to someone else by endorsing it appropriately but, whatever he or she does, your responsibility is at an end.

In any endorsement your name must be written, exactly as it appears on the check, across the left side of the back of the check. If the spelling is incorrect, write it the way it appears and then write it again, correctly, below.

BALANCING YOUR CHECKBOOK

Try to balance your checkbook within a few days after receiving your monthly statement. If you catch an error (and financial institutions do make errors) it will be much easier to correct at the outset. Many institutions, in fact, ask customers to notify them of any errors within a specified time; errors can often be corrected later, but it becomes more difficult.

The last number on your statement should be the same as the number in your checkbook for that date. If it's not the same, there are three possible reasons:

- One or more checks, written by you earlier, have not yet been returned for payment.
- One or more deposits may not have been credited.
- You or the bank has made a mistake in arithmetic.

Any or all of these things should be easy to catch. Yet balancing a checkbook is a task that throws a lot of people for a loop. (I've known people to change banks rather than reconcile a hopelessly fudged-up checkbook.) Don't let it throw you. Just follow this step-by-step method:

1. Put your returned checks in sequence by number or by date (some banks now provide statements with checks in sequence).
2. Match the returned checks against those in your checkbook. Make a list of any checks still outstanding.
3. Subtract any outstanding checks from the balance shown on your statement.
4. Check off the deposits shown on the statement against those in your checkbook. Add any deposits made after the statement date to the balance shown on your statement. Also add any interest earned, and subtract any fees charged against the account.
5. The balance shown on your statement plus any additional deposits minus any outstanding checks should equal the current balance you have in your checkbook. If it does not, check your arithmetic. And use a banker's trick if a stubborn checkbook won't balance: See if you can divide the disparity by nine. If you can, if your total is off by 45 or by 81 or by any other number divisible by nine, a simple transposition of numbers is at fault; somewhere along the way you wrote 123 when you meant to write 132 or made a similar transposition. If

you can't balance your checkbook despite your best efforts, don't overlook the possibility that the bank may have made a mistake. After rechecking your arithmetic, report the error to the bank without delay.

If you can't balance your checkbook because you can't bring yourself to do it, don't feel guilty. You won't get into too much trouble if you keep enough money in your account to cover the unexpected. At the very least, however, you should glance over your statement each month, checking off deposits and checks. I was glad I noticed the month the bank neglected recording a $400 deposit.

WHEN THE BANK KEEPS THE CANCELED CHECKS

Some banks and thrifts have stopped returning canceled checks. In a practice called truncation, or check safekeeping, the institution will keep canceled checks on file and supply you with copies you may need for such things as tax-return documentation. As a regular practice, instead of canceled checks, you get a very detailed monthly statement. Even without canceled checks to work with, however, you need to balance your checkbook. Without the checks themselves, it becomes more important than ever to keep accurate records of the checks you write. Some institutions will help in this regard by providing you with a checkbook which makes carbonless copies of checks as you write them. Others use a technology called imaging to send images of the checks rather than the actual checks, much the way some charge card issuers do.

Note: So far, at most institutions, check safekeeping is optional and you can still get your checks returned if you want them. With some institutions, however, you'll pay a monthly fee for the privilege.

WHEN A CHECK BOUNCES

If, for some reason, you don't have enough money in your account to cover a check you've written, you'll face both embarrassment and a service charge from your bank. (You may even face a service charge if you deposit someone else's check and it bounces—a good reason for depositing checks promptly.) You can avoid the embarrassment and service charges, however, if you (1) enter every check you write (and, on a joint account, get your partner to do so as well), (2) balance your account promptly each month so that you'll know your balance at all times, and (3) understand that we live in an electronic age and that it's no longer safe to write a check one day and deposit funds to cover it two days later—your check may, embarrassingly, clear in the meantime. It also helps if you understand the operating regulations banks impose (see below).

USING YOUR DEPOSITED FUNDS

You may think that once you've deposited funds to your account you can safely write checks on those funds. But you may or may not be right. Under federal rules, banks, thrifts and credit unions can hold most deposited funds for up to five days before crediting them to your account. During this time you can't write any checks on those deposited funds without running the risk of a bounce (technically, in this case, writing checks on uncollected funds, also subject to a charge).

How quickly funds must be made available to you depends on their source. In general, you can write checks against cash deposits, money orders, government checks and checks drawn on local institutions on the second business day after deposit, and tap checks written on nonlocal institutions on the fifth business day. The rules are the same whether you make your deposit at a teller's window or at an ATM, except for a specific wrinkle with ATM deposits: the second-business-day rule applies if you make a deposit at your own bank's ATM, the fifth-business-day if you use another bank's machine.

These are maximum hold periods; many banks permit more rapid access to your funds. Compare the policies of different institutions before you decide where to do your banking. Also, if you have other good reasons for using an institution adhering to the maximum hold times, ask if other accounts or certificates of deposit you hold in the same institution may be used as collateral for uncleared deposits. If not, and if you need the funds available, try converting a check to cash before you deposit it—and tell the bank that you will be drawing against those funds.

Note: Your bank, thrift or credit union can hold deposited funds for an extra four days if you redeposit a check that was returned unpaid, have over-

Q My monthly mortgage payments include property tax and homeowners insurance premiums, which my bank is supposed to pay as they come due. But the bank is consistently late in making the payments. I've received an overdue tax notice from my town, and my homeowner's insurance was actually allowed to expire. Is there anything I can do?

A Sit down with an officer of the bank and discuss the problem. Offer to pay these bills yourself directly and send the bank proof of payment; this will reduce the institution's paperwork, so agreement may be forthcoming. If not, however, and the bank continues to be negligent, contact the institution's president. If you still get nowhere, write to your state banking commission. Or contact federal regulatory authorities. There's a splintering of responsibility among agencies handling thrifts and banks, federally chartered and state-chartered institutions, but the Federal Reserve Board will take all complaints and either handle them where appropriate or pass them along to the proper agency; write to the Division of Consumer and Community Affairs, Federal Reserve Board, Washington, DC 20551.

drawn your account repeatedly in the last six months, or deposit checks totalling more than $5,000 on any one day.

STOPPING A CHECK

A persuasive door-to-door salesman has talked you into buying an elaborate set of pots and pans. You've signed a contract and given him a check. Now, after he's left, you've had second thoughts. What do you do?

The first thing you do is notify the company, in writing, that you've changed your mind about the purchase (consumer protection laws give you three days, after a purchase in your home, to change your mind and cancel the contract). The second thing you do, just to be on the safe side, is stop payment on your check. You do this by notifying your bank, first by telephone and then in writing, that you want the check stopped. With that notification the bank should refuse to release the funds if the check is presented for payment.

But the bank incurs expenses in stopping a check, and you can expect those expenses to be passed on to you. Most institutions charge $10 to $20. So take advantage of the stop-payment privilege if you've really made a mistake, but don't use it lightly. And do find out, when you open your account, what this charge will be.

Note: Be sure to ask how long a stop-payment order is effective. If the check has not come in during this period, you may want to renew the order. (Many banks will not honor a check more than 90 days old for payment, but some will. And some tellers make mistakes.)

AUTOMATIC PAYROLL DEPOSIT AND TELEPHONE TRANSFER

You may, at most institutions, make arrangements for automatic deposit of payroll and Social Security checks. This can be a great convenience.

You may also, at many institutions, arrange by telephone to have funds transferred from your savings account to your checking account. This, too, can

Q My employer uses a payroll deposit program under which my paycheck is automatically deposited in the bank he has designated. I prefer my own bank and do not feel I should have to pay a transfer or service fee to his bank. What can I do?

A Direct deposit programs like this one were, until a few years ago, limited to the single institution in which they were established. Today, with almost all of the nation's banks linked to an automated clearinghouse through which funds can be transferred by wire, all you should have to do is go into your own bank and say you want to arrange automatic transfer from your employer's bank to your bank. There should be no charge for this service.

be a great convenience, since you can keep funds earning interest until they are needed. If you have a market rate account (see page 69) or have combined your savings and checking accounts into an interest-earning NOW account, this transfer privilege may, of course, be unnecessary.

Electronic Banking

Banking by telephone and by computer was introduced with a big splash some years back, then sputtered to a stop. Most of us didn't own computers and weren't interested in changing our ways.

Today you can bank electronically without actually owning a computer, simply hooking up to your bank's computer over the telephone. Or, if you're technologically inclined, you can do your banking through your home computer. One in five of the largest banks in the United States offer some form of electronic banking, at a median monthly fee of $9.50.

If you choose to pay bills this way, you won't get back your canceled checks but you will get a detailed descriptive statement that spells out whom you paid and when, in the order in which you authorized payment. If your bill-paying is from a NOW or regular savings account, moreover, you'll earn interest on your money until the bills are paid. You also, of course, do away with the tedious task of writing checks.

Some people are nervous about telephone bill-paying, fearful they will lose control of their accounts. But specific authorization for each bill, plus a personal customer code, keeps you in charge.

But there are still some problems to be resolved before automatic bill-paying is totally worry-free. Consider these potential problems:

- Because bill-paying by telephone entails different procedures—you're not returning a bill stub with a check—some businesses find it expensive to process. Some even refuse to do so. Some banks, moreover, will make automatic payments only to companies on a predetermined list and not, for instance, to out-of-state companies. So you won't be able to pay all your bills by telephone just yet, even if you want to do so; you'll still have to use your checkbook.
- The process is not yet fully automatic, and your bank may simply write a check and mail it for you. Be sure you authorize payment far enough in advance of the due date so that you don't incur interest charges when the bank's check is slow to arrive.
- When you pay bills electronically, you can't stop payment if things go wrong. If your purchase is defective or your order is not delivered, you're in the same position as if you've paid cash; you'll have to argue it out with the vendor. (In fact, in any instance when you think

you might have a problem, charging your purchase to a credit card is the safest route.)

Paying bills by telephone is, of course, banking at home. But the use of video screens takes the process a step further.

At its best, this use of computers encompasses more than just banking. At most banks with the service, customers can authorize payment of bills, check the balance in a checking or savings account, or see how much credit is available on a Visa card—all by dialing the bank's computer and getting a visual display on a home television screen or monitor. But you don't even have to go through your own bank. Customers of Prodigy, the interactive computer service sponsored by IBM and Sears, Roebuck and Co., have a choice of two banking services: Full-service electronic banking through one of about 15 banks, if you have an account with that bank; and a bill-paying service you can use with any bank. It costs $12.95 a month or about $120 a year to enroll in Prodigy—which provides many other services as well—plus $9 to $12 a month for banking. Other free-standing services—one example is called Checkfree—offer similar bill-paying services to the technologically inclined.

AUTOMATIC TELLER MACHINES (ATMs)

Perhaps the most visible symbol of the electronic age, these teller machines stand on street corners, in office-building lobbies, and in supermarkets across the United States.

To use an ATM you must have a card and a personal identification number, both issued by your bank or thrift. You can use the card, together with the code number, to make a deposit, to transfer funds from one account to another, or to make a cash withdrawal. If you need cash at an hour when banks are closed, the ATM can be particularly convenient.

Note: When ATMs were new, banks were pushing their use; at least one briefly suggested a fee for using a human teller. Today, more and more banks are charging for using an ATM. Some banks are charging at their own machines. But the most common charges, of 50 cents or a dollar, apply when you use a machine that does not belong to your bank. A customer of one New York City bank, making three withdrawals a month at another bank's machine, could spend over $34 a year just on ATM transaction fees.

Caution Is Required

Beyond monitoring how much convenience is costing, you must be careful in using an ATM:

- Select an identification number that you can easily remember (so you won't have to write it down anywhere) but one that other people won't guess. A favorite aunt's birth date might be a good choice. Don't share the number, or someone else might be able to tap your account. Don't even let anyone look over your shoulder while you're using the machine. Be unfriendly, if necessary, but insist on privacy.

- Be doubly sure to enter every single transaction in your checkbook. Keep an accurate running tally, along with the machine-issued transaction records (be sure they're accurate before you leave the machine), and reconcile your statement promptly. Report any errors to the bank without delay.
- Notify the bank or thrift immediately if your card is lost or stolen. Federal rules limit your liability to $50 as long as you notify the bank within two business days after you learn of the loss or theft; after this two-day period, your liability escalates sharply. If you do not report the loss within two business days after you realize the card is missing, you could lose as much as $500 because of an unauthorized withdrawal. Worse yet, if you do not report an unauthorized transfer or withdrawal within 60 days after your statement is mailed to you, you risk losing all the money in your account plus any unused portion of an overdraft line of credit.

When automatic teller machines were new, they malfunctioned fairly often. When they were first introduced, too, they were particularly vulnerable to crime.

Today the mechanical aspects of ATMs have been greatly improved. But you should use common sense. If you make a cash deposit at a machine and the machine malfunctions, it may be virtually impossible to trace the transaction and get proper credit; make deposits by check at the machine and save cash deposits for a trip to the bank.

The security aspects are still an issue. Be careful. If the machine is in a locked area, don't be polite and hold the door open for others; it's locked for a reason. And stay clear of isolated or poorly lit cash machines; they're a magnet for criminals.

DEBIT CARDS

The traditional credit card enables you to make purchases, be billed for them later, and pay for them still later. The marvel of electronic funds transfer, however, makes it possible to pay for purchases instantly with a debit card used to draw funds from your bank account. (Until more merchants have the electronic technology, however, the card is used to authorize a transfer of funds; the transfer itself is not quite instant.)

The debit card is, in fact, a substitute for a check. It provides access to your account. Unlike a check, however, it may be accepted without a hassle in places where you are a stranger. Debit cards (occasionally called deposit access cards) are issued by the major credit card companies (Visa and MasterCard) and may be acquired from your local bank or thrift. They are also issued by brokerage firms and by oil companies. A monthly or annual fee may be charged.

While a debit card has some advantages for people who don't like credit (you don't "borrow" and there's no bill at the end of the month) and for people who travel a great deal, it does rob you of the "float"—that interval between a purchase by check or by credit card and the actual transfer of funds from your account to pay for the purchase. The float on a check may be just a few days. On credit card purchases it may be as long as two months. Either way, during the interval your money is working for you.

A debit card, in another sense, is like cash. If you buy something with a credit card and it proves defective, you can withhold payment until the matter is set straight. If the merchant has already been paid, you've lost a negotiating edge.

If you do use a debit card, remember to keep a written record of your transactions. Use of the card is equivalent to writing a check, but without a checkbook entry. And keep track of the card; as with ATM cards (which may some day become all-purpose debit cards), your liability for a lost or stolen card is potentially far greater than with a credit card.

 ## KEY POINTS

- As financial institutions compete for your dollars, you owe it to yourself to compare carefully. Look at service, costs, convenience, and stability.

- Open a checking account as soon as you have bills to pay on a regular basis; funnel all income and outgo through a checking account and you'll keep track of your cash flow.

- Don't keep much money in a checking account that does not pay interest, but don't open an interest-earning account unless you will earn enough to offset any fees you will pay.

- Keep accurate records and balance your checkbook promptly.

- Use new financial services such as automatic teller machines and debit cards with care; written records become doubly important when you're dealing with electronic gadgetry and instant access to your accounts.

CHAPTER 4

Savings Accounts, Time Deposits, and Other Bank Services

The passbook savings account has been the basis of American thrift for generations. Long before checking accounts became universally acceptable, savings accounts were widespread. Today, even when higher yields are available elsewhere, a great many people maintain some of their cash savings, if not all, in a savings account at a neighborhood bank or thrift. Parents pass the message on to children, who are encouraged to deposit both earnings and cash gifts in a savings account.

Q My 11-year-old daughter never wants to put money in her savings account. She says, if she does, the money just "gets stuck." How can I encourage her to save?

A Children have to learn how to spend before they can appreciate the wisdom of saving. They have to see what small amounts of money can do before they will understand that saving large amounts makes it possible to do more. Your daughter may be rebelling because her money really does get stuck. Do you ever let her take money out of the savings account? You should, because savings aren't meant to be a dead end. They're meant to be a useful tool. Take your daughter to the bank, if you haven't done so yet, and let her handle a transaction for herself. Give her a sense of participating in the banking process and she should be more interested.

Compound Interest

Your money grows in a savings account because interest is added to the principal on deposit on a regular basis. Interest is **compounded** when, at the end of each interest period, it is calculated on the sum of both principal and interest already in the account. This compounding is what makes the "effective annual yield" on a savings account greater than the stated rate of interest (see Table 4.1).

Table 4.1: The Power of Compound Interest

If you deposit $1,000 and add nothing more to it, this is what you'll have at various interest rates, compounded annually:

Years	2%	4%	6%	8%	10%	12%	14%
1	1,020	1,040	1,060	1,080	1,100	1,120	1,140
2	1,040	1,082	1,124	1,166	1,210	1,254	1,300
3	1,061	1,125	1,191	1,260	1,331	1,405	1,482
4	1,082	1,170	1,262	1,360	1,464	1,574	1,689
5	1,104	1,217	1,338	1,469	1,611	1,762	1,925
6	1,126	1,265	1,419	1,587	1,772	1,974	2,195
7	1,149	1,316	1,504	1,714	1,949	2,211	2,502
8	1,172	1,369	1,594	1,851	2,144	2,476	2,853
9	1,195	1,423	1,689	1,999	2,358	2,773	3,252
10	1,219	1,480	1,791	2,159	2,594	3,106	3,707

The power of compound interest alone will just about double your money in nine years at 8 percent, compounded annually. Even when interest rates are much lower, the power of compound interest can be impressive. Benjamin Franklin, according to the American Bankers Association, left $5,000 to the residents of Boston in 1791, with the understanding that it should be allowed to accumulate for a hundred years. By 1891 the $5,000 had grown to $322,000. A school was built, and $92,000 was set aside for a second hundred years of growth. In 1960, this second century fund had reached $1,400,000. As Franklin put it, in anticipation: "Money makes money and the money that money makes makes more money."

If you want to determine how long it will take your money to double at various rates of interest, use what bankers call the Rule of 72. Divide the quoted rate of return into 72 and you'll have the number of years required to double your money at that rate of interest, assuming that interest is compounded annually (see Table 4.2). When interest is compounded more frequently, as it often is, your money will double faster.

Table 4.2: The Rule of 72

If you divide 72 by the rate of interest on your savings, you'll know how long it will take to double your money if interest is compounded annually:

Rate of interest	Years it takes to double money
2%	$72 \div 2 = 36.0$ years
3%	$72 \div 3 = 24.0$
4%	$72 \div 4 = 18.0$
5%	$72 \div 5 = 14.4$
6%	$72 \div 6 = 12.0$
7%	$72 \div 7 = 10.2$
8%	$72 \div 8 = 9.0$
9%	$72 \div 9 = 8.0$
10%	$72 \div 10 = 7.2$
11%	$72 \div 11 = 6.5$
12%	$72 \div 12 = 6.0$
13%	$72 \div 13 = 5.5$
14%	$72 \div 14 = 5.1$

INTEREST RATES

Interest rates on savings accounts used to be regulated by law, but all federally imposed interest rate ceilings have now been removed. The removal of regulatory rate ceilings, however, does not necessarily mean an increase in the interest rates that financial institutions will pay. All it means is that they may set their own rates. Some, eager to attract and keep customers, will offer competitive rates. Others will not.

When rates are going up, some banks may raise rates on new accounts but not on existing ones; if this happens to you, close your old account and open a new one. Some customers don't think it's worth the bother to switch from a low-paying institution to one more in tune with the times. Such customers may be right if, in return, they receive other valuable services, such as free checking. Otherwise, such laziness makes little sense. You work hard for your money; you should keep your money working hard for you.

Some institutions pay a higher rate on statement savings, in order to encourage their use (they cost less to administer), than on passbook accounts. With a statement account you don't have a passbook. Instead you receive a monthly computerized record of deposits, withdrawals, and interest payments, much like a checking account statement. Look for an institution that pays a competitive rate, whichever kind of account you prefer.

Finding the Best Rate

We've seen that all savings accounts are not equal. But even those that appear to be equal may not be. Finding the best interest rate for your savings account funds, in short, is not simply a matter of going to the institution with the highest advertised rate. You have to dig a little deeper:

- Penalties and service fees can reduce your yield. Some banks impose service charges for low-balance accounts; others allow only one free withdrawal from a small savings account in a given month, then charge a fee for each subsequent withdrawal. Some banks charge a fee if an account is closed before it's been open for six months or a year.

- The more often interest is compounded, the more money you earn. Daily compounding pays more than quarterly compounding, and quarterly compounding pays more than annual compounding. While you'll do best with daily compounding, the difference is actually insignificant for most people. If interest rates scoot upward again, and if you keep many thousands of dollars in your savings account, how often interest is compounded may matter. Otherwise, don't worry about it.

- You will earn more if interest is computed on all the money you keep in the account rather than on just the lowest balance you have in the account during the interest period—a favorite ploy of some banks until recently. Under the Truth-in-Savings legislation effective in 1993, in fact, banks are prohibited from using any method that does not pay interest on the full balance in the account each day. This method—sometimes called day of deposit to day of withdrawal—is the most favorable for consumers.

Q If I invest directly, I want my money to go to activities I approve—not, for example, to companies that harm the environment. Is there some way I can control what a bank does with my money?

A In most cases, no. But a few institutions are coming up with ways to attract depositors who feel the way you do. For example, Vermont National Bank in Brattleboro, reachable toll-free at (800) 544-7108, has a Socially Responsible Banking Fund. Depositors who designate their wish to participate in this fund know that their money—whether it's in savings or checking or money market accounts, certificates of deposit or Individual Retirement Accounts—will be used only to aid organizations and individuals in the areas of affordable housing, conservation and the environment, agriculture, education and small business. Uninvested cash balances are held in socially screened investments.

Losing Your Savings

The power of compound interest works for you only as long as you keep your savings account active. You don't have to make constant transactions, but you do have to do *something* every couple of years—make a deposit or withdrawal, present your passbook to the bank or thrift to have interest credited, simply write a letter saying that you are alive and well—or you may find your name on one of those lengthy published lists of "lost" depositors. If your name does appear on one of those lists after a period of inactivity in your account (the precise period varies from state to state, but it can be as short as a couple of years) and if you fail to respond, your money will be turned over to the state under the "law of escheat."

It isn't just vagabonds who can lose their property this way. According to reports some years ago, the dormant accounts of two movie stars and the then governor of California had been turned over to the state. Interested observers thought that these particular depositors should have been easy to find.

Should you be inattentive enough to lose an account this way, you can still reclaim your property from the state. But you will need documentary proof of your ownership. And interest stops accumulating, in most states, at the point at which the property is transferred to the state. Don't let this happen to your hard-earned savings.

There's another penalty for the inattentive. Long before funds are turned over to the state, some banks and thrifts stop paying interest on dormant accounts. Others levy service charges. (There seem to be service charges these days for too much activity and for too little. I wonder if anyone has identified how much banking is just right?) Congressional hearings in 1980 focused attention on this practice and evoked a considerable protest from consumer advocates. A star witness was a 12-year-old Minnesota boy whose entire $5 account had been wiped out by service charges; the boy and his parents were

Q I switched banks to get a "free" checking account, then found that the bank charged a fee every time my balance fell below $500. Are they allowed to do this?

A Yes, but they are *not* allowed, under Truth in Savings legislation effective in 1993, to advertise such an account as free. Checking accounts can be advertised as free if they have charges for bounced checks and stopped payments, but not if they contain hidden charges such as those for falling below a minimum balance. You are entitled to accurate advertising and to full disclosure of all the terms of your bank account. Complain to your bank.

never told of this particular bank practice. Since then, if anything, fees have
gotten worse, although recent Truth in Savings legislation makes banks disclose the fees rather than keeping them secret. Moral: Pay attention to your
bank accounts, reading the small-print notices that often accompany statements, and keep those accounts active.

BANK FAILURE

Until the 1930s, if a bank or savings institution failed its depositors
would lose some or all of their money, but for more than half a century
individual banks and thrifts have protected their depositors by one form or
another of deposit insurance. There's federal insurance on banks and thrifts
from the Federal Deposit Insurance Corporation (FDIC) and on credit unions
from the National Credit Union Share Insurance Fund (labeled NCUSIF or,
sometimes, NCUA for the National Credit Union Administration that runs the
insurance fund).

All insure deposits up to $100,000 in any one person's name; you may
have several accounts in the same institution, each insured, if the accounts are
in different forms (such as an individual account, a joint account and an IRA).
All are backed by the U.S. government and all are safe, although credit union
deposit insurance has more funds backing its guarantees than the failure-
plagued FDIC does. State insurance plans and private deposit insurance, carried by some institutions, are a bit riskier in an era of institutional instability;
depositors in Rhode Island learned this the hard way not long ago when a couple of failures wiped out the state insurance fund. But keep an eye on federal
deposit insurance rules, too; some analysts believe these rules have made

Q When my husband was a little boy his uncle opened a savings
account for him. The bank book never turned up after his
uncle's death, and we don't even know the name of the bank. Is
there any way we can trace the account? And could my husband still
get whatever money is in the account?

A Write to the Controller's Office (usually in the state capital) of
the state in which the account was located (probably the state
where the uncle lived at the time you think he opened the account).
Give the name and address of the person who opened the account,
your husband's name, and the year in which you think the account
was opened. If the state can locate the account (states keep permanent records and will make every effort to do so) your husband
can still claim the funds. Interest, however, probably stopped accruing when the state took over.

Americans too complacent about placing money in institutions that aren't well managed, and that restrictions should be imposed.

Special-Purpose Accounts

In addition to regular savings accounts, banks and thrift institutions offer accounts for systematic saving, trust and custodial accounts, and various high-earnings accounts.

CLUB ACCOUNTS

Many banks and thrifts offer Christmas/Hanukkah Clubs; many also offer Vacation Clubs or other special-purpose savings accounts. For years such accounts paid no interest. Many people used them, nonetheless, for the week-by-week saving they encouraged. Today club accounts usually do pay interest, although the interest may be less than that on a regular savings account.

If you feel that you need the discipline of a regular coupon book to make you save, by all means use one of these accounts. But keep in mind that you can encourage yourself to save in other ways as well. You might try automatic payroll deductions. You might even try a "coupon book" of your own devising; just put a savings account deposit slip in with the bills you pay and write out a deposit every time you pay your bills. You'll be surprised how the savings add up.

TRUST ACCOUNTS

Savings accounts may also be opened by you "in trust for" someone else, such as a minor child. You control the account during your lifetime (and pay any income taxes due on the interest); the proceeds are payable directly to your beneficiary upon your death. Since you control the account, you may change that beneficiary at any time. You may also close the account.

CUSTODIAL ACCOUNTS

A custodial account is also a means of transferring your assets to someone else, but without the same degree of flexibility. Once you set up a custodial account, the funds in that account legally belong to the person named. Interest earned on the account is taxable to that person—except that investment earnings over $1,000, in the account of a child under age 14, are taxed at the parent's rate.

You might, for instance, establish a custodial account for a child's college funds (see Chapter 17) or to help support an elderly parent. As custodian, you have access to the account and can determine how it is to be invested (you might, for instance, want a higher-interest time deposit instead of passbook savings, or opt for an investment in equities), but you won't be able to withdraw the funds except to use for the child's or parent's benefit.

If you serve as the custodian on funds that you give, the account will be included in your estate—and possibly subject to estate tax—if you die before your parent does or before your child reaches legal age. A way around this: Name a trusted relative as custodian, then proceed as before.

TIME DEPOSITS

Time deposits (TDs) or certificates of deposit (CDs) are another form of savings account offered by traditional financial institutions. There is a wide variety available, in intervals from a single week to many years and in amounts from $100 to $10,000 and more.

The universal ingredient of these accounts is your commitment to leave your money on deposit with the institution for a fixed period of time in exchange for a rate of interest which is often higher than that paid on regular savings. In early 1982, when the interest rate on regular savings accounts was capped at 5.5 percent, some time deposits were paying over 14 percent. This spread no longer exists. In 1993, regular savings accounts pay about 3 percent and certificates of deposit up to a year or so in duration not much more. But CDs can be used to lock in yields, during a time of declining interest rates, before they fall further.

If you're unwilling to commit to specific CD maturities because you don't know where interest rates are headed, try a strategy called "laddering." Divide your investable cash among instruments with staggered maturity dates, and you can benefit whatever interest rates do. If you have $10,000 to put in CDs, for example, put $2,000 apiece into five separate CDs maturing at one year intervals. This strategy works with other fixed-income investments as well; see Chapter 5 for more details.

Q After I inherited $140,000 from my father, I deliberately took certificates of deposit at two different banks to be sure I was covered by deposit insurance. Now the two banks have merged. What happens to the insurance on my CDs?

A Customers with deposits at merging institutions have dual coverage for six months after the merger or, in the case of CDs, until the first maturity date after the end of the six month period. You're insured for the full $140,000 until the first CD matures. At that time, you may want to move one of the CDs to another institution.

Note, too, that the new owner of a failed bank can change the interest rate being paid on CDs. If the rate is changed, you should be notified within two weeks; if it's lowered below a level you care to live with, you can withdraw the funds without penalty.

There are things to know, however, before you buy:

■ The interest rate on these accounts is fixed for the life of the certificate. If interest rates are coming down, that's a good time to lock in a higher yield. If, however, interest rates are continuing to climb, you might be better off with your money in a money market fund or account.

■ Maximum yield is achieved when interest is compounded. If it's not, and you want the particular time deposit anyway, see if you can either withdraw the interest periodically or have it automatically transferred to a regular savings account, where it will compound.

■ Interest rates vary considerably, and you may find the best rate in another city. Long-distance banking can make sense on a time deposit, but you should be sure that the institution is covered by federal deposit insurance; many insolvent thrifts kept their doors open longer than they should have by beefing up deposits from out-of-state, but then folded anyway.

■ You can usually withdraw your money before the maturity date, but only with a penalty. The specific penalty depends on rules set by the individual institution. Don't buy a certificate without understanding the rules on early withdrawal. Don't buy one with money you know you're going to need. And don't buy one at an institution that won't permit withdrawal even with a penalty.

Q Interest rates are so low right now that CDs don't seem to make sense. Is there a safe investment that pays higher interest?

A Have you thought of U.S. Government Savings Bonds? Uncle Sam's familiar EE bonds pay a guaranteed minimum interest rate (currently 4 percent), a rate that compares favorably with current savings and CD rates. If market rates go up, and you've held the bonds at least five years, you earn a variable rate of interest that can be higher still. What's more, unlike CDs, EE bonds are exempt from state and local income taxes; federal tax is owed on the income but can be deferred until you cash in the bonds.

EE bonds purchased between November 1986 and February 1993 have a minimum guaranteed interest rate of 6 percent; those purchased through October 1986 earn at least 7.5 percent.

■ Institutions have different procedures when maturity dates roll around. Most, but not all, will notify you in advance. Some will automatically roll the account over into a new time deposit of equal length unless you notify them within a specified time (often ten days) that you want the funds. Find out which procedure your bank follows. And keep a record of maturity dates.

You may see ads for a variety of "new" CD products, designed by banks to retain customers turned off by low interest rates. Among them: the "rising-rate" CD, with predetermined interest-rate increases every six months over a period of two-and-a-half to three years; the "callable" CD, which pays higher-than-average rates, but can be called after a year at the bank's discretion; the "bump-up" CD, which allows you the one-time option of raising the CD's interest rate to current levels if rates rise; and the "indexed" CD, where the rate is indexed to a specific indicator such as a six-month Treasury bill or the prime rate.

These new CDs may appear attractive at first glance, but they are really marketing devices for banks and must be examined carefully. The rising-rate CD starts off with a lower-than-usual interest rate, for example, so that a traditional CD of the same length may actually have a greater overall return.

Other Bank Services

Both banks and thrifts offer a great many services beyond checking and savings accounts. As deregulation takes hold, and financial institutions move into such customer service areas as stock brokerage, the service smorgasbord will become still more extensive. Right now, however, you can find all or most of the services discussed below at your neighborhood bank or thrift.

LOANS

One of the reasons it makes good sense to do most of your banking in one place is to establish a reputation as a good customer—a reputation that can help you secure a loan.

Banks and thrifts offer many types of loans. There are those dedicated to a particular purpose: a mortgage, a home improvement loan, an automobile loan, a college loan. Most of these are secured loans—the mortgage is backed by the house, the auto loan by the car. But you can also get personal or unsecured loans at a bank or thrift. Details will be found in Chapter 7, on credit.

Always consider the value of your savings as collateral for a loan before taking out another form of loan. If, for instance, you need to withdraw a substantial amount shortly before interest will be credited to your account, you can take a passbook loan for that amount and come out ahead.

BANK CARDS

Bank cards, such as Visa and MasterCard, are nationally available and issued by both banks and thrifts (as well as by unrelated institutions, such as telephone companies, automobile manufacturers, and retailers). You don't have to have an account at a particular institution in order to get a bank credit card, but it sometimes helps, especially if you are establishing a credit record for the first time. Details on bank credit cards will also be found in Chapter 7.

SAFE DEPOSIT BOXES

Boxes of various sizes may be rented for the safekeeping of valuables. Rates are moderate and may, if the box is used to store items that produce taxable income (such as securities), be tax-deductible. But rates do vary. A 1992 survey by the New York City Department of Consumer Affairs found annual rents on the same size box varying from $17 to $35. So it pays to shop around.

Securely located in the institution's vault, safe deposit boxes are accessible only to the person whose signature is on file and who has the key necessary to open the box. It takes two keys to open each box, one retained by the vault attendant and the other by the box owner. Neither will work alone.

What should be kept in a safe deposit box? A good rule of thumb is to keep valuable items (seldom-worn jewelry, securities, etc.) and difficult-to-replace items (birth and marriage certificates, the deed to your house, etc.) in a box. An equally good rule is *not* to keep items that will be needed right after the safe-renter's death (the original of the person's will, life insurance policies, a cemetery deed or burial instructions) in that person's safe deposit box. The box will probably be sealed at the death of its owner and, although it may be

Q We made an application for a mortgage, and submitted several hundred dollars in fees, shortly before the lender went out of business and merged with another lender. What happens now?

A FDIC insurance covers only deposits, although it has a policy of making an immediate payment of up to $500 for claims such as yours. If your mortgage application fees were for more than that, you may be out of luck.

What's more, if you already had a loan in place when a bank went under, you could also be in trouble. Many loans have "call" provisions, meaning that the acquiring institution can insist on immediate payment. It's as important to look into the stability of an institution (see pp. 64-66) when taking a loan as it is when making a deposit.

opened to remove documents such as these, you may have to get a court order to do so. Laws vary from state to state, so check the rules before you rent your safe deposit box.

Check the rules, too, before you rent a box jointly, even with your spouse. In many states the box will be sealed upon the death of the first co-owner, until the tax authorities are satisfied. A better idea: Rent the box in one partner's name, with the other named as deputy with permission to enter. You'll have equal access, but you'll avoid the possible complications of joint ownership.

TRAVELER'S CHECKS

Many banks, as a convenience to customers, sell traveler's checks. When you buy traveler's checks, usually for a nominal fee of $1 per $100 of checks (although some banks offer traveler's checks free to customers while others have occasional special promotions during which the checks are free), you sign each one in the presence of the seller. Then, when you use each check, you sign it again so that the two signatures can be compared. Traveler's checks are a convenient and safe way to carry currency when you travel— although you may also want to carry an automatic teller machine (ATM) card to withdraw money from your own bank account. Some merchants won't accept traveler's checks; some (especially overseas) give less than the going rate of exchange.

And remember: there's little point in keeping extra traveler's checks on hand after you return home. You've paid for them, after all, so the only bene-ficiary of your failure to use them is the issuing company.

Q Recent news of a vault break-in, where the contents of many safe deposit boxes were stolen, made me wonder: How safe are these boxes? Is the bank responsible if a theft does take place?

A A safe deposit box in a bank vault is undoubtedly the safest place for your important documents and valuable possessions. But break-ins do occasionally occur. A few banks carry special insur-ance against this risk, but most don't; they are not responsible for a loss—as the small print on the safe deposit agreement will tell you. Your own homeowner's policy will cover loss up to its limits (such as $1,000 for jewelry) just as if the loss took place at your home. If you want additional coverage, consult your insurance agent; you may be able to purchase insurance specifically for the contents of your safe deposit box.

CERTIFIED CHECKS

A certified check is a personal check stamped "Certified" by your bank after funds are set aside from your account to cover the amount. You will probably have to pay a service charge to secure this guarantee, but a certified check may be required, for instance, when you take title to a house.

CASHIER'S CHECKS

A cashier's check is a similar guarantee of payment, useful if you don't have a checking account. In this case you pay the bank and it then makes payment out of its own funds. When you purchase this service, you specify the person or company to whom the check is to be made out. And you should keep a carbon or stub for your records.

MONEY ORDERS

Money orders are a means of transferring small sums of money without using either cash or a personal check. Like a check, the money order shows the name of the purchaser, the name of the person who is to receive the payment, and the amount to be paid. You buy a money order by paying the issuing bank (or post office) the face amount plus a small fee.

U.S. GOVERNMENT SAVINGS BONDS

Banks and thrifts sell and redeem U.S. Government Savings Bonds. These bonds (also often available through regular payroll deductions) offer a

Q My daughter moved to another state and, on my suggestion, secured a cashier's check to open her new bank account. We both thought that doing it this way would enable her to write checks right away. Instead, her checks bounced. What went wrong?

A When a new account is opened with a certified or cashier's check (sometimes even with cash), many banks insist on waiting a week or so to make sure both the check and the depositor are legitimate. To secure immediate access to funds in a new location, either buy enough traveler's checks, before you move, to cover immediate needs and to open a new account, or ask your current bank to wire fund's directly to the new bank. You can use your current bank's cash machine in your new town, but cash withdrawals are usually limited and may not be sufficient. In any case, keep your present account in force until all outstanding checks have cleared. Then you can have the balance wired to your new bank and credited to your account.

systematic way of saving small amounts. The interest on Series EE bonds accumulates and is paid at redemption; the interest rate has been raised over the years and is currently a variable yield tied to an index of 5-year Treasury bonds. The interest on Series HH bonds, a fixed-income bond often used for retirement income, is payable semiannually by check.

Other investments may earn more but you may find U.S. Savings Bonds, especially the popular EE series, a convenient and secure way to invest. If you are interested in Series EE bonds, these are the things you should know:

- Series EE bonds are now issued at a minimum purchase price of $25; this bond is worth $50 at maturity.
- Although bonds are designed as a long-term investment, you are not locked in. Bonds may be redeemed at any time after six months from issue date, although you will earn a higher rate of interest if you hold the bonds at least five years.
- Bonds earn interest from the first day of the month in which they are purchased. This means that you can earn double interest for almost a month by leaving money in your savings account or money market fund until the last business day of the month, then buying bonds.
- The bonds are exempt from state and local income taxes; if you live in a high-tax state, this could add appreciably to your yield.
- The earned interest is subject to federal income tax, but the tax on EE bonds may be deferred, if you choose to do so, until you redeem the

Q My late father bought a number of U.S. Savings Bonds in both our names. Is the value taxable as part of his estate? Or do the bonds simply belong to me, with no estate tax due?

A You automatically became the sole owner of the bonds upon your father's death. You may then keep the bonds as they are, have them reissued in your name alone or with another co-owner or beneficiary, or cash them in immediately. Whatever you choose to do, the value of the bonds (their redemption value on the date of his death) is included in your father's gross estate, and estate taxes may be due. Income taxes are something else. The income tax liability on all the interest the bonds ever earned will pass to you, and will be payable when you redeem the bonds, unless the executor of your father's estate chooses to pay the tax due on the interest earned until his death. If this is done, then you will owe income tax only on the interest earned from the date of your father's death until you redeem the bonds.

bonds. **Note:** If you are buying bonds for a child and do not expect to claim the tax exemption for EE bonds used for college tuition (see Chapter 17), it may be wise to declare the tax right from the beginning. Buy the bonds in the child's name. Then file a federal income tax form on behalf of the youngster in the first year (keep the form until the bonds are redeemed); there will be no tax due unless the child has other income, but you will establish the intent to pay the tax and no further forms need to be filed. If your child already owns bonds on which no tax return has ever been filed, you may file a return now and pay the tax on the interest earned up to this point. It's worth doing before your child leaves school for full-time employment and a higher tax bracket.

■ Although Series EE bonds are issued with a maturity date, the date on which interest stops accruing, maturity dates have usually been extended (see Table 4.3). The oldest bonds, E bonds issued during World War II, paid interest for a total of forty years. If you have older bonds which no longer earn interest, cash them in—or swap them for HH bonds, start receiving semiannual income, and defer paying tax on the accrued interest.

Table 4.3: Maturity Dates for Savings Bonds

Final maturity dates on U.S. Savings Bonds used to be a hodgepodge, as the Treasury Department extended different issues at different times. Now there is uniformity:

Series E bonds issued before December 1965 earn interest for 40 years.
Series E and EE bonds issued after November 1965 earn interest for 30 years.
Series H bonds issued between 1959 and 1979 earn interest for 30 years.
Series HH bonds issued since 1980 earn interest for 20 years.

■ You may buy Series EE bonds as an individual, as an individual with a named beneficiary, or as a co-owner. If you have either a beneficiary or a co-owner, then the bonds will not be part of your estate for probate purposes; they will still be counted, however, in calculating whether estate tax is due.

■ Bonds should be kept in a safe place, such as a safe deposit box. And you should keep a written record of the bonds you own. If you lose a bond, however, you may be able to secure a replacement. Write to the Bureau of the Public Debt, 200 Third St., Parkersburg, WV 26101. The more information you can supply—the denomination of the missing bond or bonds, the year of purchase, etc.—the faster you will receive a reply.

LIFE INSURANCE

Over-the-counter life insurance (Savings Bank Life or SBLI), frequently less expensive than comparable insurance available elsewhere, has been sold in mutual savings banks in Massachusetts, New York, and Connecticut for many years. An additional 15 or so states now permit banks and thrifts to make life insurance policies available to their customers. It may be convenient to buy life insurance through your bank, but you should compare the policy with those available through a life insurance agent (see Chapter 18).

MUTUAL FUNDS AND ANNUITIES

As part of the same competitive push to attract deposits, some banks and thrifts now offer mutual funds and/or annuities to their customers, either directly or through an affiliated company. Mutual funds are available in larger institutions in most states. As an insurance product, annuities are closely regulated by the states and are currently available in fewer than half the states. These mutual funds and annuities are similar to those offered by stockbrokers and insurance agents (see Chapters 6 and 23), but may in some instances have lower commissions and be more competitive.

Note: Mutual funds and annuities, wherever you buy them, are not covered by deposit insurance. Don't make the mistake of thinking they become insured bank products because they are sold in a bank.

Q I have quite a few E bonds I bought through payroll deduction in the 1970s. I was thinking about cashing them and reinvesting the money toward retirement, but a friend said I can convert them to HH bonds and get interest checks twice a year. Can I do this without paying income tax on the interest already earned?

A Yes. Series E or EE bonds may be rolled over into HH bonds with no tax payable on the interest already earned until the HH bonds mature (in 20 years) or are redeemed, whichever comes first. You need a minimum of $50 in E or EE bonds to do a rollover; above that amount you may either take any excess in cash or add cash to round off your purchase to the next $500.

Interest is credited to E and EE bonds twice a year; so as not to lose interest, try to do the rollover right after the interest accrual date. To find out when this is, send for a "Schedule of Interest Dates" from the Department of the Treasury, U.S. Savings Bonds Division, 1111 20th St. N.W., Washington, DC 20226.

RETIREMENT PLANS

You may set up a retirement plan for yourself at your bank or thrift or credit union via an Individual Retirement Account (see Chapter 23) or, if you are self-employed, a Keogh plan. These tax-deferred accounts may take almost any form, including time deposits.

A great many financial institutions, including insurance companies and brokerage firms and mutual funds, are vying for your retirement dollars. Shop around to determine which plan is best for you (see Chapter 23 for details), but don't overlook your neighborhood bank or thrift as you do.

 KEY POINTS

- Small amounts of extra cash still belong in a regular savings account, earning interest but accessible if needed.

- Larger amounts of cash should be put in a market-rate account, either in a bank or thrift or in a money market mutual fund.

- Special-purpose accounts, such as Christmas Clubs or custodial accounts, can help you put money aside for specific purposes.

- Time deposits with set maturity dates allow you to lock in a fixed rate of return, a good maneuver when interest rates in general are falling and when you're sure you won't need the money before the maturity date.

- Other bank services—from consumer loans to safe deposit boxes to U.S. Government Savings Bonds—may fit into your financial plan at one time or another.

Putting Your Money to Work: Investments

CHAPTER 5

Investment Strategy

Are you saving to buy a house? to open a business? to put children through college? to finance a trip around the world? to ensure a comfortable retirement? to build up the estate you'll leave for your heirs?

Your savings goal is important. But your savings method also depends on a number of variables: How many years do you have between now and the achievement of your particular purpose? Are you investing for the long term or the short term? How much risk can you afford to take, both in terms of your own temperament and in terms of the number of people dependent on you? Can you manage your own investments, or will you count on the advice and information you glean from others? What is the investment climate? Are you putting investment dollars to work in a time of galloping inflation? during a recession? in a period of economic uncertainty?

Finding the Money to Invest

Before you skip this chapter, on the grounds that while you're strenuously holding your head above water you can't possibly find money to invest, think again. Here are some possibilities:

■ Do you have money in passbook savings or money market accounts? How much money? Once you have the equivalent of three to six months' earnings on hand for emergencies (two to three months' earnings is probably sufficient if you are well insured and a two-income family), any excess should be put where it will grow.

Note: Money market funds, described in Chapter 6, are not an investment. Like savings accounts, although sometimes paying far more in interest, money market funds are a base for emergency funds and a parking place for temporarily idle cash. Your capital won't grow in a money fund (although it won't do badly when interest rates are high) and should not be left there indefinitely as a substitute for another investment.

■ Do you have a whole life insurance policy with accumulated cash value, with borrowing privileges at a low rate of interest? What better reason to borrow than to increase your capital and thereby provide for your family?

■ Could you get along if your employer suddenly imposed a salary cutback of $1,000 a year? You could, because you'd have to. You can also get along if you impose a similar salary reduction on yourself, and put the money to work.

■ Can you do without some purchases you were planning to make? If you invest the money you were planning to spend on redecorating the house, for example, you may come out much further ahead.

Q I've been told that you need at least $1,000 to invest. I can never scrape that much together at one time. Is there any way to buy stock, for example, with $50?

A Yes. Look for a program geared to small investors. One good bet is individual membership in the National Association of Investors Corporation (NAIC). Annual membership costs $32. Then, for a nominal $5 service charge on each initial stock purchase, NAIC will enroll you in a dividend reinvestment program at any of a number of participating corporations. Once enrolled, you can invest amounts of your choice at intervals of your choice. You can build a stock portfolio through NAIC's Low Cost Plan for as little as $10 a month.

Or you might start an investment club with friends, and pool $25 or $50 apiece each month for investment. Information about investment clubs as well as about the Low Cost Plan is available from NAIC, 1515 East Eleven Mile Rd., Royal Oak, MI 48067.

Another possibility: Merrill Lynch has a Blueprint Plan under which, after an initial investment of $500, stocks may be purchased for as little as $50 a month or $100 a quarter, with commission discounts from 30 to 80 percent and automatic dividend reinvestment.

■ Can you, conversely, sell no-longer-used possessions and raise some money? Many people have attics, basements, and garages crammed with outgrown toys, clothes, even appliances. It's possible to raise several hundred dollars, or more, at a well-organized garage sale.

■ Would you borrow money to buy a car? You could also consider borrowing money to invest—if you carefully evaluate the degree of risk. The interest you pay is tax-deductible, as long as you don't invest borrowed money in tax-exempt securities. "Leverage," the use of borrowed funds, increases your potential gain and your potential loss.

Do not, however, stretch your resources beyond the point of prudence in the search for investment capital. Don't invest money that you'll need if your car breaks down or if a family member is temporarily unemployed. Investment funds should be funds you can, at least for the short term, do without.

WHO IS INVESTING THESE DAYS?

Over 51 million individual men and women, or one in four adults, according to the New York Stock Exchange, own shares in American corporations. Here are some interesting current statistics about investors:

■ Investors are getting younger. In 1975 the median age of all shareholders was 53. By 1990, it was 43. Newer investors are younger still, with a median age of 33.

■ Investment portfolios are changing. In 1985, the median portfolio value in equities (stocks) was $6,200. By 1990, portfolio value stood at $11,400.

■ The median household income of shareholders rose from $36,800 in 1985 to $43,800 in 1990. Median income for all American households was $22,400 in 1986 and $32,000 in 1990. Yet you don't have to be rich to invest; 44 percent of the shareholder population in 1990 was composed of people with household income in the $25,000 to $49,999 range.

■ More individuals appear to be investing in the stock market through mutual funds these days, fewer through direct purchases of shares.

Before You Invest

Don't leap into the stock market (or any other investment) just because you have a few spare dollars. First, be sure that you have a financial cushion appropriate to your circumstances. In addition to readily accessible cash in savings accounts or money market funds, be sure that you have adequate insurance. Most important: medical coverage and the disability income insurance that will replace your income if you are laid up. Then analyze your investment temperament, your investment objectives, and the investment climate.

Worksheet 5.1: Your Investment Objectives

How would you characterize your investment objectives?

> **Growth:** appreciation of capital, with income secondary
> **Total Return:** a balance of appreciation and income
> **Income:** dividend or interest income, with some risk to principal
> **Preservation of capital:** protection of principal, with income

How would you describe your attitude toward risk?

> I want only the safest investments, even though that means lower returns
> I prefer little risk and invest only in relatively sure things
> I'll take some risks in the interest of above-average returns
> I'll take sizable risks in hopes of achieving significant gains

---

YOUR INVESTMENT TEMPERAMENT

Two people, at the same age, with the same assets, and the same investment objectives, may reach totally different investment decisions based on the amount of risk they are willing to take. Arthur T. and Keith J., for instance, each have two children in junior high school, each plan to send those children to college, and each can save about $5,000 a year. Arthur will put his $5,000 a year into certificates of deposit (CDs) at the local savings and loan; Keith will purchase the common stock of high-technology companies. Both say that they want their capital to grow. But Arthur is conservative; he wants no chance of loss. He also suspects that he lacks the time, and the inclination, to pay attention to the market. He'll settle for capital growth through the compounding of interest. Keith, on the other hand, is willing to take some risk for the sake of potentially greater capital appreciation. He likes the sense of participation he gets from watching the market and getting in and out as appropriate.

Wise investing stems from matching your own temperament and needs to your investment goals. The range of investment possibilities is enormous, from the totally risk-free vehicle of government issues to the high-flying realm of options and straddles (both are ways to bet on future stock prices). In between there are stocks and bonds and real estate and collectibles of all kinds, with varying degrees of risk.

As a general rule, the degree of profit that you can make is related to the degree of risk that you are willing to take. But, although it's not as pleasant to think about, potential loss is also related to the degree of risk. What's the point of a high-risk gamble if you won't be able to sleep at night? What's the value if you might be depriving your children of their education instead of improving their chances? Take a look at your own temperament and your equanimity in the face of loss, as well as how much money you can afford to lose, before you invest at all.

Worksheet 5.2: Investment Goals

Where do you stand:

Investment goals	Low priority							High Priority		
Return should exceed inflation rate	1	2	3	4	5	6	7	8	9	10
Principal should be safe	1	2	3	4	5	6	7	8	9	10
Investments should be liquid (accessible)	1	2	3	4	5	6	7	8	9	10
Diversification is important	1	2	3	4	5	6	7	8	9	10
I'd like professional asset management	1	2	3	4	5	6	7	8	9	10
I want to reduce my taxable income	1	2	3	4	5	6	7	8	9	10
I want to build tax-free income	1	2	3	4	5	6	7	8	9	10
I'm interested in long-term growth	1	2	3	4	5	6	7	8	9	10
I'm interested in short-term profits	1	2	3	4	5	6	7	8	9	10

Source: Institute of Certified Financial Planners.

YOUR INVESTMENT OBJECTIVES

Before you shift any money from savings to investments, think about your investment objectives. Think about the desired end result—college? a vacation home? retirement funds?—and whether your investment horizon is short term or long term. Then think about the means to each end; think about your investments in terms of current income, capital growth, and tax advantages. And think about diversifying your investments so that you reap the benefits of all three.

Current Income

You can get current income from a number of investments, some more secure than others. Beyond your insured savings account, look at U.S. Treasury bills, notes, and bonds; at other U.S. Government Agency obligations; at money market funds, especially (if absolute safety is a concern) at money market funds investing solely in Treasury issues. Blue-chip stocks and corporate bonds, bought individually or via a fund, may also be considered for current income.

Capital Growth

Capital growth occurs when you invest in something that appreciates in value, so that your underlying principal grows. You'll usually derive current income as well, in the form of dividends or interest, but the income may be lower when the opportunities for growth are greater. Capital growth can be obtained in relatively safe investments and in riskier ones, along a range from blue chip stocks to speculative new issues or, in mutual funds, from balanced or growth-and-income funds to aggressive growth funds. The riskiest investments—such as options and commodities (see pp. 168-170)—have the highest potential for profit, and for loss. They are highly speculative and not appropriate for the average investor.

TAX CONSIDERATIONS

A lot of fancy investments that used to be packaged as "tax shelters," notably certain types of limited partnerships, have faded into oblivion with recent changes in tax law. Maybe it's just as well. Too many investors got carried away with the idea of putting one over on Uncle Sam and eluding income taxes, when they weren't in a tax bracket where it made much sense to do so.

That said, there are still tax considerations to investing and tax-sheltered investments you may want to consider. The first two of the following three tax-advantaged investments are appropriate for almost everyone:

- Owning your own home yields solid tax benefits. When you own your principal residence (house, condominium, mobile home, even a boat), you may deduct both mortgage interest and property taxes from your income when calculating your federal income tax. You may defer payment of taxes when you sell the residence, if you put the profits into another residence. And you may exclude $125,000 of profit from taxes altogether if you are over age 55 when you sell. (See Chapter 13 for more details.)
- Retirement-linked tax savings are another good bet. If your employer has a profit-sharing or 401(k) plan, especially if the employer makes matching contributions, you should fund this plan to its maximum before you worry about other tax-advantaged investments. Do the

Q Interest rates have fallen so low that there seems to be no way to make any money in fixed-income investments. Yet I can't afford to take any risk. What do you recommend?

A First, some conservative fixed-income investments yield better returns than others. Treasury obligations, for example, might beat certificates of deposit. Second, consider a technique called "laddering." Using safe investments with fixed maturity dates—either Treasuries or insured CDs—divide your investable dollars into five equal amounts. Then put one-fifth into instruments maturing in each of five years. If interest rates are higher when the first maturity date rolls around, you can reinvest at the higher rate. If rates are lower, only one-fifth of your portfolio has to be reinvested at the lower rate while the rest continues to grow at the higher rate. Spreading maturities in this manner increases your yield over time.

same with an Individual Retirement Account (IRA) or Keogh plan if you are eligible. More information on these opportunities for tax-sheltered retirement savings will be found in Chapter 23.

■ Most municipal bonds are totally exempt from federal income taxes, and from state taxes in the state they are issued. Municipal bonds (see p. 158) are appropriate investments for highly taxed investors in high-tax states.

Taxes on Investments

Interest and dividends are taxable as ordinary income. But a slight differential has been reintroduced on capital gains. Long-term capital gains, profits on the sale of assets owned more than twelve months, are currently taxable at a maximum rate of 28 percent; ordinary income and short-term gains have a top rate of 31 percent. Losses may be applied against gains for the year, but if total losses exceed total gains, a maximum of $3,000 may be used to offset ordinary income; any capital losses in excess of $3,000 may be carried forward to later years.

It's important to look at taxes in developing your investment strategy. It's equally important not to let tax considerations dominate your investment decisions. All other things being equal, make an investment because it's a good investment without regard to tax advantages. All other things being equal, sell a stock (or other investment) when it's time to sell, before you sustain further losses. All other things are *not* equal, of course, when it's almost the end of the year and it will make a lot of difference to record the transaction in a different calendar year. Look at all the relevant factors before making any investment decision.

THE INVESTMENT CLIMATE

Assess the investment climate every time you're ready to invest. Periods of high inflation tend to depress the price of most common stocks, and fixed-

---

Q I'm reinvesting dividends in my stock mutual fund, rather than taking them in cash. Do I have to pay taxes on the reinvested dividends?

A Yes. If the money is otherwise taxable—it isn't coming from a tax-exempt municipal bond fund or an IRA—it doesn't matter to the Internal Revenue Service (IRS) whether you take the dividends in cash or reinvest them. But don't pay taxes twice on the same money; be sure to add reinvested dividend income and capital gain distributions to your original cost basis when it comes time to figure gains or losses on shares you've sold.

income securities such as bonds become competitive with stocks as interest rates rise. If you can afford to invest for the long term, it may therefore be wise to buy common stocks when prices are low—even if they may go lower still. Periods of galloping inflation make inflation hedges, such as real estate and gold coins, very attractive. But people with large sums tied up in such tangible assets may view the ebbing of inflation with alarm. When inflation does subside, fixed-rate securities, such as bonds and Treasury notes, become more attractive—especially to investors able to lock in relatively high rates right before the decline. Periods of interest-rate volatility knock most calculations out of the ballpark; the message then: Stay liquid.

Whatever you do, however, try to stay away from follow-the-pack psychology. The day that all your friends are talking about buying oil stocks is the day *not* to buy oil stocks. The day that the evening news commentators chortle about the new highs reached by the Dow Jones Index is *not* the day to decide to get into the stock market. Either buy when prices have been declining steadily (don't worry about waiting for the absolute bottom), or put consistent sums of money into investments over a period of time so that your purchases will average out. Consistent investing, otherwise known as "dollar cost averaging," is a very good way to achieve steady growth. See Table 5.2.

Meanwhile, don't bury your head in the sand. Be aware of the world around you and adjust your investments accordingly. If interest rates are very high, pull your money out of low-interest savings and put it in a money market mutual fund. If the money market is paying passbook rates or below, put your money back into insured savings. Shift varying proportions of your investment portfolio to and from stocks and bonds as appropriate. Above all, stay reasonably liquid so that you can be flexible.

Note: Marketability is not synonymous with liquidity. Common stocks may be sold easily at any time, but if you need to sell them when the market is down you will suffer a loss.

Table: 5.1: Investment Performance

Compound Annual Return, 1926-1992

Small company stocks:	12.2%
Common stocks in general:	10.3
Long-term corporate bonds:	5.5
Intermediate-term corporate bonds:	5.2
Long-term government bonds:	4.8
U.S. Treasury bills:	3.7
Inflation:	3.1

Source: *Stocks, Bonds, Bills, and Inflation 1992 Yearbook*™, Ibbotson Associates, Chicago, Illinois (annually updates work by Roger G. Ibbotson and Rex A. Sinquefield). Used with permission. All rights reserved.

Table 5.2: A Dollar Cost Averaging Program, Reflecting Investment in the T. Rowe Price International Stock Fund

Year Ended 12/31/91	Total of $100 Monthly Investments	Shares Purchased[1]	Average Cost per Share	Fund's Price Range: LOWEST	HIGHEST	Cumulative Market Value of All Shares Owned[1]
1982	$1,200	243.135	$4.97	$4.52	$5.67	$1,378.58
1983	1,200	197.420	6.20	5.31	7.16	3,152.18
1984	1,200	188.041	6.74	5.92	7.50	4,142.46
1985	1,200	205.053	7.00	6.08	9.04	7,536.21
1986	1,200	218.379	11.83	8.60	13.77	13,560.68
1987	1,200	791.354	9.49	8.48	16.62	15,742.51
1988	1,200	372.306	8.97	8.24	10.11	19,874.76
1989	1,200	316.964	9.90	8.89	10.77	25,934.41
1990	1,200	277.448	9.27	8.74	11.23	24,757.03
1991	1,200	329.563	9.32	8.31	10.16	29,952.44
	$12,000	3,139.663	$8.37	$4.52	$16.62	$29,952.44

Source: T. Rowe Price.

Notes: [1] Reflects reinvestment of all dividend and capital gain distributions made during the period. There was an unusually large capital gains distribution in 1987, resulting in the high number of shares acquired that year. This is a hypothetical illustration intended to demonstrate the effect of dollar cost averaging; it does not indicate future results.

UNDERSTANDING INVESTMENT RISK

Investment risk is not limited to the risk of having an investment decline in value so that you lose principal. Another risk factor is the risk of losing purchasing power to inflation; this is the risk you face when you limit yourself to fixed-income investments with little or no opportunity for growth. Over the long term, according to studies by Ibbotson Associates in Chicago, investment in stocks has yielded far greater rewards than investment in fixed-income securities (see Table 5.1). Another is interest rate risk, the risk you face in investments (such as bonds) that lose value in inverse proportion to interest rates; when interest rates go up, in other words, the value of most bonds declines. Then there's economic risk, the risk that a slowing economy will cause investments overall to decline in value. And there's the risk associated with specific companies or industries, such as the risk that changing tax laws or government regulation will harm a stock's outlook.

An Individual Investment Plan

■ Donna and George have $25,000, saved from current income, to invest. They are both 29 years old, both lawyers, earning a combined annual income of $79,000. They are still paying off college loans, however, and the $25,000 represents all their assets. They have no children, but expect to start a family within a couple of years.

■ Allison and Tom have $25,000 to invest, money they recently inherited from Tom's uncle. They are in their mid-thirties and have three children; their annual income is $34,700 and they have $3,500 in scraped-together savings.

The amount of money available for investment at a given time is clearly not the only factor to consider. Donna and George, while they plan to start a family, also have the kind of professional incomes that make repeated investments likely. They foresee no immediate need for their cash, and can afford to take a moderate amount of risk. Allison and Tom, on the other hand, have what is probably a one-shot opportunity to invest a significant sum. Without this money, they will find it very difficult to send their children to college. They need to be conservative in their approach to investment.

Your personal investment plan should be based on careful evaluation of where you are and where you want to go, with reevaluation at regular intervals. Look at yourself right now. Are you young, without dependents? Then as long as you earn enough to live comfortably and to save something for the future, you can probably take reasonable risks in the pursuit of capital growth. If you're middle-aged, without dependents, your biggest concern may be sheltering some of your income from taxation. If you have a family, you will probably want to protect that family by being more conservative in your investments. And when you reach retirement age, safety of principal and the highest possible income (along with continued growth to offset inflation) will be of paramount concern.

Before you start to tailor your own investment plan, look back at your net worth statement and your financial forecast. Then look at the following factors:

- Your current age
- Your state of health
- Present annual income (from all sources)
- Anticipated annual income five years from now (from all sources)
- Anticipated windfalls (inheritances, etc.)
- Current expenses, both fixed and discretionary
- Anticipated expenses
- Provision for emergencies (savings accounts, insurance)
- Amount currently available to invest
- Amount anticipated as available for investment
- Investment objectives:
  - Short-range
  - Long-range
- Tentative investment decisions:
  - How much can you risk?
  - How much are you willing to risk?
  - How much must have a guaranteed return?

Q I've been putting my retirement fund money into my company's stock. I don't have much invested anywhere else. Is this a good idea?

A I suspect you realize it isn't. Your employer may be a fine company, with good prospects for growth, but you're taking a major risk if both your current income and your future retirement security ride on the success of a single company. Diversify by choosing another investment for your retirement funds.

A BALANCED PORTFOLIO

Whether you'll aim primarily for income, growth, or tax advantage depends on your age and stage of life as well as your attitude toward risk and the amount of money you have to invest. Through the first half of life, for most people, capital growth is a primary target. In the second half, protection of income often becomes more important. At any age, however, you don't want all of your eggs in one basket. Diversify your investments, and do so in several ways:

■ Among the objectives of income, growth, and tax advantages, as appropriate
■ Among different investment vehicles, via one or more mutual funds or on your own
■ Among short-term and long-term investments
■ Among different sectors of the economy, government and corporate

The Investment Triangle

One approach to investing divides investment dollars into three parts:

■ Conservative "foundation" dollars, including bank accounts, money market mutual funds, certificates of deposit, insurance, Treasury bills and notes, fixed deferred annuities.
■ Growth investments, including growth stock and stock funds, growth-and-income and balanced funds, municipal and corporate bonds and bond funds.
■ Risk investments, including small-company and speculative stocks, stock options, variable annuities, raw land, limited partnerships, commodities.

When you're younger, you can afford to risk more (but never all) of your investment dollars. As you become older, especially as you move toward retirement, the balance should tip more toward conservative investment. But age is only one factor. Within each category the balance will shift among investment possibilities according to your objectives, your income, and the degree of risk you are willing to assume.

■ Donna and George, young professionals with no dependents and a solid income, might keep 5 percent of their investment money in a money market fund for ready access, put 30 percent into established growth company stocks for security, and put 65 percent into the stocks of small companies with likelihood of growth. Their primary objective: appreciation.

■ A 50-year-old with two children in college and one still at home would balance his portfolio differently. He might put 10 percent into a money market fund, 15 percent into small-company stocks, and divide the rest equally among intermediate-term corporate bonds, high-yield stocks, and established growth company stocks. Objective: to maintain current income and build funds toward retirement, while attaining some growth.

■ At 68, a retiree might balance his portfolio with 10 percent in the money market, 10 percent in growth company stocks, 30 percent in high-yield stocks, and 50 percent in intermediate- and long-term bonds. Objective: high income and low risk.

These proportions are appropriate only for these people. They'll be different for you, and will vary with the investment climate and with your temperament, as well as with your age. There are no fixed rules.

Diversifying Through Asset Allocation

"Asset allocation" is a buzzword for the 1990s, but it's really just another way of saying "diversification." The theory is the same: Spread your eggs among different baskets and they won't all be scrambled when a particular basket drops. Since some investments appreciate when others depreciate, reacting in different ways to market stimuli, diversification is a good way to minimize risk. Asset allocation—how much you put where—has been shown repeatedly to be far more important in determining investment success than either the selection of specific investment vehicles or the timing of purchases and sales.

Asset allocation models can be structured in different ways. The simplest model suggests dividing assets equally among cash, stocks, and bonds. Other models divide stock holdings between domestic and international, and add real estate as well.

Note: As you structure your portfolio, be sure to consider *all* of your investments, including those in tax-deferred accounts such as IRAs and 401(k) plans. Many investors wind up with woefully unbalanced portfolios because they ignore these accounts.

A suggestion from Sheldon Jacobs, editor-in-chief and publisher of *The No-Load Fund Investor,* apportions model portfolios by the investor's age and objectives. The three categories are "wealth builders," working investors whose goal is capital accumulation; a somewhat more conservative preretirement portfolio designed for investors within ten years of retirement; and a retirement portfolio emphasizing income and capital preservation (see Table 5.3). You'll note that all three investors own both stocks and bonds. You'll also note that all three own international equities. International investing can be an important way to diversify your portfolio, in an era when more than two-thirds of investment opportunities are available outside the United States.

Table 5.3: The No-Load Fund Investor Asset Allocation Model

A July 1993 asset allocation model in *The No-Load Fund Investor* (updated in the newsletter each month) looks like this (cash is not included in this model):

Wealth Builder Portfolio:

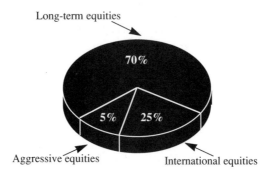

Long-term equities
70%
5%   25%
Aggressive equities   International equities

Preretirement Portfolio:

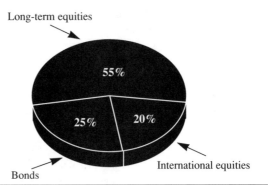

Long-term equities
55%
25%   20%
Bonds   International equities

Retirement Portfolio:

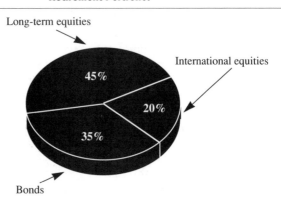

Long-term equities
International equities
45%
20%
35%
Bonds

A more complex asset allocation model (combined with a risk allocation model) is put forth by the Minneapolis-based brokerage firm of Piper, Jaffray & Hopwood. These six models are based on five categories: liquid assets (money market funds, CDs, Treasury bills), fixed income (long-term CDs, government or corporate bonds, tax exempts, unit trusts, bond funds), U.S. stocks (individual issues or mutual funds), international securities (mutual funds), and inflation hedges (oil and gas stocks, equity real estate investment trusts, gold investment companies).

The Piper, Jaffray & Hopwood categories are illustrated in Table 5.4.

Table 5.4: Piper, Jaffray & Hopwood Asset Allocation Model

YOUNG SINGLE, 20 TO 30 YEARS OLD

■ More risk-oriented; capital preservation not as critical as making money.

■ More interested in capital appreciation than in steady current income.

■ Has long-term time horizon.

■ Not averse to using leverage through margin where appropriate.

Asset Allocation

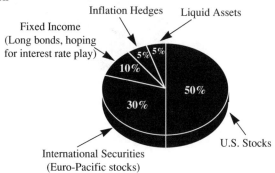

Risk Allocation

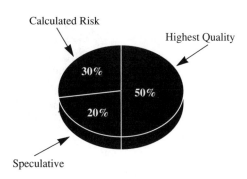

YOUNG PROFESSIONAL COUPLE, 30 to 40 Years Old, 1 to 2 Children

---

■ Feels pinched with additional responsibilities but hasn't toned down spending habits acquired while single. Mortgage, car, and credit payments don't leave much for investment.

■ Trying to start a long-term savings/investment program.

■ Each might want to develop independent portfolios.

■ Concerned about high cost of educating children, expected to reach $12,000 to $20,000 per year for public and private colleges, respectively, in the next 15 to 20 years.

■ Willing to take risk for long-term gain.

Asset Allocation

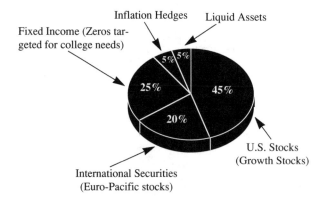

Inflation Hedges   Liquid Assets

Fixed Income (Zeros targeted for college needs)

5% 5%

25%   45%

20%

U.S. Stocks
(Growth Stocks)

International Securities
(Euro-Pacific stocks)

Risk Allocation

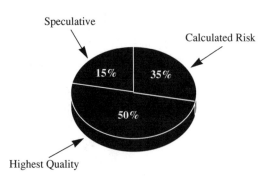

Speculative

Calculated Risk

15%   35%

50%

Highest Quality

YOUNG WORKING COUPLE, 30 to 40 Years Old, 2 Children

■ Spending habits more controlled than with young professionals. Has savings objectives: to buy a house or set up a business. Able to set aside fixed amount of income for savings/investment.

■ Risk averse. Very capital preservation-oriented; has doubts about ability to recoup losses.

Asset Allocation

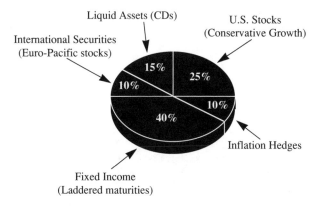

Liquid Assets (CDs)

U.S. Stocks
(Conservative Growth)

International Securities
(Euro-Pacific stocks)

15%

25%

10%

10%

40%

Inflation Hedges

Fixed Income
(Laddered maturities)

Risk Allocation

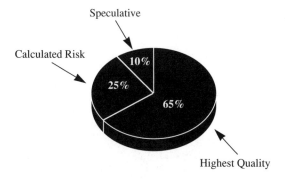

Speculative

Calculated Risk

10%

25%

65%

Highest Quality

EARLY MIDDLE-AGED, 40 to 50 Years Old, with Teenage or Young Adult Children

---

■ Approaching earnings peak; already at spending peak—height of family responsibilities.

■ Cash flow very tight; trying to pay increasing tuition costs.

■ Already might be facing responsibilities of aging parents.

■ Life-style restricts long-term savings/investment ability; just wants to get through these years.

■ Very risk averse.

Asset Allocation

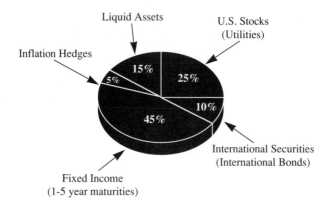

Risk Allocation

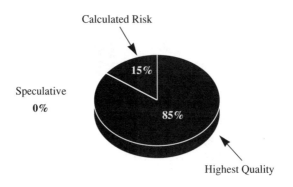

PRERETIREMENT MIDDLE-AGED, 50 to 60 Years Old

■ Most of family financial responsibilities behind; children out of school and moving from "sandwich generation" (responsibilities for taking care of children and aging parents).

■ Really interested in completing retirement planning.

■ Ability and desire to set aside large amounts for investments.

■ Modestly risk averse; concerned about lack of time to recoup losses but realizes need for growth. On balance, preservation of capital more important than maximizing investment return.

■ Tax planning increasingly critical—income and estate.

Asset Allocation

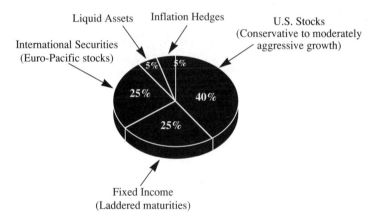

Risk Allocation

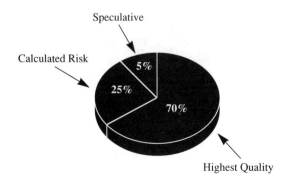

RETIREE, 60+ Years Old

- Very risk averse; can't afford to lose principal.

- Portfolio becomes much more current income-oriented.

- Worried about maintaining purchasing power.

- Beginning to have concerns about long-term disability—Will I have enough assets to take care of myself?

- Estate planning steps up.

Asset Allocation

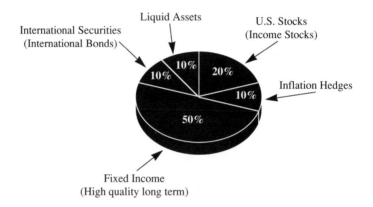

Risk Allocation

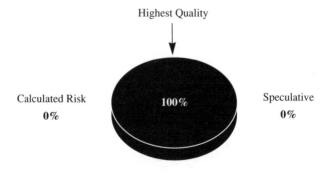

Source: Piper, Jaffray & Hopwood.

REBALANCING YOUR PORTFOLIO

Allocating assets, by whichever formula you choose, means placing a specified percentage of your assets into each category. As time passes and one category appreciates more than another, however, the balance will shift. Asset allocation, just like every other aspect of managing your money, is not something to be done once then forgotten.

But how often, and by what method, should you rebalance your portfolio? Some investors evaluate their portfolios, and make necessary adjustments, annually. Others monitor their portfolios regularly and rebalance whenever any one category fluctuates by 5 to 10 percent. According to a recent study published in the *Journal of Financial Planning,* the percentage method is the most cost-effective method. Unless you're an investor who pays constant attention, however, an annual evaluation may be more practical. Rebalancing more frequently, such as quarterly or semiannually, simply incurs greater commission costs.

AN INVESTMENT STRATEGY FOR BEGINNERS

James B. Cloonan, founder of the American Association of Individual Investors, suggests that investors who stay in the market over time reduce their risks. He suggests this strategy for a long-term investment in common stock:

1. Start by putting your money into no-load common stock mutual funds (see p. 140), until you have $10,000 to $15,000 invested.

2. Then develop a portfolio of at least seven different stocks of approximately equal dollar amounts. Do so one stock at a time, with the remaining money kept in the mutual fund.

3. Select stocks of small and medium-sized companies whose profits can reasonably be expected to grow. You'll be a winner if one company among your seven goes from being a medium-sized company to being a successful giant. If you initially buy the stock of very large established companies, you can't expect this kind of growth.

4. About four years before the accumulated wealth will be needed, whether for the purchase of a house or for a child's education, begin to sell. Sell one-quarter of the portfolio in each of the four years. Reinvest the proceeds in shorter-term, low-risk investments which will be available when the money is needed.

5. Instead of liquidating the investments, if retirement is on the horizon, begin to convert them to low-risk, interest-paying investments.

Pay Attention

Dr. Cloonan recommends holding stock for several years, through at least one business cycle. But many investors err in the other direction: they buy and then sit, ignoring changes in the business climate or the company or their own affairs that would make it advisable to sell. Don't make this mistake.

Don't invest unless you're willing to pay attention, willing to reevaluate your portfolio from time to time, and willing to make changes.

If you take a passive stance you might find yourself in the position of one of these investors:

- David M. bought a promising new issue when it was selling for $20 a share. The company prospered and grew and the stock increased in value until it was selling at $200 a share and paying a steady dividend of $4 a share. David was pleased. He was reluctant to sell, however, because he still had faith in the company's continued growth and because of the capital gains tax he would have to pay. But he didn't stop to think that although he was receiving a 20 percent return based on his cost, his return on current value was only 2 percent. When he reviewed his portfolio with his broker, he learned that the stock was considered to be overvalued at its current price and that peak growth probably had been attained. He sold the stock.

- In 1971 Mrs. K.'s husband died, leaving her a yearly income of approximately $8,000 from securities. Most of the income came from one large holding, relatively secure, but providing a fairly low yield. After the settlement of the estate, Mrs. K. sat back, content to live on the steady flow of income without investigating alternative forms of investment. Her major holding appreciated only slightly in value over the years, while the yield remained about the same. Inflation, however, steadily devoured a substantial portion of her buying power. She has begun to find it necessary to dip into capital; reinvestment in a higher-yielding security could have made all the difference.

When to Sell

Investment strategy includes deciding when to sell as well as when to buy. Too many small investors hold stocks indefinitely, afraid to admit that they've made a mistake. Losses on paper somehow seem easier to take than losses in dollars—even if sticking with paper makes the losses greater. You'll find it easier to sell if you make two basic decisions at the time you buy:

- Decide how much you expect the stock to rise and decide that you will sell when it reaches the targeted amount, even if it appears likely to continue rising.

- Decide how much of a loss you are willing to accept, and sell if the stock declines to that amount, even if you think it is likely to rebound (see Table 5.5). Set a framework for your stock, the top and bottom limits you can live with, and sell if it reaches either limit. You can make the sale automatic, and avoid temporizing, by leaving an order with your broker to sell at a specific price.

Even if you've purchased mutual fund shares with an eye to professional management, you should reevaluate your portfolio at regular intervals. You might want to review your financial holdings thoroughly every year. You also might want to review them when external or internal events dictate. The New York Stock Exchange offers these lists of factors that should prompt review:

A Checklist of External Events

■ Substantial advance or decline in the stock market
■ Change in tax laws
■ International monetary upheaval
■ Change in business regulatory laws
■ Change in attitudes of regulatory agencies
■ A shift from inflation to deflation, or the reverse
■ Political change
■ New international trade agreements, or foreign trade restrictions

A Checklist of Personal Circumstances

■ Getting married
■ Having a baby
■ Receiving an inheritance
■ Providing support for parent(s)
■ Moving into a higher tax bracket
■ Having children enter college
■ Making a substantial business investment
■ Being widowed or divorced
■ Becoming a grandparent
■ Retiring

A Checklist of Changes in Outlook of Companies Whose Shares You Own

■ Significant change in price of stock
■ New management
■ Increased or decreased earnings
■ New competitive factors
■ New products
■ Mergers or acquisitions
■ Antitrust or other government actions
■ Increase, decrease, or omission of dividends
■ New bond issue
■ Diversification
■ Purchases or sales by institutions

Table 5.5: Gain Needed to Recoup Losses

The longer you hold a losing stock, the farther behind you get. Simple arithmetic shows that it makes sense to cut your losses early. As this table illustrates, the odds that you'll recover a loss worsen rapidly if the loss gets to be larger than about 10 percent.

Size of loss (%)	Gain needed to break even (%)	Size of loss (%)	Gain needed to break even (%)
5	5.3	40	66.7
10	11.1	50	100.0
15	17.6	60	150.0
20	25.0	70	233.3
25	33.3	80	400.0
30	42.9	90	900.0

Managing Your Investments

Once you've thought about your investment objectives and promised yourself to reevaluate your investments on a regular basis, you need to keep yourself informed.

GENERAL INFORMATION

Before you invest at all, you should find out what investment is all about. This book will help. In addition, you might look at general information distributed by the securities industry. The New York Stock Exchange, for instance,

Q There was a lot of recent publicity about the failure of a stock brokerage firm. What happens to such a firm's customers?

A Few brokerage firms fail. When one does, its customers are usually protected by the Securities Investor Protection Corporation (SIPC), which covers stocks, bonds, notes, and certificates of deposit but not commodities or commodity options. Securities registered in a customer's name are returned. Then remaining cash and securities held by the firm are distributed among customers on a pro rata basis. Finally, remaining claims are settled by SIPC to a maximum of $500,000 per customer, of which no more than $100,000 may be for cash. It can take many months to settle, however, and there is no protection against market ups and downs while customer assets are frozen. A word of warning: While you can't really ascertain the financial stability of your brokerage firm, be alert to repeated bookkeeping errors and excessively slow execution of orders. These may be a signal to find a new broker.

puts out a six-booklet "Investors Information Kit," available for $12 by writing to the New York Stock Exchange, Inc., P.O. Box 5020, Farmingdale, NY 11736.

Good general information is also available through an investment course or seminar. Your local adult education program or community college probably offers such courses. So do stockbrokerage firms, although the advice may be somewhat self-serving and may need to be taken with a grain of salt. Women and retirees will find special courses designed for them.

PUBLICATIONS

There are a great many publications offering investment advice, ranging from glossy magazines available on most newsstands to special-interest newsletters available only by subscription. If you're at all serious about your investments, you should scan such publications as the *Wall Street Journal, Barron's, Business Week,* and *Forbes.* They'll tell you about the economic climate, about industry trends, and about the outlook for specific companies.

You may also want to subscribe to one or more newsletters or advisory services. Be aware, though, that "experts" frequently disagree. No one really knows when an inflationary period is ending or beginning; no one can guarantee that a particular investment will move up or down in value. All any of the advisers can do is read the economic signals and react with their own set of assumptions and expectations. So read their advice, but analyze it in light of (1) your own feelings about the economy and (2) your own individual investment strategy.

COMPANY NEWS

When you've narrowed your investment possibilities, ask for research reports on particular companies from your stockbroker. Then, once you do invest, you'll be bombarded with news and information from the company or companies in which you're participating. Read the material. Pay attention to what the figures say. Pay particular attention to the company's quarterly and annual reports.

Reading an Annual Report

Amid the dry prose and columns of figures in an annual report lie some crucial messages: Is this company doing well? Are sales increasing? Are earnings on the rise?

In order to decipher these messages, these clues to whether you should invest in the company in the first place or remain an investor from year to year, you have to review certain key elements of the report:

- ■ The company's **balance sheet** shows its year-end financial position, just as your net worth statement shows your position at a specific time. It shows the company's assets (cash on hand and in the bank, marketable securities, accounts receivable, inventories, and property, plants, and equipment) and its liabilities (accounts payable and notes payable, accrued expenses, and federal income taxes payable). It also shows stockholders' equity, the corporation's net worth after subtracting all its liabilities.

■ The company's **income statement,** sometimes called the earnings report or statement of profit and loss, is like your cash flow statement; it shows the record of operating activities over the course of the year. It matches the revenues received against all the costs incurred in running the company. The result: a net profit or loss for the year. The very first item—net sales or operating revenues—is most important. Compare this figure against the comparable figure for previous years to see how the company is doing.

■ The **independent accountant's report,** usually tucked in the back of the report, simply states that an audit has been conducted and that statements have been prepared in accordance with generally accepted accounting principles. If there are any reservations expressed in the auditor's report, be careful. This is the time to read the footnotes.

■ The **footnotes** in a financial report frequently contain extremely important information. It may be in the footnotes that you'll find such details as changes in the company's method of depreciating fixed assets, changes in the value of stock outstanding because of stock dividends and splits, details of stock option plans for officers and employees, and contingent liabilities representing pending claims or lawsuits.

Q In cleaning out some old trunks that belonged to my mother, I came across some old stock certificates. The company doesn't seem to be in existence anymore. How can I find out if the shares are worth anything?

A You may be able to trace the company and find out if it or a successor company has any assets on which the certificates have a claim. If your stockbroker can't locate the company, write to the secretary of state in the state where the company was incorporated or to the transfer agent; this information should be on the certificate. If this fails, a firm that specializes in tracing old securities may be able to help. One such firm often recommended by the New York Stock Exchange and the National Association of Securities Dealers is R. M. Smythe, 26 Broadway, Suite 271, New York, NY 10004-1701. The fee is $50 for a research report on a single company. Never send the original document when you write for information; send a photocopy. And hold on to your finds in any case; old stock certificates with no other value may be worth several dollars as antiques.

One year's annual report of one company will be informative but won't tell you nearly enough. You'll want to compare this year's figures against those for previous years; some companies make it easy by including five-year or ten-year tables in their annual reports. You may also want to compare the company's earnings against the earnings of comparable companies, particularly those in the same industry.

You can supplement this very brief explanation of annual reports by securing an excellent free guide from Merrill Lynch Pierce Fenner & Smith. It should be available at their local offices. Or write to MLPF&S, Marketing Services, 800 Scudders Mill Rd., Plainsboro, NJ 08540, and ask for a copy of "How to Read a Financial Report."

PROFESSIONAL MANAGEMENT VS. SELF-MANAGEMENT

Are you going to put in the time it takes to intelligently buy and sell individual securities? Are you going to read annual reports and financial statements, follow your securities in the daily paper, and keep yourself informed? Or are you going to do what a great many people do, and put your money into investments you will then file and forget? There is something to be said for long-range investment against in-and-out trading. But there is also a lot to be said for management of investments rather than neglect.

The super-affluent can hire money managers. But one of the best ways for most of us to attain professional management is by investing through mutual funds. By definition, these are professionally managed diversified pools of investments. Investing through funds can minimize the risks inherent in investing. You can keep costs down, and steer clear of stockbrokers at the same time, by using no-load mutual funds. (See pp. 135-146 for more information on mutual funds.)

STOCKBROKERS

If you choose to buy individual securities, you will need to buy and sell through a stockbroker. He or she can also represent you in a wide variety of other investment transactions—so many today, as brokerage firms move into real estate and insurance as well as options, commodities, stocks and bonds—that knowledge and experience in some areas may be sketchy. You pay the broker a commission for each transaction, a commission that makes brokers less than objective advisers. So while you can obtain very useful information from your broker and from the brokerage firm's research staff, you may not want to rely entirely on the broker's opinion. It is your money, and you're the only one who really cares what happens to it.

Selecting a Stockbroker

Stockbrokerage firms come in two basic flavors: full-service and discount. Both receive commissions on the financial products you buy and sell, but full-service stockbrokers generally (not always) receive higher commissions than discount stockbrokers.

If you want information and recommendations, you should use a full-service stockbroker. If you make your own investment decisions, and simply need a broker to execute your orders, you should use a discount stockbroker. Some experienced investors use both, for different situations.

Full-service Stockbrokers

Select a full-service broker the same way you would select any professional adviser. Ask friends and your other advisers (your lawyer or your accountant or your banker) for their recommendations. Then interview several candidates before you make a decision. Try to find out:

- The extent (both length and breadth) of the broker's experience. Ideally, you want a broker with several years of experience, one who has worked through market ups and downs and knows how to deal with both. You also want a broker who will admit to inadequate knowledge and who will refer you to a specialist when referral is appropriate. Your broker may be skilled in stock trades and may be able to put you into a money market fund, but he or she may not know much more about real estate syndication than you do.

- The type of clients he or she customarily handles. If most of them make larger transactions than you expect to make, who do you think will get most of the broker's attention?

- Just what the broker expects to do for you. The first thing he or she should do is ask you a lot of questions about your financial situation and your investment objectives. Steer clear of any broker who makes immediate recommendations before knowing much about you. If the broker does ask the right questions, then go further. Will she call you when an interesting opportunity comes along? Will she call you when it's time to sell, as well as when he would like you to buy?

- The broker's prior record—because, unfortunately, you can't assume you're getting the whole story. Every year, dozens of brokers and firms are fined by the National Association of Securities Dealers. But NASD won't reveal information on pending cases. Call your state investment regulation office (you can get the number by calling the North American Securities Administrators Association at (202) 737-0900) to find out if any claim has been filed against a broker or a firm you're considering doing business with.

Once you've selected a broker, give him or her a fair chance, and enough time. But always feel free to change stockbrokers if your investment goals are not compatible. Definitely make a change if you suspect that your broker is "churning" your account, buying and selling with excessive frequency. Any profits you might make will be eaten up by commissions on a churned account, and the only one to come out ahead will be the broker.

Note: Many full-service brokerage firms are pushing **"wrap" accounts,** combining professional money management with brokerage services. The good news is that these accounts carry a fixed fee, inclusive of commissions, leaving little incentive for your broker to push additional trades. The bad news is that the fee is high, typically 3 percent of assets. In most instances, you'll do better securing professional management through a no-load mutual fund.

If you think you might want a wrap account, however, ask these questions before you sign up:

- What is the money manager's track record? Ask to see performance results including only retail wrap accounts and not large institutional accounts.
- What is the average turnover in the account? Large turnover will generate capital gains taxes. Minimal turnover may mean you're paying for service you're not getting.
- Will you pay wrap account fees on cash in money market funds? You shouldn't—but some firms impose such fees; while others do not.

Q My broker lost a lot of money for me by recommending stocks which were far too risky for someone in my circumstances—recently divorced and responsible for two small children. Is there anything I can do to get my money back?

A You must realize two things: No stock market investment guarantees that you will make money; and you didn't have to follow your broker's recommendations. The final decision about what to buy was always up to you. Nonetheless, if you believe you lost money because your broker was either incompetent or unethical (brokers are not supposed to push inappropriate investments), you can sue the broker (if the brokerage agreement you signed permits you to do so) or take your case to an industry arbitration panel. The National Association of Security Dealers, the New York Stock Exchange, the American Stock Exchange, and some of the regional exchanges have inquiry, compliance, and arbitration panels. If your dispute involves less than $10,000, in fact, you may ask for arbitration by mail. Write to the Arbitrator's Office, New York Stock Exchange, 11 Wall St., New York, NY 10005.

Note: For operational problems, such as accounting snafus, your first step is to contact the branch manager of the brokerage firm.

Discount Stockbrokers

You have a right to expect some attention from a full-service stockbroker: research, telephone calls, even some hand-holding. If you don't need any of this, if you're capable of your own investment decisions, then you might want to consider using a discount stockbroker and saving from 55 to 74 percent on brokerage commissions. The size of the discount depends on two things: the fees set by the firm and the size of the transaction. Minimum fees set by some firms could wipe out any saving on small transactions.

Discount brokerage firms come in several varieties, from what analyst Mark Coler of Mercer, Inc. calls the "deep discounters" through the "big three" made up of Charles Schwab, Fidelity Brokerage, and Quick & Reilly. Some discount brokers are strictly telephone order-takers. Others are now offering some additional services: an individual to work with, a telephone alert when a stock reaches a predetermined price, a money fund for idle cash. Some run investment seminars, some offer margin accounts (see pp. 151-153). And some are moving beyond stock transactions to offer bonds, commodities, and so on. (Note, though, that using a discount broker may not save you much on a bond purchase.) Research, however, is still generally not available except from full-service brokerage firms. Decide what service you need and want, and shop around for the best price.

Note: You may be able to buy securities (often at discounted commissions) at the same place you keep your savings account, if your bank or savings and loan is one that has moved into the brokerage field. While government regulations still draw distinct lines between banks and brokerage firms, alliances are being formed that cross the lines and offer you far more flexibility. You can also buy securities directly at discounted commissions, if you're comfortable with computers, through an on-line service such as Prodigy.

Commissions

You'll pay considerably less to a discount stockbroker, by and large, than to a full-service broker. But a lot depends on the size of each transaction and on how many transactions you make. "Round lots" of 100 shares always cost less in commissions than "odd lots," at any broker. But a purchase of 100 shares is still a small transaction, one on which commission savings won't be significant. A purchase of several hundred shares, on the other hand, will probably cost significantly different sums. Note, though, that an investor who makes frequent trades at a full-service broker can ask for, and probably receive, a discount on commissions.

The annual Mercer Discount Brokerage Survey for 1993 showed this range on two typical trades:

Commission on 100 shares at $100 a share:

- At the deepest discounter: $ 24.99
- At the lowest of the "big 3": $ 49.00
- At a full-service broker: $106.00

Commission on 500 shares at $30 a share:

- At the deepest discounter: $ 25.00
- At the lowest of the "big 3": $97.00
- At a full-service broker: $314.00

Brokerage commissions were deregulated in 1975 and every firm sets its own rates, making it essential to shop around.

But don't blindly go to just any broker advertising discounts. Some discount brokers base commissions on the dollar amount of the order, and are generally less expensive when you buy low-priced stocks. Some base commissions on the number of shares purchased, and are generally less expensive when you buy higher-priced stocks. Whichever you use (and you might use both, for different types of purchases, if you are a frequent investor), be sure to compare rate schedules. And be wary of advertised discounts; some ads refer back to pre-1975 regulated rates in claiming big savings.

Some sophisticated investors use both a full-service broker, for the times when they want advice, and a discount broker, for trades initiated on their own. It isn't quite cricket, however, to take information and advice from one broker and then give the commission to another.

If your investment portfolio will contain investments other than stocks, as it should if you are to have a diversified portfolio, you may want to consider brokers specializing in certain areas. It can make sense, for example, to go directly to a bond dealer when you want to buy bonds rather than to a generalist.

Bear in mind, though, that brokers make more money on some investments than on others; the "good investment" that your broker is touting may be good for his pocketbook but not for yours. It's generally true, in fact, that the riskier the investment, the more it will cost you to buy; Treasury obligations cost under one percent of the purchase price, limited partnerships 8 percent or more. It's true that you may need more advice going into a limited partnership—but you also stand to lose more money. Don't blindly accept recommendations; always do your own homework.

Q I recently bought my first shares of stock. Can I deduct the broker's commissions on my income tax return?

A No. Commissions aren't deductible while you hold the stock, although they do reduce any taxes due when you sell the stock. At that time you subtract the commission from your profit (or add it to your loss) to determine the taxable amount, if any.

KEY POINTS

- Investments are an essential part of your lifelong financial plan; try to set aside money for investments as part of your regular budget.

- Before you invest at all, establish a readily available financial cushion of up to six months' income.

- Before you invest in any particular vehicle, evaluate it in terms of your investment temperament, your investment objectives, and the investment climate.

- Look at individual investments in terms of risk, liquidity, maturity, and tax aspects.

- Minimize risk by diversifying your portfolio, allocating assets among different investment vehicles.

- Tailor your investment plan, and balance your portfolio, in accordance with your age, income, and responsibilities; reevaluate your plan, and your portfolio, at regular intervals.

CHAPTER 6

Investment Vehicles

You can achieve your investment objectives with a variety of investment vehicles. You'll probably invest in more than one vehicle at one time, in fact, and vary your investment mix as your needs, your age, and your objectives change.

Mutual Funds

Mutual funds are pooled investments with professional management. Via a mutual fund, you can invest in common stock, corporate bonds, tax-free bonds, options, even (via money market mutual funds) money itself. You can invest for income, for growth, for safety. You can use mutual funds to get started as an investor. And you can use mutual funds, throughout your investment life, as an efficient way to diversify and balance your portfolio.

Mutual funds are certainly popular. There were 3,661 separate mutual funds in 1992, according to the Investment Company Institute, up from just over 1,000 in 1983. Perhaps the most familiar is the money market mutual fund, not strictly an investment vehicle but useful both as a cash management tool and as a between-investment place to park investment funds.

MONEY MARKET MUTUAL FUNDS

Money market mutual funds invest in money, in large-denomination short-term securities such as government obligations, corporate debt, and other high-yielding, liquid investments otherwise available only to big investors. Money funds typically come in two varieties: taxable and tax-free. Both offer safety of principal, current income, and instant liquidity. Money market mutual funds are not insured, although they are considered among the safest of investments. For a still-greater guarantee of safety (although, perhaps, slightly lower rates of return) look at money market funds that invest solely in government obligations.

Tax-exempt money market funds invest in municipal notes and bonds, tax anticipation notes, and similar items. At times the average maturity on tax-free funds may be a bit longer than the maturity on taxable funds (neither is permitted to go out more than 90 days), so these funds are slightly less responsive to changing interest rates and may be an excellent choice when rates are failing. However, yields can be considerably lower on a tax-exempt money fund than on a general-purpose money fund. Look at your tax bracket and comparative yields before you leap to the magnet of tax exemption.

Money market funds have definite advantages when it comes to cash management:

- Most money market funds are "no-load" funds; they have no sales charge or commission, just a small built-in administrative fee.
- Most money market funds offer check-writing privileges, although in many cases a check must be written for at least $500. That can include your mortgage, taxes, insurance bills, tuition ... and a monthly payment to your checking account to take care of smaller bills.
- The exact return on a money market fund is never guaranteed. But the rate is reported in the newspapers, generally on a weekly basis. When the rates go below your expectations, you can pull out without penalty.
- Many money market funds are part of a "family" of funds, with stock and bond funds, growth and income funds, managed by the same company. Most such families have telephone-switching privileges, so that moving some or all of your funds out of the money market and into, for instance, a stock fund, can be accomplished with a phone call.

Selecting a Money Market Mutual Fund

Money market funds are not all alike. You'll want to evaluate the minimum required initial deposit and subsequent deposits, the minimum amount for which checks may be written, the accessibility of information via toll-free telephone lines. Risk is also important. Look at the following factors before you decide which fund is for you:

- The composition of the fund's portfolio. While most funds invest in the same things—Treasury bills and notes, commercial paper, banker's acceptances, certificates of deposit, repurchase agreements, and guaranteed loans—some of these investments are riskier than others. Safest are government securities; riskiest are deposits in foreign currencies. Unless a fund is invested entirely in U.S. government issues, diversification is important. You'll find the fund's composition in its prospectus; the precise composition varies from day to day, but this will indicate the fund management's investment philosophy.

■ Maturity of the fund's holdings. Some stick to 30 days, others go out to 60 days or more. When interest rates are dropping, longer maturities preserve higher yields. When rates are rising, shorter maturities take full advantage of the upward trend. In general, a steady cash turnover means that even heavy redemptions won't cause an excessive drain on the fund. Maturities are found both in the prospectus and in newspaper fund listings.

Figure 6.1: Mutual Funds Can Be Grouped According to Their Level of Risk and Their Potential Return

Source: Mutual Fund Education Alliance.

OTHER TYPES OF MUTUAL FUNDS

In addition to money market mutual funds, the Investment Company Institute groups 21 types of funds by investment objective. Here are just some of the ways to meet your investment goals via mutual funds (the objectives of each fund must be spelled out in its prospectus):

■ If you want safety of principal coupled with high current income in a long-term investment, try an **income fund,** investing in corporate bonds and/or high-dividend-paying stocks.

■ If you're more interested in capital growth, to offset inflation or to build assets before retirement, look at **growth funds,** investing in high-quality common stocks. Over the past several years, the Investment Company Institute reports, equity funds with dividends and capital gains reinvested have kept their shareholders comfortably ahead of the Consumer Price Index—at a time when individual common stocks generally lagged behind. **Note:** Growth funds can be composed solely of domestic stocks, solely of foreign stocks (international funds), or of a combination of domestic and foreign stocks (global funds).

■ For still greater growth (coupled with greater risk), try **aggressive growth stock funds,** sometimes called "performance" or "maximum capital gains" funds, concentrating in speculative issues, start-up companies or specialized industries such as gold or oil exploration.

■ If you want both long-term growth of capital and current income, look at a **balanced fund,** investing in a balanced portfolio of fixed-income securities (bonds and/or preferred stocks) and common stocks. With more conservative investment policies than typical growth funds, most balanced funds do not move either up or down very rapidly. Each fund, however, has a different approach to providing a balance and to the degree of risk it will assume. Or you might consider splitting your investment dollars between two separate funds with clearly defined objectives.

■ For tax-exempt return on a longer-term basis than a money market mutual fund can offer, there are **short-term** and **long-term municipal bond funds,** investing in state and local bonds. Interest is generally exempt from federal income taxes, and from state taxes in the state in which the obligation is issued. Single-state funds are particularly popular in states with high income tax rates.

Whatever your goals, a mutual fund has distinct advantages. It affords diversification, reducing your risk by investing in many different securities. You can't manage this much diversification on your own unless you have significant sums to invest. It gives your money professional management, the skills and talents of full-time managers. It promises liquidity; shares can always be redeemed at current net asset value.

INVESTMENT STRATEGY WITH MUTUAL FUNDS

You can make the most of your mutual fund investments if you:

■ **Select a "family" of funds** with free exchange-by-telephone privileges so that you can switch your investments as circumstances dictate. *The No-Load Fund Investor,* a newsletter available by subscription (P.O. Box 318, Irvington-on-Hudson, NY 10533), recommends selecting a family by, first, analyzing the type and quality

Table 6.1: Identifying Funds for Your Portfolio

Identify funds for your portfolio in terms of objective, potential capital appreciation, potential current income, and stability of principal.

IF YOUR BASIC OBJECTIVE IS	YOU WANT THE FOLLOWING FUND TYPE	THESE FUNDS INVEST PRIMARILY IN	POTENTIAL CAPITAL APPRECIATION	POTENTIAL CURRENT INCOME	STABILITY OF PRINCIPAL
Maximum Capital Growth	**AGGRESSIVE GROWTH**	Common stocks with potential for very rapid growth. May employ certain aggressive strategies.	Very High	Very Low	Low to Very Low
High Capital Growth	**GROWTH SPECIALTY**	Common stocks with long-term growth potential.	High to Very High	Very Low	Low
Current Income & Capital Growth	**GROWTH & INCOME**	Common stocks with potential for high dividends and capital appreciation.	Moderate	Moderate	Low to Moderate
High Current Income	**FIXED INCOME EQUITY INCOME**	Both high-dividend-paying stocks and bonds.	Very Low	High to Very High	Low to Moderate
Current Income & Protection of Principal	**GENERAL MONEY MARKET FUNDS**	Money market instruments.	None	Moderate to High	Very High
Tax-Free Income & Protection of Principal	**TAX-EXEMPT MONEY MARKET**	Short-term municipal notes and bonds.	None	Moderate to High	Very High
Current Income & Maximum Safety of Principal	**U.S. GOVERNMENT MONEY MARKET**	U.S. Treasury and agency issues guaranteed by the U.S. Government.	None	Moderate to High	Very High
Tax-Exempt Income	**MUNICIPAL BONDS DOUBLE & TRIPLE TAX-EXEMPT**	A broad range of municipal bonds.	Low to Moderate	Moderate to High	Moderate

Source: Mutual Fund Education Alliance.

of its stock funds, because this is where differences in performance are most apt to appear. Then look at the variety of fixed-income funds available. Is there a tax-free as well as a taxable bond fund? Then review the group's money market funds; performance may be similar, but preferred groups have three types of money fund—general-purpose, government-only, and tax-free.

■ **Don't plan on frequent trades.** Mutual funds are not the same kind of trading vehicles as individually purchased stocks and bonds. You might sell a stock because it has gone up as much as you had hoped, but a fund can continue to grow as long as the stock market gains. Mutual funds, with one exception, should be considered long-term investments (but not indefinite; you should still keep an eye on performance and sell, or switch to another fund, if yields drop consistently). The exception: aggressive growth funds. These funds may be the best way for the average investor to invest in the stock of small, likely-to-grow companies, but they are extremely volatile and should be sold as soon as performance begins to decline.

■ **Diversify your investment** in mutual funds, just as you would in any other investment. Invest regularly, over time, to dollar-cost-average. And consider investing in two to four funds with different investment objectives and management styles. These two to four funds may be within the same fund group, if you have chosen wisely, thereby minimizing costs and inconvenience.

Investment objectives, as described above, range from aggressive growth to fixed income. Management style refers, particularly within equity (stock) funds, to a choice between "value" and "growth" stocks. Some managers pick so-called value stocks, whose prices are low when measured against per-share value of the company's earnings or assets. Others lean toward classic growth stocks. Some funds invest primarily in large blue-chip companies. Others look to midsize companies while still others, generally with more

---

Q I just found out that I'm paying a sales charge every time I reinvest dividends in my mutual fund. Is this usual?

A No. But a few mutual funds do levy the same sales charge or "load" on reinvested dividends that they do on an initial investment. Check the prospectus: If there is no charge for reinvestment, it will say that dividends are reinvested "at net asset value." If there is a charge, reinvestment will be "at the offering price"—and you may want to select another fund.

aggressive objectives, look to small emerging companies in what is called the "small-cap" sector.

Important: Management styles do better or worse as the economy moves through different cycles; investing in both value and growth funds, therefore, is a form of diversification that truly minimizes risk.

■ **Elect automatic reinvestment.** This option allows you to put fund dividends and/or capital gain distributions back into the fund to buy new shares and thereby build up new holdings. Note that reinvested dividends, like dividends you take in cash, are taxable as ordinary income.

PICKING A FUND

In addition to funds designated by investment objectives, there are a great many special funds. Some stick to one industry (e.g., chemicals). Some are organized along geographic lines (e.g., investment in the Far East). Some are "index" funds, owning all the stocks reported by one market index (such as Standard & Poor's 500) and intended to reflect the performance of the market as a whole. And some are "socially conscious" funds, investing in companies that make some contribution to the well-being of the world. Special-interest funds may follow different strategies to meet different investment objectives.

There are also significant differences among funds in purely practical terms. In addition to investment objectives, two important factors are the reputation of the fund manager and investment performance. The two are inextricably linked and, in many analysts' view, the departure of a longtime manager is a good time to sell fund shares. Funds are often reluctant to release the names of portfo-

Q I don't like the idea of my money going to industries that pollute or to companies that make weapons. Is there a way to invest more responsibly?

A Yes. Socially responsible investing, in fact, has become quite popular in the last few years. You can take part by investing in individual companies that meet your personal values. Or you can buy shares in one of a growing number of mutual funds espousing social responsibility. Some are concerned primarily with protecting the environment, others with equitable employment practices, still others with public health. Some of the mutual funds grouped in this category are Dreyfus Third Century (800-645-6561), Calvert Social Equity (800-368-2748), and Pax World (800-767-1729). Additional information is available in the books listed in the bibliography.

lio managers (although the Securities and Exchange Commission has been attempting to force disclosure), but you can often find the information in investment publications such as *Barron's* and *Forbes.* In comparing fund performance, forget quarterly reports and look at returns over at least a five-year period.

Here are some other major points to consider.

Load or No-load?

This used to be a simple distinction because funds were sold either with a "load" (a sales commission) or without. Funds offered through a stockbroker or other agency were more likely to charge a sales fee, typically 8.5 percent, while those offered directly to the public via newspaper ads and direct mail were more likely to be of the no-load variety.

Arguments have raged over whether fees have anything to do with performance. Investment advisers and stockbrokers claim that it's worth paying for good advice, while consumer advocates point out that paying hefty fees (both loads and annual expenses) means that less of your money is working for you. A 1993 study by CDA/Wiesenberger, a Rockville, Maryland, firm that compiles mutual fund data, offers some answers. When it comes to top-ranking equity funds, according to this study, expenses are not significant; management decisions can be key to investment performance. Bond funds are a different story; long-term bond funds with the lowest expenses did best, while those with the highest expenses fared poorly. The implications for income investors are important. As CDA/Wiesenberger noted in releasing the study results, "A fund with high expenses but strong performance probably earned its gains by assuming added risk—something investors should consider carefully, since these same aggressive strategies could backfire. The best choice would be a fund with above-average performance and below-average expenses."

Table 6.2: The Top-Performing Funds of All Time

Performance rankings 1/1/40 to 12/31/92.

EQUITY FUNDS

Objective	Fund	$10,000 Grew to[1]
Growth/Income	Investment Company of America	$5,314,926
Long-Term Growth	Keystone K-2	5,029,747
Long-Term Growth	Seligman Growth Fund	3,974,559
Growth/Income	Seligman Common Stock Fund	3,866,198
Growth/Income	Affiliated Fund	3,805,329
Growth/Income	Fidelity Fund	3,768,130
Maximum Capital Gain	Keystone S-4	3,066,984
Long-Term Growth	Mass Investors Group Stock	3,017,292

Long-Term Growth	Putnam Investors Fund	2,946,401
Growth/Income	State Street Investment	2,924,643
Growth/Income	Safeco Equity Fund	2,813,848
Equity Income	United Income Fund	2,674,188
Long-Term Growth	Alliance Fund	2,652,532
Growth/Income	Fundamental Investors	2,513,455
Growth/Income	Mass Investors Trust	2,342,757
Growth/Income	Alliance Growth & Income	2,063,596
Growth/Income	Financial Industrial Fund	2,042,340
Special Financial	Century Shares Trust	1,947,532
Growth/Income	Lexington Corporate Leaders Trust	1,920,669
Growth/Income	Selected American Shares	1,917,342
Growth/Income	Nationwide Fund	1,697,556
Long-Term Growth	Keystone S-3	1,579,437
Growth/Income	Eaton Vance Stock Fund	1,139,038
Growth/Income	Eaton Vance Investors	1,136,678
Growth/Income	Keystone S-1	1,038,767

BALANCED FUNDS

Balanced[2]	Delaware Group-Delaware Fund	2,603,919
Balanced	American Balanced Fund	1,424,406
Balanced	CGM Mutual Fund	1,296,278
Balanced	Putnam (George) Fund of Boston	1,252,319
Balanced	Dodge & Cox Balanced Fund	1,044,453
Balanced	Alliance Balanced Shares	1,025,156
Balanced	Wellington Fund	1,022,626
Balanced	Composite Bond & Stock Fund	799,183

BOND FUNDS

High-Yield Bond[2]	Keystone B-4	1,180,855
Income Flexible	Keystone K-1	963,165
Government Bond[2]	Lord Abbett U.S. Gov't Sec.	739,023
Corporate Bond	Keystone B-2	497,975
Corporate Bond[2]	Scudder Income Fund	463,317
Corporate Bond	Keystone B-1	179,415

Source: CDA/Wiesenberger of Rockville, Maryland.

Notes: [1] Assumes $10,000 investment made on January 1, 1940, at current sales charge (if applicable). Data is believed reliable but cannot be guaranteed.

[2] Fund had a change of policy during period.

Today the lines between load and no-load funds are blurred. There are still load funds, but relatively few charge the full 8.5 percent load at the time of purchase; more broker-sold funds now have "contingent deferred sales charges" or "back-end" fees, loads imposed at the time you sell (sometimes only if you sell within a specified period of years). Some broker-sold funds offer two classes of shares, one with a front-end load and one with a back-end load. And then there are so-called "low-load" funds, offered by brokers, by many banks (in a new move by the banking industry into mutual fund sales), and directly by mutual fund families; low-load funds have initial sales commissions of two or three percent.

Many funds also have "12b-1 fees," named after the section of the securities law that brought them into being, which levy year-after-year fees intended to cover the costs of advertising and distribution (in other words, a portion of your profits as a shareholder goes to market the fund to other investors). A 12b-1 fee can cost you more, over many years of owning shares, than a one-time up-front load of 8.5 percent.

Note: The load is a sales commission. All funds—load, low-load, and no-load—charge annual management fees, usually 0.5 percent to 1 percent of the fund's net asset value.

Pure no-load funds (with no front-end loads, back-end charges, exit fees, dividend reinvestment charges, or 12b-1 fees) still exist; a listing may be

---

Q We have some money to invest, for the first time, but don't know how to get started. A broker suggested a stock-index fund. Can you explain just what this is and tell us whether it's a good idea?

A Index funds buy and hold the stocks represented in a broad market index, such as the Standard & Poor's 500, so that their performance mirrors the stock market as a whole. They can be a good bet if you don't want to make choices among individual stocks or funds and if you will stick with the investment for a long time. But index funds do have limitations:

- Since they so closely follow the market, they can be very volatile in the short term
- Because of the way they are designed, index funds won't ever outperform the market; you must be content with average performance

Also, because that "average performance" will be further reduced by expenses, it's wise to choose an index fund with no "load" (commission) and with low operating expenses (this number, called the expense ratio, is in the prospectus).

Figure 6.2: Interpreting Mutual Fund Newspaper Listings

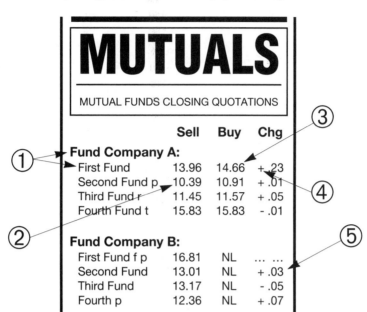

MUTUALS

MUTUAL FUNDS CLOSING QUOTATIONS

	Sell	Buy	Chg
Fund Company A:			
First Fund	13.96	14.66	+ .23
Second Fund p	10.39	10.91	+ .01
Third Fund r	11.45	11.57	+ .05
Fourth Fund t	15.83	15.83	- .01
Fund Company B:			
First Fund f p	16.81	NL	... ...
Second Fund	13.01	NL	+ .03
Third Fund	13.17	NL	- .05
Fourth p	12.36	NL	+ .07

① Funds are listed alphabetically by fund company with specific funds listed under each company.

② "NAV" means "Net Asset Value" and is the value of stocks being held in the portfolio divided by the number of the shares of the fund being held by the shareholders. "NAV" shows how much each share in the fund is worth.

③ "Offer Price" is the amount you would pay if you wanted to buy the shares and is the same as the "NAV", plus any sales charges. "NL" means it is a no-load fund and you would pay the same price per share to buy it as you would receive if you were to sell it.

④ This tells how much the net asset value of the fund has changed since the previous trading day. A plus (+) value means your shares have increased in value since the close of the last trading day by the amount indicated, and a minus (-) value means each of your shares has fallen by that amount.

⑤ Change shows the amount by which the net asset value of one share of the fund increased or decreased the day before.

Source: Mutual Fund Education Alliance.

obtained for $3 from the 100% No-Load Mutual Fund Council, 1501 Broadway, Suite 312, New York, NY 10036. A list of some 600 no-load and low-load funds, with details on their investment goals, is available for $5 from the Mutual Fund Education Alliance, 1900 Erie St., Suite 120, Kansas City, MO 64116. A directory of over 3700 mutual funds of all kinds (load and no-load) is available for $5 from the Investment Company Institute, 1600 M St., NW, Washington, DC 20036.

Newspaper listings of mutual fund quotations show "N.L." under "Offer Price" to designate no-load funds. Performance is often comparable, but you should realize that part of your money is not working for you when you go into a load fund.

What Conveniences and Privileges Does the Fund Offer?

Ask these questions before you invest:

■ How easy is it to purchase shares? What is the minimum purchase amount? The minimum amount accepted for subsequent deposits? Is there an automatic reinvestment program? You can open accounts by mail, telephone, or bank wire, depending upon the particular fund. Some will accept automatic deductions from a savings or checking account.

■ Is there an exchange privilege? by telephone? Many funds belong to a "family," a group of funds with different investment vehicles and objectives, and allow investors to switch among the funds as investment objectives or conditions change. Find out, in advance, if there is a charge for the transfer. Find out, too, if there is any limit on the number of times that you may transfer funds.

Q I read an ad for a bond mutual fund with check-writing privileges. With interest rates so low on bank accounts and money-market funds, this seems like a good way to earn more interest and still be able to write checks. Is there anything I should know before I use a bond fund this way?

A Yes. Bond funds fluctuate in value and every time you write a check you are selling shares at a different price. Each sale is a separate taxable transaction, on which you'll have to report capital gains and losses, so using a bond fund as a checking account will give you a real headache at tax time. It will reduce record-keeping problems if the fund supplies average-cost information for tax purposes. Some do, some don't, so ask before you pick a fund. And, even if a bond fund fits your investment goals, try to keep check writing to a minimum.

■ How easy is it to withdraw your money? Shares may be redeemed by letter, telephone, bank wire, or check, depending on the particular fund. Many mutual funds offer withdrawal plans under which shareholders may secure payments at regular intervals; this can be particularly useful for retirement income. For one-shot withdrawals (as, for instance, when you need to write a sizable tax check to Uncle Sam) consider opening a money market mutual fund within your fund family. Then a simple telephone call will transfer funds from a stock fund, as an example, to your money market fund—and the singular advantage of money market funds is the ability to write a check (usually in a minimum amount of $500) directly on your money in the fund.

■ How good is customer service? Many funds offer toll-free telephone numbers, but can you get through, or is the line always busy? This may seem trivial, but can generate acute aggravation.

TAXES ON MUTUAL FUNDS

The ownership of mutual funds has tax considerations both during ownership and when you sell your shares:

As a share owner you may receive dividends and/or capital gains distributions. Dividends, whether you take them in cash or reinvest them, must be reported as ordinary income. Capital gains distributions, as the fund profits from buying and selling securities, are generally received and reported annually and are also reported as ordinary income. Funds with high turnover rates (because they buy and sell frequently) generate a heavier tax burden for shareholders.

Some cautionary notes:

■ Funds are required to make year-end distributions of capital gains. If you buy shares in a fund just before that distribution is made, you will wind up paying income taxes on profits you didn't receive. To avoid

Q I had no trouble with my mutual fund until I wanted to close out the account. Now they require a signature guarantee, not a notarized signature but a guarantee, before I can get my money. I don't have a stockbroker, and I don't use a commercial bank. Where can I get a signature guarantee?

A Your savings and loan may be able to arrange a signature guarantee through an affiliated commercial bank. Or you might find a local commercial bank willing to accommodate you even if you are not a depositor. Not all mutual funds have this requirement, and it might be better, next time, to invest in one that does not.

this trap, find out the fund's distribution date, and wait to invest until just after the distribution is made.

■ When you sell your shares, remember that you've already paid taxes on reinvested dividends; don't pay taxes again on the same money by basing your profit calculations on the simple difference between your initial purchase price and your sales price. Good records can avoid this trap.

When you sell your shares, you may have either a capital gain or a capital loss. If you buy into the fund at one time and sell all your shares at one time, your arithmetic is simple (but don't forget to subtract those reinvested dividends). If you've bought in over a period of time and want to sell only a portion of your shares, your calculations become more complicated. If you keep careful records as you go along, you'll be able to sell specific shares, selecting long- and short-term capital gains or losses, to your tax advantage. If not, the Internal Revenue Service (IRS) permits you to use an average cost basis. But it isn't this simple; tax matters rarely are. Ask your mutual fund for tax-reporting information. You may also want to consult a tax adviser.

Note: Capital gains or losses must be reported when you exchange shares within a family of funds. According to the IRS, such a transaction is a sale and a purchase.

CLOSED-END FUNDS

All of the mutual funds described above are open-end pooled investments, with managers buying and selling within the fund to meet declared objectives and deal with changing market conditions. An open-end fund can issue an unlimited number of fund shares and continue to issue shares as new investors arrive on the scene. Closed-end funds are similar pools of securities, but issue a fixed number of shares in an initial public offering. Once issued, the shares are traded on a stock exchange the way common stock is traded. Closed-end funds have portfolio managers and, as of 1993, the names of those managers must be revealed to investors.

Closed-end funds include some with the same investment objectives as open-end funds. There are stock, bond, and balanced funds. And there are specialty funds, including a broad variety of regional and single-country funds. But the difference in fund structure creates a difference in pricing. The share price of an open-end fund, called the net asset value, is the value of total holdings divided by the number of shares outstanding at any one time. The share price of a closed-end fund, like the share price of common stock, is largely determined by supply and demand. While you can buy open-end mutual funds either through a broker or directly, closed-end funds are available only through brokers and only by paying a commission.

There's often a flurry of activity surrounding the initial public offering (IPO) of a new closed-end fund. A broker may tell you this is a good time to buy, because the commission is built into the price of the shares. In fact, a hefty chunk of your investment in an IPO goes to underwriting fees. Moreover, new funds typically trade at a discount after they've been available for a couple of months. It may therefore be wiser to wait.

UNIT INVESTMENT TRUSTS

There's another type of pooled investment, the unit investment trust. These trusts are closed-end but they are also unmanaged, because the portfolio (typically corporate or municipal bonds) is fixed at the time of purchase and subsequently runs its course until maturity. That maturity date might be six months from purchase date if the trust invests in certificates of deposit (CDs). It might be 20 or 30 years in a trust that invests in corporate bonds.

Unit trusts are often sold as having a fixed interest rate. But it's important to remember that unit trusts are subject to the same market risk and price fluctuations as other investments. Moreover, where a unit trust invests in bonds, bond "calls" (early redemptions by the issuer) may (and usually does) result in lower yields.

Unit trusts are sold in minimum increments of $1,000, with sales charges ranging from 2 to 5.5 percent. Interest on the trust is paid by check,

Q Someone called me recently about a new security with a guaranteed return of 12 percent. That sounded awfully good, maybe too good to be true, so I asked for a prospectus. Now I've got a fancy document. But how do I check this out?

A You're absolutely right to be suspicious. When interest rates fell to record lows in the early 1990s, a lot of scam artists came out of the woodwork to tempt people needing income. If you want to confirm the legitimacy of this particular offer, do this:

■ Call the Securities and Exchange Commission in Washington, DC (202-272-7450) and ask whether the company has filed an offering statement. If it hasn't, or if all you get in the way of information is a glossy brochure, stay away.

■ Call your state investment regulation office (for the number, call the North American Securities Administrators Association at 202-737-0900) to check on complaints against the broker. Again, if there are *any* complaints on record, stay away.

In general, it's never wise to invest in securities issued by a company you've never heard of on the basis of a telephone call from a stockbroker you do not know.

often monthly; in many trusts there is also a reinvestment privilege which enables you to compound your return.

Unit investment trusts are always sold with a load—that is, your broker gets a commission. Although unit investment trusts offer the advantages of professional portfolio selection, diversification, and simplicity, it is often more expensive to buy and sell a unit investment trust than it is to buy and sell either individual bonds or CDs or an open-end mutual fund. Don't look at trusts as trading vehicles, therefore, but as a long-term investment.

Common Stock

When you buy one or more shares of common stock you are buying a portion of the corporation that issues the stock; you are becoming an owner. You're not much of an owner, of course, and you are not going to be making any management decisions, although you will be asked to cast a vote at the annual meeting of the corporation either in person, or by mail via a proxy. But your fortunes will prosper or decline along with the fortunes of the company, with both the price of the stock itself and the dividends it pays subject to change.

WHAT ARE STOCKS WORTH?

Simply put, a share of stock is worth whatever someone is willing to pay for it. The buying and selling of common stock is based purely on supply and demand. The initial shares of a corporation's stock are sold by the corporation, to raise money. After that, for the most part, shares are sold by investors and bought by other investors.

One measure that investors use to determine a stock's value is the **price-to-earnings ratio.** This P/E ratio is the price of a share of stock divided by the company's annual earnings per share. A stock selling for $50 a share and earning $5 a share, for instance, is said to be selling at a price/earnings ratio of 10. This figure is also called the **multiple.** Whatever it's called, it's most useful as a means of comparing various securities or the same security over time.

The **yield** is another important figure, reflecting dividends as a percentage of the current price of the stock. A stock with a current market value of $40 a share paying dividends at the rate of $3.20 is said to yield 8 percent ($3.20 divided by $40).

The P/E, the yield, and other important information can be found in the stock market reports in your daily newspaper. Under the headings New York Stock Exchange Composite Index or American Stock Exchange, you'll find detailed information about each stock traded on each exchange. Separate listings are run for over-the-counter stocks, often but not always the stocks of smaller companies, under the heading NASDAQ National Market.

Here's a sample stock quotation, for Mobil Corporation (terminology may vary slightly in different newspapers):

52 WEEK High Low	Stock	Div	YIELD %	P/E Ratio	SALES 100s	High	Low	Last	Change
67 57	Mobil	3.20	4.9	21	3798	66	64⅞	65	-1

- ■ The first two figures, the **52-week high** and **low,** reflect the stock's highest and lowest values over the preceding year.
- ■ After the name of the stock, you'll find a column for its **dividend.** This figure is in dollars and represents the annual dividend, based on the latest declared dividend.
- ■ The **yield** is the percentage return represented by the annual dividend at the current price of the stock.
- ■ The **P/E ratio,** as explained above, is the number of times by which the latest 12-month earnings figure for the company must be multiplied to obtain the current stock price.
- ■ **Sales 100s** refers to the volume of sales for the day. There were 379,800 shares of Mobil traded on the day in the chart. A **z** preceding the volume figure means the sales are quoted in full.
- ■ Stock prices are stated in dollar amounts, with increments of one-eighth. The **high, low,** and **last** figures refer to the stock's prices on the particular trading day. Mobil's high was 66 ($66); its low for the day was 64 7/8 ($64.87), and its closing price, at the end of the day's trading, was 65. The **change** for the day, -1, is the difference—plus, minus, or no change—between the day's last reported price and the previous closing price.

There are other symbols in the tables. A small **s** refers to the fact that the stock has split and the price has been adjusted accordingly. When a stock splits—when, for instance, your 100 shares at $50 are now 200 shares worth $25 apiece—your holdings don't actually increase in value. The fact that a corporation has declared a stock split, however, implies that the company is doing well and its stock is becoming more valuable. This, in turn, may create more demand for the stock and drive the price up.

An **x** in front of the sales volume figure means that the stock is selling **ex-dividend.** That is, a dividend declared during this period will be paid to the seller and not to the buyer. This is usually a period of just a few days, after a dividend is declared but before it is actually paid.

STOCK MARKET AVERAGES

Listen to news broadcasts each day and you'll hear the ups and downs of the stock market referred to, more often than not, in terms of the Dow Jones Industrial Average. What is this index? And what does it tell you about the state of the economy? About whether or not to invest?

The Dow Jones Industrial Average measures the performance of the 30 largest and most prestigious industrial concerns in America. It therefore represents, for many people, the health of the American economy. But the Dow is just one among several stock market averages. Others, some observers believe, provide a more accurate measure. The Standard & Poor's Index, for instance,

Q My husband and I have bought some securities in joint ownership, with right of survivorship. Is this really a good idea?

A Jointly held assets can reduce administrative costs and speed settlement of the estate of the first to die. But jointly owned securities can also be a big headache. For example: While you're both alive, you both have to agree to a sale, precluding rapid action in the face of market shifts if one of you is ill or out of town. After one of you dies, the securities may bypass probate, but the survivor may face enormous amounts of paperwork in reregistering the stocks individually. Just as an example, one major corporation lists these required forms (all of which must be submitted with signature guaranteed by banker or broker):

■ A security "power" form, with the survivor's Social Security number and signature, and the serial numbers of the securities held
■ A death certificate, available from the funeral director
■ An affidavit of legal residence of the deceased stockholder for one year prior to death, together with affirmation that all debts, taxes, and claims against the estate have been paid; this document must be notarized
■ An inheritance tax waiver or, depending on the state, consent to transfer stock ownership

Alternatively, under new rules in some states, securities may be issued under a "Transfer on Death" (TOD) form of ownership, in which a designated beneficiary becomes the owner at the first owner's death. This method is not yet available everywhere; even where it is available by law, it is not necessarily offered by every issuer of securities.

All in all, it's probably preferable to own securities on an individual basis. You can keep things on an equal footing if you each invest approximately equivalent amounts; this is a wise move for estate planning, in any case (see Chapter 21).

measures the performance of 500 companies. The New York Stock Exchange Index and the American Stock Exchange Index measure the market value of stocks traded on the respective exchanges. And the NASDAQ (National Association of Securities Dealers Automated Quotations) Index reflects activity on the over-the-counter market.

Over the long haul, the measures should be relatively similar. In the short run, because they measure different groups and types of securities, one index may differ greatly from another. For your purposes, as an average investor, the Dow and the others will serve you best if you remember the following points:

- An index is a measure of movement in stock prices. Part of your yield, however, comes from dividends. You should keep both in mind in evaluating any stock for purchase or retention.

- Each index represents an average. On any given day, certain stocks within the measured group will rise while others will fall. Don't worry too much about day-to-day fluctuations; keep your eye on long-range trends.

- While an index may measure economic trends, your specific concern must be with your own portfolio. You should track the performance of your own securities and create your own index to guide your investment decisions.

BUYING STOCK

Most stock purchases are made on a cash basis. That is, the order is placed and payment is due, in full, within five days. After payment is made, you may choose to receive the stock, registered in your name. Or you may leave the stock with your broker, registered in "street name," for safekeeping. The latter course works well for frequent traders but makes less sense if you will buy the stock and hold it for long periods (especially because more and more brokerage firms are charging fees for inactive accounts).

Buying on Margin

You may also elect to leverage your purchase, increasing your potential profit (or loss), by buying on margin. When you buy securities on margin, you are buying on credit according to rules laid down by the Federal Reserve Board, the New York Stock Exchange, and your own broker. Those rules say that you can buy shares of stock, for example, with only part of the amount necessary to buy with cash; the difference is borrowed from your broker and secured with the stock itself. Margin requirements are changed periodically by the Federal Reserve Board. When the margin is set at 50 percent (as it is in 1993), you can buy $10,000 worth of stock with a cash outlay of $5,000. You don't have to put up any more money unless the value of your stock drops below a specified amount. The New York Stock Exchange, at this writing, requires additional cash if the stock's value drops below 25 percent (or, in this example, $2,500); many brokerage firms have more stringent requirements for additional cash. Look at this example:

You've made a $10,000 purchase with $5,000. If you then sell the stock for $12,000, the broker immediately receives the $5,000 you borrowed from him. You are entitled to $7,000 (your initial $5,000 plus the $2,000 in appreciation), minus commissions and interest on the loan. If your stock declines in value, you've got a different situation. Now you have to decide whether to sell or to hold on. If you sell for $8,000, you will receive $3,000 (the $8,000 minus the $5,000 loan), minus commission and interest. If you don't sell, and the stock continues to drop, you may well face a **margin call,** a request for more money (or additional securities as collateral) so that you will continue to meet the 25 percent rule. If you don't meet a margin call, your broker can sell your stock.

There are several lessons in this example:

- You can increase your yield (or your loss) by buying on margin, as you can with any leveraged purchase. If you bought that $10,000 worth of stock with your own $10,000 and it went to $12,000, you'd have made $2,000, or 20 percent. If you put up just half of the purchase price ($5,000), however, your yield doubles, to 40 percent. The same principle works when you lose. You can lose money when you trade stocks on a cash account, but you can lose far more when you trade on margin.
- It is difficult to make a profit on small margin purchases. The interest you pay on the loan itself (depending on how much you borrow and

Q We need additional cash to pay tuition bills, I was thinking about a home equity loan, but my broker has suggested a margin loan. What would you recommend?

A Both, at this writing, carry about the same interest rate. But there are other factors to consider. Both loans are backed by collateral: your house, in the case of a home equity loan, or your securities. Interest on a home equity loan of up to $100,000 is deductible; interest on a margin loan is deductible only if the proceeds are used for a taxable investment. A home equity loan can be written as a line of credit, so that you can write checks as tuition bills come due. Finally, and perhaps most important, while there are often fees (closing costs, points, etc.) associated with a home equity loan, margin loans usually only make sense for short-term borrowing; held for the duration of college, a margin loan could become very expensive—especially if the value of the underlying securities should drop. Between the two, I'd suggest a home equity line of credit.

how often you do so) will start at 0.75 to 2 percent above what the broker pays to borrow the money from the bank; in mid–1993, interest rates on margin accounts were in the neighborhood of 7.25 percent. This loan interest (although it is tax-deductible) plus commissions (larger, proportionately, on a small purchase) can easily equal or even exceed the appreciation on a small investment.

■ Your broker may urge you to enhance your profits by buying on margin. Before you do so, realize that you enhance your risks as well. Buying on margin is a good technique for gamblers or, at best, in-and-out traders; it holds too many pitfalls for the conservative investor who plans to hold for the long term.

DIVIDEND REINVESTMENT

Whether you are a conservative investor or enjoy the risks of speculation, you can benefit from participating in dividend reinvestment plans. Under these plans, offered by a rapidly growing number of corporations, you can choose to have your dividends applied to the purchase of additional shares. There are several advantages:

■ Dividend reinvestment is a convenient way to put small sums to work, sums you might otherwise fritter away without noticing.

■ Even when commissions are charged—and over 70 percent of companies offering dividend reinvestment absorb the cost—the commissions tend to be lower than they would otherwise be on small purchases because your funds are pooled with those of other investors.

■ Dividend reinvestment is a form of automatic **dollar cost averaging.** This is a system of stock purchase under which you purchase small amounts of stock at regular intervals, some at higher prices and some at lower ones, thereby averaging your purchase cost over the long term.

Assuming that you have made a good choice of company or mutual fund to begin with, you can compound your profits by participating in the dividend reinvestment plan. I would suggest doing so unless you are relying on your stock dividends for current income. You can also withdraw from a reinvestment plan at any time, and sell part or all of your accumulated shares, so you might consider participating even if you are approaching the years when you might look to dividends for regular income. When those years arrive, you can pull out.

As you plan your investment strategy, therefore, you might look to corporations with potential for growth plus good dividend reinvestment plans. Any dividend reinvestment plan offers the above advantages. But some offer still more:

■ With some plans you have a "cash option," the privilege of supplementing the dividend with cash and thereby purchasing additional shares at a moderate charge.

■ Some corporations (over 20 percent of those with reinvestment plans) not only absorb the commission costs on purchases through dividend reinvestment, but offer a discount on the purchase price of the shares. Such discounts, typically 3 to 5 percent, have been ruled taxable by the IRS. (The dividends themselves are taxable whether you take them in cash or reinvest them.) Note, too, that the discount may be applicable only to reinvested dividends and not to cash purchases.

KEEPING RECORDS

If you participate in a dividend reinvestment plan you will receive quarterly statements of your account: how many shares are held by you, how many shares or fractional shares have been purchased with the latest dividend, how many shares altogether the company has in your account. This information is important for tax purposes.

Your broker and the corporations in which you've invested (whether or not you elect dividend reinvestment) will send you other forms, also important for tax purposes. A confirmation of purchase and of sale will document your profit or loss for income tax purposes; these confirmation slips should be retained and kept on hand for at least three years after the filing of the tax return for the year in which you sell the stock. (That's how long the IRS has for a regular audit, as described in Chapter 20.) Year-end 1099 forms will document the income you've received during the year, whether you take it in cash or reinvest it in additional shares. Dividends and interest must be reported each year and income tax must be paid.

Q My 17-year-old son made a good bit of money with a lawn-care service this past summer and would like to buy some common stock. My stockbroker says he can't do so until he is legally an adult. Is this true?

A Yes. Because a minor can't be held to a contract, stockbrokers generally won't assume the risk of selling them securities. You could make the purchase in your son's name, but he could run into problems in selling the shares. Until your son becomes a legal adult (the age depends on the state in which you live), the solution may be ownership of securities under the Uniform Gifts (or Transfers) to Minors Act, with you or another adult as custodian. The shares would legally belong to your son, but you would have to act on his behalf in buying or selling.

It's also wise to keep your own records as the year goes by. Set up a notebook in which you record each dividend as it is received (or each paper dividend as it is reinvested). This way you'll know if a check gets lost in the mail. Record extra dividends, stock splits, and any other relevant information in your notebook, and you'll have a running tally of your investments.

PREFERRED STOCK

Preferred stock, like convertible bonds (see p. 157), combines some characteristics of both stocks and bonds. It is subordinate to any debt (bonds) which a corporation has outstanding. But, as the name implies, it usually has a claim ahead of the common stock upon the payment of dividends and upon the assets of the company should the company be dissolved.

Preferred stock also has these characteristics:

- Unlike bonds, it is traded on the stock exchange, making it easier to track your holdings and to sell.
- The dividend is usually at a set rate, so that preferred stock, like bonds, is a fixed-income investment.
- Where bonds almost always have a final maturity date, preferreds do not. But many preferreds, like most bonds, can be called in at prices set when the security was issued.
- Some preferred stocks, like some bonds, are convertible into common stock.
- Preferred stock, in general, offers steadier income, a higher return, and a lower degree of risk than investment in common stock.

Q After my father's death we were unable to find the certificates for some stock he owned. Can the certificates be replaced?

A Consult your father's stockbroker to make sure that he still owned the securities at the time of his death (he might have sold them) and that he actually had possession of the certificates (sometimes a broker keeps them). If the certificates have in fact been lost, the corporation must be notified. Most companies will put a "stop transfer" notice on the account for a three-month period during which the stock cannot be sold. You will have to file an affidavit of loss and buy a surety bond, for a premium of about 2 percent of the market value of the securities, which protects the company against any financial loss. After these steps are completed, new certificates will be issued.

Bonds

When you buy a share of common stock, you're becoming a part owner of the corporation. When you buy a bond, on the other hand, you are becoming a creditor of the corporation (or of the governing body, since bonds are also issued by state and local governments). You are loaning money to the issuer, usually in $1,000 increments; in exchange you will receive the principal sum, at maturity date, plus interest for the use of the money.

When you buy a share of stock, as an owner, you can expect to share in the fortunes of the company. If the company does well, your dividends may increase and the shares themselves may be worth more money. When you buy a bond, you are buying a fixed-rate security. The company may prosper but your rate of return is set from the beginning.

Bonds used to be called the investment of widows and orphans; their fixed rate of return made them both safe and stable. In recent years, however, investment in bonds has not been a sure thing at all. As inflation escalated in the late 1970s, new bond issues had to have higher and higher nominal yields in order to attract investors. As yields on new issues increased, older bonds lost a great deal of their value. Investors who wanted or needed to sell their bonds before maturity often sustained significant capital loss. Conversely, as interest rates fell in the early 1990s, bonds issued at higher interest rates were "called" (see p. 162) by their issuers, leaving bondholders with money to reinvest at lower rates. "Bond," in some quarters, has become a nasty four-letter word. In other, less conservative, quarters, bonds are a vehicle for aggressive investment.

Bonds of one sort or another will probably still play a role in your investment strategy. How big a role depends on your investment goals, your age, and your attitude toward risk. Here are the varieties of bonds to consider:

CORPORATE BONDS

Corporate bonds, as indicated, represent a corporation's debt to you. That debt may be backed by collateral, as when a corporation issues mortgage bonds. Or it may be backed, in bonds called **debentures,** by a promise to pay and the full faith and credit of the issuing company. Although bondholders take precedence over stockholders when it comes to repayment out of diminished assets, it's still wise to check the financial standing of a corporation before buying its bonds.

When bonds are taking a beating from inflation, corporations increasingly try innovative methods to spur investor interest. Corporate bonds generally pay more interest than municipals, although municipal issues (see p. 158) usually have the advantage of tax exemption. Some bonds are being issued with shorter maturities, five to seven years, perhaps, instead of thirty. Some are being issued with "call protection" so that high yields are guaranteed for a longer period of time.

Discount Bonds

New bonds are issued at a fixed price and fixed interest rate. Discount bonds are older bonds whose prices have declined since they were issued because interest rates have risen in the interim. So-called "deep discount" bonds are those with a significant discount. Discount bonds generally offer lower current income than new issues. But when you determine the yield to maturity, adding in the capital gains that will stem from redemption at face value, the overall return looks much better.

For example: A 35-year bond issued by Southwestern Bell Telephone, due in August 1997, was selling in mid-1992 for $935 and yielding 4.5 percent. But you could also count on a long-term capital gain of $65, in just five years, boosting the actual yield to just over 6 percent. Looking farther out, a 39-year Mountain States Telephone bond due June 1, 2005 was trading in mid-1992 at $867.50; with its yield of 5.5 percent and a capital gain of $132.50, its yield to maturity was over 7 percent.

Zero-Coupon Bonds

These bonds, which sprang to popularity about a decade ago, pay no interest at all but promise big capital accumulation by maturity. Called by such acronyms as CATS, TIGRS, and the like, zeros are available through stockbrokers. These bonds are attractive (if interest rates don't spiral upward) because the rate is locked in. But there's a catch: Even though there's no interest actually paid, the IRS assumes "imputed interest," which is taxable each year just as if it were actually paid. Taxable zero-coupon bonds are therefore most suitable for tax-deferred investments such as Individual Retirement Accounts (IRAs) and Keogh plans.

Zero-coupon bonds may be purchased either individually or in specially formulated bond mutual funds. Some have also been issued by state and local governments, which eliminates the tax problem and may make the bonds suitable for tax-sheltered investment outside your retirement plan. Some state issues, nicknamed "baccalaureate bonds," are designed for college saving (see Chapter 17).

Convertibles

Some bonds, combining characteristics of both bonds and common stock, are convertible to the common stock of the issuing corporation. Convertible bonds, marked with a "cv" in newspaper bond tables, pay interest, often more than the dividends on comparable common stock but less than the interest on comparable straight (nonconvertible) bonds. Convertible bonds offer appreciation possibilities linked to the earnings and growth of the company; they tend to rise and fall in value along with the company's common stock. Yet convertible bonds have an investment value above that of common stock. Most convertible bonds are convertible into stock at a fixed rate during the entire life of the bond. Sometimes, however, the conversion privilege expires at a set date.

Why buy convertible bonds? Common stock usually offers more opportunity for appreciation. Straight bonds usually offer more income. But your investment objectives (like most people's) may be mixed. You may be willing to sacrifice some capital appreciation possibilities for the sake of income or, conversely, give up higher income possibilities for a degree of appreciation potential.

Warrants

Warrants, like convertible bonds, are options which entitle you to purchase the common stock of the company at specified prices with the payment of cash and surrender of the warrants. With convertible bonds you turn in the bonds in exchange for the stock; with warrants you turn in just the detachable warrant, along with your cash payment, and retain the bond itself.

Most warrants are good for only a short period of time. While they are good, you can exercise them at a profit when the common stock goes up in value. You can also usually sell warrants themselves through your broker. Once they expire, however, they are worthless.

MUNICIPAL BONDS

Municipal bonds have traditionally been exempt from federal taxes and usually from state taxes in the state in which they are issued. (Some states impose a tax on out-of-state issues. If your state does so, and if it is a high-tax state, your yield will be reduced and the bond may not be worth buying. You may want to stick to bonds issued in your own state.) Municipal bonds come in several varieties:

General obligation bonds are backed by the full faith, credit, and taxing power of the municipality issuing them.

Revenue bonds are issued to raise money for a specific purpose (a turnpike, a utility system, a hospital, etc.) and are backed by funds raised by the particular project.

Moral obligation bonds are backed not by either taxes or projected revenues but by the issuer's moral pledge to make up any capital reserve deficiency.

General obligation bonds are the safest, followed by revenue bonds, and then by moral obligation bonds. In any case, although municipal bonds are generally considered just below U.S. government obligations (see p. 162) in terms of safety and quality (payments on more than 98 percent of all municipals were met during the Depression of the 1930s), they are only as good as the financial soundness of the issuing state or municipality. When local governments are in financial difficulty, as does happen, be sure to investigate thoroughly before you invest. Or buy only **insured** issues (labeled accordingly—but bear in mind that insurance guarantees principal and interest only if the bonds are held till maturity; market price is never guaranteed.

Note: For some taxpayers, income earned on municipal bonds is subject to the **alternative minimum tax** (see p. 593). Consult your tax adviser if you are unsure whether this applies to you.

Should You Buy Municipal Bonds?

If sheltering income from taxes is of major concern in your investment strategy, then tax-free municipal bonds may be right for you. But they'll only be right if you're in a tax bracket where the tax savings make sense—and if you'll stay in such a tax bracket, as far as you can tell, for the life of the bonds. Consider state and local income taxes, too, as you make your calculations. Interest of 6 percent on a tax-free bond is the equivalent of 8.7 percent taxable interest if you're in the 31 percent marginal tax bracket but only the equivalent of 8.3 percent if you're in the 28 percent bracket (see Table 6.3). Below the 28 percent bracket, forget it; tax-free bonds don't make sense.

Note: But don't forget your state income tax when doing your calculations.

To find equivalent yields of taxable and tax-free investments, divide the tax-free rate by the reciprocal of your tax bracket (the reciprocal is the number you get by subtracting your tax bracket from 100). If, for instance, a municipal is yielding 6 percent and you are in the 28 percent tax bracket, dividing 6 by 72 shows that you would have to receive 8.3 percent in a taxable issue to be competitive. You can do the same thing in reverse—multiply a taxable yield by the reciprocal of your tax bracket—to get the tax-free equivalent. You can accomplish the same thing, without the arithmetic, by asking your stockbroker for an equivalency table like the one in Table 6.3.

Table 6.3: Tax-free vs. Taxable Yields

Find your federal tax bracket based on your net taxable income:

	28%	**31%**
Joint return:	$36,901-89,150	$89,151 and above
Single return:	$22,101-53,500	$53,501 and above

To match a tax-free yield of:	A taxable investment would have to pay you:	
3%	4.17%	4.35%
4%	5.56%	5.80%
5%	6.94%	7.25%
6%	8.33%	8.70%
7%	9.72%	10.14%

Based on 1993 federal income tax tables.

Source: Fidelity Investments.

Tax-free municipal bonds may be attractive, but don't borrow to buy them. The IRS forbids deducting interest on loans made for the purchase of tax-exempt securities. If the bonds are used as collateral for a loan, moreover, then the interest paid on the loan must be offset against the income on the bond for tax purposes. You can't exclude earned interest while deducting owed interest. And don't buy municipals for your IRA or Keogh plan, designed to shelter retirement funds from taxes. It makes no sense to erect a tax shelter over tax-exempt securities.

BEFORE YOU BUY BONDS

Here are the basic facts you should know before you invest in bonds:

Bond Issuance

Bonds may now be issued only in registered form, issued in your name and with interest mailed directly to you. Bearer bonds, which were an alternate form until the 1982 Tax Act specified that all new bonds with maturities of more than one year must be registered, have coupons to be clipped on specified dates and surrendered in exchange for interest payments.

Risk and Ratings

Some bonds are safer investments than other bonds. Those issued by the U.S. government are probably the safest investments in the world. Those issued by municipalities and corporations run the gamut from very safe to very risky. Good guides for the investor are the ratings published by Moody's and Standard & Poor's; for minimum risk stick to bonds rated A and better. Lower-rated bonds (like the "junk" bonds that attained such notoriety a few years ago) may offer higher yields but with considerably higher risk.

Note: A high rating does not guarantee a return on your investment. All it does is assure you that the issuer is, as far as is known, credit-worthy with respect to the particular bond issue.

But credit risk isn't the only kind of risk associated with bonds. **Market risk** refers to the possibility that interest rates will rise after your purchase, causing your bond's price to decline to reflect the higher rates. This will only hurt if you must sell your bond before maturity. (And, of course, if interest rates should decline, your bond will be worth more.)

Table 6.4 shows what happens when interest rates rise or fall. Note that short-term bonds have far less volatility than long-term bonds.

Maturity

Bonds are issued for set periods of time. Long-term bonds may have maturity dates 20 or 30 years in the future. You are guaranteed the return of your principal if you wait until maturity to redeem the bonds; if you need the money sooner, you may lose some money. Volatility is directly related to the length of the bond; far greater price fluctuations occur in long-term bonds than in short- or medium-term.

Volatility can be minimized if you peg your bond purchases to specific needs. For example, looking ahead to retirement in 15 years, you may buy bonds scheduled to mature in 15 years. This is a good investment strategy, but only if you can be reasonably certain that you won't need the money in the interim. You can sell most bonds at any time, but you can never be sure of the price. If you know you'll need the money at a specific time, therefore, look for maturities on or before that date. In fact, in assessing total return on any bond, you must look at both current yield and appreciation or depreciation in the price.

Table 6.4: What Happens When Interest Rates Rise and Fall

The percentage change in principal value for each 1 percentage point change in overall interest rates, assuming a 6.5% coupon rate for each bond.

Maturity in Years	Rates fall 1% and prices rise by...	Rates rise 1% and prices fall by...
1	0.96%	-0.95%
5	4.32	-4.11
10	7.61	-6.95
30	14.61	-11.87

Source: T. Rowe Price.

Yield

Return on bonds is calculated in terms of both **current yield** and **yield to maturity.** If you buy a newly issued bond and hold it to maturity, your yield is fixed. But bonds are bought and sold, sometimes at a premium and sometimes at a discount, depending on prevailing interest rates. As the price changes, the yield changes as well. If you pay more than the face value of the bond, the excess amount is prorated annually over the life of the bond and subtracted from the yield. If you pay less than the face value, then the discount, also prorated, is added to the yield. Seventy dollars in interest on a $1,000 bond yields 7 percent, but $70 interest on the same bond, priced at $1,100, yields 6 percent. Exact yields, including the impact of compound interest, are found in the bond tables of most newspapers. Here's a sample bond quotation:

Bonds	Current Yield	Sales in $1,000	Last	Net Change
ATT 8 1/8 24	7.8	272	103 3/8	-1/8

Bond prices are quoted as a percentage of the par or face value of the bond, represented as 100. The name of the issuing company is in the first column, followed by the original coupon or interest rate and the last two digits of the year of maturity; the above bond pays interest at the original rate of 8 1/8 percent and matures in the year 2024. Its current yield is 7.8 percent. The **Last** (or **Close,** in some newspapers) column refers to the bond's price during the day's trading; **Net Change** is the difference between the day's closing price and the previous day's closing price. The **Sales in $1000** column simply indicates that exactly 272 of these bonds were traded on the New York Stock Exchange on this particular day.

Note: Most corporate bonds and all municipal bonds are traded on the over-the-counter (OTC) market rather than on an exchange; you will not find their prices listed in the newspaper (see below for what this means when you want to buy or to sell).

Callable Bonds

Some bonds are subject to call, which means that the issuer may redeem the bond at a stated price before maturity, often after a specified number of years. (Sizable numbers of bonds were called in 1992, when interest rates had fallen sufficiently that the issuers could float new debt at much lower cost.) Always ask whether a bond is callable and when and then, in order to reduce the risk of loss, don't buy a bond at a price well above that at which the company can call the bond for redemption.

Note: If you hold registered bonds you will be notified of a call; if you hold bearer bonds, and don't read the financial press, you may not find out until you present a clipped coupon for interest. You may, as a result, lose as much as six months' interest.

"Averaging" the Cost of Bond Purchases

It's possible to adopt a technique with bond purchases similar to dollar cost averaging in stock purchases. With bonds, the technique is called **laddering**; it entails buying a series of bonds that will reach maturity in different years. Every time a bond is redeemed the resulting cash can be reinvested to stretch the cycle still further. In addition to achieving a constant cash flow, this procedure tends to average out the effect of market price changes.

Commissions

You may find that your broker doesn't recommend bond purchases as often as stock purchases. One reason: Brokerage commissions are far smaller on bonds, and, of course, the broker is in business to make money. You can save on even this commission by buying newly issued bonds; here the broker's commission is paid by the issuer of the bond and not by the buyer.

You should be aware, though, that bond prices vary enormously; once you decide what you want, price the specific bond at different dealers before you buy. You may also want to consider buying from a specialist, from a bond dealer rather than from a stockbroker.

United States Government Obligations

You can also derive income by lending money to Uncle Sam, either directly through Treasury issues or indirectly through various agency obligations. Both are fixed-income investments, with yields calculated in advance and no opportunity for growth of capital. They are ideal for people seeking both safety and guaranteed income.

TREASURY ISSUES

The U.S. Treasury raises money through three different vehicles: bills, notes, and bonds. All are direct obligations of the U.S. government, and the safest possible investment. All are exempt from state and local income taxes, but not from federal income tax.

Treasury bills are issued in 3-month, 6-month, and 12-month maturities, in minimum amounts of $10,000 and multiples of $5,000 above this minimum. T-bills are sold at a discount, with the interest deducted in advance from the purchase price, which means that the actual yield is higher than the stated yield.

Note: Because the interest is subject to federal income tax in the year the bills mature, investors can use T-bills to bounce taxes into the next calendar year. Buy a 6-month T-bill in July, for example, and it will mature in January; income tax on the interest will be due fully 15 months later, when you file your return for the previous year.

Treasury notes are issued with maturity periods of two to ten years. Those with maturities four years or less are usually offered in a minimum denomination of $5,000; when maturities are longer than four years, the minimum denomination is usually $1,000. Interest is payable twice a year.

Treasury bonds are usually issued with maturity periods of 30 years (although the technical definition is a maturity of more than ten years), with the minimum purchase price set at $1,000, and interest payable twice a year. Fewer 30-year bonds are being issued since a policy shift to shorter-term borrowing in May 1993.

Q Short-term Treasury bills are paying so little in interest right now that I'm thinking of buying 30-year bonds to boost my income. Would this be wise?

A Don't go from one extreme to the other. Short-term T-bills offer liquidity, so they can serve a useful purpose if you need a temporary parking place for cash. Longer-term Treasuries can indeed boost income, but the longest term bonds—the 30-year bonds you're considering—carry the highest risk of loss if interest rates should rise. Stick to a middle range. Five-year to seven-year notes yield almost as much as a 30-year bond, and have done so for at least 15 years. Or, if you have a sizable amount to invest, "ladder" your investment by buying different maturities; if you split your purchase among 3-year, 5-year, and 7-year issues, for example, you'll be able to reinvest maturing amounts at then-prevailing rates and reduce risk over the long term.

How to Buy Treasury Issues

Treasury bills, notes, and bonds may be purchased directly from the Department of the Treasury, Bureau of the Public Debt, Washington, DC 20226, or from any of the 12 regional offices (and their local branches) of the Federal Reserve Bank (see p. 165). There is no charge to purchase Treasury issues through the Federal Reserve Bank, and the process is reasonably simple. Write to the nearest Federal Reserve Bank and ask for the necessary forms; submit the forms, together with full payment, by the date given for the offering in which you are interested.

Treasuries used to be issued as engraved certificates; some of these older issues may still be available on the secondary market. New Treasuries, however, are now issued only in book-entry form. Under the program called Treasury Direct, investors receive a consolidated account statement showing all Treasury holdings, interest payments are credited directly to the bank account you designate, and you may also elect automatic reinvestment at maturity. Should you wish to sell Treasury issues before maturity, however, you cannot do so through Treasury Direct; you will have to do so through a bank or broker, and pay a fee or commission.

You may, instead, buy Treasury issues through your stockbroker or through many commercial banks. If you buy in this convenient way, there will be a handling charge, depending on the institution, of about $50; this will reduce your yield.

You may also invest in Treasury issues by investing in a mutual fund which, in turn, invests only in U.S. government securities. These funds have grown in recent years in response to investor awareness that money market funds are not insured. A fund that invests solely in government issues is as safe as the U.S. government itself.

Q My bank now charges a fee for cashing the coupons I clip from Treasury bonds. Is there some way to avoid this?

A Yes. You can avoid the fee by opening a free Treasury Direct account. You'll also spare yourself the inconvenience of going to the bank and cashing the coupons (or waiting for and cashing interest checks on registered bonds), as well as any concerns about safekeeping for certificates. With Treasury Direct, interest payments are deposited directly in your bank account. Also, you can easily reinvest proceeds of maturing securities, if you wish to do so, by filling out a simple form.

There is no charge for making what the Treasury calls the "Smart Exchange." For information on what to do, call (toll-free) 800-366-3144.

AGENCY OBLIGATIONS

The U.S. Treasury issues the bills, notes, and bonds described above. A wide range of other government agencies issue notes and bonds to finance their own projects. But they are not exactly the same. Treasury issues are

Where to Find the Federal Reserve Bank Nearest You	
Federal Reserve Bank of	**Address (mark envelope "Attention: Fiscal Agency Dept.")**
Atlanta	104 Marietta St., NW, Atlanta, GA 30303 or P.O. Box 1731, Atlanta, GA 30301-1731 (404)586-8500
Boston	600 Atlantic Ave., Boston, MA 02106 (617)973-3000
Chicago	230 South LaSalle St., P.O. Box 834, Chicago, IL 60690 (312)322-5322
Cleveland	1455 East Sixth St., P.O. Box 6387, Cleveland, OH 44101 (216)241-2800
Dallas	400 South Akard St. (Station K), Dallas, TX 75222 (214)651-6111
Kansas City	925 Grand Ave., Kansas City, MO 64198 (816)881-2000
Minneapolis	250 Marquette Ave., Minneapolis, MN 55480 (612)340-2345
New York	33 Liberty St., Federal Reserve P.O. Station, New York, NY 10045 (212)791-5000
Philadelphia	Ten Independence Mall, P.O. Box 66, Philadelphia, PA 19106 (215)574-6000
Richmond	701 East Byrd St., P.O. Box 27622, Richmond, VA 23261 (804)643-1250
St. Louis	411 Locust St., P.O. Box 442, St. Louis, MO 63166 (314)444-8444
San Francisco	101 Market St., P.O. Box 7702, San Francisco, CA 94120 (415)544-2000
If unsure, write to:	Board of Governors of the Federal Reserve System, 20th and Constitution Ave., NW, Washington, DC 20551 (202)452-3000

backed by the full faith and credit of the U.S. government. Agency issues generally are not (although it's not very likely that the government would allow one of its agencies to default), so the yield on agency obligations is often a bit higher than that on Treasuries.

Some of the agencies raising funds via public offerings include the Farm Credit Bank, the Federal Home Loan Bank, and the Federal National Mortgage Association. These obligations cannot be purchased directly from the issuing agency; you must buy them from a commercial bank or stockbrokerage and pay a handling fee. You do not receive a certificate—computer records are kept by the issuer—but you do receive interest payments by check. The interest is subject to federal income tax. Interest on most issues, but not all, is exempt from state and local income tax. Ask your broker for details on different issues.

"Ginnie Maes"

Securities issued by the Government National Mortgage Association (GNMA), familiarly called Ginnie Mae, are being bought by many small investors. A Ginnie Mae certificate represents a share in a pool of government-backed mortgages and, unlike many other agency obligations, is backed by the full faith and credit of the U.S. government. The minimum size of original individual certificates is $25,000, but existing certificates may be purchased for substantially less. You may also buy shares, at $1,000 apiece, in a Ginnie Mae fund sponsored by a securities firm.

Although mortgages typically run 25 to 30 years, yields on new GNMA pools are projected to an average life of 12 years. Sometimes mortgages are prepaid and the life of the pool is shortened, increasing the yield to the investor. The yield, however, is not guaranteed.

Each month, as a Ginnie Mae investor, you receive both interest and a partial return of capital representing partial amortization of the principal on all the mortgages in the pool. These regular payments—although they will vary, depending on how many mortgages are paid off in a given month—make Ginnie Maes an ideal long-range investment for steady income, attractive to many retirees.

But Ginnie Maes do have drawbacks. Because you receive a partial return of principal each month, you get nothing back at the end. If you've frittered away your return of capital along the way, rather than reinvesting it, you won't have anything left to reinvest. Furthermore, although the government does back GNMAs, that backing does not mean you'll make money. In fact, the actual yield is somewhat of a mystery until the pool is finished—and many GNMA investors were sorely disappointed when homeowners holding high-rate mortgages refinanced those mortgages at lower rates in the early 1990s.

Annuities

An annuity contract is the reverse of a life insurance contract: Instead of paying regular premiums toward the day when the proceeds will be paid to your survivors, you pay (in either a lump sum or periodic payments) toward the day when monthly distributions will be made to you. Those distributions usually begin in retirement (although you can delay distributions, under many contracts, until you reach age 85) and continue for a lifetime, so that the annuity has traditionally been a retirement-planning vehicle purchased by people concerned about outliving their resources (see Chapter 23).

But there are two kinds of annuity, both providing tax-deferred growth. The conservative version is the fixed annuity, where you know exactly how much you will receive; that's the one I discuss in Chapter 23. Less conservative is the variable annuity, where how much you ultimately receive depends on the performance of underlying investment funds that you select. Variable annuities, as one of the last tax-sheltered investments, have been a hot product in the last few years. But that doesn't necessarily make them a good product.

The problem, in a nutshell, is fees. With a variable annuity, you pay three kinds of fees:

- Surrender charges. These back-end sales charges typically start at 7 percent, tapering off to zero after seven years. But some variable annuities have surrender charges lasting as long as 12 years. Don't buy a variable annuity if you don't plan to stay put. (If performance is truly terrible, or the insurance company runs into trouble, you can make what is called a tax-free or "1035" exchange and transfer to another annuity.)
- Contract fees, including administrative costs and insurance charges. Annuities are tax-advantaged because they come in an insurance package. Someone has to pay for the mortality calculations.
- Portfolio management fees. That insurance packaging is wrapped around a set of mutual funds. Those funds have to be managed and the managers have to be paid.

Most criticism of variable annuities has to do with these layers of fees. It's hard to make money when so much goes off the top before your money begins to work for you. You'd do better in many cases in some good no-load mutual funds. On the other hand, a variable annuity may have a place in your financial plan under some conditions:

- You plan to hold the annuity for at least ten years, not only to get past the surrender charge period but so that the tax-deferred growth has time to offset the annual cost. You also want to be past age 59½ or the IRS will get you (with some exceptions) with tax penalties.
- You will take the distribution over time, as an annuity. If you take it as a lump sum, you will pay taxes all at once.

Note: Should you die before benefit payouts begin, your beneficiary will receive the greater of the current market value of your annuity or the amount you invested; this guaranteed death benefit helps protect against a market downturn.

■ You select an annuity with solid performance in all its underlying funds, especially growth-stock funds. Once you're in an annuity, your investment choices are limited to the funds it contains. And the only reason to buy an annuity is to obtain tax-deferred growth; it makes no sense to pay annuity fees and keep the money in a fixed-income or money market fund.

■ You compare fees carefully and think about buying an annuity, if you buy one at all, from a no-load mutual fund company. Because fees are considerably lower (at this writing), a variable annuity like the one offered by the no-load Vanguard Group (800-523-0857) can be a good choice.

■ You check the stability of the insurance company. It may be many years before you start taking money out of your annuity; you want the company to be there for you when you do.

Options and Commodities

U.S. government obligations are the safest of all investments. They are also very conservative, in the sense that your money will grow through interest but not through capital appreciation. At the other end of the investment spectrum, for the investor with nerves of steel, are the risk-laden but potentially profitable areas of options and commodities.

A word to the wise, from the Securities and Exchange Commission, concerning any investment:

■ Before buying... think!
■ Don't deal with strange securities firms. (Consult your broker, banker or other experienced person you know and trust.)
■ Beware of securities offered over the telephone by strangers.
■ Don't listen to high-pressure sales talk.
■ Beware of promises of spectacular profits.
■ Be sure you understand the risks of loss.
■ Don't buy on tips and rumors... get all the facts!
■ Tell the salesperson to put all the information and advice in writing and mail it to you. Save it!
■ If you don't understand all the written information, consult a person who does.
■ Give at least as much consideration to buying securities as you would to buying other valuable property.

OPTIONS   *N.A.*

If you wanted time to make up your mind about the purchase of a piece of real estate, you might buy an option. You would pay the seller a specified amount in return for his holding the property for you at a specified price for a specified period of time. If you chose not to buy the real estate, you could simply let the option expire at the end of the time period, and the seller would keep the option fee as payment for keeping the property available to you for that length of time. If you did buy the property, the price you paid for it would be over and above the price you paid for the option.

Options on securities are a bit more complicated but work on the same principle. A price is paid, for instance, for the right to buy 100 shares of a given stock at a specified price within a specified period of time. If the right is not exercised, the option expires. The purchaser hopes, meanwhile, that the stock's price will go up (if he bought a "call," the right to buy) or down (if he bought a "put," the right to sell) by an amount large enough to pay the premium, fees, and commission on the transaction and to provide a profit as well. If the price holds steady or moves in the unhoped-for direction, the price of the option is lost. The option itself is a contract to buy or to sell, applied to a particular security.

Buying options offers a potentially large profit from a relatively small investment (the price of the option, rather than the price of the stock), with relatively little risk (the most you can lose is the price of the option). Selling options provides a hedge against a decline in stock prices. If the price of your stock goes down, you can sell it at the price set by the option. Selling options is a conservative move, if you own the stock on which you are selling the option. If you don't, then you are playing a speculative game. With a "naked" option, one where you don't own the underlying stock, you may lose your bet and have to purchase the stock for delivery at a very high price.

Either way, you should be prepared to follow the market closely, via the closing option prices listed in the daily newspapers; options have a short life span and are much more volatile than common stock. If you want to get involved, you should also find a broker who is knowledgeable about this specialized area. And be prepared: commissions are sizable.

Note: Options on stock date only from the 1970s, but new variations, mostly tied to commodities (see below), are already in the works. For the highly sophisticated risk-seeker, options may be considered on gold and silver, coffee and sugar, Treasury bills and bonds, and so on.

COMMODITIES   *N.A.*

Commodities are another highly technical and speculative investment, one where a lot of money can be made or lost. An investment in commodities or commodity futures is an investment in the future price of some basic commodity: coffee or sugar or pork bellies, Treasury bonds or gold or foreign currency. If you buy commodities, you are gambling on government policies, international market developments, and the buying patterns of consumers around the world. You can put up as little as 5 percent at the outset, but you can lose much more, sometimes in a matter of hours; it's been said, although it's hard to document, that 85 to 90 percent of all the players lose money in this game. This is not an investment for anyone trying to accumulate money for home buying, college tuition, or retirement.

It is possible, however, to invest in a commodity pool, a mutual fund formed as a limited partnership, with somewhat less risk. With a pool (unlike the margin trading of individual accounts), you can't lose more than your original investment. But you can, and very well may, lose that. At the same time, fees and commissions (although small, commodity people say, in relation to the size of the position you're controlling) can run more than 20 percent of the amount you invest. Also worth knowing: You can't buy and sell shares in a commodity pool as you would a mutual fund; instead, you put in a minimum of $2,500 or $5,000 and must leave it there for a specified period. At the end of the five years, or whatever, some pools will guarantee a return of principal; unfortunately, the way principal is guaranteed, by putting a portion of the fund into a zero-coupon bond, can sharply reduce any potential return.

Even purchased via a fund, commodities are not for the faint-hearted.

Financial Futures

One of the newer wrinkles in commodities trading is the futures contract without an actual underlying commodity. It is now possible to enter into futures contracts on Treasury bonds, on foreign currency, and on the action of the stock market itself, via an index of stock market prices. The Kansas City Board of Trade, for instance, uses the Value Line Arithmetic Index; the New York Futures Exchange uses the New York Stock Exchange Composite Index. Financial futures are a form of betting on interest rates and are not a game for amateurs. If you want to gamble, go to Las Vegas; the stakes are not as high.

Real Estate

Real estate, whether owner-occupied homes or investment properties, has declined in value in many parts of the country in recent years. Nonetheless, over the long haul, real estate may offer investment opportunities—especially if you can pick up potentially valuable properties at depressed prices. If you have money to invest, and time to devote to your investment, you might look to the profit-making opportunities and tax-sheltering incentives of a self-managed real estate investment. Just don't do so if you're looking for short-term returns; real estate is a long-term investment.

There can be a number of substantial benefits:

■ The possibility of **appreciation,** especially if inflation picks up again. Real property has traditionally been one of the best hedges against inflation. Even though prices have leveled off and, in some areas, actually declined, careful choice and careful management may still yield profits.

■ **Leverage.** Real property, unlike some other investments, can often be purchased with as little as 10 percent of the purchase price. The smaller the down payment, the more someone else's money is working for you and the greater your potential profit.

■ **Cash flow** can be consistent, although the quality of your tenants (will they stay put? pay their rent on time? take care of the property?) and your operating costs will determine the actual amounts.

■ **Equity buildup**. As the existing mortgage balance is reduced, your equity in the property—and your potential profit—increases.

■ **Tax losses** stemming from **depreciation** (the recognition, in tax law, that buildings eventually wear out). But current tax law establishes a 27.5-year depreciation period for residential real property, and a 31.5-year period for nonresidential real property. These extended periods reduce the tax advantages of real estate investment.

■ The possibility of **tax credits.** Tax credits are even better than tax deductions, because they directly reduce the amount of tax you owe, not just the amount of income on which you pay tax. Tax credits are limited today, but may be available if you invest in certain historic rehabilitation properties or in low-income housing. Don't let this tax credit blind you, however, to the true investment value of a property.

MANAGING REAL ESTATE

In order to invest actively in real estate, you need cash, time, and good advice.

■ While you can buy into a limited partnership for as little as $5,000 (but probably shouldn't; see p. 175), you'll need considerably more than that to do your own personal investing in real estate. You'll need enough money at the outset (money you won't need for anything else, because real estate is one of the least liquid of investments) to make a cash down payment. You will also need money for upkeep. And you may want to allocate funds to pay a professional manager, and to secure professional advice.

■ You aren't likely to make money from a property that isn't closely supervised. Even if you hire an on-site manager, you'll need to keep close tabs on your investment. That means frequent visits and regular supervision.

■ Good advice is essential. You'll want financial advice from your accountant and your attorney. You may want technical advice from an architect, an engineer, and/or an appraiser. And you may want to deal with a Realtor who specializes in investment property, perhaps one who is a CCIM, a Certified Commercial Investment Member of the Commercial Investment Real Estate Institute, an affiliate of the National Association of Realtors.

HOW TO INVEST IN REAL ESTATE

If you have the cash, the time, and the inclination, then, how do you go about investing in real estate? With the help of your real estate broker, investigate properties *in and around your home town.* While it's true that property is appreciating more in some areas of the country than in others, it's also true that you can't really keep tabs on an investment located in another city. You also can't really know the score. In your own home community, you know which areas are coming up and which may be sliding inexorably down. You know what's what in terms of shopping, schools, and plans for new highways. You can make a reasonably intelligent investment, based on your own knowledge, and then supervise it closely.

What type of investment? Some people have done very well with one-family houses, especially with run-down houses that can be rehabilitated and then sold at a handsome profit. Others swear by multifamily units, especially small apartment houses. And some think that profits lie in commercial buildings, in a medical office building, or small shopping mall. You can do well—or badly—with any of these. Look at all the facts and figures on any particular investment possibility before you make your decision.

Note: Be careful about investing in second mortgages, especially those not sponsored by a regulated financial institution. With the stabilization (even decline) of house prices in recent years, many investors have lost their life savings.

Raw Land

They may not be making any more of it, as the saying goes, but that does not mean that raw land is a good investment. Quite the contrary, in fact, according to those in the know. Here are the problems:

- Raw land has no intrinsic value. Its worth lies in what happens to it. Will residential development move in that direction? Will the land turn out to be a prime location for a shopping center? Might a new highway be built? The answers to all of these questions—and the potential worth of the land—are tied to political decisions and demographic factors over which you have no control.
- Raw land yields no current return and, in fact, costs money to hold. You'll have taxes to pay, year after year, whether or not the land is ever developed. You'll have interest to pay, if you took a loan to buy the property. You'll be taking your money out of circulation, if you buy with cash, and earning no return.

■ Tax advantages do not exist. Land isn't depreciable and, depending on how you structure the financing, you may not even be able to deduct the interest on your loan.

■ Newly honed environmental awareness makes it imperative to investigate raw land before buying. Areas defined as "wetlands," not always identifiable to the naked eye, can't be developed. And if anyone ever dumped a hazardous chemical on land you buy, you will be responsible for cleanup costs.

Raw land can be profitable, but you're best off considering it speculation rather than investment.

WHEN YOU SELL

Profits on real estate, like profits on any investment, are subject to tax. But your tax liability can be reduced via one of two methods:

■ Taxes can be paid as the money is received rather than in the year of the sale, with no limitations as to how much must be paid to the seller in any one year. You can reduce the tax bite by taking installment payments over several years, possibly raising the sale price of the property in exchange for allowing the purchaser to keep more of his money for this period of time. For more details, see IRS Publication No. 537.

■ You can defer taxes by swapping your property for one of "like kind," instead of selling it. The new property doesn't have to be identical, but it should also be investment property. It's even possible for sophisticated investors, with the help of attorneys specializing in real estate tax law, to get into three-way or four-way exchanges. Some cash may actually change hands, and some taxes may be due, but the bulk of that tax can be deferred.

REAL ESTATE INVESTMENT TRUSTS

Another way of investing in real estate—and a better bet for small investors—is through a Real Estate Investment Trust (REIT). These pooled investments operate somewhat like mutual funds, but the funds are invested exclusively in real estate. REITs are traded on the stock exchanges, so there is always a market and your investment is liquid.

REITs got a bad name in the mid-1970s, when a great many went under. Those that failed were primarily mortgage-based, however, and the credit crunch did them in. Today's successful REITs are equity-based, owning and managing properties rather than buying and selling mortgages. They offer some of the advantages of real estate ownership, without some of the pitfalls. Dividends tend to be good, since REITs are required to distribute to shareholders 95 percent of all ordinary income generated each year. Your initial investment, moreover, may be lower in a REIT than in almost any other form of real estate investment; some shares sell for just a few dollars. REIT prices generally rise with falling interest rates.

If you are interested in investing in a REIT, look for one specializing in a particular market segment (such as health care facilities or retail stores or a specific geographical area) and, above all, look for solid management (it's a good sign when managers own shares in the REIT) and a good track record. But be careful. Rising interest rates could dampen profitability.

REITs vs. RELPs

Equity REITs are sometimes confused with real estate limited partnerships (RELPs), another type of direct property investment. However, several important differences exist:

Operational structure	Managed by a board of directors who are accountable to the corporation's shareholders	Managed by a general partner who typically operates autonomously
Tax treatment	Considered portfolio investments. Treatment of dividends and capital gains and losses is the same as any other stock	Generally considered "passive activity" investments, which are subject to separate tax rules regarding gains and losses
Liquidity	Actively traded on the major stock exchanges and the OTC market	Most are illiquid, except for a small group of publicly traded partnerships. In some cases, you must sell at a deep discount to attract buyers

Source: Ernst & Young *Financial Planning Reporter.*

Limited Partnerships

Remember "tax shelters?" In the heyday of limited partnerships—before the Tax Reform Act of 1986 took the bloom off the rose, and off real estate in general—lots and lots of ordinary investors put megabucks into these arrangements that were supposed to provide shelter from taxes. Limited partnerships were formed to invest all kinds of exotic enterprises. The ones that were most popular, and that still survive, generally stuck to real estate, oil drilling and gas exploration, and equipment leasing.

Tax shelters as such have gone the way of the dodo bird, and limited partnerships may not be far behind. But, just in case someone comes your way with an offer you can't refuse (try hard) or just in case you already own a limited partnership and would like to get out, here is what you need to know:

In a limited partnership, whatever its investment vehicles and goals, a general partner is responsible for the business decisions; the limited partners— that's you and others like you—put up most of the money. In exchange for your investment, in the bad old days, you got shelter from taxes. Today you're better off looking for income. As a limited partner, you'll receive a share of the profits, if the enterprise has any profits. If it fails, your liability is limited (hence the term "limited" partner) to the amount of your investment (although, thanks to some arcane accounting rules, the IRS may come after you seeking taxes on phantom income).

INVESTMENT REQUIREMENTS

There are two types of limited partnerships:

Public offerings are registered with the Securities and Exchange Commission and, often, in the states in which they are sold. This registration does not imply approval or endorsement, but it does mean that the partnership must meet certain standards. Public offerings, described in a prospectus, can usually be purchased in $5,000 units or, for IRAs and Keogh plans, in $1,000 or $2,000 increments.

Private offerings, which are not registered or regulated, are described in an offering statement. They take fewer partners and usually require an investment of upwards of $50,000. Potential rewards may be greater; so is the risk.

Both public and private offerings often state minimum income and net-worth standards for investors.

SHOULD YOU INVEST IN A LIMITED PARTNERSHIP?

Probably not, for several reasons:

■ Partnerships are distinctly illiquid investments, almost impossible to dispose of before they are liquidated by the general partner.

■ Tax requirements mean a lot of extra paperwork and extra accounting fees.

■ Until the properties are sold and the partnership terminated, it's exceedingly difficult to value your holdings. (Guidelines released by the International Association for Financial Planning [IAFP] at the end of 1992 call for general partners to provide annual valuations beginning in the fourth year, along with more consistent and uniform financial reports.)

- Termination is usually scheduled for a fixed date, often seven to ten years down the road. If you're going to need the money sooner, a limited partnership is not for you. Sometimes partnerships are liquidated early—but the prevailing trend in recent years, with the devastation of real estate, has been much longer life spans than anticipated.

- "Roll-ups" of troubled partnerships, in which several partnerships were combined into a master limited partnership which could be traded as common stock, were supposed to provide liquidity. In fact, they have meant much greater losses for the limited partners. Weak partnerships often merged with stronger ones. The general partners take more in management fees. And, according to one study of 65 roll-ups, prices dropped an average of 37.4 percent on the first day of trading.

- You have very little control over your investment (the general partners make all the decisions), yet you can't get out if things go bad. (The IAFP recommends that limited partners should have a greater role in determining when a partnership's assets should be liquidated, if it's still in existence beyond original expectations.) There is a limited secondary market for limited partnerships (see below), but selling has been exceedingly difficult. Don't ever invest in a partnership with money you may need.

QUESTIONS TO ASK BEFORE YOU INVEST

If you do decide that a particular partnership is worthwhile and that you can afford an illiquid investment—that is, one that you can't convert quickly to cash—there are a number of questions to ask before you invest:

- Is it a legitimate business deal, with an expectation of profit? Do the assumptions about operating revenues and operating costs, as set forth in the prospectus or offering statement, support income and cash flow projections? (Public partnerships generally do not have projections; private placements do.)

- How much of your money will actually be invested and how much will be eaten up in sales commissions, property acquisition fees, administrative charges, and the like? The expenses can be very large on a limited partnership, and you want to know what to expect before you make a commitment.

- Will you receive a minimum return before the general partner takes part of the cash flow? That's good. Will the general partner be paid substantial fees, in advance, for services to be performed? That's bad.

■ What is the background of the general partners? Have they managed similar projects, and managed them well? Do the general partners have a financial stake in this project, with their own money invested? If so, they are more likely to pay close attention and to manage it well.

If you must invest in a limited partnership, you can minimize the risk by investing in a diversified partnership (one that invests in several shopping centers, for instance, rather than just one).

Hard Assets: Gold, Gems, and Collectibles

When inflation rates are high and the economy looks a bit unsteady, some investors turn to tangible assets. Gold and precious gems and fine art

Q In 1982 I invested in a real-estate partnership through a brokerage firm, expecting to earn tax-sheltered income, then receive a profit in seven or eight years when the properties were sold and the partnership was liquidated. Now it's more than ten years later, and there's still no sale. Is there anything I can do?

A Maybe. If your partnership has any value, you may be able to find a buyer through either a brokerage firm matching program or an informal secondary marketplace. (Of course, if it has any value, you may be better off holding on—barring an immediate need for cash.)

In early 1993 the Securities and Exchange Commission (SEC) authorized a centralized trading system for limited partnerships, expected to be operational by late in the year. At the same time the SEC granted permission for brokerage houses to match buyers and sellers, but only when the hopeful sellers originally bought the partnership units through that firm.

Meanwhile, there are a dozen or so firms that have joined forces in a Partnership Secondary Market Association. Some of the firms act as principals, buying units for their own portfolios and possible resale. Others act as agents, representing you in finding a buyer for your units. And at least one firm runs a computerized auction house for partnership units. If you are interested in selling your units through the secondary market, be sure to get several bids, because prices can vary considerably, and find out what the transaction will cost.

appear immune to the ups and downs of the stock market, the uncertainties of the bond market, and the speculative vicissitudes of options and commodities. But are they, really? Let's look at these assets as investments (apart from their role in any take-to-the-hills survival strategy) and at their possible role in your investment strategy.

As of mid-1992, these were some of the players in the secondary marketplace:

Pacific Asset Group, Inc.
215 North Marengo, Ste. 115
Pasadena, CA 91101
(800)727-7244

Cuyler & Associates
349 West Commercial St.,
  No. 1445,
P.O. Box 619
East Rochester, NY 14445
(800)274-9991

Liquidity Fund
1900 Powell St., Ste. 730
Emeryville, CA 94608
(800)548-7355

Frain Asset Management
416 North Bath Club Blvd.
North Redington Beach, FL
33708 (800)654-6110

Chicago Partnership Board
185 North Wabash Ave.,
Ste. 1900
Chicago, IL 60601
(800)272-6273

Partnership Securities Exchange
1999 Harrison St., Ste. 720
Oakland, CA 94612
(800)736-9797

Partnership Consultants, Inc.
7222 South Tamiami Trail,
  Ste. 102
Sarasota, FL 34231
(813)923-5836

Raymond James & Associates
880 Carillon Pkwy.
P.O. Box 12749
St. Petersburg, FL 33733
(800)248-8863 ext. 5055

Nationwide Partnership
  Marketplace
100 Galli Dr., Ste. 8
Bel Marin Keys, CA 94949
(415)382-3555

MacKenzie Pattersson
3685 Mt. Diablo Dr., Ste. 150
Lafayette, CA 94549
(800)854-8357

EquityLine Financial Group
9200 South Dadeland Blvd.,
Ste. 609
Miami, FL 33156
(800)327-9990

Source: Partnership Secondary Market Association.

One important point to remember about all tangible assets: You earn no interest and no dividends while you hold them; your only opportunity for profit is when you sell—if prices are up and *if* you can find a buyer. At that time you'll face dealer commissions or premiums on the sale (on top of the premiums paid when you bought). Meanwhile, you'll probably have safekeeping charges in the form of vault fees—unless you keep these assets at home, which poses other risks.

GOLD

Gold, the classic hedge against disaster, rose from $125 an ounce in 1975, when Americans could legally own gold for the first time since the 1930s, to $850 an ounce in January 1980. It then proceeded to move down, with periodic fluctuations, until it hovered around $333 in early 1993. If you had bought it at or near its low and sold it near the top, you could have made a great deal of money. But then, that's true of any investment, and easier to say than to do. The truth, in any case, is that many people who buy gold do so less as an investment than as a cushion against an uncertain future.

A cautionary note for gold bugs: James Cloonan, respected founder and chairman of the American Association of Individual Investors, thinks that gold is now no more important than commodities like platinum and copper. His reasons, in late 1992: The supply of gold is increasing; gold has not kept up with inflation in recent years; in times of war and other devastation, food is a more important unit of exchange than gold; and, last, it is extremely unlikely that the world will move to a hard-asset economy.

If you want to buy gold, here are the varieties to consider:

Gold coins, minted by several countries and sold at a small markup over the actual value of the gold content, are the safest and easiest way for the small investor to buy and own gold as a tangible object.

Bullion bars come in sizes from half-ounce wafers (that's a Troy ounce, the official measure of gold) to bars weighing hundreds of ounces. Buy from a reputable dealer, one who will give you a written promise to repurchase the bullion, to be sure that the bar is at least 99 percent pure. Gold in bars has two major disadvantages: You can't sell off part of a bar to raise needed cash; and when you want to sell the bullion, you will have to have it assayed, a procedure which will reduce any profit you might make. (However, you can avoid assaying and the accompanying charge if you leave the bars in the dealer's safekeeping instead of taking possession.)

Gold certificates are another way of buying bullion without taking physical possession. The certificate, whose value fluctuates with the underlying price of the gold, is your evidence of ownership; it is easily sold.

Gold mining stocks are a way of investing in gold and securing dividend income as well as the chance of capital appreciation. Gold stocks, however, are susceptible to government policy and political disruption, and come complete with a significant amount of risk.

Mutual funds offer a better way to specialize in gold shares, a way to diversify while leaving day-to-day management to others. As an example, the no-load Lexington Goldfund (800-526-0056) invests in gold bullion and the securities of companies engaged in mining or processing gold throughout the world.

Two cautionary notes:

■ Don't buy gold jewelry as an investment, not unless you like the jewelry and will enjoy wearing it. The reason: You'll be paying for the design and workmanship as well as for the gold itself.

■ Don't speculate on gold; that's really a game for thick-skinned experts who can afford to lose. If you buy gold, buy it with money you won't need, and be prepared to hold on. Otherwise, when you need the cash, the price of gold could be at an all-time low.

DIAMONDS

As a tangible asset and hedge against inflation, diamonds share some of the disadvantages of gold: no interest or dividends, the cost of insuring and safekeeping, and dealer premiums on both purchase and sale. They also have another disadvantage: When you buy a diamond, you pay the retail price, since the dealer has to make his profit, but when you sell a diamond (assuming that you can find a buyer), you get the wholesale price, so that the purchaser can make a profit when he resells the stone. You can't win, unless prices rise enormously.

Diamonds were a popular investment in the late 1970s, when a top-quality "D-flawless" 1-carat stone rose from $6,000 to over $60,000 in three years. But look what happened in the next two years: Between 1980 and 1982, the wholesale price of that same flawless diamond fell to about $15,000, the level it remains at in early 1993. Diamonds, like gold, are a risky investment.

If you do want to put some diamonds in your investment portfolio here are some tips:

■ Know the four keys to diamond value: color, clarity, carat, and cut. The best diamond has the least **color,** with ranks ranging from D (virtually colorless) down to X. Investment-grade diamonds range between D and J. Forget the term "blue-white"; it doesn't mean a thing. **Clarity** measures freedom from imperfection; "flawless" is best. **Carat** is the international standard for diamond weight, with 142 carats to an ounce. Each carat weighs two-tenths of a gram, but diamonds are so valuable that each carat is further divided into "points." A point is less than one ten-thousandth of an ounce. And **cut** is the design (round, emerald-cut, pear-shaped, etc.) and the perfection of that design. An investment stone should be round, rather than a shape that may be only temporarily fashionable.

■ Know the company. Never buy from a salesperson or company totally new to you. Do some investigation. Ask for trade references, bank references, supplier references.

■ Be sure that any verbal claims are in writing. Does the company promise to buy back the stone? Within what time period and at what price? (Reputable companies seldom make this claim; be cautious of any company that does.)

■ Look for certification from an independent laboratory, such as the Gemological Institute of America. This certification is not an appraisal and does not assign a value; it is an identifying report on the specific features of the stone and verifies that the diamond you buy is indeed the one you receive.

■ Get an appraisal, too, from an independent source. An appraisal from the people who sell you the diamond is worthless.

COLORED GEMS

Diamonds may be risky, but colored gems are riskier still. There are certification standards set for diamonds. If you buy from a reputable dealer, you can be reasonably certain that an E-flawless diamond is an E-flawless diamond. But there are no objective standards for colored gems, and even reputable dealers have trouble telling some varieties apart. Leave investment in colored gems to the professionals, unless you're prepared to become a professional yourself.

COLLECTIBLES, ANTIQUES, AND ART

There are stories of vast profits in a wide range of tangible items, from mint-condition comic books to contemporary lithographs. There are also stories (the ones you don't hear at cocktail parties) about losses when the wrong collectible is purchased. Such stories have become more common. In 1980, inflation had lifted prices of all types of collectibles to record highs. By the early 1990s, most collectibles had fallen on hard times. The prices of rare coins, stamps, photographs, antiques, etc., have fallen drastically.

If you are interested in collecting for profit:

■ Become knowledgeable in a particular field and concentrate on that field.

■ Pick a field you like, so that you'll enjoy living with your collection before you sell.

■ Look for quality and rarity as keys to value. ("Instant" collectibles and "limited" editions, whether plates or medallions or prints, are widely advertised and sold; they seldom increase very much in value.)

■ Be prepared to hold your collection for some years before you sell. When you do sell, expect to pay commissions ranging up to 25 percent.

■ Understand the tax treatment of collectibles. Capital gains tax applies to profits from a resale, but a loss cannot be deducted unless you can prove that you intended to make a profit. Without such proof your collection will be considered, for tax purposes, as a hobby.

 ## KEY POINTS

■ Investment in mutual funds permits diversification without a major commitment of money. Your best bets are no-load funds in a "family" of funds, with free exchange-by-telephone privileges.

■ Purchases of common stock make you a part owner of the corporation issuing the stock; the value of your investment will rise and fall along with the fortunes of the company.

■ Purchase of bonds makes you a creditor of the issuing corporation or governing body, entitled to interest for the use of your money.

■ Fixed-income Treasury issues provide safe guaranteed income but no opportunity for capital growth.

■ Variable annuities can provide tax-sheltered growth, but typically come with surrender charges (phasing out over seven or more years) and high annual fees (for the life of the contract).

■ Options and commodities are highly risky investments, suitable only for the knowledgeable investor who can afford to lose considerable sums.

■ Real estate may offer investment opportunities, but the safest route for the small investor is through real estate investment trusts (REITs) traded on the stock exchange.

■ Limited partnerships may offer income (tax "shelter" is a thing of the past) but are illiquid investments that are inadvisable for most investors. Despite an informal secondary marketplace, limited partnerships are very difficult to sell.

■ Tangible assets, such as gold and precious gems, are attractive when inflation rates are high; even then, however, they provide no income, only the chance of a profit when you sell.

Putting Your Money to Work:
Credit

CHAPTER 7

Getting Started

Several years ago a well-known statesman arrived in Washington, direct from an overseas assignment for the U.S. government. When he arrived at the airport, he tried to rent a car for the trip home. He had a pocketful of cash and ample identification (including his diplomatic credentials), but no credit cards. The result: no car.

Credit—paying for goods and services after they've been used—is a way of life for most Americans. We use credit when we pay a dentist's bill the month after a cavity has been filled. We use credit when we finance the purchase of a car or take out a college loan. We use credit when we take a long-term mortgage to buy a house. Credit is so much a way of life that it's extremely difficult to do some things, including renting a car, without it.

For better or for worse, the American economy is built on the use of credit. Outstanding consumer debt (excluding mortgages) totaled almost $722 billion in July 1992.

But the credit picture has changed. After years of steady increases in outstanding consumer debt, the total amount actually dropped from 1990 to 1991. Clearly, the recession is at least partly responsible; consumers who are fearful of holding on to their jobs are not eager to spend. Also, interest rates charged for the use of credit, despite declining rates in general, have not come down very much. In late 1992, when you were earning about 3 percent on your savings and the prime rate (the basic lending rate to business) stood at 6 percent, interest rates on bank credit cards averaged 18.4 percent.

Today, "easy credit" may be easy, but it is more expensive than ever before. So, while you'll probably still use credit, it's more important than ever to do so carefully and as part of your overall financial plan. This chapter describes the fundamentals of establishing and using credit. The next chapter describes using credit well; fitting it into your financial plan, and keeping it manageable.

You can use credit, via borrowing, when you need something and don't have the cash on hand. And you can use credit for convenience, when you do have the cash but prefer to postpone payment. But you can't use credit, in either form, unless you first establish a credit rating.

Establishing Credit

Jodi L. prides herself on always paying cash for everything, including the secondhand car she drives to her teaching job. Credit cards are a trap, she thinks, leading to impulsive buying, and she's deliberately steered clear of them. Now Jodi wants to buy a house and, with no credit history and no credit rating, is having great difficulty securing a mortgage. Jodi has learned, a little late, that it's easier to get a small first loan than a large one, easier to establish a credit rating before it's needed than at the last moment.

GETTING STARTED

The two key factors in establishing credit are (1) your **ability to repay,** based on your income and on your other indebtedness (a large paycheck, already committed to a host of other bills, does not make you a good credit risk), and (2) your **willingness to repay,** based on your previous credit record (how often you borrow, how prompt you are at repayment). Many credit grantors also look for evidence of stability: how long you've held your current job, how long you've lived in your current home, whether you own or rent that home. Some creditors use a statistical profile in making a credit decision, others rely on their own experience. Either way, the higher your income, the longer you've lived in one place, and the more you own, the easier you'll find it to secure credit—especially if your previous credit is good.

Credit grantors are not all alike, however, and it's easier to secure credit with some than with others. A good place to start, when you're seeking credit for the first time, is by maintaining checking and savings accounts without bounced checks or other evidence of fiscal irresponsibility. Then take a small loan from your bank or thrift. Repay it promptly and you will establish a credit history. Another good starting point is at a local retailer or department store. Once you have the card, use it regularly and pay the bills promptly, and you will establish a credit history. Then you can apply for a national bank card, with a reasonable chance of success.

Here are some additional tips, from New York's Citibank:

■ Answer every question on a loan or credit application. An unanswered question will usually count against you more than a not-quite-acceptable answer.

■ Don't assume that the lender already has the answer, even if you have previously applied to the same lender for a different loan. The information may be in the lender's computer, but a new file is usually opened for a new application.

■ Offer as much information as you possibly can. If you don't have an established credit rating but you've lived in the community for a long time and have a stable employment record, be sure to point it out.

SECURED CREDIT CARDS

If you have a poor credit history, or no credit history at all, you may be able to get started by depositing money in a bank account as security against possible default. These cards are tricky—many are issued by so-called "credit clinics" (see pp. 230-231) charging outrageous fees and offering very little in return. Others are good only for purchases from catalogues put out by the issuer. But secured cards can be useful if you're temporarily in a credit bind and want to use one as a stepping stone to regular credit. Before applying for a secured card, however, this is what you should know:

■ The line of credit available on a secured Visa or MasterCard is based on how much money you have on deposit; you may be able to charge amounts up to half or, sometimes, all of the amount the bank is holding as collateral. You may have a choice of regular savings, money market savings, or certificates of deposit, but the interest you earn may be lower than on accounts not backing a secured card. Furthermore, your funds will be frozen, sometimes for up to 45 days after you surrender the card and close the account. Never apply for a secured card with money you may need for other purposes.

■ Always find out exactly how much a secured card will cost. Application fees and processing fees are often charged in addition to annual fees. Many secured cards also carry high interest rates.

■ Don't take a secured card unless you are sure that your good payment record will be reported to a credit bureau. It may be worth the cost and temporarily tying up your funds, in other words, if you actually build a credit record and can move on to unsecured credit.

Sources of information for reputable secured credit cards include state or local consumer affairs offices, local affiliates of the Consumer Credit Counseling Service, and BankCard Holders of America (BHA, 560 Herndon Parkway, Herndon, VA 22070, sells a list of reputable banks offering secured cards).

CREDIT BUREAUS

Credit histories are maintained at credit bureaus. Contrary to what many people think, however, credit bureaus do not make decisions about granting credit. Such decisions are made only by the grantors of credit, by the stores and banks and oil companies that actually permit you to buy now and pay later. Those credit decisions, however, are often based on the material in your credit file. That file contains information about how promptly you pay your bills, about any prior rejection for credit, about any court judgments or bankruptcies. The file is accessible to you, under consumer protection laws. You'll find a discussion of seeing your credit file and correcting any omissions or errors on p. 189.

Although credit files contain a lot of information, they don't necessarily have everything. Most oil companies, for instance, don't report accounts unless they are delinquent. So you could hold two or three oil company credit cards and be rejected for a bank card because you "have no credit history." If this happens, you can correct the file.

Note: Credit bureau files on consumer repayment, contrary to what some people believe, do *not* include reports of moral character. They are simply a report of credit activities. Investigative reports, which do involve interviews with acquaintances about your life-style and your character, are sometimes prepared in connection with insurance or job applications. You should be notified in writing if such a report is requested.

There are approximately 800 credit bureaus around the country, several large bureaus (see p. 201) and hundreds of small local ones. To find your file, look in your local Yellow Pages under Credit Reporting Agencies or ask your bank or a department store. If you move, your credit history should follow you.

IF YOU'RE REJECTED

The creditor's written acceptance or rejection of your credit application must be given to you within 30 days of your application. If you are rejected, the creditor must tell you why. If you have been denied credit because of information furnished by a credit bureau, you have the right to find out (at no charge) what information is in your credit file. It's not required by law but, in

Q My husband has a nephew with identical first, middle, and last names. In the past month, two local stores have asked my husband to take care of bad checks actually written by his nephew. Are there any precautions we can take, before this nephew does anything further, to keep our name and our credit record good?

A You should get in touch with all your creditors, your banks, *and* the credit bureau to explain that you have no responsibility for debts incurred by this nephew. Point out any identifying features (an address or a Social Security number) which might be used to differentiate between your nephew and your husband. And ask the creditors, the banks, and the credit bureau to note your record with these distinguishing characteristics.

response to many complaints, a new procedure permits consumers to receive free or low cost reports from all three of the major credit bureaus even in instances other than rejection for credit.

You also have the right to ask the credit agency to recheck the information. If it proves inaccurate the credit bureau must remove it from your file and, at your request, notify all creditors who received the incorrect information in the past six months that the file has been corrected. If you disagree with the credit bureau's record or if the information is accurate but incomplete—if, for instance, your late payments on one account stemmed from a dispute with a merchant over defective merchandise and payments resumed once the dispute was settled—you can write an explanation (of 100 words or less) which must be added to your credit file.

If you're turned down one place, try somewhere else. Every lending institution sets its own standards for acceptance. But don't apply for too many cards at one time. Creditors may view this as an overextension of your ability to repay.

If you do in fact have a poor credit history, you should know that it will not last forever. It does, however, last for seven years (ten, if you've declared bankruptcy), which may seem like forever if you need credit. Try, therefore, to take on no more debt than you can responsibly handle.

Women and Credit

Under the Equal Credit Opportunity Act of 1975, you should not have any difficulty securing credit because you are a woman. The same criteria of

Q I'm a full-time homemaker but I would like to have credit in my own name. Is there any way I can do so?

A Credit grantors may not discriminate against women. But anyone, man or woman, must have the ability to repay in order to be creditworthy. Do you own any assets, such as stocks or bonds or an automobile, in your own name? Have you received an inheritance which you keep in a bank account in your own name? Do you work, or have you worked, part-time? Do you receive a regular monthly income from your husband? All of these factors must be considered in an application for credit. Without any of them, however, your best bet is to add your name to your husband's accounts, so that the credit history will be reported in both your names.

ability to repay and willingness to repay must be applied to both women and men. Credit grantors are not allowed to ask about birth control methods or childcare provisions, they may not consider sex or marital status in evaluating creditworthiness, and they must take all income (including alimony and child-support payments, if you choose to declare them) into account.

Note: When you apply for an individual account, solely in your own name, creditors may not ask your marital status or ask for information about your spouse—unless you live in a community property state (see p. 191).

Although discrimination is illegal, women may still encounter problems in applying for credit. Here's what you, as a woman, should know:

- ■ Use your own name on any credit application. "Mrs. John Jones" is a social title and can apply to any wife of John Jones; Mary Jones refers to a specific person. Use your own name, and use the same name all the time. Be consistent.
- ■ If you get married (or remarried) after establishing credit, and plan to take your new husband's surname, write to each of your creditors and tell them you want to maintain your own credit separate from your husband's.
- ■ Have joint accounts with your husband if you like, but see that the credit history is reported in both names. This should be done automatically on new accounts. If you have accounts opened before June 1977, notify each creditor (store or bank or mortgage lender) that you want the history of the account reported to the credit bureau in each name; then check with the credit bureau, after a couple of months, to

Q I moved after my husband died, after years of paying telephone bills promptly, and when I tried to get service in my own name the telephone company wanted an advance deposit. Isn't this discrimination?

A A utility account is a credit account (you get service now and pay for it later), and utility companies keep track of good and bad payment patterns. They may ask for a deposit if you have a bad utility credit history or if you're a new customer and if the company routinely requires all new customers to pay deposits. They may think you're a new customer because your name was not on your husband's account. If this is the case, tell the company that you had earlier service in your husband's name. The company must then consider his credit history as well. (It would be much easier, of course, if marital partners put both names on such accounts.)

be sure that these accounts are being reported in your personal credit file. If you are widowed or divorced (and 85 percent of American women are left alone, one way or the other), this credit history will be very important.

■ Creditors cannot close accounts because of a change in your marital status. They can, however, ask you to file a new application if they have reason to believe your ability to repay has changed—if, for instance, you have divorced and the original account was based on your former husband's income.

■ You may have a credit card with your first name on it that is still an adjunct to your husband's account. The only way to be sure is to ask the credit bureau for your credit history. It may cost a few dollars (unless you've been turned down for credit, in which case it's free), but it's well worth the cost.

■ In community property states (Arizona, California, Idaho, Louisiana, Nevada, New Mexico, Texas, and Washington) and in Wisconsin, where husband and wife are legally responsible for each other's debts and obligations, creditors will consider the credit history of both husband and wife in an application for an account by either one if the application bases ability to pay on jointly owned property or the income of both parties. You can still apply for credit as an individual, by specifying that you wish to be judged on your own, and you should still be sure that your credit history is maintained in a separate file under your name.

Q My ex-husband won't pay charge account bills that he was ordered to pay in our divorce settlement. The stores are coming after me because my name was on the accounts too. Is there anything I can do, before my credit rating is ruined?

A The judge's order, unfortunately, is not binding on the stores. Both you and your husband continue to have contractual responsibility for jointly held accounts until they are closed, and information on the accounts will continue to be reported to credit bureaus in both names. Get in touch with your creditors and explain the situation. Ask to have your explanation attached to your credit report. If your husband can't be found and made to honor his debt you may have to pay up (you can sue him later), but the stores should be willing to make a payment schedule you can meet. Then be sure that the accounts are closed so that no further debt can be added.

In a community property state (and in any state if you choose to have a joint account with your husband) it will be counted against you if he fails to pay his bills—and, of course, vice versa. If you divorce a spouse who has demonstrated an inability to pay bills on time, don't expect to continue your own credit based on a history of this joint account.

Young People and Credit

Most children are exposed to the use of credit at a very early age. They watch parents pay with plastic. Sometimes they buy cash-free schoolday lunches at a local luncheonette or pizza parlor under an agreement that a parent will pay for it later. Sometimes, too, older children borrow a parental credit card and, together with a note of authorization, use it to shop in local retail stores.

Local retailers occasionally offer teenagers their own charge accounts. And national cards such as MasterCard, Visa, and Discover are targeting high schoolers with educational programs designed to cement brand loyalty. A 1992 study by MasterCard found that about 10 percent of high school juniors and seniors had regular access to a credit card, either in their own name or a parent's. Such accounts can offer teens an introduction to credit responsibility. But the cards will extend the wrong lesson if parents pay all the bills. Parents may be legally responsible but when a youngster uses credit, whether a personal account or a parent's account, the youngster should pay the bills. That's the only way to learn to stay within a budget, to charge no more than can be comfortably repaid.

College students, who are often bombarded with credit card offers, need to learn the same lessons. Too many college freshmen run up bills and fall seriously into debt, ruining their credit ratings, just as they're getting started using credit. Yet the rules that can make it difficult to secure credit when you're out of school and on your own don't seem to apply in the college market. Bank card issuers are targeting a younger and younger audience. And American Express, which had a program of extending credit to new college graduates, now extends credit to virtually any full-time student at a four-year college or university. According to one study, one-third of all entering college freshmen have a credit card before they ever set foot on campus; almost three-quarters have credit before they graduate from college. The average limit on student bank cards is $1,200, against $3,500 on all bank cards.

For young adults who don't take advantage of in-school credit offers, establishing credit assumes the same dimensions as for any first-timer. Creditors are not allowed to judge an applicant by age, although they may ask age. But they do look at length of time on the job, length of residence, and the existence of checking and savings accounts. Because both time on the job and time in one residence may be short, young adults, even with responsible jobs, often have difficulty securing that first account. The tips on pp. 237-238 may help.

Older People and Credit

Older men and women have complained about being denied credit just because they were over a certain age. Others have found credit suddenly cut off or sharply reduced just because they've retired from full-time jobs. But credit discrimination on the basis of age is illegal, under the Equal Credit Opportunity Act. A creditor may ask your age. But a creditor, under the law, *may not* turn you down or decrease your credit just because of your age, ignore your retirement income in considering your application, close your credit account, or require you to reapply for it just because you reach a certain age or retire.

Your age may be considered only when it is directly relevant to your ability to repay. At the age of 64, as an example, you might be denied a 30-year mortgage with a small down payment. But the denial would have to be based on the fact that your income is about to drop after retirement; it cannot be based solely on your age. If you are denied such a loan, you may still be able to secure a smaller loan with a larger down payment, especially if you have good collateral.

If a potential creditor points to reduced income as a disqualifying factor, be sure to point out any compensating factors. You might, for instance, have a long and solid credit history indicating willingness to repay. You might have assets beyond your retirement income.

Sometimes creditors insist that older borrowers take out credit insurance (see p. 217). It is, however, illegal for a creditor who requires such insurance to deny credit to you if you can't get credit insurance because of your age.

Sources of Credit

You use credit when you make a purchase of goods or services with the promise to pay at a later date. With this form of credit you often have the choice of paying in full upon receipt of the bill or spreading payment over a period of months. You also use credit when you borrow money. Here, however, you agree in advance to a fixed repayment schedule. Both types of credit are available from a variety of sources.

RETAIL STORES

Local stores and national chains alike issue credit cards, typically good only at their own outlets. (But the lines are blurring: The all-purpose Sears Discover card functions like a bank card and is accepted in many places.)

Store cards usually do not cost anything to get or to maintain, as long as bills are paid promptly. When payment is extended, however, finance charges are levied on the unpaid balance.

Those finance charges can be high. A survey released in late 1992 by the Massachusetts attorney general disclosed retail interest rates frequently exceeding 20 percent. Retailers can justify their interest rates—they don't charge annual fees, they don't collect the "merchant fees" levied by bank cards, and they are losing money on credit operations. From your point of view as a consumer, however, it may make sense to use a bank card instead of a retailer's card to pay for purchases. (It doesn't make any difference, of course, if you pay all your balances in full.)

OIL COMPANIES

Oil companies, similarly, issue credit cards to their customers, cards which are good only at their own stations. (Some oil-company cards are also usable at certain hotels, but most are single-purpose cards.) Like retail charge accounts, these may be paid in full without a finance charge or paid over an extended period with interest.

Note: With the difference between cash and credit prices at most gas pumps, consumers appear to be more tempted to use debit cards when buying gasoline. These cards access your checking account and are like cash to the merchant, so buying with a debit card secures the cash price. See p. 79 for details.

BANK CARDS

These credit cards—Visa and MasterCard—are typically issued by financial institutions. Although they're still called "bank cards," however, more and more nonbank issuers are jumping on the bandwagon. These issuers—familiar names include AT&T, General Motors, and General

Q If I offer to pay in cash for a big-ticket item, instead of charging it, shouldn't I be entitled to a discount on the purchase price?

A You're never "entitled" to a discount, but you can certainly ask if the merchant is willing to give one. Discounts are legal, so long as they are offered to every cash customer. But, while you might think merchants would happily offer discounts to dispense with both the paperwork and the delayed payment associated with credit, many merchants think credit cards justify their use by the added business they generate. As a result, they do not give discounts for cash. But it never hurts to ask.

Electric—must work through a bank but you apply directly to the issuer for these specialty cards rather than through your bank.

Visa and MasterCard are honored at a wide range of establishments, from restaurants to retail stores to travel agencies and airlines. With these cards you have a choice of paying the full amount right away (usually, but not always, without any interest charges) or paying the bill, with interest, in installments. These cards are issued with a preset spending limit, based on your credit history. Spending limits are rarely as restrictive as they once were, however, and whatever your initial limit, it is often raised and raised again as you demonstrate your ability to repay.

Cash Advances

Bank cards may also be used to secure a cash advance. This can be a useful feature if you're temporarily in need of cash. But it can be an expensive convenience. The finance charge typically starts immediately on a cash advance; on purchases you often have a grace period before finance charges commence. The finance charge may carry a higher interest rate, and it may be accompanied by transaction fees. The effective interest rate on cash advances, as a result, may be considerably higher than you realize.

In an example cited by BankCard Holders of America (BHA), a consumer advocacy group in Washington, D.C., a consumer takes a cash advance of $300 and is charged the average fee of $2.50 in addition to one month's

Q My bank is raising its interest rates on credit cards and applying the new rate to unpaid balances. I thought that an interest-rate increase could only be applied to new purchases, not to outstanding balances. Am I wrong?

A I'm afraid you are. Under the federal Truth in Lending Act, a credit issuer can raise interest rates simply by giving cardholders 15 days advance written notice of the change (except in a couple of states, where state law requires 30 days notice). After that, at the credit issuer's option, the new rate and terms may apply to outstanding balances as well as to new purchases.

You might apply for a new card at a lower rate and, after you have the new card, cancel the old one. The bank issuing the new card might be willing (more likely, delighted) to transfer the old card's outstanding balance to the new card. Or you could use convenience checks or a cash advance on the new card to pay off the old; just be sure there isn't a fee or a higher interest rate on cash advances.

interest at 18.5 percent. If the cardholder repays the advance in full 25 days after taking it, she will have paid an effective interest rate of 32.94 percent. You read it right. That's 32.94 percent. If there is a fee for a cash advance, BHA concludes, the effective rate will always be higher than the stated rate.

Exceeding the Spending Limit

When you reach your spending limit you'll probably be denied use of the card until you've paid at least part of the outstanding bill. This can be embarrassing—especially if your card is rejected in front of a friend or a business colleague—so it's a good idea to keep track of your credit purchases and your available credit limit.

Note: Some credit card issuers will authorize specific purchases when you've exceeded your spending limit, on a case-by-case basis. If you have a specific need for additional credit, call your credit grantor.

You may use more of your authorized credit line than you know you're using, however, because of a little-known practice called "credit hold." Some creditors, mostly car rental agencies and hotels, may freeze $200 or so above the billed amount as a deposit against potential damage. They should tell you they are doing so, but may neglect to do so. They should also "unfreeze" the excess amount promptly once you've returned the car or left the hotel, but may neglect to do so. (A New York State law, which other states should emulate, requires notification, written customer consent, and prompt release of any amount over $25.)

Gold Cards

Gold cards presumably offer more "prestige" than standard bank cards. Unless you will actually use the special features, however, you probably don't

Q I heard about a company that will keep track of all my credit cards, and contact all the companies for me if my cards are lost or stolen. Is this service worthwhile?

A If making a single telephone call to report loss or theft, instead of calling each of your creditors, is worth the annual fee (usually about $12), then it's worth it to you. But the most tedious chore—making a list of all your accounts—is still one you must do for yourself. You either do it to submit to the card registry, or you do it for your own records. Keep this in mind before you sign up. And remember: Federal law limits your liability on any lost or stolen card to $50, if charges are made before the card is reported missing. If you report a loss promptly—or if the creditor fails to give you a postage-paid preaddressed form to use in notification—you won't be responsible for any charges.

Credit Card Checklist

	Card A	Card B
Is there an annual fee?	_____	_____
How much is it?	_____	_____
What is the grace period?	_____	_____
Does it begin at:		
Date of purchase?	_____	_____
Date of posting?	_____	_____
Date of billing?	_____	_____
What is the interest rate?	_____	_____
If variable, how often does it change?	_____	_____
If variable, what index is used?	_____	_____
If rate is tiered, where does it change?	_____	_____
If rate is tiered, what is the rate on		
higher balances?	_____	_____
on lower balances?	_____	_____
Is the interest rate based on:		
Average daily balance		
(including new purchases)	_____	_____
Average daily balance		
(excluding new purchases)	_____	_____
Two cycle average daily balance		
(including new purchases)	_____	_____
Two cycle average daily balance		
(excluding new purchases)	_____	_____
Is there a fee, and how much, for:		
Late payment	_____	_____
Cash advances	_____	_____
Exceeding the credit limit	_____	_____
Each transaction	_____	_____
ATM use	_____	_____
Document requests	_____	_____
Telephone account inquiries	_____	_____

Source: Credit Union National Association.

need to pay the extra price to have a gold card. Standard cards can be found with annual fees ranging from zero to $25. Gold cards cost from $20 to $50.

Gold cards typically combine a higher line of credit ($5,000 to $25,000) with a package of financial services: high cash advances, worldwide cash access via banking offices and automated teller machines (ATMs), automatic credit life insurance, automatic travel insurance when the card is used to buy transportation, and so on. This card, accepted in the wide range of places that accept bank cards, has a bank card rate of interest on unpaid balances.

But you can probably secure as high a line of credit as you'll need on a standard bank card. You may also be able to find a no-fee card (see p. 208). And, since almost everyone seems to carry a gold card these days, the prestige value is dubious.

TRAVEL AND ENTERTAINMENT CARDS

These cards—American Express and Diner's Club are the prime examples—are sometimes called pay-as-you-go or charge cards because bills must be paid, in full, when presented. They have been predominantly used for travel, entertainment, and leisure, but are now beginning to be accepted in many retail stores as well.

Although the lines are blurring (American Express also issues the Optima card, with an annual fee and interest charges), pure travel and entertainment (T&E) cards still differ from bank cards in two key ways:

■ There are no preset spending limits, which makes them useful in emergencies.
■ They have annual fees but no finance or interest charges, because payment is expected immediately.

Q I always thought bank cards were less expensive than charge cards, but with the new annual fees some banks are charging I'm not sure. How should the two be compared?

A Look at your own spending patterns. Do you pay your bank card bill in full immediately or accrue finance charges on an unpaid balance? And look at the practices of your bank. Does the card have an annual fee? When do finance charges start? Even if a bank card is free, you may face interest at 18 percent (or more) a year. If you accrue finance charges on many purchases, you could spend a great deal more on such a card than on a charge card. (With a charge card, of course, you'll be expected to pay in full when the bill is presented; so forget the comparison if you would be unable to do so.)

In lieu of finance charges, however, there are often late fees. When payments are 50 days overdue, for example, American Express charges either $20 or 2.5 percent (in most states) of the unpaid balance, whichever is greater. At 90 days, when a bill is still outstanding, the account is subject to cancellation. It will then be very difficult to reinstate.

Under some circumstances (typically in the purchase of airline or cruise tickets) you may be able to extend payment on a T&E card. Under the American Express "Sign and Travel" program, for example, you pay one thirty-sixth of the outstanding balance each month until the balance is paid off. The interest rate, adjusted twice a year, is the prime rate plus a designated amount; for the first half of 1993, the rate stood at 15.9 percent.

How Many Cards Should You Have?

A California man applied for, and received, 1,098 credit cards. He got his name in *The Guinness Book of World Records*. He also got a major headache in terms of storing and protecting his cards.

Nobody needs over 1,000 cards. But how many do you need?

One of the major bank cards is useful, not only for making purchases but for check-cashing identification. (Just try to pay for an airplane ticket by check, with no credit card for identification.) You might even want two, a Visa and a MasterCard, issued by different banks—one with a low interest rate for the balance you'll carry, one with a higher interest rate but no or low fee for the balance you'll pay in full. A local department-store card, one or two oil-company cards, and, perhaps, a travel and entertainment card should round out the package. Few people need more. And most people find too many credit cards a temptation to overspend.

Switching Cards

If you've been carrying a high-interest bank card and want to switch to a low-interest card, there are several ways to pay off your outstanding balance and make the transition. For example: Your new card (always be sure you have a new card in hand before you drop your old one) may offer "transfer" or "convenience" checks specifically for this purpose; as each check clears, it will appear as a charge on your new card's statement. (Some issuers treat these charges as purchases, others as cash advances; if it's a cash advance, you may be hit with immediate interest.)

Once you've paid off your outstanding balance, you still have to close the old account or you will continue to be subject to an annual fee and any other applicable charges. To close the account: Send written instructions to the card issuer along with the cut-up card (be sure to cut the card so that no one can copy the numbers or read the magnetic stripe). Ask the issuer to close the account and to notify the credit bureau that the account has been closed at your request. Check with the credit bureau in a few weeks to make sure your instructions have been followed.

PROTECTING YOUR CARDS—AND YOUR CREDIT

However many cards you have, take care to protect them. Don't leave your cards in your glove compartment or in your desk; these are the first places a thief will look. Make a complete list of all your cards and their expiration dates; a good way to do this is to simply make a photocopy of all your cards (but don't walk away and leave them in the machine!). And don't give a credit card number to anyone who solicits you by phone or calls to tell you that you've "won" a contest that you didn't know you'd entered. Even though your liability on any one card is limited to $50, your bank may refuse to issue a new card if there is reason to believe you've been careless.

Credit Card Fraud

Safeguard your credit identity. I can't say that strongly enough. Protect your credit identity from the hordes of criminals waiting to pounce on enough information to use your credit or to secure credit for themselves in their names. Consumer protection legislation means that you're not responsible for unauthorized charges or for more than $50 of a bill incurred with a lost or stolen card. But, and it's a big but, the headaches of straightening out a fouled up credit record will make you wish you could pay some money just to get out of the mess.

Here are some specific suggestions:

■ Keep in a safe place—and destroy before discarding—any piece of paper with your credit card number on it. This includes car rental agreements, travel itineraries and ticket receipts, credit card carbons and receipts, old credit card statements. Also shred preapproved credit card applications that arrive in the mail, before you throw them away; criminals may enter a "new" address to apply for the card, then use the credit in your name.

■ Don't write your address and phone number on credit slips, or your credit card number on checks. Some store clerks will give you grief over this stance (show your credit card if you must, but don't let the clerk copy the number), but both Visa and MasterCard forbid this usage of credit information and it's illegal in many states. Illegal or not, any crook having access to all this information can have a field day with it.

■ Never give your credit card number over the telephone, unless you've placed the call to a reputable retailer. (Even then, you can't be sure. One very reputable catalogue company recently found an employee misusing credit card numbers.)

■ Protect your Social Security number, to the extent that you can. If you live in a state where the number is your driver's license number, don't let anyone write your driver's license number on a check. (If your state allows you to use a different number for your driver's license, take advantage of the offer.)

■ Be very careful when using a calling card in a public place; thieves listen to numbers or use binoculars to pick up numbers entered on a keypad, then run up thousands of dollars in long-distance calls.

■ Check your credit record periodically, so that you don't find it full of errors *after* you've applied for a mortgage. At this writing, TRW, one of the "big three" of credit bureaus, is giving consumers one free report per year. Equifax and Trans Union Corporation charge up to about $8 per report. See below for how to contact these credit reporting agencies.

Note: Maryland and Vermont currently give consumers the right to one free copy each year of their credit reports. Elsewhere, you may have to pay the $8—but it's worth it to keep errors from creeping in.

Loans

When you want to borrow money outright, your credit rating also comes into play, but your sources may be different.

RELATIVES AND FRIENDS
These personal loans are very useful, especially if you don't yet qualify for a standard loan. But it's important to treat such loans in a businesslike way.

Where to Reach the "Big Three" Credit Bureaus:

TRW National Consumer Relations Center
P.O. Box 2350
Chatsworth, CA 91313-2350

Equifax Credit Information Services
Attn: Consumer Assistance Department
P.O. Box 740241
Atlanta, GA 30374-0241
(800)685-1111

Trans Union Corporation
P.O. Box 7000
North Olmstead, OH 44070

Even if no interest is being charged, sign a note indicating the terms of the loan: how much, when it is being loaned, and when it is to be repaid.

If you are making the loan, put the signed note in your safe deposit box; should you die, your family will know—and be able to prove—that money is owed. If you are making the loan, too, don't count on declaring the loss as a casualty deduction on your federal income tax should your relative fail to repay; the Internal Revenue Service (IRS) often considers such loans as tacit gifts.

PASSBOOK LOANS

Your own savings can provide collateral for a relatively inexpensive loan, if you can afford to freeze the amount of the loan in your account for the period of the loan.

With a passbook loan, you are borrowing against the money in your savings account. The rate is generally lower than for other bank loans because the bank holds your savings as collateral. In return for the lower rate, however, you temporarily lose access to your funds. The advantage: You continue to earn interest on the savings account while it is frozen, effectively reducing the amount you pay for the loan (but not by much, when passbook savings are paying just 2 to 3 percent in interest).

LIFE INSURANCE LOANS

Whole life insurance, if you have policies that have been in force for some time and have accrued cash value, can be a low-cost source of money. The interest rate on older policies ranges from 5 to 8 percent; newer policies generally charge variable rates, which may be higher. Life insurance loans do not have to be repaid, although any outstanding loan will diminish the amount

Q Last year I lent a boyfriend $1,200 to repair his van. I trusted him and did not ask him to sign an IOU. We're not seeing each other anymore and he won't answer letters or phone calls. Is there any way I can get him to pay me back?

A Possibly, if you take the matter to court. In some jurisdictions, you can go to Small Claims Court; in others, the amount will be too large for Small Claims Court and you'll have to go to local district court. For a nominal filing fee, however, you can handle the matter yourself. You are more likely to win, however, if you have some kind of proof: a canceled check, a money order receipt, a witness who knew about the loan. It's always best, even within your own family, to have a signed document for any loan you make.

of the death benefit. Whether or not you repay the loan balance, you should pay the interest due. See p. 493 for details.

BANKS AND THRIFTS

Both commercial banks and thrifts are authorized to make consumer loans. So are credit unions, to their members. (Loans from credit unions are often less expensive; see Table 7.1). Such loans may be secured (by some asset, such as the automobile to be purchased with the loan) or unsecured (issued on the basis of your credit rating alone). Interest rates vary with the type, amount, and duration of the loan, as well as whether or not you provide collateral and where you take the loan. (More details on the cost of credit will be found starting on p. 207).

Table 7.1: It Makes a Difference Where You Borrow

Average Consumer Loan Rates, June 1992

	Banks	Credit Unions
Auto loans	9.8%	8.7%
Personal loans	16.3	14.0
Credit cards	18.4	14.7

Sources: Bank Rate Monitor, Credit Union National Association.

Overdraft Checking

Overdraft checking, sometimes called reserve checking, is a line of credit offered by banks. You must apply for overdraft checking just as you would apply for a credit card or an installment loan. It then comes into play as an automatic loan if you overdraw your checking account. The service is free, until you use it; then interest charges are applied.

With overdraft checking, you will never bounce a check. But you should be cautious:

- While a few banks will lend you the actual amount of the overdraft, most lend specified amounts, often in multiples of $100. You could wind up borrowing, and paying interest on, more than you actually need.
- Some banks will automatically repay your loan from your next deposit. But some will deduct a portion, such as one-twentieth, each month so that your payments and the interest due are stretched over a much longer period of time. And some banks will not credit any portion of a deposit toward the loan unless you specifically request that they do so. Be sure you understand the terms of your overdraft check-

ing before you use it. It may cost you less, under some circumstances, to use a credit card instead.

More information on overdraft checking is on p. 70.

Home Equity Loans

You may be tempted to borrow against the equity in your home when you need a sizable sum. These loans have become increasingly popular now that deductibility of other consumer interest has been greatly curtailed. They are available from traditional financial institutions, as well as from finance companies (see p. 206). Some home equity loans are old-fashioned second mortgages but most take the form of revolving lines of credit; you establish a credit line, then write checks against that amount as needed.

Interest on home equity loans of up to $100,000 is deductible (if you took a larger home equity loan before August 17, 1986, you may continue to deduct interest on the entire amount). Typically, you can borrow up to 80 percent of the appraised value of your home minus the amount you still owe on your first mortgage. But this is a maximum; the amount is limited by the factors that go into any application for credit: your income and how much other debt you have outstanding. In 1992, according to a study by the Consumer Bankers Association (CBA), the average open-end home equity line was $32,095. Given an average first mortgage balance of $58,891 and an appraised home value of $133,343, the average borrower had 68 percent of the appraisal value of the home in loans or potential loans.

A few lenders are currently offering loans for more than 80 percent of equity. These loans may appeal to you if you don't have much equity in your home. But there are some catches: The maximum amount of the loan may be no more than $25,000. The interest rate is typically a couple of percentage points higher than it is on a standard home equity loan. You must have impeccable credit to qualify.

Be careful. A home equity loan (of any amount) may be cheaper than other loans, and the interest may be tax-deductible if you itemize, but it also means putting your home on the line. Don't do it to pay for something like a vacation that will be quickly forgotten while your payments go on for years. Do consider tapping home equity to make value-added investments like home improvements or putting children through college. But be extra-cautious when it comes to full-value loans; if the market value of your home declines, you may be left owing more than it's worth.

If you do want to tap this source of credit, these are some things you should know:

■ When opening a home equity line of credit, expect the closing costs that go with financing a house (although some lenders, to entice borrowers, waive most fees): an application fee, title search, appraisal, attorneys' fees, and (sometimes) points (see pp. 289-290). But some lenders charge more than others. In 1991, fees ranged from $25 to

Table 7.2: Open-end Home Equity Loans Are Used For:

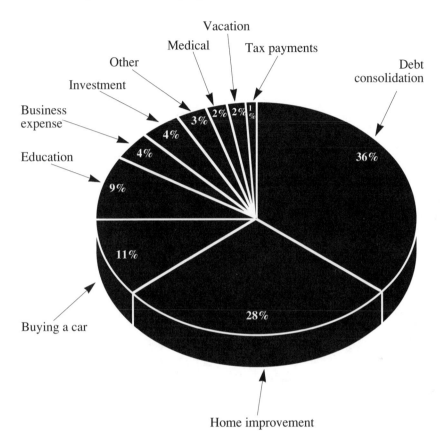

Vacation

Medical Tax payments

Other Debt consolidation

Investment

Business expense

Education

2% 2% 1%

3%

4%

4%

36%

9%

11%

28%

Buying a car

Home improvement

Source: Consumer Bankers Association.

$2,090, with an average of $380. Interestingly, according to the CBA report, two-thirds of the open-end lines were booked after the lender waived most of the fees. As always, it pays to shop around.

■ A "discount" rate is a low introductory interest rate that usually lasts only six months. Find out what the rate will be at the end of that period.

■ Most credit lines have variable interest rates. If the interest rate goes up, so does your monthly payment. Find out how often the rate is adjusted (most are adjusted monthly, but 10 percent are adjusted every day and 15 percent are adjusted quarterly) and what limitations there are on how much the payment may rise (all home equity lines of credit issued after December 8, 1987, must include a cap on interest rates).

■ Some lenders charge transaction fees every time you access the account. Find out whether your lender makes these charges, and how much they are, before you apply.

■ When you open a home equity account, you have three days to cancel the transaction, in writing. If you exercise this "right of rescission," the lender must return any money you've paid and must do so within 20 days.

STOCKBROKERAGE FIRMS

Personal loans are available from stockbrokers, often at a lower interest rate than may be available elsewhere, if you keep securities in a brokerage account. The catch: If the securities (your collateral) decline in value, they may have to be sold to pay off the loan. See p. 151 for more details on margin accounts.

FINANCE COMPANIES

Finance companies were traditionally the source of money for the "little guy," the consumer who couldn't get a loan elsewhere. But times have changed. More higher-income people are now turning to finance companies. And there has been a massive shift, according to the American Financial

---

Q My 18-year-old niece has asked me to cosign an auto loan for her. What will I be getting into if I say yes?

A You will be legally obligated to repay the full amount of the loan if your niece fails to do so. Don't cosign any loan unless you know the borrower well, have good reason to believe he or she will repay it, and are prepared to repay the loan yourself if necessary. If you do sign, make sure the contract is completely filled in and also that it specifies that you will be notified if any payments are missed. The contract should not pledge your house or car as security for the loan unless you expressly agree to such a provision. State laws vary and so do contracts, but a cosigner anywhere assumes a definite risk. Remember: Lenders ask for cosigners only when the principal borrower is a poor credit risk or has no credit rating at all.

Note: In most states, if you do cosign and your niece misses a payment, the lender can collect from you immediately without pursuing the borrower first. The lender may even collect the loan from you when there is collateral for the loan, coming after you instead of repossessing the car.

Services Association, toward larger loan amounts and toward secured loans, particularly second mortgages. At least two major finance companies no longer make loans to people who do not own their own homes. Even with this collateral, interest rates may be higher than those available elsewhere. Before you turn to a finance company, however, check into other sources of money.

INSTALLMENT LOANS

In addition to borrowing from a relative, a bank, or a finance company, you can often arrange for a loan direct from the seller of big-ticket items such as automobiles, appliances, and furniture.

But don't assume such a loan is preferable. Don't automatically finance a new car through the dealer, for example, without checking into a loan from your bank. Always compare terms carefully. Look at both the price of the item and the cost of financing the purchase. You may be able to negotiate one or the other to your advantage. Reducing the interest rate by 2 or 3 percent, for instance, may have the same net effect as cutting the price of a car by several hundred dollars. In an example prepared by the Credit Union National Association, a 3 percent difference in loan rates equaled almost a 6 percent difference in the price of a car. Put another way, if you can afford to pay $304.35 a month, you can finance a $12,000 purchase over four years at 10 percent and a $12,700 purchase at 7 percent.

Variable-rate loans, available in some areas, often start at a lower interest rate and run for a longer term. Initial monthly payments are usually lower, but be sure to ask how often and how much interest rates can change.

PAWNSHOPS

If you have no other source of funds, if you are in need of money for a short period of time, and if you have an asset to leave as collateral, you might look to a pawnshop or loan office. The typical pawnshop accepts color television sets and electric guitars. At least one such company, in Beverly Hills, California, does business with wealthy customers pawning expensive jewelry and works of art. Either way, the amount of the loan varies according to the resale value of the item, and loans may be renewed by paying off the accrued interest. Interest rates are often based on the value of the collateral. This particular "upscale" pawnshop charges about 4 percent a month. That would equal 48 percent a year, but pawnshops generally keep pawned items for much shorter periods.

Pawnshops are legitimate places of business, and are regulated by law, but they should not be your first source of funds.

The Cost of Credit

You'll fool yourself if all you look at is the monthly payment, and whether you can manage that payment. The true cost of credit is the total finance charge, how much you pay and for how long. It's important to shop for the best buy in credit as you would shop for the best buy in anything.

THE FINANCE CHARGE

This is the total dollar amount you pay to use credit. It includes interest charges and other costs such as fees, service charges, and points. And it's affected by whether or not there is a grace period and how that grace period is handled.

ANNUAL FEES

Closed-end loans usually require application and processing fees. Most bank cards charge an annual fee, typically from $15 to $25. But you can probably find a free bank card if you shop around. If you're a good customer, routinely charging a lot and carrying a balance, you may even find your card issuer willing to waive the annual fee. It doesn't hurt to ask.

Q I saw an advertisement guaranteeing a loan. When I called the "free" 800 phone number, I was passed on to a 900 number that cost $2 a minute. Then they said I had to send $200 before I could get the loan. Is this legitimate?

A Probably not. The Federal Trade Commission (FTC) has cautioned consumers against scams "guaranteeing" loans in exchange for an advance fee. Legitimate lenders may charge fees to process a loan application, but they never guarantee that you will qualify before they review your application. Fraudulent companies make lots of promises, then, typically, disappear without making the promised loans.

The FTC suggests these precautions:

■ Be wary of advertising claims that bad credit is no problem in getting you a loan. If money is not available to you through traditional lending institutions, it is unlikely to become available in response to a classified ad.

■ Be cautious of lenders using "800" and "900" numbers.

■ Never give your credit card, checking account, or Social Security numbers over the telephone unless you are familiar with the company. Once you give out this information, you're vulnerable to other frauds (see pp. 200-201).

GRACE PERIODS

Most bank cards come with a grace period. So do some loans. It sounds good: 25 days in which no interest charges accrue. But it doesn't quite work that way. Typically, you do have a grace period on new purchases if your previous balance is zero. You could also benefit from a grace period if you pay for all new purchases plus any outstanding balance by the due date. If you carry a continuing balance, as almost three-quarters of all cardholders do, you forfeit the grace period.

At some banks, moreover, finance charges begin to accrue from the date of purchase (not from the date, typically at least several days later, when the purchase is posted). Be sure you understand the rules when you apply for a particular card or loan.

Note: It may not always be advisable to take advantage of a grace period on a loan. Your mortgage company may grant you a couple of weeks after the first of the month before an additional fee is required. But that same mortgage company may (and probably does) report payments after the first of the month as late. You could be in for a surprise when you check your credit record, if you routinely make your mortgage payment after the first.

THE ANNUAL PERCENTAGE RATE

This is the key figure in the cost of credit, the true cost on a yearly basis; it's worthwhile to look at it closely.

Q I'm being billed for a suit I returned to a department store. The finance charges are adding up and I'm afraid my credit will be ruined. How can I straighten this out?

A Don't panic. And don't pay for merchandise you did not keep. Under the Fair Credit Billing Act, you have time to set matters straight without damaging your credit record. Write to the creditor (phone calls don't count) within 60 days, with your account number, a description of the error and why you believe it is an error, and the dollar amount in question. If you have a receipt for the returned merchandise, enclose a copy (keep the original) with your letter. The creditor must acknowledge your letter within 30 days; he must either correct the bill or explain why he believes it is correct within 90 days. If an error has been made, finance charges on the disputed amount will be dropped. Meanwhile, you need not pay the portion of the bill which is in dispute, although you must pay all other parts of the bill. Until the matter is resolved, the creditor may not report you to a credit bureau for nonpayment, bill you for the amount, or take any action to collect.

The annual percentage rate (APR) is not usually the same as the interest rate, although it might be under some circumstances. If, for instance, you borrow $100 from a friend at 8 percent interest and repay your friend $108 at the end of the year, you are actually paying 8 percent. But installment lending, where you repay a loan in equal monthly installments, does not work this way. If you borrow the same $100 at the same 8 percent from a commercial lender and repay it in 12 equal monthly installments of $9 each, you don't really get to use the entire $100 for the entire year. In fact, you get to use less and less of it as you make each monthly payment. Because this is so, the APR on this loan works out to 14.5 percent.

Lenders of all kinds are required to state the cost of credit in terms of both the finance charge and the APR. Both figures must be shown to you before you sign a credit contract.

Caution: BankCard Holders of America points out that most bank card issuers include finance charges in the balance on which finance charges are calculated; this compounding of interest yields a higher effective rate for the year than is apparent from the stated APR.

While the APR is the key figure, be sure that you also compare the dollar amount you will pay for credit. The dollar amount is affected by the length of the loan as well as by the finance charge and the APR. For example: A $4,000 loan for three years at an APR of 12 percent, with monthly payments of $133, will cost you $783 in interest charges. A four-year loan at the same 12 percent, with monthly payments of $105, will cost you a total of $1,056.

Q My banker said the APR was all I had to know in comparing the cost of a loan. Then he started talking about an "add-on" loan. What's he talking about?

A The APR *is* the most important thing, but it will vary according to whether the loan is figured on an add-on or a discount basis.

Look at a $1,000 loan at 6 percent simple interest, with $60 as the annual interest. With an add-on loan, the bank would add the $60 to the $1,000 loan amount at the beginning. You have the use of the entire $1,000, at the outset, but must pay back a total of $1,060 in equal monthly installments of $88.30 for an APR of 10.75 percent. With a discount loan, by contrast, the $60 in interest would be deducted in advance, leaving you an actual loan of $940. You pay a little less each month—$83.40—but, because you are paying the same 6 percent interest on $1,000 while you have only $940, your actual cost or APR is 11.75 percent.

Finance charges and annual percentage rates apply to all kinds of consumer borrowing: auto loans, home mortgages, bank cards, etc. There are also specific factors to consider in open-end or revolving credit.

OPEN-END CREDIT

This is the kind of credit, typically found in bank cards and retail charge accounts, which allows you to make credit transactions again and again, usually up to a predetermined borrowing limit. You have a choice, when you receive your monthly bill. If you pay the entire amount in full, there will be no finance charge. If you pay the designated minimum amount and defer payment on the rest, interest is charged on the unpaid balance.

When interest is charged, there are two things to consider:

When does interest begin? Most creditors allow a 25-to-30-day period in which you may pay your balance in full without interest. With this provision you can take advantage of the delayed billing; by making a purchase right after the billing date you can have up to almost two months before payment is due.

But some bank cards no longer offer a free ride even to customers who always pay their bills in full. With some bank cards, purchases now accumulate interest from the date they are posted by the bank, even if there is no balance carried over from the previous month.

Note: Some banks have advertised "free" bank cards when, in fact, they impose immediate finance charges. These charges, if you use the card frequently, can add up to more than an annual fee.

How is the finance charge calculated? Depending upon which of four methods is used, the same annual percentage rate can yield very different monthly interest charges.

Average daily balance (including new purchases). According to a recent study by BankCard Holders of America, this is the most common method. The balance is figured by adding the outstanding balance (including new purchases) and deducting payments and credits for each day in the billing cycle, then dividing by the number of days in the billing cycle.

Average daily balance (excluding new purchases). This is the least expensive for the consumer (see Table 7.4) because new purchases are not included when figuring the average daily balance.

Two-cycle average daily balance (including new purchases). This method, the most expensive for consumers who sometimes pay in full and sometimes carry a balance (it won't affect you if you always do one or the other), is calculated by adding the average daily balances for the current billing cycle and the previous one. Several large card issuers use this method.

Two-cycle average daily balance (excluding new purchases). Similar to the above, but slightly less expensive because new purchases are not included in calculating the average daily balance.

Suggestion: If you tend to carry an ongoing balance on your bank card, try to find a card using either the average daily balance or the average two-

Table 7.3: What it Costs to Finance $1,000

All figures are rounded to the nearest dollar.

Annual % rate	Length of loan	Monthly payments	Total finance charge	Total cost
8%	1 year	$87	$44	$1,044
	2 years	45	86	1,080
	3 years	31	128	1,116
	4 years	24	172	1,152
10%	1 year	88	55	1,056
	2 years	46	108	1,104
	3 years	32	162	1,152
	4 years	25	218	1,200
12%	1 year	89	66	1,068
	2 years	47	130	1,128
	3 years	33	196	1,188
	4 years	26	264	1,248
14%	1 year	90	77	1,080
	2 years	48	152	1,152
	3 years	34	230	1,224
	4 years	27	312	1,296

Source: Federal Trade Commission.

cycle balance but excluding new purchases from the calculation. This way, you get an automatic grace period on all new purchases.

There are innumerable variations on each method, depending on how finance charges, late fees, and grace periods are treated. But the net result is that you can hold several credit cards, all with the same stated APR, and be charged very different finance charges on the same purchase amounts.

Note: In a number of states cards are issued with split interest rates with, for instance, 18 percent charged on the first $500 of your outstanding balance and 12 percent on the rest. If this is so in your state, or on your bank card, you might be better off lumping your purchases on one card rather than making a number of small purchases on two or more cards. If your credit limit permits you to do so, a larger balance on a single card results in lower interest charges.

All these calculations are infinitely more complicated if you hold a bank card charging a variable interest rate. Almost 30 percent of bank card issuers offer cards with variable interest rates.

Table 7.4: Finance Charges for Different Balance Calculation Methods

In this example, a consumer starts the first month with a zero balance and charges $1,000, of which he pays off only the minimum amount due or one thirty-sixth of the balance. The next month, he charges another $1,000. He then pays off the entire balance due. This same pattern is repeated three more times during the year. The interest rate is 19.8 percent.

Average Daily Balance (including new purchases):	$132.00
Average Daily Balance (excluding new purchases):	$ 66.00
Two-cycle Average Daily Balance (including new purchases):	$196.20
Two-cycle Average Daily Balance (excluding new purchases):	$131.20

Source: BankCard Holders of America.

Note: You may be offered a card with a low introductory rate. Just be sure that you read the small print, and know what the interest rate will be after the "teaser" period is over.

MINIMUM PAYMENTS

There has been a recent trend among bank card issuers to lower the minimum monthly payment, from about 5 percent of the total balance in the mid-1980s to 2 to 3 percent today. Don't think the issuers are doing you a favor by reducing the amount you must pay each month (or, for that matter, by allowing you to skip a month). Interest continues to accumulate on unpaid balances and you will owe a lot more in the end.

Low minimum payments encourage long-term indebtedness. As a BankCard Holders of America study notes, a balance of $2,500 at the average interest rate of 18.5 percent will take a consumer more than 30 years to pay off if she makes minimum monthly payments of 2 percent or $15. That same consumer will pay over $6,650 in interest.

Suggestion: Pay as much as you can each month. And, if you are carrying a balance, try to pay your credit card bills as soon as they arrive. By paying early, you reduce both your average daily balance and your interest charges.

USURY LAWS

Federal legislation, such as Truth-in-Lending, protects consumers across the country by requiring that creditors give accurate information about interest charges. The amount that may be charged, however, is generally left to state legislation (Congress periodically addresses the possibility of overriding all state interest-rate limits on consumer loans but has so far not done so).

State-imposed limits, in any case, have more impact on consumer loans than they do on credit in general. That's because the governing law on credit cards is the law of the state in which the card is issued rather than the state where the consumer lives. Many bank card operations have moved to states (such as Delaware and North Dakota) where the law is favorable ... to them. The best word for the consumer: Shop around. And hope that competition reduces the cost of credit.

Should You Prepay a Loan?

It doesn't make sense to many consumers, but it *can* cost money to pay off a loan early. Here's why:

PREPAYMENT PENALTIES

Many loan agreements, both installment loans and mortgage loans, include a specified prepayment penalty. If you pay such a loan early you'll have to make an additional lump-sum payment. The reason: Lenders make long-range plans based in part on loans being repaid at specified intervals. If the loans are repaid early, the plans are disrupted.

Prepayment penalties are not universally applied to all kinds of loans. And they are not permitted in every state. On the disclosure statement required

Q I charged $95 on my bank card when I had my carburetor repaired. But the car is functioning as badly as it did before, and I don't think the repair was made properly. Do I have to pay the bill?

A Until a few years ago the answer would have been yes. Once the debt was turned over to a third party, such as the bank which issued your card, you would have been responsible for paying the bill no matter how defective the product or service. Your only recourse would have been to sue the garage. No more. Under the Fair Credit Billing Act, you can refuse to pay the bill (or any remaining portion of it, if you've already paid part) if (1) the amount of the bill is more than $50, (2) the charge was made in your home state or within 100 miles of your home, and (3) you made a good faith effort to resolve the dispute with the merchant.

by Truth-in-Lending legislation, the lender must indicate whether you "may" or you "will not" have to pay a penalty (see Figure 7.1). If you may face a prepayment penalty, you have a choice: Shop elsewhere for credit, or take the loan and pay it over the predesignated period.

THE RULE OF 78S

Although not strictly a prepayment penalty, this mathematical formula formerly used by some creditors sometimes (especially when applied to loans longer than four or five years) has had a similar effect. This formula, sometimes also called the "sum of the digits" (because the sum of the digits 1 through 12, representing a 12-month loan period, add up to 78), is applied when all of the interest on a loan is computed in advance. When you sign a loan agreement based on this advance computation, you agree to pay the principal plus interest in equal monthly installments.

This accounting method is prohibited by federal law for loans made after September 30, 1993. If you have an outstanding loan, however, you still have to be careful. When you decide to pay off such a loan early, the creditor uses the Rule of 78s to determine your "rebate"—the portion of the total interest charge you won't have to pay. This rebate, however, is seldom as much as you might think. That's because you pay more interest in the beginning of a loan, when you have the use of more of the money, and less interest in the later months.

The Rule of 78s has been called a form of prepayment penalty. The more you've borrowed and the longer the loan, the worse the impact. For example: You bought a recreational vehicle for $20,000, financed over 15 years at an APR of 12 percent. Pay it off after five and a half years, and your hidden penalty from the Rule of 78s comes to $1,743.

In a few states, consumer loans are made on a simple-interest basis, with the interest portion of each payment calculated on the outstanding principal

Q I took a $10,000 four-year car loan at an interest rate of 10 percent, with monthly payments of $253.62. I noticed that the payment book says the finance charges are figured by the "Rule of 78s." What does this mean?

A Nothing—unless you want to prepay the loan. Then you'll find the Rule of 78s acts as a prepayment penalty. For example: If you doubled payments from the beginning and paid off your 10 percent loan in two years instead of four, you would save $554.53 under your loan agreement. Without the Rule of 78s, you would save $1,206.28.

Figure 7.1: A Sample Truth-in-Lending Form

Friendly Bank & Trust Co.   Lisa Stone
700 East Street   22-4859-22
Little Creek, USA   300 Maple Avenue
                                                    Little Creek, USA

ANNUAL PERCENTAGE RATE The cost of your credit as a yearly rate	FINANCE CHARGE The dollar amount the credit will cost you	Amount Financed The amount of credit provided to you or on your behalf	Total of Payments The amount you will have paid after you have made all payments as scheduled
12 %	$ *675.31*	$ *5000–*	$ *5675.31*

You have the right to receive at this time an itemization of the Amount Financed.

☐ I want an itemization.   ☐ I do not want an itemization.

Your payment schedule will be

Number of Payments	Amount of Payments	When Payments Are Due
1	*$262.03ᵉ*	*6/1/93*
23	*$235.36*	*Monthly beginning 7/1/93*

Late Charge: If a payment is late, you will be charged $5 or 10% of the payment, whichever is less.

Prepayment: If you pay off early, you ☒ may ☐ will not have to pay a penalty.

Required Deposit: The annual percentage rate does not take into account your required deposit.

See your contract documents for any additional information about nonpayment, default, any required repayment in full before the scheduled date, and prepayment refunds and penalties.

_____

e means an estimate

This form illustrates an installment loan of $5,000, at a 12 percent simple interest rate and a term of two years. The date of the transaction is expected to be April 15, 1993, but the first payment amount is labeled as an estimate because the transaction date is uncertain. The odd days' interest ($26.67) is collected with the first payment. The remaining 23 monthly payments are equal.

Source: Federal Trade Commission.

(the way mortgage payments are calculated). With this arrangement, there are no late charges or prepayment penalties; you simply pay interest for the precise period of time involved and the Rule of 78s does not come into play. If your payment is a couple of days late, you pay a little more interest; if you pay early, you pay less. Lenders, not surprisingly, balance their books more easily when they can collect late charges and prepayment penalties.

Credit Insurance

Credit insurance, which pays off a loan in the event of your death or disability, is frequently offered as an adjunct to installment loans. Credit insurance benefits the lender. It can benefit your family as well, because loan payments will not have to be made on a reduced income.

But credit insurance has been harshly criticized by consumer advocates. Before you buy it, here are the things you should know:

Credit insurance is usually optional. If a creditor requires that you purchase credit insurance, the cost must be included in the finance charge. Most creditors, as a result, do not require it, but borrowers may think that they do. Don't be pressured. Make an informed decision about whether or not to make this purchase.

Credit life insurance is term insurance. Credit life insurance, the most widely sold form of credit insurance, is usually a form of declining term insurance. That is, it is issued in an amount which then declines with the outstanding balance over the life of the loan. The premium stays the same, but the face amount of the policy declines along with the amount you owe. It is usually less expensive, however—unless you are ill or over age 50—to buy decreasing term insurance directly from an insurance company. The Consumer Credit Insurance Association points out, on the other hand, that it can be difficult to buy an insurance policy for $1,000 or $2,000. If you feel that you need insurance to cover a small loan, and if you don't have other insurance or other assets that will enable your family to repay the loan, then credit insurance may be your only choice.

THE COST OF CREDIT INSURANCE

The price of credit life is usually expressed as cents per $100 of initial coverage over the life of the loan, with maximum premiums set by the respective states. In 1992 the cost ranged from about 27 cents per $100 (in New York) to $1 per $100 (in Louisiana), with a national average of around 53 cents per $100. (Credit unions, as in so many other instances, are typically less expensive.)

Whether the cost is reasonable, as the industry claims, or excessive, as consumer advocates believe, it does add to the cost of credit. Credit life insurance has been estimated to add one percentage point to the interest rate of a loan, and credit disability (or accident and health) insurance to add two percentage points. If you take both credit life and disability, according to Stephen J. Brobeck, executive director of the Consumer Federation of America, a 15 percent loan will become an 18 percent loan.

Credit insurance can, nonetheless, be worth buying under certain circumstances. Think about it if:

- Your family will be heavily burdened by paying off your debts.
- You don't have enough other life insurance and can't afford to buy it.
- You are ineligible for other life insurance because of ill health.
- You are at an age—generally over 50—where credit life insurance might be less expensive than other term insurance.
- You want to cover a small short-term loan, an amount so small that a commercial insurance company will not be interested.

If you do buy credit insurance, however, compare prices carefully and know what you're buying. And leave a note with your loan papers; otherwise your family, despite the insurance, might continue paying the loan after your death.

 KEY POINTS

- Shop around for the best terms. Remember that finance charges may differ depending on the method the creditor uses to assess them.
- Make sure you understand all the terms of your credit card or loan agreement before you sign—including any prepayment penalty.
- Pay bills promptly, to avoid high finance charges and to keep your good credit rating.
- Safeguard your cards—and your numbers—to forestall fraud.
- Keep a list of all your credit card numbers in case of loss or theft.
- Keep accurate records of all your purchases and payments.

CHAPTER 8

Staying Afloat

The use of credit has definite advantages:

■ You don't have to carry large amounts of cash, or pass up a good buy because you're short of cash.
■ You don't have to worry about whether a personal check will be rejected.
■ You get a detailed record of all your purchases.
■ You receive a single bill, for any number of small purchases, payable with a single check.
■ You can pay for essential purchases, and some luxuries too, over an extended period of time.

But the use of credit has a negative side as well:

■ The availability of credit may lead you to spend more than you should.
■ Impulse buying may become a chronic problem.
■ The spread between income and outgo may become narrower and narrower, until
■ Debt becomes a way of life.

Establishing credit is one thing; using it wisely is, for many of us, something else.

Credit Trouble

People of all ages, occupations, and income brackets run into credit trouble, as is clearly shown by the records of credit counseling agencies and bankruptcy courts. More and more people in what used to be called comfortable circumstances are running into trouble these days—sometimes because of heedless spending but sometimes because of unexpected medical bills or the loss of a job.

Even without recessionary layoffs, credit woes can surface when a family relies on multiple incomes to keep up with inflation, and one of the jobs is lost. Ironically, many families first get into trouble when a homemaker wife first goes back to outside employment. The costs of her going to work—commuting, clothes, child care, meals eaten out and convenience foods eaten in, plus an additional tax bite (see p. 567)—may be misjudged in relation to her actual take-home pay. The couple may look at the added income and, discounting the added expenses, live up to that income by charging still more.

Trouble also comes when boom times lead people to think that times will always be good. An example: The inflation psychology of the mid-1970s to the mid-1980s, in which homes steadily increased in value, led many people to tap that increased equity. Many of those who took second mortgages or home equity loans have since found themselves overextended. The loans are coming due and the value of the homes on which they are based has stopped rising. With new financing either unavailable or unaffordable, many owners have been forced to the wall.

And trouble comes when people simply spend without regard to income, using credit to fulfill emotional needs. Credit counseling offices are heavily booked in February and March with people who have overbought for Christmas. One such couple spent over $400 on gifts for their children, ages six and two. Not much, perhaps, except that they were already committed, before Christmas, to $11,000 in prior debts on an income of $30,000 a year.

And, of course, trouble doesn't wait for Christmas. Some people spend heedlessly all year round, using money (or, in this case, plastic) to win friends, seek status, cure depression, raise self-esteem.

How can you stay out of trouble? How can you use credit within your lifelong plan for financial management?

When to Use Credit

Credit can fit into your overall financial plan if you use it to get ahead. A prime example: buying a house. Few Americans ever buy a house without the help of a mortgage loan, a use of credit which produces a significant asset with relatively little cash. A comparable use would be the financing of an education through loans; here, too, the asset outweighs the indebtedness.

Credit also makes sense in other situations: When you could earn 16 to 18 percent on your money in 1981 and 1982, it made sense to finance a car at 12 to 15 percent rather than tap savings—especially if you filed an itemized federal income tax return and could deduct the interest you paid. It's another story when you are earning 2 to 3 percent on your money, car loans cost 8 to 9 percent and revolving credit costs an average of 18.25 percent, as in mid-1993, and when you can no longer deduct the interest. Still, if a washing machine will eliminate endless costly and inconvenient trips to the laundromat, it can make sense to buy it on credit. It will make still more sense, of course, if you can buy the machine on sale. A saving of 20 to 25 percent justifies finance charges of 18 percent.

But credit has become a way of life. Where once the major family debt was the household mortgage, and that was to be paid off at the earliest possible opportunity, today we think it's foolish to pay off a mortgage. And we owe money, across the board, for all kinds of consumer purchases. After all, why not buy now and pay back with deflated dollars? One good reason: Because deflated dollars are still dollars—and a deflated salary may have to pay the bills.

Ask yourself: Will you still have the item in question by the time the final bill comes due? (An education yes, a vacation no.) Will you be able to pay the bills, as they come due, out of current income? (If you are counting on a bonus that is not guaranteed, think again.) Are you assuming that creditors won't grant you credit that you can't handle? (Don't. A lending institution looks at your past record of payment; only you know your future ability to repay.) Could you save enough, over a period of time, to make the purchase in cash? (If not, don't make it on credit or you may not be able to pay the bills.) Can you comfortably manage the debt you already have? (Manageable debt differs from family to family, but everyone needs a margin of safety.)

How Much Debt Is Too Much?

Most people can easily handle short-term debt—installment loans, retail credit, etc. (everything but a mortgage)—amounting to 10 percent of take-

Q We are a family of five with annual income (before taxes) of $37,000. Our debts consist of $55,000 owed on our house (worth perhaps $86,000), loans of $2,570, and a credit card balance of $1,685. We own two cars (both paid for) but have no savings. Are we in too much debt?

A You may not be in too much debt, but you do have a serious problem. With no savings, you have no cushion for an emergency. Try to cut back on credit card use and develop a regular savings program until you build up your assets.

home pay. While still manageable, 15 percent is not quite so comfortable. And 20 percent is the danger level.

But generalizations are just that: generalizations. What is your own comfort level? How much can you manage without the stress that goes with uncertainty about paying bills? There are two ways to evaluate your situation: You can look for the warning signs that indicate you're heading for trouble, and you can calculate your own personal debt ratio.

WARNING SIGNS

In addition to a general diffused sense of anxiety, there are specific warning signs that should tell you you're heading for trouble. Are you:

- Unable to save?
- Paying your bills a little later each month?
- Afraid to figure out your total debt load?
- Borrowing to meet current bills?
- Paying only the minimum, never more, on credit cards?
- Receiving overdue notices from creditors?
- Relying on overtime or bonuses to meet regular bills?
- Taking cash advances from one credit card to cover payments on another?
- Charging everyday items like groceries?
- Using savings instead of current income to pay these bills (for everyday items) when they come due?
- Using a large number of credit cards and juggling payments?
- Always paying the interest due, but never making a dent in the principal?
- "Shaving" your bills, by paying just a little less than is due?

Any or all of these symptoms means it's time to get your spending under control.

YOUR DEBT RATIO

Here's a simple way to figure the percentage of your annual after-tax income now committed to repaying installment loans.

1. Write down your total income for this year, after tax and other payroll deductions. Include wages, bonuses, tips, interest, dividends, etc.
2. Divide the amount by 12 to find your monthly spendable income.
3. Add up your monthly payments on all consumer loans, everything except your mortgage: credit cards, auto loans, student loans, checking account overdrafts, home equity loans, and so on.
4. Divide your monthly payments (step 3) by your spendable income (step 2) and you'll get your current actual debt ratio.

In mid-1992 the average American had a debt ratio of 16.4; this was the amount of after-tax income going to short-term credit. Some people can handle this level of debt; some can't. If your housing costs are low, for example, you may be able to manage more short-term debt. If you are putting children through college, you may want to keep your other debt low.

Suggestion: Determine what is manageable for you by dividing your annual take-home pay by 10 (if you believe a 10 percent debt ratio is safest), or by 6.7 (if you believe that you can live with a 15 percent debt ratio), or by 5 (if you want to live dangerously and sustain a 20 percent debt ratio). Compare the two. How does your actual debt ratio compare with your ideal (theoretically manageable) debt ratio?

Beyond a manageable debt ratio, in percentage terms, you also need a margin of safety in dollars. Determine your current margin of safety by subtracting your current debt commitment from your theoretical manageable commitment. If your current commitment leaves only a narrow margin of safety, an almost imperceptible cushion against disaster, it's time to take stock. If it is larger than your manageable debt ratio, you're already in the danger zone.

You probably know if you're in that danger zone. The real use of these calculations is to help you determine whether or not you can safely assume additional debt. Suppose you have monthly take-home pay of $2,500 and monthly expenses, including your mortgage, of $2,100. If you have other monthly loan payments of $400, you clearly have no safety margin at all. You should not borrow again until one or more of your current loans is paid off.

Look at your current loans. The $400 in debt breaks down, let's say, into a $60 installment loan payment which will be paid off in four months, a $140

Sample "Debt Payment Burden"

Annual take-home pay	$24,000
Monthly take-home pay	2,000
Other monthly income	200
	$ 2,200

Monthly consumer credit payments (other than mortgage)

Auto loan	$300
Credit cards	100
Student loan	150
	$550

Debt payment burden

($550 divided by $2,200):   25%

Source: American Financial Service Association's Consumer Credit Education Foundation.

payment which will take another eleven months, and a $200 payment which runs for another year. In four months, then, you'll reduce your monthly outgo on loan repayment to $340, leaving a safety margin of $60. Should you take on another loan at this point? Maybe, but first look at two factors: your take-home pay and your cost of living. If your income has gone up (perhaps you've received a raise) you might consider a loan to buy the dishwasher you've been wanting. But you'd best recalculate your committed outgo of funds first; with the price of just about everything going up at a steady rate, you may not have the margin of safety you think you do.

When You Start to Fall Behind

When the warning signals start flashing, when your personal debt ratio leaves no margin of safety, don't ignore the situation and hope it will go away. It won't, not unless you take action. There are a number of things you can do once things get out of hand, from credit counseling to debt consolidation to a declaration of bankruptcy. Before taking any of these routes, however, take a good hard look at your own situation and try to establish your own debt management program.

Debt Management

Personal debt management is a three-part plan: reducing your use of credit, identifying income and outgo, and establishing your priorities.

REDUCING YOUR USE OF CREDIT

The first, and absolutely essential, step in any debt management program is to stop running up finance charges. Try to pay off all new charges each

Q I've fallen a little behind on my debt payments, but what's the big deal? Don't they all allow a grace period?

A Creditors will accept late payments, but the fact that payments are late will show up on your credit records. And they will stay on those records for seven years, possibly standing in the way of securing additional credit. Even where there is a grace period (as when mortgage lenders accept payment between the first and the fifteenth of the month without additional charge), the payment may be regarded as late. An occasional late payment may be unavoidable, but try not to get in the habit.

month, plus interest and a portion of the previous balance. It will get easier and easier, as finance charges drop. Better yet, stop incurring debt. Put your credit cards away (you don't have to destroy them, as long as you have some willpower) until you have reduced your current debt. You will never get your head above water if you continue to commit yourself to new debt before you make a dent in the old. So put the cards away. Use cash. You'll be surprised how it will reduce your spending.

But don't look at credit problems in isolation. Look at your entire financial picture. Paying off credit cards costing 18 percent or more in interest can be far more effective than seeking high yields on investable cash. Robert J. Klein, a certified financial planner in New York, suggested this tactic for borrowers with investment reserves: First pay off existing credit card balances, then open a no-fee asset management account at a discount brokerage firm. Put at least $5,000 worth of securities in the account, make regular cash deposits into the account's money market fund, and use the credit card that comes with the account to charge purchases. Then, if you charge more than the cash in your money fund, you'll wind up with a margin loan costing (in 1993) under 7 percent. (But there are some risks associated with margin loans; see p. 151.)

IDENTIFYING INCOME AND OUTGO

Income-outgo calculations are an essential part of all financial planning and play a particularly important role in debt management. The very first step in gaining control of your finances, whether for simple budgeting or for getting out of debt, is finding out exactly where you stand. So, now, repeat the exercise from Chapter 2: Write down all your sources of income, and total them up (after taxes). Then write down all the ways in which you spend money, with a total in each category.

You'll probably find it easiest to determine income and outgo on a monthly basis. If you are paid weekly, you can figure monthly income as four and one-third times your weekly rate. It would be wiser, however, to use the four-week figure in your calculations. This leaves an "extra" four weekly (or two biweekly) paychecks each year as a "bonus" that can be set aside for savings, used to meet emergencies, or put toward a vacation. (For tips on budgeting on an uncertain income, see p. 42.)

Once you identify income and outgo, analyze both. Look at income first. Can you identify any additional sources of income, funds that will help get you out of the credit trap? Do you have any U.S. Savings Bonds tucked away? How about a cash-value life insurance policy? Could you have a tag sale, and get rid of accumulated possessions while taking in some cash? Do you have time, at least temporarily, for a second job? If you do find these or other sources of funds, use them to pay off current debt. Don't take on more.

Now break down the outgo category into essential and optional. If you're over your head in debt, you'll have to cut down on those optional expenditures. But first you have to determine your own priorities.

DETERMINING YOUR PRIORITIES

One person's luxury is another person's necessity. If you're going to make a debt management plan you can live with, you have to clearly identify your own optional and essential expenditures. Be realistic. If dinner out once a week, just you and your spouse, is essential to save both your sanity and your marriage, don't treat it as a dispensable luxury. But do consider a less expensive restaurant. Or if you are so far in debt that dinner out is temporarily out of the question, schedule personal time for dessert and coffee. Meanwhile, look at other areas in which you may be able to cut back. Do you really need a new suit for business wear? Or is your current wardrobe usable for another season? Is the family's second car essential? Or is it a convenience which, with a little juggling of schedules, you could do without? Are cigarettes or soft drinks or lunches out adding unnecessarily to the outgo side of your ledger?

The *only* way to gain control of your spending is to identify your personal priorities ("personal" in this instance includes your spouse as well; if you don't agree on priorities, you have some negotiating to do). Look at your life-style. How much of the way you live, and the things you spend money on, is a result of habit? How much really matters to you?

There's another important sorting out of priorities to do, if you're already beyond your depth in debt: You must decide which creditors should be paid first when you can't manage to pay them all. Many people in this situation play by some instinctive rules—they continue to pay the mortgage and the installment loan on the car, juggle department-store bills, and put off the doctor and the dentist. Don't act by instinct. Make a plan.

Dealing With Creditors

Make a list of all your creditors, with the amount of the loan, the monthly payment, the balance due, whether or not the loan is secured by your property, and the amount of interest you're being charged. This last point is important. Some loans are at a level rate of interest. Others may have no interest at all until they are overdue, and then accrue significant amounts. Now determine how much you can manage to repay. Can you pay any of the loans in full? Or would you be better off attempting to reduce and extend payments across the board? Figure out what will work best for you.

Then discuss the situation, face to face, with each creditor. Tell your creditors the facts: that you're having difficulty (and give them the reason: that you've lost your job, are facing extensive medical bills, or are simply overextended), and that you would like to work out a repayment plan you can manage.

Most creditors will go along with a reasonable plan. They would prefer to be paid, even if slowly, rather than repossess your furniture or take you to court. And if you've been a good customer in the past, they have reason to hope that you will be so again.

You may find, however, that not every creditor will go along with your own carefully worked out plan. You may have to do some rearranging if Creditor A insists on being paid in full, while Creditor B wants a percentage of the balance due before consenting to extended payments. If you've worked out your own plan and then talked to your creditors, you should be able to rearrange things to everyone's satisfaction. Whatever you do, don't ignore bills or notices from creditors. Doing so will only make matters worse.

Dealing With Debt Collectors

Once an overdue bill has been turned over to a debt collection agency, trouble assumes serious proportions. Now, unless you can come up with a satisfactory repayment plan, you face the possibility of legal action.

After sending you a written notice telling you how much you owe, the name of the creditor to whom you owe the money, and what action to take if you believe you do not owe the money, debt collection agencies may pursue you in an effort to collect. They may write to you and they may telephone. But they are not permitted to harass you. Federal law (the Fair Debt Collection Practices Act) is very clear on this point. A debt collector may:

■ Contact you in person, by mail, telephone, telegram, or fax
■ Contact other people, including your employer, in order to locate you

A debt collector may *not:*

■ Call you repeatedly, or at night, or at work if you ask him not to do so
■ Tell your employer or anyone else that you owe money
■ Use a postcard or an envelope which would identify the writer as a debt collector
■ Use obscene or profane language
■ Misrepresent who he is, who he works for, and what he is doing

Q I don't have the money to pay a hospital bill for emergency room care, but I do intend to pay eventually. In the meantime, how can I stop the collection agency that the hospital has hired from pestering me?

A Send a certified letter, return receipt requested, telling the debt collector to stop contacting you. Once you do this, the debt collector may not contact you again except to say that there will be no further contact or to notify you that the collection agent intends to take a specific action against you. But don't stop there. Talk to the hospital and see if you can work out a manageable repayment plan.

■ Use threats of violence or harm against your person, property, or reputation

■ State that you will be arrested, your wages garnished, or a lawsuit filed—unless these actions are both legal and intended

If a debt collector violates the law, don't be intimidated. Report the illegal practices to the Federal Trade Commission, Debt Collection Practices, Washington, DC 20580. The FTC does not intervene in individual disputes but can use the information to document a pattern of abuse on which it can take action.

Note: The federal Fair Debt Collection Practices Act defines a debt collector as anyone who regularly collects debts for others. The federal law generally does not apply to creditors (although the laws of some states do). If a department store is after you for nonpayment of its bills, this means that its credit department may legally call you at work. If the store has turned the account over to a debt collector, however, the collector may not call you at work once you advise him that it is inconvenient for you to receive calls there.

If you fail to pay your bills, for whatever reason, and fail to work out a satisfactory repayment plan, debt collectors may (depending on state law) take additional measures. Two such measures are repossession or garnishment.

Q About five years ago, before I knew my husband, his wages were garnisheed. Now no one will give us credit. Is there any way we can clear this from his credit record? Or, since I had good credit before I married my husband, would I be able to get credit through my name even though I'm not working now?

A The fact that your husband's wages were garnisheed will remain on his credit record for a full seven years, although he may find a creditor willing to extend credit before the time is up. Another possibility: You may be able to secure credit on your own if you currently have a dependable source of income *or* if you continued your credit history from before your marriage. Write to your local credit bureau, giving your maiden name, and ask for a credit report (it will probably cost a few dollars). Tell the credit bureau that you want to continue this good record under your married name. Then apply for a credit card (your best bet is probably with a local department store). Make sure you apply for an individual account; if you apply for a joint account with your husband, his negative record will be counted against you. And once you get the account, be sure to pay the bills promptly.

REPOSSESSION

If your debt is secured by an article of property—a car, for instance, or furniture—that property may be repossessed by the creditor. This may not, however, be the end of your problems. Sometimes (especially when the creditor is a little less than honest) the article is sold after repossession, at a price that will not pay off the loan. You are then without your property *and* you still owe the creditor the balance due.

If repossession appears inevitable, see if you can sell the item yourself, particularly if it's an automobile with some resale value. This way you'll be able to repay the loan with the cash from the sale and, not incidentally, you'll keep repossession off your credit history.

GARNISHMENT

When the loan is not secured, and when the creditor sees no other means of collecting, wages may be garnisheed. Through a legal procedure, your employer must then withhold a portion of each paycheck and remit it to the creditor. Although you can't be fired for garnishment for a single debt, employers don't like the paperwork ... and they may also lose their good opinion of employees who get in such a fix. It also does your credit record no good.

Before this happens to you, see what you can do about setting up a debt management program. If you can't do it alone, get outside help.

Credit Counseling

Howard A. knew he was getting in over his head when he owed over $13,000 to 11 different creditors. Instead of looking at his finances or dealing with the debt on any kind of realistic level, he went out and got a second job. That didn't do the trick—not surprisingly, since he continued to use his credit cards—so he took a second mortgage on his house. In effect, Howard was trying to borrow his way out of debt. He finally sought help, at a consumer credit counseling agency.

Consumer credit counseling agencies exist in cities, large and small, across the country. Over 750 are part of a national network headed by the National Foundation for Consumer Credit (for the one nearest you, if you can't find a local listing, call (800) 388-CCCS from a touch-tone phone). Others are affiliated with Family Service Agencies (look in your local telephone directory) and other social service agencies. Still others are profit-making ventures; be careful about these.

The typical Consumer Credit Counseling Service (CCCS) client is 35 years old, slightly more likely to be male than female, has a monthly *pretax* income of $2,056, and owes an average of $18,312 to 11 creditors. When this client comes to a consumer credit counseling service affiliated with the National Foundation for Consumer Credit he will be offered a self-management program in which the agency helps him set up a budget and payment plan. This is often done at no cost. If self-management won't work, either because the client is seriously overextended or because he lacks the discipline, the agency will work directly with creditors. Under these repayment (also called debt liquidation) plans the agency will run interference with creditors, negotiating a repayment schedule, collecting from you and paying the creditors. This service may cost $10 to $12 a month.

The agency may be able to get creditors to agree to delayed payment or to a reduced schedule of repayments. One such prorated plan is based on a "fair share" percentage of the regular payment. Suppose you have the following debts:

Creditor	Balance Owed	Monthly payment
Second National Bank	$3,000	$100
Ace Finance Company	1,500	60
Dr. Welby	300	20
Fred's Collection Service	200	20
TOTAL	$5,000	$200

After subtracting necessary living expenses from income, you can only make $150 per month available for debt payments. This is 75 percent of regular payments. Therefore, each creditor is offered a prorated payment, 75 percent of the regular monthly payment:

Creditor	Regular payment	Prorated payment
Second National Bank	$100 (x .75)	= $75
Ace Finance Company	60 (x .75)	= 45
Dr. Welby	20 (x .75)	= 15
Fred's Collection Service	20 (x .75)	= 15
		$150

Whether you go for budget counseling or for debt liquidation, the consumer credit counseling agency will do two things:

■ Request complete information about your income and about your debts. Just making this list will help you see where you are, an essential first step in making any financial plan.
■ Cut up your credit cards; the only road to fiscal solvency is a cash-only road.

The National Foundation for Consumer Credit and its affiliated agencies have received some criticism because they are funded by business. They are therefore most interested in seeing that creditors get their due and less likely, some observers feel, to suggest bankruptcy (see following pages) even when it might be the right solution. But this network of agencies has, nonetheless, rescued a great many people. Howard A. was able to get back on his feet over a three-year period. He made regular monthly payments of $370 to the agency. The agency, in turn, arranged with Howard's creditors for delayed payments and canceled penalty charges, and paid the creditors from Howard's monthly payments.

Note: Watch out for profit-making agencies and so-called "credit clinics" that charge large fees. (They are prohibited in some states but still exist in others.) They will only put you further in debt.

DEBT CONSOLIDATION

When the consumer credit counseling agency took over payment of Howard's debts, as he paid the agency a monthly sum, the effect was debt consolidation. But there's another form of debt consolidation, one that may or may not work to your benefit. This is when you take a new, large loan in order to pay off all your outstanding loans.

Consolidation loans can serve a worthwhile function, but it's important for you to do the arithmetic before you take out a new loan or refinance an old one. What will your monthly payments be? for how long? If your payments are going to go up, when you were having trouble paying the existing debt, a consolidation loan won't make sense. Don't be victimized into rolling a loan over and over, for an eternity of debt.

Q I saw an ad for a company that promises to fix my credit record for a fee of $400. Is this legitimate?

A No. There is no quick and easy fix for a poor credit record, and nothing such a company (or "credit clinic") can do that you can't do for yourself. Accurate information about late payments or bankruptcy cannot be removed from your credit record, no matter what anyone says, until seven to ten years have passed. Inaccurate information can be challenged and corrected, by you, once you've reviewed your credit record.

If you find an error, notify the credit bureau of the problem and provide full information about exactly what is wrong. The credit bureau must then, at no charge to you, reinvestigate the disputed information. It must correct any mistake or delete any information it cannot verify and, if you so request, send a copy of the corrected copy of your report to anyone who saw the incorrect version within the past six months. If the dispute is not resolved, you may file a written statement of up to 100 words with your credit report.

Bankruptcy

Can a man who owns a personal residence valued at $300,000 be bankrupt? Yes. This particular case occurred in California, as the result of a second mortgage which could not be refinanced when it came due. But this upright citizen is not alone. There's the printer making $32,000 a year who decided to open an ice cream shop—and failed. There's a county administrative assistant who was out of work for ten months after a knee injury. There's a policeman faced with the overwhelming cost of divorce. People of all income and educational levels have declared bankruptcy in recent years. Personal bankruptcies skyrocketed between 1981, when 315,832 Americans filed for personal bankruptcy, and 1992, when more than 900,000 people filed.

There are a number of reasons for the increase: In the early to mid-1980s, it was double-digit inflation. More recently, we've had deepening recession and rising unemployment. All along, we've had increasing reliance on credit and an increasing acceptance of debt as a way of life. People of all ages are affected, but baby boomers may be among the hardest hit. One study of several major metropolitan areas found that people between the ages of 28 and 45, making up 42 percent of the population, comprised 58 percent of those filing for personal bankruptcy. Nearly half had experienced layoffs, illnesses, or other breaks in income. Many had divorced.

Many carried too many cards and too much debt. A study by MasterCard in 1991 found that three months *before* declaring bankruptcy the typical borrower carried three bank cards with a total of $7,775 outstanding and had another 15 credit lines, from gasoline cards to home equity loans. Worse yet, after being up to date on all payments for at least six years, bankruptcy came with little or no warning.

Q After losing my job, I've cut back on spending everywhere I can. But it's been a year and a half, and I can't find another job. I'm afraid I'll have to declare bankruptcy. Must I lose my home if I do?

A It all depends on why you file, which chapter of the bankruptcy code you file under, and where you live. If you can't keep up payments on either a mortgage or a home equity loan, then your home may ultimately be lost. If you file under a Chapter 13 repayment plan, however, the courts may impose a repayment schedule allowing you to keep your home. If you file under Chapter 7, some or all of your home equity may be protected from creditors—but, again, not if those creditors hold loans secured by the home. Consult a competent bankruptcy attorney to determine your options.

There are two forms of bankruptcy and, while you may choose, the bankruptcy court may override your choice; it may require you to file under Chapter 13 and, at least in part, repay your debts.

Chapter 7 Bankruptcy

This is straight bankruptcy, under which your assets will be sold to repay as much of your debt as possible, with a court-appointed trustee overseeing liquidation. It's not quite as harsh as it sounds, however, because the federal bankruptcy law permits you to keep specified property, including (double each figure for a husband and wife filing jointly):

- Up to $7,500 in equity in your home (if this is not used, up to $3,750 may be applied to other property)
- $1,200 in a car
- $750 in professional implements or tools required for your trade or business
- Household goods, clothes, appliances, and books, up to a total of $4,000
- Up to $500 worth of jewelry (but jewelry and other luxury goods bought within 40 days of your filing the petition for bankruptcy may not be eligible for this exclusion)
- About $4,000 in a "wild card" exemption which you can apply as you wish

State law may allow different exemptions, either more or less generous. In thirteen states and the District of Columbia you may choose between allowable federal and state exemptions; elsewhere, state law (generally more liberal) applies.

Note: Filing under Chapter 7 probably won't make sense if most of your debts are in the form of back taxes, student loans, alimony or child support;

Where you can choose between federal and state bankruptcy exemptions:

Connecticut	Minnesota	Texas
District of Columbia	New Jersey	Vermont
Hawaii	New Mexico	Washington
Massachusetts	Pennsylvania	Wisconsin
Michigan	Rhode Island	

Source: American Bankruptcy Institute.

none of these loans will be forgiven and you'll be worse off than when you started. On the other hand, a Chapter 7 filing does permit you to keep exempt assets; if you have a state that permits a lot of exemptions, you may be better off under Chapter 7. Talk to a knowledgeable attorney.

Chapter 13 Bankruptcy

Under Chapter 13 of the Bankruptcy Code, you get to keep your property. In exchange, a portion of your income will be assigned to repay your debts. You must submit a monthly budgeting plan to the court, indicating how much you can afford to pay after living expenses are met. The actual decision is made by the bankruptcy judge, after reviewing all the information about your assets, income, and obligations. Sometimes debtors repay as little as 10 cents on the dollar; sometimes they are required to pay their debts in full (in which case the only thing they have to show for the filing is additional debt, for the lawyer's fee, and a blot on their credit record). Repayment under Chapter 13 is generally for a three-year period, with occasional extension to five.

Note: If you've had friends or relatives cosign any credit application, those cosigners will be liable for your debts when you file for bankruptcy. Under Chapter 7, your creditors can demand immediate repayment from your cosigners. Under Chapter 13, they must wait until it becomes clear that they will not be fully repaid under the court-approved plan. They may then collect the amount required to make up the full amount of the loan.

Note: You can't file under Chapter 13 if you owe more than $350,000 in secured debt (backed by your home and/or your car) and more than $100,000 in unsecured debt. An alternative here is filing under Chapter 11, formerly reserved for business bankruptcies but now available to individuals as well. A filing under Chapter 11 is a debt restructuring—but your creditors have a say in the process, which can become expensive as it drags on over time.

Q In 1989, after I was ill and out of work for months, I had to declare bankruptcy. For the last few years, I've had a job and have been able to pay my bills. But I couldn't save much, and now I've been laid off. Can I declare bankruptcy again?

A If you filed a "straight" bankruptcy under Chapter 7, turning over many of your assets under court order, the answer is no; you generally can't file more than once every six years. But if the 1989 bankruptcy was under Chapter 13 and you repaid your debts, you can declare again. Talk to a lawyer about your situation and consult a nonprofit consumer credit counseling agency to see if you can avoid bankruptcy.

CONSUMER PROTECTION

Whichever way you file, the law includes consumer safeguards:

■ Creditors must leave a debtor alone. As soon as a petition for bankruptcy is filed, under either Chapter 7 or Chapter 13, creditors may no longer contact you about missed payments or other financial obligations.

■ Debtors still have the option of reaffirming their debts (agreeing to pay them, despite the bankruptcy), but the affirmation must be public and the bankruptcy judge must agree that it is in your best interests. Even then you have 60 days in which to change your mind and rescind the agreement. This provision forestalls pressure to pay off old, legally discharged debts in exchange for the promise of new credit—an exchange that could put you right back in deep water.

IF YOU FILE FOR BANKRUPTCY

Chapter 13, if you must file at all, is probably preferable to Chapter 7. It indicates to creditors a desire to pay your debts and hence may not be as severe a blot on your credit record. But bankruptcy under either Chapter 7 or Chapter 13 should be considered only as a last resort. It's never as easy as it looks. Here are some of the pitfalls:

Q I understand that I can file for bankruptcy by myself, without a lawyer. Is there any reason why I should use a lawyer?

A You can file by yourself, for a nominal fee (see *How to File for Bankruptcy* by Stephen Elias, Albin Resnauer, and Robin Leonard, Nolo Press, 1991). But if you have any property, a lawyer can show you how to protect it. A lawyer may also be able to tell you whether a Chapter 7 or a Chapter 13 filing would be best in your circumstances. If you do use a lawyer, be sure to select someone who:

■ discusses the alternatives to bankruptcy, such as counseling,

■ tells you how to retain secured property,

■ advises you fully about both Chapter 7 and Chapter 13 (Chapter 7, because it's a one-step procedure, is sometimes recommended by lawyers reluctant to embark on a time-consuming Chapter 13 proceeding; your lawyer should recommend what's best for you),

■ informs you about both federal and state exemptions, and

■ is open about his or her fees.

■ The slate can never be wiped completely clean. Debts linked to property, such as a home or an automobile, must be paid in full or you will lose the property. Under Chapter 7 (Chapter 13 is more lenient), some legally enforceable debts, such as taxes, alimony, or child support, are never forgiven. If most of your debts fall into either or both of these categories, bankruptcy won't help.

■ Unless you learn to keep your finances under control, bankruptcy will provide only temporary relief. (Some 20 percent of those who declare bankruptcy do so again. Some 50 percent face financial problems within two years.)

■ The fact of a bankruptcy declaration remains on credit records for ten full years. During this ten-year period, you may find it very difficult to take out a loan, open a charge account, or establish credit in any form. Even after the ten years, creditors may ask whether you've *ever* declared bankruptcy.

■ You may not be ready for the psychological fallout of going bankrupt. Bankruptcy may not have the stigma it used to, but it doesn't exactly boost your self-esteem either. Nor does it do much for family relationships.

Circumstances sometimes make bankruptcy inevitable. If this happens to you, use the bankruptcy law and start again. But don't use it unless you must. Those who have been through bankruptcy tend to agree that it isn't quite as easy to live with as it is to declare.

Q I knew when I filed for bankruptcy that it would take a while to get credit again, but I didn't realize how hard it would be to live without it. Now I've heard about a way to establish a new credit identity and start all over. Should I do it?

A No. This is another scheme perpetrated by people out to make a quick buck at your expense. The problem is, the technique is illegal. It is a federal crime to make any false statements on a loan or credit application. You could even be charged with mail or wire fraud if you use the mail or the telephone when you apply for credit with false information. You could face fines or even a prison sentence. If you receive a letter from a company offering this "service," contact your state attorney general or consumer protection office.

Reestablishing Credit

Bankruptcy may mean a fresh start, but that start means doing without credit, at least for a while. Although a study by the Purdue University Credit Research Center found that more than half of bankruptcy filers get credit again within five years, creditors are not obligated to extend credit at all. Many won't for the ten year period in which bankruptcy remains on credit records.

Some debtors seem to believe that they should immediately be entitled to credit. Not so. Why should a creditor, given a demonstrable record of nonpayment of debts, want to throw money away? Why should he think he'll be repaid?

In order to reestablish credit, however many years have gone by, you have to demonstrate to creditors that you will repay your debts. There are several steps you should take:

■ When you have built up your savings, take a passbook loan and pay it back promptly. The loan will be secured by your savings (your account—or at least the amount you've borrowed—will be frozen for the duration of the loan) so you should obtain it without difficulty. Prompt repayment will demonstrate your intent to handle credit responsibly.

■ If you have access to a credit union, you may be able to borrow money and repay it via payroll deduction. This, too, would demonstrate your intent to be responsible.

Q I had to declare bankruptcy several months ago, after an extended period of hospitalization left me with loads of bills and no income. It was the worst decision I ever made, but I simply had no choice. But no one cares about that. First my lawyer said I would have to wait about four years to get some credit back again. Now he says seven. What's the real number? And is something I did out of desperation, not out of a desire to get away with something, going to ruin my chances for home ownership or any credit at all forever?

A Not forever, but probably for ten years. That's the amount of time that bankruptcy remains on credit records. (Other delinquencies—a repossession or a wage garnishment—stay on file for seven years.) But you may be able to explain your circumstances to potential creditors (they do care that your bankruptcy was the result of hospitalization rather than high living), and you may be able to reestablish your credit rating without waiting the full ten years. The best bet: Talk, face to face, with a local retailer and explain your situation.

- When you are ready to apply for a credit card, do so with a local retailer. Save the national bank cards for later.
- You may have to be willing to make a larger down payment (on, for instance, an auto loan) or to provide a cosigner.

All of these steps, you'll notice, closely resemble the steps you take when you establish credit the first time around. That's because you're in precisely the same position, after your "fresh start," except that you're actually one step further behind. You now have a blot on your record that you must erase. But you'll be able to do so, if you're patient *and* if you're responsible. Don't bounce a check. Don't take a loan, any loan, unless you can repay it promptly.

Note: If you are in fact a responsible citizen whose bankruptcy was caused by a serious but temporary problem (such as your own illness or the need to care for aged parents), tell your creditors. They will probably be responsive. If you've gotten into trouble out of sheer irresponsibility, however, don't expect the welcome mat to be out the next time around. You really will have to prove yourself.

 KEY POINTS

- Most Americans use credit, and it's a useful thing to have. But misuse can disrupt the best-laid financial plans, and care must be taken to manage credit well.
- Use credit when it fits into your long-range financial plans. Try not to use it on impulse, or to buy things you really don't need. Try not to leave yourself without a margin of safety.
- If you do start to fall behind, stop using credit and try to follow a structured repayment program. If you can't do it alone, seek help from a not-for-profit consumer credit counseling agency.
- If you must deal with a debt collector, be aware of your legal rights. And if you reach the point of considering bankruptcy, be sure to consider all its implications. It won't be easy to reestablish credit.

Spending Your Money: Housing

CHAPTER 9

Housing Decisions

Home ownership is the American dream, and has been for 45 years. Dreams die hard. Despite the recession, despite a leveling off of house values in many regions and actual decline in others, despite the fact that houses in many areas are selling at a loss when they are selling at all (a boon to shelter-oriented buyers but a potential problem for the investment-minded), 80 percent of us still identify the traditional single-family detached home with a yard as the ideal place to live.

A house can be a tax shelter and a hedge against recurring inflation. Even when pure financial analysis stacks the deck against buying a house, it may be emotionally desirable. Either way, it is probably the biggest purchase you will ever make.

Before you buy your first house, or your second, you owe it to yourself to evaluate your personal housing needs, determine where you want to live, and decide whether to rent or to buy. First, however, a quick look at the American housing scene today may prove helpful.

HOUSING IN THE 1990S

Housing patterns are shifting, largely as a result of the changing social and economic patterns of American life:

■ After rising steadily since World War II, the rate of home ownership is down. The number of Americans owning their own homes peaked at almost 66 percent in 1980 and is now hovering at about 64 percent.
■ Later marriages and delayed childbearing, combined with more divorces and more single-parent families, mean that fewer people are living in each household, down from an average of 3.1 people per

household in 1970 to 2.7 in 1990. In 1990, moreover, 23 million adults lived alone; this is more than twice the number in 1970.

■ The costs of owning a home are down but incomes are down as well, and the down payment and closing costs are insurmountable hurdles for many want-to-be homeowners.

■ Regional contrasts in housing markets are increasingly sharp. House prices in the Southwest appear to be coming back after bottoming out in 1991. (House prices in Houston dropped almost 40 percent between 1982 and 1991, according to a study by the Joint Center for Housing Studies of Harvard University). Sky-high house prices in southern California, as the recession lingers, are still dropping as this is written.

■ Many homeowners are remodeling rather than moving to a bigger and better home. Almost $31 billion was spent on additions and alterations in 1991.

The seemingly ever-higher cost of housing, the spiral that became the norm in the late 1970s, has come (at least temporarily) to a screeching halt. Even while monthly housing costs seem to reach dizzying new heights (property taxes often go up as municipalities attempt to compensate for declining assessed values), the purchase price of houses has in fact slowed its incessant rise. In the early 1980s house prices were up on paper but down in fact, after adjusting for inflation and for price discounts offered as incentives to move stagnant inventory. In the mid-1980s, with inflation at a low, house prices leveled off in many parts of the nation and began to drop in others. In 1993, prices have begun to come back in some regions but are still falling elsewhere, notably in California and the Northeast. That last phrase is key; there is enormous regional variation in how much (or how little) house prices appreciate.

If you are looking for a first house when or where the market is depressed, you're at an advantage because bargains may be available. This may be why, according to an annual study by the Chicago Title and Trust Family of Title Insurers, first-time buyers made up almost 48 percent of all buyers in 1992. If you are trying to sell a house, however, you may find that your selling price must be reduced and that your investment has not appreciated nearly so much as you had expected. This may be why the same study shows a decline in "seasoned repeat buyers," those who have purchased three, four, or more homes over the years. If you'd simply like to stay put, you may find the loss of a job making it impossible; foreclosure rates are up everywhere, with the highest rates, at the end of 1992, in New Jersey, Massachusetts, Oklahoma, and Connecticut.

The lesson in all of this: Buying a home is still worthwhile, *if* you plan to stay in one place for a number of years and if you don't over-extend yourself in making the purchase. Excessive debt is out, in the 1990s, and that includes home purchases riding on minimal down payments and two salaries.

Your Personal Housing Needs

Before you decide where you want to live or what kind of housing you want to live in, take a look at your housing needs in terms of your position in the life cycle.

Table 9.1: Home Sales Prices by Buyer Characteristics

	1988-89		1991	
	Median	**Mean**	**Median**	**Mean**
Household Composition				
Married Couple w/ Children	$115,000	$149,000	$99,000	$121,500
Married Couple w/o Children	96,000	119,900	94,300	114,700
Single Female w/ Children	86,000	114,600	60,500	71,700
Single Female w/o Children	82,000	94,000	73,900	82,400
Single Male w/ Children	85,000	195,100	104,800	87,800
Single Male w/o Children	73,000	89,100	77,000	85,900
Unmarried Couple w/ Children	79,800	90,900	114,500	83,800
Unmarried Couple w/o Children	110,300	143,600	78,500	85,300
1st-Time Home Buyer	76,000	86,100	76,000	84,200
Repeat Home Buyer	120,500	153,200	106,500	129,600
New-Home Buyer	109,500	135,300	116,800	137,300
Existing-Home Buyer	91,000	124,800	83,000	101,600

Source: *The Homebuying and Selling Process, 1991,* National Association of Realtors.

SINGLES AND LIVE-TOGETHERS AND THE NEWLY MARRIED

At this stage, you seldom need much space, probably prefer simplicity of living, and want to minimize costs. The solution, for most, is a rental apartment.

But you may want to buy a house or a condominium. Although home ownership has long been associated with meeting the needs of a growing family, both childless couples and singles of all ages are more and more often becoming homeowners. In 1970 it was relatively rare for a single individual to buy a house; in 1991, according to the National Association of Realtors, almost one in five home buyers were single.

The Mingles Market

More and more single people, both friends and couples, with platonic relationships and romantic ones, are teaming up to find affordable housing. Some share the rent on apartments. Some buy detached homes or condominium units.

State laws on such purchases vary a great deal, so it's vitally important to check the law in your state. In addition, says Kristelle L. Petersen, author of *The Single Person's Home-Buying Handbook* (published in 1980 by Hawthorn/ Dutton but still a good reference if you can find it in your library), sign a contract with your partner before you take title to the property. The contract should spell out:

- How the property will be owned. (In most states, the best ownership arrangement for unrelated owners is as tenants in common, without the right of survivorship.)
- Each person's contribution to the purchase price and each person's contribution to the mortgage, insurance, taxes, and maintenance.
- What happens if either partner falls behind in payments.
- Who will be allowed to live in the house (both partners' consent should be secured before either can bring in another resident).
- What happens if the house is sold: How will the property be divided? What happens if only one partner wishes to sell? The other partner should be given the first option to buy, with the method of payment designated in the contract.
- What happens to the property if one partner dies. (Be especially careful here if one of you has children and the other does not.) If title to the property is without right of survivorship, be sure that you each write a will.
- What happens in the case of the disability of one partner. (If you give each other a power of attorney with respect to the property, each will

Q I bought a house jointly with a friend and then, almost immediately, her job required a move to another state. I can't handle the payments alone and don't know anyone who might want to share. Will I be forced to sell?

A Not if you're fortunate enough to live in an area with a house-matching service sponsored by a community or public agency. Most of these services are designed to find housing for people who need help in finding reasonably priced housing—initially mostly older adults, now often younger ones as well—while providing a source of income for homeowners who face mounting bills. Most, as a result, match renters with owners. Through such a service, however, with its careful screening of applicants, you should be able to find a renter to share the financial burden. If you prove compatible, you might then move on to a co-ownership arrangement.

be able to make necessary decisions without the other should it become necessary.)

■ What happens if you no longer wish to live together, but both wish to remain in the house. Will you flip a coin, with the winner to buy the other out?

■ Who owns property within the house, such as appliances purchased either individually or jointly.

Table 9.2: Neighborhood Characteristics Important to Buyer (Percentage Distribution)

Level of Importance

	Most 1	2	3	4	Least 5	Total	Not a Reason
Near parks and recreation facilities	7%	16%	24%	27%	26%	100%	36%
Near good schools	29	27	21	14	9	100%	33
Near good transportation	10	21	23	24	22	100%	53
Near my place of work	26	26	21	14	13	100%	32
Near health facilities and public services	7	13	23	28	29	100%	49
In a better neighborhood/less crime	29	28	20	15	8	100%	21
In an area within my/our price range	39	23	18	12	8	100%	8
Will provide good rental income	15	20	20	18	27	100%	63
Near homes of friends/family	16	24	22	22	16	100%	40
Near shopping	3	12	24	29	32	100%	30

Source: *The Homebuying and Selling Process, 1991,* National Association of Realtors.

FAMILIES

Families with children begin to need more space; they also want good schools and adequate play facilities. As apartment living begins to seem too cramped, home ownership may become increasingly desirable. But home ownership is also costly. Among married couples buying a first house in 1992, almost 90 percent relied on two incomes. This can become a problem if one spouse loses a job or if one wants to stay home for a while with children.

As children grow and as income nears its peak, a larger home may become both desirable and affordable. Again, the purchase may take two incomes. Among repeat buyers in 1992, according to the annual study by The Chicago Title and Trust Family of Title Insurers, more than three-quarters had two incomes. An alternative, if your home is in a good location: remodeling to make it suit your needs (see p. 261).

Single-Parent Families

Single parents are also child-oriented in their search for housing but, if it is death or divorce that has created single parenthood, may find it necessary to move from a larger home to a smaller one. Profit from the sale of a first house, even if it must be divided, may make it possible to buy a second house, but the ability to make mortgage payments is often limited by the need to support a family alone.

The Empty Nest

Once the children are grown, you may choose to move to more compact quarters. Move or not, money freed from child-rearing may be spent on more lavish living (although these are the years when you should be building retirement reserves). "Adult" communities may be popular among those who want to shed the cares of individual home ownership; most, but not all, of these communities take the condominium form of ownership (see Chapter 14). Such communities, however, fail to interest those who prefer the stimulation of mixed-age living. Think it through carefully before you decide on such a move.

OLDER ADULTS

The elderly, alone or as a couple, generally want reduced housing costs and ease of maintenance. Some move to a moderate climate. Most, contrary to popular belief, prefer to stay exactly where roots have been put down. But maintaining the family home can be difficult, both physically and financially. Once income is fixed, housing costs consume an ever-larger proportion of that income. Even when a mortgage has long since been paid off, rising taxes and the costs of maintenance (especially when doing it yourself has become difficult) are forbidding obstacles to home ownership. (See pp. 331-334 for information on tapping the equity in a house you own.) Health considerations often become an issue, too; see Chapter 23 for information on more housing choices in later life.

Accessory Apartments

The empty nest can provide a golden egg, as the National Council on Aging puts it, if empty space in the hard-to-manage houses of older adults is converted to rental apartments. Such "accessory" apartments are being created in suburban houses across the country, often in violation of local zoning codes, as people in need of both income and companionship put in second kitchens and rent out space.

There is a lot of opposition in some communities, as residents fear lowered property values from rental units. But the trend seems sure to grow—current estimates range from 500,000 to 3 million such apartments—and communities can control the growth with laws regulating conversion. Some such laws provide that either owner or renter must be over the age of 62, prohibit absentee landlords, and require a renewable permit.

Conversion benefits young adults eager to find affordable suburban housing as well as older adults in need of income. The existence of rental apartments also benefits young families otherwise unable to afford the purchase of a house.

Where Do You Want to Live?

Americans are, by and large, a mobile group. We move to meet changing family needs. We move to secure new job opportunities. Between March 1990 and March 1991, about 17 percent of the adult population changed residences. Younger adults move still more; about a third of those in the 20-to-29 age group moved during the same period. Put another way: The average length of residency per house, measured by mortgage length, is frequently reported as seven years.

So your first housing choice probably won't be your last. Nonetheless, your housing priorities deserve careful thought. Work out your personal and family needs before you look at your first house or apartment: How much space do you want? How much space do you actually need? Is more than one bathroom a must? What about storage space? Do you need a garage? Do you entertain frequently?

Some of the answers to these questions will dictate where you want to live. If you need a garage and want lots of outdoor play space for the children, a high-rise apartment or an urban brownstone may not be for you. If you like the stimulation of city life and prefer compact easy-to-care-for quarters, on the other hand, you might find an apartment, owned or rented, just fine. If your family is large, you may require the kind of living space that only an older suburban house can offer. If there are just two or three of you, however, you can probably find suitable housing just about anywhere.

In making your housing choices, look at region, at city or suburb or exurb, and then at particular communities and neighborhoods.

CHOICE ONE: REGION

Unless you are locked into one area because of family or job commitments, you may want to think about a long-distance move. Maybe you'd prefer the Southwest to the winter cold of the North Central states. Maybe you could find cold weather exhilarating and would like to live in New England. Maybe, on the other hand, the Pacific Northwest has the combination of ingredients you'd like to call home. Think about your personal inclinations. Think, too, about costs.

The Cost of Housing

The median prices of homes purchased in 1992, according to Chicago Title's annual survey, ranged from $102,600 in the South to $166,800 in the West. Mortgage payments as a percentage of household income were highest in New York City, at almost 40 percent, and lowest in Phoenix, at 28 percent.

The highest average monthly mortgage payment, in dollars, was $1,611 in Los Angeles; the lowest was $697 in Cleveland (both lower figures than in 1991). Clearly, your pocketbook is affected by where you live.

But median prices tell only part of the story. What if you want to compare the same house on the same-sized lot in the same sort of middle-income suburb in different parts of the United States? Where would you get the best value for your housing dollar?

In a study of 250 communities released in 1992, Coldwell Banker evaluated the cost of a four-bedroom, two-and-one-half-bath, 2,200-square-foot detached house with a family room and two-car garage, the kind of house that might be bought by a corporate middle-management transferee. The cost of this house ranged from a low of $75,750 in Oklahoma City to a high of $1,184,167 in Beverly Hills, California. Despite the top-heavy median price in Beverly Hills, the national median price in 1991 was $198,007, about 1 percent less than the national median in 1990.

By the time you read this, prices may be down still further. But at the end of 1991, when prices in Beverly Hills were out of sight, a comparable house could be bought in San Jose, in northern California, for $380,625, in suburban Chicago for $387,833, and in Norfolk, Virginia, for $136,000.

Rental prices vary by region and city as well as by type of building. The typical 850-square-foot apartment in an elevator building rented for $609 a month in 1991, according to the Institute of Real Estate Management, while the same size unit in a garden apartment costs $646. Rents are higher in the Northeast, Mid-Atlantic, and West Coast regions (see Table 9.3).

The Cost of Living

Look beyond the cost of housing to the cost of maintaining your style of living in different areas. You won't have many heating bills in much of the South, for example, but your air-conditioning bills may be substantial. You may not need to own a car in New York City, if you rely on mass transit, but

---

Q Our house cost $180,000 in 1987. We sold it recently and could get only $156,000. Since we would have had to pay capital gains tax if we had made a profit, can we claim a tax deduction because we suffered a loss?

A No. There is no tax benefit from a loss on your personal residence (see Chapter 13). You could claim a loss only if you had converted the residence to a rental property. In that case, though, there are special rules to follow and you should consult a tax adviser.

housing costs will be high. The Bureau of Labor Statistics indicates in its regular regional comparisons that the Northeast and the West Coast have the highest overall living costs, while it costs less to live in the South and the Midwest.

Table 9.3: Average Annual Rental Costs in 10 Most Expensive and 10 Least Expensive Locations Nationwide, 1993

Location	Annual Rental Costs	Index
Most Expensive:		
Honolulu, HI	$12,480	244.7
San Francisco, CA	9,320	182.7
Washington, DC	8,920	174.9
New York, NY	8,810	172.7
Boston, MA	8,780	172.2
Los Angeles, CA	7,910	155.1
Chicago, IL	7,370	144.5
Philadelphia, PA	6,900	135.3
Providence, RI	6,900	135.3
San Diego, CA	6,840	134.1
STANDARD CITY, USA	5,100	100.0
Least Expensive:		
Corbin, KY	$2,460	48.2
Newport, TN	2,760	54.1
Hennessey, OK	2,880	56.5
Scottsboro, AL	2,940	57.6
Casper, WY	3,000	58.8
Midland, TX	3,300	64.7
Roanoke Rapids, NC	3,360	65.9
Rangely, CO	3,480	68.2
Hobbs, NM	3,540	69.4
Lafayette, LA	3,600	70.6
STANDARD CITY, USA	5,100	100.0

The annual rental values shown in the above table are based on an 800-square-foot, 3-room, 1-bedroom, 1-bath rental unit. This accommodation is typical for a single renter earning $25,000 in annual income at Standard City, USA. Rental units are typically located in communities surrounding the core city. The ranking is based on an analysis of 200 population centers nationwide.

Source: Runzheimer International.

In determining cost-of-living values for specific locations, Runzheimer International, a management consulting firm in Rochester, Wisconsin, establishes a hypothetical "Standard City, USA" with an index of 100. Against this index (see Table 9.4), Los Angeles had a high of 129 in 1992, while Memphis, Tennessee, scored 92.5. In dollar numbers, based on a family of four with a $60,000 annual income, the cost of living in Los Angeles is $77,454 (yes, more than the income) while the cost of living in Memphis is $55,492. The figures assume that the family lives in a 2,400-square-foot mortgaged home, owns two cars, and pays all appropriate income and sales taxes.

Table 9.4: Cost-of-Living Values in Selected Locations

Location	Total Annual Costs	Index
Los Angeles, CA	$77,454	129.1
New York, NY	74,706	124.5
Washington, DC	71,967	119.9
Chicago, IL	66,353	110.6
Atlanta, GA	63,925	106.5
Minneapolis, MN	63,227	105.4
Seattle, WA	62,745	104.6
Miami, FL	60,437	100.7
STANDARD CITY, USA	60,000	100.0
Dallas, TX	57,982	96.6
Denver, CO	57,713	96.2
Phoenix, AZ	55,718	92.9
Memphis, TN	55,492	92.5

Source: Runzheimer International.

State and local taxes are a major reason why people with comparable incomes can't afford the same life-style in different locations. Before you pick a state, if you're not already settled, look at:

Income Tax. Forty-four states and the District of Columbia have a personal income tax. The exceptions (in 1993) are Florida, Nevada, South Dakota, Texas, Washington, and Wyoming. But the taxes are very different. Some states tax all income at a flat rate, others assess a flat percentage of the federal income tax in a piggyback tax, and some have a steeply progressive tax on graduated income. With states facing financial crises, actual tax rates are changing rapidly. But you can be sure of one thing: where there are state income taxes, your take-home pay will be noticeably lower. (Where there are state income taxes, too, your *pension* income may also be lower; even if you move, some states tax pensions earned out-of-state. See Chapter 23.)

Sales taxes. Levied by most but not all states, these also make a noticeable dent in your budget. Two things to look for: the **rate** of the tax and **what it covers.** Some states exempt food, clothing, and prescription drugs; others exempt one or another but not all three. Some municipalities add a local sales tax over and above the one set by the state.

Property taxes. These vary from place to place; so does the method of valuation. Consider tax rate, full or partial valuation, and frequency of reassessment.

Inheritance and estate taxes. These vary considerably and may be of particular interest if you are picking a retirement home (see Chapter 21).

Special taxes. Some states tax interest and dividends; some tax capital gains. Some localities also turn to special use taxes, such as an automobile tax, to raise funds.

The combination of state and local taxes turns out to be a major part of your tax burden. State and local general tax collections averaged $1,234 per capita in 1991, according to the Tax Foundation. Alaska collected the most in taxes on a per-capita basis (although the oil industry paid most of the tab), with Hawaii coming in second. New Hampshire residents paid the least. Taxes are lower in the South, as a rule, but per capita income is lower too.

CHOICE TWO: CITY OR SUBURB OR EXURB

There's a trade-off in convenience. There's also a trade-off in costs. You'll get more for your housing dollar, as a rule, the farther you are from a major population center. If you move too far, however, to a remote rural area ("exurbia"), you may find that your commuting-to-work costs increase significantly. You'll also probably find that the costs of transportation may make food and clothing and all the necessities of life very expensive. In a big city, converging transportation lines and large numbers of consumers combine to make goods available at less cost.

Political Shock

Newly elected members of Congress, moving to Washington, D.C., in early 1993, faced the "sticker shock" of living costs. According to Runzheimer International, many of them found that the annual Congressional salary of $129,500 wouldn't stretch very far. This was particularly true for new arrivals from Bismarck, North Dakota, Springfield, Illinois, and Boise, Idaho. In the nation's capital, it cost $153,368 to sustain a standard of living comparable to what $122,290 would buy in Bismarck. Is this how Congress gets used to deficit spending?

252 THE LIFETIME BOOK OF MONEY MANAGEMENT /segment

In the suburbs, where most Americans have congregated in recent years, there are no hard-and-fast rules ... except that it may cost a considerable amount to heat a rambling suburban home and to get from that home to your job. Other costs will depend on the size and density of your community, its closeness to distribution centers, and its economic level. High-income suburbs, not uncommonly, have stores with prices geared to those high incomes.

CHOICE THREE: COMMUNITY

What's the most important factor when you buy a home? Location, location, and location, say real estate authorities. Consider your location carefully before you move. Making a mistake can be costly.

One young couple were, wisely, more cautious than most. They had long dreamed of a certain Connecticut community as their ideal location. But they weren't quite sure enough to go out and buy, so they rented an apartment first. They learned several things: The commute was long and tiring. The neighbors were intensely dissatisfied with the schools. The parks were vandalized by bored local youngsters. And the picture-postcard rural community was simply too isolated to suit their tastes. They bought a house, when they bought, in suburban New Jersey.

Once you've narrowed your choice by region and by state, you'll have to look at particular communities. If you have no ties and are picking blind, here are some hints that may help:

- Subscribe to a local newspaper for several weeks or months before you make a final decision. A careful reading of the news and features will show you the prevailing politics of the community, the variety of religious groups on hand, the social and cultural activities which can be found. An equally careful reading of the ads will show you what merchandise is available and what prices are like.
- Talk to people in the local planning and zoning and tax offices. What's happening to the population? Is it growing, with younger families, so that educational and recreational facilities may become crowded and money will have to be raised (via taxes, of course) to build new schools and playgrounds? Is the population getting older, so that the school you are considering for your children may be closed for lack of enrollment within a short time after you move in? What's the tax base of the town? Is there industry, light or heavy? Are there shopping centers and office buildings? Or does the entire tax burden fall on homeowners? Are sewers and sidewalks in place? Or will you face this cost as well? Does the community have zoning regulations? Or could a factory be built on the nicely wooded lot directly behind your prospective home?
- What amenities and services does the community offer? Do the schools have a good reputation? Are there parks and recreational facilities? Is there a good library system? Your property taxes may be

higher, depending on the tax base, to support such services but the value of your property may be higher as well. Is there an adequate police force? Is there a paid professional fire department? A volunteer fire department (no matter how dedicated and how diligent) may cost you less in property taxes, more in fire insurance.

■ How stable is the neighborhood? Look for well-maintained property. Be careful, if you plan to buy, about an area with a great many "for sale" signs sprouting on the lawns (although, in recessionary times, these may simply be a sign of bargains to be had), or a lot of rental property in an area of one-family homes. Be alert to rapid turnover and/or many vacancies in an apartment building or development. All may be a sign of deterioration.

To Rent or to Buy or to Remodel

Until the end of World War II the majority of Americans lived in housing owned by others. Since the late 1940s, however, the scale has tipped dramatically in the other direction. Today almost 64 percent of Americans own their own homes. Some own throughout their adult lives. Others, perhaps more typically, rent, then own, then, perhaps, rent again. Some choose to rent as a permanent way of life. Many factors, some financial and some not, enter into the decision. Here are some things to consider.

IF YOU RENT

Renting may be a first step as you save money on the way to home ownership. Renting may also be appropriate if you are located temporarily and expect to move. Renting may be the solution for small households. And renting, for some of us, is simply a perfect way of life.

There are both positive and negative aspects to renting:

In Favor of Renting

You'll have more control over your living expenses. And those expenses may be lower than the expenses associated with ownership. Your rent, if you have a lease, will probably remain stable for several years. Your commitment will be limited to the term of your lease.

If you rent an apartment, moreover, you can call on someone else to shovel walks, remove trash, and fix balky plumbing. If you rent a house, you may be responsible for routine maintenance and minor repairs, but the landlord will probably assume responsibility for major items such as roof or plumbing repair; be sure to clarify responsibilities before you sign the lease. Apartment or house, you'll be unlikely to sink money into costly improvements to property that is not your own. You can invest your savings in liquid

assets yielding a reasonable return instead of tying up your money in not-nec-
essarily-easy-to-sell real estate.

Negative Aspects of Renting

As a renter you do without the investment value of real estate; you build
no equity and you take no tax deductions. You usually can't alter the unit to
suit your preferences. You may well have less space and less privacy in an
apartment than in a house. You may also be subject to restrictions imposed by
the owner. Rental units, moreover, are becoming increasingly scarce (and
often increasingly expensive) as fewer multiple-unit buildings are built, more
and more buildings convert to condominium ownership (see Chapter 14), and
more and more single-person households come into being.

The Financial Commitment of Renting

Although your financial commitment to rental housing is usually far less
than your financial commitment to a house of your own, there are pitfalls for
the unwary. Be sure that you:

- Read your lease carefully. What happens if you must move before the
  lease expires? Are you allowed to sublet the apartment? What are
  your obligations with respect to maintenance? What is the landlord's
  obligation? Is there a clause permitting the landlord to pass along
  increases for fuel, utilities, taxes, etc.?

- Consider the cost of utilities if they are not included in your monthly
  rent. Will your apartment be separately metered, or will an allocation
  of costs be made by the landlord or the utility company?

- Understand any applicable rules and regulations. Are you allowed to
  paint or paper the apartment? to add shelves? to put in a washing
  machine or a dishwasher? If you're not, and you do, what will be your
  financial liability?

- Know local laws with respect to health and safety in residential housing. Most cities now have housing codes which set minimum standards, and tenants in many areas are allowed to repair defects ignored
  by the landlord and then to deduct the cost of those repairs from the
  rent.

- Understand any deposits you are requested to make. A **damage
  deposit** must be returned when you leave unless you caused physical
  damage beyond normal wear and tear or, depending on the terms of
  your lease, unless you caused economic damage to the landlord by
  failing to give adequate written notice about moving. A **security
  deposit** is sometimes used the same way, but it can also be more complicated; it might require that you rent the unit for a specified period
  of time in order to receive a refund of the deposit. A **cleaning deposit**
  is a separate deposit, usually not refundable, used for cleaning the

premises after you move out. Local laws may regulate deposits and their return; in some areas, landlords must keep deposits in interest-bearing accounts with the interest payable to the tenant.

Inspect any rental premises thoroughly before you move in, making a written record of any damages. Ask the landlord to attach a copy of this record to your lease, and keep a copy yourself. This record will document the condition of the apartment, and substantiate your claim for return of a damage or security deposit when you move out.

IF YOU BUY

Ownership also has its positive and negative aspects:

On the Positive Side

With home ownership you'll find, as a rule, greater space and privacy along with the freedom (within local zoning laws and building codes) to improve and change your property. You'll also secure tax advantages and (depending on when you buy and when you sell) the opportunity to realize a profit when you sell. You'll have an investment that provides a hedge against inflation (as long as property values continue to increase).

If you take an adjustable-rate mortgage, you may be able to buy more house (see Chapter 11), but you won't have the two-part inflation hedge that combines a true increase in the value of the house with a fixed-rate loan that is paid off in ever-cheaper dollars. However, you will still own a tangible asset and benefit from any appreciation in the value of that tangible asset—although lower inflation and a slower economy have at least temporarily reduced house price appreciation. Prices on existing homes increased by 5 percent from 1990 to 1991, but by just over 3 percent from 1991 to 1992; prices on new homes actually dropped in the same period. Living in a house may be nice, but it isn't necessarily a surefire investment.

Q I sublet my apartment, in accordance with the terms of my lease, when I went away for the summer. Unfortunately, my subtenant has proved to be unreliable. He neglected to pay the rent, and the landlord is dunning me. Do I have to pay?

A If your landlord agreed to an "assignment" of your lease to your subtenant, then the subtenant is legally responsible along with you. If, however, you turned the place over as a straight sublease, you remain completely responsible.

Table 9.5: The Median Price of Houses, 1969-1991

	New homes	Existing homes
1969	$25,600	$21,800
1970	23,400	23,000
1971	25,200	24,800
1972	27,600	26,700
1973	32,500	28,900
1974	35,900	32,000
1975	39,300	35,300
1976	44,200	38,100
1977	48,800	42,900
1978	55,700	48,700
1979	62,900	55,700
1980	64,600	62,200
1981	68,900	66,400
1982	69,300	67,800
1983	75,300	70,300
1984	79,900	72,400
1985	84,300	75,500
1986	92,000	80,300
1987	104,500	85,600
1988	112,500	89,300
1989	120,000	93,100
1990	122,900	95,500
1991	120,000	100,300

Source: National Association of Home Builders, National Association of Realtors.

Negative Aspects of Ownership

But home ownership also entails some disadvantages. Both the initial and the ongoing costs are high. Some, if not all, of the costs are variable, making it difficult to plan and to budget. And you should make a commitment to stay for an extended period of time—at least four years, according to some studies—if your initial costs are to be recovered and equity realized. If you must move earlier you may lose part of your investment.

Things to Consider Before You Buy

When you buy, rather than rent, the financial equation becomes more complicated. After the initial purchase price and related transaction costs (to be discussed in detail in Chapter 10) you'll have to look at:

■ Monthly mortgage payments
■ Utilities
■ Heat
■ Property taxes
■ Property insurance
■ Services, such as trash pickup and snow removal
■ Landscaping and maintenance
■ Possible assessments for streets, sidewalks, and sewers
■ A reserve against repairs

Table 9.6: House Price Changes Compared to Inflation, 1979-1992

Percent Increase

	Consumer Price Index (all items)	Average sales price of existing homes
1979	11.3%	14.4%
1980	13.5	12.6
1981	10.3	6.7
1982	6.2	2.1
1983	3.2	3.7
1984	4.3	2.9
1985	3.6	4.2
1986	1.9	6.4
1987	3.6	6.9
1988	4.1	4.0
1989	4.8	2.6
1990	5.4	2.6
1991	4.2	5.0
1992	2.9	3.1

Source: Bureau of Labor Statistics; National Association of Realtors.

Some of these costs, of course, are affected by where and what you buy. Insurance, for instance, may cost more on a frame structure than on a brick one; it may also cost more in areas without a professional paid fire department. Services are provided by municipal taxes in some communities; elsewhere you'll pay separately, for instance, for private trash removal. The larger house costs more in property taxes, more to heat. The older house costs more for maintenance and repairs.

The key factor, however, may be that few of the costs of home ownership are fixed. Monthly mortgage payments will be a stable element in your budget if you take a fixed-rate mortgage, but with an adjustable-rate mortgage monthly mortgage payments will be unpredictable. Electricity and heating oil and the gasoline used for commuting have all risen sharply in recent years. Repair costs are unpredictable; just when your budget appears to be under control, the water heater may give way or the roof may spring a leak. Do the best you can to come up with an all-inclusive list of expenses before you decide to buy.

The "Real Costs" of Owning vs. Renting

You could simply compare monthly rent to monthly home ownership costs, and make your decision accordingly. But economists don't simply look at dollar outlay, or even at interest rates, in calculating real costs. These hard figures have to be modified by other factors before a valid financial comparison can be made between monthly rent and monthly home ownership costs. You should look at other factors as well:

Imputed Rent

"Imputed rent" is the value of your owned house as living space, the amount you might pay for it in rent if you were renting instead of buying. Because you are, in effect, paying yourself when you own, that is money gained. But there's more to the equation: If, instead of living in your own house, you rented it to someone else, you would have to pay income tax on your rental income (after deducting operating expenses). If you live in the house yourself, you don't pay this rent and you don't pay the taxes on rental income. This can be a saving of several thousand dollars a year.

Opportunity Costs

If you decide to buy a house, however, you forgo the opportunity to invest the money you commit to the house in other ways. If you commit

Q I'm retired, living comfortably on a total of almost $1,800 a month from Social Security, pension, and stock dividends. I also have $62,000 invested in a money market fund. I rent an apartment, for $445 a month, but am thinking of buying a $55,000 condominium to cut my income taxes. Would this be a good idea?

A Don't look to tax savings without regard to anything else. If you buy a condominium unit, you'll be reducing your yearly income by the interest on the sum you use for the purchase. You'll also have to face costs—rising costs over the years—for taxes, assessments, and utilities. You may be better off continuing to rent.

$10,000 to a down payment on a house, as an example, and you could have earned 8 percent a year in interest on that $10,000, that's a first-year opportunity cost of $800 (minus, of course, the income taxes due on that interest income). If the interest was reinvested each year, for a compounded return, your lost opportunity costs would be significantly greater over time. Your home may, of course, appreciate in value by at least as much. But there's no guarantee that it will, and even if it does, you won't realize the gain until you sell.

Tax Considerations

Because mortgage interest costs are deductible, costs of ownership are directly affected by your income tax bracket. (If you rent, your landlord gets the tax breaks and you get none.) The higher your income, and the higher your tax bracket, the more you will save by owning your own home. The married couple filing jointly with a taxable income of $90,000 is, according to 1993 federal tax tables, in the 31 percent bracket. For each dollar of mortgage interest payments deducted from their taxable income, they will reduce the amount of taxes they pay by 31 cents. The married couple with a taxable income of $35,000, by contrast, currently has a marginal tax rate of 15 percent. Reduction of their taxable income by a dollar's worth of mortgage interest reduces their income tax bill by only 15 cents.

Much is made of the tax advantages of home ownership. But you should be aware that you receive the tax benefits of ownership only if you itemize deductions. More important, the full tax benefits are available only if your other itemizable deductions are at least as much as the standard deduction. The standard deduction for a married couple filing jointly in 1992 was $6,000. Unless your non-housing-related deductions (for state and local taxes, charitable expenses, medical bills, and so on; see Chapter 20) exceed $6,000 you're not getting the full benefit of your housing-related deductions. The reason: The housing-related deductions may push you over the $6,000 mark and thus make it advantageous to itemize, but some of those deductions would be covered by the $6,000 standard deduction if you didn't itemize; only the amount of deductions *over* $6,000 can be considered an extra saving of tax dollars. (Conversely, of course, adding housing expenditures may make it possible to benefit from other potential deductions.)

Assuming that you can and do itemize your tax deductions, the advantages of home ownership are substantial. During the early years of a mortgage, a much greater share of the monthly payment goes to interest than to principal. The interest is directly deductible.

Note: A tax credit for first-time home buyers, an on-and-off proposal in Congress, would make home ownership still more advantageous—if it is ever passed.

Length of Occupancy

How long you expect to stay in one place is also a critical factor in your decision to rent or to buy, not only because it may not seem psychologically worthwhile to buy a house if you're planning to move again shortly but because it is probably not economically sound to do so. The longer you will stay in one place, economists agree, the more cost-effective it is to own your residence.

One way of viewing the decision to <u>buy or to rent</u> is to ask what the rent would have to be to equal the same return on investment you would receive from owning. What, in other words, is the <u>break-even point</u> in terms of your personal finances? Here's one way to do the calculation:

- Write down the purchase price and financing terms on the house you're thinking of buying, including the down payment, closing costs, and points.
- Estimate your total monthly costs, including utilities, maintenance and repairs.
- Figure out your net monthly outlay, determining the tax savings from deducting mortgage interest and property taxes.
- Project what you might be able to get for the house if you sell it after 5 years, 10 years, or 20 years. Figure appreciation at a conservative 4 percent per year. *100.000 =b 4.000/yr. !! NOT ...R I.!*
- Write down what your rent would be, in total, for the same period of years.
- Calculate how much you could earn on the amount otherwise spent on a down payment and closing costs.
- Compare the two sets of figures.

The Impact of Inflation

You might, although this is more difficult, also consider an inflation factor in your calculations. One of the advantages (to homeowners, but not to lenders) of the traditional fixed-rate mortgage has been in paying off a mortgage loan in cheaper and cheaper dollars. With adjustable rate mortgage loans this advantage disappears.

But you can still adjust your mortgage loan, mentally, to get a "real" cost of interest in terms of inflation. For instance, if your mortgage loan is at 8 percent in a year when the Consumer Price Index is at 4 percent, then your real rate of interest is 4 percent. Figure in the tax savings and your real rate of interest is lower still. With inflation plus tax deductions, in fact, your real rate of interest may even be negative. At the same time, the value of your house may continue to rise. Although appreciation has slowed (existing homes rose in value by almost 7 percent from 1986 to 1987, by about 3 percent from 1991 to 1992), any increase in value must be calculated. If your "real cost" is below the annual increase in value, you are making money by owning your own home.

Note: Don't forget the value of leverage, the fact that you put up relatively little of your own money when you buy a house, thereby increasing your return when you sell (see p. 298). You may even come out ahead if house prices decline.

If You Remodel

The Stantons felt very fortunate when they moved from an apartment to their first house in 1985. The house wasn't perfect—it was, after all, a "starter" house, with three bedrooms and one bath—but it was just right for a young couple with one small child. Today the Stantons have three children, and a growing sense of frustration over their inability to afford a larger house. They feel lucky, by comparison with friends who failed to buy a starter house at all. But they also feel trapped in a house that is too small for a growing family.

The Emersons' problem is similar but different. Bob Emerson recently retired, and the couple would like to move to the condo they own in Florida. But the depressed housing market in New England has made it almost impossible to sell their 46-year-old suburban home.

The solution for both couples: Remodel. By remodeling, the Stantons expand the house they own and make it livable. By remodeling, the Emersons can make their house more attractive and find a buyer.

If you're thinking of remodeling, you have some hard questions to answer. Which improvements are most cost-effective in terms of adding to resale value? How should you finance expansion? How can you find workmen who are both competent and honest?

Table 9.7: Most Popular Home Improvements in 1991

Type of improvement	Proportion of remodeling jobs
Remodeled kitchen	34%
Remodeled bath/powder room	30%
Replace/add deck or patio	24%
Added bath/powder room	23%
Added family/living room	20%

Source: National Association of Home Builders Remodelors Council.

Whatever you do in the way of home improvement, some general rules apply:

■ Don't improve your house so much that it's far above neighboring homes in value. You shouldn't expect to sell a $135,000 house, when it comes time to move, in a neighborhood of $80,000 homes. An appraiser's rule of thumb: Don't improve a house by more than 30 percent of its current value—unless you've bought a "handyman's special" in a neighborhood of expensive homes and are bringing your home up to neighborhood standards.

■ Improvements should be consistent with the character of the house and of the neighborhood. A modern addition on a Colonial-style home may never blend into its surroundings. A swimming pool, in a neighborhood that has no others, may be a drawback rather than a plus.

■ Keep resale value in mind, if you expect to move in a reasonably short time; otherwise design your improvements to suit your family. If you are simply sprucing up your home in order to make it appeal to potential buyers, then cosmetic improvements are the most cost-effective in normal markets: the quick coat of paint, higher-wattage light bulbs, a new bed of flowers. When a lot of houses are competing for a few buyers, you may need to do more. One northern California real estate broker told *Remodeling* magazine that "Remodeling can make the difference between selling at your price and not selling for any price." A minor kitchen update alone can make all the difference. Modernizing an old bathroom, or adding a bathroom to a house with only one is also helpful.

■ If you are remodeling in order to postpone the financial ordeal of moving, however, then added value is almost beside the point; what you want is a house to live in comfortably. Don't expect a dollar-for-dollar return on any home improvement (although some, as we'll see, do better than others); do expect added enjoyment in living. The Stantons spent $27,000 and added a second floor with two bedrooms and a bath, thereby making their home comfortable for their growing family—and at considerable less cost than moving to a larger house.

■ Keep accurate records of home improvements, because money spent to improve a house (as contrasted to money spent on maintenance) reduces the taxable gain when the house is sold (see Chapter 13).

Cost-Effective Improvements

Although you'll improve your house to suit your family you will also, if you plan wisely, get a portion of your expenditure back when it's time to sell. Some improvements, of course, add more to resale value than others. Those that will enhance any family's way of life, logically enough, provide the most financial payoff; most people want at least three bedrooms and are willing to pay for them. Those that fit a purely personal interest have the least; a swimming pool or hot tub, to many people, is a liability rather than an asset.

BRINGING YOUR HOME UP TO DATE

The most cost-effective improvement, according to remodeling contractors, is the minor kitchen make over; painting kitchen cabinets and installing new appliances, adding new lighting fixtures or windows to brighten up a dark room brings a return, nationally, of 104 percent. Spend the national average of $6,234, in other words, and you can expect to recoup $6,511 when you sell. A major kitchen remodeling, something you may have to tackle if your floor plan doesn't work or your cabinets aren't structurally sound, returns a national average of 94 percent of dollars spent (see Table 9.8).

Note, though, that there is a difference of opinion here. Home improvement contractors say that modernization is a sound investment. Real estate appraisers, on the other hand, believe that such modernizations are seldom cost-effective, unless the original room is so antiquated as to be virtually useless. The reason: While an old-fashioned kitchen or bath is viewed as a negative by potential buyers, a modern room is simply taken for granted. (Nonetheless, modernization may be essential if you hope to sell a house in a tough market.)

Note, too, that there are sizable regional variations. The kitchen refurbishing that will yield 119 percent of value on the West Coast produces a 93 percent return in the Midwest.

Table 9.8 indicates how much you can expect to get back, on a national average, on specific remodeling projects.

Table 9.8: Cost-effective Remodeling Projects

Project	Average cost	Resale value	Cost recouped
Minor kitchen make over	$ 6,234	$ 6,511	104%
Adding a bath	10,552	10,020	95%
Major kitchen remodel	19,261	18,021	94%
Bath remodeling	7,207	6,109	85%
Adding a family room	28,455	24,069	85%
Master suite	22,060	18,320	83%
An attic bedroom	21,904	17,715	81%
Adding a deck	5,731	4,456	78%
New windows	7,315	5,289	72%
New siding	9,052	6,403	71%
Adding a sun space	24,929	17,416	70%

Source: *Remodeling,* October 1992.

ADDITIONAL LIVING SPACE

Added space is a big plus on the home improvement menu. An extra bedroom or a family room, in a house that is otherwise too small for most buyers, can be a cost-effective improvement. Adding a family room adds $8.50 to a home's value for every $10 spent. In some parts of the country (regional considerations always play a major role), you may actually get full value back when you sell. If your house already has four bedrooms, however, adding another may overprice the house for a contemporary market consisting mostly of smaller families. If you do need a fifth bedroom, think about placing it so that it can function as a study or a den. You may not use it that way just now (although you might look ahead to an eventually emptying nest), but the next owners may like the idea.

Be imaginative as you consider extra space. You may not need to add a wing, and you may not spend as much money, if you can convert an unused attic or little-used garage to a bedroom or study. (Watch local ordinances, however; you may have to have a garage.) If you don't have convertible space, you may save some money by making use of existing exterior walls. If your house forms a corner, for instance, would it make sense to tuck an extra room into that corner, thereby using two existing walls? Could you, perhaps, raise the roof to secure extra living space above? Talk to an experienced home improvement contractor before you make a final decision; tips on choosing one will be found on pp. 266-269.

PERSONAL CHOICE

The least cost-effective home improvements are those that may be categorized as personal interest items. Some people like hot tubs and saunas, greenhouses and tennis courts; others find them an expensive nuisance. Your family may relish a backyard swimming pool; a potential buyer, small children in tow, may look on it as dangerous and unnecessary. So put in such amenities if you will stay in the house for a while to enjoy them, but don't expect to recoup your investment.

ENERGY-SAVING IMPROVEMENTS

Energy-saving improvements, although often less immediately apparent, can reduce your living costs right now and can also attract potential buyers when you are ready to sell.

Forget expensive and complicated installations along the lines of active solar technology, with its rooftop collectors; until the price of heating oil hits the stratosphere again, it's simply not economically attractive. Passive solar elements—such as large window areas on the south-facing wall to take advantage of the winter sun—can be cost-effective. But so are smaller adjustments. For example: You can probably reduce your annual heating bills by significant sums if you add insulation (attic insulation is both effective and easy to install) and put in storm windows and doors. Such improvements cost some money at the outset, but pay for themselves in fuel savings in a fairly short period of time.

Try these home improvements:

■ Add insulation to your attic

■ Install storm windows and doors

■ Have the burner on your furnace tuned so that it operates at top efficiency

- Install a shower flow restrictor, which will cut the cost of heating hot water
- Air-dry the dishes in your dishwasher instead of consuming the fuel to dry them by machine
- Caulk and weatherstrip leaky window frames
- Install insulation around your hot water heater
- Use an automatic thermostat to lower the heat at night and, if you're out at work, during the day as well

How to Finance Home Improvements

Improving your home may add to its value in the long run, but it does call for an initial outlay of funds.

Before you embark on any home improvement project, find out what it will cost. Get several bids, and understand your financial commitment. Then, if you need to borrow money, you'll be able to be specific with the lending

Q Five years ago we paid off the mortgage on our small but comfortable home. Four years ago we replaced the roof, installed metal siding, painted, and put in new windows. The cost: $8,000, obtained through a bank loan. Now, looking at retirement two years ahead, we'd like to add a spacious master bedroom and bath. We think it will greatly increase the value of the house. But how should we meet the cost? Through a bank loan for the entire amount? Through borrowing against insurance policies? Or should we use cash savings in our money market fund to pay for as much as possible, then borrow for the rest?

A If you take cash from your money market fund or from other investments, you have to calculate the value of lost interest. If, on the other hand, you take a bank loan or a life insurance loan, you'll have to pay interest. A home equity loan, a revolving line of credit based on the accrued equity in your home, might be the best bet. You can take such a loan, establishing a line of credit up to about 80 percent of your equity, and the interest on the loan will be fully tax-deductible. Moreover, because it's actually a line of credit, you can draw on such a loan as needed, for home improvements or any other purpose.

institution. You may be able to borrow on an unsecured basis, if you're planning a relatively minor repair. For most sizable remodeling jobs, however, most homeowners turn to home equity loans. Home equity loans are available from credit unions, banks, stockbrokers, and other financial institutions (see p. 204). In 1992, 28 percent of home equity loans were used for home improvements. Almost all carried a variable rate of interest.

Remember: If you can't make the payments on a home equity loan, for any reason, you stand to lose not only the amount of the loan but your entire investment in your home. If home prices continue to decline, moreover, you may not have as much equity as you think you do.

Rather than take a home equity loan or line of credit, the 1990s version of a second mortgage, you might refinance your first mortgage. When interest rates are high, this can be a costly way to finance a home improvement. If you need $15,000, you may be borrowing $50,000 and at interest rates that may be considerably higher than your original mortgage loan. You'll be paying for many years. You'll also have closing costs to pay.

But when interest rates are low, as they are today, refinancing a first mortgage may be a smart move. In 1993, as home mortgage interest rates dropped to their lowest point in years, homeowners flocked to lending institutions for refinancing. As a rule of thumb, an interest rate at least 2 points below your original rate makes refinancing worth considering. You can reduce your monthly costs while raising money for home improvements. Just be sure to consider all the related costs (points, etc.) before you make your decision (see p. 329-331).

A new "HomeStyle" mortgage loan, introduced at the end of 1992 by the Federal National Mortgage Association, provides financing for home repairs, remodeling, and rehabilitation. HomeStyle mortgages may take the form of either first or second mortgages, although the greatest demand is expected to be for refinanced or second mortgages. Initially, only selected lenders will be involved; ask around among local lenders to see if any are participating.

Choosing a Contractor

Whatever home improvement you contemplate, you have a basic choice: do it yourself or hire a contractor. You can save money by doing many things yourself, if you know what you're doing. For most major jobs, however, most homeowners are better off hiring professional help.

But make sure that the help you hire is both competent and honest. (And *never* do business with an itinerant contractor who comes along with a deal "too good to refuse.") Only 7 percent of home improvement contractors are dishonest, says the Federal Trade Commission, but those 7 percent do a lot of harm.

COMPARISON-SHOP FOR PRICE

Ask several contractors to submit bids, in writing, for the specific job you want done. But don't jump at the lowest bid; it may omit essential work or be based on less than the best in materials. If four contractors submit bids ranging from $8,500 to $9,500 to remodel your kitchen, and a fifth quotes $6,200, you should probably stay away from the fifth. You'll get what you pay for. Reputable bids should be reasonably close, so you may want to drop the

Q My brother had central air conditioning installed in his house. It never did work properly, so he told the contractor he would stop paying until repairs were made. The next thing he knew, he received a foreclosure notice on his house. He had to pay the contractor or he would have lost his house, even though the contractor never did make the repairs. How could something like this happen?

A Your brother must have signed a contract which included a "lien-sale" provision. This clause allows a contractor to foreclose on a house if the customer fails to pay his bills. It is being used increasingly by dishonest contractors who do shoddy work—many of whom, not incidentally, prey on senior citizens. The Consumer Federation of America, in a detailed report on home improvement frauds, points to lien-sale contracts as a major problem. When they lead to foreclosure, as they can, the consumer stands to lose the entire investment in his house. Once foreclosed, the house is sold to repay the debt. In theory, at least, the homeowner should receive the difference between the debt and the selling price of the house. But some swindlers go a step further: In the "private sales" permitted by many states, the house is sold, at a very low price, to the creditor or to a friend of the creditor. The loan is paid off, the consumer gets nothing, and the swindler sells the home for a huge profit. California state law (much of this fraud has taken place in California) now protects the consumer from having a lien placed on a home by a contractor; it does not offer the same protection to loans placed with financial institutions. The result: Some contractors are now marching homeowners to financial institutions for direct loans.

Your brother had little choice once he signed this contract; he had to pay the contractor or lose his house. The best defense against this kind of practice is to be an alert consumer and not sign such contracts in the first place.

lowest and highest you receive, if they are far apart from the others, and concentrate on selecting one from the middle range.

Buying home improvements is not like buying a car. You can't pick out the model you want with the options you want, and price it at a number of dealers. Each remodeling contractor has a different way of arriving at the price. You may have to probe to find out just how each bid has been figured. In an example supplied by Peter Johnson, former president of the National Remodelors Association, a homeowner secured three bids for insulation. One was $1,700, the second was $1,550, and the third was $1,200. He eliminated the lowest bidder, because he suspected that the bid was too low to assure good quality. Then he had to decide between the other two contractors. After further investigation, the homeowner discovered that the highest bidder had specified six inches of insulation, while the other bidder had specified four. It turned out, in this instance, that the best value was found in the highest bidder. Sometimes, however, estimates are simply miscalculated. And occasionally a good but busy contractor will deliberately overestimate a job to discourage a homeowner from adding to his workload. When times are tough, on the other hand, as they have been recently, quality homebuilders are doing renovations they might turn down if they were busy building houses.

COMPARISON-SHOP FOR QUALITY

Price is far from the only factor to consider. Before you select a contractor, ask several:

- Do they have offices in your community? (Stay away from itinerant workmen operating out of the glove compartment of a car; stay away from traveling salespeople offering "bargains" ... they'll travel and you'll be left with the "bargain.")
- Will they give you the names of satisfied customers? (Talk to them and be sure the work was completed both satisfactorily and on time.)
- Who are the company's banks and suppliers? (Talk to them, and to the Better Business Bureau as well, about the contractor's reputation.)
- Is the contractor a member of a trade association or professional group? of local civic or fraternal organizations? (You want someone who has roots in the community, and a reputation to protect.)
- Do they carry adequate insurance, both worker's compensation and property damage/liability? (If not, and there is an accident, you can be financially liable.)
- Is the contract specific, spelling out the work to be done, the materials to be used (by brand name), and the date for completion? (Verbal promises are worth the paper they're written on.) It's up to you to make sure the contract includes everything important to you, such as complete cleanup and removal of debris.

■ Will they give you a precise cost for the job? And is that cost reasonable? (It should be within 10 percent of most bids submitted, and include the materials you specify.)

■ Will the contractor secure all the necessary permits? A major renovation usually requires several permits; your contractor should know what's required in your town and should do the paperwork. The National Association of Home Builders (NAHB) Remodelors Council strongly recommends that you *not* apply for the building permit yourself; the person who obtains the permit is considered to be the contractor and is liable if the work fails to comply with building codes.

■ Do they take part in a warranty or arbitration program? Many good contractors do not, but if your contractor does, you have an added assurance of quality. Home Owners Warranty Corporation has a five-year warranty-plus-insurance program for remodeling contractors.

AFTER YOU SIGN A CONTRACT

Once you've picked your reputable contractor and signed a contract, there are additional things you should know:

Q A contractor has bid $24,500 to add a family room and bath to our house. We think the bid is reasonable and are prepared to go ahead. But he wants half the money—$12,250—before he starts work. He says he needs it to buy materials, but we're uneasy. Should we give him the money?

A No. The NAHB Remodelors Council suggests a down payment of no more than one-third of the total contract price, followed by a schedule of payments (spelled out in your contract) pegged to the completion of various phases of the work. State or local laws may govern the amount of down payment, but remember: If you pay a great deal up front, you are extending an invitation to the contractor to take the money and run. In fact, Tom Philbin, author of *How to Hire a Home Improvement Contractor Without Getting Chiseled* (St. Martin's Press, 1991), strongly suggests that no more than a few hundred dollars should be paid up front. If he needs money for supplies, pay the money directly to the supplier; alternatively, protect yourself by having a bond posted guaranteeing completion of the job, or get a lien release from suppliers and subcontractors. And always, Philbin says, keep a portion of the agreed-upon fee until you are sure there are no problems with the completed work.

■ The contractor may offer to secure financing for you. Compare the terms of this loan with the terms of loans from other sources before you agree; the convenience of the contractor's loan may be a trade-off for additional cost. Be sure, if you take the contractor's loan, that you receive all the written information required by law: notice of your right to rescind (see next item), and information about the terms of the transaction—the annual percentage rate, the finance charge, the amount financed, the total number of payments, and the payment schedule. Note that if the contractor arranges the loan, with your approval, the money will probably be paid directly to him. This may deprive you of the leverage you need if the job is not done as promised.

■ If you sign a contractor's contract which includes financing and uses your home as collateral for the loan, federal law gives you three business days in which to change your mind. If you decide the next morn-

---

Some warning signs of possible trouble ahead with a contractor:

■ You can't verify the contractor's name, address, telephone number, or credentials. You are unable to verify that the contractor is licensed or insured, where required.

■ The salesperson tries to "high pressure" you into signing a contract by using scare tactics, intimidation, or threats.

■ The company or salesperson says that your home will be used for advertising purposes (as a model job, or show house, or by display of their sign) and that for this you will be given a special low price.

■ The contractor tells you that this is a special price available only if you sign the contract today.

■ The contractor doesn't comply with your request for references or the references have some reservations about the contractor's work.

■ You are asked to pay for the entire job in advance, or to pay cash to a salesperson, instead of paying by check or money order to the company itself.

■ You are asked to sign a completion certificate for the job by appeal, treat, or trick, before the job is properly completed.

Source: National Association of Home Builders Remodelors Council.

ing that you didn't check the contractor's references sufficiently or you realize a day later that you can get a better interest rate elsewhere, you may cancel the contract and get your money back. During those three days the contractor should not start work or deliver any materials. You are allowed to give up this right of cancellation (technically known as the "right of rescission"), but you shouldn't do so, unless you have a genuine emergency—such as a damaged roof which needs immediate repair—and unless you have satisfied yourself that the contractor is reputable.

■ If work is to be sublet, the contractor should post a bond assuring that he will pay his subcontractors. If he does not do so, you may pay him but he may not pay his subcontractors. They could then put a lien on your home to collect.

■ To protect yourself further, match your payments to the progress on the job. Never make a final payment or sign a certificate of completion unless and until the work is entirely completed according to the terms of the contract.

SHOULD YOU BUY A HOUSE AS AN INVESTMENT?

The spiraling price increases of the late 1970s made many Americans scurry to get on the home ownership carousel, to grab the brass ring and move on to the next and larger house. No matter how insane the price of housing, it seemed, you couldn't lose. The spiral just kept moving upward as houses became more and more valuable. But the carousel has slowed and, in some parts of the country, come to a screeching halt. Houses in some areas are worth less today than they were a year ago. People who bought at the height of the price spiral, and who now must sell, are forced to take a loss.

Should you, in view of these developments, continue to look on home ownership as a worthwhile investment?

Yes. People who bought their houses before the price run-up of the 1970s and early 1980s have clearly done well. Those who bought at the peak of the market, in 1986 or 1987, could lose money (at least in some parts of the country) if they sell now but may still come out ahead if they stay put. But don't assume that a decline in current price necessarily means a net loss on your investment. *The State of the Nation's Housing, 1992,* a report by the Joint Center for Housing Studies of Harvard University, describes this scenario: A house purchased in 1983 in Pittsburgh for $45,990 declined in value by 10 percent by 1991. Nonetheless, the family's original equity in the home (their down payment of $9,198) became $21,427 (after the payment of principal plus nominal appreciation), an increase translating into 6.9 percent of real annual growth—not at all bad when compared to returns on other investments in the early 1990s.

For the last 17 years, the Harvard study concludes, "home ownership has been a very good savings vehicle" in most places. No one can predict the future, but home ownership (assuming that it meets your need for shelter) is likely to remain a good investment, particularly if you can remain in the house long enough to ride out short-term fluctuations in the market.

Don't speculate when you buy your home. Be aware that the rate of appreciation of house prices is likely to continue to be slower than it was, and that adjustable-rate mortgages (if you choose to take one) mean that you don't keep as much of the appreciation in value as you might have in the past.

Look at the purchase of a house as a shelter for your family first and an investment second, and you'll be making a wise purchase.

 KEY POINTS

- Don't make any housing decisions until you evaluate your personal housing needs. Your age and your stage in the life cycle are important factors in where and how you live.

- Different regions, states, and communities have different things to offer. Look at both the quality of life and the impact on your pocketbook before you decide where to make your home.

- Renting living space may be appropriate for you at one stage, ownership at another. Look at all the positive and negative aspects of each before you decide what to do at any particular time.

- Additional living space is the most cost-effective home improvement, returning almost dollar for dollar of your investment. Personal-choice additions, such as swimming pools or greenhouses, are the least cost-effective.

- If you remodel, get bids from several reputable contractors and compare financing terms carefully before you sign any home improvement contract.

- Home ownership is an investment, but look at it first as an investment in a way of life rather than as an investment for capital appreciation.

CHAPTER 10

Buying a House

You've evaluated your personal housing needs, decided where to live, and determined to buy rather than rent. Finding an affordable mortgage may be the next thing on your mind. But there are other factors to consider before you seek a mortgage: What, besides mortgage payments, should you look at in doing your arithmetic? What kind of house do you want to buy? Should you use a real estate agent? How do you negotiate a price? What, at last, will happen at the closing on the house, when you actually take title? This chapter will focus on these matters; the next will deal with financing your purchase.

How Much Can You Spend?

You may have heard that you can afford to buy a house costing two to two and one-half times your annual income. Another time-honored rule of thumb is that monthly expenses on housing should run no more than 25 percent of your take-home pay. Forget it. Back in 1974, the average buyer spent 24 percent of income on housing. In the 1990s, according to an annual survey conducted by the Chicago Title and Trust Family of Title Insurers, the average buyer spends about 34 percent of income on monthly housing payments. First-time buyers spend a bit more, repeat buyers somewhat less. If you bought a house some years ago you are probably spending far less of your income on housing. If you buy a house today, you can expect to spend more.

What you must ask is this: How much can you spare each month, month after month, with some cushion for emergencies, and how much can you commit to housing? Your answer will not be the same as your neighbor's. One 28-year-old, with a wife, a child, and another child on the way, earned $39,000 a year when he set out to buy a $92,000 house. According to his bank, he should have been able to manage $970 a month on housing. He convinced the bankers, however, that he could manage over $1,500 a month on housing. It meant no movies, no meals out, no extra clothes, and a carefully drawn budget projected several years into the future. It didn't hurt that the 28-year-old was an accountant.

You must draw up your own budget, establish your own priorities. You can't stretch to the limit to buy a house if you're already deeply in debt for your Alfa Romeo and the clothes on your back. Most lenders still prefer that the portion of your income committed to housing not exceed 28 percent. Another common prescription is that your total monthly debt payments, including mortgage payments, should not exceed 36 percent of your income.

These rules, like all rules, are somewhat elastic and depend a great deal on the size of your family and on the life-style you choose. A two-person, two-income household, assuming that the two incomes are stable, can safely spend a larger proportion of income on housing than a one-income family with several mouths to feed. If you like macaroni, moreover, you can devote more of your income to housing than if you insist on roast beef. And if owning a house is more important to you than anything else, you may, like the 28-year-old above, be willing to forgo almost all luxuries for its sake.

As always, where you live makes a difference. You'll spend more on housing, as a rule, if you live in a large city and less if you live in a small town; see Chapter 9 for some specific examples.

What you buy makes a difference as well. Condominium units generally cost less than individually owned houses. Mobile homes cost less than condos. Older houses cost less, by and large, than new ones.

The amount of money you decide you can spend will influence your decision about the type of housing you buy. Condominium ownership is very popular today, particularly among first-time buyers and among older adults with empty nests, because condominium ownership (see Chapter 14) can be both less expensive and less troublesome than conventional ownership. If you want the traditional individually owned single-family detached house, you'll have to decide, at the outset, between an old house and a new one.

In general, older houses can be purchased for lower prices than brand-new houses. The median national selling price in 1992 was $121,100 for new houses and $103,700 for existing ones. This difference may account for the recent surge in purchases of older homes. Determine your own preference, then shop your own market carefully, keeping the following information in mind.

The New House

In general, new houses may be more expensive, but a lower down payment may be possible and easier financing may be available. Builders and developers have their own steady sources of financing and can often save you the time and trouble of shopping around to secure a mortgage commitment (although price shopping is always a good idea). In today's housing market, in fact, many builders are offering special financing (see Chapter 11). With the one-to-one arrangements in purchasing an older house, you're often left to do your own legwork (although here, too, sellers may help with financing).

New houses are also up-to-date. Appliances will be new, kitchens and baths will be modern, air conditioning may be built-in. New systems, however, may need a shakedown period before they function faultlessly. And, in some ways, there may be additional costs with a new house that there might not be with an older one. Builder-provided landscaping is often sketchy, and you may have to spend a good bit on your grounds. Screens and storm windows and such necessities as trash cans won't be available from a previous owner; you'll have to buy your own.

If you decide to buy a new house, there are two subspecies to consider:

The Builder-Built House

Far and away the most common, these houses may be in a massive tract of look-alike houses or in a handful of houses tucked into an existing neighborhood. Builder-built homes have a lot to offer. Because a builder deals in quantity, he can keep prices down on everything from lumber to appliances; because a builder-built house is built on speculation (built, that is, before it has a buyer), it is designed to appeal to as many people as possible and will therefore be easier to resell. But don't fall for the model home with all its appealing extras; try to be realistic about the house you'll actually buy.

The Custom-Designed House

This is a new house built just for you by a builder or an architect. A builder will tailor stock plans to suit your preference; his profit will be built into the cost of the house. An architect will design a house expressly for you, with a fee based on a percentage of the building cost; fees vary, but you can expect to pay about 15 percent. A skilled architect, however, can save you that much and more.

Either way, the custom-designed house is built just for you and is likely to suit you better. But, unless you're careful, it may be more difficult to resell. Your pet greenhouse or hot tub may represent a pain rather than a plus to a potential buyer.

The individually designed and built house is also likely to be more expensive. Construction materials will not be bought in quantity; they'll have to be bought as needed. As their prices rise, so will the cost of your house. Your natural inclination, too, will be to build the best, and the best, as a rule, costs more.

If you embark on either a builder-built or a custom-designed house, try to restrain the impulse to change things as you go along. It is extremely expensive to move doors or windows or closets once they are even roughly in place.

A TALE OF A NEW HOUSE

Buying a new house, even from a reputable builder, requires vigilance. One couple, very happy with their development house on one and a half acres in rural northwestern New Jersey, tells what happened:

- Construction was slower than expected (as it often is), and closing was postponed from March 1 to July 20. Since the couple had given up their apartment on July 1, and since storing furniture was very expensive, they put their furniture in the basement of their unfinished house while they moved in with her parents. The furniture was not insured and they were lucky to have only minor water damage.
- Construction workers are human; they make mistakes. Regular visits by this couple—and early detection of mistakes—made corrections possible. "We realized one day, even though the ceiling sheet rock wasn't in place yet, that there was no cathedral ceiling in the living room. If we hadn't caught it then, the builder might not have been able to correct it." If you can't keep track during construction, or have someone do it for you, you're bound to run into trouble.
- Some things always remain to be done after moving day, and the New Jersey couple, wisely, had $1,500 of the purchase price put into an escrow fund until work was complete. Even so, it took several months before the front porch, the driveway, and promised plantings were finished. Nails will continue to pop and walls to crack for quite a while. The contractor will send workers back after the house has settled, in about a year, to do the necessary repairs, which will mean more plaster dust, more mess.

This couple had relatively little trouble. Post-construction defects were minor, and their builder made the necessary corrections. Not all home buyers are so fortunate. You, as a home buyer, should (1) seek a reputable builder (see p. 266) and (2) look for a house with a warranty.

WARRANTIES

If you buy a can opener and it turns out to be defective, you can take it back to the store and ask for a replacement; most stores, although not obligated to replace the can opener (they could refer you to the manufacturer), will do so. But what happens if you buy a new house and it proves to be defective? Beyond the obvious impossibilities of returning a house for a replacement, what are your chances of getting the builder to set things right?

There have been many complaints about builders over the years, from the builder who can't be bothered to come back to fix sticky windows to more serious instances of a builder's refusal to mend leaky roofs or cracked foundations. One Federal Trade Commission survey of a few years ago indicated that the average newly built house has defects costing nearly $1,000 to repair; 62 percent of new-house owners in this survey had at least one construction problem that the builder wouldn't resolve; and 20 percent reported a "serious disagreement" with a builder.

The HOW Program

In 1974, in an effort to combat consumer dissatisfaction with builders (and to forestall government regulation of the industry), the National Association of Home Builders established the Home Owners Warranty (HOW) program. Now an independent corporation with 10,000 builder participants, HOW has provided warranties against structural defects for almost 3 million houses. The program isn't perfect; some homeowners complain bitterly that their problems remain unresolved, and some builders have dropped out in dissatisfaction (some have joined other warranty programs; see p. 279) or been dropped for failure to respond to the homeowners' complaints. Nonetheless, HOW does offer protection where little existed before.

For example, in a case from the HOW files, a newly built Florida house with a cathedral-ceiling-high stone fireplace began to settle. The fireplace separated as much as a full inch from the walls; the frightened homeowners were justifiably afraid that it would topple.

Because the builder refused to repair the damage, HOW insurance came into force. The insurance investigation revealed that the foundation had been laid without footings and with one of the essential supporting piers in each row omitted. The insurance carrier had the house moved from its foundation, the old foundation bulldozed out, and a new one installed. The home was then moved back and the interior damage repaired. The total cost amounted to some $36,000. The cost to the homeowners: $250.

HOW is not the only warranty program for new homes but, as the first such program, it has become synonymous with the concept. The HOW program is available to consumers in every state but Alaska. As a combination warranty and insurance program, this is the way it works:

A warranty covers the first two years. In the first year, the builder warrants the home to be free from defects in workmanship and materials in compliance with the program's standards. This is the time, under the "free from defects" provision, for the homeowner to catch those persistent problems of sticking windows or blistering paint or incomplete landscaping. During the second year the builder continues to warrant against major structural defects and against malfunctioning of the wiring, piping, and ductwork in the electrical, plumbing, heating, and cooling systems.

In these first two years, the builder is required to come back and repair the covered defects. If, however, the builder fails to perform—if he's gone out of business or is simply uncooperative—the warranty is backed by the HOW Corporation and HOW makes the repairs, subject to a $250 deductible paid by the homeowner on each claim.

In the third through tenth years, the home is directly insured against major structural defects, again with a deductible of $250. If your foundation shows signs of cracking, HOW insurance should take care of repairs.

Other things you should know:

■ HOW coverage is available through builders; it is not available directly to consumers.

■ The builder who enters the HOW program pays the fee for coverage. The fee may, of course, be passed on to the buyer in the price of the house.

■ HOW coverage is transferable. If you buy a covered house within the warranty/insurance period, the coverage will transfer to you. If you sell, similarly, your buyer will pick up the protection.

■ When a builder does not agree that any repairs are necessary, the homeowner may refer the disagreement, at no cost, to HOW's dispute settlement procedure.

■ Builders must meet HOW standards in order to join the program. If a builder fails to perform he is expelled from the program, although he can continue in business. In New Jersey, with a tough state-mandated warranty program, builders who fail to perform may lose their registration and therefore their right to do business in the state.

■ Some builders advertise their participation in HOW, but some do not; you'll have to ask. Be sure, in any case, to choose a builder very care-

Q I've heard several terms applied to joint ownership of property. Can you explain the difference?

A The biggest difference among the three forms of joint ownership is what lawyers call the "right of survivorship." When one joint owner dies, in other words, depending on the form of ownership, the other owner may or may not automatically own the property. There are three types of joint ownership:

Tenancy in common does not have the survivorship right, and is more often used by business partners than by spouses.

Joint tenancy has a right of survivorship, but either owner can sell his or her interest and force a division of the property.

Tenancy by the entirety, permitted only between spouses, has the right of survivorship and also requires joint action. Neither partner can sell his or her share, so that this form provides the most protection to both. Tenancy by the entirety, moreover, is the assumed form of ownership by husband and wife in some states, unless the ownership papers specifically spell out a different arrangement.

fully, as outlined below. Building houses is an economically perilous way to make a living. Many builders, even with the best of intentions, fail to make a go of it. These are the builders who may cut corners in an effort to stay afloat. These are also the builders who may simply go under, leaving their buyers to fend for themselves.

■ For more information about the HOW program, call toll-free 800-CALL HOW (for people who hate these acronyms, as I do, that's 800-225-5469) or write to HOW, 1110 North Glebe Rd., Arlington, VA 22201. For information about two other nationwide programs, contact the Home Buyers Warranty Program at 800-776-4296, 2313 East Atlantic Blvd., Pompano Beach, FL 33062 and the Residential Warranty Program at 800-247-1812, 5300 Derry St., Harrisburg, PA 17111.

PICKING A BUILDER

Choosing a builder isn't quite as important as choosing a good surgeon, says the National Association of Home Builders, but it's far too important a decision to trust to a walk through the Yellow Pages. You've heard the stories of endless construction delays, lost deposits, and badly built houses. You've seen the need for a Home Owners Warranty program. So don't trust to luck at all. Do your homework:

■ Check out the builder's reputation. Talk to previous customers (ask for names of people in houses built earlier and knock on doors if the development you are considering is already partially occupied); find out what these homeowners think of the builder's skill and performance, especially post-sales performance.

■ Ask the builder how he stands behind his work. If he offers a warranty, ask what it does and does not cover. Ask him what responsibility he assumes for subcontractors and others who work for him. Find out if he belongs to the Home Owners Warranty program or any other organized warranty/insurance program.

■ Find out how long he has been in business and under what name. A family name is a better indication of permanence than a corporate name; be especially wary of a builder identified only through his current project ... how will you find him once the project is completed? Find out where his main office is located, and don't do business with a builder who operates out of a truck or a post office box. Ask your local Home Builders Association and/or Better Business Bureau about his reliability and professional standing. Ask local suppliers about the builder's reputation. You might even ask your bank to run a financial check; it may cost you a few dollars but they will be dollars well spent.

Be extra vigilant when times are tight (as they have been recently), and builders are in danger of losing their financing in mid-project. If you're buying in a development, look for one that is at least three-quarters completed before you make a commitment. Make sure the builder has put up a performance bond with the local governing body, to ensure completion of roads, sewers, and so on. Have an attorney review sales documents and ensure that your deposit is kept in an escrow account. And stick to a builder sizable enough to be able to show you an audited financial statement. It might even be worth having your own financial adviser review the statement, to alert you to potential signs of trouble.

YOUR AGREEMENT WITH THE BUILDER

Once you've satisfied yourself about the desirability of the house and the reliability of the builder and are ready to make a commitment, get everything in writing. Don't rely on spoken promises. The contract itself should spell out all the details:

- The total sales price and how it is to be paid
- The completion date for the house and the date title is to be transferred
- Any special features to be included in the house; any changes from stock plans
- Any builder-provided amenities, such as streets, sewers, or sidewalks, and when they are to be completed

Then, when the house is finished and you're ready to move in, be sure you have the necessary documentation: a Certificate of Occupancy, warranties from all manufacturers for equipment in the house, approval of plumbing and sewer installations, and any applicable certificates of code compliance.

The Older House

Strictly speaking, an older house is any previously occupied house. A one-year-old custom-built house thus qualifies as an "older" house although it is technically more correct to call it a resale. The significant difference in buying an older home of any vintage: You buy from an individual. This means two things:

- The purchase price is negotiable. An individual, eager to sell and move on, may come down several thousand dollars from the original asking price—especially if the house has been on the market for some time or if a death or a divorce has disrupted the family.
- You must secure financing on your own rather than rely on a builder package. This financing, these days, may be obtained with the help of the seller (see p. 326).

The Advantages of an Older House

The true older house, several years old and in an established neighborhood, has certain advantages. For one thing, the neighborhood is established. You're unlikely to be surprised by the need for new sewers or new schools; taxes are therefore more stable. The house itself is probably complete with lawn and trees, screens and storm windows. It may offer considerably more space for the money than a new house, and may (although not always) be better constructed. The house, if it is an older design, may also offer more interesting architecture, spacious rooms plus nooks and crannies, maybe even the charm of an old-fashioned front porch.

A young resale is considered by many to be a "best bet." Under five years old, these houses are contemporary and up-to-date. Yet such a house has been through its shakedown cruise and the quirks, if any, are out of its systems.

The Disadvantages of an Older House

You may find, on the other hand, that considerable work is needed to bring an old house up to your standards. The kitchen and bathrooms may be outmoded and in need of expensive modernization; they may also have been remodeled by someone without your taste. There may not be a bathroom on the main floor. Closet space may be inadequate. Basic systems, if the house is over 20 years old, may be in need of repair or renovation; even the best heating plant doesn't last forever. That interesting architecture may mask hollow walls, with no insulation to keep heating bills down.

The disadvantages of an older house will be most apparent in the **handyman's special,** the house that may strike you as having considerable charm at low cost, well worth the trouble and expense to fix it up.

Many homeowners, indeed, have reaped profits by improving rundown houses. But go into such a venture with your eyes wide open. Find out, before you buy, exactly what will need to be repaired or replaced and how soon. Hire an engineer or home inspection service (see below) to give you a written report. Then find out exactly what it will cost to make the essential changes; add that figure to the cost of the house to determine what you are actually paying for the house. And don't forget your own sweat. You may not be able to put a dollar value on it ... or want to, when it's your dream house over which you're laboring. But stripping woodwork can lose its charm when weekend after weekend is spent doing little but stripping woodwork. At that point, you may feel driven to hire help. Will you have the funds to do so?

APPRAISALS AND INSPECTIONS

If you're thinking of buying an older house, you may want to have it appraised, to be sure a fair price is being asked. You should definitely have it inspected, preferably by a qualified structural engineer or home inspector, to be sure there are no hidden defects. You may buy a house even if you know the electrical system has to be replaced, but you should be able to buy it at a lower price. In any case, if you're forewarned by an inspection, you won't be faced with a costly surprise later on. The inspection itself may cost approximately $300 to $400 (more if you want potential environmental hazards evaluated as well), well worth it considering the magnitude of the purchase.

But be careful in selecting the inspector, because only Texas has a law requiring home inspectors to be licensed. In the absence of licensing, membership in a professional organization is at least an indication of competence. For a referral to a home inspection professional in your community, call the American Society of Home Inspectors in Arlington, Virginia, at (703)524-2008, or the National Academy of Building Inspection Engineers in Portland, Maine, at (207)828-1977.

Resale Warranties

Warranty programs are also available on many resale homes, typically through real estate brokers but sometimes through home inspection compa-

Q Our real estate agent has suggested that we purchase a one-year warranty contract on the house we're buying, at a cost of $385. Would this be worthwhile?

A A warranty or service agreement covering both major mechanical systems (heating, plumbing, and electrical) and built-in appliances can provide peace of mind—particularly if you're buying an older home that hasn't been upgraded.

But before buying a warranty, be sure you understand its provisions, particularly:

- Costs; a one-year contract can cost from $350 to $450, putting your quoted price at the low end of the scale
- Deductibles, which can run $35 to $200 for each service call
- Exclusions. Warranties, for example, almost never cover structural elements such as roofs
- Limitations on preexisting conditions. You will still need an inspection, because warranties generally do not cover problems existing before you buy the coverage
- Extra costs, to cover nonstandard items such as swimming pool equipment

And, before you pay for the warranty, ask if the home's seller or your real estate agent will pay all or part of the cost.

nies. Many are local, but some are national; the National Home Warranty Association currently represents eight resale warranty programs. The cost (often paid by the seller) is typically $350 to $450 for a one-year contract, with a deductible on each service call of $35 to $200. (If your real estate broker can't tell you about a warranty program, call the National Home Warranty Association at 800-325-8144.)

One of these programs, as an example, is available through ERA real estate brokers just about everywhere. ERA's Buyer Protection Plan provides a one-year warranty on plumbing and electrical systems, heating and cooling systems, water heaters and water softeners, and built-in appliances. At an additional cost, "extras" such as swimming pools and hot tubs can be covered as well.

Whether or not your home comes with a warranty, be sure to hire an independent inspector and have the house given a thorough inspection.

THE AGREEMENT TO BUY

When you have found the house of your dreams and agreed on a purchase price, you will make a deposit and sign a purchase agreement (called by various names: a binder, bid, contract, or offer to buy). That agreement is a legally binding document that will govern your title to the house; be sure it itemizes every condition of the sale:

■ The purchase price and how it is to be paid

Q I signed a purchase agreement to buy one house, then found another house I like better. The owner of the first house does not want to return my deposit and, in fact, is insisting that I have to go through with the purchase. Do I have to?

A You might. Buyers and sellers alike often look at the binder or purchase agreement as simply a temporary agreement pending the formal contract of sale. But, and it's a very big but, courts in some states have held that a binder is in itself a legal contract. One buyer unwittingly agreed to an all-cash deal because only the purchase price, and no mention of financing, appeared in the binder. Another signed a binder that committed him to paying the seller's share of closing costs. And a New York seller who changed his mind about moving was forced by the courts to complete the transaction initiated by the binder, to sell the house, and to move. Talk to your lawyer about the agreement you signed; you may find a way out. And next time, make up your mind before you sign any document that can be legally enforced.

■ The date title is to be transferred, and any contingencies that may delay that transfer (you may want to be sure you have sold your current home, the seller may want to be sure his new house is ready, but don't leave the date of transfer open-ended)

■ What is to be included in the purchase price, with a detailed list of specific fixtures and furnishings the seller has agreed to leave for the buyer as part of the sale (appliances, curtain rods, lawn furniture, and so on)

■ Responsibility for fire and other possible damage until the date of the closing

■ A provision that your deposit will be held in escrow until you take title to the house

■ The condition that the purchase is subject to your obtaining a mortgage commitment within a specified period of time

Real Estate Brokers

It is possible to buy or sell a house on your own. Most people, however, find it helpful to use a broker.

WHEN YOU ARE THE BUYER

A broker knows the community and the houses in the area you prefer. He or she can give you information about taxes, schools, zoning, etc. (But confirm these facts elsewhere. Brokers have been known to refer to the "one train a day" on nearby tracks; home buyers later learned, after they moved in, that the trains were considerably more frequent.) He or she can help secure financing, and refer you to attorneys, surveyors, and title insurance companies. (But you may get a better price if you shop for these services yourself.) Most important, perhaps, a knowledgeable broker, tuned in to the local real estate network, will know of many more homes for sale than you can find out about on your own.

A broker can be very helpful but remember, if you're buying, *the broker works for the seller* (unless you use one of a relatively new breed of "buyer brokers" or "single agency brokers"; see below). In a practical sense, this means that the broker may tell you that the roof leaks, but not tell you that the purchase price can be lowered to compensate. More important, it means that while the broker must tell the seller your top dollar offer, if you've shared that information with him, he isn't going to tell you if a lower offer might be accepted by the seller. Not only would such advice be against his client's best interests, it would also (since the broker's fee is based on the selling price) be opposed to the broker's best interests as well. It's difficult, in other words, for the most ethical of brokers to avoid some conflict of interest in trying to represent both seller and buyer. Most, as a result, represent the seller—although they will help you, the buyer, in your search.

Note: Most states now require agents to disclose the agency-client relationship in writing at the outset.

Brokers for Buyers

In a departure from traditional practice, more and more brokers limit their representation. Some, called "single agency brokers," may represent either a buyer or a seller but will not represent both buyer and seller in a single transaction. Others, called "buyers' brokers," represent only buyers. With no conflict of interest, either type of buyer's representative can actively work toward lowering the purchase price and improving the terms for the buyer. This means, for example, that your broker can legitimately negotiate to get the seller to fix that leaky roof and pass a warranty on to you.

The brokerage fee should be included in the transaction, so you should pay no more to use a broker who represents your interests. Be aware, though, that sometimes the buyer's broker and the seller's broker will share in a commission based on the sales price of the property.

Single agency and buyers' brokers have faced resistance from other brokers but are beginning to catch on. As long as they are licensed real estate agents and members of the local Board of Realtors, they should have access to the Multiple Listing Service run by the Board. In fact, if you face a recalcitrant broker, do two things: Point out that the National Association of Realtors now supports full written disclosure of whom the broker actually represents. And walk away from any broker who won't commit to representing you and only you. To find a buyer's broker or single-agency broker:

- Check display ads under "real estate" in your telephone directory,
- Call the Consumer Division of Buyer's Resource (a franchise of buyer broker offices) in Denver (toll-free, 800-359-4092),

---

Q In selling one house and buying another, we've been dealing with the same broker. A friend says we'd do better using a "buyer's broker" for purchasing the new home. Why?

A Many people don't realize that, unless specifically stated otherwise, brokers are legal representatives of sellers. This means that, while they can be very helpful in showing you houses, they can not legally negotiate on your behalf. A buyer's broker, representing only the buyer, may be able to secure a better price and better terms.

■ Or send a stamped self-addressed envelope to the Single Agency Realty Association, c/o McTighe, 20561 Shadyside Way, Germantown, MD 20561.

Before you hire a buyer's broker, however, find out:

■ How is the fee calculated? If there is a commission, you may wind up in the same conflict of interest situation that you would have with an agent representing either the seller alone or, in what is called "dual agency" representing both seller and buyer. Try to negotiate a flat fee arrangement rather than a percentage of the sales price.
■ Will you owe the entire fee, or some portion of it, whether or not you actually purchase a house? Will you owe the entire fee, or some portion of it, if you purchase a home that you find by yourself?
■ Will you have to sign an exclusive contract? If so, try to limit the duration of the contract. And include an escape clause giving both you and the agent an opportunity to void the contract, after a specified period of time, if either is dissatisfied with the arrangement.

When Something Goes Wrong

Buyers' brokers are still few and far between in many parts of the country, which means that it's still generally "buyer beware" when you buy a house. But it's more common now for sellers to fill out disclosure forms disclosing any defects they know about; some states actually require such forms. Disclosure or not, courts are beginning to uphold home buyers' claims against both sellers and real estate brokers. When defects are discovered these days, it's not uncommon for a home buyer to sue. In recent cases:

■ An Alabama buyer sued a broker for failure to disclose a water leak, claiming that the broker knew about it all along.
■ In Minnesota, a buyer wanted the seller to pay for fixing a basement leak—even though the sellers had filled out a disclosure form indicating that the basement sometimes leaked.

Q The only way we can buy a house is by watching every penny. Won't it cost us less if we find a house that's being sold without a broker?

A Not necessarily. Most sellers who go through the trouble of selling on their own, without a broker, do so to save the commission for themselves. But shop carefully; you may find a seller willing to split the savings if not give them up entirely.

- A California home turned out to be on less acreage than had been claimed; the buyer sued the broker.
- In another California case a home was advertised as having a magnificent view; when another house went up nearby, blocking the view, the homeowner sued the broker.
- And, in a well-publicized case in New York State, buyers backed out of a signed contract on the grounds that they hadn't been told the house was haunted. The sellers lost a considerable amount of money.

Although courts are upholding some of these claims, and some are settled out of court, it's still both expensive and troublesome to sue. Know what you're doing beforehand. Hire your own lawyer; have your own independent home inspection; get your own title company and your own title insurance (see p. 291). And remember: The broker, unless as a buyer you hire your own, represents the seller.

WHEN YOU ARE THE SELLER

A broker can help you to determine the appropriate asking price, based on market conditions in your community. He or she will advertise the house, screen out "lookers" with no serious intent to buy, show the property, handle negotiations, and take care of the paperwork that goes with a sale.

Most brokers work on commission, and that commission, paid by the seller, is usually a percentage of the sale price of the house. Although it is illegal for real estate brokers to fix commissions, the force of custom (and pressure by some brokers on other brokers) has combined to keep commissions throughout the country at 5 to 7 percent. But commissions are negotiable. You should always discuss the broker's fee before signing a contract. Ask exactly what the fee covers; perhaps there are some services you don't really need and won't have to pay for. You might show the property yourself, for instance, while the broker advertises the property, sends potential customers your way, and helps your buyer obtain financing.

Q We sold our house last year and paid the real estate agent a commission of $3,810. Can this commission be deducted on our federal income tax return?

A No. But the commission you paid, along with money spent on permanent improvements to the house over the years you owned it, reduces your profit on the sale. Be sure to keep receipts documenting such expenditures.

Note: In a tight real estate market, brokers are working very hard to make sales, and many feel that they fully deserve the commissions they charge. As a fact of life, although commissions are negotiable, brokers may be understandably less inclined to push a house on which the commission is lower.

How to List Your House for Sale

You can list your house in several ways:

- You can give the broker an **exclusive agency listing,** usually for a period of three to six months. This gives the broker considerable incentive to sell the property. Be careful, though, that you don't give an exclusive right to sell; under this arrangement, you could owe the broker a commission even if you sell the house with no assistance at all from the broker.
- With an **open listing,** the house may be listed with several brokers at one time; only the selling agent gets a commission, so that brokers tend to devote the same effort to such listings.
- **Multiple listing services,** under which brokers pool house listings, provide wide exposure to potential buyers. The commission is shared between the office obtaining the listing and the office arranging the sale. (But multiple listing services have been criticized, in a number of areas, for excluding discount brokers.)

You can also sell a house yourself, in what's called a "fizzbo" (for sale by owner) transaction. But you have to be prepared for unfamiliar and time-consuming chores. You have to be available at all times, to all comers. And you have to take the chance that the effort will cost you money rather than save you money, unless you are a good negotiator and a skillful salesperson.

When You Take Title

You've found your house, negotiated its price, obtained a mortgage (see Chapter 11), and now you're ready to take title. You'd also best be ready to spend some more money.

SETTLEMENT COSTS

Settlement costs, or closing costs, include all those miscellaneous items that go with taking title to property. They vary from region to region, and from lender to lender, but typically include three types of costs:

- Charges for establishing and transferring ownership, including a title search, to be sure the seller has the right to sell, and title insurance, to protect the mortgage lender (you may want to buy a separate policy to protect your own interests; see below for details). Attorney's fees (you may have to pay for the lending institution's attorneys as well as your own) fit in this category as well.

■ Charges by state and local governments, including transfer taxes, recording fees, and prepaid property taxes. These charges can be significant; in some New York counties, for example, the mortgage recording tax is 1.75 percent of the loan amount—or $1,750 on a $100,000 mortgage loan.

■ Charges associated with securing a mortgage loan, including a survey, to determine the precise location of the house and the property, and an appraisal, to satisfy the lender about the value of the property. Lender's fees also include charges for preparation of documents, a

Q I've been transferred to another city, but can't sell my house. I certainly can't afford to carry two mortgages. Any suggestions?

A You might try renting out your house until the real estate market picks up. If rental income exceeds deductible expenses, you'll have to pay taxes on the difference. If rental income does not cover your expenses, you *may* be able to claim a loss—but only if the conversion to rental property is permanent (see below). Be sure to consult a knowledgeable tax adviser before you make decisions, but here are some things to consider:

■ In order to preserve the right to defer taxes on the sale of your home, you must move from one principal residence to another. This means that the conversion to rental property must be temporary rather than permanent. Keep records documenting your efforts to sell the house before renting it, and be sure you have an agreement with your tenant allowing you to show the house to prospective purchasers.

■ In order to defer paying taxes on the profit you make on your house when you do sell, you must sell the old house within two years of the time you buy a replacement home. If you are over age 55, and seeking the once-in-a-lifetime exclusion of $125,000, you must live in the house for at least three of the five years before you sell.

■ Being a landlord involves significant headaches—screening tenants, collecting payments, making repairs. You can avoid some of these headaches by hiring a rental agent to manage the property.

credit report, prepayment of hazard insurance, and points or origination fees (a one-time charge, sometimes called a loan discount, to
increase the mortgage yield for the lender; each point equals 1 percent
of the mortgage amount). You'll find more information on points in
Chapter 11.

You may also be required by the lender to have a termite inspection, to
pay for recording the documents, to pay for keeping funds in escrow pending
adjustment of taxes, and so on and on.

It can add up to a not-so-pretty penny, with fees totaling 3 percent to
almost 7 percent of the purchase price of a house. The exact amount depends
on where you live. It also depends on whether you shop around, and whether
you negotiate. The seller might be willing to pay for the termite inspection, for
example, or to share the cost of transfer taxes. See Table 10.1 for an illustration of the range of closing costs, provided by the Mortgage Bankers
Association of America.

Table 10.1: Closing Costs Can Vary Considerably

	Down Payment	
	10 percent	20 percent
Loan Application Fees	$75 to $300	$75 to $300
Loan Origination Fees	$675	$600
Points	$675 to $2,025	600 to $1,800
Mortgage Insurance	$338 to $675	—
Title Search/Insurance Fees	$450 to $600	$450 to $600
Attorney's Fees	$500 to $1,500	$500 to $1,500
Appraisal	$100 to $300	$100 to $300
Adjustments	?	?
Homeowners Insurance	$300 to $600	$300 to $600
Inspections	$175 to $350	$175 to $350
Survey	$125 to $300	$125 to $300
Notary Fees	$10 to $25	$10 to $25
Recording Fees	$40 to $60	$40 to $60
State/Local Transfer Fees	$75 to $1,125	$75 to $1,125
TOTAL:	$3,438 to $8,235	$2,950 to $7,260

Source: Mortgage Bankers Association of America.

Keeping Closing Costs Down
Some closing costs are required by law; some are pretty much fixed in
price. But some can be greatly reduced, maybe even eliminated, by careful

shopping and by thinking ahead. You may be able to skip a new survey, for instance, if you can get the seller to give you the existing survey plus an affidavit that no changes have been made to any structures that would overlap the boundaries. A title insurance company may give you a lower rate if it recently wrote a policy on the same property or if it writes your policy at the same time it writes the policy for the lending institution. Insist on choosing your own lawyer, title company, and surveyor—don't leave this choice to the broker— and discuss their fees before you make a final selection.

RE-
ISSUE?

The lender must inform you of the anticipated closing costs, in writing, three days after receiving your mortgage application. You'll receive a final statement at the closing itself, and you may review it the day before. You'll have to have the money in hand on the day of the closing. (In most parts of the country, you'll meet face-to-face with the seller on closing day; in some places, however, the transaction is handled by a third party called an escrow agent.)

You'll also have to adjust various costs with the seller when you take title: for the oil in the tank that he paid for and you'll use, for the taxes he's paid on the house you'll now occupy, and so on. And you'll have to pay a mortgage insurance premium, if mortgage insurance is required by the lender, and a premium for hazard or homeowners insurance as well. You may be able to include all of the payments in a single substantial check, or you may write check after check. Either way, you'll need enough money in your checking account to cover the closing costs in full.

Note: Some mortgage lenders won't give a mortgage commitment until they're assured that you can cover these closing costs. Some will require certified checks at closing.

TITLE INSURANCE

You may look at title insurance as just one of the many nuisance items for which you write a check on the day you take title to your house. But title insurance deserves a somewhat closer look, because it can, under certain circumstances, protect your investment in your property.

A title search should clear up most questions about clear title to the property, and some consumer advocates claim that a title search is all that's necessary. But there can be problems despite the most careful search: An anxious seller may conceal unpaid debts to contractors; those contractors may be able to place a lien on the property. The existence of an estranged wife may similarly be "forgotten"; under the law in some states, she would continue to have certain rights in the property. A not-quite-valid will two generations back could cast doubt on the legal transfer of title. Mistakes may simply be made. In a situation in New York State, a parcel of land that had actually been deeded to an heir of the seller was also mistakenly included in acreage sold to a developer. Five families who had purchased houses in the developer's subdivision were ordered by a court to return the land, including the improvements (their houses), to the rightful owner.

Worksheet 10.1: Calculating Personal Housing Costs

STEP 1. CALCULATE MONTHLY INCOME.

Income from employment after deductions	$_____
Interest and dividends	+ $_____
Other income (second job, business, etc.)	+ $_____
Total income	= $_____

STEP 2. CALCULATE MONTHLY NON-HOUSING EXPENSES.

Food, beverages (home and work)	$_____
Entertainment and recreation	+ $_____
Clothing and grooming	+ $_____
Transportation and automobile expenses (auto loan, insurance, gas, oil, etc.)	+ $_____
Medical care	+ $_____
Child care	+ $_____
Education	+ $_____
Gifts	+ $_____
Insurance (life and health)	+ $_____
Installment loans (charge accounts, credit cards)	+ $_____
Savings	+ $_____
Other	+ $_____
Total monthly non-housing expenses (add)	= $_____
Subtract non-housing expenses from total of Step 1.	= $_____

STEP 3. ESTIMATE MONTHLY EXPENSES.

Proposed mortgage payment or rent	$_____
Allowance for property taxes	+ $_____
Allowance for utilities (heat, water, phone, electricity)	+ $_____
Allowance for maintenance and repairs (including garbage removal, gardening and lawn service, etc.)	+ $_____
Allowance for insurance	+ $_____
Other (association dues? street/sidewalk assessments?)	+ $_____
Total monthly housing expenses (add)	= $_____

STEP 4. Compare estimated monthly housing expenses (Step 3) with income available for housing (Step 2). If income available does not equal or exceed monthly housing expenses, then you must reevaluate your budget and resources.

These things don't happen often, given the vast number of real estate transactions that take place in this country, but they do happen. That's why your mortgage lender takes a title policy (for which you pay) protecting his investment in the property. That's also why you may want to consider a title insurance policy of your own. Your lender's policy does not protect you. It doesn't even cover the full value of the property, just the amount of the mortgage loan. You should consider a policy that will protect your title—it's inexpensive, as a rule, if taken at the same time as the lender's.

The five Long Island families ordered to return their land had court costs paid by the developer's title insurance company. But that land included their homes and they still faced substantial loss. Four of the five families had their own title insurance policies. The fifth did not have an owner's policy. In the end, after considerable anxiety, the legal owner agreed to a settlement and the settlement was paid by the title company.

Other Costs

The 28-year-old with the $92,000 house described at the beginning of this chapter faced monthly payments for mortgage and taxes of just over $1,000. His total out-of-pocket housing costs, however, month after month, came to over $1,500. He had to include—and you might too—the costs of utilities, garbage removal, homeowners insurance, and mortgage insurance. He also had monthly dues (required, not optional) for a community recreational facility.

Be sure that you include every possible expenditure as you look at housing. Use the Personal Housing Cost Worksheet (p. 292) to determine how much money you can comfortably spend. Be honest with yourself about outgo on housing, and about your own income. Do not commit uncertain income, such as overtime or bonuses.

In addition to ongoing costs, there are also up-front costs that you should be sure to consider. These include moving, decorating, and an emergency fund.

MOVING COSTS

Although the trucking industry has been deregulated and moving companies can now compete for business, moving may still cost more than you expect. Be prepared to pay hourly charges on local moves, distance and weight charges on interstate moves. And be sure that you shop around. Some movers will now offer binding estimates, some give discounts, some will guarantee pickup and delivery within a specified number of days.

Ways to Save on a Move
- Do it yourself, if you have the time and the energy.
- Get at least three estimates if you decide to use a professional mover; check references with previous customers and check for complaints

with your state transportation department, local consumer affairs office and/or the Better Business Bureau.

■ Move in the second or third week of the month, and try not to move in the popular summer months.

■ Pack as much as you can yourself (although it's not a bad idea to let the movers pack fragile items and take the responsibility for them).

■ Be there when the moving truck is weighed, both before and after your belongings are loaded. On the first weighing, be sure the fuel tanks are full and that heavy equipment such as dollies and chains are in place. At the second weighing, see that no husky movers jump aboard at the last moment.

■ Arrange for adequate protection in case your belongings are lost or damaged. Your homeowners insurance policy may cover you during a move; check with your agent or company to be sure. If it does, or if you choose to purchase a special liability policy to provide protection during the move, you can sign an agreement with the mover for what's called "released value"; if you do, there is no charge to you but the mover's liability for damage is limited to a maximum of 60 cents per pound per item. If a painting that weighs 10 pounds but is worth $1,000 is damaged, you'll collect $6.00. Don't sign this release unless

Q My washing machine hasn't worked properly since I moved, and now it's failed altogether. I'm sure it was damaged in the move, but the mover denies responsibility. Is there anything I can do to collect the cost of repairs?

A Under a program of the American Movers Conference, the industry trade group, you and the mover can agree to submit your dispute to binding arbitration. As long as you submitted your initial claim to the mover within nine months after delivery—the mover must acknowledge your claim within 30 days, and take action within 120 days—you can request arbitration by writing to the American Movers Conference, Dispute Settlement Program, 1611 Duke St., Alexandria, VA 22314-3482. The move must have been made interstate, the mover must participate in the program, and you must write within 60 days of the company's denial of your claim. Include your name, address, and phone number, the identification number of the shipment, dates and location of pickup and delivery, and any assigned claim number. Most cases are decided on the basis of written documents submitted by both parties; sometimes (for a fee) an oral hearing is arranged.

you are sure you have other protection. If you don't, the mover is required by the Interstate Commerce Commission to assume liability at $1.25 per pound times the weight of your shipment; if your shipment weighs 4,000 pounds, the mover will be liable for loss or damage up to $5,000 (you can obtain additional coverage, if your shipment is worth more, by paying $5.00 for each $1,000 of declared value). Under this arrangement, you could collect the full $1,000 for your 10-pound painting.

■ Don't sign a receipt for delivery until after you check the inventory and make sure that everything has been delivered in good condition.

DECORATING COSTS

You'll have to make your new home livable, so, unless you already own a complete houseful of items that will fit in your new surroundings, be sure to calculate the cost of furniture, appliances, carpeting, wallpaper, etc. You may be able to postpone some purchases (many a family has lived in the family room, with an empty living room, for months or years), but you may need to make others right away. Figure out these costs as realistically as possible, before you commit your funds.

AN EMERGENCY FUND

Don't allocate every penny in advance. As you should realize by now, homeowning is an expensive proposition. An emergency fund, to pay for everything you didn't expect, should be part of your financial plan. No matter how carefully you estimate, there will be unanticipated expenditures. Be sure you have a cushion of at least several hundred dollars, more if you can manage it, to soften the impact.

 KEY POINTS

■ New houses, in general, cost more than resales but may be easier to finance. Older homes cost less, as a rule, but may cost more to put into livable shape.

■ Your purchase contract, for new house or old, should spell out all the details; don't leave anything to unwritten agreement.

■ Real estate brokers can be very helpful, but remember, if you are the buyer, that the broker represents the seller—unless you use a "single agency" or "buyer's broker."

■ Evaluate how much you can spend on housing in terms of your entire budget, and remember to allow enough money for settlement costs, for moving and decorating, and for an emergency fund.

CHAPTER 11

Financing a House Today

The drastic changes in housing finance in the last decade or so have placed home buyers on an emotional and financial roller coaster. Mortgage interest rates peaked at 18 percent in 1982, when fewer than 5 percent of all American households could afford to buy a median-priced house. By 1993, after recession slam-dunked the American economy, house prices were down and the interest rate on a 30 year fixed rate mortgage hovered at 7.5 percent, the lowest rate in 20 years.

Nonetheless, there's an apparent contradiction: At the same time that housing has become more affordable (prices in many parts of the country are still heading downward), many first-time buyers are still either priced out of the market or are relying on two incomes in order to buy a home. The situation *has* improved as interest rates have come down. In the fourth quarter of 1992, when the median priced "starter house" sold for $87,600, the interest rate on a 30 year fixed rate mortgage stood at 7.74 percent; even with an added premium for the private mortgage insurance that permitted a lower down payment (see p. 300), monthly mortgage payments on this house were $578. Compare this to the fourth quarter of 1990, when the median priced starter house sold for $78,400; with interest rates then at 9.92 percent, the monthly payment was $628. Nonetheless, more than 86 percent of all first-time buyers, according to a 1992 study by the Chicago Title and Trust Family of Title Insurers, needed a second income to qualify for their mortgage loan.

If you're a repeat buyer, moving upward and onward by shopping for a second house (and can manage to sell the first), you are, relatively speaking, on easy street: You can put the appreciated value of your first house toward your second. Repeat buyers, as a result, can and usually do buy more expensive homes. But what if you've not yet bought your first house? Can you afford to do so? And is now the time to try?

Economists speak of affordability on a national scale. But you have to look at your own personal situation, at your income (both current and potential), and at your life-style. What do you have in current savings to apply toward a home purchase? How much of your current monthly income can you spend on housing? Is your income likely to grow? Or are you worried about losing your job? Or, perhaps, have you reached a life stage where income expectations have pretty much leveled off?

Table 11.1: How Much House You Can Buy

If you can afford to spend $500 a month on housing, here's how much house you can buy (assuming a down payment of 20 percent) at various rates of interest.

6%	$104,245
7%	93,942
8%	85,177
9%	77,676
10%	71,219
11%	65,629
12%	60,761

Source: National Association of Home Builders.

As you answer these questions, also look at what homeownership can do for you. With the tax benefits that Uncle Sam provides for homeowners (see Chapter 13), you can effectively reduce your taxable income. At the same time you are building equity in a tangible asset.

But should you think about buying a house right now? Won't interest rates come down still further, making a purchase easier? Interest rates may indeed come down, although no forecaster has a clear crystal ball, but it can be argued that it won't help if you wait until they do. The reason: While you wait, house prices may start to rise, requiring larger down payments, larger mortgage loans, and, even at lower interest rates, larger monthly payments.

A lot depends on your expectation of interest trends (and your willingness to gamble), but you may, if you postpone a purchase till rates fall still further, find yourself in the position of racing after a bus you've missed. When mortgage interest rates fall and more money becomes available, more people will be ready to buy; increased demand, in turn, will inflate housing prices once again.

Unless you have to wait because you can't afford to get a toe in the door at all, think about buying now. Think about buying in terms of your two major financial commitments: the down payment and the mortgage loan.

The Down Payment

A down payment may be 20 percent or more of the purchase price. It may be 10 percent. And it may, under certain programs (such as Veterans Affairs [VA] and Federal Housing Administration [FHA] guaranteed mortgages and mortgages secured by private mortgage insurance), be 5 percent or less. Which is right for you?

SMALL DOWN PAYMENT OR LARGE?

The lower down payment has significant advantages. Its biggest advantage, clearly, is that it may make it possible for you to buy a house. With a 20 percent down payment on a $100,000 house, you would need $20,000 in cash right up front; with 10 percent down, you'd have to come up with just $10,000. Beyond this simple arithmetic, however, a lower down payment may make sense if you would otherwise borrow at still-higher installment loan rates to buy, as an example, new furniture for your new home. You would also come out ahead if you were able to invest the difference between a high and low down payment in a high-yielding investment.

You may also find that a lower down payment actually increases your rate of return on the house as an investment. That's because the increase in value of the house is calculated in terms of money you've actually invested in the house. This is what real estate investors call leverage: using small amounts of money to make large amounts. It works like this: If you buy a $100,000 house with a $10,000 down payment, and later sell the house for $150,000, your profit, $50,000, is five times your cash investment. If you've bought the same house with a 20 percent down payment of $20,000, your profit on the

If you're a first-time home buyer, see if your state has a program to make home buying affordable. Many states do. As an example, in March 1993 New Jersey announced its "Welcome Home" program, financed by tax-free mortgage bonds sold by the state, to provide below-market fixed rate loans to first-time buyers. The loans are available through participating lenders, and have these features:

- Down payments as low as 3 percent, backed by private mortgage insurance to protect the lender.
- Subsidized interest rates at one to one-and-a-half percent below the market rate.
- Grants or loans of up to $10,000, depending on income level, family size, and location

sale is only two and one-half times your actual investment. (This is a simple example. In fact, the higher monthly payments on a low-down-payment loan would reduce the profit.)

The majority of first-time home buyers in the last few years have purchased houses with down payments of under 20 percent (see Table 11.2). If you want to do so, however, you may find it difficult. In the wake of rising numbers of mortgage defaults, as people in financial difficulty walk away from homes in which they have little invested, mortgage lenders and insurers are pulling back, tightening the rules and making fewer loans with 5 percent down payments.

Table 11.2: Average Down Payments

	1992	1991	1990	1976
Down payment as % of sales price				
Average down payment	21.4%	22.6%	23.3%	25.2%
First-time buyers	14.3	14.7	15.7	18.0
Repeat buyers	28.0	29.1	28.9	30.8
Down payment of:				
10% or less	42.2	39.0	40.3	26.9
20% or less	68.3	66.3	66.5	60.2
More than 50%	9.8	9.8	10.6	12.9

Source: The Chicago Title and Trust Family of Title Insurers.

A lower down payment, in any case, has disadvantages as well as advantages. Chief among them: You will pay a lot more each month to carry a larger mortgage loan; be sure you can manage these higher payments before you elect the lower down payment. Remember that the larger payments will go on month after month until the mortgage loan is paid up or until you sell the house; the difference over a period of years may be many thousands of dollars. Many mortgage lenders, moreover, charge a slightly higher interest rate for low-down-payment loans, thereby increasing your monthly costs still further.

SOURCES OF FUNDS FOR A DOWN PAYMENT

If you have enough cash on hand to choose between a low down payment and a higher one, be sure you consider all the factors (including the other costs involved in a home purchase; see Chapter 10) before you make your decision. If you have to scrape the money together for any sort of down payment, however, look at all the available sources of funds (but bear in mind that lenders are increasingly wary when borrowed money is the source of down payments):

Your Own Savings

Money you've saved and invested is still your primary source of funds for the purchase of a house. If you are looking forward to your first house (this is where life cycle planning proves its worth), you should be putting aside all

Q My husband and I have found a house we like for $75,000. We can manage the monthly mortgage payments, but we haven't saved enough to make the required down payment of 20 percent, or $15,000. Have you any suggestions?

A There are four possibilities:

1. VA-backed loans, which require no down payment at all, are available for eligible veterans.

2. FHA-backed loans, available through most lenders on homes costing a maximum of $124,875, typically require a down payment of 5 percent.

3. Pilot programs, under such names as Affordable Gold (backed by Freddie Mac) and the Community Home Buyer's 3/2 Option (backed by Fannie Mae), have minimum down payment requirements of 5 percent, with up to 2 percent of the required five coming in the form of a gift. Without such special programs, limited to home buyers earning up to 115 percent of the household median income for their areas, gifts toward down payments are looked at with suspicion by mortgage lenders.

4. Private mortgage insurance (PMI) may enable you to reduce your down payment to 5 or 10 percent. Private mortgage insurance requires an initial premium payment of 0.5 percent to 1.0 percent of the mortgage amount plus an additional monthly fee. PMI is available in every state; most lenders have master policies with one or more companies. If neither your lender nor your real estate agent can help you, however, write to the Mortgage Insurance Companies of America (MICA) for names of lenders in your area who offer private mortgage insurance; the address is 805 15th St., N.W., Washington, DC 20005.

Note: Don't confuse private mortgage insurance (see p. 300) with mortgage life insurance, which pays up your mortgage if you die. Private mortgage insurance protects the mortgage lender if for any reason you default on your mortgage payments.

surplus funds, in the highest-yielding investment possible, toward that down payment. Even with inflation eroding the value of savings, disciplined savings works: If you can save just $2,000 a year toward your house, by brown-bagging your lunch and seeing fewer movies if that's what it takes, you would have a $6,500 down payment in just three and a half years. That's if you put your money in the mattress and it earns no interest. If the money is invested at money market rates, you could have your $6,500 a lot sooner.

Life Insurance Loans

If you've been paying premiums on a whole life insurance policy, that policy has been amassing cash value. That cash value is yours. You may borrow it, under the terms of most older contracts, at an interest rate of 5 to 8 percent; the precise rate is spelled out in your insurance contract. (New policies typically have a variable loan rate, and may not be an inexpensive source of money, but if you have an older policy, the rate can't be changed.) Chapter 18 has the details on life insurance and life insurance loans. All you need to know here is that (1) an older life insurance policy is an excellent source of low-cost funds, and (2) a life insurance loan does not have to be repaid.

Relatives

First-time buyers often find it necessary, especially in today's housing market, to turn to parents for help with a down payment. Almost one in four first-time buyers relied on loans and gifts to make up the down payment in 1991, according to the National Association of Realtors, in a trend that has become so widespread that some economists refer to it as the new G.I. Bill: Generous In-laws.

Q With a combined income of $75,000 and a scheduled wedding date a year from now, my fiance and I think we can afford a $200,000 house. But we don't have enough saved for a 20 percent down payment of $40,000 and, if we put down less, monthly payments will be too high for comfort. Any suggestions?

A Put yourselves on a lean budget, temporarily, to boost your savings as much as possible. For example: Can one or both of you live with parents and save money on rent? Can one or both of you earn overtime? Find a temporary evening or weekend job to boost income? Can you agree to live on an austerity budget, cutting out restaurant meals and weekend trips and extra clothing, until your down payment fund is built? A bare-bones budget should be tolerable if you keep your eye on the target, and if you know it's temporary.

But generosity sometimes has strings attached. If you do need parental help:

■ Try to keep the arrangement businesslike. Borrow the money, and sign a note agreeing to the terms. Your parents may decide to forgo repayment when the time comes, but then again they may need the money and find it awkward to ask for it. This breeds resentment and ill-feelings. Put your agreement on paper.

■ Take them with you, if you can, while you look for a house. Otherwise they may be shocked and disapproving at the amount of house you are able to buy for the amount of money you are spending. They may be reading the newspapers about today's housing prices, but it won't hit home until they compare your first house with their own. Cushion the blow by taking them along so that they see what is actually available and what it costs.

■ Think about a formal "partnership mortgage," with relatives or with outside investors, to ease the financial burden of the down payment and/or the mortgage itself; see pp. 324.

If you are the parent of first-time home buyers, and want to help, keep the above advice in mind. In addition:

Q We would like to help our daughter and her husband buy a house, but we can't afford to make them a gift of several thousand dollars. Is there some way we can help them out and be sure of repayment, without setting the scene for a family squabble?

A Yes. If you use a "pledged account" you can reduce your daughter's cost of homeowning, while keeping your funds in your own name and earning a fair return on your investment. Here's how it works: You place your "contribution" in a certificate of deposit (CD) at the lending institution that grants your daughter's mortgage loan. You earn an agreed-upon rate of interest (if you take a lower rate of interest, your daughter's monthly mortgage payments will be lower) and, depending on your agreement with the lending institution, may be able to withdraw the interest on a periodic basis. At the end of the term, you can withdraw your funds from the CD, and your daughter's mortgage rate will be renegotiated. Or, if you wish to continue to help, you can roll over the CD and maintain the below-market interest rate on the mortgage. Talk to your daughter, her real estate broker, and her lender, to see if a pledged account can be arranged.

■ If you can afford it, think about an outright gift. You are allowed (at this writing; the law may change) to give $10,000 per person per year to as many people as you like, free of federal gift tax. This means that you and your spouse could give as much as $40,000 in one year to your child and his or her spouse. Don't do it if you may need the money. But if you are sure you won't need it and the money is going to go to the younger generation later on, anyway, think about doing it now.

■ Alternatively, you could cosign a loan. Be careful, here, though. Your own good credit will be on the line if, for any reason, your child defaults on the loan. Your child may be honorable, and have the best of intentions, but jobs can be lost and marriages can dissolve.

■ Look for a lender with an institutionalized arrangement for parental sharing of costs. Some banks, for example, will offer a mortgage loan for 100 percent of the purchase price if parents take a certificate of deposit for 20 percent of the purchase price and leave the money on deposit until the mortgage balance drops to 80 percent. Similarly, Merrill Lynch has a "Parent Power" program providing 100 percent mortgage loans where parents put up over 30 percent of the loan amount via securities in a Merrill Lynch brokerage account or a home equity line of credit. These alternatives can be costly, however, and it may be worthwhile having an accountant or financial planner review the arrangement before you make a commitment.

The Mortgage Loan

There was a time, not very long ago, when an individual in search of a mortgage loan would go to a financial institution (usually a savings and loan association or mutual savings bank, traditional mortgage lenders) and secure a commitment. It was a good idea to compare interest rates and provisions at different institutions, but the basic terms didn't differ very much.

This all changed within the last decade. In the face of enormous pressure generated by the higher-than-ever interest rates paid out to depositors in the early 1980s, the nation's financial institutions were forced to develop new mortgage forms to generate higher rates of return on their investments. Most of these new mortgage forms shift the risk of fluctuating interest rates to the buyer, making it all the more important to compare mortgage provisions. Even though the lower mortgage interest rates of the last few years have generated a return to the traditional fixed-rate mortgage, you still have to decide which kind of mortgage is best for you and where to apply for that mortgage. Don't think it doesn't matter. HSH Associates, a publisher of mortgage information, notes that in any given week, no matter where you live, the spread between the highest and lowest 30-year fixed rate is about 2 percent.

SOURCES OF MORTGAGE LOANS

Bear in mind, as you start your search for financing, that not every type of mortgage is available from every lender. Federally chartered institutions operate under one set of rules, state-chartered institutions under another. Then there are private mortgage lenders. Some are eager to make mortgage loans, others, especially when the cost of money is high, are not. You may have to do considerable shopping around to get a mortgage commitment at all—especially when high interest rates restrict the flow of funds, or you have had personal credit problems in the past (a mortgage broker may be useful; see p. 305). You certainly should shop around, at any time, to get the best possible terms. Look into these sources of funds:

- Savings and loan associations, savings banks, and (in the 17 states where they exist) mutual savings banks, traditionally the consumer's source of mortgage financing
- Credit unions, beginning to make mortgage loans in increasing numbers
- Commercial banks, moving more intensively into mortgage lending
- Mortgage bankers, no longer necessarily more expensive, and likely to have mortgage money available when others do not
- Insurance companies and mutual fund families have begun to offer some mortgage loans
- The seller of the house you want to buy (seller financing, at times when other mortgage money is unavailable or overpriced, is a popular option; see pp. 326).

QUALIFYING FOR A MORTGAGE

As a general rule of thumb, lenders want no more than 28 percent of your gross monthly income devoted to mortgage payments (including princi-

Q I know that mortgage rates and terms can be very different from place to place. Can I apply for a mortgage loan from any lender anywhere?

A Not really. With the exception of a few national lenders (and even those don't operate in every state), mortgage lending is really a local operation. And you can see why this is so, if you think about it. Every housing market is different, and lenders must deal with local real estate appraisers, title search companies, attorneys, etc. You should still shop for your mortgage loan, but I'm afraid you'll have to keep your shopping local.

pal and interest, taxes, insurance, plus condo fees, owners association fees, and mortgage insurance premiums, where applicable. Although the rules are occasionally bent, where a borrower has an excellent credit record, no more than 36 percent of gross monthly income should go toward mortgage payments plus all other monthly credit obligations (automobile loans, credit cards, and so on). See Table 11.3.

Want to bend the rules, with the blessing of your lender? Apply for an "energy efficient mortgage." Under these little-known plans, buyers of energy-efficient homes can obtain mortgages under more lenient qualifications (meaning more debt is permitted) and buyers of homes that are not energy-efficient can finance energy improvements. The mortgage loans are available in several varieties, under the sponsorship of the whole alphabet

Q We've found the perfect home but are worried about qualifying for a mortgage because we had credit problems a few years ago. Is there anything we can do to smooth the process?

A You might try applying through a mortgage broker rather than directly to a mortgage lender. Mortgage brokers deal with a large number of lenders, including those in other states, and can make it easier not only to find a mortgage but to find the right mortgage for your circumstances. Mortgage brokers can also be helpful for people who are too busy to shop around.

It shouldn't cost you any more to use a mortgage broker than to find a mortgage on your own. But be sure the broker you choose is qualified. Ask:

1. Are you licensed (if your state has a licensing procedure for brokers), or are you certified by the National Association of Mortgage Brokers?

2. How many lenders have you closed loans with over the past year? (Good brokers represent at least 10 lenders.)

3. If an application fee is required, under what circumstances will it be refunded? (An application fee should be $300 or less.)

4. How long will the advertised interest rate be in effect? (If you arrange for the rate to be locked in for a specified period, be sure it is the lender—not the broker—who guarantees the rate.)

soup of federal housing agencies: FHA (Federal Housing Administration), VA (Department of Veterans Affairs), Fannie Mae (Federal National Mortgage Association), and Freddie Mac (Federal Home Loan Mortgage Corporation). The rules differ, and there can be considerable red tape, but an energy efficient mortgage may be an option for first-time home buyers.

Table 11.3: How Much You Can Spend on Housing and Meet Lender Requirements

Gross annual income	Monthly mortgage payment (at 28%)	Monthly credit obligation (at 36%)
$ 20,000	$ 467	$ 600
30,000	700	900
40,000	933	1,200
50,000	1,167	1,500
60,000	1,400	1,800
70,000	1,633	2,100
80,000	1,867	2,400
90,000	2,100	2,700
100,000	2,333	3,000
130,000	3,033	3,900
150,000	3,500	4,500
200,000	4,667	6,000

Source: Federal National Mortgage Association.

MORTGAGE CALCULATIONS

If you find mortgage payments confusing, you're not alone. But the arithmetic is simpler than it may seem. Each monthly mortgage payment consists of two parts: (1) the interest, which is what you pay the lender to borrow the money, and (2) the principal, which is the portion of the loan itself you are paying back. With your principal payment, you are increasing the portion of the house you own and decreasing the portion the lender owns. But it is the interest payment that is the key to understanding how most mortgages work.

The interest portion of your monthly payment is the monthly interest rate on your loan times the outstanding balance of the loan. The monthly interest rate is simply the annual interest rate divided by 12. If you had a mortgage loan with an interest rate of 12 percent, your monthly rate would be 1 percent. It's harder to calculate the decimals with less easily divisible interest rates, but the point to remember is that whatever the interest rate on your mortgage loan, you are paying far more interest in the early months and years and very little toward principal, with the balance reversed toward the end of the loan.

As an example, supplied by the National Association of Home Builders, suppose you have a $100,000, 30-year fixed-rate loan at 8 percent. Your monthly payment would be $733.76. This payment remains the same for 30 years, but the portions you pay toward principal and interest change each month. In the very first month, you owe the lender an interest payment of $666.67. The remaining $67.10 goes toward reducing your loan balance, making it $99,932.90. Your second payment consists of $666.22 in interest and $67.55 in principal, reducing your loan balance to $99,865.35.

The same thing happens throughout the life of the mortgage loan (whether you have a fixed-rate or an adjustable-rate mortgage (ARM), although it's a lot harder to be sure lender calculations on an ARM are correct; see p. 320) until the final payment, consisting almost entirely of a contribution to principal, is enough to pay off the loan. The final payment of this 30-year mortgage, in fact, consists of $4.86 in interest and $728.91 in principal. Because the initial payments go almost entirely toward interest, most of your mortgage costs at the outset are tax-deductible. Later, as the loan matures, you have less tax deduction but more equity in the house.

Points, often calculated as part of closing costs (see p. 288), are either separate fees or prepaid interest charges that raise the effective yield to the lender without raising the stated interest rate on the loan. If you pay $2,000 (two points) in borrowing $100,000, you are really borrowing $98,000—but

---

Applying for a mortgage? You can speed the process by bringing:

■ Names, addresses, and telephone numbers of current and prior employers, for the past two years

■ W-2 forms for the last two years, and pay stubs for the current year, to document income

■ Tax returns for the last two years (especially important if you are self-employed)

■ Verification of other income (if it will be needed to qualify for the mortgage), including Social Security, pension, interest and dividends, rental income, alimony, etc.

■ Bank account numbers and location of account(s)

■ Credit card and installment loan information: the creditor's name and address, your account number, and the amount of both the outstanding balance and your monthly payment

■ The purchase offer (earnest money agreement) for the house you are buying

Table 11.4: Monthly Mortgage Payments

Monthly mortgage payments (principal and interest) for a 30-year fixed-rate mortgage at different interest rates and loan amounts.

Interest Rate	Loan Amount								
	$50,000	$60,000	$70,000	$80,000	$90,000	$100,000	$120,000	$140,000
6%	$300	$360	$420	$480	$540	$600	$719	$839
7%	$333	$399	$466	$532	$599	$665	$798	$931
8%	$367	$440	$514	$587	$660	$734	$881	$1,027
9%	$402	$483	$563	$644	$724	$805	$966	$1,126
10%	$439	$527	$614	$702	$790	$878	$1,053	$1,229
11%	$476	$571	$667	$762	$857	$952	$1,143	$1,333
12%	$514	$617	$720	$823	$926	$1,029	$1,234	$1,440
13%	$553	$664	$774	$885	$996	$1,106	$1,327	$1,549
14%	$592	$711	$829	$948	$1,066	$1,185	$1,422	$1,659
15%	$632	$759	$885	$1,012	$1,138	$1,264	$1,517	$1,770

Source: National Association of Home Builders.

you'll pay back the full $100,000 face amount of the loan plus interest. Another way of looking at it is that each point is equivalent to 1/8 of a percent in interest.

You may be offered a choice between, for example, a mortgage loan at 7.5 percent with three points and one at 7.75 percent with one point. Which should you take? The answer depends on how long you will live in your home. The longer you intend to stay, the less impact points will have.

Note: Points paid on a first mortgage (other than prepaid interest) are deductible in the year you take out the loan. Prepaid interest on a first mortgage and all points paid on a refinancing must generally be deducted over the life of the loan.

Fixed-Rate Mortgages

Fixed-term, fixed-rate mortgages are the traditional mortgage loans, the loans that made housing available for generations of Americans and that have

Q I received notice that my mortgage has been transferred and payments are to be sent to a different company. Does this sound legitimate?

A Mortgages are frequently sold or transferred from one servicing company to another. But you are right to be cautious because there have been instances of fraud, where homeowners have been told to send payments elsewhere when no transfer had actually taken place.

Don't rely on a letter from a new company. Insist on notification from your original lender. Under federal legislation, on mortgages issued after March 1991, lenders must notify you in writing at least 15 days in advance of a transfer. On mortgages issued before then, if you don't get an official letter from your original lender, be sure to ask for one before sending payments elsewhere.

Note: After a transfer of mortgage servicing companies, there is a 60-day grace period during which you cannot be charged a late fee if you mistakenly send your mortgage payment to the old mortgage servicer instead of the new one. As part of the same rule, the new servicing company cannot report such a late payment to a credit bureau.

made housing such a rich investment. With a fixed term (often 30 years, although 15-year terms are increasingly popular) and a fixed interest rate (established when the contract is written, then remaining stable for the length of the mortgage), these mortgages provide budgetary stability for homeowners. They also act as a cushion against inflation and against the possibility of rising interest rates. When interest rates drop, conversely, holders of higher-rate fixed-rate mortgages can wind up paying more than necessary—unless they go to the trouble and expense of refinancing.

When interest rates were high, fixed rate mortgage loans became increasingly difficult to secure, for one very simple reason: As lending institutions had to pay ever higher interest rates to entice depositors (thereby making money available for mortgages), they became ever more reluctant to commit investment dollars to investments with a rate of return locked in place for many years. (Commitments to old single-digit mortgages, in fact, were largely responsible for the plight of many savings institutions in the double-digit 1980s.) When mortgage rates reached double digits, adjustable-rate mortgages (see p. 316) became more popular. Today, with lower interest rates, the pendulum has swung back. Fixed-rate mortgages accounted for 70 percent of all mortgages issued in 1992.

FIXED-RATE TERMS

When you take a fixed-rate mortgage you agree to pay the same amount toward the mortgage principal and interest each month; if interest rates go up after you take the mortgage, you're ahead of the game. When interest rates are

Q We've secured a good mortgage rate, but are worried about what may happen to interest rates while the loan is being processed. Would it be a good idea to take a mortgage lock-in?

A A lock-in (also called a rate-lock or a rate commitment) is a lender's promise to hold a certain interest rate (and sometimes a specified number of points) for a specified period of time. A lock-in can protect you against rising rates. But there is often a fee associated with a lock-in, and that fee may or may not be refundable if you withdraw your application, if your credit is denied, or if you do not close the loan. The fee may be a flat fee, a percentage of the mortgage amount, or a fraction of a percentage point added to the rate you lock in. Be sure to ask if there is a fee and how much it is, how long the lock-in will apply, and what happens if interest rates drop in the meantime. You might also ask if you can let your interest rate float for a while, and then lock it in; this can be advantageous if interest rates are dropping but not, obviously, if they are likely to rise.

low, as they have been for the last few years, 30-year fixed-rate mortgages are the best loans for home buyers who plan to remain in the house for more than six or seven years.

With a fixed-rate mortgage loan, the lender agrees that the rate of interest and hence the monthly payments will remain the same over the life of the loan; if rates subsequently fall, the lender benefits. It's a gamble (although, if interest rates fall sufficiently, you can always refinance your loan; see p. 329). But the biggest single benefit that the fixed-rate mortgage loan offers to the home buyer is its predictability. With this mortgage, you can budget your biggest housing expense and know exactly where you stand.

Fifteen-Year Mortgages

If you want to dramatically reduce the amount of interest you pay over the life of your mortgage loan, while building your equity much faster, you may want to consider one of the increasingly popular 15-year mortgages. Monthly payments are higher, but more of each payment goes toward reducing the principal (see Table 11.5). In the example we used earlier, of a $100,000 mortgage at 8 percent, the monthly payment on a 15-year loan would be $927.01 (instead of $733.76 on a 30-year loan). But a much larger portion ($302.01 instead of $67.10) goes directly toward reducing the principal. As the principal is paid down, subsequent interest payments are smaller and smaller. With a mortgage rate of 8 percent, a borrower with a 15-year loan has $33,231 in equity at the end of five years; a neighbor with a 30-year loan will have just $7,523 in equity at the end of the same five years.

Table 11.5: Interest and Principal Paid on Mortgages

The following data show the interest and principal paid over seven years on a $100,000 mortgage amortized over 30, 20, and 15 years.

	30 years at 8%	20 years at 7⅞%	15 years at 7½%
Monthly Payment	$734	$829	$927
Interest Paid in 7 Years	$54,114	$50,368	$44,638
Principal Paid in 7 Years	$7,523	$19,241	$33,231

Source: Federal Home Loan Mortgage Corporation.

But don't leap into a 15-year mortgage. Interest savings may be advertised as being many thousands of dollars over the life of the loan. And they are. But those interest savings have to be measured against two other factors: (1) your tax bracket, because the higher your bracket the more you have to gain from making larger interest payments and the less you have to gain from reducing those payments, and (2) the amount of investment income you'll forgo by putting money into your mortgage instead of into another investment.

The 15-year mortgage (or its cousin, the 20-year mortgage) may still be right for you, if (1) you can meet the higher monthly payments (for some people, this may mean buying a less expensive home), (2) you won't invest elsewhere and your mortgage is a form of forced savings, (3) you want to reduce your debt load, or (4) you want to pay off your mortgage before retirement or before, for example, a child starts college.

If you are intrigued by the idea of a short-term mortgage, but already have a mortgage, take heart. It may be worth refinancing, if the difference in interest rates is significant; see p. 329.

Biweekly Mortgages

With this variation of the fixed-rate mortgage loan, you make a mortgage payment every two weeks—typically, to avoid lapses, in the form of an automatic transfer from your bank account. By making the equivalent of one extra monthly payment each year, you can pay off your loan in about 20 years instead of 30.

The advantage of a biweekly payment schedule, in addition to more rapid payoff, may be a slightly lower interest rate. The disadvantage may lie in locking yourself into these extra payments. As noted below, you may prefer the flexibility of taking a 30-year loan and prepaying additional amounts as money becomes available.

Prepaying a Mortgage

Instead of taking either a 15-year or a biweekly mortgage loan, with their contractual commitment to more rapid payoff, you can accomplish much

Q We have three months to go on our 30-year mortgage. What will happen when it's paid off? What kind of documentation should we expect from our lender?

A You should receive the original mortgage note, marked "paid," and a "satisfaction" of the mortgage. Instead of the satisfaction, if you live in a state where deeds of trust are used, you can expect a release of the deed of trust. You should also receive an accounting from the lender for any escrow balances.

If the lender has not recorded the mortgage satisfaction or release with your county recorder of deeds, you should see that this is done. And, if the lender has been paying taxes and homeowners insurance premiums on your behalf, you'll be taking over these obligations and should make sure the bills are sent directly to you from now on.

the same thing by making extra payments toward principal. Making just one extra monthly payment a year can finish up a 30-year mortgage in under 22 years. The advantage of prepaying, in fact, is that you can put in varying amounts at varying intervals, as your pocketbook permits—so long as you meet your obligatory monthly mortgage payments. Those you can never skip—even if you've made extra payments along the way.

Note: Many states don't permit prepayment penalties but, before you apply extra payments to your mortgage principal, check with your lender to be sure it's okay.

Balloon Mortgages

These loans are usually based on 30-year amortization tables but are due and payable after a preset period of either five or seven years. When the balloon comes due, you have the choice of refinancing the mortgage or paying it off. These mortgages make the most sense if you plan to sell your house and move within a few years. If you wind up staying, you run the risk of refinancing at higher rates or of losing your house.

Two-Step or Balloon Reset Mortgages

This cross between a convertible adjustable loan (see p. 319) and a balloon loan involves less risk than pure balloon mortgages and is also appropriate if you think you'll move within a few years. Structured as 30-year loans, these mortgage loans start out at one interest rate, then adjust to a new rate after either five or seven years. There are no conversion fees or refinancing costs, there is usually a cap of 6 percent on how much the interest rate can rise, and it will rise only once. Bear in mind, though, that these mortgages start at a rate slightly lower than the rate on a 30-year fixed-rate mortgage but change, after the adjustment, to a rate that is higher than the prevailing rate on a 30-year fixed-rate loan. If interest rates have risen in the meantime, you could wind up with much higher monthly payments and an advanced case of sticker shock.

Two-One Buydowns

This is another variation that surfaces when mortgage rates start to rise. Here a lender gives you a mortgage loan with an interest rate initially discounted below current rates. The rate will go up at the end of the first year and again at the end of the second year, leaving you paying the next 28 years at a rate slightly higher than the current market rate. For example, if mortgage interest rates were at 8 percent and you started with a discounted rate of $6\frac{1}{2}$ percent, you would pay $7\frac{1}{2}$ percent in the second year and $8\frac{1}{2}$ percent for the balance of the loan. It makes it easier to get your foot in the door, to qualify for a loan, but you pay for it longer. Again, all of these arrangements make more sense if you plan to move within a few years.

FHA and VA Mortgages

Government-backed FHA and VA mortgages are essentially like conventional mortgages, with these exceptions:

- There is a ceiling on the amount of an FHA mortgage loan (in 1992 it was $124,875 on a one-family house), which makes these loans particularly appropriate for people buying a starter house.

Q I earn $23,000 a year and my husband earns $29,000. We made a bid on a $73,000 house and were turned down for a mortgage on the basis of "insufficient income." I suspect the bank just didn't want to count my income. Is there anything I can do?

A If you are right, you may have a complaint under the Equal Credit Opportunity Act (ECOA), a federal law which prohibits discrimination against an applicant for credit on the basis of sex, marital status, race, color, religion, national origin, or age. You should know that:

- You can't be refused credit just because you're a woman ... or single, or married, separated, divorced, or widowed.

- You can't be refused credit because a creditor won't count income you receive regularly from alimony or child support.

- You can't be discouraged from applying for a mortgage loan.

- You can't be offered a loan on terms different from those offered to other people. You can't be asked for a 20 percent down payment, for instance, when others are offered mortgages with a 10 percent down payment.

- Your income, if you are a married woman, must be counted in full, even if you work part time (but you should be prepared to show that your income is reliable). The lender, moreover, may not ask you about birth-control methods and/or childbearing plans.

ECOA requires the lender to notify you about the status of your loan within 30 days after your application is complete. It also requires you to be given a specific reason if your loan is denied. If you are not satisfied with the reason, you should have an opportunity to challenge the lender and make your case again. And, if you are convinced you are the victim of discrimination, you may file a complaint.

■ Lower down payments (in some instances, on VA mortgages, no down payment) are required.

■ Interest rates are often lower than prevailing rates, but points may be added by the lender to raise the actual rate.

■ There is no prepayment penalty so, if mortgage rates drop, you can refinance the mortgage at a lower rate (although you may have to pay additional closing costs if you refinance).

One drawback to FHA and VA mortgages is the extensive paperwork they require, which makes lenders reluctant to issue them, the mortgages themselves slow to obtain, and sellers often unwilling to wait.

Table 11.6 shows monthly mortgage payments at various interest rates under a fixed-payment loan. When interest rates are high, as shown, you may not be able to afford much house for your money—especially since you must also manage monthly outlays for taxes, insurance, heat, utilities, and maintenance. When house prices are also high, you may be squeezed out of the market altogether ... unless one of the mortgage forms developed in the last era of double-digit interest rates makes a return appearance.

Table 11.6: Monthly Mortgage Payments and the Income Needed to Qualify

Interest rate	Monthly payment	Minimum annual income
6%	$ 570	$27,340
7%	632	30,338
8%	697	33,460
9%	764	36,691
10%	834	40,017
11%	905	43,426
12%	977	46,905
13%	1,051	50,443
14%	1,126	54,030

In 1993, the average home buyer borrowed $95,000. With interest rates lower than they had been in years, many more borrowers could qualify. Monthly payments on a $95,000 30-year mortgage at 8 percent are $697, requiring an annual income of $33,460. The same mortgage at 11 percent costs $905 a month and requires an annual income of $43,426.

Source: National Association of Home Builders Economics Division.

When You Comparison-Shop for a Mortgage Loan, Find Out:

■ What additional fees or charges must you pay? These may include charges for appraisal, credit report, photographs, various statements or papers, or an origination fee or service charge.

■ Is there a late-payment charge? How late may your payment be before the charge is imposed?

Note: When payment is due the first of the month, you may be allowed until the fifteenth to pay without a late charge. But don't be deceived. Payments after the first may still show up on your credit record as late payments.

■ If you wish to pay off the loan early, must you pay a prepayment penalty? Does this apply when you move and sell the house?

■ Will the lender allow the loan to be assumed by someone else (see p. 326)? At what interest rate? Will there be an assumption fee?

■ Will you be required to pay into a special escrow account from which the lender will pay your property taxes and your homeowners insurance premiums? If so, how large a deposit will be required at the closing? Will interest be paid on the account?

Adjustable-Rate Mortgages

It hasn't been very long since interest rates exhibited wild volatility, reaching unprecedented highs in the early 1980s. When interest rates shoot skyward, lending institutions suffer enormously from being locked into long-term fixed-rate mortgage loans written when rates were low. During the high-interest-rate years of the late 1970s and early 1980s many mortgage lenders, fearing still-higher rates yet to come, were understandably reluctant to issue

Q After living together for three years, we would like to buy a house. We talked to a real estate agent, who said we should conceal our unmarried status in applying for a mortgage. We see no reason to lie. What do you think?

A Don't lie. Not only is the purchase of real estate by unmarried live-togethers accepted almost everywhere, you may even find it easier to secure a mortgage. Some lenders will be delighted to find buyers with two incomes and separate credit identities.

fixed-rate mortgage loans. Their answer: adjustable-rate mortgages (ARMS) which share the risk of fluctuating interest rates between lender and borrower. Although interest rates have subsided since the heady days of 1982, and increasing numbers of fixed-rate mortgages are currently being issued, adjustable-rate mortgages still suit some home buyers' needs.

Adjustable-rate mortgages are generally offered at lower initial interest rates than fixed-rate mortgages, but that rate, by definition, is not guaranteed for the life of the mortgage. It can and will change, according to the adjustment period specified in your contract, as prevailing interest rates change. As you compare mortgage loans, consider the following factors:

The Index

The index will be the keystone of your mortgage interest rate, and it's very important to ask which index will be used, how often it will change, how it has behaved in the past, and where it is published. Possibilities (although almost any public index of interest rates may be used) include:

- The Federal Home Loan Bank Board's (FHLBB) "cost-of-funds" rate
- The 3-month or 6-month Treasury bill rate
- The yield on Treasury securities maturing in one, three, or five years

Note: Do not accept an index pegged to the individual institution's cost of borrowing or a regional cost of borrowing.

Which index you choose can make a considerable difference. The Consumer Federation of America, in a study of what would have happened under existing interest rates if an adjustable mortgage had been issued in 1976, found that payments on a $60,000 mortgage starting at an initial rate of 9 percent would have risen by 1981 by a minimum of $117 a month (when tied to the FHLBB's cost-of-funds rate) to a maximum of $389 a month (when tied to the 3-month T-bill rate).

It's not necessarily true, of course, that one index will always lead to smaller increases and another to larger ones—although you should ask the lender to show you some recent examples of how each index has moved. It depends on both the volatility of the index and the state of the economy. Some indexes reflect short-term changes in interest rates; others reflect longer-term trends. Short-term indexes usually fluctuate more sharply than longer-term indexes, so mortgage payments may change dramatically. Longer-term interest rates and indexes tend to be more gradual in their movements, but also tend to be higher than the short-term indicators. There's a trade-off between the volatility of interest and payment levels and locking in payments for a longer period at possibly higher levels. You will have to make the choice.

Note: Given the inaccuracy of many adjustable mortgage calculations (see p. 320), it's important to have a mortgage tied to a frequently published index. You may still find the calculations complicated, but at least you'll be able to track the basic index.

The Adjustment Period

The interval at which rate adjustments will be made is also significant. In theory, under an ARM, payments could change every month. In practical terms most ARMs are written with an adjustment period of one year, three years, or five years.

Think about your income potential, about the frequency with which you can reasonably expect your income to increase, before you agree to frequent unlimited changes. Remember, if the payments increase beyond your capacity to meet them, you could run the risk of default. But think, too, about the length of time you anticipate living in the house. If this is your "starter" house and you expect to move on in a few years, it might be worth securing an adjustment period long enough to lock in your payments for those few years—even if you have to pay a slightly higher rate of interest to do so. It depends, of course, on what you think interest rates will do.

The Margin

The margin, which is usually fixed for the life of the loan, is added to the index rate by the lender to determine the interest rate on the loan. Different lenders use different margins (the range, in early 1993, was typically 2.5 to 3.25), and these will determine your payments. On a $65,000 loan when the index is at 10 percent, for example, a 2 percent margin will produce an interest rate of 12 percent and a monthly payment of $668.60; a 3 percent margin will produce an interest rate of 13 percent and a monthly payment of $719.03. It's just as important to check on the margin as on the index.

Caps

Interest-rate caps, currently built into ARMs by most lenders, reduce the risk of major fluctuations in your monthly payments and are a major consumer safeguard. An **interest-rate cap** may limit the interest-rate increase from one adjustment period to the next, it may limit the interest-rate increase over the life of the loan, or it may do both. Typical caps are 2 percent per adjustment period and 5 or 6 percent over the life of the loan.

Payment caps limit the amount of payment increase at each adjustment to a percentage of the previous payment; they have the disadvantage of leading to potential negative amortization—a situation in which the caps do not permit monthly payments to be large enough to pay all of the interest that is due. When this happens, the interest shortfall is added to the debt and interest may be charged on that amount, so that you may owe the lender more later in the loan term than you did at the outset. Payment caps have pretty much fallen out of favor and are currently found only on monthly adjustables and, for the most part, only on the West Coast.

Conversion Features

Many adjustable-rate mortgages permit you to convert to a fixed-rate mortgage at a specified time, often between the second and fifth years of the loan. This can permit you to lock in a lower-rate fixed-rate mortgage if rates drop. But weigh the feature carefully. It may cost you slightly more in interest. And, if you have to pay a higher rate of interest on a fixed-rate mortgage obtained through conversion as well as a fee of several hundred dollars to exercise the conversion privilege, you may come out ahead by refinancing your adjustable to a fixed-rate mortgage instead. Before you refinance and pay closing costs, though, think about how long you will stay in the house. And see p. 329 for more information on refinancing.

Should You Take an ARM?

There is little doubt that the fixed-rate, fixed-payment mortgage offers stability that the ARM does not. But the ARM does have some advantages when interest rates are high. When they are low, as they have been recently, ARMs have a lot less to offer.

In the long run, whether an adjustable mortgage loan turns out to be a good buy or a bad one depends on (1) how soon you plan to sell your house and move, (2) whether interest rates are on their way up or down when you obtain your loan, and (3) what happens to interest rates over the life of your mortgage. With an adjustable mortgage loan, you have to be a bit of a gambler.

Questions to Ask Before You Take an ARM

- Can you qualify? Although you need less income to qualify for a lower interest-rate mortgage, and adjustables have lower rates, it can be tougher to qualify for an adjustable rate mortgage because lenders may want to see income sufficient to cover a rise in interest rates and an increase in monthly payments.
- What index will be used to adjust the payments? Ask the lender for a table showing movements in that index over several years, to give you an idea of how your payments might change.
- What is the initial mortgage rate? Does it reflect a special discount? Some initial discount rates are lower than the sum of the index and the margin, so that the rate may rise at the first adjustment period even if the index remains the same. If this is the case, you may be in for "payment shock" when your payments increase sharply. Don't take this kind of loan without thinking about your ability to make payments in the future.
- How often will the mortgage be adjusted? The shorter the adjustment period, the more you and the lender share the risk of fluctuating rates; in return for your sharing that risk, you may have a lower interest rate on a shorter adjustment period. The longer the adjustment period, the better you will be able to plan ahead.

■ Which elements of the loan can be adjusted? The lender should give you a full explanation of how interest rates, payments, the loan balance, and the term to maturity may be adjusted and how adjusting one element may affect the others.

■ Is the loan assumable, so that you can pass it on to a qualified buyer when you are ready to sell? Is it convertible, so that you can change it to a fixed-rate loan at designated times?

■ What is the margin? Are there payment or interest-rate caps? Can negative amortization take place? Are there prepayment penalties?

MAKING A DECISION

As you decide which mortgage form is right for you, these are some of the factors to weigh:

■ Your age and your income potential. If you are in your twenties, with relatively low current income but great expectations, an ARM with a

---

Q My adjustable-rate mortgage has just been adjusted for the first time, and I'm baffled by the new payment figure. How can I determine if the lender is correct?

A It isn't easy, especially since regulators find that many lenders have been making mistakes with the complex calculations. First, check the published index figure and be sure the lender used the correct date. Add on the lender's margin, and be sure it's rounded in accordance with the terms of the contract; an eighth of a percentage point can make a substantial difference over 30 years. Then, and this is important, ask a senior lending officer for a full explanation.

If you have trouble doing all this—and it wouldn't be at all surprising if you did—consider using one of the firms that have sprung up to assist homeowners with these complex calculations. For a fee (be sure to ask how much it is, and exactly what the firm will do in return), one of these auditing services may be able to help:

■ Consumer Loan Advocates   800-767-2768 or (708)615-0054
■ LoanChek   800-477-6166 or (619)455-7570
■ Loantech   800-888-6781 or (301)330-0777
■ Mortgage Monitor   800-283-4887 or (203)853-3636

Worksheet 11.1: Mortgage Checklist

Ask your lender to help fill out this checklist.

Basic Features for Comparison	Mortgage Amount	
	Mortgage A	Mortgage B
Fixed-rate annual percentage rate (The cost of your credit as a yearly rate which includes both interest and other charges)	_____%	_____%
ARM annual percentage rate	_____%	_____%
Adjustment period	_____	_____
Index used and current rate	_____%	_____%
Margin	_____%	_____%
Initial payment without discount	$_____	$_____
Initial payment with discount (if any)	$_____	$_____
How long will discount last?	_____	_____
Interest rate caps: periodic	_____%	_____%
overall	_____%	_____%
Payment caps	_____%	_____%
Negative amortization	_____	_____
Convertability or prepayment privilege	_____	_____
Initial fees and charges	$_____	$_____

Monthly Payment Amounts

What will my monthly payment be after 12 months if the index rate:

stays the same	$_____	$_____
goes up 2%	$_____	$_____
goes down 2%	$_____	$_____

What will my monthly payments be after three years if the index rate:

stays the same	$_____	$_____
goes up 2% per year	$_____	$_____
goes down 2% per year	$_____	$_____

Take into account any caps on your mortgage and remember it may run 30 years.

Source: Federal Reserve Board/Federal Home Loan Bank Board.

low introductory rate might be right for you. If you're in your fifties or sixties, with fixed-income years looming ahead, you might prefer a short-term fixed-rate mortgage even if it costs a bit more.

■ The number of years you will stay in the house. If you'll be there only a short time, again, it could be preferable to take an adjustable-rate mortgage. But ARMs are typically written with one-year adjustment periods these days and you might be better off, in this case, with a balloon or two-step loan. If you're planning to stay for the foreseeable future, however, and are worried about the long-range prospects for interest rates, you might try to secure a fixed-rate mortgage with its guarantee of stability.

■ Your willingness to accept risk. Are you a gambler? Or does uncertainty make you nervous? If you think interest rates will stay level or come down, and are willing to gamble on that assumption, you might want to take your chances with an adjustable-rate mortgage. If the inability to budget definite mortgage payments from year to year will give you sleepless nights, you might pay a bit more to get a fixed-rate mortgage.

If you take an adjustable-rate mortgage and interest rates rise, housing may consume more and more of your income. If interest rates come down, however, you could be better off with an ARM than with the fixed-rate variety (especially if you got stuck with a fixed-rate loan at an interest peak). It's not an easy decision, since no authorities, least of all economists, agree on the direction interest rates will take.

Evaluate your own needs and your own temperament, then shop around in your community. Remember, as you shop, that financial institutions are

---

Q We got a refund on our adjustable-rate mortgage last year after finding that we had been overcharged for several years. Our lender tells us we'll owe taxes on this refund. Is this so?

A Yes. If you deducted the mortgage interest in the year in which you paid it, then the refund of excess interest is considered taxable income. Whether you take it in cash or apply it to your mortgage, you must report it on this year's federal income tax return.

Note: If you were *undercharged* by the lender (it does happen, more often than you might think), or if you were overcharged but did not claim a mortgage interest deduction in prior years, you don't need to do anything.

governed by a variety of federal and state regulatory agencies; some permit one mortgage form, some another. Remember, too, that rates may vary widely within the same community. Unless you enjoy throwing money away, it's imperative to shop around.

Alternative Mortgage Forms

Some of the wild-and-woolly mortgage variations of the 1980s have gone the way of the dodo bird. Most mortgages these days, as we've seen, are of the plain-vanilla fixed-rate variety. Second in popularity are balloon and two-step mortgages. At the bottom of the popularity list, at least for now, are adjustables.

But it might not be a bad idea to keep the following mortgage forms in mind. Some lenders are offering them now. More will undoubtedly do so when interest rates, and hence the mortgage climate, change.

THE GRADUATED PAYMENT MORTGAGE (GPM)

The GPM is a fixed-rate mortgage (an adjustable version is also some-times offered) designed for home buyers who expect their incomes to rise. It has monthly mortgage payments which start low, then rise gradually over a period of five to ten years before leveling off for the rest of the mortgage period. Payments change, in other words, but you know in advance exactly when and how they are going to change.

The lower initial payments enable you to qualify for a GPM with less income than you would need for a comparable level-payment loan. Put another way, you can buy more house for your money. This is attractive to young home buyers with low salaries and high potential.

But there are some drawbacks. Your income may not rise as expected, so that increased payments are difficult to meet. Or one of your two incomes may turn out to be less stable than expected. Even if incomes continue and increase, you'll pay out considerably more over the life of the loan (if you stay in the house that long) than you would with a traditional fixed-rate mortgage. If you sell early, on the other hand, you may not have much equity, maybe not even enough to make a down payment on another house. If you sell early enough, you may even owe the lender additional interest because of negative amortization.

THE GROWING EQUITY MORTGAGE (GEM)

Sometimes called the **Rapid Payoff Mortgage,** this is a fixed-rate mort-gage with payments that change over time; since the schedule is fixed in advance, there is no uncertainty about how they will change. The major differ-ence between the GEM and the GPM is that you start paying the same amount as you would for a level-payment fixed-rate mortgage, with increases in payments used entirely to reduce the principal. The increases in payments enable you to pay off a 30-year mortgage in 15 to 20 years. A more popular substitute these days is the biweekly mortgage, or simply making additional periodic payments to principal on a 30-year fixed rate mortgage.

PARTNERSHIP MORTGAGES

High homeownership costs (whether high in fact or high in terms of a potential purchaser's pocketbook) can be made manageable if someone else shares the burden. That someone else can be a third party, such as a lender or an outside investor. Or it might be (and more often is) a family member. That third party shares in the cost of buying the house, in its potential appreciation and, meanwhile, in the tax benefits of ownership.

But partnership mortgages are extremely complex and should not be undertaken without sound legal advice and a carefully drawn agreement. That agreement should specify the ownership share and form of ownership ("tenants in common" is the usual approach), the terms of the rental agreement (the occupants must pay a "fair market rent" for their share of the property or the Internal Revenue Service may disallow tax deductions), when the arrangement will end in the form of sale or refinancing (seven years is typical, with a provision to extend the agreement by mutual consent), how profits will be split at that point, and what happens, meanwhile, if either partner defaults. All of these points apply whether the investor/owner is an outside investor or a relative. But a relative has an interest, other than financial, in the occupant-owner. An outsider does not. If you enter into a partnership mortgage with an outsider you should ask some additional questions:

■ What happens if you, the home buyer, want to make improvements in your home and the investor does not agree? Some shared mortgages give the investor veto power over home improvements, and you might wind up living with kitchen cabinets you don't like and without the patio you want.
■ What happens if the house fails to appreciate in value, or to appreciate very much? Will whatever profit there is be shared equally? Or will either the house's occupant or the investor come out with a loss?
■ What happens if the investor needs to sell? Can his share of the property be sold without forcing the house's occupant to sell as well?

Look at all aspects of equity sharing very carefully, and get competent advice, preferably from an experienced real estate attorney who has handled this kind of arrangement before.

LAND LEASING

Another way of reducing housing costs involves separating the house and the land. With a land-leasing arrangement, you buy the house alone and pay annual rental on the land. This reduces your down payment by as much as

25 percent, as well as your monthly carrying costs. If a house with its land is priced at $95,000, the house alone might be priced at $75,900. A down payment on house plus land, at 10 percent, would be $9,500, while a down payment on the house alone would be $7,590.

In addition to monthly mortgage costs on the house, however, you would have to pay monthly lease charges on the land. The total may be less

Q We are taking on a massive mortgage commitment with our new house, and I'm concerned about what will happen to my family if anything happens to me. I was all set to take out a **mortgage insurance policy** when I heard that there's more than one kind. What are the differences and which is the type I should buy?

A Mortgage insurance is essentially a type of decreasing term insurance; you pay the same amount in premiums each year but the amount of the policy decreases along with the mortgage. You can buy this kind of coverage in three ways: via a group mortgage policy issued by your lender, via an individual mortgage policy you take on your own, or via a regular decreasing term policy. The first two would be tied to the amount of your mortgage; the last could be taken out in any amount you choose.

Before you buy any policy, however, consider these facts:

■ It's more important to have adequate life insurance, to cover all your family's needs, than to buy mortgage insurance alone. Even with the mortgage paid off, your survivor would still have to pay taxes, utility bills, and all the other costs of running a household.

■ On a group policy issued by a lender, the lender is usually the beneficiary. Should you die, the mortgage would be paid off. But what if your survivor would prefer to continue making mortgage payments and use insurance money for other costs of living? An individual mortgage policy or regular decreasing term would permit that choice.

Note: Don't confuse mortgage life insurance with the type of mortgage insurance (**private mortgage insurance,** or PMI) you may be required to take on a low down payment mortgage loan; the latter protects the lender in the event you default on the mortgage and is required because, with a low down payment, you have little equity and therefore less incentive to continue making payments.

than a mortgage on both house and land, but be wary: Lease charges usually start out low, so that the total monthly payments are lower, at the beginning, than they would be with a conventional mortgage, but the rental portion (often tied in with an option to buy) often has an escalation feature. If the rate is tied to inflation, you could find rapidly rising costs. Ground rents, moreover, unlike mortgage interest payments, are not tax-deductible.

Land leasing is still relatively rare in the United States. Where it is offered, it is generally by developers of new homes. Before you decide on a land lease, however, ask some hard questions: When and how often can the payments increase? at what rate? Does the contract include an option to buy the land? at what price? with what limitations? Are local mortgage lenders willing to finance a home with a land lease? And, not least, what are the resale prospects?

OWNER FINANCING OF RESALE HOMES

So-called "creative financing" played a major role in home sales in the early 1980s, as owners who were desperate to sell and move on became involved in providing mortgage financing through a variety of innovative techniques. Seller involvement is far less common when interest rates are down, but you may still encounter one or more of the following:

Mortgage Assumptions

When the buyer can take over an existing mortgage with a lower rate of interest, it can be very helpful to both the buyer and the seller. Mortgages used to be readily assumable. Today this is not necessarily the case, as lenders press

Q After several months of looking for a house, we are totally bewildered by today's financing terms. If and when we actually decide on a particular house, will anyone explain all the financial details so that we can understand them?

A Your lender, if you secure a conventional fixed-rate or adjustable-rate mortgage, should explain the details. If you use seller financing through a builder or an individual, however, you may be largely on your own. Protect yourself: Refuse to sign any contract until you fully understand the annual percentage rate (with all extra fees, such as points, factored in), the total financing charges (over the entire course of the loan, even if earlier payments are lower), and the amount of the final payment and when it is due (you don't want to be surprised by a large "balloon" payment due at the end). Your accountant or other financial adviser should be able to help.

to enforce the "due-on-sale" provisions that say a mortgage must be paid off when the property changes hands. Adjustable-rate mortgages are often assumable, but it isn't much help when the interest rate will reflect rising rates. Fixed-rate mortgages are sometimes assumable, but you'll have to check with the lender to be sure.

Even where an assumption is permitted, the old mortgage may be fairly small by the time the house is sold. The buyer must, therefore, either come up with additional cash for a substantial down payment or find additional financing, which may be secured via a second mortgage.

Second Mortgages

The purchase money mortgage or second mortgage involves the assumption of a first mortgage by the buyer and the issuance of a second mortgage (or deed of trust, as it is called in some parts of the country) by the seller to cover the difference between the first mortgage and the amount the buyer owes. The seller-issued mortgage is usually at an interest rate lower than that on a new mortgage, and is issued for a shorter term. (Second mortgages may also be obtained from lending institutions, but then the rate will usually be higher than that on a first mortgage.)

When the seller issues (takes back) the second mortgage, the buyer pays the original mortgage lender the monthly amount due on the first mortgage and pays the seller a monthly sum on the additional loan. The combined mortgage loans create a financing package that is generally (but not always) less expensive than a new mortgage would be. A second mortgage may make it possible for you to buy (or sell) your house—especially when lenders are appraising property conservatively and offering smaller loans. But be aware that:

- Payments are generally calculated on a 25-to-30-year basis but with a single large payment, a "balloon," due at the end of an agreed-upon loan period—usually three to five years but sometimes as much as 15 years. (For you, as a buyer, the longer term is preferable; for you, as a seller, the shorter term works best.)
- The terms of the first mortgage on the property may forbid secondary financing without the lender's consent. If you go ahead anyway, you may find yourself in default.
- The IRS requires that mortgage interest payments be reported; if you receive mortgage interest, therefore, you will have to issue a year-end statement to the borrower.

The Lease-Purchase Option

These "contract sales" allow a buyer to occupy a house before actually taking title. Under an option agreement, typically for 12 months, a sales contract may be executed with a closing date which coincides with the expiration of the lease. In this case the price of the house is set in advance, and the seller should try to assess realistically, as far as possible, what the house may be worth in a year's time. The buyer pays option money, which can be applied to the down payment, and can move into the house without a major expenditure. The buyer also forgoes the tax advantages of ownership during the lease period; rent is not tax-deductible (although, depending on the terms of the agreement, it may be applied in whole or in part to the purchase price of the house). The seller gets the option money as well as the lease or rental payments, and keeps the tax benefits of homeownership until the option is executed and the house is sold.

THE RISKS OF BEING CREATIVE

Creative financing is an invention born of necessity. You won't be likely to use it when conventional financing is both affordable and available, but if it becomes necessary, you should be aware of the risks involved and do what you can to protect yourself.

To Protect Yourself, If You're the Buyer

■ Negotiate. Take advantage of the seller's eagerness to sell, and get the lowest price possible. See if the seller will accept a completed deal, at a lower price, rather than embark on creative financing.

■ Evaluate what you can afford at each critical point: for the down payment, when a balloon payment is due, etc. Don't overestimate your ability to pay, or count on bonuses or overtime that may not happen.

■ If you sign a balloon payment loan, make the period as long as you possibly can; five years is better than three, seven is better than five. (Seven is considered optimum by some analysts because it's the length of most business cycles, thereby taking in low interest rates as well as high.) Try to include a clause stipulating that the loan will be extended for a specified period if interest rates haven't dropped to an affordable level by the time the loan comes due.

■ Ask for the right of prepayment without penalty, so that you can refinance the loan when money does become available.

■ Insist, meanwhile, on notification by the primary lender if the seller fails to make any payments for which he is still responsible. If the seller moves away, skips payments, and you're not informed, you could lose your house.

If You're the Seller

■ Think about reducing your price instead of getting involved in creative financing, if it will mean that the buyer can get his or her own financing and you can invest the cash for a comparable return. If you do help the buyer:

■ Insist on an adequate down payment, at least 10 percent, 20 percent if you can get it. The more stake buyers have in the property, the more likely they are to keep up payments.

■ Don't be patient with chronic late payments. Insist on prompt payment, and have your loan agreement include a provision for a penalty when payments are late.

■ Find out if the buyer is creditworthy. Ask for credit references.

■ Keep the term of the loan as short as possible.

■ Realize that if you need the cash before the loan is due, you may have to sell the note to an investor at a substantial discount.

■ Be aware that foreclosure, if you're forced to that point, is both slow and very unpleasant. If you hold a second mortgage, moreover, you're second in line after the holder of the first.

■ Think about including a due-on-sale provision so that the buyer can't sell the house, and your loan along with it.

For Buyers and Sellers

Whether you're the buyer or the seller, consult a knowledgeable real estate attorney before embarking on any creative financing arrangements. The attorney should help you:

■ be sure that the particular form of financing is legal in your state

■ determine that your financing is acceptable to the primary lender, if any, under the contract terms

■ find out whether there is any conflict with state usury laws where they exist (when a private seller sets the interest rate on a mortgage loan, there is the potential for such conflict)

■ assess the degree of risk and be sure that it is acceptable

■ draw up documents to protect your interests

With creative financing there are no standard mortgage documents. Each deal is negotiated individually. Whether you are the buyer or the seller, therefore, you'll want to protect your interests in this very complex negotiation. Don't rely on a real estate agent to protect your interests; many are simply not trained in the complex mathematical and legal ramifications of creative financing. Use a lawyer skilled in real estate transactions in your state.

REFINANCING A MORTGAGE

There was a mad rush to refinance home mortgages in 1991 and 1992, when interest rates dropped to their lowest level in almost two decades. But refinancing isn't for everyone. Before you jump into refinancing, consider:

■ Will your present lender modify or renegotiate your current loan without a complete refinancing? If not, you don't have to stay with your present lender. You are free to shop around for the best terms, but be prepared to pay the closing costs and up-front fees you would pay if you were taking a mortgage for the first time.

■ What are the after-tax implications of refinancing your loan? Remember, interest on a home mortgage is one of the few tax deductions left. If tax brackets go up, as it seems likely they will (and don't forget state taxes when you do your calculations), that tax deduction may be even more worthwhile.

■ Will you stay in your home long enough to break even on the costs of refinancing, typically 4 percent to 6 percent of the amount borrowed? If you plan to move within two or three years, it probably doesn't pay to refinance.

■ If you do refinance, will you want to roll an existing home equity line of credit into your new mortgage? It can make sense to do so if you are paying a variable rate of interest on your home equity line and expect rates to go up.

■ If you do refinance, will you want to move from a 30-year mortgage to a 15-year? There can be advantages in doing so, but reread the pros and cons of 15-year mortgages (on p. 311) before making your decision. What about refinancing from one adjustable-rate mortgage to another? This can make sense if the first-year rate on a new ARM is considerably lower than the rate you have; you could save considerable sums in the first year of the new loan—and put new, lower caps on the interest rate you'll pay in the future.

Q We were eager to buy a house, and we thought interest rates would keep going up, so we took a mortgage loan at 10 percent. Then rates fell. Are we stuck with our high-priced mortgage, or can we somehow take advantage of the new lower interest rates?

A You can refinance your loan. And you should certainly consider doing so if the mortgage interest rate differential is at least 2 percentage points. Ask your current lender, first, if it will renegotiate your loan and, if it will, whether it will reduce or eliminate closing costs and prepayment penalties.

Do some careful arithmetic. Monthly payments on a $100,000 mortgage drop about $83 for every percentage point drop in the interest rate. But you have to balance this saving against the additional fees you'll pay for refinancing and the mortgage interest deduction you'll lose. How long will you have to stay in the house to come out ahead?

Note: Remember what we said earlier about how much of your monthly payment goes to interest and how much to principal? A rule of thumb offered by the newsletter, *100 Highest Yields,* suggests that if you have less than 12 years left to pay off a 30-year mortgage, or 6 years left on a 15-year, you won't save much by refinancing.

Equity Conversion

A 72-year-old widow, a retired laboratory technician, lives in a northern California house worth $152,000. But she lives on Social Security and a small pension and can barely make ends meet. That is, she could barely make ends meet until she became one of the first recipients of a "reverse" mortgage which will pay her over $500 a month, based on the value of her home, for the next ten years.

First-time home buyers are not the only people with problems of housing affordability. Elderly homeowners, buffeted by rising costs and fixed incomes, often have difficulty remaining in their homes. A house may be worth a great deal, but that value can't be tapped to keep the household going. Finally, after years of one step forward and two steps back, elderly homeowners in most states can tap the equity in their homes and use it for living expenses without having to sell or to move.

Table 11.7: Monthly Payments Under a Reverse Mortgage

Monthly payments under a reverse mortgage are linked to your age and the amount of equity you have in your home.

	Maximum monthly payment		
Age	**A house worth $50,000**	**$75,000**	**$100,000**
With payment for life, under an FHA-insured plan:			
65	$ 90	$162	$234
75	154	259	364
85	272	438	604
With payment for a 10-year term:			
65	$146	$262	$378
75	233	391	549
85	340	547	755

Source: Federal National Mortgage Association.

There are three kinds of plans currently available, and another on the drawing board:

FHA-insured plans permit you to receive a monthly check for a fixed term or for as long as you live in the house, a line of credit, or monthly payments plus a line of credit. Although you pay no interest while you are receiving payments, the interest is typically variable and can affect how quickly the loan balance grows over time. FHA-insured loans are limited at this writing to a maximum of $124,875, and are available from local lenders.

Lender-insured plans offer monthly loan advances, or monthly payments plus a line of credit for as long as you live in your home. Interest may be fixed or variable. These loans may be larger than FHA-insured loans, but may involve greater costs.

Uninsured plans are dramatically different, typically offering monthly payments for a fixed number of years. The big drawback here: You will have to repay the loan at the end of the fixed term. If you are unable to do so, you may have to sell your home and move.

Annuity plans, on the verge of being introduced in early 1993, differ from the other plans in three key ways: You receive monthly advances for as long as you live, wherever you live; you always have some equity left at the end of your loan; and the loan is structured to be an attractive investment for large investors such as insurance companies, which means that these loans may be more widely available. But there's a cautionary note, raised by Ken Scholen of the National Center for Home Equity Conversion (for an excellent primer on equity conversion, see his book, *Retirement Income On the House* [NCHEC Press, 1992]): Lifetime income may mean inadequate income, especially because annuity payments are taxable. And, because your money may be coming from an insurance company, you have to make sure the company is stable and solvent.

At this writing, annuity plans are not yet available. Before you take any of the existing equity conversion plans, consider:

- Reverse mortgages are loans that get bigger and bigger, because the interest is added to the principal loan balance each month.
- There can be sizable fees associated with these loans—origination fees, closing costs and, in some instances, insurance premiums and mortgage servicing charges. You may be able to finance these costs, but that will add to the total amount that is owed.
- Some plans offer fixed-rate interest, others are adjustable.
- Interest on reverse mortgages is deductible for income tax purposes until it is actually paid.
- Taking a reverse mortgage means leaving less to your heirs. When you move out of the house, you (or your heirs) will have to repay the loan, typically from the proceeds from the sale of the house.

Table 11.8: A Summary of Popular Mortgage Varieties in the 1990s

Type	Description	Considerations
Fixed-rate mortgage	Equal monthly payments over a long time, often 30 years.	Provides stability and tax advantages. Interest rates may be higher than other forms of financing. Rarely assumable.
15-year fixed-rate mortgage	Higher monthly payments, so that mortgage is fully paid after 15 years.	May be lower interest rate than 30-year. Has faster accumulation of equity, but higher monthly payments. Tax deductions are lower because interest is paid over the mortgage term.
Balloon mortgage	Monthly payments based on 30-year term, but payments may cover interest only with principal due at the end of 5 to 7 years.	Low monthly payments but may be no equity until loan is fully paid. When due, loan must be paid or refinanced. Refinancing poses high risk if rates climb.
Two-step	Monthly payments fixed for 5 to 7 years, then adjusted for balance of 30-year loan.	Lower interest rate at beginning, higher for the second phase.
Adjustable-rate mortgage	Interest rates are adjusted at preset intervals, often at one-year intervals, pegged to a predetermined index.	Interest rate may be below market initially but may rise as much as 6 percent over the life of the loan.
Reverse mortgage or equity conversion	Borrower owns property free (or almost free) of debt. Lender makes monthly payments to borrower, using property as collateral.	Can provide needed cash. Available for specific term (in which case borrower must repay the loan and may have to sell) or for life. More monthly income is available to older borrowers.

Source: Federal Trade Commission.

Taking all the disadvantages together, you may be better off trading down—selling your house, moving to less-expensive quarters, and investing the difference. But this is in purely economic terms; consider a reverse mortgage instead of selling if you have an emotional attachment to your home and want to remain there.

On the plus side, of course:

- Equity conversion can make it possible for you to live comfortably and remain in your home.
- The monthly payments under a reverse mortgage (unlike the new annuity plans for equity conversion) are not taxable, and do not affect your Social Security or Medicare benefits.
- Your legal obligation to pay back the loan is limited by the value of your home at the time the loan is repaid. This could include increases in the value of your home, if it appreciates after the loan begins. But, under insured programs, you are protected in case the value of your home falls; you will never owe more than the equity in the home at the time the loan concludes.

 KEY POINTS

- Because mortgage loans are available from a number of different sources with varying down payment requirements, interest rates, mortgage terms, and fees, comparison shopping is vitally important.
- Fixed-rate, fixed-term mortgages offer certainty in monthly payments, but adjustable-rate mortgages, usually available at a lower initial interest rate, are a popular alternative.
- Interest or payment caps can protect you against excessive interest rate swings on an adjustable-rate mortgage, but it's also important to understand the index, the margin, and the adjustment period in order to assess your ability to make larger payments in the future.
- Creative financing, unnecessary when mortgage loans are affordable and available, may become useful once again if interest rates rise. But creative financing has pitfalls for both buyer and seller; before embarking on any form of creative financing, be sure to secure competent advice.
- Refinancing a mortgage loan can make sense when there is a spread of two or more percentage points between the rate of interest on your current mortgage and the rate available on a new mortgage loan.
- Equity conversion, or reverse mortgage loans, can enable elderly homeowners to tap home equity and provide cash with no need to repay while they remain in their homes.

CHAPTER 12

Insuring Your Property

- Your kitchen catches fire and newly installed cabinets are destroyed.
- A neighbor's child runs across your lawn and trips over a garden hoe. A concussion leads to impaired vision, and the child's parents sue.
- A burglar ransacks your home, vandalizing what he doesn't steal.
- You're on vacation and your luggage is stolen.
- While your daughter is walking the family dog, several blocks from home, the dog bites a passerby.
- A massive tree limb cracks and falls, severely damaging your home's roof and chimney.

These unfortunate events have just one thing in common: Protection against financial loss stemming from any of them is provided in a homeowners insurance policy.

Whether your kitchen catches fire or a tree limb falls on your roof, you need protection against **physical damage** via a homeowners policy. Whether your neighbor's child is injured on your property or your dog bites someone anywhere, you need protection against **liability** claims via a homeowners policy.

Homeowners Insurance Forms

If you own your own house you have a choice among homeowners insurance packages. All include protection against liability claims, usually

Table 12.1: Perils Against Which Properties Are Insured Under the Various Homeowners Policies

					Perils
Broad HO-2	Special HO-3	Renter's HO-4	Unit Owner's HO-6	Older Home HO-8	
					1. Fire or lightning
					2. Windstorm or hail
					3. Explosion
					4. Riot or civil commotion
					5. Aircraft
					6. Vehicles
					7. Smoke
					8. Vandalism or malicious mischief
					9. Theft
					10. Damage by glass or safety glazing material which is part of a building
					11. Volcanic eruption
					12. Falling objects
					13. Weight of ice, snow, or sleet
					14. Accidental discharge or overflow of water or steam from within a plumbing, heating, air conditioning, or automatic fire protective sprinkler system or from within a household appliance
					15. Sudden and accidental tearing apart, cracking, burning, or bulging of a steam or hot water heating system, an air conditioning or automatic fire protective sprinkler system, or an appliance for heating water
					16. Freezing of a plumbing, heating, air conditioning, or automatic fire protective sprinkler system or of a household appliance
					17. Sudden and accidental damage from artificially generated electrical current (does not include loss to a tube, transistor, or similar electronic component)
					All perils except flood, earthquake, war, nuclear accident, and others specified in your policy. Check your policy for a complete listing of perils excluded.

Dwelling and Personal Property   ▨   Dwelling only   ▨   Personal Property only

Source: Insurance Information Institute.

with a standard $100,000 limit which you may raise (and probably should; see p. 349 for details). All also include protection against physical damage to your property resulting from fire, theft, windstorm or hail, explosion, riot or civil commotion, aircraft and vehicles, smoke, vandalism and malicious mischief, and the breakage of glass.

Progressively more expensive policies cover more of what the insurance industry calls "named perils." Table 12.1 will help you to sort out the details of the various plans but, briefly, the Broad (HO-2) Form adds to the basic list with falling objects, weight of ice and snow and sleet, collapse of building, sudden breakage of a heating system or plumbing system or appliance, freezing of plumbing, heating, and air-conditioning systems, and sudden injury from electrical appliances or wiring. The Special (HO-3) Form, sometimes called "all-risk" coverage (although there is no insurance policy, whatever the title, that really covers absolutely everything), insures you against property damage from everything except specified exclusions: flood, earthquake, war, nuclear accident, and whatever else your particular policy excludes; an endorsement extends this comprehensive coverage to the contents of your house.

If you've amassed possessions over a number of years, carefully evaluate the value of those possessions before settling for less-than-complete coverage. One suburban house went up in flames when a spark from a gas water heater ignited a solvent being used to put down basement floor tile. Insurance enabled the family to rebuild the house, but the standard contents coverage (50 percent of the insurance on the house itself) was far less than adequate. See pp. 347-348 for more details on coverage of contents.

Be careful, in any case, about the "bargain" coverage of the Broad (HO-2) Form, especially if you live in the northern states. This policy does not cover

---

Q Lightning struck a tree in my yard, tearing off a limb that damaged my neighbor's house and shrubs. His insurance company says my insurer must pay the bills, but my insurer says his company should pay. Who is right?

A Your insurer. In most cases (unless you neglected a rotting tree) you are not at fault; your neighbor's homeowner's policy should cover his damage. But you don't have to argue with your neighbor. The insurance companies should resolve the matter between them.

Note: If the lightning-struck tree on your property must be removed, your own insurer may pay up to $500 under your homeowner's policy toward the cost.

water damage to ceilings and walls caused by leakage. It does cover water damage, but only if your roof actually collapses from the weight of snow and ice; most damage is caused by water seepage. If you upgrade your policy to HO-3, you'll increase your yearly premium in most states by just about 5 percent.

THE ELEMENTS OF HOMEOWNERS INSURANCE

All homeowners forms have basic elements in common, although specific details will differ in accordance with state law and the issuing company. All include both property insurance (usually with a built-in $250 deductible; you pay the first $250 it takes to repair any damage) and personal liability coverage (with no deductible). All cover:

- The house itself, in the amount you designate (that amount—unless your company requires 100 percent coverage—should be at least 80 percent of the replacement value of the house; see p. 340)
- Other structures on the same property, such as a detached garage or a toolshed, to 10 percent of the insured value of the home (**Note:** If you maintain an office or a business in a separate structure on your property, it is not covered by your homeowners insurance.)
- Personal property, the general contents of your house, usually up to half the insured value of the house (unless you arrange for more; see p. 347), but with a strict dollar limit on valuable items such as furs and jewelry
- Additional living expenses, should you have to house your family elsewhere while repairing damages caused by an insured risk
- Damage to trees, shrubs, and plants (but generally not from wind) up to 5 percent of the value of the dwelling, with a maximum of $500 per item
- Losses of personal property away from home, usually up to 10 percent of value and limited to certain conditions
- Personal liability, in case someone slips on your icy sidewalk or trips over a garden tool, typically to a maximum of $100,000 per occurrence
- Medical payments to people injured on your property, without regard to fault, up to $1,000 per occurrence (this amount, too, may be increased)
- Damage to the property of others, regardless of fault, up to $250 (useful if your child puts a softball through a neighbor's window)

Table 12.2 shows the type and amount of coverage for a typical dwelling under a Broad Form (HO-2) homeowners policy. Special insurance packages are designed for condominium owners (see p. 381), for mobile home owners (see p. 397), and for tenants (see p. 354).

Table 12.2: Homeowners Coverage, Assuming a House With an $80,000 Replacement Value

	Insured to replacement value	Insured to 80% of replacement value
Property coverages		
Dwelling	$80,000 (full value)	$64,000 (80% of full value)
Other structures on property	8,000 (10% of dwelling)	6,400 (10% of dwelling)
Unscheduled personal property	40,000 (50% of dwelling)[1]	32,000 (50% of dwelling)[1]
Loss of use	16,000 (20% of dwelling)	12,800 (20% of dwelling)
Liability coverages		
Personal liability	$100,000 (each occurrence)[1]	$100,000 (each occurrence)[1]
Medical payments to others (regardless of fault)	1,000 (each person)[1]	1,000 (each person)[1]
Damage to property of others (regardless of fault)	250 (each occurrence)	250 (each occurrence)

Source: Insurance Information Institute.

Note: [1]Larger amounts are available; some policies may have lower standard amounts.

Q A delivery truck ran out of control down our street and across my lawn, destroying an old and beautiful oak tree that shaded our house. How can I establish the value of the tree for an insurance claim?

A Your insurance company will probably want to send someone to look at the downed tree, so don't have it removed before you call your agent or the company. You might also want to call a local nursery or landscaper for an independent appraisal. It will help, too, if you have pictures showing the tree shading your house. The tree might be worth a great deal and, if it was very large, be impossible to replace, but an appraisal will focus on its species, size, condition, and location.

PROPERTY DAMAGE COVERAGE IN THE HOMEOWNERS POLICY

Whichever homeowners package you choose, it is absolutely vital that you buy enough insurance in the first place and that you keep your coverage up to date. "Enough" insurance means at least **80 percent** of the **replacement value** of your house. Don't settle for the amount of insurance required by your mortgage lender to cover the mortgage loan. If you do and disaster strikes, the bank will be protected by insurance but your own investment may be unprotected. "Up to date" means regular review and increase for inflation (see below) *and* for any improvements, especially any additions you make to your house.

The amount of coverage you purchase on your dwelling becomes the base for the percentage amounts assigned to other structures on the property, to household contents, to additional living expenses, and so on. More important, **the amount of insurance on the dwelling itself determines whether you will receive full or partial reimbursement in the event of a partial loss.** With a total loss of your property, of course, you are covered up to the face amount of the policy. But most insurance claims are for partial loss: a kitchen fire, an electrical storm that topples a tree onto the roof, and so on.

The 80 Percent Rule

If your house is not insured to 80 percent of its replacement value, then you will be reimbursed only for the actual cash value of depreciated property at the time of loss. With 80 percent coverage, you'll be sure of reimbursement for the full cost of repairing any damage or replacing any damaged item, without regard to depreciation, up to the full face amount of the policy. But check with your agent or company to see if 80 percent (instead of 100 percent) is allowed.

The amount of coverage you have makes a significant difference. For example: If it would cost $80,000 to rebuild your house from the foundation up, then $64,000 of insurance would meet the 80 percent requirement. If a fire damages your kitchen, with its 8-year-old cabinets and appliances, the insurance company will pay the claim on the basis of what it costs to put the kitchen back together at today's prices. If you have less than 80 percent coverage on the house, however, payments for partial loss are reduced, with the calculations made in one of two ways. If you are carrying $40,000 in insurance, instead of the $64,000 you should have to meet the 80 percent rule, you would collect either forty sixty-fourths of the loss (on a $5,000 loss, that would be $3,125) or the actual cash value (replacement cost less depreciation), whichever is larger.

If you sustain a total loss—if, for example, your house burns to the foundation—you will be reimbursed only up to the face amount of the policy. If it will cost $80,000 to rebuild and you are insured to $64,000, you'll be out of pocket for the difference. Total disaster, fortunately, is rare, but it's devastating when it does occur; just ask the victims of the Oakland fire and the Florida hurricane. Consider full coverage.

Household Insurance at Different Life Stages

Property insurance needs relate to how much property you own rather than to your stage of life, but your insurance should be reviewed and changed as necessary as you move through various life stages.

■ As a young single or just-married, your primary insurance need, if you own a car, is probably for automobile insurance. Beyond this expensive possession, however, you may have other items worth protection. A tenants policy will cover your household contents. A blanket valuables endorsement or personal articles floater can list a camera or a coin collection or an engagement ring.

■ Live-togethers should be particularly careful about insurance as they amass possessions. Some companies will cover you both on a single tenants or homeowners policy; others won't. It can be a shock if you discover, after a theft, that your stereo wasn't insured because the tenants policy was in your partner's name.

■ When you buy your first house, you'll get your first homeowners policy, insuring your home to at least 80 percent of its replacement value. The Broad Form (HO-2) may well be recommended, with the standard 50 percent coverage on household contents, but you might want to consider more extensive coverage with a larger deductible to reduce premium costs. You may also want a floater policy, covering individually valuable items such as jewelry or furs.

■ As you move to a bigger house and more possessions, you may want an HO-3 policy with an all-risk contents endorsement, 70 percent contents coverage and a larger deductible. Replacement cost coverage on contents will be more desirable. You'll still need a floater policy and you may want safe deposit coverage as well. Umbrella liability coverage may become necessary, if you haven't purchased it earlier.

■ If you sell your house when you retire and move to a condominium or to a rental apartment, you will change your property insurance to the Condominium Owners Form or to the Tenants Form. You'll also want to consider reducing insurance costs by taking larger deductibles. Consider dropping umbrella coverage if you're no longer vulnerable to expensive lawsuits.

Replacement Value

Don't think about the market value of your house when you think about insurance. Replacement value, or rebuilding cost, is the key. When you rebuild, you don't need to consider the value of the land or even of the foundation. On a brand-new house, replacement value may be close to market value. In most cases, however, it's not at all comparable. Your home may very well be underinsured, in fact, because market prices have leveled off but repair costs have continued to rise.

Automatic adjustments for inflation (see below) will protect your pocketbook in most circumstances. But a replacement cost provision is well worth considering to cover you in case of catastrophe. If your home would cost $100,000 to replace today, it could cost $140,000 to replace tomorrow—if overnight a hurricane, for example, devastated your city and drove the cost of lumber and other building supplies sky-high. With replacement cost coverage, your insurer would pay for rebuilding your home even if that rebuilding cost more than the face value of the policy.

Q Our home is worth less now than it was a few years ago. Can we at least save some money by reducing our homeowners insurance to reflect this?

A Probably not. The key factor in homeowners insurance is **replacement** value, not market value. In other words, you want enough insurance to rebuild your home if it were completely destroyed—and chances are that the cost of building materials and labor has gone up even if the market values of real estate have gone down in your area. Try to insure your home to its *full* replacement value (excluding land and foundation)—and talk to your agent or company about inflation protection to keep your coverage up to date with rising costs.

Important: If your community has adopted new zoning or building codes since your house was built, you may also want to consider a special policy rider that would cover the higher cost of rebuilding to meet the new standards.

For more information, send a stamped, self-addressed, business-size envelope to the Insurance Information Institute, 110 William St., New York, NY 10038. Ask for "Insurance For Your House and Personal Possessions: Deciding How Much You Need."

INFLATION PROTECTION

You can keep your homeowners coverage in line with current replacement costs in one of two ways:

■ Review your coverage on a regular basis, upgrading it as necessary.
■ Buy a policy with an "inflation-guard" provision, or add such a rider to an older policy.

It's safer by far, given human nature and our disinclination to pay attention to such things, to have the increases built into the policy. With inflation-guard protection, depending on the practices of your insurance company, your coverage will be automatically increased each year, typically by an index of actual construction and labor costs in your area.

A number of companies provide these index services to insurers, based on square footage, number of floors, type of construction, and additional features such as extra baths, fireplaces, and central air conditioning. Total rebuilding cost is then adjusted for locality, to reflect the tremendous differences across the country in the cost of labor and materials.

A Cost Analysis

Here's how a typical cost analysis might look, based on data supplied by Marshall & Swift Insurance Services Group, which prepares computerized analyses of individual home replacement value for insurance companies. This particular system is based on a square foot cost, a cost which would be different for different types of homes. In this example, the house is a two-story Colonial, frame construction, with 1,200 square feet of living space on the ground floor (not including deck or garage). The base figure in 1992 was:

1,200 square feet x 94.10 = 112,920
Additional features add to this base figure:

A half-bath	$ 1,260
One-car attached garage	7,210
Brick fireplace	3,840
Deck, 100 square feet	700
Full unfinished basement	9,050
Total replacement cost	**134,980**

This figure, $18,800 more than the replacement cost for the same house in 1986, is a national average. Using the "location modifiers" supplied by Marshall & Swift, here's what the same house would cost to rebuild in three sample locations:

Shreveport, LA:	$ 102,585
Spokane, WA:	125,531
Pittsburgh, PA:	133,630

These locations are not the extremes. The lowest replacement cost, in June 1992, was to be found in the Hugoton, Kansas, area, where this same house would cost $86,387 to rebuild. The highest cost in the continental United States (Alaska and Hawaii, because so much must be imported, pose special situations) was in New York City, $179,523.

The Marshall & Swift service is not available to consumers; talk to your insurance agent about securing an analysis of your home. Should you want to do the arithmetic to get an idea of your home's current replacement value, however, here is a simplified formula to use; it is based on the "unit method" and does not require square foot calculations. (Remember, though, it will only approximate the actual replacement value of any individual house; the square foot method is more accurate.)

1. Determine the construction grade and quality closest to your house:
   a. Economy (Class I). Low-cost tract homes, with minimum materials and workmanship. No extras, such as dens or family rooms.
   b. Standard (Class II). The majority of homes. Standard plans, simple design, with average-grade materials and workmanship. Has extra rooms, such as dining room or den, and ornamentation.
   c. Custom (Class III). Built from special plans or modified standard plans, with good-quality materials and workmanship. Typically includes dining room, family room, den, and foyer. Exceeds building codes.
2. Count each full room and each of the following as one unit: finished basement; full bathroom(s); brick or stone exterior; central air conditioning; aluminum siding; attached two-car garage; a full-wall fireplace; large enclosed porch; other special features. Count each of the following as a half unit: half bath (powder room or lavatory); large open porch; standard fireplace; unfinished basement; attached one-car garage; utility or laundry room; brick or stone veneer on the front only; unfinished attic with full headroom. Then adjust your count to reflect extra rooms or extra large rooms.
3. Use Table 12.3 for the type of construction and the number of units in your house; the figure shown will be the approximate replacement cost. However, note that this calculation provides a very rough estimate. It is not as accurate as a calculation by the square foot method, and it does not include location modifiers, so it is an average figure rather than one specific to your location. Also, this calculation won't work at all for houses built before 1940, homes worth more than $300,000, or for multifamily dwellings.

WHEN YOU FILE A CLAIM

If you do suffer a loss to your home or property, the New York State Insurance Department suggests that you take the following steps:

Table 12.3: Approximate Replacement Costs of Homes

Use the following table for homes built after 1940:

Construction Units	Class I	Class II	Class III
5	48200	60400	76900
5.5	51900	64300	81400
6	55900	68400	85700
6.5	59500	72200	90100
7	63200	76100	94600
7.5	67100	80100	98800
8	70800	83900	103200
8.5	74600	87800	107500
9	78300	91800	111900
9.5	82200	95600	116300
10	85900	99600	120600
10.5	89700	103600	124800
11	93400	107300	129200
11.5	97000	111200	134100
12	100600	115000	138500
12.5	104300	118900	143300
13	107800	122600	148000
13.5	111500	126600	152500
14	115000	130300	157200
14.5	118500	134100	161900
15	122100	137900	166500
15.5	125900	141800	171100
16	129400	145500	175800
16.5	133000	149400	180400
17	136400	153100	184900

For construction grades falling "in between," interpolate on a judgment basis. Costs include markups for contractor's overhead and profit, taxes, insurance, and general conditions.

Source: Marshall & Swift.

■ Notify your agent or insurance company, without delay. They will arrange for an adjuster from your insurance company to look over the damage and give you an estimate on the cost of repairs or replacement. They will also help you fill out the claim forms and gather the materials you need to prove your loss.

- You should also get an estimate from your own contractor, to compare with the company's estimate. Your contractor may charge a fee for this service, but he probably will credit it to your bill if he gets the repair job.
- If there is considerable fire damage, you may want to call in a public adjuster, a licensed professional who will act as your agent in negotiating a settlement with your insurance company. The fee for this service is generally a specified percentage of your insurance settlement, based upon a retainer you agree on in advance in a signed contract. Be cautious, however, about signing up with the first public adjuster who appears on the scene after your house burns down. Gather your wits before you sign a binding agreement.
- Protect your property against further damage. If windows are broken, for instance, have them boarded up to protect against vandalism and weather damage. The cost should be covered by your homeowners policy, so save receipts for these temporary repairs.

Q We bought an old Victorian house, with built-in cupboards, carved stair posts, and original gingerbread trim. The house cost us $66,000 but would probably cost three times that to restore if it were ever damaged. There's no way we can insure it to 80 percent of its replacement value. What can we do?

A Depending on where you live, you have a choice. You may be able to buy a Market Value homeowners policy (HO-8) which would provide for reconstruction with materials used today. The policy insures against basic risks but with the special provision that property will be returned to usable condition rather than to its original condition. This means that you may wind up with wallboard after a fire rather than with the plaster walls of the original, but you will have a usable home and a policy with a manageable premium. Or, in most states, you can add an endorsement to a standard replacement cost homeowners policy to reduce, without penalty, the amount of insurance required. Coverage can be modified to 50, 60, or 70 percent instead of the usual 80 percent. With this endorsement, you would recover the full cost of replacement in case of partial loss or damage to the house up to the policy limit, as long as the agreed-on percentage was met. If there were a total loss, the policy would cover the cost of rebuilding using modern materials and methods. Talk to your insurance agent about what is available in your state and which approach is best for you.

■ Be patient. Don't have permanent repairs made until the insurance company has inspected the property and you both agree on the cost of the repairs. The company has a legal right to inspect the property in its damaged state and can refuse to reimburse you for any damage repaired prior to its inspection.

INSURANCE ON HOUSEHOLD CONTENTS

The standard coverage of household contents under every form of homeowners policy is limited to 50 percent of the amount of insurance on the house itself. You can, if you elect to do so, increase contents coverage to 70 percent. Whatever the maximum, however, these are the limits:

■ Some types of personal property, such as motorbikes or golf carts, may be excluded under some policies. Other types of property, such as coin collections or silverware, may be severely limited in the dollar amount of coverage. Specific valuable items may be covered by a separate personal articles floater (see p. 349) or, from some companies, a blanket "valuable items" endorsement (see pp. 351-352).

■ "Mysterious disappearance" is covered under some policies, typically the more inclusive policies, and not under others. If you're not quite sure what happened to a gold chain—did you lose it because the catch broke, or did someone steal it?—you may or may not be able to collect.

■ Business-related property may or may not be covered. If you run a business from your home, talk to your agent about a "permitted incidental occupancies" endorsement. Under this coverage, which may add as lit-

Q I bought a small computer which my children use for both homework and video games and I use for my part-time business of writing advertising copy for local merchants. Is the computer covered under my homeowners policy?

A Many insurance companies now cover home computers used for business, up to a total of $2,500. Some have higher limits. Check with your own company or agent—especially if your business-related equipment is worth more.

Note: If your employer is supplying a computer (or other equipment) for you to use at home, your homeowner's policy probably won't cover theft or damage. Verify this with your own insurer or agent, then talk to your employer about providing coverage.

tle as $20 a year to your homeowner's premium cost, business equipment would be covered to the full personal property limit on your policy. You would also be protected against liability for a computer repairman, for example, tripping on your steps. ("Incidental" coverage does not apply if you run a full-scale business from your home, complete with clients or patients coming and going; if this is your situation, consult your insurance agent for the appropriate coverage.)
■ If you leave your house vacant for more than 30 consecutive days before a loss, you may not be covered. If you plan extensive travel, therefore, you might want to consider hiring a responsible house-sitter.

Replacement Cost Coverage

Coverage of household contents is generally based on current value less depreciation, an amount which may not be nearly enough to replace cherished possessions. Today, however, more and more companies are offering replacement cost coverage. If you elect to pay the additional premium (roughly 10 percent more on a standard homeowners policy), this insurance would generally provide enough to replace the stolen or damaged item at current prices. It's worth considering. After all, your living room furniture may have cost $1,800 and now be worth $350 (used furniture is worth very little). Yet it would cost at least $3,200 to replace at current prices. With replacement cost coverage your insurer has the option of repairing a damaged item, replacing it with a similar item, or reimbursing you for the amount necessary to do your own shopping.

Some possessions are often excluded from replacement cost coverage. For example: Memorabilia, souvenirs and collectors' items are usually covered for actual cash value rather than replacement value. So are particular valuable items, such as antiques and paintings. If you possess such valuables, consider taking blanket valuable items coverage or a scheduled personal articles floater; see pp. 350-352.

Note: You can turn down your insurer's offer to replace the item and insist on cash. But don't expect the full retail value. Since the insurer could probably use wholesale sources to replace your stolen or damaged property, you are more likely to be given the wholesale price.

LIABILITY COVERAGE IN THE HOMEOWNERS POLICY

All forms of the homeowners policy include liability coverage designed to protect you against financial loss resulting from personal liability, medical payments to others, and physical damage to the property of others.

The liability coverage in your policy will protect you against a claim for damages if you misjudge the distance in taking down a diseased tree in your backyard and the tree falls on your neighbor's house. It will protect you if someone is injured on your property and files suit. Legal defense is provided under the terms of the policy whether or not you are legally at fault. But damages are not paid unless it is determined, often in a court of law, that you are legally responsible.

The standard limit, as noted earlier, is $100,000. This may well not be enough. Damage awards in personal injury suits today are often considerably more. If your savings might be wiped out by a personal injury lawsuit, or your future earnings threatened, it's worthwhile to consider taking out extra liability coverage. You can take extra coverage under your homeowners policy. You might consider $300,000 in liability coverage on both your automobile and homeowner's policies. And, if you are a professional or a business executive with high or potentially high earnings that might be susceptible to a lawsuit, you should also consider a separate umbrella liability policy.

Umbrella Liability Coverage

These policies, which usually sell for under $200 for the first $1,000,000 in coverage, pick up where your homeowners and automobile policies stop. If your homeowners policy has the basic $100,000 in liability protection, the umbrella policy will pick up after your basic policy has paid the $100,000. These policies also provide primary coverage for situations not covered by other insurance. If you're sued for libel or wrongfully evicted, for instance, an umbrella policy would provide protection above a specified amount; $1,000 is frequently specified, but some companies set a $250 threshold while others use $2,500.

For example:

■ A school board member, along with the rest of the board, was sued by a teacher for defamation of character. The member was covered by her umbrella liability policy.

■ While driving a rental automobile in Jamaica, British West Indies, a vacationing American was involved in a fatal accident. He had limited coverage from the rental company, and his own automobile policy excluded foreign coverage. The personal liability policy provided coverage.

■ A tourist browsing in an antique shop broke a valuable Chinese vase. Her homeowner's policy would have paid just $500 toward the damage; her umbrella liability policy paid the full $11,700 cost of the vase.

Additional Insurance You Might Want

The homeowners policy, even in its broadest form, has certain limits. It covers personal property only up to designated amounts. It does not cover damage from flood or earthquake at all. It may not be available in high-crime areas. Special policies fill the bill in these circumstances.

PERSONAL ARTICLES COVERAGE

The homeowners policy has a strict dollar limit on coverage of valuables. Jewelry, for instance, might be covered (depending on your company) only up to $1,000, silver flatware to $2,500. If you own valuable items such as furs or jewelry or camera equipment, you may want a personal articles floater.

Issued either separately or as an endorsement to your homeowners policy, a floater covers listed items, to the designated amounts, wherever they are located when a loss occurs. If a diamond falls out of your engagement ring on your way to the movies, your homeowners policy will not provide reimbursement; a personal articles floater will. If a camera is destroyed by water when an overeager amateur photographer aims at the surf, your homeowners policy will not provide reimbursement; a personal articles floater will.

Most personal articles floaters contain a provision for automatic coverage of newly acquired property (within already listed categories) for 30 days. If you forget to notify your insurance agent before leaving for your vacation about a newly purchased camera, and it's lost or stolen or hit by a wave, you will be covered—if you notify your agent of the loss right away.

The personal articles floater also contains a "pair and set" clause, under which coverage on certain items is limited to the difference between the actual value of the intact pair or set and the actual cash value of what's left after a loss. If, for instance, you own a set of five irreplaceable commemorative medals, each of which is worth $500 but which together are worth $5,000, the loss of one would make the insurance company liable for $3,000. That's the difference between the value of the entire set ($5,000) and the value of the remaining medals ($500 x 4, or $2,000). The same principle applies to a pair of earrings; you may not be able to wear a single earring, but you haven't lost full value with the loss of just one.

Q Because I work full time, I hire a baby-sitter to be with my 7-year-old son after school every day. Should I be carrying any special insurance in case she's hurt in my home?

A It's important for you to be financially protected in case anyone you hire—baby-sitter, handyman, houseworker—is injured in your home. Outside contractors should have their own insurance; check to be sure. Regular workers need to be covered by you, but the type of protection you need depends on where you live. In some states your homeowners policy will provide coverage; in others you need a separate workers compensation policy. Ask your insurance agent.

The Cost of Coverage

Premiums are based on value but vary according to the items listed and where you live. Insurance on silver flatware, for instance, generally costs about 50 cents per $100 of value. Jewelry coverage runs about $2 per $100 of value, in most parts of the country, but costs considerably more in high-risk urban areas. Insurance companies set their own rates, and it may pay to shop around.

Your insurance company will probably want an appraisal to back up your opinion of the value of the listed items (on newly purchased items, the bill of sale should be sufficient). And you'll probably want to update that appraisal regularly, especially with regard to jewelry, in an era when gold and silver prices fluctuate with the daily papers.

Pick your appraiser carefully (membership in the American Society of Appraisers is a good sign) and stay away from those who charge a percentage of the appraised value. Such a fee—instead of the preferable flat fee or hourly rate—is a temptation to the appraiser to inflate the value. You'll then wind up paying more than necessary, both for the appraisal itself and for your insurance.

BLANKET VALUABLE ITEMS ENDORSEMENT

Expensive jewelry, cameras, and furs may be worth listing individually on a personal articles floater. But what about less-costly jewelry, silverware, musical instruments, golf clubs, and all the cherished possessions that you would want to replace if they were stolen or destroyed in a fire or other cataclysmic event?

Some companies now provide a form of coverage midway between the general contents coverage on your homeowner's policy and a scheduled per-

Q I increased the insurance on my gold jewelry when gold went to over $800 an ounce. Then the price fell and it's been up and down ever since. Should I reduce my insurance when the price goes down? If my jewelry were stolen, would I collect the amount it's insured for even if it's worth less?

A You will never make a profit on your insurance, because you can collect only the actual value of the jewelry in case of a loss (up to the amount of the coverage). The insurance company would, if possible, replace the missing item through its own wholesale sources. If replacement weren't possible, it would pay you the market value, as long as it wasn't more (it might be less) than the face amount of the policy. Don't worry too much about the per-ounce price of gold, but do keep an up-to-date appraisal on file with your insurance agent or company.

sonal articles floater. Kemper, for example, has introduced a Blanket Valuable Items endorsement under which jewelry, furs, silverware, and fine arts can be insured for up to $20,000, with a maximum of $5,000 per item. Cameras, musical instruments, golfer's equipment, and guns are covered up to a total of $5,000, or $2,500 per item. A category called china/crystal also goes to a total of $5,000, with a $500 limit per item. The advantage of this coverage: no deductibles, no appraisals, and low cost.

SAFE DEPOSIT COVERAGE

If you keep your valuable jewelry in a safe deposit box, you probably won't need full-time insurance coverage. But if you don't insure it, what happens when you take it out to wear? Few, if any, companies still write insurance combining inexpensive long-term in-vault coverage with short-term out-of-vault coverage for occasional wear. Ask your agent about this coverage, but if you wear valuable jewelry often, you'll probably want a personal articles floater.

Although a safe deposit box is the safest place for your valuables, thefts do occasionally take place. The contents of your box are not usually insured by the bank. Your homeowners policy, as noted earlier, limits coverage of jewelry and of securities, so you may want to check into safe deposit coverage. Or leave your securities with your stockbroker and take out a personal articles floater on your jewelry.

FLOOD INSURANCE

If hurricane-driven flood waters damage your home, and you don't have flood insurance, you may collect under your homeowners policy only if you

Q Recent hurricane warnings off the coast have made me worry about our low-lying home. If a hurricane were to come through here, would we be covered for damage under our homeowners insurance?

A Homeowners insurance covers wind damage from a hurricane but not flood damage. Damage from water would be covered only if wind made it possible for the water to enter—if, for instance, wind blew a tree through your roof, allowing wind-driven rain to destroy your furniture. The only way to secure insurance against flooding is via a special federal program, if your community qualifies. If you're eligible (you can find out by calling, toll-free, 800-638-6620), you can buy flood insurance from almost any insurance agent.

can prove that wind damage occurred first and made it possible for the water to gain entry. Nonetheless, Hurricane Andrew, which struck the Florida coast in August 1992, has had a devastating impact on property insurers; at least eight smaller companies were driven out of business, while larger companies sustained sizable losses. The likely result: Companies will not write insurance in coastal areas. And premiums for homeowners insurance, wherever you live, will go up.

If you live in an area susceptible to flooding, ask your insurance agent about the federal flood insurance program. If you build or purchase a home located in a designated flood plain, you may be required to purchase flood insurance. Otherwise, it's optional, but, very possibly, a good idea.

Coverage is provided in two phases. In the first, or emergency, phase, limited amounts of insurance are available at fixed rates. In the second, or regular, stage, which begins once a community has undertaken a comprehensive flood-management program, increased coverage is available at rates determined by amount of risk. There are deductibles on both building and contents.

There is limited coverage on vacation homes located in flood-prone areas. If you occupy the house less than 20 percent of the year, full coverage can't be claimed. Instead, only actual cash value, which takes depreciation into account and is less than replacement cost, will be provided.

And there are some drawbacks to flood insurance: It doesn't cover the decks and docks and shrubbery typically washed away. It won't cover "finished" basements, but only foundations, utility connections and mechanical equipment situated below ground level. And valuables, including works of art and jewelry, are covered to a negligible amount.

EARTHQUAKES

Earthquakes, like floods, are specifically excluded as insured risks on standard homeowners policies, even on the "all-risk" variety. But earthquake coverage may be readily obtained, wherever you live, as an endorsement to your homeowners policy. Rates will vary in accordance with state regulation and with your actual exposure to earthquakes. And, no matter how much you pay, you'll never receive the full amount necessary to rebuild because deductibles are much higher than with other types of insurance.

Note: Damage from volcanic eruptions has been included in standard homeowner's policies since Mount St. Helens erupted in 1980.

CRIME INSURANCE

Residents of high-crime areas, such as inner cities, have often had difficulty securing theft insurance. Under the Federal Crime Insurance Program homeowners who meet specified requirements, including the installation of protective devices on their homes, may qualify for subsidized insurance against robbery or burglary. But the program is very limited (maximum coverage is $10,000), and very few states currently participate. Six states withdrew from the program in 1992 and another three in 1993, so the program may effectively be winding down. To find out if coverage is available in your state call 800-638-8780.

FAIR PLANS

If you have trouble getting property insurance at all, for any reason, ask an insurance agent or your state insurance department about a FAIR Plan. FAIR Plans, comparable to assigned risk pools for automobile coverage, are available in 29 states plus the District of Columbia. They are generally limited to fire and extended coverage, although some, depending on the state, offer full homeowners insurance. With more property insurers pulling out of states ravaged by the floods, hurricanes, tornadoes, and blizzards of the early 1990s, more and more homeowners may be forced to secure homeowners coverage (and pay more for the privilege) through these risk pools.

Tenants Insurance

If you rent your dwelling, you still need insurance. A lot of tenants don't seem to think so. While 96 percent of owner-occupants carry property insurance, only about 26 percent of the tenants surveyed by the Insurance Information Institute in late 1989 carried fire insurance and a similar proportion insured their household contents.

Q I was flabbergasted at the belongings my daughter carted off to school: computer, stereo, television, bicycle, as well as small appliances like a corn popper and hair dryer. Is all of her stuff insured under my homeowners policy?

A Property owned by a member of your family and maintained in a temporary residence, such as a college dorm or an apartment, is generally insured up to 10 percent of the households contents coverage in your homeowners policy. Your household contents coverage is usually limited, unless you elect replacement cost coverage, to half the assigned value of your house. If you carry $60,000 in insurance on your house, with $30,000 in contents coverage, your daughter's belongings will be covered to $3,000. Check your policy, though, and watch for any exclusions; jewelry and cash are often covered to very limited amounts. And all coverage may cease if the student leaves property on campus during an extended vacation.

Yet a landlord's policy covers only the building and any property belonging to the landlord. Your own possessions, should there be a fire (and a fire can start in someone else's apartment and spread throughout the building), will have no protection at all unless you have your own insurance. The tenant's form, HO-4, will provide reimbursement for loss of your worldly goods, from the risks itemized in HO-2. It will also provide additional living expenses should you need to seek temporary housing while your own premises are being repaired after insured damage. Costs are moderate; ask your insurance agent.

Owners of cooperative apartments may use either the renter's (HO-4) policy or the special form (HO-6) designed for owners of condominium units (see Chapter 14).

Cutting the Costs of Insurance

Insurance is an inexpensive way to protect an expensive investment. According to the Bureau of Labor Statistics, homeowner's insurance represents just 5.3 percent of the total costs related to home ownership (see Table 12.4).

Table 12.4: Household Expenditures Related to Owning a Home

Mortgage interest:	61.5%
Property taxes:	19.8%
Maintenance:	13.3%
Homeowners insurance:	5.3%

Percentages do not add up to 100% because of rounding.

Source: Alliance of American Insurers, Bureau of Labor Statistics.

Clearly it would be the ultimate foolishness to cut corners on property insurance. Without adequate insurance, you stand the chance of losing the biggest investment of a lifetime. A few dollars a month can make all the difference.

But this does not mean that you want to waste money on insurance either. There are legitimate ways to keep costs down while having proper coverage.

PREMIUM CONSIDERATIONS

Homeowners insurance premiums are based on several factors:

■ The rates approved in your state. There's not much you can do about this.

■ The loss experience of your particular company; you can shop around for a company with lower premiums. Bear in mind, however, that you want a company that provides good service as well as a company with low premiums; ask friends for recommendations based on personal experience. But premiums for the same house in the same location have been found to vary among companies by as much as 50 to 60 percent; comparisons are certainly in order.

■ The construction of your house. Brick or stone houses, because they are not as vulnerable to fire, are often less expensive to insure. The addition of smoke and/or fire detectors to your home, whether the house is brick or frame, will probably earn you a discount; the discount is larger if the alarm is connected to a central station.

■ The type of fire department and the nearness of a water supply. You'll generally pay less for insurance if your community has a paid professional fire department; you're also better off with a hydrant in front of your house or a fire department within a mile of your home.

■ The type of policy you buy and the amount of coverage you select. Here's where you have the greatest control and can save the greatest amount of money. But don't stick to bare-bones protection without evaluating all your options. You can have more extensive coverage, and save some money, if you are willing to pay for some portion of potential losses yourself. Deductibles are the key.

Deductibles

Take the largest deductible you think you can manage over and above the standard $250 deductible in most homeowners policies and put your insurance dollars to work against the catastrophic situation, the situation that could impoverish you and your family. A $500 deductible, depending on the amount of insurance on your house and which company you use, might save you from 5 to 10 percent of the annual premium.

For example: According to Kemper National Insurance Companies, the annual premium on a $130,000 frame house in Arlington Heights, Illinois, a suburb of Chicago, would be $269 a year with the standard $250 deductible and $100,000 of liability coverage. The cost would go up by about $10 a year if you raise the liability coverage to $300,000, and by another $27 if you elect replacement cost coverage on your contents. It would come down by 10 percent, to $242, with a $500 deductible, and by about 25 percent, to $202, with a $1,000 deductible. The savings might be used to buy additional liability protection or to add coverage for valuable items.

ONCE YOU HAVE INSURANCE ON YOUR PROPERTY

It's not enough to buy insurance and put it aside. In addition to periodic updates to compensate for rising home values, you should:

■ Read your policy, and understand your coverage. It isn't always easy, even though more and more policies are now written in what the insurance industry calls "plain English." But it's worthwhile to understand your policy before you're faced with filing a claim.

■ Keep your coverage up to date, notifying your company or agent of changes or improvements to your home.

■ Keep track of your possessions with an ongoing inventory. Itemize what you buy, when, and for how much. Write down serial numbers of appliances, photographic equipment, etc. Keep the list, along with purchase receipts and a photographic record of valuables, in a safe place away from home. In case of theft or fire, you'll need this documentation for the insurance company. Without an up-to-date inventory, in fact, you'll find it almost impossible to reconstruct the contents of your own home. Try to picture one entire room, right now, from memory, and you'll see, upon checking, how much you've probably missed.

■ Buy whatever extra coverage you need. If your inventory shows, for instance, that you have valuables that won't be covered beyond minimal amounts on your homeowners policy, take out a personal articles floater or a blanket valuables endorsement. It doesn't cost a great deal, and it's worth it for peace of mind.

■ Keep your policy, or a copy of it, in a safe place away from home. You can get a copy from your insurance company, but if you do have a fire you'll want to be able to refer to that policy in a hurry.

■ If you do have a loss, let your insurance company know without delay. If you suspect theft, report it to your local police department; that report, whether or not the police can do anything to recover your property, will help to back up an insurance claim.

If you have questions about property insurance, the National Insurance Consumer Helpline (call 800-942-4242) will provide you with answers to most questions about household or automobile insurance as well as health and life insurance. If you are dissatisfied with insurance company service after you make a claim, the helpline will assist you by contacting the company directly. If you are still dissatisfied, contact your state insurance department.

KEY POINTS

■ Homeowners insurance covering property damage and liability comes in several forms. If you own your own house, consider buying a comprehensive HO-3 policy.

■ Insuring your home to at least 80 percent of its replacement value will ensure full reimbursement for partial losses. It's far safer, however, to insure your home to 100 percent of replacement value and have inflation adjustments built into the policy.

■ Standard coverage of household contents is 50 percent of the amount of insurance on the house itself; you can increase this coverage to 70 percent. Replacement cost coverage on contents will enable you to replace stolen or damaged property at current prices.

■ Some types of personal property are excluded from household contents coverage; others are covered but to a limited extent. You may want a personal articles floater or other special policy to fill these gaps.

■ Umbrella liability coverage can provide additional protection above the limits in both your homeowners and automobile policies.

■ Floods and earthquakes are not covered under standard homeowners policies, but may be covered separately.

CHAPTER 13

Taxes and Homeownership

Owners have tax advantages over renters. Why? Not because Uncle Sam loves homeowners (although it sometimes seems that way), but because the income tax structure of the United States has long favored borrowers of money. The tax advantages of most borrowing have been wiped out but not the advantages of the borrowing most people do, in the form of a mortgage, to buy a house or a condominium. Mortgage payments consist partly of principal and partly of interest; the portion that is interest (on mortgage loans up to $1,000,000) may be deducted from your taxable income, thereby reducing the taxes due.

The deductibility of mortgage interest is probably most important, but there are other reasons why owning a home is financially more appealing, for most people, than renting:

- Property tax payments are deductible.
- The tax due on profit from the sale of a house may be deferred.
- Sellers over age 55 may sell their homes without paying any tax on sizable sums.
- Equity in your home can be tapped for other purposes, such as paying for college (see Chapter 17) or providing income for the elderly (see p. 331). The interest on a home equity loan of up to $100,000 may be deducted from federal income tax returns.

All these benefits hold true despite massive recent changes in tax law. Virtually all other areas of the tax code have undergone dramatic change, but the tax advantages of home ownership remain (at least for now) almost unscathed. There are still tax advantages when you buy a house, while you own it, and when you sell. Overlook any of them, and you can be out considerable sums of money.

When You Buy a House or Condominium

Right at the outset there are two major tax benefits: the tax-deductible portions of closing costs and the potential tax deductions if you've moved for job-related reasons, both available to all buyers who itemize deductions.

CLOSING COSTS

The costs of taking title fall into three categories. Some may be deducted from your taxable income in the year you make the purchase. Some are totally nondeductible. And some may be added to the "basis," the initial cost of your house for tax purposes; this figure becomes important when you sell the property.

Deductible Closing Costs

The closing costs you may deduct in the year you take title include real estate taxes, interest, and points. Each point is one percent of the loan amount. (Note, though, that points may be fully deductible in the year you take title only on an initial mortgage for a primary residence; they must be spread over time for refinancing and for vacation homes.)

Real estate taxes are usually divided between buyer and seller. If you take title on September 1 and the seller paid part of the year's property taxes on August 15, your settlement costs would normally include a proportionate share of those taxes for the period you own the house. You may deduct that share on your federal income taxes for the year. Even if you don't reimburse the seller for that amount, you are still permitted to deduct it on your return. If you don't reimburse the seller, however, you must reduce the basis of your property by the amount the seller paid on your behalf.

Q We recently bought a time-share property, financing the purchase through the developer. May we claim the interest as a mortgage deduction on our income tax?

A Yes, if you bought the time-share in what's called "fee simple" ownership—meaning you received a deed. No, if you simply bought the "right to use" the property. Where a deed is issued, time-shares qualify as a secondary residence under Internal Revenue Service (IRS) regulations. That means that you may deduct the interest on your loan—even if you use the property only for a week or two a year and even if you swap it for the use of other facilities.

For more information on time-shares, see pp. 387-390.

Interest charges on the mortgage to the date of settlement also normally appear on the closing statement and are deductible.

Points charged by a lender as a fee for granting the loan are deductible if they are solely for the use of money and therefore constitute interest. If the points are compensation for specific services such as an appraisal fee or document preparation, then the payment is not interest and may not be deducted. The determination depends, to some extent, on established practices in your area. As in other complex tax areas, it is always wise to consult a knowledgeable tax adviser.

Nondeductible Items

The settlement-day checks you write that are purely out-of-pocket expenses, with no tax benefit, include homeowners insurance premiums, mortgage insurance, charges for the use of utilities, and other fees or charges for services related to the occupancy of the house.

Closing Costs that Affect Your Tax Basis

Just about all other closing costs may be added to your basis, the official cost of your house for tax purposes, thereby reducing the capital gains tax due when you later sell the house at a profit (see pp. 370-371). These items include attorney's fees, abstract fees, surveys, transfer taxes, title insurance, and anything actually owed by the seller that you agree to pay, such as recording or mortgage fees, charges for improvements or repairs, and a commission to a real estate agent.

HOUSE-HUNTING AND MOVING COSTS

If you move because you've changed the place where you work, you may deduct certain allowable expenses, but only if you itemize the deductions on your federal income tax return. You may do so even if you are a tenant rather than a homeowner. See pp. 574-576 for details.

Q I accepted a new job 600 miles away, without thinking about how expensive it would be just to find a place to live and make the move. Are any of these costs tax-deductible?

A Yes, if your move is necessitated by a job you've already secured, you may deduct the cost of house-hunting trips, of temporary living expenses, and of the move itself, up to specified limits. You don't actually have to buy a house to make a house-hunting trip deductible, but the trip's principal purpose must be to find a place to live.

The costs of selling and buying a house or condominium in a job-related move may be applied to your tax advantage in one of two ways: You may deduct them as moving expenses, or you may use these costs to reduce the gain on the sale of your old home or to increase the basis on your new home. The IRS suggests that it may be preferable to deduct them as moving expenses; if you reach the allowable ceiling on moving expenses, then turn to the second choice. But do the arithmetic and see what works best for you.

Note: At this writing, pending federal legislation would limit total deductions for moving expenses to no more than $5,000. In some cases, particularly longer moves, this might not cover anything beyond the cost of transporting your household goods.

While You Own a House or Condominium

One big tax advantage of home ownership is the deductible interest you pay on your mortgage loan. Another advantage lies in the deductibility of real estate taxes from federal, state, and local income taxes. The higher your marginal tax bracket, the more you save. Other tax benefits for some homeowners include casualty loss deductions and an office at home.

PROPERTY TAXES

Local taxes on real property pay for schools, for police, for fire protection and parks, and all the expenses of running local government. Some towns keep residential property taxes down by encouraging industrial and commercial development; others keep taxes down by providing minimal services; some, no matter how hard officials try, can't keep taxes down at all. Evaluate a prospective community carefully before you decide to buy, because local real estate taxes can be a major ongoing expense of home ownership.

Property taxes seem to rise inexorably, even in an era when property values are, at best, holding steady. Money collected in property taxes on the local level rose almost 8 percent from 1991 to 1992. The areas with the highest property taxes (you know, if you're a resident): the District of Columbia, Alaska, Connecticut, New Hampshire, New Jersey, and New York. The lowest tax burden is carried by residents of Alabama, Arkansas, Kentucky, New Mexico and West Virginia.

One way to evaluate property taxes is strictly dollars-and-cents; how much will you pay out of pocket each year to your local government? Another involves measuring property taxes in terms of personal income. According to the Tax Foundation, a nonprofit research and public education organization based in Washington, D.C., property tax burdens relative to personal income increased in 24 states and the District of Columbia from 1980 to 1990. Another involves looking at property taxes as a percentage of your home's market value. A 1992 study of some 200 cities nationwide by Runzheimer

International revealed some interesting relationships between taxes and market values; see Table 13.1.

THE EFFECT OF DECLINING PROPERTY VALUES

Local real estate taxes are based on assessments of market value. Periodic assessments (exactly how often depends on the local community) establish market value; the tax (at so many dollars per $100 of value) is then pegged at full market value or at a specified percentage thereof. When assessments are down, because market value is down, the tax **rate** is generally increased to provide the necessary tax revenues.

Either way, assessments usually lag behind volatile real estate costs. The lag helped homeowners, by keeping taxes down to earlier levels, when home values were rising rapidly. In a housing recession, however, values rise less rapidly, level off, or even fall, and today's assessments may be based on yesterday's higher market value.

You may, as a result, find your property overassessed and overtaxed.

Q Property taxes on our house and quarter acre come to about $2,800 a year, or $700 every three months. We've always scraped the money together when each payment is due. Now we're refinancing and the lender has offered to collect money each month, along with the mortgage payments, to hold and apply to our quarterly tax payments. Is this a good deal for us?

A You're lucky to have the choice; most lenders insist on collecting both property taxes and homeowners insurance premiums and keeping them in an escrow or trust account. Should you accept the lender's offer? If you find it difficult to make the payment each quarter, you may find it easier to pay your taxes to the bank in monthly installments. Find out, however, whether or not your lender will pay interest on money held in the property tax escrow account. If not, you could be better off (if you can discipline yourselves to do so) putting the money each month into an interest-earning savings account.

Note: If your monthly payment to your mortgage lender includes an amount placed in escrow for real estate taxes, you may not simply deduct the total of these amounts as your real estate taxes for the year; you must report the amount actually assessed and actually paid by the lender on your behalf. Ask your lender to supply you with this figure if you don't receive it at year-end.

When You Want to Appeal Your Assessment

Even though the tax rate may go up when assessments go down, you owe it to yourself to be sure your home is fairly assessed. If it's not, you should file a tax appeal. The steps in an appeal are as follows:

1. Find out if your house has been accurately evaluated. It's not uncommon for homeowners to discover, when they ask, that their house has been listed as, for example, larger than it actually is. It's not uncommon to find a half bathroom listed as a full bathroom, or a brick facade translated into an all-brick house. Some busy appraisers simply don't take all the time they should.

2. Then, if the evaluation has been accurate and you still believe that your assessment is too high, you have to provide evidence to change the assessor's mind. Talk to neighbors with similar houses and find out if their appraisals were similar; look at property tax records in your town office to see comparable houses and their assessments; review records of recent sales in the office where deeds are recorded, again looking for comparable houses and their valuations; talk to real estate agents for an estimate of current market value.

   If you believe that there are specific physical conditions that should reduce your assessment, take pictures to show the assessor. A flooded basement, cracked walls indicating settling, old plumbing fixtures ... all may prove your contention that your assessment is too high. (Personal financial problems, such as unemployment or overindebtedness, are not grounds for the reduction of an assessment.)

3. Then request a meeting with the assessor. Explain your case, and show your evidence. Your appraisal may be reduced right then and there. If not, and if you are not satisfied, you can appeal upward, first (depending on the community and state in which you live) to a county board and then, perhaps, to the state level. Your last resort is the courts.

Be sure to follow the timetable set by your town. And don't decide, without a try, that it's not worth the effort. The appeal procedure is simple. You don't need a lawyer (unless you choose to go to court and, even then, some special tax courts permit you to present your own case). And, it's estimated, a significant proportion of this country's homeowners are paying more property tax than they should be.

Table 13.1: Real Estate Taxes Related to Home Market Values

Location	Home Market Value	Annual Real Estate Taxes	% of Home Market Value
High Tax Areas			
Battle Creek, MI	$131,600	$4,792	3.64%
Racine, WI	163,000	5,350	3.28
Syracuse, NY	187,600	6,120	3.26
Kankakee, IL	128,000	3,886	3.04
Waterloo, IA	165,100	4,769	2.89
Low Tax Areas			
Monroe, LA	$106,000	$ 269	.25%
Decatur, AL	118,500	405	.34
Honolulu, HI	465,400	1,571	.34
Huntington, WV	129,800	449	.35
Seaford, DE	117,500	466	.40

The home market values shown above are based on a 2,400-square-foot, 8 room, 4 bedroom, 2.5 bath home in communities in or around the central city where families in the $60,000 income bracket reside. Real estate taxes are obtained directly from the local tax office in each community or county in which the homes are located.

Source: Runzheimer International.

CASUALTY AND THEFT LOSSES

If you're unlucky enough to suffer financial loss via casualty or theft, you can, at least, claim certain tax deductions.

Q My husband is only 38 but he's been disabled and unable to work for over two years. My friend said we don't have to pay property taxes because of his disability. Is she right?

A It depends on where you live. Some communities have property tax exemptions or, more often, specified reductions for senior citizens and/or the disabled. Look on the back of your next tax bill, or call your local tax assessor for information.

Casualty Loss

To qualify as a casualty loss, damage, destruction, or loss of either real or personal property must result from an identifiable event that is sudden, unexpected, or unusual. Some qualifying events: earthquakes, fires, hurricanes, tornadoes, floods, storms, sonic booms, vandalism, and volcanic eruptions. Structural damage from termites is not a casualty loss because it takes place over a period of time; structural damage from a flash flood, however, generally qualifies. Smog would not, as a rule, qualify. But it may, if a sudden and severe concentration of chemical fumes in the air damages the paint on your house.

Until changes in the tax law in 1982, uninsured losses exceeding $100 could be deducted in full on your federal income tax return. Now, although the $100 base remains intact, losses are deductible only to the extent that they exceed 10 percent of your adjusted gross income. If your adjusted gross income is $30,000, your loss has to exceed $3,000 before you can claim a deduction. This means that it's now more important than ever before to carry adequate insurance.

Here are the current rules for claiming a casualty loss:

■ Reduce the loss by $100 and by any insurance compensation. If you have $400 of storm damage, and your insurance company settles your claim for $300, you are left without a casualty deduction.

■ Deduct the loss in the year the casualty occurs, unless you expect reimbursement that is later refused. In this case, you may deduct the loss when your claim is rejected.

Q I had some jewelry soaking in a cleaning solution, in a glass by the kitchen sink. When my son washed the dinner dishes, he dumped the jewelry into the sink and turned on the garbage disposal. The jewelry, which was not insured, was ruined. Can I take a casualty deduction?

A In a similar case the Internal Revenue Service said no, because the person dumping the glass was negligent, but the Tax Court reversed the decision and allowed a full deduction. The IRS itself gives a similar example of a qualifying deduction. A car door is accidentally slammed on your hand, breaking the setting of your diamond engagement ring (the IRS doesn't mention what happens to your hand). The diamond falls from the ring and is never found. The loss of the diamond is a deductible casualty (with the deductible amount determined by its value in relation to your adjusted gross income).

■ Prove the loss, by collecting appropriate documentation as soon as possible after the loss occurs. Pictures of the damage, or newspaper photographs and reports, are helpful.

■ The amount you may claim is based on the decrease in fair market value of the property after the loss. Bear in mind, however, that no matter how much your property may have increased in value since its purchase, you may never claim a loss greater than the original cost plus improvements. Keep purchase slips, appraisals, photographs, and any evidence which will document property value.

Theft Loss

To qualify as a deductible theft loss, personal property must have been unlawfully taken under the laws of your state via larceny, robbery, embezzlement, extortion, or other criminal means. Accidental loss or disappearance may sometimes qualify if it results from a sudden or unusual event or if circumstances strongly indicate that theft may have occurred.

The same rules apply for theft as for casualty losses: The loss must be reduced by $100 and any insurance reimbursement; the loss must be deducted in the year it occurs; the amount you may claim may never be more than the original cost of the property; the deductible amount of the loss must exceed 10 percent of your adjusted gross income.

Proof may be even more important where theft is concerned, since the IRS does not generally allow accidental loss to qualify. Make a report to the police if you suspect a theft, even if neither you nor they can prove a theft actually took place. The police report itself will provide documentation.

Q I gave a builder a $5,000 deposit on a new house. The foundation was dug; then the builder went bankrupt. It doesn't look as if I'll get my money back. Can I claim a theft loss on my income tax return?

A You can't claim a theft loss unless fraud was involved, but you can claim a nonbusiness bad debt deduction. Even though your deposit was not actually a loan to the builder, you do have a legitimate claim for repayment of your money. As tax experts at Prentice-Hall point out, that creates a debtor-creditor relationship and you can take the deduction. A nonbusiness bad debt is treated as short-term capital loss and is deductible to the extent of any capital gains you may have plus $3,000 of ordinary income. Any excess can be carried forward from year to year, reducing taxes due, until it is used up.

IF YOU MAINTAIN AN OFFICE AT HOME

If you work at home, you may qualify for a home office tax deduction. But the IRS is tough on this one; you must meet stringent requirements: The part of your home that you use for business must be used *exclusively* as your *principal* place of business or as a place of business used for meeting with patients, clients, or customers. There are only two exceptions to the "exclusive use" test: using your home as a day-care facility, or using part of your home for storage of inventory.

This means that if you use a den in your home to prepare legal briefs for a part-time legal practice but also occasionally use it as a guest room, you may not claim a tax deduction for its business use—unless you've divided the room and can clearly identify the separate space used for work. If you work at another location five days a week and at home on evenings and weekends, you can't claim a deduction for work you do at home for your employer, but you can claim a deduction if your home office is your principal place of business for a sideline business. And, if you are a traveling salesperson or self-employed consultant, on the road most of the time, you can no longer claim a deduction for your home office because it is not (under a new and stringent interpretation) your "principal" place of business.

If you qualify for a home office deduction, you should use form 8829 to document your deductions; this form, introduced in 1992 for the 1991 tax year, supplements the Schedule C filed by sole proprietors. Deduct **direct expenditures** in full; an example would be the cost of painting your office. (Some direct business expenditures, such as the purchase of equipment and supplies, are deductible as business expenses whether or not you qualify for the home office deduction.)

Deduct **indirect expenses** in an amount proportionate to the percentage of your home that is used for business. Indirect expenses include painting the outside of your home or repairing the roof; note, though, that landscaping and

Q In addition to my full-time work as a nursery school teacher, I've just set up a typing service in my home. If I start keeping records now, will I be able to deduct expenses for my home office?

A Not long ago, the answer would have been no. But recently relaxed IRS regulations make it possible to take home office deductions for a secondary business. You must follow the same rules as if you ran a full-time business from home: You must set aside a portion of your home to be used exclusively and on a regular basis for your typing service. And you must make some money for your efforts; deductions may not exceed your income.

lawn care are not deductible. Nor is any portion of the rental charge for the first telephone line in your home, although itemized toll calls do qualify; in order to deduct the full cost of your business phone, put in a second line. The proportion of indirect costs may be figured as square footage or, if your rooms are approximately equal in size, on a per-room basis.

If you set aside 10 percent of your home for your office, therefore, you may deduct one-tenth of such items as real estate taxes and mortgage interest (the balance of these two items is deductible on your regular income tax return), outside painting, fuel costs, and so on. But you must make your deductions in sequence: (1) taxes and interest, up to the extent of income; (2) operating expenses allocable to the office; (3) allocable depreciation.

For example: You set up a former breakfast room, which is one-tenth of the total floor space in your house, as an office for your typing service. Net income from the typing service in your first year is $500. You had the following expenses:

	Total	10% for business
Taxes	$1,500	$150
Interest	2,500	250
Operating expenses of home	1,500	150
Depreciation	1,000	100

According to the IRS, you figure your deductions for business use as follows:

	1. Business net income		$500
Less:	2. Taxes	$150	
and	3. Interest	+ 250	400
	4. Balance		$100
Less:	5. Operating expenses of home		$150
and	6. Depreciation		100
	7. Total		$250
	8. Deduction (line 4 or 7, whichever is less):		$100

In general, your total home office deductions in any one year may not exceed your net income from the business. And watch out for another rule: In order to exclude deductions in connection with hobbies, the IRS requires that you show a profit for three or more years of any consecutive five year period.

You'll have to file a Schedule C, Profit (or Loss) from Business or Profession, along with your federal income tax return. You might want to consult IRS Publication No. 587, *Business Use of Your Home,* one of a lengthy series of specialized tax advice booklets published by the IRS and revised annually. And, because this area is extremely complicated, you would do well to consult a competent tax adviser.

Selling a House With a Home Office

When you sell a house on which you are taking a home office deduction, your tax situation will be complicated. You have to treat the sale as if you sold two pieces of property, one a residence and the other a business. The deferral of tax applicable to the residence portion (see p. 372) will not be applicable to the business portion; you will have to pay any tax due in the year of the sale And, just to go a step further, if your new home will contain an office, you must treat the purchase (for tax purposes) as if you were buying two pieces of property.

Note: The Tax Code does contain a loophole. If the home office deduction is not taken in the year of the sale, no matter how many years it's been taken before, the entire profit from the sale may be rolled over into a new residence. This is considered an aggressive stance by some tax advisers, one that might subject you to an audit. But others believe that this is acceptable so long as you can document that the room previously used exclusively for a home office is now used for other purposes (you've moved the family television in, or the kids' toys).

When You Sell a House or Condominium

The Landons bought their Brooklyn brownstone in 1968, when the area was just reverting to single-family occupancy, for $26,000. They've put another $40,000 or so into the house over the years, putting in new plumbing and an entirely new kitchen, stripping and refinishing walls and floors, and so on. It was a financial struggle for a long time, with rent from a basement apartment helping to defray the costs. Now, however, the neighborhood is very desirable and the house is worth $420,000.

Here's the big tax payoff, the place where Uncle Sam really demonstrates his affection for homeowners. Under normal circumstances the sale of property on which you've made a profit leads to a substantial tax liability; profits, after all, are grist for the tax man's mill. If the Landons' $66,000 investment had been an investment in the stock market, they would owe tax on the $354,000 in profit. But when the profit is made on a house, there are a number of legitimate ways to reduce the tax, postpone the tax, or avoid it altogether. First, however, you have to understand how the profit on a house is calculated.

HOW TO CALCULATE THE PROFIT WHEN YOU SELL YOUR HOUSE

Don't just subtract the purchase price from your sales price, or you'll pay more tax than necessary. The Landons paid $26,000 for their house and sold it for $420,000, which looks like a profit of $394,000. But they also put additional money into the house. Even if you haven't performed the extensive renovations necessary on an old brownstone, you've put money into your house too.

Here's how to perform the calculations:

1. Determine the **basis** or tax cost of the house you've sold. Take your original purchase price and add to it (a) fees paid at the closing for title insurance, legal services, etc., and (b) the cost of any capital improvements (such as a new deck or central air conditioning) that enhanced the value of the house. Reduce the basis by any tax credits or deductions previously claimed for residential energy credits (based on installing approved energy-saving devices) or casualty losses (from theft or natural disaster; see pp. 366-367).
2. Determine the **adjusted sales price** of the old house by taking the sales price and subtracting broker's commissions, legal fees, and any allowable fix-up costs (such as painting the house, within ninety days of entering into a sales contract, to make the house more salable).
3. The difference between the basis and the adjusted sales price is your taxable profit.

Reducing the Tax on House-Sale Profits

If you find yourself in the position of owing taxes on the profits in your home, the rules on installment sales may prove helpful. Under these rules, you close the deal as you otherwise would but spread the payments over time, paying tax as the money is received. As long as you receive at least one payment after the tax year in which the sale took place, the transaction qualifies as an installment sale. The size of the down payment no longer matters, as it once did. Nor do you have to report your decision to the IRS; the installment method of reporting will be assumed unless you state otherwise.

In an example provided by tax attorney Julian Block, suppose you realize a profit of $45,000 on a home you sell for $150,000. If you are not buying another house, you can't roll over the profit. Take the entire $45,000 in one year, add it to your other income, and you will owe more in income tax than

Q After a contractor quoted almost $1,700 to insulate our basement walls, I did the job myself for under $600 in materials. I've also done a lot of other work around the house. How do I determine what to add to the tax cost of the house?

A Do-it-yourselfers have to resign themselves to saving money on their original work. The IRS won't recognize the value of your own labor or the market value of the job. All you can add to the basis of the house is the actual cost of materials for improvements that enhance the value of the house.

you care to think about. But suppose you divide the $150,000 purchase price in thirds, taking $30,000 as a down payment in December of the first year, $45,000 in January of the following year, and $75,000 the year after that. In effect, since the December and January payments are so close, you're spreading payment over two years. For tax purposes, however, you now have three years in which to pay your due to Uncle Sam. Instead of reporting the entire $45,000 profit in a single year, you wind up reporting $9,000 the first year, $13,500 the second, and $22,500 the third; the figures are based on the 30 percent portion of profit (the profit of $45,000 divided by the sale price of $150,000) in each installment, plus interest income.

This means that you can arrange the sale of your house to suit your tax picture. If you are under 55 and can't take the one-time exclusion, and if you do not plan to buy a larger house (see below), you might arrange to spread the payments for your house over a period of time. You might even sell the house this year and choose not to receive any money at all until next year. The whole flexible arrangement (spelled out in IRS Publication No. 537) allows you to minimize the tax bite on the sale of a house. Again, however, it would be a good idea to consult a competent tax adviser.

Deferring the Tax on House-Sale Profits

Tax on the gain from the sale of your home is postponed if you buy another home whose price is at least as much as the adjusted sales price of your former residence. Here are the rules:

Q We bought our home in 1987, just at the peak of the market, for $187,000. Now we have to move to another state because of a job transfer, and we don't think the house will bring more than $130,000. That's less than we still owe on our mortgage. Can we take the loss as a deduction on our income tax return?

A No. While Uncle Sam is happy to tax home-sale profits, he grants no favors to homeowners forced to sell at a loss. And don't get any idea that you can walk away from your remaining obligation on the mortgage, simply letting the lender take over the house. The lender can—and probably will—come after you, garnisheeing your paycheck, if necessary, to collect on its loan. And, if the lender decides not to collect, the IRS will say you owe taxes on the lender's "forgiveness of debt"—even though you're actually losing money on the deal. Perhaps you can rent out your house until the housing market rebounds.

■ Both the old house and the new house must be your principal residence. A condominium, a cooperative apartment, a mobile home, or a houseboat qualifies as well as a single-family detached house. A vacation home does not.

■ You must move into the new residence within two years of the sale of the old residence. There are no exceptions to the time test; if the house you are building burns down just before you are ready to move in, the IRS will not take pity on you. (Certain adjustments are possible only if you are on active duty in the armed forces.)

■ Your investment in the new house must equal or exceed the selling price of your old house, the adjusted sales price defined earlier, if you are to defer tax on the entire gain. If the cost of the new house is less, you are taxed on the difference. You may count capital improvements to your new house (such as landscaping or a new deck) as part of its costs, as long as they are paid for within the two-year period.

You may defer the payment of the tax no matter how many times you buy and sell (except that, unless a move is job-related, you are limited to one deferral in a two-year period), as long as each new house is at least as expensive as the one before. You don't have to invest the cash proceeds from the sale into the new house either. The deferral takes place even with a no-down-payment mortgage. When the time comes for a smaller and less expensive house, the tax will be due ... unless you are then over age 55.

The Over-55 Exclusion

Eventually, for most people, the time comes when you want a smaller house instead of a bigger one. This time typically arrives when the children are grown and you're nearing retirement. The tax code, oddly enough, recognizes this particular human need; tax on up to $125,000 of profit is eliminated alto-

Q My wife inherited her parents' home and we plan to live in it, but it needs major renovation before we can move in. We'll sell our current home and use the money to remodel. Can we deduct the remodeling cost from the profit on our home sale?

A Yes, but you will owe capital gains tax on any profit in your current house to the extent that it exceeds the amount you invest in remodeling the house you inherit. You can't use the value of the inherited house itself to reduce the taxes you'll owe (even though you'll use it as your primary residence) because you're not actually buying the house.

gether if either you or your spouse is over 55 on the date of sale. (However, you may still owe state tax; consult your tax adviser.) Here are the rules for the federal exemption:

- The 55th birthday must take place before the date of sale; if your birthday is in April, don't sell your house in February.
- You must have owned and lived in the house, as your principal residence (vacation cottages and rental property don't count), for at least three years out of the five years preceding the date of sale. (**Note:** This requirement is reduced to an aggregate of one year out of the prior five years if the taxpayer has been confined to a nursing home.)
- You and your spouse must agree on the exclusion, even if you file separate returns and even if only one of you owns the house.
- You must never before have taken this exemption. This is a once-in-a-lifetime deal for you and your spouse. You can't use part of the $125,000 on one house and part on another. You can't use it with one spouse and then, after widowhood (or divorce) and remarriage, use it with another. If you're over 55 and planning to marry someone who's already used the exclusion, be smart: Sell your house and take your tax exclusion before you marry. Otherwise, you'll lose it forever.

Note: If you take a loss when you sell your house, it is not deductible under current rules. However, a bill is currently pending in Congress that would permit taxpayers to use losses from the sale of a principal residence to reduce their basis in their new homes; this would have the effect of ultimately reducing any gain that would otherwise be reported.

Special Situations

There are other tax ramifications of property ownership. The biggest, perhaps, is that associated with the death of a property owner. Estate planning with respect to property ownership, including the sticky question of who should own what (it's no longer always necessarily wise to own property jointly, even if you are happily married), is discussed in detail in Chapter 21. Tax questions also arise in cases of divorce and around the ownership of vacation homes.

DIVORCE

Do you own your family home jointly? Are you getting a divorce? Watch out for the tax consequences.

Several different things can take place. Sometimes one spouse (perhaps the husband wants to remain in the family home while the wife takes an apartment) will buy out the other's share. This is a clear-cut purchase by one and sale by the other, and the appropriate taxes are due—except that, under new rules, buyouts within one year of divorce, or directly related to divorce, result in no taxable gain or loss to either party.

In other instances, one spouse (often the wife) will take sole title to the house as part of the divorce settlement in place of alimony or other portions of the marital property. When this was the case, until recently, the IRS treated the transaction as a sale and a purchase; a tax based on appreciated value of the property was immediately payable—even though no cash changed hands and the "seller" might not have had the means to pay. Today the rules are different. There is now no gain or loss to either party when property is transferred as part of a divorce settlement. The transfer is considered a gift. Should the recipient sell the property, however, tax will then be due.

There are also state tax ramifications, but they depend on where you live. In some situations, if you and your spouse are on relatively good terms, it may be wise to split property before you split the marriage. In others it would be a big mistake. Be sure, if you are contemplating divorce, to get good legal and financial advice. It's extremely difficult to change agreements once they are made.

VACATION HOMES

A second home can provide a welcome change of scenery; it may also provide a valuable tax shelter. But the shelter has been leaking a bit since the Tax Acts of 1976 and 1986 greatly tightened the tax deductions that could be taken on second homes. Here are the rules:

Personal Use

If you use your second home solely for your family's personal pleasure, you may deduct interest, taxes, and casualty losses as you do on your year-round home. Personal use has become a lot more popular since lower tax rates and restricted tax advantages combined to curtail investment benefits.

Q I inherited a house which my parents had lived in for thirty-five years. I'm planning to sell and know that it will bring many thousands of dollars more than they paid for it back in the 1940s. How do I calculate the tax?

A Any increase in value between the date of original purchase and the date of the owner's death is forgiven for tax purposes. You must calculate your tax on the basis of the increase in value between the date of death (or six months thereafter, as determined by the estate's executor) and the date on which you sell the property.

Note: You may rent out the property for up to 15 days in any one year and still claim exclusive personal use. If you do so, you need not report any rental income and you may not deduct any rental expenses.

Rental Property

If you own the home primarily as a profit-making venture and don't use it yourself for more than 14 days during the year (or 10 percent of the time the house is available for rent if greater than 14 days), then you may also shelter some of your rental income via deductions for depreciation and maintenance. If your expenses exceed your income for the property, in other words, and if you actively manage the property, as much as $25,000 of the loss may be used to offset some of your other income. The $25,000 amount is phased out as your adjusted gross income goes from $100,000 to $150,000; once you earn that much, you can't claim any loss. These income levels apply to both single taxpayers and married taxpayers filing jointly. But you can't double the benefit by filing separately if you're married.

You are allowed to visit the property to fix it up, without counting such time as part of your "personal use" time. You're even allowed, since the IRS relented a bit, to have family and friends along while you work.

Both Personal Use and Rental Property

If you use the house for more than 14 days yourself *and* if you rent it out for more than 15 days during the year, then matters (and the taxes you owe) get complicated. Here's what you have to do:

Q My husband and I are negotiating a property settlement as part of our divorce. He wants his money out of our house, but I want to keep living here. If I take out a loan to buy his share of the house, can I deduct the interest on my tax return?

A Yes, so long as the loan is secured by the house and you buy out your husband within 90 days of taking the loan. But talk to an attorney or accountant knowledgeable about the tax consequences of the transfer. Because the IRS will treat it as a property settlement and not as a purchase, your "tax basis" in the house remains the same and you may owe more in taxes when you eventually sell the house.

Your husband won't have to pay taxes on the amount you pay him, so you may want to even things out, if possible, by negotiating a lower payment to buy him out.

1. Determine the amount of expenses attributable to rental activity. To do this, multiply your expenses for property taxes and mortgage interest by the number of rental days and then divide the result by the total number of days the house is in use.
2. Subtract the amount you get in step one from the gross rental income. If the figure is negative, stop here. You can deduct all of the interest and property taxes, just as you do for your primary residence, but you can't claim any other deductions. In other words, you can't deduct more than you earn in rent.
3. If the result of step two is positive, you can claim deductions for operating expenses such as insurance, repairs and utilities. But you must apply the same fraction you arrived at in step one until you meet the level of your gross revenue. You cannot create a tax loss.

Suggestion: If you have the cash to do so, it can make sense to pay down the mortgage on your vacation home. You'll lose the mortgage interest deduction, but you'll pick up other deductions that you might not otherwise be able to claim, up to a point. For example: You have a vacation home that you use about one-third of the year and rent out the other two-thirds. Your operating expenses—insurance, utilities, etc.—come to $6,000. You can deduct about $4,000 of the $6,000 in expenses, based on the two-thirds of the time you rent out the property. If you're deducting mortgage interest, that deduction may take up a good portion of the allowable $4,000; if you've paid down the mortgage, you may be able to claim other operating expenses instead. Do the arithmetic, with the help of your tax adviser, to see how it works out for you.

Q I own a cottage which I used to use as a family weekend and summer retreat. It's winterized and perfectly suitable for year-round living. We don't use it much anymore, however, and I'm thinking of renting it out on a year-round basis and taking the tax deductions that go with rental property. At the same time, my wife's parents need a place to live. Am I allowed to rent the cottage to them and still take the deductions?

A The Internal Revenue Service has had a very tough policy of disallowing deductions on rental to relatives, but that policy, after a lot of protest from taxpayers, has been amended. Now, as long as you charge a fair market rental (the equivalent of rents charged on similar accommodations in the local marketplace), the property should qualify for all normal deductions. Keep accurate records, however, and be able to show the IRS that no special favors changed hands.

Be careful in your calculations. Vacation home deductions are scrutinized by the Internal Revenue Service.

Record-keeping

There's so much money at stake in your home, so much potential tax liability, that record-keeping is enormously important. You may never run a business from home or sustain a casualty loss. But virtually everything you spend on your home (other than normal maintenance) will have some tax impact, either now or when you sell the house.

From the day you move in, therefore, keep a file with bills and receipts for every penny you spend on anything related to the purchase itself and to improvements to the house. Document every expenditure from closing costs to new storm windows to a deck or swimming pool. Don't forget to include receipts for the few dollars here and there for lumber or electrical outlets you install yourself; these expenses add up over time. This documentation may well reduce your tax liability when you sell the house.

Under most circumstances, documents to substantiate tax claims need to be kept for only three years after the date of filing. But receipts for the purchase or improvement of property on which taxes may be due when the property is sold should be kept until three years after the year in which that property is reported sold. With a house, where the basis of your old home is used for computing the basis of a new home, thereby postponing tax on the profit from the sale of the old home (no matter how many homes you buy in the course of a lifetime), keep the relevant records indefinitely. Those records include the purchase contract, settlement papers, and receipts and canceled checks for any improvements and additions to the property.

 KEY POINTS

- The income tax structure of the United States is designed to encourage the owning of property.
- The biggest tax deductions most people have are mortgage interest and property tax payments.
- Taxes may be deferred when a primary residence is sold, as long as another residence of at least equivalent value is bought.
- People over age 55 may avoid paying tax altogether on up to $125,000 of home-sale profit.
- Adequate records are essential if you want to take full advantage of home-related tax deductions.

CHAPTER 14

Condominiums, Cooperatives, and Mobile Homes

Housing choices go well beyond the issue of whether to rent or to buy. Once you decide to buy, you may want to consider a condominium unit, a cooperative apartment, or a form of manufactured housing. All three—because they tend to be less expensive than conventional single-family detached houses—are popular among first-time home buyers and among retirees. But there are fundamental differences among these housing forms, both in financial and in physical terms.

The Condominium

A condominium is actually a form of ownership, not a type of housing. Condominium ownership is found in high-rise apartment buildings, in attached townhouses and garden apartments, in vacation lodges, and in all forms of housing in retirement or "adult" communities.

If you buy a condominium, you will individually own and maintain the enclosed space you occupy. You will also share ownership, along with your neighbors, of the "common elements" of the property—the exterior of the building or buildings, hallways and utilities, landscaping and recreational facilities.

In many ways, owning a condominium is like owning a conventional single-family detached house: You secure your own mortgage and pay your own taxes (taking the appropriate tax deductions), you have a deed to your property, you may remodel and decorate its interior as you please, and you may sell it when you choose to move. In another way, owning a condominium is more like renting an apartment: You'll be in close proximity to neighbors; you will have to abide by community association rules about exterior decoration, use of the grounds, and so on; you won't have to care for those grounds yourself. Shoveling snow and mowing lawns will be the responsibility of the condominium owners association. You will have to pay a monthly maintenance fee toward the upkeep of the common elements, and you may also face periodic special assessments. If the roof or furnace needs replacing, you, as one of the owners, must share in the bill. (And if your neighbors fail to pay their assessments, you may have to pay their share as well. You will not, however, be responsible for their mortgages if they default.)

THE WIDE APPEAL OF CONDOMINIUMS

■ Jean holds a responsible job and works long hours. She wants to build equity instead of continuing to pay rent but does not, as a single woman with little leisure time, want to cope with home maintenance and repair. Her solution: an apartment condominium.

■ The Stulls have had many years of home ownership, upkeep, and repair. Now, as they near retirement, they want their own space (with room for grandchildren to visit) but they also want to be free to pick up and travel without worries about leaving property untended. Their solution: a townhouse condominium.

■ Marylou and Paul have their hearts set on a single-family detached house with a fenced play yard for the family they've just begun. But housing prices and mortgage interest rates are beyond even Paul's solid income as a corporate comptroller. Their solution, as a "starter" house: a detached condominium unit in a development.

In 1991, almost one in five first-time buyers bought a condominium; slightly more than one in ten repeat buyers did so as well. Singles and young childless couples often turn to condominiums because they are less expensive than detached single-family homes. But the National Association of Realtors reports that 42 percent of condominium purchasers in 1991 were age 55 and above, reflecting a trend by "empty-nesters" to scale down housing as they near retirement.

PRICE FACTORS IN A CONDOMINIUM PURCHASE

Condominiums, in general, cost less than individually owned houses. (They also, very often, contain less living space.) The median cost of a single-family home in 1991 was $118,700, according to an annual survey conducted by Chicago Title and Trust, while the median cost of a condominium unit was $109,500. The median is the midpoint of the price range; half sell for more, half for less. Apartment condominiums, however, are often far less expensive; these units, frequently the result of apartment conversions, play an important role as starter homes.

Mortgages on condominiums are exactly like mortgages on conventional housing, and median monthly housing expense for condominium owners is almost exactly the same as for house owners. Many specific costs are lower, according to one survey, but mandatory monthly assessments make the total just about the same. Recent increases in utility costs, maintenance and repair costs, taxes, insurance, and overall operating expenses have forced assessments up. Median monthly assessments for all types of condominium units stood at $136 in 1991, according to the Institute of Real Estate Management, while assessments for high-rise condominium unit owners are about $244.

The Condominium Assessment

As a condominium owner, you face two distinct sets of costs: assessments for upkeep, and maintenance of your own unit. As an owner, you are responsible for a proportionate share of operating and maintenance expenses on the common elements, including:

- Utilities
- Heating and air conditioning
- Management costs
- Garbage removal
- Janitorial service
- Grounds maintenance
- Security services
- Maintenance of recreational facilities
- Reserves for future expenses

Find out, before you buy, exactly what your assessment will cover. Is there a security patrol? Are new recreational facilities in the works? The most important thing to know: **Your assessment must be paid.** It is not voluntary. If you don't want a swimming pool and don't use it but your monthly assessment includes swimming pool maintenance, you must pay your share.

In addition to the assessment, you will be responsible for the costs of maintaining your own unit. This includes your mortgage payments and real estate taxes, remodeling and decorating, interior repairs and maintenance, and homeowners insurance.

INSURANCE ON YOUR CONDOMINIUM

The owners association should carry insurance on the common elements, the structure itself and the areas you share with your neighbors. Be sure that your association does carry fire, theft, worker's compensation, and liability insurance. Be sure, too, that you secure your own insurance to fill in any gaps.

You'll probably want an HO-6 policy, the Condominium Owners Form of homeowners insurance, to cover your own unit, including any additions or alterations not covered by the association's policy. When you own a condominium, even one that looks like an apartment, you are not simply renting an apartment. You may own, and need to protect, depending on the bylaws of your particular condominium, all the space in your unit within the outer walls of your building. That could include interior walls and fixtures such as kitchen cabinets in addition to your household goods.

You also need adequate liability insurance, including a clause that will protect you if the association itself is sued for more insurance than it carries. If this should happen—if someone is seriously injured, for instance, in a diving accident in the community-owned pool—each unit owner could be assessed to cover the amount of damages above and beyond the association's insurance. A loss assessment provision, now a standard part of most HO-6 policies, will protect you against such potentially costly loss. It will also protect you against loss from physical damage to the common property, above and beyond the association's coverage. An example might be the bursting of a hot water heating system or extensive roof damage from ice. Ask to see the association's policy, then arrange for your own coverage to pick up where it leaves off.

Note: If this provision is not part of your policy, ask your insurance agent about adding a loss assessment endorsement.

BEFORE YOU BUY

Condominium ownership is no longer a new concept in the United States, and many early problems with take-the-money-and-run developers have been resolved through state consumer protection laws. With or without consumer protection laws, however, it's up to you to protect yourself. Remember that a condominium purchase is a home purchase. It may be even more complex in its legal aspects than the purchase of a conventional house.

Q My husband has been out of work for some time, following an accident. My own salary isn't enough to pay all our bills. What will happen if I pay the mortgage but put off paying the monthly assessment on our condominium?

A You run the risk, in many states, of losing your unit through foreclosure by the condominium association. If your assessment is what the courts would define as reasonable (your association hasn't decided to put in an Olympic-size swimming pool), you are obligated to pay or you'll put an unfair burden on the other owners who will have to pick up your share. Talk to your association's board of directors, and work out an arrangement to pay your assessment over a period of time.

Take at least the same time and care in buying a condominium unit that you would in buying any house.

Read All the Documents

Read the master deed or declaration (the "constitution" for the condominium community, requiring unanimous vote for change), the bylaws (the operating rules and regulations), and the sales contract. Together these documents will probably amount to hundreds of pages of fine print, but this fine print will, if you buy, govern the way you live. Hire a lawyer, experienced in the specialized field of condominium law, to review the documents before you sign anything.

A careful reading of these documents will provide the answers to a number of important questions. Just what, for instance, will you actually own? A balcony may be part of the individual unit or it may be a common element; if it's a common element you may not be able to fix it up as you choose. Parking spaces may be individually owned, or they may be common elements, in which any owner may park in any spot. The land and recreational facilities may be owned as a common element or leased to the owners association by the developer at a cost which may become increasingly prohibitive. Commercial property within the development may become an albatross around owners' necks if the bottom drops out of the market for commercial space. Find out before you buy.

Familiarize yourself with the association bylaws. They may restrict your right to have visitors or to keep pets, to put up a fence or to paint your front door in a color of your choice. They may restrict your right to rent your unit to someone else, or they may simply require that any tenant abide by the rules and regulations. The homeowners association may amend these bylaws by majority vote, but don't count on amendment in a direction of your choice; you will have to abide by the regulations in force when you make your purchase and those enacted after you move in by majority vote of all the owners.

Scrutinize the Operating Budget

The Warners calculated their budget to the last penny before they signed an agreement to buy their high-rise condominium unit. Within the first year, however, their careful calculations—and their budget—were obsolete. A structural engineer found that stonework on the building's facade was cracked, posing a danger to pedestrians below. Repair work was urgent, and repair bills, which had to be apportioned among the unit owners because the association lacked an adequate reserve fund, were high.

It's very important to analyze the operating budget and see if it's realistic. Look at both operating costs and reserves. Maintenance costs on a new project are sometimes "lowballed," deliberately underestimated by a developer eager to attract buyers; they may then rise sharply when the development is fully sold. Reserve funds on an existing project may also be low, in part because the association board tries to keep assessments low and in part because it simply fails to realize that every building needs repairs after a certain number of years. Either way, if the reserve fund is inadequate, special assessments will almost certainly become necessary later on.

The condo issue for the 1990s is the issue of adequate reserves. This shouldn't be surprising; many condominium developments began in the 1970s and are approaching the need for major repairs. Before you buy:

- Find out what reserves have been created. Median annual reserves, according to the Institute of Real Estate Management, currently average $232 per unit or 16.6 percent of total operating expenses, less in high-rise buildings and considerably more in townhouse developments. If reserves are much less, be very wary of buying.
- Ask for the record of assessments over the life of the condominium development. You want to know the rate of increase in maintenance assessments over time, as well as how often special assessments have been necessary. You might also ask if there are ceilings on annual increases.
- Ask what the maintenance schedule is, who has responsibility for what, whether the association is or has been or is likely to be in litigation (if so, owners must pay the legal costs), and what the relationship is between the condominium and associated structures (such as stores). Some high-rise condominiums in the Midwest have been badly hurt by retail vacancies in ground floor stores.

Find Out How the Homeowners Association Functions

What are your rights and responsibilities as a voting member of the association? A very large association may hire a full-time resident manager. Medium-sized developments may contract with an outside management firm for specific services. Small condominiums may rely to a larger extent on the

---

Q We own a condominium unit in a development with eighty owners. Last year, after a fire destroyed the roof of our clubhouse, we were each assessed sizable sums to cover the cost of a new roof over and above the amount of insurance the association received. Shouldn't the association's insurance have covered the entire cost?

A Standard policies cover only depreciated value. Suggest to your board that it purchase a replacement-cost policy, which will cover repair or replacement at current prices, and save on costs by taking a sizable deductible.

volunteer labor of residents, with rotating teams of snow shovelers, sidewalk sweepers, and trash emptiers.

The kind of services you receive, and the amount of your assessment, will depend on the kind of management; the management, in turn, depends on the association. You can participate in the association in a number of ways: by voting for the board of directors and on community issues, by serving on a committee, by running for office yourself. But you should plan to participate, on some level, because the association will be your local government, maintaining and protecting the way of life you have chosen by moving into a condominium.

CONDOS: NEW, OLD, OR CONVERSION?

When you buy a condominium unit, you may purchase a new unit in a new development. You may buy into a building being converted to condominium ownership. Or, as is increasingly likely, you may purchase a resale unit. All of the above guidelines apply in each case. But there are also special conditions:

The New Condominium Unit

Before buying a new condominium unit, try to evaluate the quality of construction. If the unit is in a multiunit building, and the building is already occupied, talk to residents; ask, particularly, about noise transmission between units. Or visit a development built earlier by the same company and talk to residents there. Consult the local Association of Home Builders, the Better Business Bureau, and consumer protection agencies to determine if there have been complaints.

Look closely at management. Is the developer, in a new condominium, acting as manager? Has he hired a management firm? When control is transferred to the owners association, will the association be free to make its own arrangements? Or will it be locked into a "sweetheart" agreement made by the developer? When, exactly, will unit owners take control?

Previously Owned Unit

If you buy a condominium unit as a resale, be sure to get all the documents that the original owner received at the time of purchase; ask for them if they are not offered. Consult the association to be sure that all outstanding assessments have been paid. And find out if the previous owner has made any unapproved changes; if so, you may find yourself paying to remove the glass enclosure on the balcony or to repaint the front door.

Most important: Ask hard questions about the financial condition of the association. Are there any special assessments pending? Any upcoming repairs or improvements which will add to your costs? Are there adequate reserves to pay for both normal upkeep and capital repairs?

Find out, too, whether the owners association has the right of first refusal when you want to sell. Although this is no longer permitted under federal regulations, some condominiums, especially those built in the mid-1960s

and early 1970s, restrict sales by including this right (common to cooperatives) in the bylaws; the association can then buy a vacant unit itself or refuse
a potential buyer.

The Condo Conversion

If you're considering buying a unit in a building being converted from
rental to condominium status, an engineer's report could be your most important document. Buildings 20 years old or older have the best potential for conversion, from the landlord's point of view, and may also provide a good buy
for you, but they may also be in serious need of repair.

Hapless residents have discovered, sometimes after purchase, that heating plants or wiring need a major overhaul to extend the building's useful life.
Insist on an engineering report that estimates remaining useful life and
replacement cost for plumbing and electrical systems, the heating plant, and
the roof over your head. Be sure, too, that there is an adequate reserve fund
against repairs; this is particularly important in an older building.

COPING WITH CONVERSION

If you currently rent an apartment which is being converted to
condominium ownership and you think you might like to buy your apartment,
here's what to do:

- Read the offering plan very carefully; it spells out both the sponsor's
  offer to sell and all the legal ins and outs of the offer.
- Get together with your fellow tenants to find out as much as possible
  about the plan and its impact on you. Ask for a meeting with the sponsor, as a group, to get the answers to all your questions.
- Understand that the first plan is usually an offer, subject to negotiation, and be prepared to negotiate. "Insider" prices, the selling price
  for tenants, may be cut; reserve funds may be raised; debt burdens
  may be lowered ... but you have to negotiate.
- Evaluate the economics of the deal. Look at the building as a whole:
  Is the estimated budget adequate? What kind of loan burden will the
  association face at the outset? And figure out what your own apartment's net carrying cost will be if you buy. Don't just compare the
  purchase price with the purchase price of other available apartments,
  or the monthly carrying charges with the rent you now pay. Look at
  your purchase price and your monthly maintenance costs and adjust
  them for the tax benefits you'll secure as an owner. Then compare
  that net cost to the costs of other housing.

If You Don't Want to Buy

If you currently rent an apartment which is being converted to
condominium ownership and you can't afford to buy or simply don't want to
buy, what (other than moving) can you do? Consider the following steps:

■ Form a tenants' organization. Work together to get information and to negotiate with the landlord. Hire a lawyer to represent the group. Hire an engineer to inspect the building, *before* you enter into negotiations.

■ Ask your attorney, your state attorney general's office, a local consumer protection agency, or a real estate board about local law with respect to condominium conversion. Some jurisdictions require that a specified percentage of tenants agree to conversion; others protect the rights of tenants, or of certain groups of tenants such as the elderly, who want to stay on as renters.

You may be able to delay the conversion. Or you may be able to negotiate, as a tenants group, so that the purchase price becomes manageable. You will, in any case, gain some time in which you can make a reasonable decision about whether to buy or to move.

TIME-SHARING

The Drews enjoyed their week's vacation on Florida's west coast so much that they decided to return. They also decided to buy a time-share, a January week every year, in a one-bedroom condominium apartment. The purchase price was $9,000 and the annual maintenance cost was $350. The price was right but a problem arose the very first year: Dan couldn't get his usual week off in January and they were unable to use the apartment. They were also unable to rent it to anyone else.

Time-sharing is based on a simple premise: Instead of paying many thousands of dollars to own a vacation home that you may use for a couple of weeks a year, you pay a small fraction of that amount to use the property for a

Q For $14,500 plus annual maintenance costs of $450 we can buy two weeks a year at a vacation resort we enjoy. Would this be a good buy?

A The only way to tell is to look at the weekly rates charged by other resorts and apartments in the vicinity. One rule of thumb is that a time-share price should be about ten times the weekly rate for comparable accommodations; don't compare one room in a hotel with a two-bedroom condo. If it's more, you might think about simply renting instead of buying. Another guideline is that your vacations should be paid for, and you should start to save money, after about seven years. But you should be aware that those maintenance costs are far from fixed; as the cost of maintenance rises, which it will, so will your assessment.

specified week or weeks each year. The concept has grown in popularity; about 440,000 time-share intervals were purchased in 1991, up from about 100,000 in 1980. One week cost an average of $9,500 at the end of 1992, with annual maintenance fees ranging from $200 to $1,000.

What to Know Before You Buy

- There are two kinds of time-sharing arrangements. Under one arrangement, far more common today, you actually take title to the property; you get a deed and have some rights even if the developer disappears (be sure you actually receive the deed and that it has been recorded). Under the other, you buy the "right to use" the property for a specified number of years and should be sure that you're reserving a specific unit; you should also be reasonably certain that the developer is going to remain in business.

- Outright ownership is preferable. If you can't get title, however, be sure to ask what the developer has done to ensure that you will be able to use your property for the promised term. There are a couple of ways to protect purchasers. One would be the inclusion of a "nondisturbance clause" in the contract (required by some states), so that you would retain the legal right to use your unit even if the developer goes under and someone else takes over management. Another would be an escrow account to provide management funds even if the developer runs into financial trouble.

- Whatever the form of ownership, your resort will be a good place to visit for years to come only if it is properly run. Before you sign on the dotted line, ask for a copy of the current maintenance budget, ask for a maintenance schedule, and find out how often furnishings are replaced and units redecorated. With up to 50 different occupants a year (two weeks are often reserved for renovation), apartments get much harder use than a one-family residence.

- The developer's reputation is more important than anything else. Talk to buyers at other resorts operated by the same developer; if there are no others, be wary. And stay clear of high-pressure sales tactics; some developers are notorious for strong-arming potential buyers.

- Exchange privileges are often promised, under which you may swap your unit for someone else's somewhere else; this makes it possible to enjoy a Florida beach vacation one winter, a Colorado ski vacation the next. But such exchanges are not guaranteed; they depend strictly on someone else's interest in your unit. If you want to be able to exchange, you'd best buy in a popular area at a popular season; don't expect to buy an off-season week in an undesirable resort and trade up to a peak location at a peak time. And ask whether your time-share development belongs to one of the two big associations; membership in Resort Condominiums International and/or Interval International makes it easier to arrange a swap.

■ If you don't plan on swapping or may be unable to do so, be sure to pick an area you're going to enjoy year after year. The money you spend on your share may preclude your vacationing anywhere else for

Q We bought a time-share unit that we enjoyed for a few years. But the maintenance fees keep going up, I've been laid off, and we'd like to sell. An agency says it can sell the unit, for a listing fee of $400 plus a sales commission. Should we do this?

A Not without asking some hard questions, because some agencies have been known to collect fees and never make any attempt to sell the units. Insist on knowing the agency's success rate, including how long the typical unit stayed on the market, what it listed for, and what it sold for. Find out if your fee will be refunded if the unit doesn't sell. In addition, the Federal Trade Commission suggests that you take these precautions:

■ Ask the caller to send you written materials to study. And never agree to anything over the telephone until you've had a chance to check out the company.

■ Ask for names, addresses, and telephone numbers of consumers who have used the service.

■ Ask where the company is located, and in what state it does business.

■ Ask if the company's salespeople are licensed to sell real estate by the state where your time-share is located; then check with the state licensing board to make sure this is so.

■ Ask the Better Business Bureau, state attorney general's office, and local consumer protection agencies whether any complaints have been lodged against the company.

Most time-share resales, like most time-share sales, are accomplished by word of mouth. Lend your unit to a co-worker or friend and you may find a buyer. Or use your unit one more time, sit by the pool every day and see if you can find a buyer among the visitors. But, if you can't sell, don't abandon your obligation; the developer may foreclose and may even be able to secure a personal judgment against you for the money you owe.

some years to come. And the nicest vacation area can begin to seem dull when wanderlust strikes.

■ If you're in the market for a time-share at an established resort, consider buying from an owner who wants to sell or an agent representing such an owner. You'll probably pay considerably less than if you buy directly from the resort.

■ Buy your time-share to enjoy and not as an investment. The industry says about 16 percent of owners are actively trying to sell their units; some estimates are closer to 60 percent. With a glut of intervals on the market, and a slow economy, it can be very difficult to dispose of an unwanted unit. It can be impossible, even if you do find a buyer, to get all your money out. (If death or an illness makes you unable to use your unit, your developer may do you a "favor" and take it back, with no money changing hands.)

The Cooperative Apartment

When a brownstone building on Manhattan's West Side was converted to cooperative apartments in the late 1970s, the Smarts bought a two-bedroom duplex apartment, with the use of the rear garden, for $45,000. The building corporation, with eight apartment units, has 4,000 shares assigned by the developer. Because the Smarts occupy the largest apartment, they own the largest number of shares in the corporation, 785. Their monthly mortgage-and-maintenance assessment, therefore, is considerably more than that of their neighbors, as the necessary outlay is divided by 4,000 and then multiplied by each resident's shares. The building is small, so the residents do most of their own maintenance, keeping costs down. And Dorothy Smart, because she is a writer who works at home (and because she is a natural organizer), sets up the building schedules for trash removal, sidewalk sweeping, and snow shoveling. The co-op has increased in value. It has also turned out to be a satisfactory way of life.

Cooperatives are relatively rare, found primarily in major cities such as New York and Chicago, and mostly in older buildings. Most new construction in shared housing takes the condominium form. The two are vastly different.

When you buy a condominium unit, you buy an actual piece of property. When you buy a cooperative apartment, you buy a share in a corporation which owns the building. The share sometimes, but not always, is based upon the size of the unit you occupy. (The Smarts own 785/4,000ths of their building; they could, if ownership was per-unit, own one-eighth.) There is a single mortgage and a single tax bill for the entire building, with payments toward each divided among the residents; a proportionate share of the mortgage interest and taxes may be taken by each resident as a tax deduction.

With a co-op, unlike a condominium, you are not taking individual title to a specific piece of property. You are becoming a joint owner, with rights as a lessee. You are, in effect, your own tenant. This joint ownership, however, creates special complications:

ASPECTS OF COOPERATIVE OWNERSHIP

- Instead of a mortgage (because you have no individual real property to pledge as collateral), if you need financing you may have to take a personal loan. Such a loan may be (1) difficult to secure, and (2) more expensive than a mortgage (although some New York City banks, for example, do offer co-op loans similar to conventional mortgages). The interest on the loan, however, along with your proportional share of the interest on the corporation's mortgage, will be a deductible item on your federal income tax. (A cooperative corporation may conduct a stringent review of your financial situation before allowing you to purchase shares, and may require that you finance no more than 50 percent of the purchase price.)

- Monthly carrying charges, because they include the building's mortgage loan and real estate taxes, are generally higher than monthly carrying charges on a condominium unit. According to the Institute of Real Estate Management, the median monthly assessment in 1991 for a cooperative townhouse was $220, the median monthly assessment for a condominium townhouse was $124 (with a condominium, of course, you would probably also be paying your own mortgage). If one resident defaults, moreover, the others must make up that share or the mortgage on the entire building will go into default. This is not the case with condominium ownership, where each owner has a separate mortgage.

Q My son has been living with me for many years in the co-op apartment I own. I plan to leave him the apartment in my will. A friend said this isn't good enough, that the co-op board may give him a problem about staying on. If this is true, is there anything I can do now to protect his interest?

A Owners of condominium units can generally leave their apartments as they please; owners of cooperative apartments sometimes do run into posthumous trouble with board approval. The proprietary leases of most co-ops in New York City, for example, give spouses an automatic right to take over an apartment. Children, other relatives, and friends may be another matter. An attorney familiar with co-op law and procedures may be able to help you reach a solution.

■ You may have to secure permission from your co-owners before making structural changes to your own unit.

■ You may not be totally free to sell your unit when you want to move out or even to bequeath it in your will; the corporation, in the interests of protecting a mutual investment, may want to screen potential residents (as you may have been screened before your purchase). Some cooperative apartments, moreover, built under specific provisions of the law, limit the amount of profit a seller can make.

■ The corporation may impose a "flip tax" whenever an apartment changes hands. This fee helps to build the corporation's financial reserves.

WHEN YOU BUY A CO-OP

Buying a cooperative, however, is in some respects like buying a condominium unit. You will be buying into a community. Before you buy a cooperative:

■ Review the operating budget and financial statements. There should be adequate reserves for repairs and replacement of building systems.

Q We are all set to buy a cooperative apartment but have been told that the corporation owns only the building and not the land beneath it. Our lawyer advises us not to buy into a building on leased land. What should we do?

A Buying a coop on leased land can pose certain problems. The cooperative corporation itself may find it difficult to secure financing for improvements to the building. The ground rent may be increased, with a resulting hike in maintenance fees. You, as a tenant-owner, will have to pay real estate taxes on both the land and the building but may be able to claim as a tax deduction only a proportionate share of the taxes on the building. Most important, even though such leases typically run for 99 years, the value of your investment may be significantly diminished. At the end of the lease period all rights to the property and anything on the property (including the building itself) revert to the landowners. Unless the cooperative corporation has purchased the land in the meantime, the apartment may be worthless. If the apartment is a good buy, however, and if you don't plan to live there forever and then pass it on to your heirs, you may be justified in making the purchase. Just think it through carefully, and get good legal advice, before you do.

■ Ask if there are any liens on the building, any litigation against the corporation, and any unpaid property taxes. Any of these situations may result in extra assessments against tenant-owners.
■ Find out how often the carrying charges have been increased. What are provisions for future increases?
■ Read the bylaws. Can you live with the rules and regulations?
■ Talk to residents and see if they are satisfied with management. How much control do residents have over management decisions, if there is an outside manager? How willingly do residents pitch in if they've agreed to do the work themselves?
■ Find out if you can remodel your unit, sublease it, and freely sell it when you are ready to move on.

CO-OP CONVERSION

Most new construction of shared housing takes the simpler condominium form. In cities where cooperatives are well established, however, older apartment buildings are often converted to cooperative ownership. Such conversions may be good for you if you are a potential buyer. But what if you are a tenant faced with a conversion? Whether or not you want to buy your present rental apartment, consider the suggestions, on pp. 386-387, for those faced with conversion to condominium ownership.

Bear in mind, too, that if you buy you will become your own landlord as well as your own tenant. The mix can take some adjustment. You may have to take care of your own plumbing repairs, and you may have to agree with assorted neighbors on the pattern of the wallpaper for the lobby. If you prefer to call the superintendent for repairs and complain about the wallpaper the landlord selects, don't buy a co-op; stick to renting an apartment instead.

Manufactured Housing

Manufactured housing is factory-built housing; it is also sometimes called prefabricated housing. This does not mean that manufactured housing is all alike or instantly identifiable; it does mean that each house is built in the factory, trucked to its site, and assembled. The house itself, once assembled, may look like a ranch house or like a two-story Colonial or, as you might expect, like a mobile home on wheels.

Manufactured housing is affordable housing because it costs less to mass-produce in a factory than to build individually on site. It costs less to buy materials in bulk and to install those materials in assembly-line fashion. Even when the prices of conventional houses leveled off and began to drop, in the late 1980s and early 1990s, factory-built housing remained a very affordable option, coming in (depending on just where you live) at 25 percent to 33 percent less per square foot than site-built housing. Look at the figures: The average newly built conventional site-built house cost $149,000 in 1990; the average resale cost $118,000. In the same year, the average factory-built house cost $27,800. Factor in land at the average price of about $45,000 for a one-quarter to one-third acre site, and you have a total price of $62,800.

Manufactured housing suits both the young and the old. Thirty-five percent of all sales are made to people in their twenties and thirties, a third to those over age 60. Forty-two percent, across the age range, are single, either never-married, separated, divorced, or widowed. Two-thirds are one- or two-member households.

There are two broad categories of factory-built housing: modular and manufactured. Both are made in the factory and transported, virtually complete, to the site where they will be installed. Both come in units 12 to 16 feet wide and up to 80 feet long; both can be doubled or tripled in width and in living space by placing units side by side. Both have just about everything in place before leaving the factory, from the heating system and plumbing to the carpeting on the floor.

But there are major differences as well.

MODULAR HOUSES

Modular houses are usually purchased and financed, like conventional site-built housing, along with land. They are treated in all respects, in fact, as conventional housing: They must be placed on a permanent foundation, they must conform to local construction codes, they are taxed as real property. Modular houses, like other houses, often appreciate in value. Their assembly-line construction, at the same time, results in costs that are considerably less than conventional site-built housing.

Transportation costs (getting the house to the site) sometimes eliminate the initial price advantage. But builders are interested in speed; the faster a home can be occupied, the lower the carrying costs and the higher the profit margin. More and more builders, therefore, are teaming up with manufacturers to offer modular housing.

A factory-built modular house may appeal to you if you're looking for less expensive housing. It may also appeal to you, if you want a new house, on the basis of speed. From foundation to completion, a site-built house can take six to nine months; a factory-built house, by contrast, can be in place within a few weeks.

Because modular housing is exactly like conventional housing, with the exception of construction techniques, financing and insurance considerations are exactly the same. The information in Chapters 11 and 12 applies to factory-built homes as it does to site-built homes.

MANUFACTURED HOMES

Manufactured homes are another story. (You may think of them as mobile homes, but within the industry this term is generally reserved for factory-built homes built prior to June 1976 when a federal building code went into effect; homes built since then, under the Department of Housing and Urban Development [HUD] code, are called manufactured homes.) These homes, although they are seldom mobile at all, are built with a chassis and wheels, axles and brakes and have traditionally been regarded as motor vehicles; they've been placed on rented lots, financed with short-term high-interest installment loans, and taxed as personal property, depreciating in value. All of this is beginning to change.

- Manufactured homes are now being built in a variety of styles, including luxury models with cathedral ceilings, sunken bathtubs, and fireplaces. Some cost $80,000 and more. Some, with pitched roofs and shingle siding, look very much like conventional houses.

- Some states are beginning to tax manufactured homes as real estate, especially when they are placed on individually owned land. In mobile home parks, on rental lots, homes are still more often taxed as personal property. Either way, manufactured homes are now more likely to appreciate in value (although still not as much as conventional houses). So you won't necessarily lose money when you sell.

- At least 19 states, too, have ruled that exclusionary zoning is illegal. In these states a community cannot exclude a manufactured home or restrict its location just because it is a manufactured home. Local jurisdictions may, however, require that all the houses in a given area (including manufactured homes) conform to compatible standards.

- New manufactured home developments are more and more often planned to look like suburban housing developments, with sidewalks, underground utilities, and recreational areas. Increasingly, too, residents own their land as well as their homes. About half of all mobile homes are placed on individual lots, usually in rural areas. Manufactured home subdivisions involve the sale of land with homes, and manufactured home condominiums, like other condominiums, involve individual ownership of home-plus-lot and joint ownership of common elements.

All of these changes in mobile homes have led to changes in the financial picture as well.

Financing a Manufactured Home Purchase

Manufactured homes, like automobiles, have generally been financed with relatively short-term installment loans. Most lenders require a minimum down payment of 10 percent, with loan terms generally no more than 15 years although some will go out as far as 25 years. Interest rates are often 2 or 3 percentage points above those for conventional home mortgages. Loans are available from mobile home dealers or from lending institutions; many purchasers take the easy route and finance through the dealer, although it's always best to compare terms and interest rates.

As manufactured homes become more and more like site-built houses in their size and the amenities they offer, there is a national trend toward financing them like site-built houses. This is particularly true when the manufactured home will go on land you own, and where it is a larger multi-section home.

If you are financing a manufactured home purchase, shop around:

■ Go to savings and loan associations, banks, and credit unions as well as to the mobile home dealer.

■ Find out how your state taxes manufactured homes. In the states where they are taxed as real estate rather than as personal property, it is more likely that you will be able to finance your purchase through a loan resembling a conventional mortgage.

■ Be aware that you will probably owe a sales tax on the purchase of a new manufactured home. If you buy a used mobile home directly from an owner, you may or may not, depending on the state, owe a sales tax. If your home must be moved to its site, however, new or used, you will have to pay a motor vehicle registry fee.

■ Do not sign any financing agreement unless the terms are carefully spelled out. The lender must tell you the annual percentage rate you are being charged, in simple interest terms.

■ Look into financing backed by the Federal Housing Association (FHA) or the Department of Veterans Affairs (VA). Both guarantee loans on manufactured homes; both steadily liberalize their criteria. The FHA, as of mid-1992, will insure up to $40,500 for 20 years on a single-wide or multi-section unit; it will insure up to $54,000 for 20 years on a single unit plus land and the same amount for 25 years on a multi-section unit plus land. For eligible veterans, the VA will guarantee up to 50 percent of a loan (40 percent where the home is not permanent) to a maximum of $20,000; maturities are 20 years on a single-wide unit, 23 years on a multi-section.

■ Find out if your state has a special program to help manufactured home buyers. At the beginning of 1993, for example, the Rhode Island Housing and Mortgage Finance Corporation, concerned that potential purchasers were being priced out of the market, began to offer mortgages at 4.45 percent for buyers with household incomes of up to $32,480 and at 7.45 percent for families with at least three members whose household incomes are up to $46,690.

■ There are generally no closing costs or attorney's fees to pay in financing and insuring a mobile home. A title search is not required either, unless you are buying land as well as the home itself.

Ongoing Costs

If you decide to buy a manufactured home, you will be responsible for:

■ Monthly payments of the principal and interest on either an installment loan or a mortgage, if you finance your purchase

■ Monthly rent, if your home is in a park or development (and this rent can go up very steeply; residents in one Massachusetts community found their rents increased by 20 percent two years in a row)
■ Property taxes, if you own your own lot
■ Property and liability insurance
■ Utilities
■ Maintenance and repairs

BEFORE YOU BUY A MANUFACTURED HOME

Manufactured homes, despite vast improvements, are still not the precise equivalent of conventionally built homes. So you may not pass a manufactured home on to your children and your grandchildren. But it may provide reasonably comfortable and affordable housing right now.

Before you buy:

■ Be sure you have a place to put your home. Local manufactured home parks may be full, or may require that a home be purchased through the park. Zoning regulations may not permit placement on private property.
■ Understand the rental fee if you will rent a lot. The average rental fee nationally is around $200 a month, but rents vary from $150 to as

Q We've bought a new double-wide manufactured home which will be placed on a lovely grassy site in a well-run park. What kind of insurance do we need?

A You want protection against damage to your personal property, the contents of your home, as well as against damage to the home itself. Many large insurers offer special homeowners policies for the owners of manufactured homes. Be aware, though, that differences in construction, especially susceptibility to wind damage, may make manufactured home policies more expensive than comparable policies on conventional houses. Having a properly installed tie-down may reduce your premium. Older mobile homes, bought used, are even more difficult and more expensive to insure.

Manufactured homes, by the way, often fare reasonably well in earthquakes; one insurance company representative told me that they "roll right off the foundation" and can be put back. Manufactured homes, on the other hand, are not the best place to be in hurricane-force winds.

much as $500 or more a month. One community in Malibu, California, is rumored to cost as much as $1,000 a month. Get a lease if you can, and find out how often the lot rental has been raised and can be raised. (One of the persistent complaints about manufactured home living has been the arbitrary authority of park operators. In most cases, residents have little say about regulations and little redress if rents are raised.)

■ Understand the rules and regulations of any manufactured home community you are considering. Will you be permitted to have a pet? (In one Virginia park, residents are allowed one small pet, up to 10 inches high at the hips and 26 pounds, at an extra $5 in lot rental per month.) Will you be required to buy all equipment from the park operator? Can you be evicted at the owner's pleasure?

■ Find out what the base price includes, which appliances and what furnishings. If you don't want to buy the furniture, you may get a discount, but it won't be equivalent to the retail value of the furnishings.

■ Find out what extras you will have to cover. Many manufactured home communities require steps with handrails, skirting to conceal the wheels, foundation supports, anchoring to the ground. These costs typically add about 15 percent to the purchase price of the home.

■ Decide what other options you might like. Air conditioning and a patio are pleasant additions, but be sure to calculate their cost before you commit yourself to a purchase.

■ Be sure that your home conforms to the 1976 HUD standards, providing for fire safety and wind resistance (about 50 percent of all homes currently inhabited were built prior to this protective code). A newly built home will meet the standards; an older home bought as a resale may not. Multi-sections, in general, are sturdier than single-wides. An older home, too, may have building components containing formaldehyde, suspected of cancer-causing emissions.

■ Find out what warranty you have on the house itself and on any appliances and equipment. Find out who will honor the warranty if any work is required. And be aware that a used mobile home may have no warranties at all, on either the home itself or its contents.

WHEN YOU WANT TO SELL

When you're ready to sell your manufactured home and move on, you'll probably have little difficulty if you own the land on which it stands. If you are renting in a mobile home park, however, you may have to obey the regulations of the park. Find out what those regulations are (recognizing that they are subject to change) before you move in.

As manufactured homes are becoming more and more the nation's affordable housing, eager buyers are likely to be found—except where steep increases in lot rentals deter potential purchasers or where a regional economic downturn has affected housing costs in general. Manufactured homes in one northeastern state sold for $40,000 in the late 1980s; by 1992, many owners couldn't find buyers even at a drastically reduced $20,000. The problem in selling, if there is one, will stem from the home's location.

 KEY POINTS

- A condominium may look like an apartment or like a house. It is a form of ownership which combines the ease of apartment living with the advantages of homeownership. When you buy a condominium unit, you buy an actual piece of property.

- Cooperative owners do not own individual units. When you buy a co-op, you buy a share in the corporation that owns the building.

- Factory-built housing includes modular or prefabricated houses built in a factory but assembled on an individual lot and sold, financed, and taxed as individual homes.

- Factory-built housing also includes manufactured homes, factory-built and factory-assembled, and placed on an individually owned lot or on a rental lot in a mobile home community. Manufactured homes, although more and more resembling conventional houses, are still often financed with short-term installment loans and taxed as either vehicles or personal property.

Spending Your Money: An Automobile

CHAPTER 15

Owning, Leasing, or Renting an Automobile

If home ownership is the number one American dream, automobile ownership must rank a close second. In fact, 86 percent of households in the United States have at least one car; 38 percent have two or more cars.

While owning a car is essential for most Americans (outside a few large cities, adequate mass transit simply doesn't exist), owning and operating a car is expensive. So more and more people are refraining from buying new cars, holding on to their old cars, and driving less.

What about you? Are you in the market for a new car? A used car? Should you have a car at all? This chapter will focus on the costs of car ownership, on alternatives to ownership in the form of renting and leasing, and on how to buy and pay for a car if you decide to do so. The next chapter describes the ins and outs of automobile insurance.

What It Costs to Own a Car

In 1972, the last full year before the Arab oil embargo (remember those lines at the gas pump?), driving cost 12.1 cents a mile and cars were driven an average of 10,362 miles a year. Total cost: $1,256 for the year. In 1993, according to the American Automobile Association and Runzheimer/ International, driving a new car for 10,000 miles cost an average of 47.0 cents per mile, for a total of $4,000. Drive the same car for 15,000 miles and the average per-mile cost drops to 38.7 cents, for a total of $5,805.

The costs of automobile ownership come in two parts: purchase price and operating costs.

INITIAL PURCHASE PRICE

The average new car, with the most popular options (power steering, power brakes, automatic transmission, and air conditioning), sold for $17,127 at the end of 1992. Purchase prices on secondhand cars are considerably less. A pick-of-the-crop year-old car with relatively little mileage on it may sell for 25 percent less than the same car brand-new, while a seven-year-old model may run as much as 90 percent less. Specific prices, of course, depend on the age and condition of the car, as well as its model (some models hold value bet-

Q My new car has a warranty for three years or 36,000 miles. The dealer is offering an extended warranty for five years or 50,000 miles. Would this be worth buying?

A Maybe. But be sure you understand what you're buying. First of all, according to the Federal Trade Commission, an extended warranty is actually a service contract and not a warranty as defined by federal law. The service contract may duplicate coverage you already have under the warranty.

Before saying yes, find out:

■ Who backs the service contract? The manufacturer? The dealership? An independent company? Is the contract backed by an insurance company? (This is required in some states.)

■ How much the contract will cost. You can expect anything from several hundred dollars to more than $1,000. You may also have to pay a deductible every time the car is repaired under the contract.

■ Exactly what is included. Some service contracts exclude many specific items. Others have a "depreciation factor" and you may receive only partial reimbursement based on mileage.

■ Must you return the car to a specific location for service under the contract? This could be very inconvenient if you run into trouble away from home.

■ Can the contract be transferred if you sell the car while it is in force?

ter than others), but the average price of a secondhand car sold by a new-car dealer in 1992 was $8,310.

OPERATING COSTS

How much it costs to operate your car depends, at least in part, on the kind of car you buy. Runzheimer International calculates that the annual cost of operating a compact Ford Escort LX, purchased new in 1993, comes to $6,612; the annual cost of operating a full-size Cadillac DeVille, also bought new in 1993, comes to $11,638. Since Runzheimer deals primarily with business travel, both figures are based on driving 20,000 miles per year for three years; the average motorist, who commutes to work by car, drives about 15,000 miles a year.

Table 15.1: Where Does Your Automotive Dollar Go?

Cost as a Percent of the Total

Cost Component	1992
Depreciation and Interest	55.7
Gasoline	16.5
Insurance	15.1
Maintenance	6.8
Tires	2.5
License	0.3
Other	3.1

Source: Runzheimer International.

Whatever the total, the costs of maintaining your car can also be viewed in two parts: fixed and variable.

Fixed Costs

These "standing" costs are those that remain essentially the same whether your car is driven 15,000 miles a year or left sitting in your driveway. They include licensing, taxes, insurance, interest, and depreciation (the difference between the resale value and the initial purchase price). They may also include such ongoing expenses as monthly garage rent or inspection fees. These figures are fixed, once established, but they are affected initially by the kind of car you buy (taxes, licensing, insurance, and depreciation) and by the way you buy it (interest costs). Fixed costs, according to an annual survey by the Motor Vehicle Manufacturers Association, came to an average of $12.43 per day in 1992, almost double the 1984 figure of $6.43. These costs usually amount to two-thirds to three-fourths of your total annual outlay; the more you drive, however, the lower fixed costs become on a per-mile basis.

Table 15.2: The Cost of Driving a 1993 Mid-Size 6-Cylinder Car

Operating costs	Cost per mile
Gasoline and oil	6.0 cents
Maintenance	2.4 cents
Tires	0.9 cents
	9.3 cents

Ownership costs	Cost per year
Comprehensive insurance ($250 deductible)	$ 107
Collision insurance ($500 deductible)	232
Property damage/bodily liability ($100,000/$300,000/$50,000)	385
License, registration, taxes	183
Depreciation	2,883
Finance charge (20% down; loan at 10%, 4 yrs)	696
	$4,486 ($12.29 per day)

Cost per mile

Based on the above figures, a motorist driving 15,000 miles a year would pay:

15,000 miles at 9.3 cents	= $1,395
365 days at $12.29	= 4,538
	$5,881
COST PER MILE:	39.2 cents

Source: American Automobile Association, Runzheimer International.

Variable Costs

These "operating" costs are those directly related to how much or how little you drive: gasoline and oil, service and repairs, tires, batteries, sparkplugs, as well as bridge and tunnel tolls, sporadic parking charges, and traffic tickets. Some of these costs, of course, are also tied to the kind of car you buy. In the Runzheimer example, the 1993 Ford Escort LX cost $1,630 a year in variable operating costs while the Cadillac DeVille cost $2,520.

Fuel efficiency, in particular, can have a significant impact on the amount you spend on gasoline in the course of a year. But fuel efficiency, despite the considerable attention it's received in recent years, is but one of several factors and should be weighed accordingly. If you get hung up on fuel efficiency, you may wind up spending more overall on automobile operating costs.

For example: Suppose you are trying to decide between a new $15,000 car that is supposed to average 26 miles per gallon and a used $10,000 car that may average 13 miles per gallon. Suppose, also, that gasoline costs $1.00 a gallon. If you drive 10,000 miles a year, you would spend about $384 on gasoline per year for the $15,000 car and $764 per year for the $10,000 car. Clearly, your gasoline expenditures will be cut by about half if you buy the more fuel-efficient vehicle. But what about the initial purchase price of the car? the additional interest charges on a bigger loan? the higher insurance premiums on a new and expensive car? You will have to drive the fuel-efficient car for seven years before you recover the additional cost in savings on gasoline alone. And if you drive fewer miles, fixed costs will be proportionately more important than variable costs such as gasoline; the operating cost differential between large and small cars becomes, as a result, less significant.

If you decide to buy a car, after calculating how much it will cost (use Worksheet 15.1 to do your calculations), several elements will enter into your calculations: how much you can afford, what size car you need, how to get the most car for the best price (old car or new), and how to pay for your purchase.

How Much Can You Afford?

The answer to this crucial question depends on your budget (see Chapter 2), which, in turn, depends at least in part on your stage of life.

Average driving costs per year (when you drive a new car) are about $6,000, over and above the initial purchase price of the car. Where does this figure fit in your income-outgo picture? And, beyond the dollars-and-cents answer to that question, beyond your practical need for transportation, how important is it to you to own a car? What are your other goals? If you're single, with few responsibilities, you may be willing and able to put more money into an automobile than cold hard figures would otherwise indicate. If you've just

Q We don't use our family car for business. Is there any way that any of the owning and operating costs might be tax-deductible?

A Yes. If you use your car for *medical* (trips to the doctor) or *charitable* (including volunteer activity on behalf of a charity) purposes, you may deduct either the actual costs of operating the car (gasoline, oil, and maintenance) or the standard per-mile rate permitted by the Internal Revenue Service (IRS). (In 1992, the rate was 9 cents a mile for medical care and 12 cents per mile for charity.) You may also claim tolls and parking fees. Accurate records are essential.

Note: Total medical costs (including per-mile costs) must exceed 7.5 percent of adjusted gross income in order to qualify for a deduction. See Chapter 20 for more information.

Worksheet 15.1: Calculating Car Ownership Costs

Costs in Your Locality

1. Amount paid for your car $_____
2. Cost of accessory items $_____
3. Cost of a tire to fit your car $_____
4. Price of gasoline per gallon (including tax) $_____
5. Price of oil per quart (including tax) $_____
6. Annual cost of your insurance $_____
7. Estimated cost of your daily parking $_____
8. State registration fee for your car $_____
9. Sales/titling, and/or personal property tax $_____
10. Mechanic's labor charge per hour $_____
11. Monthly interest cost
     (monthly payment x number of months
     for loan less amount of loan/number of months for loan) $_____
12. Term of your auto loan   _____
13. Your mileage for the year   _____

Estimated First-year Cost

Ownership costs (first year)	Total	Cost per mile (total column ÷ line 13)
14. Depreciation (25% of line 1)	$_____	_____
15. Accessories (line 2 ÷ 12)	$_____	_____
16. Insurance (line 6)	$_____	_____
17. Registration fee (line 8)	$_____	_____
18. Financing (12 x monthly interest cost)	$_____	_____
19. Sales/titling, and/or property tax (line 9)	$_____	_____

Operating costs (first year)

	Total	Cost per mile
20. Gasoline (annual gallons used x line 4)	$_____	_____
21. Oil (line 13 ÷ owners manual change requirements x line 5)	$_____	_____
22. Snow tires (2 x line 3 x .25)	$_____	_____
23. Maintenance and repair (based on line 10)	$_____	_____
24. Parking (250 x line 7) or actual days parked x daily cost	$_____	_____
25. Tolls	$_____	_____
26. Total cost (add lines 14-25)	$_____	_____

Source: Federal Highway Administration.

started a family, a car may be essential but strictly on a no-frills basis. And if you've retired on a limited and fixed income, transportation may play a definitely secondary role.

Start by reviewing your cash flow and deciding what you can afford. The Credit Union National Association suggests this step by step procedure: Add the total of the down payment, any rebate the manufacturer offers, the value of your present vehicle, and the money you can afford to borrow. Then find out how much you can borrow at current loan rates. For example: You've saved $2,500 for a down payment, the car you want comes with a $1,000 rebate, and your old car is worth $4,000 if you sell it yourself. You can comfortably repay $200 a month for four years. That $200 a month in repayment would permit you to borrow about $7,600 at an annual percentage rate of 11.5 percent. Add up the figures and you have the resources, given this set of assumptions, to buy a car worth about $15,000. Use the following checklist to calculate your resources:

	Example	**You**
Down payment	$2,500	_____
Rebate	1,000	_____
Existing car value	4,000	_____
Loan	7,600	_____
Total:	$15,100	_____

Source: Credit Union National Association.

HOW MUCH CAR DO YOU NEED?

Will you be using the car for daily stop-and-go commuting? Or solely to transport camping gear on an occasional weekend jaunt? Do you stick to

Q I'm planning to buy a new car and take advantage of an advertised manufacturer rebate. Someone told me I'll have to pay sales tax based on the entire price of the car, including the rebate. It seems to me I should have to pay tax only on the price I actually pay. Which is correct?

A It depends on where you live. Until recently, most states collected sales tax only on the net price of the car, after any rebate or trade-in allowance. Today, with growing budget shortfalls, more states are collecting sales tax on the entire price before any rebate or trade-in. Ask your dealer how the transaction will be handled.

superhighways? Or travel a rutted country road to a retreat in the hills? Must you accommodate only yourself? Or must you also comfortably seat a spouse, a car pool crowd, a couple of small (or large) children? Smaller cars are generally less expensive to operate, but the answers to all these questions should dictate the size and type of the car you buy.

Look at all your needs, at how often you do what. Don't buy a wagon or a van to hold your camping gear if you go camping once a year; a roof rack may do just as well. Don't buy a small car with a small engine, in the interests of fuel efficiency, and then find that the steep road to your favorite vacation hideaway is an almost insurmountable obstacle. Don't buy a sporty two-door model when you know that you'll be taking three or four passengers back and forth to work each day; the trip will become distinctly uncomfortable.

Psychological Needs

A two-door car may be uncomfortable for your car pool, but if it's the only model that suits your racing-car self-image, you may buy it anyway. Emotional needs often play a major role in automobile selection.

A "psychographic" marketing study by the Opinion Survey Center of Toledo, Ohio, measured the elements that go into the decision to buy a particular car. Just about half the car-buying population, the survey found, is practical, making logical step-by-step pocketbook-in-mind decisions. The other half, which tends to be younger but includes people of all ages, is more emotional, swayed by newness, snob appeal, or image.

Are you practical? Do you focus on price and value, reliability and durability, over and above the image a car conveys? Do you look at a car as first and foremost a means of transportation? Then you may be happy (and your budget will certainly be better balanced) with a modest sedan, new or secondhand.

Or are you more emotional, seeing your car as a personal statement, a reflection of yourself? Are sexy looks more important than practicality? the newest model better than the tried-and-true? Then you're likely to want the sporty two-door model, regardless of your passengers' comfort.

It's possible, of course, to buy the same car for different reasons. A sports car may be racy to one driver, a well-engineered automobile to another. But if you understand your own motives when it comes to buying a car, you'll do your pocketbook as well as your ego a favor.

Old Car or New?

If you're in the market for a car, should you buy a new vehicle or an old one? It will cost you less to run an old car than a new one. Most Americans have learned this lesson well. The average age of cars currently on the road is 7.9 years, the highest average since the Korean War years of the early 1950s. At the same time, as more and more people keep their cars longer before trading them in for newer models, it's becoming increasingly difficult to buy a good used car.

Fixed and variable costs for brand-new cars driven 10,000 miles a year, taken together, range upward from 39.1 cents a mile for compacts to 57.4 cents a mile for full-sized cars. If you drive more over the same four years, the per-mile figure drops while the dollar outlay rises. If you keep your car longer, your overall costs go down.

A new car, well maintained, should provide 100,000 miles of driving. Forty to 45 percent of all cars are still on the road after ten years of operation, with a sharp drop-off between the tenth and the fifteenth year. With regular maintenance and good driving, and the luck to stay clear of accidents, you should be able to expect ten years and 100,000 miles from almost any car.

Table 15.3: Annual Fixed and Operating Costs for a 1993 Mid-Size Car in Selected Locations

Location	Fixed Costs	Operating Costs	Total Annual Costs
Los Angeles, CA	$6,281	$1,635	$7,916
New York, NY	5,104	1,605	6,709
Chicago, IL	4,514	1,658	6,172
Washington, DC	4,023	1,628	5,651
Orlando, FL	3,904	1,418	5,322
Sioux Falls, SD	3,630	1,358	4,988

The costs above are based upon a 1993 mid-size 6-cylinder, 4-door sedan equipped with automatic transmission, power steering, power disc brakes, tinted glass, AM-FM stereo, cruise control, and air conditioning. Costs include operating costs: fuel, oil, tires, and maintenance; and fixed costs: insurance, depreciation, taxes, and license fees. Factors are based on a 4-year/60,000 mile retention cycle. Vehicles are driven within a 50-mile radius of the city.

Source: Runzheimer International.

Whatever type of car you drive, regional considerations will affect your operating costs. Urban areas are generally more expensive places to keep auto-

Q My husband has always put the family car in his name alone. Is there any reason why our car shouldn't be registered in both our names?

A It's generally not a good idea to own an automobile jointly. The reason: If either of you is involved in an accident and the car is jointly owned, you could both be sued. Assets belonging to each of you individually could then be subject to any court judgment. It's best to have the family car registered in one name, either name.

mobiles, but urban areas are not all alike. Variables include the factory-to-destination price of the automobile, the risk of accident and hence the cost of insurance, repair and maintenance costs, parking costs, and tolls.

IS IT TIME TO REPLACE YOUR CAR?

Your four-year-old car is beginning to show signs of wear. Should you foot the bill for increasing repairs? Or is it time to turn it in for a new model? How do you decide?

Fixed ownership costs (depreciation, insurance, finance charges) typically fall as a car ages. Variable operating costs (gas, oil, maintenance and repairs) typically rise. But new car payments, according to Runzheimer International, are the deciding factor. If you financed a new 1992 car instead of keeping a similar 1988 car, it will cost an additional $8,864 over a four year period. See Table 15.4 for the details.

BUYING A NEW CAR

If you've decided to buy a new car, you'll have, in addition to a choice of models, a choice of options. Here, too, you'll be best off thinking it through before you set foot in a showroom. Are anti-lock brakes a must? What about power steering? intermittent wipers? air bags? A basic no-frills car costs considerably less, a couple of thousand dollars less, than the same car "loaded."

Your initial choice of automobile, moreover, will affect the options you need. Expensive extras on some cars are basic included-in-the-sticker-price elements on others. A careful reading of the annual automobile issue of *Consumer Reports,* published each spring, will spell out the details and help you decide what's worthwhile. The dealer may offer you a "package" of options at a bargain price. The price may indeed be lower than all the options purchased separately, but it won't be a bargain unless you need and want all the individual items.

Once you know what you want in a new car, be prepared to negotiate. Most car prices are negotiable, although some are more negotiable than others. If it's the end of a month ... if a model is moving slowly ... if the dealer has a lot of cars on hand ... you're more likely to find a better price. Comparison-shop among different dealers, and don't be pressured into buying before you're ready.

Remember:

- Finance costs vary considerably; don't take dealer financing on the assumption that it's less expensive. If you do take dealer financing, be firm about wanting just financing; don't pay extra, over the life of your loan, for credit insurance, an extended warranty, a dealer's service package, or any other "extras" the dealer may try to include.

- Dealer preparation charges, taxes, licensing fees, and destination charges, which can add up to hundreds of dollars, must also be added in.

Table 15.4: The Cost of Financing a New Car vs. Keeping an Older One

These figures are based on 1988 and 1992 6-cylinder, four-door sedans. The older car originally cost $12,597 and produces 21.0 miles per gallon. The new car costs $15,448 and produces 21.0 miles per gallon. Our figures are based on certain assumptions (see below). Your cost should be determined by your circumstances.

	Year One		Year Two		Year Three		Year Four		Four Year Total	
Accumulative Mileage	75M	15M	90M	30M	105M	45M	120M	60M		
	Old	New	Old	New	Old	New	Old	New	Old	New
Car Payment Principal[1]	—	2,585	—	2,856	—	3,155	—	3,484	—	12,080
Interest On Car Loan[2]	—	1,092	—	821	—	522	—	192	—	2,627
Fuel & Oil[3]	917	900	917	900	924	900	924	900	3,682	3,600
License, Registration & Miscellaneous Taxes[4]	235	433	232	357	231	327	224	311	922	1,428
Insurance[5]	894	952	855	932	855	932	855	894	3,459	3,710
Repairs, Maintenance, Tires[6]	640	350	647	342	1,844	855	929	350	4,060	1,897
Resale Value of Car	3,177[7]	8,953	1,821[7]	7,120	466[7]	5,614	149[7]	4,504	—	—
Total Expenses									12,123	25,342
Minus Final Resale Value of Car									149	4,504
Total Costs[8]									11,974	20,838
Difference										$8,864

Source: Runzheimer International.

Notes: [1] Assume the older car is paid off. The total car payment principal ($12,080) equals the cost of the new car + average sales tax at the beginning of year one ($16,366) minus the resale value of the older car at the beginning of year one ($4,286) which is used for the down payment. [2] The interest is calculated for four years at 10 percent. [3] Based on 15,000 annual miles, fuel priced at 122.4¢/gallon, 20% full-serve/80% self-serve fuel blend. [4] Reflects average license, registration, and personal property/excise taxes. [5] $100 deductible Comprehensive, $250 deductible Collision, $50,000 Property Damage, $100,000/$300,000 Bodily Injury and Uninsured Motorist. Commutation coverage, clean driving record. [6] Covers normal repairs and preventative maintenance plus tire replacements, repairs, rotations, and balancing (costs are higher for years in which tires are replaced). [7] At the end of years 5, 6, 7, and 8 of the old car's life. [8] Reflects projected total costs over the 4 year span.

■ If you don't feel comfortable negotiating, consider using a buying service, a car broker, or one of the newfangled dealers offering fixed prices. Discount prices are available through some American Automobile Association affiliates, through some credit unions, and through national car-buying services such as Car/Puter (800-221-4001; in New York State, 800-522-5104 or 718-455-2500). Important price information is available in the form of printouts through *Consumer Reports* (Box 8005, Novi, MI 48376) and *Money* magazine (800-777-1880).

■ A trade-in of your old car, if any, should be negotiated separately. Find out what the bottom-line price is on the new car you want; then talk trade-in value (and sell privately if you want top dollar and don't mind the hassle).

■ You're going to want service from the dealer as well as delivery; keep this in mind if you find the best price at a dealer 30 miles away or through a discount buying service.

Tactics to Avoid

In your price-shopping, be wary of the high-pressure sales tactics engaged in by some dealers:

■ In **lowballing** the dealer meets your price, then suddenly "remembers" some extra charges he failed to include. Don't agree to a price that goes up after a deal is made.

■ In **highballing,** by contrast, the salesperson offers you a terrific trade-in price on your old car, then turns around and increases the price on the new car to make up the difference.

■ **Turnover** tricks involve wearing you down with sales pitches from one salesperson after another.

■ You're **locked in** when you turn over a temporary "deposit" or the keys to your old car; then, when you decide you've had enough, you may not be able to retrieve your property to leave. Don't sign anything or turn over keys (you can go along on a test drive) until you're sure the deal is the one you want.

BUYING A USED CAR

Used cars, as noted, cost considerably less than new cars, both in initial purchase price and in operating costs. It shouldn't surprise anyone that many people, especially younger people, buy and drive secondhand cars.

But there are other factors to keep in mind:

■ A new car can be ordered with the options you want; a used car will be an as-is proposition.

■ As people keep cars longer, to avoid the costs of trading up, good used cars are both harder to find and more expensive.

■ Repair costs increase along with the age of the car, although the slowed rate of depreciation, in many people's opinion, does a lot to compensate. (If you keep the car past the first set of repairs, moreover—past the three-year mark—you probably won't face major repairs again for another three or four years.)

■ Warranties, where available at all (it depends a great deal on where you buy the car; see below), may provide minimal coverage.

■ Financing may cost more on a used car (although overall costs will be lower) because some lending institutions charge higher rates and offer shorter loans on older cars. In 1991, the Motor Vehicles Manufacturers Association reported that the average new car was financed at 12.4 percent for a term of 55 months; the average used car was financed at 15.6 percent for a term of 47.2 months. Since the financed amount was lower on the used car ($8,884, on average, against $12,494) monthly payments were also lower ($253, on average, against $298).

Where to Buy a Used Car

All things being equal, you will save money by buying a secondhand car. If you decide to do so, comparison-shop among new-car dealers, used-car dealers, rental or leasing agencies, and private individuals. Keep the following distinctions in mind:

Q My new car has been at the dealer for repairs more often than it's been in my driveway ready for use. They can't seem to make it work properly, and I know I've got a lemon on my hands. Is there anything I can do?

A The manufacturer's warranty should provide repairs of defects, but it does not oblige the manufacturer to replace the car or offer a refund if the defect can't be fixed. You do have the right, under federal law (the Magnuson-Moss Warranty Act of 1975), to sue for a replacement or a refund, plus attorney's fees, if the car remains defective after a number of attempts at repair. You may do better, however, under your state's "lemon law" protection for new-car purchasers. In 1991, 48 states and the District of Columbia (every state but Arkansas and South Dakota) had some form of lemon law. Under the New York law, for example, failure to repair substantial defects in four attempts means that the manufacturer or the dealer will be required to either refund the purchase price or replace the vehicle. If he fails to do so, the buyer can sue for refund or replacement after first submitting to arbitration.

■ A new-car dealer resells the best of the used cars he takes in trade-in. His prices are often higher than those of other used-car sources, but he has service facilities and may offer a written warranty.

■ Used-car dealers often have a wider variety of cars on hand, from the best to the worst. They often do not have service facilities and are less likely to offer a warranty.

■ Some rental agencies sell their used cars directly to consumers after about a year of use. Rental cars tend to run up 18,000 to 22,000 miles in a year, but they are also usually well maintained and come with warranties. Prices are generally lower than dealer prices, but they are also generally nonnegotiable.

■ The big rental agencies (Hertz, Avis, Budget, National) have been lured from the direct-to-consumer market by manufacturers' buy-back programs. Under these programs, designed to provide high-quality used cars for dealers to sell, manufacturers buy back rental cars after three or four months of use, then auction them to dealers at wholesale prices. You can buy one of these "nearly news" direct from dealers, at a price that may be (depending on the model) 30 percent less than the original sticker.

■ If you buy from an individual car owner you may strike a better deal, but you're also completely on your own—no service, no warranty, no

---

Q I bought a used car and the brakes failed almost as soon as I left the lot. The salesman says I bought the car "as is," but isn't the dealer responsible for repairs when something happens so soon?

A That depends on the terms of your sales contract and on the state in which you live. If the contract says that the dealer "disclaims all warranties" or that you bought the car "as is," then the dealer is not responsible. The only exceptions: Some states require dealers to make cars fit to pass inspection. If you live in one of these states, the dealer will have to repair the brakes; otherwise you must foot the bill yourself. And some states include used cars under lemon laws, spelling out the warranty terms for cars of different prices and with varying odometer readings. In New York State, for example, new vehicles are covered under lemon laws for the first 18,000 miles or two years, whichever comes first. Used vehicles are covered for 90 days or 4,000 miles, whichever comes first, for cars with 36,000 miles or less at purchase, and 60 days or 3,000 miles for cars with more than 36,000 and less than 80,000 miles.

recourse if things go wrong. Your best bet if you buy privately: Buy from someone you know, someone who has probably kept the car in good repair.

Paying for Your Car

Most cars, new and used, are financed at the time of purchase. The average new-car loan in 1992 was $13,109, according to the Consumer Bankers Association, while the average used-car loan was $8,704. If you're planning to take a loan to pay for your car, you should know that:

■ While more and more people are financing automobiles through home equity lines of credit, on the theory that the interest is deductible, this isn't necessarily a brilliant idea. Home equity should be tapped, ideally, for appreciating assets (such as an improvement to your home, or a college education for your children) rather than for a depreciating asset like an automobile.

Table 15.5: Manufacturer Financing vs. Bank Financing

Given a choice between manufacturer's reduced-rate financing and a cash rebate, it is sometimes possible to save money by using the rebate to add to the down payment and financing through a bank. For example:

	Manufacturer Financing	Bank Financing
APR[1]	6.9%	9.5%
Price	$14,000	$14,000
Down Payment	$ 2,500	$ 2,500
Mfr. Rebate[2]	0	$ 1,500
Loan Amount	$11,500	$10,000
Repayment Term	48 months	48 months
Monthly Payment	$ 274.85	$ 251.23
Total Payment	$13,192.80	$12,059.04
Total Savings		$1,133.76

Always compare financing costs, looking at the total cost over the life of the loan, before you decide where to take a loan.

Source: American Bankers Association.

Notes: [1] Figures are for illustration only and may not reflect current rates. [2] Applied as additional down payment.

■ Automobile loans, like other loans (see Chapter 7 for a full discussion of credit), are available from a number of sources. If you take the financing agreement offered by the auto dealer without first comparing costs at a variety of lending institutions (banks, savings and loans, credit unions), you may spend more than necessary ... except, perhaps, if the manufacturer or dealer is offering a temporary bargain rate as an incentive to sales. Even then, you should do a careful comparison of costs.

■ Interest rates vary from lender to lender. The figure to get, and to compare, is the annual percentage rate or APR. Federal law requires lenders to give you this figure. Use Worksheet 15.2 to compare financing alternatives.

■ Look at the total interest cost over the life of the loan; don't be misled by monthly figures, which will vary with the length of the loan and with the APR. For example, if you finance $9,600 at 11 percent for three years (which used to be the standard length of an auto loan), you will pay $314.29 a month or $1,714.50 in total interest over the life of the loan. If you finance the same amount at the same rate for five years (rapidly becoming the industry standard), you will pay $208.73 a month and a total of $2,923.64 in interest over the life of the loan. That's $1,209.14 extra for the privilege of spreading payments over the additional years. At higher interest rates (and a five-year loan often costs at least a half percent more), the differential is greater still.

■ Almost 60 percent of new-car loans now run four to five years. Think carefully, however, before taking a loan of more than three years. Recognize that, with depreciation, you may then face a period of well over a year when the actual value of the car is less than the amount outstanding on your loan. If you trade in the car during this period, you probably won't get enough to pay off the loan. If the car is wrecked or stolen during this period, your insurance (see Chapter 16) will probably cover only the depreciated ("book") value of the car (less any deductible); if the book value is less than you owe, you will be liable for the difference.

■ You do not, as a rule, have to accept or pay for credit insurance as part of your loan. If a lender tells you that it is required, check with your state insurance department or consumer affairs department. In most cases, for most people, credit insurance is overpriced and unnecessary. See Chapter 7 for more information on credit insurance.

PAYING CASH

Skipping a loan and paying cash for your car, if you have it to pay, usually saves money. But you should always do the arithmetic. Look at:

■ The interest you will lose on the money you withdraw from investments to pay for the car

■ The rate of inflation, and your own opinion about paying back a loan in what may be less valuable dollars

Financing can make sense if you need cash for other purposes, don't want to drain your savings, or can buy a better car by borrowing the money. But be aware that dealers make commissions on financing they arrange. And don't be fooled by fancy footwork. The Federal Trade Commission has sued a distributor of computer software used by many car dealers to "prove" that you

Worksheet 15.2: Comparing Lender Financing

Don't undercut any savings you've obtained in negotiating the price of the car by automatically taking dealer financing. Shop around, among dealers, banks, and credit unions. Use this worksheet to compare:

	Lender A	Lender B	Lender C
Amount financed	_____	_____	_____
Down payment	_____	_____	_____
Total finance charge	_____	_____	_____
Total cost of car	_____	_____	_____
Monthly payment	_____	_____	_____
Loan length	_____	_____	_____
Annual percentage rate	_____	_____	_____

You might also compare other factors that may cost money or affect satisfaction:

	Car A	Car B	Car C
Warranty (time/mileage limits)	_____	_____	_____
Resale value	_____	_____	_____
Crash-test performance	_____	_____	_____
Fuel economy	_____	_____	_____
Insurance rate	_____	_____	_____
Maintenance costs	_____	_____	_____
Frequency of repair history	_____	_____	_____
Dealership	_____	_____	_____
Convenience of location	_____	_____	_____
Service reliability	_____	_____	_____
Reputation	_____	_____	_____

Source: Credit Union National Association.

can save money by financing a car at one interest rate while investing the cash not spent in a certificate of deposit earning a lower interest rate. Computer printouts notwithstanding, it is impossible to come out ahead by paying more on a loan and earning less on your savings.

Whether you pay cash or take a loan, you can reduce your dollar outlay for a car by paying as little as possible for the car in the first place (see pp. 414-415).

Should You Lease?

At one time, leasing was pretty much restricted to corporate fleets and to individuals such as salespeople who were on the road much of the year and who could deduct a leased vehicle as a business expense. Today, as a result of rising new-car prices, the loss of the tax deduction for consumer interest, and manufacturer and dealer leasing incentive programs, almost one-quarter of new cars are leased instead of purchased.

Before you lease a car, however, there are a few things you should know:

- If you drive less than 10,000 miles a year, leasing probably does not pay. Unless you drive a lot, in fact, leasing may work out to be more expensive than owning.
- If you keep your cars longer than three or four years (remember, you can expect to get 100,000 miles out of a well-maintained car), you're generally better off buying.
- If there's any chance that you must end the lease early, be sure you understand what penalties apply; they can be sizable.
- Leases are written on the basis of assumed mileage. If you lease a car and drive more than the agreed-upon amount, you will pay a sur-charge.
- When you've finished with a lease, all you own is a piece of paper. When you finish paying off an auto loan, you own a physical asset that can be sold.

Nonetheless, leasing has some advantages for some people:

- If your driving is business-related, leasing provides documentation for income tax purposes and may be slightly more convenient than owning your own car. On the other hand, if you buy a car for business use, you can take advantage of depreciation deductions.
- Do you need or want a bigger, more expensive, or newer car than you can otherwise afford? By eliminating the down payment (although you may have to pay up to two months' leasing fee as security), leasing makes it possible to buy more car for the same monthly payment.

■ If you trade in your cars every three or four years, leasing may make sense.
■ If you don't want to worry about eventually selling the car, then you might want to think about leasing.
■ Can you earn a substantial return on money otherwise committed to a down payment on a car? If so, leasing may make financial sense for you.

LEASING CONTRACTS

Leasing got a bad name when open-end leasing contracts left many consumers holding the bag at the end of the lease for sizable excess charges. Today, however, almost all automobile leases are closed-end leases with a fixed residual value. With a closed-end lease, you can hand in the keys at the end of the lease period and, assuming that the car is undamaged (be sure you understand the leaser's definition of undamaged), walk away. You won't have to be concerned with its current market value.

An open-end lease, just in case you run across one (but don't take it), involves a bet with the leasing company: If the resale value of the car is higher than the company expects it to be at the end of the lease, you come out ahead; if the car is worth less, you'll owe some additional money (but usually no more, according to federal law, than three times the monthly lease payment). If you're going to consider an open-end lease, do so only with a car known to hold its resale value. And consider a lease with an option to buy. If you like the car, at the end of the lease period, you'll be able to acquire a good (because you've taken care of it) used car.

Q I've been happy with the car I've leased for three years. But how do I decide if it makes good financial sense to buy it when the lease period ends? Might I be better off leasing another new car instead?

A Good financial sense in buying a leased car depends on whether the residual value of the car (the amount you agreed upon at the outset) is approximately the same as the current market value. If you're going to owe another few hundred dollars or even more, do you want to pay the money and then not have the car? Start checking newspaper classified ads a month or two before your lease ends to see the retail value of the car you have; then compare that figure to the figure on the lease. But remember: If you're happy with the car, if it's running well and serving your needs, that may be the most important factor.

Before you lease a car, or even indicate to the dealer that you are considering a lease, do the same comparison shopping you would do if you were buying a car. And negotiate just as hard. If you don't negotiate, the selling price (on which your lease payments are based) is likely to be too high. Be aware, too, that you will pay a hefty surcharge if you surrender the lease early.

With any lease you will assume at least some of the variable expenses of car ownership: gasoline, oil, and so on. You may have to pay sales tax on the lease payments, and you may have to pay state registration fees as well. You also, under some if not all leases, buy your own insurance.

Where you rely on your own auto insurance, ask your dealer or leasing company for "gap insurance." This will supplement your regular policy and make up the difference between the car's depreciated market value (the amount your policy will pay) and the amount you still owe on the lease (which you will still have to pay if the car is stolen or totaled in an accident).

Where the leasing company provides the insurance, be sure that it covers everyone who may drive the car. Sometimes drivers under age 25 are excluded; such a clause can be a real nuisance if you need your 24-year-old to drive you to the airport.

Leases also vary with respect to **maintenance:**

- A full-maintenance lease has the leasing company providing complete service, from batteries to tires.
- A non-maintenance lease leaves you in charge.
- There are also some partial maintenance plans.

The more maintenance you have the leasing company assume, the more you will pay. A general rule of thumb is that maintenance packages don't become cost-effective unless you will put more than 20,000 miles a year on a car.

COST COMPARISONS

It's very difficult to make dollar-for-dollar comparisons between owning and leasing. Too much depends on whether or not you finance a purchase, and at what interest rate; too much depends on the number of miles you drive and how long you keep the car. But with today's incentive programs, the cost can be very close. (See Table 15.6.)

Note, though, that a small move one way or the other could dramatically change the cost comparison in this table. Pay an extra 1 percent in interest charges, get hit by a big repair bill, and the equation shifts. Buying a car with home equity dollars, giving you interest deductions on your income tax, reduces the overall cost of buying. Keep the car more than four years, for a period in which you don't pay finance charges, and you're better off buying. Better yet, pay cash, eliminate finance charges altogether, and you're definitely better off owning. And don't forget: At the end of the leasing period the driver owns nothing; at the end of the loan period the same driver does own a car.

Table 15.6: Buying vs. Leasing an Automobile

The costs of buying a 1992 mid-size versus leasing the same vehicle. The mid-size costs $16,000 with financing at 9 percent and a down payment of 20 percent.

Purchase

	Year 1	Year 2	Year 3	Year 4	Total
Down Payment	$3,200				$ 3,200
Yearly Payment	3,372	$3,372	$3,372	$3,372	13,488
Tax Benefit	—	—	—	—	—
Trade-in	—	—	—	(5,280)	(5,280)
Total Cost	$6,572	$3,372	$3,372	($1,908)	$11,408

Lease

	Year 1	Year 2	Year 3	Year 4	Total
Deposit	$ 235				$ 235
Yearly Payments	2,820	$2,820	$2,820	$2,820	11,280
Tax Benefit	—	—	—	—	—
Deposit Refund	—	—	—	—	(235)
Total Cost	$3,055	$2,820	$2,820	$2,820	$11,280

Source: Runzheimer International.

If you decide to lease, after weighing all the variables that apply to your situation, you have several choices of leasing agent, among them banks, rental companies, leasing companies, and automobile dealers. Some offer only one type of lease; others offer you some choice. Shop around, after you decide which type of car you want, comparing costs among at least three vendors and two types of leaser.

CONSUMER PROTECTION IN AUTO LEASING

Federal law, in the form of the Consumer Leasing Act, protects you when you lease personal property such as automobiles, furniture, or appliances for more than four months. The law has the following provisions:

■ You must be given a written statement of costs before you agree to any lease, including (1) the amount of any advance payment, such as a security deposit; (2) the number of payments, the amount of each one, and the dates they are due, as well as the total amount of those payments; and (3) the amount you must pay for license, registration, and taxes, as well as for any other fees such as maintenance.

■ You must be told the **terms** of the lease, including (1) what kind of insurance you need; (2) who is responsible for maintenance and service; (3) any penalty for default or late payment; (4) how you or the leasing company may cancel the lease, and the charge for doing so;

and (5) whether you can buy the property and, if you can, when and at what price.

■ You must be helped to **compare** the cost of buying on credit with the cost of leasing, by being told the total amount you are responsible for under the lease, the value of the property at the beginning of the lease, and the difference between the two.

Note: If you are leasing a car exclusively for personal use, don't agree with a salesperson's suggestion that you may also occasionally use it for business. Business use, such as calling on clients, excludes you from the protection of the Consumer Leasing Act.

Do You Need a Car?

If you live in a community with good, safe, dependable mass transit, you may very well be able to do without a car. If you live in a built-up urban area, moreover (the kind of area most likely to have good mass transit), you may find the costs of car ownership prohibitive. Parking garages alone, in New York City, can cost more than many people are accustomed to paying for housing. If you can walk to the supermarket, bank, and library, and use a bus or subway or bicycle to commute to work, you probably don't need a car. Your occasional need for a car, largely on weekends and for vacations, can probably be met, less expensively, by renting (see below).

If you find yourself behind the wheel virtually every day, however, chances are that you do need a car ... unless a lot of the driving is more from habit than from necessity. This may be particularly true if you're driving the household's second car. Would it be worth it to you to consolidate errands, share a ride to work, and generally do without the convenience of car ownership in order to save some money?

Renting a Car

The car that you own costs you money 24 hours a day, 365 days a year, whether you are using it or not. You continue to pay for insurance, interest, and the intangible but very real depreciation even while the car sits idle in your driveway or at the curb. The only car that costs you money only while it's actually being used is a rental car.

Most people think about renting for personal use only while on vacation. But if you live in a city where garaging is expensive, you may save money by renting even if you use a car every single weekend plus two weeks a year. However, it's impossible to look at owning versus renting in financial terms alone. There's a psychological element as well. The cost of renting for the year may be favorable, but you are likely to look at the cost per weekend and decide that your planned activities are not worthwhile. If you are going to spend $40 or more to rent a car for a day, a picnic in the country may begin to look like expensive fresh air.

If you do decide to rent, whether for vacation or for year-round use, be very careful to compare costs carefully.

RENTAL COSTS

There are three kinds of basic rates to compare before you rent a car:

■ Time plus mileage, in which you pay so much per day plus so many cents per mile. Some companies have two-tier mileage rates, where you pay one rate for each mile up to a specified number of miles, then a higher per-mile cost for each additional mile.

■ Unlimited mileage plans, now much more common, under which you'll pay more per day or per week, but that's it. With no extra mileage charges, these plans are often (depending on how far you'll drive) more economical than time plus mileage. There are also some combination plans available, under which a specified number of miles is included with extra charges for extra miles driven.

■ Special rates. Every car rental company has a confusing variety of special plans. Rent a car in Florida during vacation season and you'll probably find a special rate. Rent a car on your way to a city where the rental company needs the car and you may get a special rate. Watch the ads, and ask the rental companies, to see what's available when you plan to rent a car.

In addition to these basic rates, the ones featured in advertisements, there are often additional costs (which are supposed to be spelled out in ads, but may be in small print). Examples are fuel charges, surcharges, airport access fees, and extra charges for a second driver. Always be sure you get a complete picture when you compare car-rental costs.

Cost-Cutting on Rentals

You'll save money if you compare rates carefully, in terms of your own particular needs. You'll also save some money if you:

■ Take advantage of discounts. Almost every corporation, association, and fraternal group seems to offer a car rental discount to its members. But don't take a discount without making some comparisons: The largest car rental companies, with the highest base rates, offer the largest discounts; you may under some circumstances be better off with a different company and no "discount." You also can't take both a special rate and a discount; in some cases you'll save more money with a special rate.

■ Rent the smallest car you can comfortably use. Rates at all companies go up with the size of the car. (If you've reserved a specific size car ahead of time, you get the rate for that car, even if the company gives you a larger car.)

■ Understand all the terms of the agreement. If you're an hour late in returning the car, will you be charged for an extra day? What happens if you take a weekly rate and return the car a day early? How much insurance is included (see below)?

■ Understand any extra charges and, if possible, work around them. Rental companies typically charge more than pump prices for gasoline, for example, so fill up your car's tank before you return it. If you select a less-expensive rental from a company based off airport grounds, be prepared to pay an airport access fee—or (after checking that it will actually save money) use some method of transportation other than the one the rental company provides to get to the rental location.

■ Rent an older car, if you don't care too much about looks. In many cities mechanically sound older cars are available at a much lower cost from rental agencies going by such names as "Rent-a-Wreck" or "Lease-a-Lemon."

INSURANCE ON RENTAL CARS

When renting a car, you want to have both **liability** insurance to protect you against injury and damage claims from others and **collision** coverage to protect you against the costs of damage done to the rental car itself. Both may be provided through your own automobile insurance, assuming that you carry insurance, but you may also want to purchase extra coverage. Here's what you need to know:

The major car rental agencies carry personal injury liability insurance, which protects you, up to specified limits, in case of an accident. But those limits may be the minimum required by the state. With most companies, you can supplement this basic protection through buying supplemental liability insurance (which ups the limit of liability coverage to, typically, $1 million).

These same agencies will also ask you to waive collision coverage or to pay an extra $7 to $13 a day for this coverage (except in the handful of states that forbid the sale of these collision damage waivers or limit their cost). Before you decide, find out whether your own auto insurance covers you or whether your credit card issuer provides this protection.

Note: Don't expect double protection. Buying the collision damage waiver may void credit card coverage.

Whether or not you take additional coverage, keep the basic liability coverage in force by:

■ Having everyone in your group who might drive the car sign the rental agreement. Others, especially family members, are sometimes allowed to drive without advance signature—although some companies now charge extra for each driver, and cancel insurance if an unauthorized driver is at the wheel. Drivers under 21 or, sometimes, under 25 may not be allowed to drive your rental car at all. Be sure you read the contract carefully before you turn the wheel over to your child.

■ Understanding and abiding by the basic provisions of your rental agreement. It may, for instance, forbid towing. It may not allow driving in another state, or on an unpaved road. Read the small print in your rental agreement, even if you're in a hurry.

 KEY POINTS

■ It costs less to buy and to run an old car than a new one.

■ Compare financing costs carefully before you buy, especially when rebates and special deals are offered.

■ Leasing a car is another option, and may be worthwhile if you drive more than 10,000 to 12,000 miles a year and will keep a car no more than four years. Compare costs carefully, however, before you decide to lease.

■ Think about whether you need a car at all. It may be cost-effective to rent a car on an as-needed basis instead of owning one all year round.

CHAPTER 16

Automobile Insurance

Auto insurance consumes a relatively small proportion of family budgets, an average, for most people, of about 2 percent of total outgo. In dollars and cents, the cost looms larger; the average household with auto insurance spent $953 on premiums in 1991. Many people (especially those who live in congested urban areas, or who have teenage drivers in the household) spend considerably more. Auto insurance, depending on where you live, your family makeup, and the kind of car you drive, can come to thousands of dollars a year. You can keep those costs under control, at least in part, by careful shopping.

Even if automobile insurance is expensive, you can't do without it. Automobile coverage protects you against potentially tremendous financial loss stemming from accidental injury to other people or to property. Most states require motorists to carry some automobile insurance. But, whatever the law in your state, you should carry automobile insurance; you should also consider carrying more than the mandated minimum of liability coverage.

Basic Auto Insurance Provisions

Automobile insurance comes in six basic parts, some of which are essential and some of which are optional.

BODILY INJURY LIABILITY

Bodily injury liability coverage is absolutely essential (and required in most states). It provides financial protection against legal liability (up to the limits stated in your policy) for injury or death resulting from an accident involving your automobile. It applies whether the injured person is in your car, in someone else's car, or a pedestrian. It applies to injury caused by your car, no matter who is driving, as long as the person driving your car has your permission to do so. And it applies when you or members of your family are driving someone else's car, as long as the driver has the owner's permission.

Bodily injury liability coverage may be written as a single number, the maximum your insurer will pay per accident. But it is often written with what insurers call a "split limit"—with maximum amounts per accident and per person. If you carry $300,000 in bodily injury coverage per accident, for example, a "split limit" policy would typically provide $100,000 for injuries suffered by each person involved in that accident.

Suggestion: Regardless of your state's liability limits, buy as much bodily injury liability protection as you can afford. Jury awards in accident cases can be very high, and without enough insurance you can be wiped out.

PROPERTY DAMAGE LIABILITY

John intended to back out of his driveway, but put his car in drive by mistake. As he shot forward, he demolished his neighbor's fence. The fence was rebuilt with money received from John's automobile insurance company.

Property damage liability applies, up to the stated limits in your policy, when your car damages the property of others. Damaged property is most often a car (John could have sideswiped his neighbor's car), but the coverage applies to any property (except your own): fences, lampposts, buildings, etc. Protection is in force no matter who is driving your car (with your permission) and while you or members of your family are driving someone else's car (with the owner's permission).

Property damage coverage is often expressed as the third part of the liability formula: 50/100/10. Again, your state may have minimum requirements, but you may want to consider additional coverage.

No-Fault Insurance

Your automobile insurance policy will pay personal injury and property damage liability claims when you are at fault. In many accidents fault is not easy to ascertain (three cars pile up in an intersection and you're caught in the middle; whose fault was it?), leading to extensive and expensive lawsuits. A number of states, as a consequence, have adopted "no-fault" auto insurance.

Under no-fault laws, ideally, your own insurance company will pay for bodily injury losses resulting from an accident, including medical and hospital expenses and lost income, no matter who is at fault. Details of coverage vary from state to state, however, especially with regard to the amounts to be paid and conditions governing the right to sue. No-fault laws generally permit lawsuits if injuries meet the law's threshold of "serious," a threshold which may be expressed in dollar numbers or in descriptive terms. No-fault was intended to keep costs down, but watered-down laws permitting lawsuits even in minor accidents, have undermined the effort.

MEDICAL PAYMENTS

This coverage in the basic automobile policy covers medical, dental, and surgical bills resulting from injury sustained in an auto accident; it's generally available in amounts ranging from $500 to $10,000 per person per accident. It covers you and all members of your family who live with you (not an adult son or daughter resident elsewhere) while riding in your car or someone else's car, or when struck by a car while walking. It also applies to guests in your car.

Medical payments are made without regard to fault, and the coverage is not available in some states where no-fault insurance is the norm. It also may not apply where you are covered under group medical insurance.

Note: If you regularly drive your children's friends to Little League or nursery school, check your automobile insurance policy to make sure it includes medical payments coverage. Some states require this coverage. If yours does not, and if you choose to save money on your premium by skipping medical payments coverage and letting your group health insurance pay any accident-related medical bills, you may want to reconsider. Group health insurance generally covers only your own family, not other people's children.

PERSONAL INJURY PROTECTION

This form of medical coverage is typically offered in states with no-fault insurance, either instead of or in addition to medical payments coverage. It covers medical bills. It also replaces income lost due to injuries sustained in an auto accident, and it pays for essential services, such as housekeeping, that an injured person can't perform.

Personal injury protection (PIP) is generally optional and, if you have good health insurance coverage, you may choose to forget it. But it doesn't add much to the cost of your auto insurance, and it may be worth having to protect non-family members injured in your car.

PROTECTION AGAINST UNINSURED MOTORISTS

This coverage applies mainly to bodily injuries for which an uninsured motorist or a hit-and-run driver is legally liable—the kind of situation where

---

Q May I use my car in a car pool, without changing my automobile insurance policy?

A Yes. As long as the car pool is not a business conducted for profit (it's okay to collect expenses from your passengers), your insurance will apply. If you are regularly carrying several passengers, however, it might be a good idea to consider increasing the limits on your bodily injury liability coverage.

another driver runs a red light and puts you in the hospital for several days, then out of work for several weeks, and you find he has no insurance.

Despite state financial responsibility laws and mandated liability coverage, some estimates indicate that at least one of every twelve motor vehicles on the road today is not insured. Unless your state has no-fault insurance, in which case you will be compensated by your own insurance company, becoming the victim of an uninsured motorist can leave you financially destitute as well as physically injured. Even with no-fault insurance, uninsured motorists coverage can provide additional protection in instances where your coverage limits aren't high enough to cover all the bills.

Uninsured motorists protection is optional (as is underinsured motorists coverage in some places). Unless you are adequately covered under other forms of insurance for any potential financial liability, give serious thought to including it in your basic automobile policy.

There is no excuse for being an uninsured motorist. Every driver can get insurance. If insurance is not available on an individual basis because of a poor driving record, lack of experience, or the situation in your state (many companies refused to write any auto insurance in New Jersey, for instance, when the state refused to allow rate increases), it is available through an "assigned risk" plan. Shop around first and then, if necessary, ask an insurance agent about assigned risk. Rates may be higher, depending on the state and on your own record, but you will have insurance. And you may be able to move to regular coverage after an accident-free interval.

COLLISION INSURANCE

Steve was slowing for a red light when the driver in front jammed on his brakes. With quick reflexes, Steve was able to stop, without hitting the car in front. But the driver in back was not so lucky, or so skillful. His left front fender tangled with the right rear fender of Steve's car. The repairs to Steve's 1990 Chevrolet cost $2,380. Steve filed a claim with his own insurance company and collected $2,180 (the cost of repairs less a $200 deductible) under his

Q My 22-year-old son, who is on his own and working and living in another city, does not have his own car and drives ours when he comes to visit. Should we still carry him on our auto insurance?

A As long as he is no longer a student and is living away from home, you probably don't have to keep him on your policy; he should still be covered if anything happens while he is driving your car, so long as he has your permission to do so. But check with your own agent or company representative to make sure.

collision insurance. Since the other driver was clearly at fault, he was able to collect the rest later, when the other company settled with his company.

Collision coverage pays for damage to your car regardless of responsibility, whether you run into a tree or another driver runs into you. If you are involved in an accident in which the other driver is legally at fault, the collision insurance you carry on your own car will enable you to collect from your own insurance company and have your car fixed without delay. Without collision coverage you have to wait for payment until the other driver's insurance company agrees to a settlement.

If you do collect under your own collision coverage when another driver is at fault, your own company will then "subrogate" your claim—that is, submit it to the other company for payment. When it is paid, you will receive your deductible.

Collision coverage, which is optional, is written on a deductible basis, with premiums based on the year, make, and model of your car. It is generally worth carrying when your car is new and not worth carrying on a car that is several years old and greatly diminished in value. (If you have a loan on your car, however, the lender will probably require that you carry collision insurance.)

COMPREHENSIVE PHYSICAL DAMAGE

Mary's windshield was cracked by a flying stone. Andrew's car was stolen from a busy suburban shopping mall. Both were covered under the physical damage portion of their auto insurance policies.

Comprehensive, as it's usually called, protects you against financial loss stemming from a wide array of perils (other than accidents): fire, theft, glass breakage, flood, falling objects, missiles, explosion, earthquake, windstorm, hail, water, vandalism or malicious mischief, riot or civil commotion, or collision with a bird or animal. It does *not* apply to damage incurred in a collision with another car or object and it does not include wear and tear, engine failure, or mechanical difficulties.

The coverage is written with a deductible, and with premiums based in part on location. There are more car thefts in some areas than in others. Wind and hail storms, similarly, are more frequent in some areas than in others.

Replacement Cost Insurance

When Marilyn took a skid on an icy Nebraska road, her yearly budget hit the skids too. She learned it would cost her more to repair her 1989 auto than it was currently worth. Her insurance company totaled the vehicle and gave her a claim settlement of $5,300, its current value, which was less than she still owed on the loan she had taken to buy the car. Marilyn had to dip deeply into her already none-too-healthy savings account to purchase the 1993 model of the same car for $13,400.

A car is deemed a total loss by an insurance company not only when it is impossible to repair but also, as Marilyn found out, when it would cost more to repair than the car is currently worth. With escalating repair costs, this situation is confronting more and more drivers. In 1971 only 3.5 percent of all damaged autos insured by one major carrier were totaled; by 1991 the figure was 9.8 percent. According to the Alliance of American Insurers, a 1989 Nissan Maxima that cost $17,499 new would cost $60,755 for parts and paint alone, without labor, if it had to be rebuilt.

One answer: replacement insurance, similar to the replacement insurance on household contents described in Chapter 12. Under a Kemper plan, for example, the insurer will pay to repair the car even if repair costs exceed its current market value, up to the cost of a comparable new car. If the car cannot be repaired for less than the price of a comparable new car, the company will pay the cost to replace the damaged auto with a new car of the same make with the same equipment.

How would this coverage work for Marilyn? Because a replacement car of the same type cost $13,400, the insurer would have paid up to $13,400 for

Q I may drive to Mexico for vacation and I was told that I need special automobile insurance. Doesn't my regular insurance apply?

A No. Mexico has special rules, requiring that nonresident drivers purchase auto liability insurance from a Mexican insurance company. The rules are very stringent (a Mexican endorsement attached to a U.S. policy is not sufficient), and failure to comply could leave you in serious trouble. Your car could be impounded, your driver's license could be revoked, you could even be imprisoned. You can buy a short-term "Special Automobile Policy for Tourists" from a Mexican insurance company in most American border cities. Don't leave home without it.

If you're crossing the border in the other direction, however, and traveling to Canada, you'll find life a bit easier. Your American insurance policy does apply, although you'll need a "Non-resident Interprovince Motor Vehicle Liability Insurance Card." This card, which proves that you do have auto insurance, may be easily obtained from your own insurance company or from a provincial or territorial government office of Canada.

If you intend to drive a car overseas, talk to your insurance agent before you go.

repairs to her car even though the car was "worth" only $5,300. If repair was not possible, the insurer would have provided up to $13,400 for the purchase of a replacement vehicle.

Replacement coverage is not available in every state, or sold by every insurer; where it is offered, some restrictions and coverage limits may apply. As a rule, however, replacement insurance must be elected within 30 to 90 days of your purchase of a new car. It does not apply to damage caused by fire, theft, or larceny. It may, however, be worth investigating. At a modest additional cost—Kemper's coverage is priced at an extra 10 percent of the combined comprehensive and collision premium, or an average of $18 per six-month policy period for the average mid-size car—you could be protected against the significant financial loss you could face if your car was severely damaged. That loss could entail both the inflated price of a new car, while your old car was still providing good transportation, and the continuing cost of paying off an auto loan on a car you no longer have.

Auto Insurance Rates

While automobile insurance still makes up a fairly small segment of most family budgets, rates in many areas have risen sharply, fueled by more accidents, higher repair costs, more lawsuits, and more expensive medical care. If your own driving record includes some accidents, if you live in an urban area and if you have a teenage driver in your household, you don't have to be told about high-priced auto insurance.

Many car owners feel that auto insurance is overpriced. Some state regulators agree. For the last few years there has been a tug-of-war between regulators and insurance companies about premiums and how they should be set. Bear in mind, though, that the cost of insurance is a bargain compared to the cost of settling most claims. This is not a place to pinch pennies.

But you don't need to waste money either. It's possible to keep your own automobile insurance premiums down. It helps, to start with, if you understand how rates are established.

Where You Live

The overall cost of insurance is determined by the experience of insurance companies: the number of claims they receive and the cost of resolving those claims. Because this claims experience varies from place to place, automobile insurance rates have traditionally been based in large part on where you live. The other two elements in rate-setting typically involve who you are (your age, gender, marital status) and the kind of car you drive.

A rating territory may be an entire city, or a part of a large city, a suburb, or a rural district. Rates are based on the claims involving cars kept in the particular territory, regardless of where an accident or theft actually takes place. A

Tennessee driver responsible for an accident in California affects Tennessee rates, not those levied in California.

In general, for obvious reasons, it costs more to insure a car in Los Angeles, California (or any large city), than in Clinton, Iowa (or any small town or rural district). There have been arguments, however, that the whole territorial classification system is unfair. Why should a middle-aged driver in Newark, New Jersey, with a spotless driving record, have to pay more for auto insurance than a younger (and more careless) driver in a Princeton suburb?

Some state regulators have moved to remove residence from the rate-setting process, but with little result. California is the only state currently relegating territory to the tail end of a list of relevant factors in setting auto insurance rates; New Jersey made a similar effort, but its law was overturned.

Driver Classification

Claims experience also varies in accordance with personal characteristics: driving record, age, sex, and marital status. In general, the younger the driver, the higher the rates, with still-higher rates for single males and the highest of all (based on nationwide accident experience) for young single males who own and operate their own cars.

There's been a lot of discussion about whether this age, sex, and marital status categorization is fair. Four states currently ban rate classification based on age, seven prohibit classification based on sex, and two won't let insurers consider marital status.

But insurance companies point out in their own defense that it's been well documented that unmarried males under the age of 25 are responsible for proportionately more accidents than young women or older adults of either gender. Even where age is eliminated as a rating factor, insurers can (and do) levy higher premiums on inexperienced drivers.

Q Can my insurance company insist that I put my 24-year-old son's car on my auto policy and make me responsible for premium payments? He's buying the car and registering it in his own name, but he lives with me.

A No. In fact, most insurance companies would insist that he have his own policy. Perhaps your agent believes that combining the cars on one policy would save money by making you eligible for a multicar discount. But the higher cost for a young driver would probably outweigh any discount and, at least with some insurers, you would have to own his car in order to qualify. Tell your agent that your son wants his own policy.

Until this controversy is resolved (if ever), bear in mind that insurance companies are competitive in setting rates. If you shop around, you may find very different premiums charged for a person who fits your description.

The Car You Drive

Because some cars suffer more damage than others in the same kind of fender-bender, because some cost more to repair, and because some are more tempting targets for thieves (a sports car is six times more likely to be stolen than a station wagon), the kind of car you drive can make a big difference in the premiums you pay for auto insurance. The Highway Loss Data Institute (HLDI) compiles annual reports on how various models perform. Many insurance companies use HLDI reports in setting premiums (see Table 16.1).

Table 16.1: Comparing Insurance Costs

Vehicle	HLDI Ranking Collision	Collision premium ($200 deductible)	Comprehensive premium ($50 deductible)
1991 Buick Century, 4-door	69[1]	$112	$56.50
1991 Chevrolet Beretta, 2-door	131[1]	$163	$97.50

Premiums are for six months based on cars used for pleasure driving by a 30-year-old male living in Mount Prospect, Illinois.

Source: Kemper National Insurance Companies.

Note: [1] Rankings below 70 are substantially better than average; rankings above 130 are substantially worse than average.

Be aware, too, that some cars, notably high-performance and sports cars, may cost you more to insure; the assumption is that you won't buy all that power unless you mean to use it. Luxury cars, too, attractive to thieves and expensive to repair, may also cost more to insure. Before you buy a new car, compare rates on different models with your insurance agent or company.

Other Factors

Where you live, what you're like, and the car you drive are the major factors that enter into the setting of rates. But there are others:

- Whether the vehicle is driven for business (and exposed to more traffic and more potential accidents) or solely for pleasure
- The number of miles driven each year (less is better)
- Whether or not the car is kept in a garage (and thereby protected from the elements and, somewhat, from theft)

Table 16.2: Sample Automobile Insurance Rates

	Average student living at home	Good student living at home	Average student away at school[1]	Good student away at school[1]
50/100/25 liability				
$50 deductible/comprehensive				
$200 deductible/collision	$577	$433	$480	$384
50/100/25 liability				
$100 deductible/comprehensive				
$500 deductible/collision	509	383	424	340
100/300/50 liability				
$50 deductible/comprehensive				
$200 deductible/collision	612	460	509	408
100/300/50 liability				
$100 deductible/comprehensive				
$500 deductible/collision	544	410	453	364

Comparative rates on automobile insurance for a Dublin, Ohio, family of three—a 42-year-old husband, a 40-year-old wife, and their 19-year-old son. The father, who is the principal driver, commutes 12 miles to work in the family's 1993 Ford Taurus. The son has taken a behind-the-wheel driver education course. Each of the three drivers has a good driving record. Rates are for six months, effective November 1992.

Source: Kemper National Insurance Companies.

Note: [1]More than 100 miles away from home.

■ Your occupation (considered as a rating factor by some companies, in some states)

Typical rates are shown in Table 16.2.

KEEPING COSTS DOWN

You can keep your automobile insurance costs down by driving less, by garaging your car, and by buying a well-rated model. You can also keep your auto insurance costs down by taking larger deductibles and by taking advantage of available discounts (ask your company which discounts it offers; it may not volunteer the information).

Larger Deductibles

Think about how much you can afford to "self-insure," to pay out of your own pocket, and buy insurance with the appropriate deductibles. Collision insurance, for example, is often written with a deductible of $250. Raise your deductible to $500 and you could save 15 percent to 30 percent on your collision insurance; a $1,000 deductible could mean a savings of 40 percent. Comprehensive insurance may be written with deductibles from $50 to $250; choosing the $50 deductible instead of full coverage could save you 8 to 12 percent.

Discounts

These are some typical discounts; not all are offered by every insurer:

■ Safe driver plans, for drivers with good records

■ Anti-theft devices, and air bag or automatic belting systems

■ Farm discounts, for cars or trucks owned by a farmer or rancher

■ Driver education discounts, for high school and college students who maintain good grades

■ Away-from-home discounts for students living at school over 100 miles away (this discount does not apply to students who own their own cars and carry their own insurance; it's always less expensive to register your child's car in your name and to include the child on your insurance policy)

■ Good student discounts, for high school and college students who maintain good grades

→ ■ Multiple-car discounts, for households owning two or more passenger cars and insuring them with the same company

■ Nonsmoker and nondrinker discounts, offered by some companies

■ Senior citizen discounts, offered by some companies

■ Car pool discounts, for those who share the driving to work

Car Pooling

Car pooling saves money, in several ways:

- On auto insurance. Premiums may drop from 10 to 25 percent if you share the driving with others. Even with companies which do not offer specific car pooling discounts, lowering driving mileage may place you in a lower premium classification.
- On actual dollar outlay. If you drive a one-way distance of 10 miles, in a standard-size sedan, you save at least $500 a year by sharing the driving with just one other person. Rotating drivers among a larger group would save proportionately more.
- On time. Many cities have car-pool lanes on highways and toll bridges, speeding commuting time to work. Many employers, too, now offer preferential parking to car poolers.
- On car upkeep and maintenance. Driving your car less means less wear and tear.

Dropping Unnecessary Coverage   COLLISION !

Consider dropping collision insurance altogether when your car is four or five years old. Chances are that its book value at this point is far less than you would collect should the car be damaged. The car may provide adequate transportation for your family, and therefore cost a good bit to replace, but its book value is what counts. No company will pay more in repairs than the car was worth before the accident, minus any salvage value (unless you have replacement insurance; see p. 000).

Note: You may want to carry collision insurance longer if you drive a model that retains value. And you will probably have to continue collision coverage as long as you are paying off the loan you took to buy the car.

Don't duplicate coverage. If you carry umbrella liability insurance (described in Chapter 00), you may not need as much personal injury liability coverage. If you have adequate health and accident insurance, you may not need medical payments coverage (unless you're driving a children's car pool; see p. 000). If you belong to an auto or travel club, you may not need towing insurance (or, if you have towing insurance, you may not need to belong to an auto or travel club). Review all your policies carefully to narrow any gaps while reducing overlapping coverage.

Shopping Around

Rates vary widely; it pays to comparison shop. But look at a company's claims record as well as its rates. The April issue of *Consumer Reports* magazine often lists insurance companies by service as well as cost. And you may be able to secure comparative claims information from your state insurance department. The New York State Insurance Department, for example, issues an annual ranking of automobile insurance complaints. According to the 1991 ranking, judged on the number of upheld complaints per million dollars of premium, the poorest performers were American International Group (AIG), Country-Wide Insurance Company, and Eveready Insurance Company. The three best performers were

AMICA Mutual Insurance Company, Exchange Insurance Company, and Tri-State Insurance Company. Note that these are companies doing business in New York State. Note, too, that smaller companies may provide better service—but these smaller companies may not write policies in every state or write policies, where they are available on every applicant.

Worksheet 16.1: Choosing an Insurer

Price You Will Be Charged for One Year of Coverage

	Company/ Agent 1	Company/ Agent 2	Company/ Agent 3
Minimum amount of insurance your state requires you to carry for:			
Bodily injury liability: _____	_____	_____	_____
Property damage liability: _____	_____	_____	_____
Personal injury protection (if you live in a no-fault state):	_____	_____	_____
Uninsured motorist: _____	_____	_____	_____
TOTAL for required coverages:	_____	_____	_____
Amount of coverage you would like to carry for:			
Bodily injury liability: _____	_____	_____	_____
Property damage liability: _____	_____	_____	_____
Medical payments: _____	_____	_____	_____
Personal injury protection (if you live in a no-fault state): _____	_____	_____	_____
Collision			
$100 deductible:	_____	_____	_____
$250 deductible:	_____	_____	_____
$500 deductible:	_____	_____	_____
Comprehensive			
with no deductible:	_____	_____	_____
$50 deductible:	_____	_____	_____
$100 deductible:	_____	_____	_____
Uninsured motorist: _____	_____	_____	_____
Underinsured motorist: _____	_____	_____	_____
TOTAL for desired coverages:	_____	_____	_____

Source: Insurance Information Institute.

It may also pay to give one company both your auto and your homeowners insurance business. As a bigger customer, you may be eligible for a discount. And you will avoid the gray areas that can occur between coverages ... the kind of situation, for instance, that might develop if a passenger trips while getting out of your car and injures himself in your driveway, and two insurers fight over who should pay.

But don't be penny-conscious to the extent that you leave yourself vulnerable. Keep your coverage in step with inflation, particularly in the areas of property damage liability, medical payments, and uninsured motorists coverage.

Note: Insurance companies have long been known as stable financial institutions. Today, however, some have fallen victim to the same economic problems and imprudent investments that have challenged banks and thrifts. Before you decide where to place your automobile and homeowners insurance, check the insurer's ratings from A.M. Best, Standard & Poor's, and Moody's; two of the three should give the company their top rating before you sign on the dotted line.

If your company does run into trouble: In most cases, another insurer takes over and business continues as usual. If not, you will be protected (but not necessarily immediately or fully) by the insurance guaranty fund in your state (the District of Columbia and Puerto Rico also have guaranty funds). They don't work exactly the same way, but the underlying principle is that solvent insurers cover claims against insolvent insurers. As a consumer, the presence of a guaranty fund is comforting. It's preferable, however, to pick a solvent well-run company in the first place.

Keeping Your Insurer Up-To-Date

Keep your insurance agent or company informed of changes in your life that may change your insurance premiums. Tell the company if you move, stop driving to work, join a car pool, reach the age of 25, get married, or have a child go away to college. All of these things make a difference.

 KEY POINTS

- Bodily injury liability insurance is absolutely essential, whether or not it is required by your state.
- Buy as much bodily injury liability protection as you can afford, against the risk of injuring anyone with your car.
- Save money on auto insurance by taking sizable deductibles on collision and comprehensive protection, and dropping these coverages altogether as your car ages.

■ When you buy auto insurance (or any insurance), pay attention to the stability of the company, as well as to competitive rates and quality service.

Spending Your Money: Higher Education

CHAPTER 17

Financing an Education

Bill Taylor is the father of three children, ages 10 through 14. He's aware that college costs a lot of money, but never sat down to actually calculate what college will cost. Now he's learned, to his horror, that four years at the average state university currently cost about $32,000 while four years at the average private university are in the neighborhood of $68,000. If all three children attend a state university, the total cost, at today's fees and without regard to inevitable yearly increases, will be $96,000. But today's costs, as Bill well knows, won't be tomorrow's costs. What's more, with three children in a span of four years, the Taylor family will face overlapping expenses. At Bill's current income of $43,200, the next ten years look bleak indeed.

Education beyond high school is an expensive proposition. But it is also an investment in the future. Whether you are a parent planning for the higher education of your children or an adult planning your own advanced education, you'll want to think through the best ways to finance that education and to make the most of the opportunities open to you. This chapter will focus on college costs and on ways to meet those costs. The first section of the chapter deals with funding your children's educational expenses, first when you have a long-term investment horizon and then when college is around the corner; the second focuses on economical ways to educate yourself.

What Does College Cost?

College comes in many shapes and sizes, from the highly selective and high-priced institutions of the Ivy League to local low-cost community colleges where students live at home. In between are universities and colleges in

Table 17.1: Expenses, by Region, for Resident Students, 1991-92

	Tuition and fees	Additional out-of-state tuition	Books and supplies	Resident			Commuter		
				Room and board	Trans-portation	Other costs	Board only	Trans-portation	Other costs
National									
2-year public	1,022	2,396	480	—	—	—	1,543	902	966
2-year private	5,290	—	476	3,734	519	895	1,529	786	925
4-year public	2,137	3,309	485	3,351	464	1,147	1,468	793	1,153
4-year private	10,017	—	508	4,386	470	911	1,634	795	1,029
New England									
2-year public	1,749	2,783	467	—	—	—	1,405[1]	1,115[1]	931[1]
2-year private	7,835	—	404	5,038	398	617	1,592	724	703
4-year public	3,439	4,224	502	3,972	300	1,086	1,593	988	1,068
4-year private	13,487	—	501	5,344	360	815	1,533	864	960
Middle States									
2-year public	1,812	2,639	477	—	—	—	1,431	909	792
2-year private	7,098	—	477	4,056	402	1,049	1,875	835	819
4-year public	2,770	2,851	506	3,747	403	1,013	1,376	731	1,156
4-year private	10,469	—	503	4,964	356	882	1,626	726	1,017
South									
2-year public	804	2,194	487	—	—	—	1,609	1,062	1,027
2-year private	4,617	—	458	3,246	530	913	1,609	840	1,160
4-year public	1,873	2,874	489	3,027	485	947	1,557	905	989
4-year private	8,478	—	493	3,744	608	886	1,497	802	908

Midwest

2-year public	1,273	2,456	460	—	—	—	1,628	890	976
2-year private	4,541	—	496	2,808[1]	494	849	1,357	896	975
4-year public	2,348	3,024	449	3,090	396	1,323	1,334	738	1,146
4-year private	9,446	—	500	3,650	479	873	1,772	857	1,082

Southwest

2-year public	665	1,236	458[1]	—	—	—	1,484	934[1]	979[1]
2-year private	—	—	—	2,874	890	1,384	—	990[1]	977[1]
4-year public	1,284	2,715	453	2,911	738	1,101	1,410	941	1,056
4-year private	7,106	—	492	3,474	648	1,078	1,423	862	1,014

West

2-year public	477	2,830	500	—	—	—	1,502[1]	727[1]	1,023[1]
2-year private	2,714	—	537[1]	—	944	1,093	—	685[1]	1,031[1]
4-year public	1,673	4,911	520	4,027	551	1,502	1,602	707	1,357
4-year private	9,793	—	579	4,760	572	1,212	1,665	790	1,142

Sample Expense Budgets

	Resident	Commuter
2-year public	—	$4,913
2-year private	$10,485	9,006
4-year public	7,584	6,036
4-year private	16,292	13,983

Source: College Entrance Examination Board, *The College Cost Book, 1993*, 1992.

Note: [1] Sample too small to provide meaningful averages.

a wide range of sizes, of quality, and of cost. Whatever school you look at, however, whatever kind of school it is and wherever it is located, there's no doubt about one thing: College costs are up.

In the 1970s, college costs actually rose at a rate well below the rate of inflation. But financial pressures have caught up with colleges in a big way and, for more than a decade, the overall cost of college has increased by much more than the Consumer Price Index. At the same time, family incomes have risen at a far slower pace. According to the College Board, the cost of college just about doubled from the 1982-83 academic year to the 1990-91 academic year; median family income in the same period rose from $23,433 to $35,353.

There are many reasons for the increase in college costs: Deferred maintenance and crumbling physical facilities, higher fuel costs, faculty pressures for better salaries, higher administrative costs, including the cost of computerizing, and less support from state governments facing financial pressures of their own. For hard-pressed parents, of course, the reasons don't matter. What does matter is that college is expensive, and giving your children the head start on life that college confers may well be painful to your pocketbook.

On a nationwide basis, for the 1992-93 school year, according to an annual survey taken by the College Board, resident students at public four-year colleges paid an average of $8,071 a year for tuition and fees, room and board, books and supplies, personal expenses and transportation. At private four-year colleges, the average total reached $17,027 a year. Two-year colleges are less expensive, with commuting students at public institutions spending about $5,282 a year and those at private colleges about $9,444. Commuting students spend less, as a rule, at any school—between $1,800 and $3,000 less each year than their on-campus classmates.

There are regional variations as well; colleges in New England, by and large, are more expensive, and those diagonally across the nation, in the Southwest, are less expensive. In 1992-93, according to the College Board, one year at the average four-year private college in New England (not Harvard; it cost over $25,000) cost $20,500 while a comparable college in the Southwest cost just under $13,000 (see Table 17.1).

How Will You Meet These Costs?

The days are past when children could be expected to work their way through school without help from parents; the college price tag is simply too high. The time is also pretty much past when full scholarships could be expected to pay for four years of higher education. A parental contribution, of some magnitude, is virtually a necessity. And that contribution—particularly if you are an older parent facing the triple threat of college costs, your own looming retirement, and the increasing need of your own aging parents—may be a painful burden.

Before you decide how to shoulder that burden in the least painful way, decide how you feel about paying for college.

Some parents want to provide everything, including a college education, to get their children off to a good start in life. Others believe that some things, including college, mean more to the child who contributes to the cost. Most college financial aid offices today require contributions from both parent and child. Decide on your own position.

As your child earns money during the high school years, for instance, will the child be able to spend that money? Or will you insist that some portion of the child's earnings be set aside for college? (If you do, be sure that college is the child's goal as well as your own.) Once your youngster is in college, will you continue to provide a regular allowance? Or will the student be expected to contribute to his or her social life, if not to tuition itself?

Some parents have always scrimped and saved to put money aside toward college education for their children. Others, out of choice or necessity, have spent money on current need while assuming that college costs would somehow be met. Under many college aid formulas, as we'll see a bit later in this chapter, the parent who has saved and accumulated assets may be penalized. Even without penalties, however, the combined influence of higher college costs and widely available financial aid has created a fundamental shift: Where parents used to believe in the virtue of savings, in paying for college out of past income, many now turn to borrowing, to paying for college out of future income. Where do you stand?

Where you stand may depend, to some extent, on the ages of your children. If you have preschoolers and are told that the current cost of college, at a state-supported public institution, may run to a minimum of $25,000 for each child for four years, you may just throw up your hands and assume that you can't possibly save enough to meet the dollar figure that those costs will reach in 15 years. If you have teenagers, on the other hand, you may already have had lengthy discussions about meeting college costs in the almost-here-and-now, and you may have decided that you've missed the boat, that it's too late to start saving in any meaningful way.

But whatever the ages of your children, now is the time to start planning ahead. If you have preschoolers, it's not too soon. If you have teenagers, it's not too late. Start now.

One Family's College Funding

Here's the way college costs shape up for the Taylor children. Based on a steady rate of inflation in college costs of 7 percent, four years at a public college for the three children will require a total outlay of $151,702. That's if the Taylor family pays each bill as it comes due, without advance planning. Table 17.2 shows how the figures look, based on an analysis prepared by Harold Evensky of Evensky & Brown, financial advisers in Coral Gables, Florida.

Because the three Taylor children are spaced two years apart, twelve years of college have to be paid in an eight-year period. A range of $9,887 to

$27,734 will be required each year between 1996 and 2003 if bills are paid as they come due.

Table 17.2: Projected College Expenses

Projected college expenses for the three-child family discussed in the text, assuming that they attend four-year public colleges.

Child's name and present age:	Chris, 14	Nikki, 12	Barry, 10	Total annual outlay
1993	0	0	0	0
1994	0	0	0	0
1995	0	0	0	0
1996	$ 9,887	0	0	$ 9,887
1997	10,579	0	0	10,579
1998	11,320	$11,320	0	22,640
1999	12,112	12,112	0	24,224
2000	0	12,960	12,960	25,920
2001	0	13,867	13,867	27,734
2002	0	0	14,838	14,838
2003	0	0	15,877	15,877
Total	$43,898	$50,259	$57,542	$151,699

Source: Evensky & Brown.

Q I would like to use some securities I've accumulated over the years to pay my grandson's way through college. I don't want to give him the money. I also don't want to sell the stock and pay the tax. Can you suggest an approach that will help my grandson, while minimizing taxes due?

A Donate the stock itself to the college, with the provision that the earned income be used to fund your grandson's tuition and that income earned after his graduation be used to establish a scholarship fund. You'll get several tax breaks. The gift itself is a charitable contribution. You're removing the asset from your taxable estate. And, if the university sells the stock rather than your selling it, you won't have tax to pay on the appreciated value. Any college or university will be happy to help you make the necessary arrangements, but be sure to get advice from a tax professional as well.

But there's no reason to wait until Chris' freshman year to get started. The burden can be spread over 12 years if the Taylors start now. See Table 17.3.

Note: Table 17.3 assumes a 9 percent return on investment. This may be unrealistic for Chris because he is too close to college for the family to take advantage of the growth potential inherent in equities without running undue risk that the money won't be available when needed. More conservative fixed-income investments will probably yield a lower return and therefore require larger annual deposits.

Table 17.3: Possible Solution to College Expenses

A possible solution for the three-child family described in the text, based on an annual contribution to an investment fund earning 9 percent.

Year	Opening balance	Annual deposit	Annual withdrawal	Annual earnings	Closing balance
1993	$ 0	$12,360	$ 0	$ 0	$ 12,360
1994	12,360	12,360	0	801	25,521
1995	25,521	12,360	0	1,654	39,535
1996	39,535	12,360	0	2,562	54,457
1997	54,457	12,360	11,320	3,529	59,026
1998	59,026	12,360	12,112	3,825	63,099
1999	63,099	12,360	25,921	4,089	53,627
2000	53,627	12,360	27,735	3,475	41,727
2001	41,727	12,360	29,676	2,704	27,115
2002	27,115	12,360	31,754	1,757	9,478
2003	9,478	12,360	16,988	614	5,464
2004	5,464	12,360	18,177	354	0

Source: Evensky & Brown.

Note: Numbers are not exact because of rounding.

Clearly, it's easier for most people to lay out $12,360 every year for 12 years than to come up with $27,735 in a single year. But both models assume that the Taylors are paying the entire bill. In fact, it's reasonable to assume that your children will have some savings of their own, that they will work during summer vacations and apply that money toward college, and that they will get at least some financial aid in the form of loans if not outright grants. It's also reasonable to assume that you will be able to fund at least part of the cost of college out of current income or through tapping the equity in your home. So don't be put off by the apparent need to come up with enormous sums (those staggering numbers in the Taylor tables apply only to public college; the costs of private college are more than double) because you don't have to come up in advance with the total cost of college.

Long-term Planning

The Taylors are getting started when Chris is just four years from college. If your children are still at least ten or twelve years from the starting gate, you have the advantage of a long-term investment horizon. With time on your side, you can accumulate the money for college through a variety of investment vehicles. Systematic savings, as I've discussed throughout this book, are the key to reaching all your financial goals, including college.

Systematic savings can work for you, no matter when you begin, although the earlier you start the easier you will find the task. If you start to save just $45 a month at 4 percent when your child is 4 years old, you'll have $10,112 saved in 14 years, when your child is ready for college. If you wait until the child is 16, you'll have to save $401 a month to have $10,000 for freshman year (see Table 17.4). A mere $10,000, of course, won't go very far. But if you already have it in hand when your child starts college, you won't have to take it out of current income that year.

Table 17.4: Amount You Would Need to Save to Have $10,000 Available When Your Child Begins College

If you start saving when your child is	Number of years of saving	Monthly savings	Principal	Interest earned	Total savings
			Amount available when child begins college		
(Assuming a 4 percent interest rate.)					
Newborn	18	$ 32	$6,912	$3,187	$10,099
Age 4	14	45	7,560	2,552	10,112
Age 8	10	68	8,160	1,853	10,013
Age 12	6	124	8,928	1,144	10,072
Age 16	2	401	9,624	378	10,002
(Assuming an 8 percent interest rate.)					
Newborn	18	$ 21	$4,536	$5,546	$10,082
Age 4	14	33	5,544	4,621	10,165
Age 8	10	55	6,660	3,462	10,062
Age 12	6	109	7,848	2,183	10,031
Age 16	2	386	9,264	746	10,010

Source: U.S. Department of Education, "Preparing Your Child For College."

Start as early as you can to save as much as you can. Be methodical. Get in the habit of regular saving or investing, via one or more of the following vehicles (and refer back to Chapter 6 for additional investment ideas).

GROWTH INVESTMENTS

Many parents, fearful of taking chances with college money, think only in terms of fixed-income investments when saving for college. In fact, as pointed out in Chapter 5, there is more than one kind of risk. You can lose a lot of purchasing power over time if your investments don't outpace inflation. And the only investment vehicle that has consistently outpaced inflation, at least since 1926, is common stock.

If you have at least ten or twelve years before your children will be ready for college—enough time to ride the inevitable ups and downs of the market—equities can be a very good choice for a college fund. You can, of course, invest in individual common stock. But mutual funds offer the distinct advantage of professional management coupled with diversification. Either way, start moving out of the stock market and into a safe liquid investment vehicle (such as certificates of deposit or a money market mutual fund) when your youngster is within four years of starting college. Aim for growth in the early years, in other words, and safety when college is on the horizon.

Note: When it's time to trade growth for stability, consider giving the shares to your child. When the child then sells the shares, assuming he or she is over age 14 and will therefore be taxed at his or her own rate rather than yours (see p. 457), the tax bite will probably be smaller than if you sell the shares yourself.

Any solid growth-and-income or balanced equity fund can be a good choice for college savings, but some mutual fund families offer special programs. The primary benefits are typically lower investment requirements and reduced fees. As examples:

- Fidelity Investments offers a College Savings Plan either through a brokerage account or through its mutual funds. In the first version, investors have access to a full range of brokerage products (stocks, zero-coupon bonds, U.S. Treasuries, etc.) at discounted commissions. In the second, four specific mutual funds are available with no sales commission and a $1,000 minimum initial investment, instead of the usual $2,500, or by committing $100 a month through automatic transfer from your bank account.
- Twentieth Century Investors has a College Investment Program combining a growth fund investing primarily in common stocks and a money market fund to provide liquidity when college nears. As little as $25 a month can be invested, through automatic transfer from your bank account. Then, starting four to six years before freshman year (your choice), money is gradually moved to the money market fund to preserve capital and provide the liquidity to pay college bills. The advantage to this program is this automatic "rebalancing" of the

account; you don't have to think about it, once you've made your initial decision as to timing, and you don't need to do anything. The disadvantage, and it's a potentially serious one, is that shares are bought and sold every other month during the several years of rebalancing. These transactions are taxable events, in the eyes of the Internal Revenue Service (IRS), and you will have to be able to document the purchase price of the shares (not necessarily easy, when dividend reinvestment buys different shares at different times) and account for any capital gains or losses.

Twentieth Century Investors has another option, particularly popular among grandparents and godparents. Giftrust is a special fund, accepting initial investments of at least $250. The money is placed in an irrevocable trust for a minimum of ten years or until the child becomes a legal adult, whichever is longer. Many grandparents choose maturities timed for college (age 18), for the purchase of a house (age 30), and even for the grandchild's eventual retirement (age 65). The fund invests aggressively, and entails some risk; the idea is that the long time frame makes for potentially sizable rewards.

Note: The giver of a Giftrust must file a United States Gift Tax Return, even on an investment as small as $250, although no tax need be paid until cumulative gifts exceed the lifetime exemption amount (currently $600,000 on gifts and estates combined). Because Giftrust is a trust, investments do not qualify for the annual gift tax exclusion.

FIXED-INCOME INVESTMENTS

Investments with a fixed rate of return are most appropriate in the years just before college. They're also most appropriate when maturity dates are pegged to the start of each college year. But fixed-rate investments do have a role in any diversified portfolio. And some parents are just too nervous to go with stocks. So here's a look at some fixed-income investments that may play a role in your college funding:

U.S. Government Savings Bonds (EE bonds) issued since January 1, 1990 may be completely free from tax if the bonds are owned by a parent or parents over the age of 24, if the proceeds are used for college tuition (not room and board), and if you meet income limitations when the bonds are redeemed. The income limitations are indexed to inflation; in 1993, EE bonds were totally exempt from taxes for single parents earning no more than $44,150 (in adjusted gross income) and for married couples filing jointly earning no more than $66,200. There are gradually reduced tax benefits at income levels up to $60,706 for singles and $99,300 for couples. Note, though that the interest on the bonds is included in your income calculation in the year you redeem the bonds; a large redemption could push you over the income limit and disqualify the tax exemption.

If you don't expect to qualify for the federal tax exemption (EE bonds are always exempt from state income taxes), you may want to consider EE bonds anyway. They pay a minimum of 4 percent interest if held at least five years and, because they pay a variable rate of interest after that, will keep pace with inflation should interest rates start to rise. If you're absolutely sure you won't qualify for the tax break, consider buying the bonds in your child's name; any tax due at redemption will then be payable at the child's presumably lower rate. For more information on EE bonds, see pp. 93-95; on children's tax rate, see p. 457.

Zero coupon bonds (see p. 157) are popular among parents because they pay a fixed amount at maturity and can be pegged to college entrance. But zeroes have some drawbacks:

- Zeroes are volatile. If you do need to sell them before maturity, you could lose a portion of your principal.
- Zero-coupon bonds pay nothing as they go along but return the entire yield at the end. With zero-coupon corporate bonds, however, you'll owe tax on the "imputed interest," on money you haven't actually received.
- Zeroes are frequently callable. If your bonds are called before maturity, you will have to reinvest the money at what is likely to be a lower rate of return (bonds aren't called when rates have moved higher).

So-called **baccalaureate bonds,** municipal bonds issued by about half of the states specifically for college saving, get around this last problem. Baccalaureate bonds usually aren't callable. They are also issued in small denominations to make them more accessible. In some states, there's an added bonus paid if the student attends a state college. More important, although the bonds are sold as a form of college financing, the money can actually be used for anything.

Tuition guarantee programs, offered by a few states, allow parents to put up a specific sum of money in advance; that sum is then guaranteed to cover the cost of a year of college whatever that year actually costs when the

Q I want to buy an EE bond for my grandchild, to use toward college. But I'm confused about how to fill out the form. If I make my son the owner of the bond, where do I include the child's name?

A You're right to name one of your grandchild's parents the owner of the bond; this will make the money nontaxable if it is used for college tuition and if the parents meet income limits at the time. Put your grandchild's name down as a beneficiary, and be sure to check the box marked beneficiary. if you leave it blank, the child will be assumed to be a co-owner of the bond and the tax exemption will be lost.

time arrives. Tuition guarantee programs haven't caught on as anticipated, largely because the IRS issued adverse tax rulings against the bellwether Michigan program. But there were other drawbacks as well: What if your toddler turned out to be a budding astrophysicist who needed a program unavailable in your state? You would probably get your money back, but any interest on that money would probably be minimal. Tuition guarantee programs made more sense in states like Michigan, with a wide range of public institutions; they may make less sense in states like Wyoming, with a single state university. Because guarantee programs have built-in limitations, baccalaureate bond programs have become more popular.

The six states offering tuition prepayment in spring 1992 were Alabama, Alaska, Florida (the only state with separate prepaid contracts covering housing as well as tuition), Kentucky (actually a savings plan where money can be applied to any school in the United States), Ohio, and Wyoming (a single contract including tuition, room and board).

The **CollegeSure CD,** issued by the College Savings Bank in Princeton, New Jersey, is another alternative. Heavily advertised, and competing head-on with both zero-coupon bonds and EE bonds, the CollegeSure CD guarantees to pay the cost of the college or type of college you pick. A minimum interest rate of 4 percent is guaranteed; if the college inflation rate is higher, the CD

In evaluating college prepayment and savings plans, ask these questions:

■ Are there minimum or maximum amounts that can be contributed?

■ Can the proceeds be used anywhere? Or only at certain institutions?

■ Can the proceeds be used by another family member if plans change?

■ Is the yield from the plan guaranteed? In what way?

■ Is the plan insured? Can the investment be recovered if the plan sponsor goes out of business?

■ Are there residency requirements for eligibility? What happens if the family moves?

■ Does the plan cover all college costs, or just tuition?

■ Will money be refunded if the student doesn't go to college?

■ Are plan benefits taxable?

Source: Adapted from guidelines provided by The College Board.

will pay more. An account can be opened with an initial investment of $1,000; additional deposits may be $250 or more. The CD pays a rate tied to an index that measures future college costs; since the actual rate paid to depositors is less than the index (that's the bank's profit), parents must invest more up front to make up the shortfall. Taxes are due on the interest as earned. There are penalties for early withdrawal of the principal, but interest can be withdrawn without penalty during a specified period each year.

Critics note that better yields are often available elsewhere. But securing those yields presupposes that you actually make and track investments. If you prefer a cut-and-dried, no-hassle approach to college funding, the CollegeSure CD may appeal to you.

In Whose Name: To UGMA or Not To UGMA

Whether you choose to go for growth or for a fixed return, you have to decide how you'll make the investment: in your name or your child's. Many parents automatically opt for custodial accounts, via the Uniform Gift to Minors or Uniform Transfers to Minors Act of their state. But don't do so without thinking it through. There are both advantages and disadvantages, but the latter may actually outweigh the former.

The big advantage of custodial accounts in the past was the ability to shelter income from taxes; because the money was held for the child, interest and dividends were taxed at the child's rate. Today, thanks to the "kiddie tax," interest and dividends in excess of $1,200 (the amount is indexed, and goes up each year) earned by children under age 14 are taxed at their parents' higher rate. If you do choose to use a custodial account, therefore, consider one of two approaches:

■ Invest in the custodial account only until annual interest exceeds the amount taxed at the child's rate. In 1993, when that amount is $1,200, you could invest $1,000 every year for 11 years, in an account earning 6.5 percent, before the interest would be taxed at your higher rate.

Q I opened a custodial account for my three-year-old, intending to save for her college education. Then I lost my job, and need money to pay bills. Can I close the account and take the money?

A No. Once the money is in a custodial account, that money legally belongs to your child until she becomes an adult and can use it herself. But you do have one way out: You may withdraw money from the account so long as it is used for the benefit of the child (for her food, clothing, or day care costs, for example).

■ Invest in growth stocks, skipping current taxable income in favor of potential capital growth. By the time the stock is sold, the child will be over 14 and the taxes will be payable at a lower rate.

Before you open a custodial account, however, here's what you need to know:

■ With a custodial account, you control the money until the child reaches legal age but at that point the money is legally the child's. If Sally decides to run off with a rock band, or Junior wants to buy a red Corvette instead of going to college, they can take the money and run.
■ Money in the child's name is assessed far more heavily than money in a parent's name when it comes to calculating financial aid (see p. 468). So putting too much of your college savings in the child's name, if you expect to qualify for financial aid, may resemble shooting yourself in the foot.
■ A tax return will have to be filed for the child. You are permitted to combine the child's income with your own, rather than filing a separate return, but this may raise your taxable income and eliminate some deductions you could otherwise take. It may also result in higher state income taxes.
■ Before establishing a custodial account, find out what regulations apply in your state. In most cases, the custodian may retain control of the funds until the child turns 21 (even if the legal age of majority in the state is 18), but some states require that control be relinquished at the child's 18th birthday. Do you want your youngster to control the money then?

When an Ohio couple inherited $25,000 in 1976, they thought ahead to the college education of their two children, then ages 16 and 13. They established four custodial accounts for each of the children. Each account contained $3,000 and took the form of a bank certificate of deposit (CD); each CD was timed to mature in each of the four years of college for each child. Although not one of these accounts paid over 8 percent, before taxes, the accounts made it possible to send the children away to school.

When the first $3,000 account matured after a year and a half in August 1977, in time for their son's first year at college, it returned $3,393. The fifth certificate, redeemed in August 1981, in time for their daughter's first year of college, returned $4,278. Since the son's first year cost about $7,000 and the daughter's almost $9,000, each maturing CD paid just under one semester's bills.

■ Money, once given, stays given. You can't put money into a child's name and then take it back again. Don't give money you can't afford to give.

■ If you name yourself as custodian for your child, and die while the custodial account is in effect, the money becomes part of your taxable estate. If your taxable estate will be $600,000 or more in value, large enough to be subject to federal estate taxes, think about naming someone else as custodian: a relative (required in some states) or a trusted friend.

■ If assets in a student's name earn enough income (once the child reaches age 19, and with or without his or her own earnings) to provide more than half of the student's support for the year, you lose the student as a dependent on your federal income tax return.

■ Money and securities are most often given under a custodial arrangement; some states with the more inclusive Uniform Transfers to Minors Act also permit gifts of insurance policies or real estate.

Table 17.5: Projected College Costs, 1993-1997

Type of institution	1993-94		1994-95	
	Resident	**Commuter**	**Resident**	**Commuter**
4-Year Private	$19,000	$16,310	$20,520	$17,620
2-Year Private	12,730	10,500	13,750	11,340
4-Year Public	8,930	7,100	9,550	7,600
2-Year Public	7,820	5,780	8,370	6,190

Type of institution	1995-96		1996-97	
	Resident	**Commuter**	**Resident**	**Commuter**
4-Year Private	$22,160	$19,020	$23,940	$20,550
2-Year Private	14,850	12,250	16,040	13,230
4-Year Public	10,220	8,130	10,940	8,700
2-Year Public	8,960	6,620	9,580	7,080

Source: "Don't Miss Out," Octameron Associates.

When College Is Just Around the Corner— Short-term Planning

But what if you haven't planned well in advance? Will you be able to send your children to college? Yes, somehow you will, through a combination of current income, financial aid, home equity loans (see pp. 202-204), and whatever else it takes. Before you start filling out financial aid applications, however, try to get a handle on exactly what college will cost for your particular child. Refer to Table 17.5, then consider:

■ Where your children can get a good education. It isn't necessarily a high-profile expensive institution. Many good colleges, less well-known than the Ivies, offer excellent educational opportunities (how much your children actually learn, of course, depends on how well they take advantage of those opportunities).

■ Where your children will get the best education to meet their particular needs. If you have a budding physicist or musician, the choices may be limited; for the average nondirected teenager, the choices are generally more extensive.

■ Current college costs at the type of school each child will need. Add an inflation factor of 7 percent (inflation may subside, but it's unlikely to be totally eliminated).

■ How many children you will have in school, for how many years. Overlapping years need extra weight in your calculations. (Overlapping years can also help in financial aid applications; if you will have two or more children in college at the same time, be sure to note that fact when you apply for aid.)

Worksheet 17.1 lists a wide range of possible college funds. Which are applicable to you?

Worksheet 17.1: College Funds

Fund source	Amount you can expect per year
Savings	
Parents	$ _____
Student	$ _____
Income	
Parents	$ _____
Student, summer	$ _____
Student, school year	$ _____
Scholarships/grants	
Need-based	$ _____
Academic merit	$ _____
Special interest/talent	$ _____
Athletic	$ _____
Community	$ _____

Loans

Government-backed	$	_____
College	$	_____
Private	$	_____

Other

GI Bill	$	_____
Military (ROTC, etc.)	$	_____
Borrowing against life insurance	$	_____
Refinancing a home	$	_____
Home equity loan	$	_____
Gifts from grandparents	$	_____

Miscellaneous Expenses

Don't forget the "extras" when preparing a student budget. Many parents, understandably, focus on paying for the major elements of a college education: tuition, room, and board. But there's a lot more at stake when young people are sent off to live on their own. Figure on $1,500 to $2,000 for transportation, books, supplies, and personal items. Some students, of course, spend considerably more. Some of the big dollar items: food (those late-night pizzas and their accompaniments can add up to hundreds of dollars a year) and telephone calls (today's students call their far-flung friends; they don't seem to write). Owning and maintaining a car on campus, for those who do, is another major expense.

What's the best way for parents to handle this outgo? Encourage your child to plan spending over a semester. If you're supplying spending money, do so on a semester basis and don't plug the gaps that may occur in between. If the youngster is depending on his or her own earnings (summertime or year-round part-time) it will be even easier; you can just bow out of the personal-spending question and let the student manage. It won't necessarily be good management—middle-class college students are notoriously irresponsible about spending money, especially while they're busy adjusting to college life—but it's the only way they'll learn. If you supply money on an as-needed or as-requested basis, life in the real world after graduation will be a tremendous shock.

KEEPING COSTS DOWN

An essential part of meeting college costs is keeping those costs as manageable as possible. In recent years parents and students have been told to pick the best school for the student, regardless of cost, and then figure out how to pay for it. The rationale for this approach is that schools will create financial aid packages for students they want, in a "need-blind" approach to admissions. This was true and may still be so at some schools but because (1) not every student has a single "best" school (most don't) and because (2) federal aid to education is being drastically curtailed, it's not a bad idea to look at ways to keep those costs down. Here are some tips.

Accelerated Programs

Bright students, in particular, may get as much as a full year's college credit on the basis of Advanced Placement (AP) courses and examinations completed in high school (but be sure the college of choice permits this alternative; some put an AP scholar in higher-level classes but still require four years of study). Diligent students may do four years of college in three, or make up a semester by attending a lower-cost summer school.

Cooperative Education

The federal government has work-study opportunities; so do some private institutions. With some variation among individual programs, a student may alternate semesters of work and study, work part time during the school year, or, in rare instances, even work solely during summer vacations. Under most of these programs the course of study takes a bit longer but, since students can earn up to $7,000 a year, savings are considerable.

Attending a School in Your Home State

This can be a double money-saver: First, if you go to college within your home state, especially a public institution, you'll probably find tuition and fees lower for state residents. And, second, within your home state you may be eligible for grants, scholarships, or loans offered only to residents. Note, though, that costs at hard-pressed public institutions have risen faster than those at private institutions in recent years and that state legislatures are less willing to subsidize the education of those who can afford to pay.

Community Colleges

These two-year institutions are generally the least expensive educational option of all. Perhaps for this reason, more than half of all entering college freshmen in the fall of 1992 were enrolled in community colleges.

Many students live at home and hold down a part-time job while attending a community college. Then, armed with an associate degree after two years of study, the able student can transfer to a four-year institution to complete work toward a bachelor's degree. Unfortunately, the cost crunch affecting all colleges in the 1990s is also affecting community colleges; fees have been raised, sometimes significantly. And, for the first time, many community colleges are turning students away.

Note: While tuition and fees are generally much less at a community college, it is not necessarily true that living at home with parents costs less than living in a dormitory or apartment on a college campus. Food costs may actually be higher: The student will consume his or her usual quantities at the family table and will also need on-campus meals (when there's no time to get home between classes or between class and an evening activity) and snacks (for social time). Transportation, to and from campus on a regular basis, may cost close to $1,000 a year. Do your arithmetic carefully before assuming that commuting to college is cost-effective.

Employer-Paid Plans

If you work for a company with generous tuition benefits, you may be able to attend school at your employer's expense. Job-related study is most often reimbursed (when it isn't, you can still secure tax benefits; see p. 579), but some companies pay for undergraduate and graduate education as well. Under a law that expired June 30, 1992 (but periodically expires and is then extended retroactively), the first $5,250 of such educational assistance was tax-free. If the law is extended, as expected, the ambitious high school graduate can seek a job with educational benefits and save almost the entire burden of college costs.

Note: Some tuition assistance may be taxable as income.

Q My daughter will need a checking account for the first time when she goes off to college. What's the best way to set it up? Should we have a joint account, at a bank near home, so I can make deposits for her when necessary? Or would it be better if she opens an account at school?

A Long-distance management is difficult. If her account is near her school, where she'll be living most of the year, she'll easily be able to verify her balance and handle any problems that arise. She'll also find it easier to cash checks from the same community; out-of-state check-cashing can be very difficult. Wherever the account is opened, however, tell your daughter how important it is to keep accurate records and to balance her checkbook. Tell her, too, that it's better to keep her money in an interest-earning NOW account, to make the most of what she has. Tell her to compare minimum balances and service charges before picking a bank or savings institution. And be sure she understands (it's surprising how many college freshmen don't) that cash can't come out of a cash machine unless there is money in the account.

Your daughter will probably need a credit card, too, especially if she must travel any distance between home and school. Despite her lack of a credit history and her undoubtedly inadequate income, she shouldn't have any trouble getting a card once she arrives on campus. Credit card grantors, in fact, are actively soliciting on college campuses and many students are finding themselves overextended. Caution your youngsters about the importance of paying bills on time, and try not to bail them out if they get in trouble. The idea is that they learn to be financially responsible.

The Military

The highly competitive service academies (West Point, Annapolis, and the Air Force Academy) are free although open to very few. But there are other ways to use military assistance for education. There are ROTC scholarships, educational benefits for joining the Reserves or the National Guard, and educational programs for enlisted men and women.

Correspondence Courses

Expensive on-campus time can be shortened if a student moves ahead via home study. Be sure, however, that the correspondence school is accredited and that its credits will be accepted for transfer at the college you plan to attend.

Special Programs

Some colleges reduce tuition costs for siblings (and some allow parents of students to attend school for free or at reduced costs). Some, eager to attract able students, reduce tuition for good grades. Some even guarantee the four-year cost of education, if the entire bill is paid in advance. In asking questions of colleges, ask about such special programs as well.

APPLY FOR FINANCIAL AID

The moment of truth will dawn during your youngster's senior year of high school. If savings don't add up to enough, you'll have to turn to other sources. One such source might be a second mortgage on your house or a home equity loan (interest on home equity loans of up to $100,000 is at this writing fully deductible). Another might involve borrowing against life insurance, although interest on such loans is no longer tax-deductible. But the first step, for many people, will be an application for financial aid. (You might want to defer taking a home equity loan until you know the results of your financial aid application; equity in your home doesn't count in the federal aid formula but cash coming from that equity can reduce your eligibility.)

Q My parents are divorced and each says the other should fill out the financial aid application for my colleges. What do I do now?

A Tell the parent with whom you lived for the greater part of last year that it's his or her job to fill out the form. If you lived on your own, or shared your time equally between your parents, then the job falls to the one who provided the bulk of your basic support (housing, food, clothes, medical care, etc.). An individual college may also require a financial form from the other parent, and may consider that parent's current marital status and other obligations.

Financial aid may be undergoing a major transformation, as the Clinton administration wrestles with funding college in an equitable manner. Check with high school guidance counselors and college financial aid offices when your child is ready to apply, because the rules may have changed. For now, this is the picture.

Financial aid is generally designed to meet what's called "demonstrated need," the difference between total college expenses and the amount your family is able to contribute. Note that demonstrated need is not a fixed amount; since the sum the family can contribute remains essentially the same, a student will usually receive more in aid from a more expensive school.

Note: Aid packages from comparable schools have tended to be comparable. In the aftermath of a federal court ruling that a number of eastern colleges violated antitrust laws by sharing financial information about applicants, school financial aid officers are no longer putting their heads together. As a result, a student may receive very different offers from similar schools and may be able to play one off against the other to get the best financial aid package.

Whatever the amount, financial aid generally comes in three forms: jobs, grants, and loans. The proportion of each in the total package depends on the amount of demonstrated need. It also depends on the philosophy of the particular college. Some, believing in student self-help, give jobs and loans first; others start out with grants. Overall, however, by far the largest proportion of financial aid comes in the form of loans. In the 1963-64 school year, loans made up about 21 percent of all financial aid; by 1991-92, the proportion was 52 percent.

Table 17.6: Student Aid by Source, 1991-92

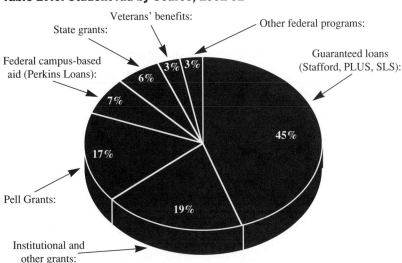

Veterans' benefits:

State grants:

Other federal programs:

Federal campus-based aid (Perkins Loans):

Guaranteed loans (Stafford, PLUS, SLS):

3% 3%

6%

7%

45%

17%

Pell Grants:

19%

Institutional and other grants:

Source: The College Board.

The Need Analysis

All financial aid is based on a need analysis, a detailed (very detailed) look at your family's financial profile. The need analysis, based on your honest answers to a long list of questions (backed up, in case you're tempted to fudge, by your tax returns), provides the answers to the fundamental questions: How much can you, as parents, contribute to your child's yearly educational costs? How much can the child contribute? And how much remains to be made up from outside sources?

The forms are complex and are based on tax data, but don't put off submitting them until tax-filing time in April. The available pool of aid is limited, and you don't want to miss out by getting in line late. Check each school's filing dates and follow instructions.

How much you can contribute is not a question answered simply by a look at your annual income. Other factors include the number of children in your family, and how many of them will be in college at the same time; your age, and how close you are to the fixed-income years of retirement; and special expenses you may have, such as medical bills for an aged or chronically ill member of the family.

How much you can contribute is also linked to your assets, and here is a point of some controversy. Should the parents who have saved toward college costs, perhaps depriving themselves along the way, be expected to fork over much more than the parents, with an identical income, who have lived life to the hilt, spending every penny? (If you've saved toward college, on the other hand, why not expect to spend for college?) Should home equity be counted as an asset, so that parents who are house-poor may be relied on for a far larger contribution than those with more limited but more liquid funds? (If you own a home, on the other hand, you may not have liquid cash, but you do have more financial flexibility.)

Note: Colleges have two choices when it comes to determining your contribution: They may use the detailed need analysis approach (called the

---

Q Our son received far less financial aid than we expected, so we don't know how we'll be able to send him to college this fall. Can we appeal the college's decision?

A Yes. You can ask the financial aid office to review the aid package. Do so as soon as possible, since most financial aid is allocated early. You are most likely to succeed if you have a good reason: if a breadwinner has died, become disabled, or lost a job, for example, or if you have a child in a private secondary school or have incurred unreimbursed medical expenses. Be prepared to document any claim in writing.

Congressional Methodology) or, if your income is under $50,000 and if you've filed federal income taxes on a 1040EZ or a 1040A (with no itemized deductions), they may use a simplified need test based on income alone and

Financial Fix-up

Sally is a high school junior and you realize that, given your current financial picture, she probably won't qualify for much financial aid. Here are some last-minute tips, many of them courtesy of Octameron's useful annual publication *Don't Miss Out,* that may help:

■ Reduce the value of the assets you report. You can do this by:

1). Making major capital outlays, such as a new car or a new roof, before you apply;

2). Use savings to pay down your home mortgage because, starting with the 1993-94 school year, home equity is no longer a reportable asset under federal need analysis. (Schools can still ask questions about home equity, however, and may expect you to borrow against a paid-up home.)

3). Shifting assets from your child's name to your own, because your own assets will be assessed far less drastically; you can't take money out of a custodial account if that's where you stashed it, but you can use the money to buy Sally the computer or car she'll need for college.

■ If you still have too much money in your child's name, ask her if you can use that money to pay the entire family contribution for freshman year; doing so will improve chances for financial aid in succeeding years.

■ Defer year-end bonuses during Sally's junior year of high school, if you can, so that reportable income will be lower. Need analysis looks at the prior year's income so junior year is critical.

■ Try to either accelerate capital gains from the sale of property to two years before college, or postpone such gains until after Sally is enrolled. Capital gains count as income and, again, the junior year of high school is critical.

■ Consider buying tax deferred annuities or boosting other retirement funds as a way of moving assets out of the financial analysis. But be careful. Trying end runs can sometimes lead to disaster, as tax laws and financial aid rules change. Get competent advice before you proceed.

ignoring assets. If you meet the criteria and are asset-rich (perhaps because you live in an area with inflated real estate values), then you may want to ask the financial aid office to determine your contribution both ways, and to use the one most favorable to you.

How much your children are expected to contribute hinges on both earning power and assets. Most students are expected to be able to save $900 toward college costs from summer earnings just before the freshman year and at least $1,000 in each succeeding summer. If there is need for financial aid, moreover, the student may be expected to work part-time during the school year as well (and a job may be provided by the college).

Assets are another matter. Students are expected to contribute a sizable portion of their accumulated assets (35 percent against 5.6 percent of parental assets) to the cost of education. The assumption is that students, unlike parents, have few other demands on assets combined with greater long-term replacement potential. The result may be, however, that assets placed in your child's name to save tax dollars may later reduce the amount of outside financial aid available.

Your remaining need, the difference between college costs and the amount that you and your child can jointly contribute to the costs (not what you think you can contribute, but what the colleges think you can contribute),

Q My son has been offered financial aid from two schools. Either school would suit him fine. But the aid packages are so different that it's like comparing apples and oranges. What should we focus on in making a decision?

A Assuming that your need is fully met by each college and that your estimates of reasonable family contributions agree with the figures used by each college, then look at the proportion of each package made up of gifts (scholarships and grants which do not require repayment) and of self-help (loans, which must be repaid, and work opportunities). And remember two things: (1) Your first choice should be the college which best meets educational needs. (2) A financial aid package can be appealed. If the package at the first-choice school has more self-help and less outright help, for instance, talk to the financial aid office and see if the package can be changed. Don't hesitate to mention the offer from the other school; if the schools are comparable, this is a form of leverage that may get you more aid. If not, or if your son would really be equally happy (and equally well educated) at either school, go with the school offering the best overall aid package.

is the amount that needs to be made up in a financial aid package. That package, as noted, consists of jobs, loans, and grants. Jobs may come from the financial aid office or, for the motivated, from an independent job search. Grants and loans are more complex.

Student Grants

Scholarship grants are available from a number of sources. Some are based purely on merit but most are based on need, with specific income limitations that vary from time to time.

- Uncle Sam's Pell Grants, the foundation of student aid, are restricted to applicants from families below a specified income level (about $40,000, given a large family, in 1993) and are limited in amount (the maximum award is currently $3,700, and is expected to reach $4,500 by 1997—but those are the authorized amounts; the amount actually available at this writing is no more than $2,300 and no one really expects Congress to come up with a lot more money). It's important to apply for a Pell Grant, even if you think you're not eligible, because the application itself may make you eligible for other grants and loans. Apply early (a good word of advice for all grants and for loans as well); available funds can run dry.

- Supplemental Educational Opportunity Grants (SEOG) provide additional funds (up to $4,000 a year) to needy students. Funds are provided by the federal government but distributed by the colleges.

- State governments also offer need-based grants, many restricted to in-state study; contact your own state office of higher education for details.

- Colleges offer individual grants as well. Again, most are based on need but some, particularly at middle-level colleges eager to attract top-of-the-line students in a buyer's market, are based strictly on merit. As just one example, Lebanon Valley College in Annville, Pennsylvania, has offered half-price tuition to entering freshmen from the top 10 percent of their high school classes, and a one-third tuition discount to freshmen from the top fifth of their high school classes.

- National Merit Scholarships, which have both college sponsors and corporate sponsors, are awarded on the basis of scores in the Preliminary Scholastic Aptitude Test given each fall to high school juniors.

- Employers, civic and fraternal organizations, professional and trade associations, unions, and alumni organizations ... all may also be potential sources of grants. Many are open only to those involved in some way with the sponsor: the sons and daughters of employees, of union members, etc. Others are open to anyone, based on need or on the writing of an essay, on citizenship, or on athletic ability.

Grants, unlike loans, do not have to be repaid (although a portion may be taxable); clearly you are ahead of the game if grants make up a larger portion of your financial aid package. Some advisers suggest that once you're accepted at the college of your choice, the proportion of grants to loans can be negotiated with the financial aid office.

Note: Don't think the game is finished once the freshman year is under way. More aid becomes available to students once they have demonstrated ability on the college level. Keep grades up, and apply again. Also, if you were denied aid with one child in college, apply again when you have two or more.

Table 17.7: Federal Loan Limits, 1993-1994

	Stafford	Supplemental (SLS)	Perkins
Undergraduate			
Annual limit:			
1st year	$ 2,625	$ 4,000	$ 3,000
2nd year	3,500	4,000	3,000
3rd/4th year	5,500	5,000	3,000
Aggregate debt:	$23,000	$23,000	$15,000
Graduate student			
Annual limit:	$ 8,500	$10,000	$ 5,000
Aggregate debt:	$65,500	$73,000	$30,000

Source: The College Board.

Student Loans

College loans are available from a variety of sources, including some colleges; some schools, in fact, are developing innovative programs to fill gaps left by reduced federal spending. But the biggest programs by far are two federally subsidized loan programs: Perkins Loans and Stafford Loans.

Note: If one of President Clinton's proposals is adopted, all student loans may be made directly by colleges without lending institutions acting as intermediaries. This may change some of the rules but, for now, the following holds true:

Perkins Loans are need-based loans of up to $3,000 per undergraduate year, subsidized by the federal government but distributed directly by the colleges. They carry the lowest rate of any loan program, currently 5 percent, and repayment of the interest need not start for six months after the student leaves school.

Stafford Loans (formerly Guaranteed Student Loans) are the biggest student loan program of all. Loans are provided to the student (not to parents) by a local bank or thrift institution, guaranteed by a state agency and insured by the federal government, with an interest rate generally below market rates (the government makes up the difference to the lending institution). Repayment does not begin until six months after the student leaves school.

From 1965, when the GSL program began, until 1978, GSLs were available only to students below a specified income ceiling. Then all ceilings were removed and GSLs became available to all students. The rationale was good: Only a small percentage of students had been excluded under the needs test and the necessary paperwork made banks and thrifts reluctant to become involved in the program at all. But the result, in an era of rising interest rates, was that many families realized that they could borrow at GSL's 7 percent interest rate and put the money into a money market fund earning 17 percent. The outlay of federal funds grew enormously and, in 1981, income ceilings were reimposed. At the same time, interest rates were raised to 9 percent and origination fees of 5 percent (which effectively reduce the loan amount) were imposed.

Now there have been further changes. The biggest change is that income ceilings have been redefined; the program is now open to all families, regardless of income, but students with demonstrated need will receive interest subsidies while they are in school and students without such need will not. The interest rate since October 1, 1992 is 3.1 percent above the bond equivalent of the 91-day Treasury bill, with a 9 percent cap. Freshmen may now borrow up

Q Is it worthwhile to pay a computerized search service to help me find a scholarship?

A Probably not. You are very unlikely to find a scholarship through one of these profit-making computerized search services. When the Better Business Bureau of Metropolitan New York studied search services in late 1992, it issued unsatisfactory ratings to 20 out of 21 firms. The reasons: Very few students actually found scholarships, and the companies rarely made good on promises of cash refunds. The Federal Trade Commission has charged at least one large service with questionable marketing techniques. With a little effort, you can conduct your own search. Your high school guidance counselor or college financial aid office can supply extensive information. And, now that many schools and libraries have electronic data bases, you can probably do a computerized search yourself.

Note: You should also be aware that winning a scholarship or outright grant will make no difference at all in the amount your family is expected to contribute toward college. The financial aid office will simply subtract your hard-won prize from its financial aid package.

to $2,625, sophomores $3,500 and juniors, seniors, and fifth year undergraduates may borrow up to $5,500 per year.

On unsubsidized loans, students must either pay the interest while they are in school or have it added to their loan amount after they leave school. On unsubsidized loans, moreover, there is a hefty 6.5 percent loan origination and insurance fee.

Note: Whatever interest rate is in effect when you take your first loan is the rate that remains in effect for all subsequent loans under the program. Loans taken at 7 percent, 8 percent, or 9 percent prior to October 1992 will be renewed at the same fixed rate. But stay tuned: one proposal floating around Washington as I write would put all loans on a variable interest rate.

Repayment of Student Loans

President Clinton has proposed a program under which college loan recipients could pay off their loans either through community service or as a percentage of income; presumably this would encourage graduates to take low-paying public-service jobs. Assuming that the money is found to fund the program, it will take several years to fully phase in.

Meanwhile, the minimum annual payment on a Stafford Loan is $600, and repayment may be made over five to ten years (see Table 17.8). But one of the reasons that loan programs are being reevaluated is that too many people

Q Banks seem to write college loans only for their depositors. But my bank doesn't write them at all, and the bank where my son has an account will make loans only to college juniors. We must have help or he won't be able to start school. Is there anything we can do?

A Contact your state's Department of Higher Education, probably in the state capital, for the name of the agency supervising government-guaranteed student loans in your state. (A complete list of guaranteeing agencies may be found in *College Loans From Uncle Sam,* available for $3 plus $1.75 for postage and handling from Octameron Associates, P.O. Box 2748, Alexandria, VA 22301.) That agency should be able to tell you which institutions in your area are making loans. In some states, the agency will actually match student and lender. Lending institutions, while they must meet federal standards, can decide whether or not to participate and can set their own rules about eligibility. Don't wait until the last moment. Shop around before you need a loan, and if you'll have to open an account, do so as early as possible.

have walked away from this obligation; too many have looked at the loans as a free gift from Uncle Sam. Student loans must be repaid, and the government is intercepting tax refunds of defaulters. It is also garnisheeing wages.

Table 17.8: Monthly Repayment Schedule for Stafford Loans

Loan amount	Number of months	Monthly payment (7%)	Monthly payment (8%)	Monthly payment (9%)
$2,625	60	$52.00	$53.23	$54.49
$6,000	120	$69.67	$72.80	$76.01
$10,000	120	$116.11	$121.33	$126.68
$17,125	120	$198.83	$207.78	$216.94
$23,000	120	$267.05	$279.06	$291.36
$40,000	120	$464.44	$485.32	$506.71
$65,500	120	$760.51	$794.70	$829.74

Source: "College Loans From Uncle Sam," Octameron Associates.

Repayment on federally subsidized student loans may be deferred for a maximum of three years under certain conditions, such as service in the armed forces or the Peace Corps, returning to school full time, or being unemployed. If you don't qualify for deferment, but are unable to make monthly payments, you may ask your lender for forbearance; if it is granted, you will owe the interest that accumulates during the forbearance period. Cancellation is another story. Under most circumstances, only death or permanent total disability eliminates the responsibility to repay the loan; bankruptcy does not. Student loans, in other words, must be taken seriously as a debt obligation.

Q If I declare myself financially independent of my parents, can I secure more financial aid for college?

A Independent undergraduates may be eligible for more aid, because their resources are generally limited, than students who receive help from their parents. If you want to be considered independent for federal financial aid (colleges may set their own rules), you must be at least 24 years old. If you are married, have legal dependents other than a spouse, or are a veteran, you are automatically considered independent. Financial aid administrators may exercise their own judgment in unusual circumstances.

Loans, especially low-interest loans, are an appealing way to finance college. But interest on college loans is no longer tax-deductible. And a great many young adults, especially those with post-college graduate or professional education, are starting their working lives with an extremely heavy debt load. (One way private colleges look at it, according to Joseph Re of Octameron, is that it's okay to graduate with a debt load equivalent to the cost of a car; instead of financing a car, in other words, the new graduate can pay several hundred dollars a month toward repaying student loans.) While loans may be the only way you can attend school, be sure you understand what you're taking on. You don't want to be paying for your own college education up until the time your own children apply for college loans.

Loan Consolidation

Congress formally authorizes loan consolidation for student loans. Under current rules, the minimum loan amount that can be consolidated is now $7,500 and the maximum repayment period is now 30 years (a 30-year repayment schedule, however, could indeed have parents paying the college costs of two generations at once). See Table 17.9 for examples of how loan consolidation works.

In addition, under legislation enacted in 1992, married couples can consolidate loans together, borrowers with delinquent or defaulted loans can consolidate, and parents who have PLUS loans (see p. 475) can now consolidate them, either by consolidating PLUS loans for each of their children into a single account or by consolidating their own student loans with PLUS loans for

---

Q My daughter will graduate from college next spring with nearly $16,000 in student loans to pay off. She probably won't earn very much on her first job. Is there any way to reduce the monthly payments, at least during her first years out of school?

A Yes. Loan consolidation can mean lower monthly payments for a longer period. For example, instead of paying $200.79 each month for 10 years on $15,500 in student loans, she might pay $157.21 each month for 15 years. Other options permit even lower payments for the first few years.

To find out about loan consolidation, she must first contact the current holder of the loans (the original lender can tell her who this is); if that institution has a consolidation program, it must be used. If not, she should call either Sallie Mae at (800) 524-9100 or Nellie Mae at (800) EDU-LOAN for details on their national student-loan consolidation programs.

their children. Parents can not, however, consolidate PLUS loans for their children with student loans taken by those children; students are responsible for repayment of their own loans.

Table 17.9: Loan Consolidation

The table shows how a level-payment loan consolidation plan can reduce monthly payments. Note that consolidation relieves cash flow problems; it doesn't reduce the debt. In fact, the total amount of interest owed for the life of the loan becomes larger with consolidation. Both Sallie Mae and Nellie Mae offer graduated payment options that can reduce the monthly payment still further but at the cost of higher total interest.

Before Consolidation

Principal balance	Loan type	Monthly interest rate	Payments to each lender	Length of repayment	Total interest
$ 9,750	Stafford	8%	$118.29	10 years	$4,444.80
$ 5,750	SLS	12%	$ 82.50	10 years	$4,150.00
$15,500			$200.79		$8,594.80

After Consolidation

Principal Balance	Interest rate	Monthly Payment to Nellie Mae	Length of repayment	Total interest
$15,500	9%	$157.21	15 years	$12,797.80

Source: Nellie Mae.

Parent Loans

These "auxiliary" loans, known as PLUS loans (for parents) and SLS loans (for graduate students and independent undergraduates) are meant to provide additional funds for educational expenses. (They are also occasionally called by their former title, Auxiliary Loans to Assist Students or ALAS loans). Parents may borrow an unlimited amount, although they may be subject to a credit check before they can borrow at all. Undergraduates may borrow up to $4,000 per year for the first and second year, $5,000 a year thereafter to a maximum of $23,000. Professional and graduate students may borrow up to $10,000 per year to a maximum (including any SLS undergraduate loans) of $73,000.

PLUS and SLS loans are available from financial institutions; they are not subsidized by Uncle Sam. The interest rate, adjusted each year, is pegged to a Treasury index; in the 1992-93 school year the rate was about 6.3 percent but it can rise to a maximum of 10 percent on PLUS loans and 11 percent on SLS loans. Repayment must begin within 60 days, although student borrowers may defer repayment until they are out of school.

Note: The interest clock continues to tick even if repayment is delayed. As a result, you could wind up owing more than you anticipate.

PLUS loans may be more help to parents than to students themselves. They should, nonetheless, be on your list of avenues to investigate. If local banks cannot provide information, consult your college financial aid office or your state office of higher education.

FUNDS FROM PRIVATE SOURCES

There are two other sources of college money to consider: Private loans, and tuition payment plans.

Private Loans

In addition to the loans available from federal, state, and college sources as formal financial aid, loans may also be taken from banks and other private lenders. These loans are made to parents, based on creditworthiness. For example, Nellie Mae offers direct undergraduate and graduate loans in addition to its consolidation loans, in amounts from $2,000 up to the annual cost of education; the interest rate may be fixed or variable and repayment, which may extend over 20 years, may consist of both principal and interest or be interest-only for up to four years while the student is enrolled in school.

Tuition Payment Plans

While not strictly financial aid, any plan that allows parents to spread out the burden of college costs is a big help. Remember, college bills are usually due twice a year, once for each semester. With costs of $8,000 or more (often much more) per year, you face a hefty out-of-pocket cost every few months (usually in August and then again in December). Tuition payment plans can help.

There are a number of prepayment and installment plans available, through colleges themselves or through private agencies. For example:

- Some colleges offer parents the opportunity to pay the year's costs in eight or ten monthly installments. There may be no interest at all, just a nominal administrative fee. (The college starts getting its money two to four months earlier than it otherwise would, so it comes out ahead.) If spreading payments over a longer period of time will be important, look for a college which offers this option.

- Some commercial programs do charge interest, but may allow you to spread payments over additional years. Some of these programs are limited to students at particular colleges (you'll get a mailing on these once your child has enrolled); others are open to everyone. One of the best-known nationally available plans, administered by Knight Tuition Payment Plans in Boston, offers two programs (in addition to a straight budget program available through specific colleges). In the Insured Tuition Payment Plan, you place money in a money market deposit account, earn interest, and Knight pays the college directly; you also pay a monthly service fee of a couple of dollars for the convenience of budgeting. The Extended Repayment Plan is a loan program which can be secured with home equity in most states to provide a tax advantage; repayment begins immediately but the plan permits spreading four years of college costs over ten to fifteen years.

■ Some commercial banks offer tuition payment plans via a line of credit and extended repayment. Interest on these loans—and they are loans—is charged when checks are written against the line of credit. The interest, however, may be at the rate of interest being charged on other consumer loans; this is not a low-cost source of money.

Note: Most installment plans offer an insurance feature, either built-in or as an optional extra. If the parent who signs the loan dies or becomes disabled, the remainder of the bills may be forgiven. This insurance feature means that it's a good idea to have just one parent, preferably the parent with the larger income, sign the installment agreement.

When You Are the Student

One-third of all the college students in the United States is over the age of 25. Whether you are attending college for the first time, seeking a second degree in a different field, or going back to school to resume an interrupted education, you are part of a growing movement.

Forget age, however, and there's not much difference between older students and students of "traditional" college age. Most of the financial advice extended earlier in this chapter applies equally to the adult student. Federal grants and loans, as one instance, have no age limitations. But there are some special things to say as well:

■ The student with dependents, at any age, has special needs and must make those needs known to the college financial aid office. Extra money can sometimes be made available for expenditures such as child care which may make it possible for an adult to attend school, but the school must first know that the need exists.

■ You do have to attend school at least half-time in order to qualify for most financial aid programs. A course at a time won't count, although some programs require as few as six credits a semester to qualify. Under many programs, where aid is available to the part-timer, it may be available for a longer period of time. Find out if the institution or program to which you are applying will extend aid eligibility beyond the usual four years.

■ Each school has its own policy when it comes to awarding aid to part-time students. Many restrict scholarships and grants to full-timers, leaving only loans to help the part-timer. Others simply allocate about 10 percent of available funds for part-time applicants. Be sure to apply to a number of schools that meet your educational needs, recognizing that you may receive financial aid from one and not from another.

■ Some financial aid programs are expressly designed for adults returning to school. You owe it to yourself to find out about such programs and apply for the ones that are appropriate.

COLLEGE OPTIONS

There is an almost bewildering array of options open to the adult student seeking a college education. Some are accepted by one school and not by another. Narrow your choice of schools in terms of the education you want to receive. Then see which of the schools you would like to attend accepts which of the following:

■ The College-Level Examination Program (CLEP) tests knowledge acquired outside of the formal classroom. More than 2,800 colleges recognize CLEP exams by extending either course credit or exemption from introductory courses. The tests, given at regular intervals at more than 1,200 testing locations around the country, include two types of examination: General Examinations in five broad areas (English composition, humanities, social science/history, mathematics, and natural science) and Subject Examinations in a wide array of specialized subjects from accounting to Western civilization. For more information, write to CLEP, P.O. Box 6601, Princeton, NJ 08541-6601, or call (609) 951-1026.

■ External degrees are granted by programs in several states; you may enroll in these programs no matter where you live. The Regents External Degree program in New York and the Thomas A. Edison College in New Jersey, as examples, offer degrees for all kinds of documented learning: courses taken at other colleges or at home by videocassette, noncollegiate courses evaluated and found comparable to college courses, military education programs, correspondence courses, proficiency examinations, and individual assessments of knowledge and skills. CLEP exams usually result in a year or two of credit, so that a student can enter an on-campus program at an advanced level; external degree programs (sometimes called "colleges without walls") make it possible to earn a college degree without ever attending college in person. For information about external degree programs, write to the American Council on Education, One DuPont Circle, Washington, DC 20036, or call ACE at (202) 939-9475.

■ "Life experience" is given credit at a number of colleges. Students, under the guidance of academic counselors, usually prepare a presentation documenting what they have learned through work or volunteer experience. A longtime bookkeeper might get credit for a course in accounting, while a nursing home volunteer might amass credits in gerontology and in administration. Each school decides how much educational credit is given for life experience.

■ Weekend programs have been designed by some colleges specifically to aid the person who is attending school while holding down a full-time job. Such programs typically entail intensive on-campus work one weekend a month, with extensive home study assignments in between. Such programs are available for specialized graduate work as well as for undergraduate studies. For more information on weekend programs, contact the American Council on Education, as listed above.

If you take advantage of one or more of these programs, you can save a lot of money. A 59-year-old Connecticut man, for example, had dropped out of high school to enlist in World War II. Forty years later he took, and passed, a high school equivalency examination and signed up to "take a few courses" at a local community college. There he heard about CLEP and about the external degree program. Within 18 months, via a combination of night courses and examinations based on life experience, he earned a bachelor of arts degree. Total cost: $598.

In addition, consider the following:

■ There are special grant programs designed for women (particularly women in midlife returning to school) and for members of minority groups. Consult your college financial aid office and community organizations for the names of specific programs.

■ If you are a veteran, or the dependent of a deceased or disabled veteran, you may be eligible for some educational benefits under the G.I. Bill.

■ If you want to take a couple of courses rather than enroll as much as half-time, and if you are over the magic age called "senior" (which may be as low as 60 in some areas), you may be eligible for free courses or reduced tuition. Ask at the college you want to attend. (And don't forget courses given by local libraries, community centers, Ys, museums, recreation departments, evening high schools....)

■ Employer-paid tuition benefits are particularly appropriate for the older student. Ask your personnel benefits office about your employer's policy.

As an employed adult, you may also enjoy tax breaks by furthering your education. If the courses you take are required by your employer or by law, or if the course maintains or improves skills needed on your present job, you may deduct the costs of tuition, fees, books, and necessary travel on your federal income tax return; you must file an itemized return, and the deductible expenses must exceed 2 percent of your adjusted gross income. You may not deduct educational costs if you are unemployed or if the courses will equip you for a new and different job.

If you are a full-time student, with a working spouse and children under age 13, you may claim a tax credit for a portion of child care expenses. Tax credit may also be claimed for the care of an aged or disabled dependent. You do not have to itemize deductions to claim this credit.

KEY POINTS

- Long-term savings for college are best done through growth investments; short-term ways to pay for college, if you've waited till late in the high school years to think about college, include borrowing against home equity and life insurance as well as applying for financial aid.

- College savings can be accumulated in either your own name or your child's. Custodial accounts can save on taxes, particularly for children over the age of 14 whose investment income is taxed at their own lower rate, but money in the child's name can also reduce eligibility for financial aid.

- Financial aid from federal and state governments and from individual institutions consists of grants, loans, and jobs. Be sure to file an application, and file it early, even if you're not sure you qualify.

- College costs can be cut in a variety of ways: accelerated high school programs, attendance at local community colleges, correspondence courses and, for the adult student, through credit for life experience.

- Adults returning to school may qualify for regular financial aid; they may also qualify for special programs designed for returning students, for women, or for minorities.

Protecting Yourself: Insurance

CHAPTER 18

Life Insurance

■ Jonathan T., new Bachelor of Science degree in hand, is solicited by a life insurance salesman. The message: Buy protection cheap, while you're young and insurable.

■ Anne and Will K. are both 28 years old, both climbing the executive ladder. An insurance salesman Will meets at the gym tells him that each should carry life insurance to protect the other.

■ Eric P., 32 years old and a first-time father, receives several telephone calls from eager insurance agents while his wife and newborn son are still in the hospital. The message: You have responsibilities now, responsibilities you can carry out through life insurance.

■ The Taylors, in the midst of calculating college costs for three teenage children, are told that life insurance can build an education fund.

■ The Elmers, now that the nest is almost empty, are thinking about a divorce. In addition to the already-in-force life insurance that Mrs. Elmer will take over as part of the property settlement, an insurance agent suggests that she buy additional insurance on her husband's life. Then, if anything happens to him, her income will continue.

■ Tom A., 12 years from retirement, hears that life insurance can provide retirement income.

■ Peter M., the owner of a small business, is 67 and has been urged to carry life insurance to pay estate taxes, thereby protecting the business for his heirs.

Does life insurance actually fulfill all of these functions? Do all of these people need life insurance?

Life insurance may be used to meet a variety of financial planning goals. New types of life insurance, in fact, are being promoted as investment vehicles. But life insurance is fundamentally one thing and one thing only: **income protection.** If and when you buy life insurance, buy it to protect the people who are dependent on you from financial loss resulting from your death. Other purposes are strictly secondary.

When you buy insurance—of any kind—you are entering a pool with other people. All of the people in the pool pay a specified sum (based, in the case of life insurance, primarily on expectations of mortality), and the insurance company pays out, from the combined premiums of all the policyholders, the benefits due to those who die while they are insured.

The same principle applies to all insurance. In automobile insurance, an insured individual can repair a damaged car with insurance proceeds; the proceeds come from the reserves built up by the insurance company from premiums paid by all policyholders. In the case of life insurance, of course, the insured is no longer present to collect. Policy proceeds are paid to the person or persons the insured has named as beneficiary. Life insurance can't keep you alive; it can ease the economic damage done to your survivors' lives by your death. Life insurance, to repeat, is income protection.

The purchase of life insurance, almost more than any other part of your personal financial plan, is tied to your life stage. Your age and, even more important, the number of your dependents affects not only how much life insurance you need but whether you need it at all.

How Much Life Insurance Do You Need?

You have dependents you'd like to protect. You've decided that you do need life insurance. Now you'd like someone to tell you how much you need and what kind to buy. There are no pat answers to either question. How much life insurance you need depends on your personal situation: what you want life insurance to do and what other assets you have. What kind to buy is a related but separate question, to be considered a bit later; your choices may be limited by how much you can afford. The first decision you should make is the basic decision: how much.

Income Replacement

There was a time when a flat income multiple, such as five times annual income, was offered as the all-purpose solution. But to look solely at income is to ignore the fact that one woman making $35,000 a year is a single mother, supporting two children and an aged mother while another, at the same income level, is part of a two-income couple with no dependents. Their insurance needs are clearly different, and an all-purpose answer does not work (although you can certainly use this income multiple as a rough approximation).

In order to determine how much life insurance you actually need, you (and/or your insurance agent) should look at both the actual income needs of your family and the other assets your family can draw on to meet those needs. This "personalized needs" approach takes a bit more time but provides a far more accurate answer.

Income Needs

In assessing how much income your family will need to replace your income, think about specific times and specific purposes. Here are some of the things life insurance can do:

Immediately (with no wait for probate):

■ Provide ready cash for funeral and other final expenses, including any uninsured medical expenses, probate fees, and estate taxes.

■ Pay off any debts left after your death. In addition to uninsured medical and hospital bills, this might include a mortgage on your home (if continuing to pay the mortgage would be a burden for your survivor and if the family wanted to continue living in the home), an automobile loan, or any other consumer debt.

On an ongoing basis:

■ Provide money to cover housekeeping expenses. If you are the homemaker, it will cost your surviving spouse considerable sums to provide day care for children, cleaning and laundry services, and so on. If you are a wage-earner with a stay-at-home spouse, your survivor will incur these costs upon return to the labor market. If both of you are currently working, the costs of these services may already be built into your budget. But will they be manageable on a single income?

■ Provide replacement income for your family, in different amounts at different intervals:

1. A readjustment period of two or three years after your death, during which the family reshapes its financial affairs and during which your spouse might secure additional training to reenter the job market or might move from part-time to full-time employment. (Even if your spouse is already working full-time at a substantial income, there will be a period of readjustment while the family adjusts to one paycheck instead of two—and to the added expenses that might result from your absence. If, for instance, you were handy around the house, an electrician or a carpenter might now have to be hired for occasional tasks.)

2. The period while children are still at home and dependent, and Social Security survivor benefits may supply part of the family's income needs.

3. The college years, when Social Security has ended and expenses have become heavier.
4. The years between the time the youngest child turns 16 and the surviving spouse reaches retirement age. For most people, there are no Social Security benefits during this period and, as a result, there is additional need for life insurance to fill the gap.
5. After the survivor reaches retirement age and starts to receive Social Security retirement benefits and/or regular pension checks.

You'll find a worksheet on which to make your own personal calculations on p. 487. Before filling it in, however, evaluate all your sources of income.

Other Sources of Income

Life insurance is not the only source of support for your family. You'll need just enough life insurance to plug any gap between existing assets and your family's needs. (As assets grow, in fact, the need for life insurance diminishes.) So, at this point, you must evaluate those existing assets. Consider:

- Cash on hand, in bank accounts and money market funds, which could be used to pay final expenses
- Securities, such as stocks and bonds, which your family might sell or might retain to add to regular income
- Existing life insurance, including any on-the-job group life insurance provided by your employer, group insurance purchased through a fraternal group or trade association, and any already-purchased individual policies
- The value of your home, if it would be sold, and of other potentially salable assets such as jewelry or coin collections

Q Do you recommend buying a life insurance policy on an infant?

A Some people believe that buying life insurance for a baby gives him or her a start in life—by building cash values, ensuring insurability, and providing low insurance rates. Or parents may want to have money for final expenses if the baby should die. But, really, your first responsibility to the baby is to provide for the future if anything should happen to you or your spouse. Before you spend money on insuring the baby, be sure that you both have adequate life insurance so that the baby would be cared for into adulthood.

Worksheet 18.1: Insurance Needs

Final Expenses (lump sum)

Funeral costs	$_____
Uninsured medical expenses	$_____
Probate fees	$_____
Estate taxes	$_____

Debt Repayment (lump sum)

Mortgage	$_____
Auto loan	$_____
Other	$_____

Housekeeping Expenses (monthly amount x number of months)

Childcare	$_____
Other	$_____

Replacement Income (monthly amount x number of months)

For a readjustment period	$_____
For dependent children	$_____
For the college years	$_____
For a surviving spouse, preretirement	$_____
For a surviving spouse, post-retirement	$_____
TOTAL	$_____

This total represents your best guess as to the amount of money your family will need. The largest sums will be for ongoing expenses of housekeeping and replacement income. But, as mentioned earlier, you already have assets on hand to meet some of these needs. Add up these assets:

Assets

Cash on hand	$_____
Securities	$_____
Existing life insurance	$_____
Lump-sum pension benefits	$_____
The market value of your house and other possessions	$_____
Social Security survivor benefits (monthly amount x number of months)	$_____
TOTAL	$_____

Now subtract your total assets from the total needs you calculated above. The result is the amount of life insurance your family needs ... if your spouse is not employed. If there is another income in the family, calculate that income for the number of years the children will be dependent.

Income needs:	$_____
- Assets on hand:	$_____
- Spouse's income (yearly income x number of years of children's dependency)	$_____
= ADDITIONAL INSURANCE NEEDED:	$_____

Table 18.1: Approximate Monthly Social Security Survivors Benefits if the Worker Dies in 1993 and Had Steady Earnings

Worker's Age	Your Family	Deceased Worker's Earnings in 1992				
		$20,000	$30,000	$40,000	$50,000	$57,600 or more[1]
35	Spouse and 1 child[2]	$1,120	$1,506	$1,688	$1,870	$1,952
	Spouse and 2 children[3]	1,396	1,758	1,970	2,182	2,278
	1 child only	560	753	844	935	976
	Spouse at age 60[4]	534	718	805	891	931
45	Spouse and 1 child[2]	1,118	1,504	1,678	1,810	1,854
	Spouse and 2 children[3]	1,394	1,754	1,958	2,112	2,162
	1 child only	559	752	839	905	927
	Spouse at age 60[4]	553	717	800	863	883
55	Spouse and 1 child[2]	1,118	1,490	1,618	1,702	1,730
	Spouse and 2 children[3]	1,394	1,737	1,887	1,986	2,019
	1 child only	559	745	809	851	865
	Spouse at age 60[4]	553	710	771	811	825

Source: Social Security Administration.

Notes: The accuracy of these estimates depends on the pattern of your actual past earnings. [1] Use this column if the worker earned more than the maximum Social Security earnings base. [2] Amounts shown also equal the benefits paid to two children, if no parent survives or surviving parent has substantial earnings. [3] Equals the maximum family benefit. [4] Amounts payable in 1993. Spouses turning 60 in the future would receive higher benefits.

- Lump-sum pension benefits, such as the balance in an Individual Retirement Account, payable to your survivor
- Social Security benefits for a surviving spouse and dependent children (see Table 18.1). These benefits can be substantial, adding up to more than $1,000 a month for a family in which the wage-earner has always earned the maximum amount subject to Social Security tax.

YOUR LIFE INSURANCE NEEDS

Needs change, and this exercise can't be performed just once and then forgotten. But the only way to determine how much life insurance your family will need is to make calculations based on the assumption that you will die tomorrow. If you did, how much money would your family need to carry on? Make your best estimates as you fill in Worksheet 18.1.

Women and Life Insurance

Once upon a time, Prince Charming needed life insurance to provide income for Cinderella and the children. Today Cinderella is probably earning an income of her own. Although more and more women are buying life insurance to protect their families against the premature loss of their income, many women are still woefully underinsured.

The same rules hold for women as for men. If you are earning an income that your family would be hard-pressed to do without, you need insurance. If you are not currently earning an income, but it would be a hardship for your family to pay for the services you provide, you also need life insurance. Whether you are male or female, you need to determine just how much life insurance your family needs.

Q I let my life insurance lapse when I lost my job, but now I have another job and want coverage again. Can I get the old policy back?

A You can usually reinstate a lapsed policy within five years by paying the back premiums plus interest and passing a physical exam. It may be worth doing if you initially took out the policy some years back, because yearly premiums could be much less. A $50,000 whole-life policy for which you paid $420 a year starting at age 25 could cost you $1,200 yearly if you take it out at age 47. If you decide not to reinstate a lapsed whole-life policy, you can still turn it in for the remaining cash value or convert it to a paid-up policy in a reduced amount. Whatever you do, don't ignore that policy; it probably still contains some valuable benefits.

In performing these calculations for your own family, you may find it helpful to enlist the help of a professional insurance agent (see p. 512-514). Whether you use an agent or not, however, it's very important to decide how much life insurance you need before you think about what kind to buy.

What Kind of Life Insurance Should You Buy?

Life insurance goes by a lot of names but comes in two basic varieties: term and permanent. It's important to understand the difference.

TERM INSURANCE

Term insurance provides pure income protection, without any savings or investment features. As its name implies, term insurance is written for a specific term; the term may be one year or five years or more. The death benefit is payable if you die during the specified term. If you don't, that's it. There is no cash value, no "savings" feature, no built-in loan provisions. Term insurance, as a result, is less expensive than permanent insurance. That is, it's far less expensive when you are young. Premiums are based on age and rise at each renewal interval, rising sharply later in life. (Some combination policies—see p. 500—get around this problem.)

For young parents, needing maximum protection for a minimum outlay and only until children are on their own, term insurance (either alone or, if you think you will want lifelong protection, in combination with permanent insurance) is often the best bet. Look at it this way, in an example from one major insurer: If you can afford to spend $300 a year on life insurance and you are a

---

Q I'm raising three sons alone and am worried about what will happen to them if anything happens to me. I have some group life insurance through my job but probably should have some individual insurance as well. I can't afford very much. What would be the best kind to buy?

A You'll get the most protection for the least amount of money—which is what you need while your sons are dependent—from term insurance. Buy guaranteed renewable term, so you'll be able to renew it when the term expires. Buy term with a conversion privilege and you'll be able to convert it to a whole life policy without a medical examination should you decide to do so when your children are grown and your life insurance needs change.

35-year-old nonsmoking male, you can buy about $22,000 worth of whole life insurance. With the same $300 you could buy about $250,000 of annual renewable term insurance, convertible, without a medical examination, to permanent insurance. Clearly, if $300 is all you can afford, you'll buy more protection for your family with term insurance.

In buying term insurance, buy a policy that is:

- renewable, without regard to your health, up to at least age 70 (longer, if you think you'll want lifetime coverage), and
- convertible, without a medical exam, to permanent insurance; this option must usually be exercised at a specified interval before the term period ends.

Both features, although they may increase the premium by a small amount, are worthwhile.

Low-cost term insurance may be available through your employer (in addition to the amount provided in your benefit package), through an association, or at a savings bank. It is, of course, sold by insurance companies—although most would prefer to sell you costlier whole life insurance (see below).

Variations on Term Insurance

Declining balance term insurance, also called decreasing term, keeps the premium the same each year for the specified period while the face amount of the policy declines. This kind of policy is often used as mortgage insurance, to cover the decreasing balance of the mortgage on your home. It may be used for other purposes as well, such as insuring a homemaker's life during the diminishing period when children are dependent.

Ideally, the money needed by your family to pay off the mortgage should be included in your total insurance needs, rather than covered separately. If you plan carefully, and buy one large policy instead of several small ones for different purposes, you may save some money.

If you do buy decreasing term insurance to cover a mortgage, perhaps because you already have an insurance program by the time you buy a house, be sure that the beneficiary is your family and not the bank that holds the mortgage. If the bank gets the proceeds it will pay off the mortgage. But perhaps your family would prefer to keep the mortgage in force, live in the house, and invest the money elsewhere. You should give your family the option of making the choice.

If you buy decreasing term insurance, be sure to find out when and under what circumstances you may convert the policy to whole life or renewable term.

Credit life insurance, often sold (with or without your full awareness) as part of a consumer loan (see p. 217), provides insurance for the loan balance. The idea is to pay off the loan if you die, sparing your survivors the burden of debt (and sparing the lender the burden of collecting). Credit life insurance tends to be expensive and most people can accomplish the same purpose at less cost via regular term insurance.

PERMANENT INSURANCE

Lifelong, level-cost protection is provided by permanent insurance, also called whole life or straight life or cash value insurance. Both the face amount of the policy (the death benefit) and the premium (the amount that you pay) are fixed at the time you buy. Neither will change, despite the fact that the chance of death increases with age. Insurance companies compensate for this increasing risk of death by charging more than necessary in the early policy years, less than necessary in the later years. Thus the premium remains level. See Table 18.2 for an illustration of how the cost of term and whole life can differ.

Table 18.2: Life Insurance Premiums

Typical premiums for a 35-year-old male buying $100,000 of life insurance:

Attained Age	Whole Life	Annual Renewable Term
35	$1,100	$ 140
45	1,100	210
55	1,100	590
65	1,100	1,600

Source: National Insurance Consumer Organization.

Note: Rates vary from company to company. The crossover point in this illustration is age 61.

Cash Value

The "extra" premiums that you pay in the early years contribute to the reserves that the insurance company is building up against the increasing likelihood of paying out a death benefit. They also, in part, form your cash value in the policy, an amount that accumulates with interest and that is always available to you either as cash surrender value should you cancel the policy or as a policy loan while the insurance remains in effect.

Life insurance agents often like to call this cash value element of permanent insurance a "savings" feature. The cash value earns interest. That interest is tax-free while the policy remains in force, when you cash the policy in (except to the extent, if any, that the cash value exceeds the premiums you've paid over the years), and when your beneficiary receives it as income.

Note: It may also be tax-free, under a recent Internal Revenue Service ruling, if paid out during your lifetime as an "accelerated" benefit because of severe illness; see p. 495.

Policy Loans

You may borrow against the accrued cash value, at relatively low interest rates. (But critics point out that the cash value is your own money. If it represents "savings," they say, why need you pay interest at all?)

Policy loans on older policies are available at interest rates as low as 5 percent; newer policies may have fixed loan rates, often at 8 percent, or may have variable rates tied to current market rates and fluctuating periodically during the life of the loan. You should also be aware, as the National Insurance Consumer Organization (NICO) points out in its invaluable book, *Taking the* ✗ *MT,* *Bite out of Insurance* (1991), that the true cost of a life insurance loan may be more than the stated interest rate. That's because the dividend rate is usually adjusted downward when a loan is taken; in one instance cited by NICO, a company's stated 8 percent interest rate on policy loans became an actual 11 percent.

Policy loans can be a convenient source of cash, especially if you have an older low-interest policy. They do not have to be repaid, although any outstanding loan will be deducted from the death benefit. But it's important to pay the interest each year, if at all possible. If you don't pay the interest on the loan as it

Q I bought the largest term insurance policy I could afford when my children were small and I needed maximum protection. Now, as I reach my fifties, the premiums are becoming prohibitive. My kids are on their own, so I probably don't need as much life insurance. Should I drop the policy? Convert it to whole life?

A You may not need as much life insurance once your children are grown, but the first thing you have to decide is whether you need life insurance to protect your spouse or to provide liquidity in your estate. If you do, and you have any health problems, your choices will be limited; you'll have to keep your term policy in force or convert it to a whole life policy. If you are in good health, you have more choice. If your insurance needs are short-term, shop for a new term policy; you may find lower rates at your current age than your existing policy provides. If you want life insurance in force for a lifetime, consider a whole life policy or a combination of whole life and term. But don't buy a whole life policy, at any age, unless you plan to hold on to it for at least 15 years. ✗

comes due, the company will deduct the interest from the policy's remaining cash value, adding it to the principal of the loan, so that you'll end up paying interest on the interest and, possibly, losing any advantage you may have gained.

Automatic Payment

Most policies levy an automatic loan against accrued cash value to keep the policy in force if you fall behind on premium payments—but only if there is sufficient cash value built up in the policy. The provision can be useful if, for instance, you fall ill and forget to make a scheduled payment. (You also have a "grace period" of 31 days, after each premium due date, in which to make the payment without penalty.)

Long-Term Rights

Nonforfeiture provisions reinforce your rights to the cash value in the policy. If you drop a permanent life insurance policy, in other words, it doesn't just lapse. You retain rights to the accumulated cash value, and may tap those rights in one of several ways:

- By taking the accumulated cash value in a lump sum payment
- By using the cash value for as long as it lasts to pay premiums and keep the full amount of the insurance in force
- By using the cash value to fully pay a policy with a smaller face value

These rights may be exercised at any time (although they won't make much sense early in the policy, before much cash value has built up). They

Q In 1983, when my son started college, I borrowed $10,000 from my life insurance policy at an interest rate of 5 percent. I've just let the loan ride but now I wonder: Should I think about paying it back?

A Probably. It made sense to carry the loan when the interest was tax-deductible and when you could invest the money elsewhere for a higher return. Today neither situation applies. The $500 in annual interest (5 percent on $10,000) cost you $335 after taxes if you were in a 33 percent tax bracket; today, with no tax break for consumer interest, it costs you the full $500. At the same time, where you could have been earning 12 percent or more on safe investments in the early 1980s, today's return is more like 3 to 4 percent. Keep the life insurance loan if you have other high-interest loans, such as revolving credit finance charges, to pay off. Otherwise, consider repaying the loan.

may be particularly useful at retirement, when you no longer wish to pay premiums.

Note: If you let the policy lapse without choosing one of these options, the company will automatically use the cash value, as long as it lasts, to pay premiums and keep your coverage in force.

Should You Buy Permanent Insurance?

Whole life insurance can meet specific needs. It can provide cash to cover estate taxes, for affluent individuals whose assets are tied up in illiquid investments. It can protect a spouse whose resources would otherwise be limited, or protect children born to a late-in-life marriage, beyond the age when term insurance is cost-effective.

But it also has disadvantages, primarily the high initial cost. While the internal rate of return is better on newer policies (it used to be appallingly low) and the tax-free nature of the interest helps the cash value in comparison with many taxable investments, the Federal Trade Commission has pointed out that because the cash value builds very slowly (administrative costs and sales commissions bite very deeply at the beginning), the average annual return may actually be negative until the policy is at least ten years old. (See p. 515 on low-load policies.) Since almost half of all purchasers let their policies lapse

Q My cousin is very ill and desperately needs money to cover medical costs. Is there some way he can tap his life insurance policy?

A Yes. Assuming that he has a cash value policy, he can always take a loan against the policy. But he may be able to get more money if he is insured with one of the more than 150 insurers now offering accelerated or "living" benefits within life insurance policies. Typically, these benefits kick in when an insured has a specific catastrophic illness, an organ transplant, permanent nursing home confinement, or a terminal illness with limited time left to live. Depending on the policy, benefits may be taken as a lump sum or in periodic payments. Depending on the policy, too, the benefit is the (discounted) death benefit, available at no extra cost, or a rider available at an additional premium.

Note: Until recently, there were tax consequences in tapping policy proceeds in advance of death. Now that the IRS has proposed that accelerated benefits be treated as normal death benefits, more companies are expected to offer these benefits.

within the first ten years (they didn't really need all that insurance, they can't afford the premiums, they gave in to the urgings of a salesman ...), the only winners are the insurance companies.

The insurance industry disagrees, pointing out that cash value should not be considered savings but should be regarded as similar to equity in a house, building slowly and available to you when you need it. But there's another parallel: The longer you live in a house the more of your own money (as contrasted to the mortgage lender's) is invested in the house and the smaller the return you receive when you sell. The longer you live, similarly, the more of your own money will be returned to your survivors in the life insurance death benefit. The cash value, even if you never touch it, is not added to the policy proceeds paid to your beneficiary; it is used by the insurance company, along with other reserves if necessary, to pay those proceeds. The insurance company, in other words, assumes more risk earlier in the policy's life, less later on. Put another way, you're buying more protection at the beginning, less and less with the passing years.

Variations on Permanent Life Insurance

That said, I have to point out that some new insurance products offer the opportunity for a better return on your money—albeit with fewer guarantees and hence more risk. Attitudes toward life insurance changed in the high-interest rate environment of the late 1970s and early 1980s. As more consumers became aware of the high rates they could earn on flashier investments, life insurance companies began to create new interest-sensitive products that could compete for consumer dollars. Some of these policies make the policyholder take considerable investment risk. (These new interest-sensitive products are also, at least in part, responsible for some of the solvency problems insurers have faced in recent years.)

On a scale from the most conservative to the riskiest of whole life insurance policies, the basic whole life policy is the most conservative, with a fixed premium, a fixed death benefit, and a fixed cash value. Beyond this basic policy, this is what you will find (bearing in mind that insurers offer their own policy variations):

Variable Life

Variable life offers the opportunity for a policy to grow in value. The premium is usually fixed (**variable appreciable** policies, offered by some companies, offer flexibility in premium payments similar to that in universal life) but policyholders control the investment of their cash values, with options among equity and fixed-income funds. If investments do well, both death benefits (the face value) and cash values can grow. They can also decrease, but the death benefit typically won't fall below a floor fixed in the policy; the investment risk is concentrated in the cash value. There is, as a result, no guaranteed cash value.

Variable life, like any investment based on the performance of the stock market, is a gamble (there's little point in buying variable life and choosing a fixed-income portfolio; the only way to overcome management fees is through portfolio gains). Before you decide to take that gamble, ask yourself these questions: Do you expect the stock market to go up or down? Do you want an insurance company to manage your investments for you (you can choose your own investments within a variable life contract, but many investors choose a "managed account" and leave the decisions to the insurer)? And are you willing to pay the hefty charges (administrative expenses, brokerage fees, ongoing annual sales charges ... all in addition to a first-year sales commission of as much as 50 percent of the premium) associated with that management?

That said, there are advantages to variable life policies: Capital gains on the underlying investments are not taxed so long as they remain within the life insurance contract. And the policy's cash values are held in separate accounts rather than commingled with the general assets of the insurer; should the insurer run into trouble, your money is protected. But the National Insurance Consumer Organization (NICO), a consumer watchdog based in Washington, D.C., cautions that annual premium variable life policies take 15 or 20 years to pay off. Buy a single premium policy, and a 10 year holding period may do the trick.

Table 18.3: A Quick Check of Life Insurance Features

Term

- Protection for a specified period of time
- May be renewable and convertible to whole life insurance
- Low initial premium
- Premium rises with each new term
- Typically no cash value

Whole Life

- Permanent protection
- Fixed premium
- Fixed death benefit
- Fixed cash value
- Earnings generated by the policy are not taxed while the policy is in force

Universal Life

- Permanent protection
- Flexible premium
- Flexible death benefit
- Cash value reflects premiums paid and market conditions
- Earnings generated by the policy are not taxed while the policy is in force

Variable Life

- Permanent protection
- Fixed or flexible premiums
- Policyholders control the investment of their cash values in separate stock, bond, money market, or other accounts
- Death benefits and cash value vary in relation to the performance of invested funds
- Earnings generated by the policy are not taxed while the policy is in force

Source: American Council of Life Insurance.

Universal Life

Universal life offers a flexible premium (subject to certain limits, you can essentially pay premiums in any amount at any time) and a flexible face amount. The insurance company guarantees a minimum return on the cash value, usually not less than 4 percent, with actual rates depending on investment performance. In addition, you may choose between a fixed and a flexible death benefit. Universal life became very popular when interest rates were high, garnering 38 percent of the market in 1985. That share was down to 26 percent by 1991, when interest rates were considerably lower.

The policy offers a number of advantages in addition to its potentially high yield:

- It is extremely flexible; it's possible, for instance, to skip premiums without causing the policy to lapse (although you may then wind up with a large, and unmanageable, premium). And it's possible to change the face amount of the policy, to raise and lower premiums, and to withdraw part of the cash value without interest charges.
- Disclosure goes far beyond typical life insurance practices, with universal life issuers sending policyholders an annual statement spelling out the amount of protection they have, the fees, and the interest rate.

Universal life also has some disadvantages, less likely to be noted in promotional material:

- There is often a first-year charge of several hundred dollars plus annual administrative fees of 5 to 7 percent of your premium. These charges, like those on a load mutual fund, reduce your effective yield.
- It's difficult to compare policies and make the best buy because both rates of return and administrative charges vary over time.
- When interest rates fall, premiums are likely to go up—a fact not always made clear in an agent's presentation. Some people who bought universal life in the 1980s now find themselves paying 20 percent or more in extra premiums in order to keep benefits at the desired

level. (See p. 509 for more information on policy illustrations.)

■ When interest rates fall, in any case, universal life loses its competitive edge. In fact, according to NICO, rates of return of many dividend-paying insurers (see p. 509) currently exceed current interest rates on universal life. Interest rates on universal life tend to reflect short-term rates, which are typically lower than the long-term rates used to determine portfolio return on traditional whole life policies.

Variable Universal Life

This combination of variable and universal policies might be the most aggressive way to purchase life insurance. It offers virtually no guarantees, except that the death benefit typically cannot fall below the original face value of the policy. Don't buy variable life or variable universal life unless you are prepared to invest in equities and stay invested for the long term; it makes little sense to choose conservative fixed income investments within the framework of a life insurance policy on which you must pay commissions and administrative fees.

For most people, life insurance should be life insurance. This means choosing term insurance or a basic plain-vanilla whole life policy or, maybe, a universal life policy. For the affluent or for those who are willing to gamble on how much money they'll be leaving to their dependents, one of the variable products might be considered.

Note: Be wary of policy illustrations demonstrating what you can expect under a universal or variable policy (or, for that matter, under any policy where premiums can change; see p. 509). Until new guidelines are established (and both the Society of Actuaries and the National Association of Life Underwriters are studying the issue in 1993), there are just too many elements that a company or agent can fudge. Projected cash values and death benefits hinge on company expenses, investment return, and actual experience in paying death benefits. Minor adjustments in any one of these can dramatically affect an illustration of what might happen under the policy. Just remember: An illustration is not a guarantee.

Q When I took out a life insurance policy recently, I was 34 years old. Why did my policy list my age as 35?

A For insurance purposes age is often calculated on the nearest birthday, which may not be the last one. If your next birthday was less than six months away when you took out the policy, your age was correctly listed as 35.

Other Options

First-to-die whole life insurance is now being offered by some insurers, as a lower-cost option appropriate for two-income childless working couples where both need insurance to give the survivor liquidity but can't afford premiums on two separate policies. First-to-die typically costs about 25 percent less than two equivalent policies. A policy that pays only when the first insured dies can also make sense for business partners, where the survivor will need cash to buy out the business and keep it going.

Note: First-to-die policies are not for everyone. A working couple with children, for example, probably needs insurance on both lives. First-to-die policies build less cash value, so should be used primarily for the death benefit and not to build a reserve fund for other purposes. And first-to-die policies can be an expensive mistake if you divorce; don't even consider one if your marriage is at all shaky.

Second-to-die insurance, which can come in any of the whole life varieties, insures two lives and pays only upon the second death. This is most useful for affluent married couples where the surviving spouse won't need the money but his or her beneficiaries will need cash to pay estate taxes. For more information on this specialized form of life insurance, see Chapter 21.

Limited payment plans provide lifelong protection, but the premium period is shorter. Under 20-payment life, for instance, the policy would be fully paid-up after 20 years. You'd pay more in premiums in each of the 20 years, however, because there are fewer payments overall. Another example is paid-up-at-65, under which you pay premiums each year until you reach age 65, then have paid-up insurance in force; again the premiums are higher. With the higher premiums under limited payment plans, there are also higher cash values. Limited payment plans are still available, but have generally been replaced by the "vanishing premium" concept applied to whole life policies (see p. 509).

COMBINATION POLICIES

Permanent life insurance serves certain purposes. Term insurance serves other purposes. Which should you buy? Just to muddy the waters (and your decision), there are also combination policies to be found (and a growing trend toward buying them):

Whole life insurance may be bought with a term insurance rider, thus offering both permanent protection and cash values along with a larger death benefit at a lower total premium. The term rider can be level term to boost your total protection package. Or it can be decreasing term, to cover, for instance, the declining risk of dying before your children are grown.

A **50/50 policy** offered by some insurers is made up initially of half whole life and half term insurance. For a 35-year-old nonsmoking male, the policy would cost half as much as a whole life policy in the same amount but twice as much, in the first year, as a term policy. As time goes by, dividends buy more whole life coverage. By the twentieth year, when the policy is made up almost entirely of whole life insurance, it would cost about 25 percent less than term coverage.

Family income policies use a combination of permanent life insurance, to provide a death benefit, and declining balance term insurance, to provide monthly income during the years when children are small. The declining balance in this instance is pegged not to the amount of a mortgage, but to the declining years of dependency. As, each year, the number of years of dependency diminish, so the need for insurance diminishes. The monthly benefit remains the same, depending on what you purchase, but the number of years over which it will be paid diminishes with the life of the policy.

Note: Don't confuse the family income policy with so-called family plans. The latter provide insurance in varying amounts on each member of the family; you want to concentrate your insurance on the breadwinner(s).

Life Planning

Now let's look more closely at the cast of characters introduced at the beginning of this chapter and see where life insurance fits into their lives.

THE COLLEGE GRADUATE

Jonathan T. is 22 years old, fresh out of college, and on his way to a management trainee job he's lined up halfway across the country. His parents, who have put him through school, are in comfortable circumstances. Nonetheless, college was expensive and they're now looking forward to having money available for travel.

Does Jonathan need life insurance? No. He might, if his parents were dependent on him and his death would deprive them of needed income. Or he

Q The benefits package at my company includes the right to buy additional life insurance at group rates. A co-worker insists this is a good deal. Is she right?

A Maybe—if you work for a large company, are a smoker, or are in poor health. If not, this "group rate" insurance may actually cost more than an individual policy you can buy on your own. There can be advantages to buying additional life insurance through your employer—you probably won't have to pass a medical exam and you can pay premiums through payroll deductions—but do some comparison shopping before you decide.

might want some coverage if he had few assets and his death would burden his family with debts and last expenses. But Jonathan's parents are not dependent on him and he will probably have enough group life insurance built into his new job to cover a funeral and any final expenses.

What about the argument of cost and insurability? The sales agent has told Jonathan that he should buy life insurance while he's young and healthy because (1) it will be cheaper if bought when he's younger, and (2) he knows that he's insurable; if he's later stricken with a serious and lingering illness, he might find it difficult to purchase life insurance. Both statements are true, as far as they go. Life insurance is cheaper per dollar of coverage when bought at a younger age. But it won't be cheaper over a lifetime of premium payments. And why buy a product, any product, that you don't need? Most 22-year-olds are insurable by any health definition, but so are most 32-year-olds. In the unlikely event that Jonathan's health deteriorates in the next decade to the point where no individual life insurance is available to him, he should still be able to convert his on-the-job group life insurance to an individual policy. Such conversion, although expensive, can be made without regard to the policyholder's health.

TWO INCOMES, NO CHILDREN

Ann and Will K. have no dependents other than each other. Yet each is earning a young professional's salary and could clearly continue to do so if left alone. Do they need life insurance? Probably not. But they might want to buy some life insurance if the death of one would leave the other with a major financial burden.

For example, suppose Ann and Will recently bought a condominium in ski country. They hope to rent it out part of the year and make back some of their expenses. Meanwhile, rented out or not, there are hefty mortgage and assessment payments to be made each month. Those payments would be too much for either partner to carry alone. The condominium could, of course, be sold. But if the survivor would like to keep it, life insurance may make it possible to do so.

They have several choices: They could each buy a fixed-sum policy, either permanent or term, on the other's life or on their own. They could each buy a decreasing balance term insurance policy, to cover the remaining amount on the condominium mortgage. If Ann earns $39,000 a year to Will's $32,000, and if Ann kicks in proportionately more toward the mortgage payments, then a larger policy might be taken on Ann's life.

If their incomes are roughly equal, on the other hand, they might take insurance policies in the same amounts. Or, in still another option, they might consider a first-to-die policy, a single policy on two people which pays the face value only on the first to die. Since Ann and Will's purpose in purchasing life insurance is to protect their mutual investment in the condominium, first-to-die would serve the purpose.

NEW PARENTS

Our first-time father is another situation entirely. Eric has earned a good salary. But so has Nancy, his wife. Nancy is planning to stay out of the work force for several years now, until both children (they plan to have two) enter school. What happens if Eric should die while the children are preschoolers? When Nancy does reenter the labor force she will have lost ground and her salary will probably be lower than it might have been; it will almost certainly be lower than Eric's. She will also face childcare costs. And what happens to the family if Nancy should die, either before or after she returns to work?

This family needs life insurance, probably a good deal more life insurance than they realize. Eric needs enough insurance on his life to provide an income for Nancy and the child(ren); he can provide the most protection through term insurance but might want to consider a combination policy with a whole life component. Nancy should have enough insurance on her life, right now, to replace her childcare and household management function in the home. When she returns to work she will want enough insurance to cover both lost income and childcare.

Eric and Nancy do not, however, want life insurance on the newborn child. Despite the urgings of the life insurance agent, that child is best protected by spending available life insurance dollars on protecting the parents who will raise the child to secure adulthood.

MONEY FOR COLLEGE

The Taylors, with three teenage children, have been urged to use life insurance to fund the children's college education. A good idea? Maybe, but probably not through a policy designed specifically for that purpose. The Taylors need life insurance for the same reason Eric and Nancy do: to provide replacement income to support the family until the children are grown. Part of that support includes funding a college education. If both Taylors live and can continue their savings plan, the children will be able to attend college. But what if a wage-earning parent dies? Life insurance on that parent's life could then make it possible for the children to continue their education. Ten years of low-cost term insurance will see the three teenagers through school.

ON THE EDGE OF DIVORCE

Bob Elmer has a total of $195,000 on his own life: two individual policies of $40,000 and $55,000, and a group policy of $100,000. Dorothy expects to assume ownership of the $55,000 policy as part of the property settlement. Her insurance agent has suggested that she also buy a new $100,000 policy on Bob's life, to ensure some income if he dies and maintenance payments cease. (Dorothy is working, but she just returned to work after the children entered high school; she needs some alimony to make ends meet. She also wants to be sure that their youngest child, 19 years old, will be able to finish college.)

Let's look first at the transfer of ownership in the $55,000 policy. The transfer of that policy as part of the property settlement may subject Dorothy to unnecessary and possibly sizable taxes. It may be possible to avoid that tax by transferring the policy to Dorothy *before* the divorce. But the only sure way around taxes in the transfer of ownership is via a policy with no cash value. Either Bob transfers an existing term insurance policy to Dorothy, or he takes out a brand-new policy with Dorothy as the owner. There's also another solution: Bob doesn't transfer a policy at all, but sets up an arrangement whereby his estate must use the insurance proceeds to continue alimony payments after his death.

Dorothy can also buy a policy on Bob's life, either before or after the divorce. (Even afterward she has what is legally called an "insurable interest" in Bob's life; she will suffer financially from his death.) She can buy a policy and pay the premiums. Or she can make the purchase and have Bob, under the divorce agreement, responsible for making the premium payments. Whichever course they choose, life insurance can ensure that their youngster can finish college and that Dorothy will have an adequate income.

PRERETIREMENT

Tom A. is 53 years old and plans to retire in 12 years. His wife, Jeannette, is 47; after staying at home while the children were young she returned to school for a master's degree in social work. Today she works three days a week on the child guidance team in a nearby school district and sees private patients at home on the other days. Tom has been carrying $100,000 of individual life insurance on his own life (in addition to the $50,000 of group life provided by his employer), faithfully paying the premiums as they come due for 28 years. Jeanette has $20,000 of group life insurance through the school where she works.

Tom has been told that life insurance can be designed to provide retirement income. It can, but just as the Taylors found in examining their need for college funds, Tom and Jeanette find that a short-term life insurance policy is not necessarily the best approach to retirement income. In fact, with no dependents and with adequate income-producing assets, Tom and Jeanette should reconsider their need for life insurance. Why should Tom continue to pay premiums for $100,000 of individual coverage? He'll have his group coverage while he works and, since his employer is progressive when it comes to employee benefits, will continue half of his group coverage, or $25,000, when he retires. Why spend other dollars on life insurance at this stage of life, dollars that could profitably be invested elsewhere?

Young families with dependent children need life insurance. Older people often do not. Yet just as many people buy life insurance and let it lapse when they shouldn't, other people buy life insurance to meet specific needs and then proceed to pay premiums forever, without a second thought, when the need no longer exists. There are other options:

■ Tom might cancel his policy, take the cash value, and invest it in short-term bonds. Or he might use the cash value to purchase an annuity, from the same or a different company, to provide monthly income during the retirement years. Such a purchase may or may not be wise, depending on the state of the economy. (More information on annuities will be found in Chapter 23.)

■ Tom might keep the policy in force but convert it to a paid-up policy, reducing the amount of insurance in force but also eliminating the need for further premium payments. With this choice the built-up cash value remains intact and Tom retains the option of borrowing against it, still keeping the policy in force, or, at a later date, surrendering the policy.

THE BUSINESS OWNER

Peter M., widowed some years ago, owns and runs a small carpet-cleaning business. His children are grown and self-supporting. He continues to carry life insurance, primarily to pay estate taxes due when he dies. Does he need this life insurance? Not anymore. His business and personal assets, together, are worth less than the $600,000 that can pass free of federal estate taxes. (See Chapter 21 for a full discussion of estate taxes.) His children won't have to sell the business to pay the taxes due; they may sell it, if they choose to do so, or they may carry on. Estate taxes will probably not be a factor in their decision.

But there is another factor in Peter's insurance calculation. His mother is 87 and widowed. She's managing now with the money her husband left and occasional help from her children. But what if she outlives Peter? What if she outlives her inheritance *and* Peter? He may want to continue some life insurance coverage in order to protect her. Since term insurance is prohibitively expensive for a man in his sixties, if it can be obtained at all, Peter's best bet is to continue paying premiums on one of the whole life policies he originally bought with estate taxes in mind.

YOU AND YOUR LIFE INSURANCE

As you calculate your life insurance needs, keep three things in mind:

■ If inflation resumes at the high levels of recent years, your calculations may be quickly out of date. The amount you may now determine as adequate to provide college for your children may well not be adequate five or ten years from now. The same holds true as you project needed retirement income for your spouse. Try to include an inflation factor in your calculations, based on the number of years ahead and on whether you think the cost of living will outstrip investment income. (But don't forget that your income will probably go up as well.)

■ Your life insurance needs will change as your family grows and their needs change. You'll probably need considerably less life insurance, as an example, once your children are finished with school and are on their own. You may need more if an elderly parent becomes financially dependent on you.

■ Your life insurance needs also change as your assets change. Life insurance provides an "instant estate." That estate, the amount of money you'll leave to your family, should gradually be supplanted by an estate built up through growing net worth. Life insurance, in other words, should be part of your total financial plan. <u>Your goal should be to build your income-producing assets to the point where you no longer need life insurance.</u>

Policy Riders

A number of additional provisions may be built into insurance coverage, many at nominal cost. Some are worthwhile; some are less so.

Waiver of Premium

These provisions are built into some policies, are available as separate riders on others. With some variation (all insurance provisions vary from company to company and from policy to policy), the waiver of premium provides that your policy will be kept in force by the company, with no further premiums necessary, if you become totally disabled before a specified age. In general this provision is <u>worth having. But,</u> before you buy, find out:

■ What is the age cutoff?
■ How long is the waiting period before the rider takes effect?

Q My husband purchased a $5,000 insurance policy in 1956 and has been paying the premiums for 37 years. Dividends are applied to purchase additional paid-up life insurance. He's 59 now and we would like to know: Should we continue to pay on this policy? If so, for how long?

A The only reason to continue paying is if you want to keep the policy in force to provide the $5,000 to your husband's beneficiary. Otherwise (especially since most of that $5,000 is now made up of your own accumulated cash value), I would suggest that the policy be either cashed in or converted to a paid-up policy with no further premiums due. Ask your agent or the company for the necessary forms.

■ How does the company define total disability?

■ Does the waiver then continue for life? until recovery? for a specified number of years?

■ How much does the rider add to the cost of the policy?

Disability Income

This can be purchased as a rider on your life insurance policy. It provides payment of a monthly income (often stated as a percentage of the face amount of the policy) while you are totally disabled, after an initial waiting period. Before you buy this rider, ask the same questions you would ask about the waiver of premium provision: How does the company define total disability? How long is the waiting period? How long does the income continue? And compare costs. You probably will want some disability income protection. But in most instances you'll be better off with a separate income replacement policy. (See pp. 552-558 for a full discussion of disability coverage.)

Accidental Death Benefits

So-called "double indemnity" pays double or even triple benefits if you die by accident rather than by illness. Some specify multiple benefits only for death in an airplane, train, or bus.

Should you look for double indemnity? No. Such riders make very little sense, unless you have some reason to think that your family will need far more money to live on after you die in an accident than after you die in bed. Spend your insurance dollars on increasing your total coverage. (But if you already have this coverage, be sure your family knows about it. And don't bother buying special trip insurance when you travel.)

Note: If you pay for tickets via a charge or credit card, you may also have automatic trip insurance; be sure your family knows about this too.

Guaranteed Insurability

As its name implies, this provision guarantees the right to buy additional insurance, without regard to the state of your health, up to a specified age. Such riders are most often available on whole life policies, and provide for the purchase of more whole life insurance. They seldom, if ever, apply on term insurance.

Questions to ask:

■ Up to what age may you buy additional insurance?

■ At what intervals may the purchases be made?

■ What are the minimum and maximum amounts you may purchase?

■ What is the cost of coverage?

Other Considerations

Perhaps the biggest cost differential in life insurance is the difference between permanent insurance and term insurance. You will have to decide, at the outset, which type of policy or combination of policies best suits your needs. But there are other considerations as well:

INSURABILITY

Because the cost of life insurance is based in part on mortality, insurance companies need to know the state of your health before they issue a policy. You will be asked to fill out an application, including basic information about the state of your health. Answer the questions accurately; misinformation, if it comes to light, could invalidate your coverage. (In a recent instance, a beneficiary failed to collect because the insurance company learned that the policyholder was a smoker when he claimed he was not—even though the cause of death had nothing to do with smoking.)

In many instances—with group life insurance and with relatively small individual life insurance policies—this application form may be all that's necessary. If the application form triggers some concern at the company or if you are applying for a large amount of coverage, however, you may have to have a medical examination.

If you are found to be a higher-than-average risk, you can probably still buy life insurance, but it may cost you more. Since different companies have different underwriting standards, it is entirely possible that one company would charge you a standard rate even while another charges you more. This is another good reason for using an agent; in fact, if you know you have a health problem, it might be wise to use an agent specializing in high-risk cases. An extra premium, in any case, does not have to last forever. If your health improves, or if you have been without evidence of disease for a period of time, talk to the company; it's entirely possible that the "rating" would be eliminated or reduced (it can't be raised, so you needn't fear additional cost).

If, on the other hand, you take good care of yourself, you may be entitled to lower-than-usual rates. Most companies, for instance, offer lower premiums to nonsmokers.

Extra premiums are sometimes charged for certain occupations deemed to be risky: acrobats and astronauts, lion tamers and sandhogs, mountain-climbing guides and miners, all may be asked to pay additional premiums for life insurance coverage. But the days are past when certain occupations would exclude you from life insurance; today virtually everyone in any line of work—even astronauts—can find a company willing to write insurance.

PARTICIPATING AND NONPARTICIPATING POLICIES

Some policies pay dividends; they are called "participating" policies. Others do not; they are called "nonparticipating." Here are the differences:

Participating

The participating (or "par") policy generally has a higher premium; if the investment experience of the insurance company is good, portions of the premium are returned to policyholders in the form of dividends. Because those dividends are a return of excess premium, they are not treated as taxable income by the IRS. But interest on dividends, if you leave the dividends with the company to accumulate, is something else; it must be reported on your federal income tax form.

The holders of participating policies have some options when it comes to dividends: They may take them in cash, use them to reduce premium payments, or leave them with the insurance company to accumulate interest (that interest, as noted, is taxable). All of these options apply to dividends on both permanent and term insurance. Holders of permanent insurance have an additional choice: They may use the dividends to buy additional paid-up insurance (or, with some companies, may use the dividends to purchase one-year renewable term insurance). Buying additional paid-up whole life insurance is a good way to combat inflation by building up the value of your policy. Whichever option you choose, you may change your mind at a later date (although if you choose to buy additional insurance you may then find yourself having to pass an insurability test).

Note: Dividends on participating policies, because they depend on investment performance, are never guaranteed. The insurance company will

If an agent offers you a "vanishing premium" policy, a whole life or universal or variable policy under which dividends are expected to pay the premiums after a number of years, be sure both you and the agent understand the illustration. Ask what happens under varying interest rate scenarios. If rates drop, will you have to pay premiums for a longer period? lose the policy? start paying premiums again after stopping? The problem here is that policy illustrations showing just when premiums will disappear are only estimates based on certain assumptions that may or may not hold; policyholders who rely on implicit "guarantees" in these illustrations may be sorely disappointed. Many people who bought these policies in the high-interest rate days of the mid-1980s, confident that they would stop paying premiums within five to seven years, are now finding that they must continue paying sizable premiums for at least several more years.

Note: "Vanishing premium" is not the same as "paid-up" insurance; the latter guarantees continuation of coverage regardless of interest rates or other policy assumptions.

show you a projection of dividends. If the economy stagnates or enters a prolonged recession, or if the company's investment managers lose their touch, your dividends may not be forthcoming.

Nonparticipating

"Nonpar" policies do not return a dividend to policyholders. Where the holder of a par policy does not know in advance what insurance costs will actually be, because the price on these policies is the premium less any dividend, the holder of a nonpar policy has traditionally had the advantage of guaranteed costs—along with the disadvantage of not reaping the benefit of favorable investment returns.

In a variation of the nonpar policy, designed to give issuing companies a competitive edge (after companies were criticized for failing to pass on higher earnings and reduced mortality experience to their customers), some policies are now written with a **variable premium** (not to be confused with variable life, where the premium is fixed but the investment return may vary; see p. 496). In most such policies, the initial premium is lower than it might otherwise be; this low initial premium may be guaranteed for a base period, such as two years. If the investment outlook then changes, the premium may then be raised or lowered. Limits on such policies (how often the premium may be changed, and to what extent) vary from company to company.

COMPARING COSTS VIA THE INTEREST-ADJUSTED METHOD

Perhaps the most complicated question facing any potential purchaser of life insurance is the question of price comparison. Given the differences among insurance companies and among insurance policies, how can a rational comparison be made? You can't simply look at the premium you're asked to pay. You have to be sure, first of all, that all policy provisions are the same. For example, is waiver of premium in the event of disability built in to each policy you're considering? Or will you pay for it separately?

Assuming that two policies are identical in their provisions, you can compare their costs over a period of years by looking at:

- The sum of the premiums you'll pay over the years (a figure affected by how long you live and by how long you keep the policy in force)
- Any dividends you may receive (a figure which will vary with the company's investment experience)
- What cash value is available (a sum affected by the varying rates at which cash values build up in different policies)

Then, in order to make a valid comparison, you would also have to consider an interest factor based on the "time value" of money—the interest you could earn on your money if you did not use it for this particular purchase.

All of these factors are analyzed for you, and distilled to an index number, in the interest-adjusted costs now routinely prepared by life insurance

companies. Ask your company or agent to show you the "20-year interest-
adjusted surrender-cost index" for the particular policy you are thinking of
buying. Although the index is based on some complicated mathematics, you
won't need any mathematical skill to interpret it. Just remember: The lower
the index number, the lower the overall cost.

NET COST INDEX

How to Buy Insurance

While your first order of business should be to determine how much life
insurance you need and the form that insurance should take, you'll also have to
decide how to buy it.

CHOOSING A COMPANY

Many people buy life insurance from whichever company a friendly or
persistent agent happens to represent. But there are great differences among
insurance companies, and you'll be a wise consumer if you select your company rather than let it select you.

You'll want to consider:

■ A company with a top rating from at least two of the four rating agencies: A.M. Best, Duff & Phelps, Standard & Poor's, and Moody's.
Their reports can be found in most well-stocked public libraries.

Note: You can secure A.M. Best ratings, for a fee, by calling (900)420-
0400 on a touch-tone telephone; before you call, have the A.M. Best or
National Association of Insurance Commissioners identification number

Q Last year I borrowed about $1,900 from my six-year-old
$25,000 whole life insurance policy. Now I'd like to drop the
policy and buy term life insurance instead. If I do, do I still have to
repay the loan?

A Not in cash. But the outstanding loan and any interest due on the
loan will be deducted when you surrender the policy and you will
get very little back. Think twice before dropping an existing whole life
policy. While term insurance is often a better buy for people under age
55, you'll lose most of the money you've already paid in premiums.
Also—very important—be sure you're still insurable. It's a good idea,
in fact, to have a new policy in force before dropping an old one.

(which the agent or company can give you) for the company you wish to check.

■ Whether or not the company is licensed to do business in your state. You might also consider, no matter where you live, companies licensed by New York State. New York's high regulatory standards are a definite plus for any company which meets them.

■ The reputation of the company for service. Ask around among friends, read the most recent survey in *Consumer Reports,* and check with your state insurance department. Are claims settled promptly? Are employees courteous and responsive? Can you get through to the company when necessary?

If you buy your insurance through a life insurance agent, you may have less direct contact with the company. But payments, and decisions about payments, come from the company. Pick a company that will, as far as you can tell, remain solvent. Pick one licensed in your state so that a complaint, if one is necessary, can be filed with your state insurance department. Pick a company with a reputation for good service.

USING AN AGENT

Most life insurance policies are bought from insurance agents ... largely, as the industry puts it, because life insurance is sold rather than bought. While most of us recognize the value of life insurance, in other words, very few of us go out to buy it; we wait until a life insurance agent persuades us to buy. We

Q We carefully picked a well-rated life insurance company, only to find out after a few years that the company sold our policy to another company. They didn't even give us any advance notice. What do we do now?

A First, check the rating of the new company. If it's good, stay put. If it's not, and if you are in good health, consider transferring your coverage to another insurer. In some states (and under a proposed regulation of the National Association of Insurance Commissioners) consumers have a right to be notified of policy transfers and to refuse them. Meanwhile, policy transfers (technically called assumption reinsurance) are becoming more common. You can protect yourself by always reading mail from your insurance company, and calling both the company and your state insurance department with any questions you may have.

also wait for the agent to tell us how much insurance we need and what kind of policy it should be.

Agents, good agents, serve a purpose. They can be enormously useful in helping you to analyze your life insurance needs. But you should realize that the income of a life insurance agent is based on commissions. Some types of policies, notably the permanent variety, pay substantially higher commissions than other types. Take the advice you get, therefore, but weigh it against your own best interests as you understand them. Before you consult an agent, think through the kind of protection your family needs and think through the dollars that you can afford to spend on this protection. Then consult an agent to help you work out the best program within your own individually selected guidelines. Better yet, consult three agents and compare their recommendations.

How to Select an Agent

What should you look for in an agent? What should you expect the agent to do for you?

- Pick an agent as you would pick your attorney or your accountant: through recommendations from trusted friends, business associates, and other professional advisers, and through an examination of his or her credentials. What kind of training has the agent had? How much experience? Does the agent look at insurance as part of your total financial plan? Is he or she willing to meet with your attorney or tax adviser? Does the agent keep up, through ongoing training, with developments in insurance and in related areas such as tax legisla-

Q I know how much life insurance I want to buy, and I know what kind of policy I want. If I don't want to interview agents and compare their proposals, is there some way to get comparative information on my own?

A Yes. There are several insurance quote services, most focusing on term life insurance policies. Some of the services are free, making their profits by selling insurance. For example, SelectQuote (800-343-1985) provides information on term life insurance policies offered by the companies it represents. InsuranceQuote (800-972-1104), LifeQuote (800-776-7873), and TermQuote (800-444-8376) are similar. Others do not sell insurance, but charge a modest fee for screening policies and making recommendations. Insurance Information, Inc. (800-472-5800), for example, charges $50. A newer service, QuoteSmith (800-556-9393), charges $15.

tion? Has he or she met the stringent requirements to become a Chartered Life Underwriter (CLU)? Many competent agents are not CLUs (and not every CLU would be the best agent for you), but the designation is a useful one.

■ Pick an agent whose personal style you like and trust. Pick one who will spend time with you analyzing your insurance needs and objectively suggesting varying approaches to meet those needs, one who will be clear about both cost and coverage. There is no one answer, no one single ideal policy; be wary of an agent who suggests that there is.

■ Pick an agent who will provide the ongoing service you need, not one who will sell you a policy and disappear. The agent should keep you informed of new developments and should keep informed of your situation; he or she should review your life insurance needs every few years in terms of your changing family or finances.

BUYING DIRECT

Life insurance need not be bought through an agent. It can be bought directly from some insurers, through associations or, in a handful of states, over the counter in savings banks. It can also be bought, often with much lower commissions, through fee-based financial planners (of course, you then have to pay the planner).

Directly from insurers: Some superior companies, such as USAA Life, Ameritas, and AMICA Mutual, sell directly rather than through agents. With no agent force to support through sales commissions, policies may be less expensive. Then again, they may not. Always compare policies and costs before a purchase is made.

Association coverage: Group insurance by mail, offered to you because you belong to an association or carry a certain credit card, has several drawbacks:

■ The amount may be limited, and may not be as much as you may need.

■ Premium rates are not guaranteed.

■ Choices are limited; these policies are generally term insurance, with no cash value buildups or loan provisions.

■ You lose the insurance if you leave the group.

Association coverage may be less expensive because of the economies of scale afforded by the group. But it is often more expensive than comparable insurance purchased elsewhere because cost savings may be passed on to the association rather than to policyholders.

Association coverage also has an advantage if you're in poor health: You can't be turned down. You can generally secure insurance simply by being a member of the group, with no questions asked and no medical examination.

Use group insurance, therefore, as a supplement to your life insurance program but not as your total program. And compare costs carefully before you decide to buy.

From a savings bank: Savings Bank Life Insurance, available in New York, Massachusetts, and Connecticut, may be either permanent or term. It is sold in limited amounts as individual coverage, although much more coverage is available through so-called "group" coverage sold by some banks. Savings bank life insurance is often, although not always, less expensive than comparable coverage.

Through a financial planner: Most whole life insurance is sold with hefty commissions; as much as all of the first year's premium (sometimes even more) may be paid to the agent who sells you the policy, leaving you with little or no cash value in the early years. This commission structure may be okay if you understand what's happening, if the agent is truly helpful AND if you'll keep the policy for at least 20 years. But after 20 years, according to the Life Insurance Marketing and Research Association (LIMRA), only 25 percent of policyholders still have whole life policies in force. So there is a move, albeit a small one, toward selling whole life insurance on a "no-load" or "low-load" basis, much as some mutual funds are sold direct. If you're interested in such a policy, though, you'll probably have to pay a fee to a financial planner or certified public accountant to find it for you. This could be cost-effective in the long run, if the policy meets your needs and is favorably priced.

Note: To find a fee-based planner offering no-load insurance policies, call the Life Insurance Advisers Association (800-521-4578) or Fee For Service (800-874-5662).

Q A life insurance offer that came in the mail promises that I can't be turned down for insurance, regardless of my health, as long as I return the application by the specified date. Is this really so?

A Yes, you can hold the company to its promise. Group life insurance policies, the kind offered by mail to members of associations or other affinity groups, do not usually require proof of insurability; although they may be expensive, they may fill a need if you are in poor health and otherwise uninsurable. Both state insurance commissions and the Direct Marketing Insurance Council, moreover, say that promises made in writing in any insurance advertisement or mail offering are legally binding and must be honored. Should a promise not be kept, notify your state insurance department.

SHOULD YOU SWAP AN OLD POLICY FOR A NEW?

As interest rates rose through the late 1970s, insurance companies earned more on their investments. The result: lower premiums on new policies. The holders of older policies, unless those policies were the participating variety that returned excess premiums in dividends, were often left holding an excessively expensive policy.

This development led consumer advocates to rethink the formerly firm advice never to switch one insurance policy for another. Today, under some circumstances, you might be wise to cancel an old policy (especially an old nonparticipating permanent life policy with a poor rate of return) and buy a new one. Such a move might save you considerable sums.

Before you say yes to the next life insurance agent urging such a swap, however, do a very careful comparison of both policy features and interest-adjusted costs. Get out your old policy and read it over, then write to the company for a detailed cost breakout: premiums, cash surrender value, death benefits, plus the index figure for this policy. Get the same information on the new policy you are thinking about buying. Then ask the agent who sold you the old policy to tell you why you should keep it in force. Weigh the arguments on both sides carefully, bearing in mind:

- The biggest commission and administrative costs come out of your premium in the first year. This means two things: The agent may want to sell you a new policy because he gets a nice big commission, and your cash values build up very slowly at first, much faster later on. If you cancel a permanent contract before it is ten years old, you may be forfeiting much of its potential cash value.
- Every life insurance policy has a two-year "incontestability" clause; during these first two years the insurer may cancel the contract if it turns out that you made any untrue statements on your application. During these same two years, as a rule, no benefits will be paid in case of suicide. If you take out a new policy, you'll face a new two-year period of possible challenge.
- If you decide to swap policies after weighing all the arguments pro and con, be sure you've passed the medical exam and that your new policy is firmly in force before you cancel your old one. You could otherwise find yourself sadly uninsured.

Or, instead of swapping, think about (1) keeping the old policy in force and buying additional coverage at new lower rates, or (2) borrowing against the cash value of the old policy and using the proceeds to buy term insurance at favorable rates. If you're underinsured, as a great many people are, either approach might be better than an outright swap.

WHEN SHOULD YOU DROP LIFE INSURANCE COVERAGE?

The easy answer is, when you don't need it any more. If you bought a term insurance policy to provide college funds for your children, and your children have now finished college, you may just want to let the policy lapse. If you own a whole life policy, however, the answer is a bit more complicated. You may no longer need the death benefit but if the policy offers a competitive rate of return, it may be worth keeping.

How can you tell? Peter Katt, a fee-only insurance adviser, suggests dividing the next year's projected cash value by the current-year cash value plus the next premium. Ask your insurance company for what it calls an "in-force illustration" based on current dividends and you'll have the numbers to work with. Katt provides this example, in an article in *AAII Journal:* If the current-year cash value is $71,960 and the next scheduled premium is $1,822, the total of $73,782 is divided into the next year's projected cash value of $80,036. The yield is 8.5 percent, which may make this particular policy worth keeping. Remember that the cash value grows on a tax-deferred basis, and that it can be tapped if you need to put your hands on some money.

Note: Don't buy life insurance, file it, and forget it. As you review your life insurance periodically to make sure it still meets your family's needs, you should also review it to make sure it is paying a competitive return.

KEEPING PREMIUMS DOWN

The most obvious way to keep premiums down is to shop around among insurance companies before you buy. This is also the most significant, since some policies cost twice as much as others (or thousands and thousands of dollars over a lifetime) for essentially the same coverage. You can also save some money, although not as much, by:

■ Paying premiums annually if at all possible. More frequent payments add up to higher premiums. (One study indicated actual interest rates on monthly premiums ranging from 4.9 percent to 29.3 percent—although automatic deduction from your checking account, the way in which monthly premiums are most often collected these days, does not cost as much.

Q I'm making a college loan to my nephew for the spring semester, and while I expect him to pay it back, I would like payment guaranteed if anything happens to him. What would you think about his taking out a life insurance policy and naming me as beneficiary?

A It's a good idea. Better yet, so that he can't change the beneficiary without your consent, have him designate you as the beneficiary irrevocably. You may also want to make arrangements so that you'll be notified by the insurance company if the premiums aren't paid.

■ Buying as much as possible at one time—within, of course, the boundaries of your budget and your insurance needs. Larger policies often sell for less-per-thousand than smaller ones.

Your Beneficiary

You will be asked to name a beneficiary for your life insurance, the person or persons you wish to receive the policy proceeds when they become payable. It's also wise to name a contingent beneficiary, in case you outlive the first beneficiary. Make a specific election here, rather than simply having the proceeds payable to your estate; if you do the latter, the insurance money will have to go through the probate process along with the rest of your estate, delaying its receipt by your family.

Keep your beneficiary informed about the kind of insurance policy you have (a great many beneficiaries never collect because they simply never knew the policy existed) and where you keep the policy (preferably not in a safe deposit box, which in many states will be temporarily sealed at your death). Be sure your beneficiary knows the name of your insurance company and agent. Keep the company informed as to the whereabouts of your beneficiary.

You have the right to change your beneficiary (via a form obtainable from the insurance company) and should remember to do so if your circumstances change. You may, for example, name a child as a contingent beneficiary (after your spouse), and forget to add her later-born brother. But if you've looked ahead to the eventuality of having more children, you could have named "children of the insured, John Smith." If you've done this, no further change will be necessary. But be careful: "Children of the insured, John Smith" might mean that your wife's daughter by a previous marriage, whom you meant to include, is in fact excluded. If you make it "children born of the marriage of John and Ann Smith" you may be excluding adopted children. Think it through carefully.

And think through the unlikely possibility that one or more of your children may predecease you. You can anticipate this possibility by phrasing the beneficiary provision so that any children of such a child (your grandchildren) will share in the proceeds with your other children. This can be done either **per capita,** by equal shares, or **per stirpes,** along family lines. If you have two children and one of them predeceases you, leaving two children, a per capita distribution of your insurance would give one-third each to your surviving child and the two children of your other child; a per stirpes distribution would give one-half to your child (the same half he or she would have received had your other child survived) and divide the other half (their parent's share) between the two grandchildren.

It's very important to anticipate as many situations as possible and to review your beneficiary provisions regularly. You probably won't want proceeds to go to an ex-spouse (unless, of course, such a distribution is part of the divorce agreement), but it can happen. It can happen if you (1) have your beneficiary designation simply read "wife/husband of the insured" without a specific name, or if (2) you forget to make a beneficiary change when it's appropriate to do so.

SETTLEMENT OPTIONS

Your beneficiary doesn't have to take the proceeds of your policy as a lump sum. There are other choices, to be elected either by you or by your beneficiary when the time comes.

Interest income options allow the company to hold the proceeds and pay out interest on the proceeds, either for a specified period or for the beneficiary's lifetime. The interest paid will be based on a rate stated in the policy. Under some policies, portions of the principal may be withdrawn along with the interest.

Income for specified period or income of specified amounts may be elected to provide payouts of both principal and interest on a predetermined schedule and at a predetermined rate.

Life income provisions guarantee income for the life of the beneficiary, with the amounts based on the age and sex of the beneficiary at the time of the policyholder's death. If the beneficiary lives longer than mortality tables would indicate, the principal plus interest will be collected. If the beneficiary dies early, however, a substantial portion of the principal may be forfeited, unless the election has included a guarantee of a specified number of payments.

You may be urged to select one of these options, on the grounds that you can best determine the eventual use of your insurance proceeds. Before you do, however, bear in mind:

Q I just found out that the beneficiary listed on my husband's life insurance policy is his mother. My husband says he did this in case we should both die in an accident and that his mother knows the money is mine. I say it leaves me with nothing. Shouldn't my name be on the policy?

A If your husband wants you to receive the money, then your name should be on the policy as the beneficiary. If he is worried about what might happen if you were to die in a common accident, he can name his mother as contingent or secondary beneficiary.

- ■ Your election of a settlement option constitutes a binding contract between you and the insurance company. Your beneficiary will not be able to change your election, no matter what may happen in the future.
- ■ Your beneficiary may do much better financially if he or she can take the lump-sum proceeds, use what is necessary for immediate need, and invest the rest for maximum return. Some insurance company interest rates are notoriously low.
- ■ Your beneficiary will almost certainly do better psychologically by having control of that money. Either leave the decision to be made by your beneficiary, therefore, to suit his or her needs at the time, or elect a lump sum payment, which will accomplish the same purpose.

WHO SHOULD OWN YOUR POLICY?

Life insurance proceeds are not subject to income tax. But they are included in your total estate for the purposes of establishing the amount of estate tax which may be due. They can be excluded from your list of owned assets if you do not in fact own the policies. For many years, therefore, financial advisers have been suggesting that people with sizeable estates have their life insurance owned by a spouse (or, in some situations, by a trust set up for the purpose).

Transfer of ownership to a spouse may be worth considering, provided that the marriage is expected to last. A transfer is irrevocable. An owner has full rights to the policy: to borrow against the cash value, name the benefi-

---

Q Among my father's papers after his death we found a note with the number of a life insurance policy. We never found the policy and don't know the name of the company. Is there any way to find out who wrote this policy?

A A first step would be to look through your father's canceled checks and receipts; you may find a record of payment to the insurance company. You might also call the personnel department of the company where your father last worked, in case it was a group policy. And, if these steps are unproductive, send a self-addressed stamped envelope to the American Council of Life Insurance, Lost Policy Department, 1001 Pennsylvania Ave., N.W., Washington, DC 20004. ACLI will circulate the information among 100 or so companies; if one of them was your father's insurance carrier, it will be in touch. But be patient; the process takes several weeks.

ciary, elect settlement options, even cancel the policy altogether. (If you transfer ownership but retain any of these rights, the IRS will conclude that the transfer is simply a tax dodge.) Transfer of an existing policy, moreover, may have tax consequences of its own; gift taxes (equivalent in amount to estate taxes) may be due on the value of the policy at the time the policy is transferred. A brand-new whole life policy, or a term policy of any age, has no cash value and hence no tax consequences. But giving up such a policy still means giving up control of an asset; this is not a step to be taken lightly.

Transferring ownership may no longer be necessary, in any case, unless your total estate exceeds the $600,000 that can pass free of federal estate tax under current law. (States have their own death taxes. Many exempt all or part of life insurance proceeds.) It may not be necessary if you're leaving all the proceeds to your spouse, under the unlimited marital exemption that permits any amount to pass to a surviving spouse tax-free. Review your own total estate carefully (see Chapter 21, on estate planning), and get expert advice to minimize any tax consequences, before you decide that someone else should own your life insurance.

KEY POINTS

■ Life insurance serves different purposes at different times. But its most important function is to protect those who depend on you from financial hardship resulting from your death. Take care of income replacement as you plan your insurance program, before you do anything else.

■ Determine how much you need and how much you can spend before you think about what kind of life insurance to buy. Compare costs and policy provisions before you make a decision, and buy as much protection for your family as you can afford.

■ Review your coverage regularly, at least every five years and more often if there is a change in either your family constellation or your financial circumstances. You may find that you need a different amount or type of life insurance to reflect a new marriage, additional children, changes in income, a move to a new house, or a different job. You may need more insurance at some periods, less at others. Your life isn't static. Your life insurance program should not be static either.

CHAPTER 19

Health Insurance

We've all heard the horror stories:

- The professional baseball player whose daughter was left a quadriplegic by an automobile accident—two months after she turned 20 and was no longer covered by the family's health insurance
- The 34-year-old fitness instructor who feels locked into her job for life because, after a prior bout with breast cancer, she is uninsurable and doesn't dare switch jobs
- The single mother of two, healthy herself, who can't get family coverage because her little girl has only one kidney

The costs of health care keep going up, partly because of technological advances and partly because we're living so much longer. But the system of health care coverage we've had to date has fallen woefully short. Far too many people are uninsured. Far too many fall between the cracks.

As I write this, in June 1993, we appear to be on the verge of a major reform in our system of paying for health care. But the details are not yet in place and, even when they are, a new system will probably take several years to phase in. So, right now, you need to know what health care reform may accomplish; you also need to know how to protect your family during the inevitable transition period.

The average family of four spent $3,708 for health care in 1980 ... and $11,268 in 1991, a figure that includes both health insurance premiums and out-of-pocket expenses. Exactly how much you spend may depend in part on where you live (see Table 19.1) and in part on whether your employer pays all or a portion of your health insurance premiums or whether those premiums come solely out of your own pocket. Your age is also a factor. Younger people generally spend less; older people, even with Medicare, often spend considerably more. You have different health concerns, and different expectations of health care's place in your budget, at different life stages. But wherever you are in the life cycle, however much or little you may earn, whatever the number of your dependents, health insurance deserves a prominent place in your financial planning.

Table 19.1: Regional Variations in Costs

Health care costs vary considerably from place to place. As an example, here are typical charges for selected surgical procedures in 1992:

Procedure	New York City	Philadelphia	Atlanta
Caesarean section	$4,984	$2,247	$2,360
Coronary bypass (triple)	8,312	6,273	5,031
Appendectomy	1,934	1,026	964
Hysterectomy	5,123	2,484	2,202
Vasectomy	717	473	404

Chicago	Denver	Dallas	Los Angeles
$2,463	$2,102	$1,973	$2,521
5,983	4,792	5,802	7,006
1,216	909	1,009	1,377
2,647	1,746	1,996	2,830
460	356	375	502

Source: Health Insurance Association of America.

What are your current concerns?

■ As a young single leaving your parents' nest, you need first-time coverage of your own. Will you have it through your employer? If you do, will it be enough?

■ As a two-income couple, your primary concern may be supplementing rather than duplicating each other's on-the-job group coverage. Do you have a choice about which fringe benefits to accept?

■ A family has wide-ranging concerns, from paying the initial costs of childbearing to replacing a disabled breadwinner's earnings. Can you find adequate protection in one package? Or do you need several different policies?

■ Divorced and widowed women, suddenly on their own after years of coverage under a husband's group health insurance, have special needs. Should you try to continue coverage under the group plan in which your spouse was enrolled? Where can you find individual health insurance at a price you can afford?

■ Retirees need to supplement Medicare. And early retirees face the difficult task of filling the gap between employee benefits and the Medicare starting date. If you've thought of retiring early, have you also thought about the difficulties of finding health insurance at age 55 or 60 or 62?

Proposals for Reform

Many of these questions may be answered, once the system is reformed. Pending congressional tinkering with the Clinton proposals, it looks as if we can expect a system of "managed competition." This new bit of jargon refers to a system combining government controls (to keep prices down) with market forces (competition among health care providers). Instead of a system of national health service, such as the one that appears to be working well in Canada, the administration's proposal envisions "health purchasing alliances" (or cooperatives) able to lower prices through bargaining power; these alliances could consist of large employers with their own group insurance plans or, for those not working for a large employer or not working at all, state-organized groups. Health care providers, similarly, would be organized into networks similar to health maintenance organizations (HMOs; see p. 541).

There will probably be a basic package of benefits for all Americans, with some optional extras for people willing (and able) to pay more. Insurance companies will probably be required to cover everyone without regard to age or preexisting conditions. Individuals will be required to buy insurance, so that young and healthy individuals who may currently skip the cost of health insurance (not a brilliant idea anyway, since you never know when you may be hit by a car) will have to budget for health insurance premiums.

There is even a possibility, although this one stirs up a political firestorm, that Medicare, workers' compensation, and health benefits currently paid under automobile insurance policies will all be combined in the new national system. If they are not included, the goal of reducing the national cost of health care won't be met. If the Clinton administration tries to include them, the whole package may run into solid opposition. This one is still up for grabs.

Also still up in the air, at this writing: who pays the tab. Current thinking includes a payroll tax on employers along with an employee-paid tax on some portion of employer-paid health insurance premiums. The federal government may also pay a share of the cost, possibly through increased "sin" taxes on things like alcohol and cigarettes. A trial balloon for a national sales (value added) tax seems, at least temporarily, deflated.

Without waiting for Washington, several states have already enacted similar legislation (and, it appears, the states may have wide latitude even under a new national system). Both Washington State and Florida, for example, are phasing in purchasing cooperatives to pool the resources of thousands of people to buy health services from certified plans. Hawaii, Vermont, and Oregon have legislation designed to insure health coverage for all. Maryland has approved cost controls on physicians' fees. New York State no longer allows insurers to charge higher premiums for people with preexisting conditions; as a result several insurers no longer offer health insurance in New York. Whatever the federal government does, it seems clear that the nation is ready for reform.

Until reform is in place—and, I repeat, it will probably take several years for full implementation—you need to protect your family against the high cost of health care. Health insurance, of course, can't guarantee good health any more than life insurance can ensure that you will keep on living. Both protect you and your family against financial loss. That loss, in the health insurance arena, comes in two parts: the out-of-pocket costs of health care, which (especially for hospitalization) are outdistancing inflation; and (too often overlooked) the costs of income lost when you are ill.

What kind of health insurance do you need?

Types of Health Insurance

Health insurance, unlike automobile or homeowners insurance, comes in a bewildering variety of shapes and sizes, with no standardized forms to ease the confusion. But there are several specific types:

- Basic protection includes hospitalization, surgical, and medical benefits.
- Major medical insurance provides coverage against the financial costs of catastrophic illness. It may be designed to take up where basic protection stops; more often, today, basic protection and major medical are purchased together in a single comprehensive policy.
- Health maintenance organizations (HMOs), while not strictly insurance, can take the place of basic and major medical coverage by providing economical prepaid preventive and treatment services through a network of doctors and hospitals.
- Medicare supplement insurance, often called "Medigap," as its name implies, provides older people with the coverage that Medicare lacks.
- Long-term care policies, relatively new kids on the block, insure against the costs of long-term custodial care.
- Hospital indemnity policies, often sold by mail, provide direct cash benefits when you are hospitalized.

■ "Dread disease" policies pay benefits only for a specific, named condition.

■ Disability income policies provide you with a percentage of your earnings if you are disabled through illness or injury and unable to work.

Here's what you should know about each:

BASIC COVERAGE

Your basic health insurance package pays all or part of the medical and hospital bills associated with short-term illness or injury. It covers hospitalization, surgical procedures, and doctor visits.

Hospitalization includes payment toward room and board and regular nursing care while in the hospital, plus certain hospital services and supplies such as X-rays, laboratory tests, and medication.

Note: Your policy should include payment of hospital room and board charges at the full daily rate (semiprivate) for 60 to 120 days. It's best to have a policy based on service (that is, current charges for a semiprivate room, whatever those charges are), since benefits will then rise along with hospitalization costs. When a policy has fixed "inside limits" restricting the dollar amount of reimbursement, the benefit schedule may be out of date before the ink on your signature is dry.

Surgical procedures, both in and out of the hospital, should also be covered in this basic protection package. Some policies include a schedule of fees which will be paid for various surgical procedures. This schedule should be updated at relatively frequent intervals or it, too, may rapidly become outdated. More and more policies, instead, provide reimbursement of a surgeon's fee up to the "customary and reasonable" charge for the particular procedure. Customary charges vary by region and also by doctor. (Many consumer complaints stem from inadequate reimbursement ... and at least part of what patients consider "inadequate" reimbursement comes from using a surgeon more expensive than most in the area.)

Doctor visits are the third portion of the basic health insurance policy. Reimbursement for diagnostic procedures and laboratory tests may also be covered, but preventive care, including checkups, often is not (under the traditional fee-for-service policy, which makes health maintenance organizations or HMOs more attractive; see p. 541).

At one time a basic health insurance package might have been all you needed. Today, with escalating health care costs (especially hospital room and board costs), this is no longer so. In fact, it's more important for most people to have coverage against catastrophic illness. You can budget for Band-Aids, or for the costs associated with a respiratory illness. You can't really budget for open-heart surgery or the ongoing expenses associated with cancer. (Bypass surgery costs about $30,000 per patient, according to the U.S. Department of Health and Human Services, while treatment for lung cancer costs about $29,000.)

Major Medical

Major medical is the all-important protection that picks up where basic protection stops; alternatively, it may include basic protection under comprehensive coverage. This is the insurance that covers you against the steep and ongoing costs of a major illness or accident. It's the insurance that protects you against financial devastation. If you can afford only one type of health insurance, major medical should be the one.

Major medical and comprehensive coverage do not cover all costs. Both come with deductibles and coinsurance.

Deductibles

Major medical and comprehensive policies come with a deductible, a fixed amount that you must pay before your benefits begin. If you carry basic health insurance in a separate policy, the deductible can be linked to those basic benefits so that you have no exposure at all (beyond designated coinsurance amounts). If you don't carry basic coverage, or if you prefer to save some premium money by having a "corridor" between your basic and your major medical coverage and self-insuring these costs, you can select a larger deductible.

Deductibles on comprehensive policies may start at $100 per family member, or $300 for an entire family group. Deductibles on major medical policies can run from $1,000 to $10,000; the larger the deductible, the lower the cost of your insurance. Look at the deductible amount as the amount you are willing to self-insure, the amount you can manage to pay without bank-

Q My 38-year-old sister lost her health insurance and can't afford the kidney dialysis she needs. She applied for Medicaid but is over the income level. What can you suggest?

A The Medicare program of health insurance for people age 65 and over also covers dialysis patients of any age. To qualify, your sister must be covered as either a worker or a dependent under Social Security or the Railroad Retirement Act, and must have her doctor certify that she needs dialysis on a regular basis due to "end stage renal disease." Her local Social Security office can provide an application form. If she qualifies, Medicare will pick up 80 percent of approved charges (after a $100 annual deductible) starting with the third month after dialysis begins; it will also pay most of her other medical bills. Medicare starts with the first month for patients trained in self-care dialysis.

rupting your family. Taking the largest deductible you can manage will reduce your premiums.

The deductible should, ideally, apply to the entire year rather than to each illness. But watch out for high deductibles on each family member starting in January of each year, even if an illness began the month before. Good policies have a carry-over provision. Good policies also often apply the deductible to a family rather than to an individual. If a family of four or more carries a policy with a $100 per-person deductible, for example, the deductible might be considered fully satisfied for the entire family once three members of the family have each reached $100 in covered bills.

Worksheet 19.1: Major Medical Coverage

In considering a policy, are these medical services covered?

- ■ Inpatient hospital services   _____
- ■ Outpatient surgery   _____
- ■ Physician visits (in the hospital)   _____
- ■ Office visits   _____
- ■ Skilled nursing care   _____
- ■ Medical tests and X-rays   _____
- ■ Prescription drugs   _____
- ■ Psychiatric and mental health care   _____
- ■ Drug and alcohol abuse treatment   _____
- ■ Home health care visits   _____
- ■ Rehabilitation facility care   _____
- ■ Physical therapy   _____
- ■ Hospice care   _____
- ■ Maternity care   _____
- ■ Chiropractic   _____
- ■ Preventive care and checkups   _____
- ■ Well-baby care   _____
- ■ Dental care   _____
- ■ Other   _____

Source: Health Insurance Association of America.

Coinsurance

Major medical also comes with a coinsurance feature, under which you pay a percentage (often 20 percent) of costs and the insurance company pays the remainder. With a 20 percent coinsurance provision, a medical bill of $10,000 in eligible expenses would leave you paying $2,000 (plus the deductible) out of your own pocket.

Good policies also contain a "stop-loss" provision, under which you have to pay the coinsurance amounts only up to a specific amount and no more. If you have a stop-loss clause specifying $1,500 out-of-pocket costs, then the insurer will pay 100 percent of all remaining expenses after that level.

Major medical policies also specify a maximum amount payable, preferably in lifetime terms. More than four-fifths of employer plans have lifetime benefits of $1,000,000 or more. If you're shopping for insurance, look for a limit of at least $1,000,000. The costs of a catastrophic illness can be catastrophic; in one case (and this was a few years ago), 26 days of hospital care for a young woman with a rare blood disease came to $358,942.88. Even the best health insurance leaves the patient responsible for a percentage of the costs; the percentage, in such a case, unless your policy contains a stop-loss clause and a very large lifetime limit, can be devastating.

MEDICARE SUPPLEMENT OR "MEDIGAP" POLICIES

This insurance is specifically designed to fill in the gaps in Medicare coverage. Before you decide whether or not you need such supplementary coverage, however, you have to understand what Medicare does and does not do.

Medicare

Major changes may be in the works if Medicare is folded into the new health care system proposed by the Clinton administration. For now, Medicare comes in two parts: Part A, hospital insurance; and Part B, medical insurance. Both have deductible and coinsurance provisions. Both become available when you reach age 65 if you are retired; if you keep working between ages 65 and 70, your employer's group plan provides primary coverage.

Q My son will graduate from college in June. Can he still be covered under my health insurance policy?

A Maybe. Some policies cover dependent children to age 24; in order to qualify, your son would have to be going on for further schooling and remaining financially dependent on you. If not, his coverage under the family policy may end when he graduates and/or reaches his 19th or 21st birthday. Your policy may have a conversion privilege, however, under which he may obtain individual coverage without a medical exam, if he does so within a specified time. Even if it does not, if your health insurance is through your job and if you work for a company with more than 20 employees, your son may be entitled to continued coverage under your policy for a limited period. This "COBRA" coverage (it's named for the Consolidated Omnibus Budget Reconciliation Act of 1986) could continue for up to three years, but you will have to pay 102 percent of the premium (that's the full premium plus 2 percent for administrative costs).

You are entitled to **Medicare Part A** if you have worked long enough under either the Social Security or Railroad Retirement programs. If you retire at age 65 or over, and you are not eligible under one of these plans, you may buy this hospitalization protection (but only if you also buy Medicare Part B). It pays for a specified number of days of full hospital care for each illness after an initial deductible, and everything over a specified amount per day for a succeeding period. It also has lifetime "reserve" days, which you can draw on when other benefits are used up.

You may buy **Medicare Part B** at age 65 for a monthly premium. After you have reached the deductible amount, Medicare will pay 80 percent of doctor bills incurred in connection with illness or injury; routine checkups are not covered. The 20 percent that you must pay, moreover, is based on what Medicare designates as "reasonable fees." If you use a "nonparticipating" doctor, one who does not agree to accept Medicare fees, you may wind up paying considerably more than just 20 percent.

Medicare currently covers only 35 to 45 percent of your health care costs. Some expensive items are excluded: private duty nursing, custodial nursing home care costs, out-of-hospital drugs, dental care, routine immunizations, foot care, eye examinations and eyeglasses, hearing aids, etc. That's why many older people feel the need for additional supplementary health insurance.

Medicare Supplement Insurance

Because Medicare has sizable deductibles, coinsurance, and exclusions, many retirees supplement Medicare by buying additional insurance. Medicare supplements, often called MedSup or Medigap policies, are specifically designed for this purpose. (Long-term care policies and hospital indemnity

Q My uncle is in his late seventies, but he insists he's not eligible for Medicare. Isn't everyone covered?

A Most people over age 65 who have paid into the Social Security system or who have had a spouse covered under Social Security are eligible for Medicare. But there *are* some exceptions. For example: If your uncle retired from a civil service job before those jobs were included under Medicare, he might not be automatically covered. Even so, he can sign up for Medicare Part B, medical coverage, by paying the current monthly premium plus a surcharge for delaying application past age 65. He can also sign up for Medicare Part A, hospital coverage, but this is expensive and may be less attractive. His local Social Security office can provide details.

policies, described below, play an additional but more limited role in supplementing Medicare benefits.)

Medigap coverage is available through private insurance companies, Blue Cross-Blue Shield plans, and some retirement associations. After years of abuses, in which many older people were sold expensive overlapping coverage, new rules now protect consumers. Every company must now offer a "core" policy designed to plug specific Medicare gaps. This core policy, designated "Plan A," covers the copayment under Medicare Part A, the 20 percent copayment of allowable physician charges under Part B, and it pays for the first three pints of blood.

Up to nine other policies may be offered (see Table 19.2), each building on this core package with a different combination of additional benefits. Although not every policy is offered by every company or in every state, you can probably find policies covering the copayment for skilled nursing home care, at-home recovery, and prescription drugs.

Consumer protections include:

- An insurance agent or company can be penalized for selling duplicate coverage. If you apply for a new policy and already have a MedSup policy, you must sign an agreement promising that you will drop the existing policy when the new one is issued.
- You cannot be denied a policy based on preexisting conditions for the first six months after you turn 65 and become eligible for Medicare. Don't miss this open enrollment period; if you do, and you have a preexisting condition, you may not be able to get the coverage you want.
- If you switch policies, an insurer can't impose a waiting period for a preexisting condition if you've already satisfied a waiting period for the same condition under the prior policy. If the new policy has

Q My mother's doctor has always billed her for the amount of his charges above what Medicare pays. I heard that he's not supposed to do that any more, but my mother doesn't want to question him. Am I right?

A Yes and no. "Participating" physicians under Medicare (those who accept Medicare as full payment) are not allowed to bill for additional charges other than any deductibles or copayments. "Nonparticipating" physicians could charge considerably more but, since January 1, 1991, have been limited to billing patients for no more than specified amounts over and above what Medicare pays. If your mother has any questions, she should talk to her doctor.

Table 19.2: Medigap Benefits by Plan

Standardized Medigap Insurance Plans

Medigap Benefits	A	B	C	D	E	F	G	H	I	J
Basic Benefits	✓	✓	✓	✓	✓	✓	✓	✓	✓	✓
Part A: Hospital Deductible		✓	✓	✓	✓	✓	✓	✓	✓	✓
Part A: Skilled Nursing Home Copayment			✓	✓	✓	✓	✓	✓	✓	✓
Part B: Deductible			✓			✓				✓
Foreign Travel Emergency			✓	✓	✓	✓	✓	✓	✓	✓
At-Home Recovery				✓			✓		✓	✓
Part B: Excess Doctor Charges						100%	80%		100%	100%
Preventive Screening					✓					✓
Outpatient Prescription Drugs								Basic	Basic	Extended

Source: Health Care Financing Administration; United Seniors Health Cooperative.

Notes: States may allow only some of the ten benefit plans to be sold. States may approve innovative additional benefits plans under certain circumstances. These standardized benefit plans do not apply to policies sold in Massachusetts, Minnesota, and Wisconsin.

broader benefits, though, a waiting period of up to six months may apply for those new benefits.

- Newly issued Medigap policies must be guaranteed renewable; they can't be canceled unless you fail to pay your premiums or significantly falsified information on your application.

Long-term Care Insurance

Medicare and Medicare supplements cover skilled nursing home care, to a limited extent, when prescribed by a doctor following hospitalization. They do not cover long-term custodial care, assistance with daily living either at home or in a nursing facility. Long-term care may be needed by people of any age who have been in an accident or suffered a debilitating illness, but it is most likely to be needed by older people.

Long-term care can be expensive. One year in a nursing home costs, on average, more than $30,000; in some high-cost urban areas, the cost for one year can exceed $100,000. Using home health aides to provide similar services at home can cost $8,000 to $10,000 a year for part-time help, and as much as a nursing home if round-the-clock care is required. Yet this is the one aspect of health care for which, until very recently, there was no insurance at all.

Today more than 130 insurance companies sell long-term care insurance. Most are individual policies, although some companies offer group coverage as well; typically, employees pay the entire premium on a group policy but may find a policy at less cost than one they can buy on their own. Many group policies, too, allow employees to insure other members of their families, including parents and in-laws.

Q I recently retired and am covered by Medicare, but I know I need more. What would you say to joining a health maintenance organization instead of taking a Medigap policy?

A HMOs are actively soliciting retirees in some states, and can be a good deal. But be sure you know what you're getting, and what you're giving up. In some Medicare HMOs, you give up the right to Medicare reimbursement for medical care outside the HMO. In others you retain that right, and the flexibility to go to specialists outside the network, but you will pay Medicare's usual copayments and deductibles as well as excess physician charges. Be sure you fully understand the rules, before you sign up, and talk to people enrolled in the plan to see if they are pleased with the service. If you're dissatisfied with an HMO, you can always quit and take a Medigap policy—but you may find yourself limited to a more expensive policy with fewer benefits.

Most long-term care policies are "indemnity" policies paying a fixed dollar amount (typically from $40 to $100) for each day you receive specified care either in a nursing home or at home. The daily benefit for at-home care is usually half the benefit for nursing home care. Any fixed-dollar amount pur-

---

Worksheet 19.2: Long-term Care Policy Checklist

What services are covered?
- Skilled care _____
- Custodial care _____
- Home health care _____
- Adult day care _____

How much does the policy pay per day for:
- Skilled care _____
- Custodial care _____
- Home health care _____
- Adult day care _____

How soon do benefits begin?
- In a nursing home? _____
- At home? _____

How long do benefits last?
- In a nursing home? _____
- At home? _____

Are preexisting conditions covered?
- After what waiting period? _____

Does the policy require:
- Physician certification of need? _____
- An assessment of activities of daily living? _____
- A prior hospital stay for:
  - Nursing home care? _____
  - Home health care? _____
- A prior nursing home stay for home health coverage? _____

Is the policy guaranteed renewable? _____

Does the policy offer an inflation adjustment feature? _____
- Is there an additional cost _____

What does the policy cost? _____

Source: Health Insurance Association of America.

chased today, however, is likely to be inadequate by the time benefits are paid; most policies provide an inflation adjustment feature to keep benefits in line with inflation.

More information on long-term care policies will be found in Chapter 22, but here are some things you should know:

■ Premiums are generally based on your age when you purchase the policy. The younger you are, the lower the annual cost. In 1991 a policy paying $80 a day for nursing home care and $40 a day for home health care, with a 20-day deductible and maximum nursing home benefits paid for four to five years, cost $480 at age 50, $1,100 at age 65, and $3,990 at age 79. But the younger you are when you take the policy, the more years you will pay the premiums.

■ You can keep premiums down by electing a deductible (sometimes called an elimination period, referring to how many days you must wait for benefits to begin) of up to 100 days.

■ Most policies now cover Alzheimer's disease and other organic cognitive disabilities, but some exclude mental disorders that do not have an apparent organic cause.

■ Some policies require a specified period of hospitalization before you are eligible for nursing home benefits; others require a nursing home stay before you are eligible for home care benefits. Others (the kind you want) will pay for nursing home care whether or not you have first been hospitalized and home care regardless of prior hospitalization or skilled nursing home care.

■ Good policies pay benefits not only if you are ill but if you are unable to perform specified activities of daily living.

Should You Buy a Long-term Care Policy?

This form of insurance, in the opinion of many analysts, is most appropriate for people with assets (excluding their home) worth a total of more than $100,000 and less than $1,000,000. People with less than $100,000 in assets will quickly become eligible for Medicaid, the federal-state program that pays medical bills for those who meet income and asset limitations. People with more than $1,000,000 in assets should be able to save enough to pay their own nursing home and home care bills.

Other factors to consider include your gender (women live longer than men and make up a larger proportion of the nursing home population), your marital status (married people can usually remain in their own homes longer), and your family history (long-lived ancestors who remained healthy are a good omen; several relatives with Alzheimer's or Parkinson's disease may indicate the need for a long-term care policy).

Hospital Indemnity Policies

Hospital indemnity policies (see pp. 537-539 for details) pay daily cash benefits when you are hospitalized. But hospital indemnity policies are often very limited, and should not be your first choice as a Medicare supplement.

Your postretirement health insurance needs may also be met by membership in a health maintenance organization (see pp. 541-543).

What to Do Before You Retire

The best time to think about the health coverage you will need after 65 is long before you reach 65, while you may still be covered by on-the-job group insurance and while you have more options. Here's what to do:

- Ask your employer whether your group insurance benefits can continue beyond retirement. Some employers will continue to pay all or part of the cost of continued coverage. Others won't, but will let you sign up and pay for coverage yourself. It's a good idea to continue group coverage, even if you have to pay the premiums, because such

---

COBRA Benefits

Most health insurance in this country is provided through employers. If you lost your job, or lost a spouse who had the job, you also lost your health insurance. Now, under provisions of the Consolidated Omnibus Budget Reconciliation Act (COBRA) of 1986, workers and dependents can retain health insurance benefits under specific conditions. Most companies with more than 20 employees must comply with these rules and provide continuation coverage to:

- Employees who leave voluntarily or involuntarily, or are put on part-time status, for 18 months.

- Former dependents, for 36 months; this category includes separated and divorced spouses, children who lose dependent status either because of age or because they get married, and survivors of employees who die.

The employer must notify you if you are eligible for COBRA benefits; you must reply within a specified time and you must pay the entire premium, up to 102 percent of the premium paid by the employer. COBRA coverage ends after the 18 month or 36 month period, or earlier if you become covered under Medicare or under a new employer group plan. Note, though, that you can continue under COBRA (and may want to do so) during the period that a new employer's group plan excludes preexisting conditions.

coverage is usually cheaper than other health insurance. (You'll probably find the premiums less expensive than you expect, because Medicare will pick up much of your basic health coverage.) It may even work out to your benefit to continue a less-than-perfect group plan and take supplemental insurance to fill in any remaining gaps.

■ If you cannot continue in the group health insurance plan, find out if you can convert it to an individual plan, or use COBRA provisions to extend your group coverage. The premiums will be higher, but the advantage is that there won't be any waiting for preexisting conditions to meet a qualifying test of time. You will also be sure not to have any time lapse in coverage.

■ Whether you continue in the group plan or convert the group plan to an individual policy, find out whether you can get additional benefits under the company policy; some have riders, for example, permitting you to buy additional days of hospital coverage. Also find out whether your spouse will continue to be covered after you die. If not, it's very important for your spouse to look into individual coverage before reaching age 65.

■ Several months before you reach 65, make sure that your Social Security records are in order and that you apply for Medicare. Benefits are not automatic. You must apply, and you are well advised to do so early. If you do not sign up for Medicare Part B when you first become eligible, you may do so only during the first three months of each succeeding year. You'll also pay more with each succeeding year.

■ Think about your postretirement plans. Medicare's coverage is limited to the United States, including Puerto Rico, the Virgin Islands, Guam, and American Samoa. If you plan to do much traveling after retirement, be sure that you have private insurance which will pick up any burdensome health care costs. Some of the standardized Medigap policies described above include coverage overseas.

■ If you are planning to purchase a supplemental policy, do so early. Remember that the guaranteed open enrollment period, without regard to preexisting conditions, is a narrow window starting at your 65th birthday. You will be able to buy a Medicare supplement if you wait, but you may not be able to get the specific coverage you want.

HOSPITAL INDEMNITY POLICIES

Although hospital indemnity policies are used by some retirees to supplement Medicare, they are available, often by mail, to people of any age. Benefits under these policies, designed to reimburse you for out-of-pocket health care costs, are paid to you directly, in cash, on a per-day basis. You've seen the ads, in newspapers and in magazines and in your mailbox: $30 a day, $50 a day ... for each day of hospitalization after the first three, or five, or eight....

There are a couple of things to keep in mind about these policies:

- They are not designed to provide primary health insurance coverage. Any per-day cost, spelled out in dollars, is inadequate in an era when the average semiprivate hospital room costs more than $300 a day. These policies can, however, provide extra dollars that you can use as you see fit, whether for extras in the hospital or to help out at home. They can also be very useful if you are otherwise uninsurable.

- Limitations on preexisting conditions can range from six months to as much as two years. What's worse, some companies refuse all claims during the limitation period for illnesses which can be shown to have

Q I retired recently at age 62 and then discovered that health insurance is almost impossible to buy at this age. Supplemental policies to tie in with Medicare are available, once you reach 65, but what about those of us between 62 and 65? I'm working 15 hours a week (and can't work more without losing my Social Security retirement benefits), but these few hours leave me ineligible for group health insurance. What can I do?

A You are not alone. Individual policies are hard to find in your age bracket. But you do have some options:

- You may be able to extend your group plan for 18 months after retirement, or convert it to an individual policy (talk to your former employer quickly; it may be too late to do either, if you've already retired).

- Some insurers do accept applicants in their sixties, usually for a major medical policy that converts at age 65 to a Medicare supplement. You can keep your premium within reason by self-insuring with a sizable deductible, thereby putting limited dollars to work as protection against catastrophic illness.

- Some Blue Cross-Blue Shield plans have annual open enrollment periods, when anyone may secure individual coverage regardless of age or state of health.

- Health maintenance organizations may also have open enrollment periods for those under 65.

- As a last resort, consider a hospital indemnity policy which pays daily cash benefits in case of hospitalization; it won't cover all your health needs, but it will be something.

Whatever you do, look into post-65 health insurance before you turn 65, and secure full coverage as soon as you can.

originated before the policy was purchased—whether or not you knew you had the condition at the time of purchase. At best, a preexisting condition clause can be tricky; the longer the period, the less the policy costs, but the longer you are vulnerable to significant out-of-pocket costs.

■ The elimination period, or the amount of time you must wait before benefits begin, significantly affects premiums. You will pay more for first-day coverage, and you may not need it while Medicare is paying most of your bills (unless you want to build up a reserve against later illness).

■ These policies pay benefits *only* while you are in the hospital and only, as a rule, after a specified number of days in the hospital. Since the average hospital stay is just eight days (twelve days for older people), such policies prove useless to the vast majority of people who buy them. If, of course, you are in the hospital for an extended period of time, an indemnity policy could prove helpful. If you decide you want an indemnity policy with immediate or almost immediate payments, you can probably find one. But the premium cost will be higher.

■ Most of these policies pay cash benefits for one to two years, as long as you remain hospitalized; others will extend benefits (usually in a lower amount) to skilled nursing home care following hospitalization.

Take care of your primary health insurance needs before you consider buying a hospital indemnity policy.

DREAD DISEASE POLICIES

Health insurance policies are sold, often by mail, for a number of specific ailments. Most prevalent, however, is cancer insurance. For a relatively small sum, these policies promise to pay the costs associated with hospitalization for cancer. Are they a good buy? Most insurance experts think not. Here's why:

■ The premium may be low, but 60 percent of it, on the average, is retained by the company in salespeople's commissions, administrative expenses, and profit. Less than 40 percent, according to a study by the House Committee on Aging, is paid out in benefits. This contrasts with an average 80 percent payout on standard health insurance policies.

■ Some of the sales pitches for these policies are downright deceptive. They may claim that the policies pay "extended benefits" for hospital confinements over 90 days ... but don't say that the average stay for cancer patients is 14 days. They may say that they pay for "definitive cancer treatment" ... without noting that this means nothing is paid for much of the cost associated with cancer treatment: pathology reports, rehabilitation, etc.

Even if benefit payouts are good, and sales pitches are forthright and honest, most objective observers believe that any money you would spend on insurance against a single dread disease would be better spent in improving your overall health insurance. Cancer does strike a lot of people. But so does heart disease. Why insure against only one disease?

Health Insurance Trends

Whether or not the Clinton proposals succeed in totally reordering our health care system, certain trends are bound to continue. The most important of these trends: cost containment through networks of providers, described under the phrase **managed care.** Managed care is not exactly the same as managed competition, although it can take place within managed competition. Managed care is defined by health insurers as "systems that integrate the financing and delivery of appropriate health care services to covered individuals by means of:

- arrangements with selected providers to furnish a comprehensive set of health care services to members;
- explicit criteria for the selection of health care providers;
- formal programs for ongoing quality assurance and utilization review; and
- significant financial incentives for members to use providers and procedures associated with the plan."

In plain English, what this means is that your health insurer wants to keep costs down by encouraging you to use doctors and other health care providers preselected as part of an approved network such as (but not limited to) a health maintenance organization (HMO). It also means that insurers are playing a larger role in medical care, forming provider networks of their own, and reviewing procedures and hospital stays to determine if they are medically necessary before agreeing to pay the bills.

This is very different from the traditional health insurance policy, which is a fee-for-service arrangement. You go to the physician or other medical provider of your choice, the provider bills you, and you (or, in some cases, your doctor) then submit a claim to your insurance company for reimbursement. How much you actually receive depends on the deductible under the policy and whether it has been met, the coinsurance provisions of the policy, and whether the policy pays in full or according to a specific schedule of benefits or those considered "reasonable and customary" in your area. Preventive services such as checkups are frequently not covered because the emphasis in most traditional fee-for-service policies is on treatment rather than prevention.

With managed care, a network of providers—typically doctors, nurses, and hospitals—provide comprehensive medical services to people enrolled in the particular plan.

NETWORKS OF PROVIDERS

The most familiar network of providers is the **Health Maintenance Organization** or **HMO.** These prepaid health service plans are not strictly insurance, but they serve much the same purpose. They also do much more. They provide comprehensive health care, both preventive care and treatment, in exchange for a fixed monthly fee. That fee is often less than the usual combination of insurance plus out-of-pocket medical expenses; the average family premium in 1991 was $335 per month. It also may be paid by your employer, since prepaid group plans or HMOs are an alternative to group insurance (an alternative that must be offered by your employer if your company has 25 or more employees, if any health insurance is offered as a benefit, and if there is an HMO in your area). Any extra expenses, if you belong to an HMO, tend to be minor. Some HMOs, for instance, charge members a few dollars for each doctor visit and/or a dollar or two for each prescription.

By 1992 41 million Americans were enrolled in HMOs, up from about 19 million in 1985. Most are enrolled through groups; only 25 percent of HMOs accept individual applicants. HMOs are more popular in some areas, however, than in others. Fully one-third of California residents belonged to HMOs at the end of 1992, but not a single resident of Alaska, Mississippi, West Virginia, or Wyoming belonged. (The absence of HMOs in these states and the relative scarcity in other states—including Idaho, Iowa, Maine, North and South Dakota—may make it more difficult for any health care reform based on participation in provider networks.)

Members of HMOs receive comprehensive health services, with no worries about unexpected medical bills. In federally qualified plans (three-quarters of HMO enrollees belong to federally qualified plans) these services must include:

- Physician services (including consultant and referral services)
- Inpatient and outpatient services
- Medically necessary emergency health services (if you must go to another facility in an emergency)
- Short-term (not to exceed 20 visits) outpatient mental health services for evaluation and crisis intervention
- Short-term physical therapy
- Medical treatment and referral services for addiction to or abuse of drugs or alcohol
- Diagnostic laboratory and therapeutic X-ray services
- Home health services
- Preventive health services including immunizations, well-child care from birth, periodic adult health evaluations, family planning, and children's eye and ear examinations

Table 19.3: Benefit Comparisons

The percentage of covered expenses paid under a typical group indemnity (fee-for-service) insurance plan is often less than the percentage paid under the average HMO plan.

Covered Expenses

	Indemnity Plan	HMO Plan
Hospital	95%	100%
Surgical	85	100
Medical	82	85
Drugs	81	90
Mental Health	40	25
Preventive	0	85
Dental	80	80

Source: Hewitt Associates.

Note: The typical coinsurance level for indemnity plans is 80 percent; the table shows higher levels in some instances because limitations on out-of-pocket expenses ("stop-loss" provisions) increase average amounts reimbursed for high-cost items.

Other services may also be covered (and frequently are, especially in employer-sponsored group plans):

- Prescription drugs
- Adult eye examinations
- Dental care
- Extended mental health care
- Extended physical therapy
- Occupational therapy

The primary advantages of an HMO are low cost and comprehensive service. The elimination of the paperwork associated with insurance and Medicare claims is also a plus. A major disadvantage in the past was the frequently impersonal nature of the service, with little or no choice of doctors. Today most HMOs allow you to choose—and change—your primary-care physician. Another potentially serious criticism focuses on what has been described as a tendency to control costs by limiting care; doctors in some networks receive financial incentives for not hospitalizing patients or referring them to specialists. Nonetheless, most studies show HMO enrollees to be satisfied with the care they receive.

Selecting an HMO

Some health maintenance organizations provide more services than others; look into this carefully before you join. Some are strong and stable organizations, while others have folded after a promising start. Find out as much as you can before you sign up. Ask these questions:

- Are doctors board-certified or board-eligible? Are they well established in the community?
- How are doctors paid? (Some HMOs have been criticized for trying to keep costs down by offering doctors incentives to see patients less often, spend less time with them, and restrict referral to specialists.)
- What is the turnover rate among physicians? (The answer to this question indicates how happy doctors are with the plan and, as a result, how likely you are to see the same doctor over the years.)
- How soon can I get an appointment? (for routine visits? for emergencies?)
- Where do I go after normal office hours?
- Which hospitals does the HMO use? Is one conveniently near me?
- Where are difficult cases sent? (Transplant patients, for example, are often referred to specialized facilities.)
- How are complaints handled?
- Who else uses this HMO? Are they satisfied? (Ask them yourself.)
- Exactly what is covered, and what is not?
- What happens if you take ill or are injured while away from home?

Be aware, too, that many HMOs do not deal with Medicare and will not enroll people over 65, or continue service to those previously enrolled when they reach 65. Other HMOs (see p. 533) do want Medicare patients. Again, the time to arrange for post-65 medical coverage is before you turn 65.

Health maintenance organizations used to be headquartered in a specific location; patients had to visit the HMO facility to receive medical care. Today this is true of only one-third of HMOs. The rest operate through networks of individual practitioners; doctors belong to a network, sometimes called an **individual practice association** or IPA, but you visit the doctors in their individual medical offices.

There are also hybrid arrangements, in which your employer or insurer may offer you the choice of seeing a physician within the network or outside the network. This gives you the flexibility of using a doctor of your choice, but it will generally cost you more out-of-pocket to do so. These plans may be called **preferred provider organizations** (PPOs) or **point-of-service** (POS) plans.

Quality Assurance and Utilization Review

In an effort to contain runaway costs, insurers are becoming more involved in the kind of medical care that is delivered. Whether you have a traditional fee-for-service plan or are a member of a provider network, your insurer may play a growing role in determining what treatment you may receive, whether or not you may be hospitalized, and so on. This can mean that a clerk or, at best, a nurse at the other end of the telephone may second-guess your doctor about the treatment you may receive. You may be required to secure a second opinion before certain types of surgery or get the insurer's authorization before being admitted to a hospital, for example, and you may find that procedures or pharmaceuticals deemed "experimental" by your insurer (but possibly valuable by your doctor) may not be covered.

Note: You don't have to take no for an answer. You can appeal a negative decision, using the appeals procedure spelled out in your coverage booklet. A study by the U.S. General Accounting Office found that fewer than 12 percent of those denied coverage by utilization review companies appeal the decision—but more than one-third of those who do appeal have the decision reversed.

Utilization review may also include "case management," a review process designed for the most challenging cases. Utilization review (and managed care in general) has been criticized for undue interference in medical decisions, and there are plenty of anecdotal examples of mismanagement leading to needless suffering and even death. But there are occasions when the flexibility implicit in case management may be helpful to patient and insurer alike. A good example is the pregnant mother of two children, diagnosed with a blood disease likely to cause premature delivery. Instead of hospitalizing her for the duration of her pregnancy, her managed care program provided homemaker services and child care (not normally covered under health insurance) so that she could follow her doctor's orders for total bed rest while remaining at home with her preschoolers. She delivered a full-term baby, with less disruption to her family, and the plan saved $70,000 by avoiding her hospitalization.

WHERE TO BUY INSURANCE

If you're fortunate, you have health insurance through your job. If not, you must try to secure health coverage on your own. The latter is not an easy task, although it's been made easier in the states that have mandated coverage (and may, if we actually pass health care reform, become easier no matter where you live).

Group Insurance

The most extensive and least expensive health insurance is the health insurance you buy through a group, especially the group formed by your fellow workers. (Even if you have to pay all or part of the premiums, on-the-job group insurance will generally cost you less than anything you can buy on your own.) It may be very important when you're comparing job offers, therefore, to take a close look at the fringe benefits being offered. A good health insurance package can be worth several hundred to a couple of thousand dollars in salary; an inadequate package may need to be supplemented.

A good group policy will include the basic and major medical provisions outlined earlier. It may also contain extras (unlikely to appear in individual policies at any price) such as dental insurance. It should be relatively inexpensive, compared to individual coverage, although there is a trend toward having employees pay a larger share of the costs. An advantage to you, even if you must pay part of the premium, is insurability. In a true group plan you should not be excluded because of problems with your health—although some insurers are beginning to raise rates for sick members of a group (especially small groups), thereby in many instances forcing them out of the plan.

With these trends in on-the-job group coverage, and with the uncertainty surrounding many jobs today, you may want to supplement your group health insurance either by buying an individual policy (see p. 548) or by joining an HMO.

Reimbursement Accounts

Your employer may offer a **flexible spending** or **reimbursement account** as part of a benefits package, allowing you to pay health and dependent care costs with pretax dollars. These plans typically cover expenses not included elsewhere, such as eye exams, dental visits, hearing aids, even deductibles and copayments. **Dependent care accounts** cover day care centers and after-school baby-sitters, so long as the expenses are incurred in order for you to work.

The big advantage lies in the tax savings: If you are in the 40 percent combined tax bracket for federal and state income taxes and put $5,000 into a dependent care account, you would have the full $5,000 to spend on day care

Q I discovered that I was pregnant just a month after my employer changed group insurance companies. Now neither company will pay my bills. The first says it is no longer responsible. The second says it is not responsible either, because the pregnancy began before the policy did. Is there anything I can do?

A Talk to your employer's benefits department; most companies do make some provision for continuing coverage in this type of situation. Next, if your employer has not made such provision, get in touch with your state insurance department (probably in the state capital) and find out if your state is one of those that requires that a successor group-insurance plan, if it replaces an existing plan within 60 days, provide continuous coverage.

instead of the $3,000 you would otherwise have left after taxes. Another advantage is that you can put the money into your account slowly, over the entire year, but have the full amount available to you in January.

On the down side, you forfeit any excess in the fund if you guess wrong about how much you'll actually spend during the year. Try to calculate your spending needs very carefully before you make a commitment. And, if you plan to use the money for child care, compare how much you would receive under the child and dependent care tax credit (see p. 581) against how much you could get from a reimbursement account.

Coordination of Benefits

When 17-year-old Jack fractured his ankle playing football, it didn't cost his parents a cent, even though each of their on-the-job health insurance policies contained standard deductible and coinsurance provisions. The reason: Under a "coordination of benefits" provision, Jack's father's insurance company paid his medical bills as if it were the only coverage. Then his mother's insurance company paid the remaining charges.

Group insurance plans usually contain a coordination of benefits feature. That means that you cannot collect twice for the same ailment under different policies. You may be able to collect the deductible and coinsurance amounts

---

Q My husband and I both work for companies with excellent health benefits. Our employers used to pay the whole premium, but now we must pay an increasing share of the cost. Since we can each be covered as a dependent under the other's policy, should one of us drop coverage?

A Not without very careful thought. Group policies typically cover employees without regard to preexisting conditions only if they sign up for coverage when they are first eligible. If the one who kept the coverage should lose his or her job, or voluntarily move to a company with little or no health coverage, the other might have to prove insurable in order to go back into the group plan. If an intervening illness made you uninsurable, your whole family could suffer.

And watch out for this wrinkle: If one spouse opts out of an employer's health plan, the other employer may nonetheless coordinate benefits with whatever coverage you could have had. This provision could dump big medical bills in your lap, so you may want to remain enrolled in both company plans even if it appears as if you are receiving little benefit from doing so.

from one policy under the other although some employers, trying to cut costs, are restricting this benefit. You and your spouse, if you are both employed, should watch out for overlapping and duplicative coverage but try to have one policy extend the other, if at all possible.

When You Leave Your Job

Don't let your group insurance lapse if you lose your job; that's just when you are most vulnerable to the costs of illness. Most policies contain a conversion provision, which allows you to convert the policy to an individual basis. The cost will typically be much greater and the benefits far less extensive, but if you have any preexisting medical conditions and if you don't expect to rejoin a large group in the near future you may find conversion very worthwhile. Another possibility, if you expect to land another job within a reasonable period of time: continuation coverage under COBRA provisions (see p. 536).

Caution: If your employer is self-insured, as an increasing number of large companies are, you may not be eligible for COBRA continuation coverage. Ask your benefits office.

You can also buy short-term **interim** coverage (up to six months and, from some companies, renewable for an additional six months) to cover you for any medical claims starting during the contract period. Interim coverage can be useful for anyone temporarily without health insurance, including people who are between jobs and college graduates delaying full-time employment for several months while they travel.

ASSOCIATION GROUP

If you can't get a job with health insurance benefits, you may be able to purchase insurance through a group. If you are a member of a trade or professional association, fraternal or business group, labor union or civic organization, you may be eligible for health insurance through that group. Such health insurance will usually, but not always, be less expensive than insurance you buy on your own.

Caution: Group insurance (other than through your job) is not always true group insurance. Where an organization cannot collect and remit premiums, its members may nonetheless be seen as a natural market for solicitation. When the group agrees that its mailing list may be used, it may do one of two things: pass the premium savings on to members or use them as a money-making method for the group's treasury. There's nothing wrong with a group making insurance available to its members and at the same time enriching the group as a whole, but you should understand that mail-order insurance offered to you because you are a member of such-and-such a group may not necessarily be the best buy when it comes to insurance. You'll have to compare prices carefully to be sure.

Note: Some health care consumers, especially older people covered by Medicare and a supplemental policy, find an independent claims service useful in filling out multiple claims forms and cutting through red tape. For referral to an independent claims processor near you, write to the National Association of Claims Assistance Professionals, 4724 Florence Ave., Downer's Grove, IL 60515; include your name, address, and zip code and, if you're in a rural area, the name of the nearest city.

Individual Insurance

There are a number of circumstances in which you may find yourself without group insurance. You may be between jobs, voluntarily or involuntarily, or working for an employer with no insurance plan. You may have outgrown coverage under your parents' insurance. You may have retired. Or you may have been recently widowed or divorced, and your COBRA benefits and conversion options have run out. Whatever the circumstances, you may be in

Q What can I do if my health insurer refuses to pay for something I know is covered?

A First, go back to your policy booklet or your employee benefits office and confirm that you *are* covered. Make sure that you didn't skip an essential step under your plan, such as a second opinion or preadmission certification. Then call the insurer and ask why the claim was rejected. If it was a clerical error, such as a miscalculated deductible or an incorrect procedure or diagnosis code (you may have to ask your doctor to check that the codes on the claims form are accurate), it should be relatively easy to correct (that is, if the doctor's staff cooperates; I once had a bad experience with a doctor's secretary who refused to correct a coding error).

If the rejection wasn't due to a simple clerical error, but you are still convinced you are right, file an appeal. Include any additional information you or your doctor can supply about why the particular procedure was necessary or why the fee was as much as it was. (If your surgeon repaired an ulcer while removing your gall bladder, through the same incision, reimbursement could be substantially more; watch out, though, for doctors who "unbundle" services and charge for each separately in order to receive more money.) If your first appeal is rejected, go to a supervisor; then to the medical director of the insurance company. If all else fails, the consumer affairs division of your state insurance department may be able to help you.

trouble. Individual insurance can be both hard to get and expensive. Health care reform may provide a national solution. Until it does, if you don't live in one of the states mandating coverage, try to line up individual coverage before you need it most. You don't want any lapse in protection. Just one illness or accident, when you are financially vulnerable, could wipe you out.

Individually purchased health insurance can provide essentially the same type of protection as group insurance, although benefits may be more limited and premiums may be substantially greater. Individual insurance is available from local Blue Cross-Blue Shield organizations and from commercial life and health insurance companies. Coverage may also be obtained through a health maintenance organization, if a nearby HMO accepts individual applicants.

What you need to know:

■ Preexisting conditions may be specifically excluded from coverage, or covered only after a specified period of time
■ If a preexisting condition can be controlled (hypertension is a good example), you may be covered but have to pay a higher premium
■ If you will be relying on an individual policy, look for one that guarantees renewal
■ If cost is a problem, look for a "no frills" or "bare bones" policy; these packages of basic benefits are available in about half the states.

Blue Cross-Blue Shield

Blue Cross covers hospital bills and Blue Shield covers the costs of medical/surgical care.

Although Blue Cross-Blue Shield exists throughout the United States, local Blue Cross-Blue Shield plans are autonomous and offer different plans in different areas. Many Blue Cross-Blue Shield plans sponsor HMOs. The Blues used to take all applicants; today this is the case only in eleven states (New Hampshire, New York, Virginia, Pennsylvania, Michigan, Maryland, New Jersey, Vermont, Rhode Island, Massachusetts, and Alabama) and the District of Columbia. And the Blues, which used to tie premiums to where you live (so-called "community rating") now are more often like commercial insurers in basing premiums on age, sex, and state of health ("experience rating").

Nonetheless, the Blues have certain advantages:

■ With a single-person rate, a two-person rate, and a family rate covering a family regardless of size, most Blues have a pricing policy which makes them a good buy for a large family.
■ Blue Cross plans are based on services; whatever the bill is, it will be paid directly to the hospital. With commercial insurers you may have to pay the bill and then wait for reimbursement. That reimbursement, depending on your policy, may or may not cover the entire bill.

■ Most policies issued by the Blues are guaranteed renewable, which is not always true of commercial insurance.

Some Blues, however, have recently suffered financial difficulties. Some have actually closed, leaving policyholders stranded. In the midst of a Senate investigation into the Blues, the Blue Cross and Blue Shield Association announced in early 1993 that it will scrutinize its members more closely.

COMMERCIAL INSURERS

A number of commercial insurers write health insurance, primarily major medical, on an individual (nongroup) basis. These policies have premiums based on age, sex, and where you live as well as the deductibles and benefits you select. They are also, by and large, selective, excluding those people who may make major claims (the very people who often most need health insurance the most). Such policies, for these reasons, may be a better buy than the Blues for a young and healthy single person.

Most commercial insurers, moreover, because of rapidly rising costs, have pulled out of the basic protection area. If you want basic hospital/medical insurance you may have to buy it from Blue Cross-Blue Shield (or obtain coverage through a health maintenance organization). But the commercial insurers do have one advantage: If you want a major medical policy (the kind of protection that's most important), you'll probably have to buy it from a commercial insurer; the Blues, with a few exceptions, offer major medical only to

Q My 24-year-old brother has multiple sclerosis. His only health insurance was through the college he was attending when he got sick. Is there any way he can get health insurance now that he's out of school?

A Pending passage of universal health coverage, if your brother lives in a state with guaranteed health insurance (write to your state insurance commissioner to find out) he can buy individual health insurance from a private health insurance company regardless of the condition of his health. About half the states now have such "risk pools."

Otherwise, your brother may be able to get group coverage through an organization or, if he is able to hold a job, an employer. He may also be able to secure individual coverage during an open-enrollment period (watch for advertised dates) held by Blue Cross and Blue Shield or a local health maintenance organization.

groups. If you want both basic hospital/medical protection and major medical insurance your best bet may be a combination of a basic Blue Cross policy and major medical coverage from a commercial insurer. Keep costs down by electing the largest deductible you can handle.

Note: Don't assume that you are uninsurable because you have had a serious disease. Some companies are more concerned with heart disease, others with back problems. Many will insure people who have had some forms of cancer, after enough time has gone by. Find a good independent insurance agent, one who writes policies with a number of companies, and discuss your situation.

What to Look For

Whether you purchase health insurance through a group or on your own, through a Blue Cross-Blue Shield plan or from a commercial insurer, there are certain things you should look for. Find out:

What Is Covered?

You'll know whether the policy covers doctors' bills. But you may not know, unless you ask, whether payment is limited to specific kinds of doctors. Some policies, for instance, exclude chiropractors. Other possible exclusions to find out about, in advance: Is coverage limited to certain hospitals? Are preventive or diagnostic measures covered? What about out-of-hospital treatment? Nursing home care? Are psychiatric benefits provided? Are newborn infants covered from the day of birth? At what age will children be excluded from a family policy? What about maternity costs and, more important, any complications of pregnancy?

Is It a Managed Care Policy?

Are second surgical opinions and preadmission certification required? (About half of all the people covered by employer-sponsored health care programs in early 1993 were enrolled in some form of managed care plan.) If so, be sure that you follow the rules or you may find yourself with sizable bills that won't be reimbursed. Your policy may require that you not visit the emergency room, for example, even if you're in pain, until you or someone else calls your insurer for permission. Also be sure you know the answers to these questions: Are you covered with any medical provider you choose? Only if you use a network of providers? Or do you have a choice between a network and, typically at a higher cost to you, your own physician?

How Are Preexisting Conditions Defined?

Be sure your policy refers to conditions that you know about; otherwise, you could be refused claims for conditions that took a long time to develop but were undiagnosed when you purchased the policy.

If you're thinking of switching to a lower-cost policy, remember that you may have to start all over again to satisfy a preexisting condition clause. Your existing policy may now cover everything, without regard to preexisting conditions, and may be worth keeping even if it costs a bit more.

What Is the Company's Loss Ratio?

The loss ratio is the percentage of premiums returned to policyholders in benefits. Although the figure is not definitive (a company with a favorable loss ratio may still go out of business and leave you stranded), you'll usually get a better deal where there is a higher loss ratio. The Blues generally have a loss ratio of about 90 percent. Group plans written by commercial insurers should be able to show loss ratios in the 80 to 90 percent range. On individual coverage (where administrative costs are necessarily higher), look for a company with a loss ratio of 60 percent or more.

Is the Policy Guaranteed Renewable?

Such a policy cannot be canceled under any circumstances. Rates may be raised, but only if they are raised for an entire class of policyholders. Without a guaranteed renewable policy, you may be left at any time without health insurance protection.

Is the Company Solvent?

No one used to question the stability of insurance companies. Today, unfortunately, you must. Financial difficulties have troubled a number of formerly solid companies. Some foundered on junk bonds, others on real estate investments that soured in the recession. In the case of companies writing both life and health insurance, the introduction of interest-rate sensitive products such as deferred annuities and guaranteed investment contracts led to reduced earnings when interest rates declined. Although insolvent insurers are often taken over by other insurers, and although state guaranty funds may step in to protect policyholders when companies are not taken over, you should try to buy insurance from a stable and solvent company. Before you buy, check ratings given by A. M. Best Company, Standard and Poor's, and Moody's; all should be available in your local library.

DISABILITY INCOME

This form of insurance, important but often overlooked, provides you with an income should you become sick or injured and unable to work. It protects your family from the financial deprivation that could result if a breadwinner is out of work for any substantial period of time or (under some policies, from a few companies) if a homemaker is unable to care for the family. Disability income protection is an essential form of health insurance. Before you rush out to buy it, however, look at other forms of disability income you already have:

On the Job

Many employers provide some form of disability income. It may be a limited number of sick days with pay. Or it may be a full-scale disability income policy on a group basis. You're in good shape if your employer provides a full-scale group policy covering long-term disabilities. But you should find out exactly what benefits are provided, how soon they would begin after you became disabled, and how long they would last.

Some companies do not provide disability income coverage as such, but do have group health insurance policies for their employees under which a disability income rider can be added by the individual for a modest premium. If you have this option, you should consider taking it. Disability income protection is important insurance to have, and this is an inexpensive way to make the purchase.

Social Security

If you are covered under Social Security for retirement benefits, you are also covered for disability benefits. Those benefits are substantial and may be the most important part of Social Security for younger workers.

Under this program, you can count on a monthly benefit if you are disabled for an extended period. Those benefits, moreover, are calculated as if you had retired at age 65 in the year the disability began. As of January 1993, the average monthly payment to a disabled worker was $627. Benefits are based on age, and the maximum individual monthly benefit at age 35 was $1,293; the maximum monthly family benefit for a 35-year-old disabled worker was $1,940. These benefits can be significant for someone who is unable to work. But Social Security disability is increasingly hard to get. You really must be unable to hold a job.

These are the things you should know:

- Benefits for permanent or indefinite disabilities begin with the sixth month of disability; they continue for life, as long as you remain disabled.
- After 24 months of benefits you qualify for Medicare, which helps pay your medical bills.
- You must file a claim, and that claim must be approved before you can receive any benefits. It's important to file a claim as soon as you think you might be eligible, as soon as you've been told that you can no longer engage in "substantial, gainful activity." If you forget to file, you can claim retroactive benefits for up to 12 months, but you and your family may lose some benefits.

Other Benefits

Depending on where you live and where you work, other disability benefits may be available to you:

- Worker's compensation, for a job-related disability
- Veterans Administration pension disability benefits
- Civil Service disability benefits
- Black lung benefits
- State welfare benefits and Aid to Families with Dependent Children
- Group union disability benefits
- Automobile insurance which includes benefits for disability resulting from an automobile accident
- Credit insurance which includes the paying off of an installment loan if you become disabled (not necessarily recommended—see p. 217—but if you did buy it, don't forget that you did)
- Waiver of premium provisions under life insurance, under which you will owe no further premiums should you become disabled

Add all these benefits together. If they come to approximately 70 percent of your after-tax income, you may not need any private disability income insurance. If they fall far short, you should definitely consider the purchase of an individual policy. The risk of a disabling accident between the ages of 35 and 65 is a lot greater than the chances of dying. The risk of a *permanently* disabling accident is slim. But the risk of an accident or illness that may put you out of commission for at least 90 days is not slim at all.

When You're Underinsured

Having disability insurance on the job is a big step in the right direction. But it may not be enough. The Health Insurance Association of America offers this example:

Bob and Ann Jackson, the parents of a 6-year-old girl, live in a small city in Nebraska where Bob, age 31, earns $32,000 as a computer salesman. His monthly take-home pay is $1,994.50. After staying home for several years to care for their daughter, Ann is now working part time as a saleswoman in a local boutique. She brings home $338.42 a month. All is going well . . . until Bob develops a degenerative muscle disease and is unable to work. His physician certifies that he is totally disabled. Carl has no prior military or civil service that might qualify him for government disability programs. He hasn't worked long enough to be covered by Social Security disability benefits. And the illness is not job-related, so there will be no worker's compensation.

This couple thinks they are covered and will be able to manage; Bob's employer, after all, provides a long-term disability benefit of 60 percent of his gross salary, or $1,600 a month. But this amount will be reduced by $193 in federal income taxes and $99.97 in state income taxes (because his employer paid the premium, the benefits are taxable). He must also pay $481 a month, which his employer paid before, to continue the family's group medical policy. With Ann's earnings, the Jacksons now must live on a monthly income of $1,645.45, considerably less than their former comfortable income of $2,334.92. Moreover, because the group policy does not include a cost-of-living adjustment, the

Jackson's buying power will diminish each year. An individual disability income policy containing a cost-of-living adjustment would have gone a long way toward assuring this family an adequate standard of living.

Individual Disability Insurance

There is great variation among individual disability policies. Be sure to buy this kind of protection from a company that specializes in the field; a good agent can provide guidance. Here are the things you should know:

- Many individual policies require that you be totally disabled before benefits begin. Where benefits are provided for partial disability, the partial disability must usually follow a period of total disability for the same cause.
- The definition of disability within the policy is crucial. Be sure you find out exactly how it is defined or you may be in for an unpleasant surprise when you file a claim. There are two things to watch for. First, disability can be defined as being unable to perform your customary occupation (e.g., as a practicing dentist), any related occupation (e.g., teaching dentistry), or any occupation at all (e.g., stuffing envelopes at home). You may want to limit your choice to a policy providing benefits when you can't work at an occupation you're trained for. Second, disability can also be interpreted as requiring total in-hospital or in-house confinement. Even ill people can get out for some fresh air, however, and you don't want a policy so narrowly restricted.
- You may select the amount of your benefit, up to a point. Most insurers will limit benefits from all sources to no more than 60 to 70 percent of your gross salary. The companies don't want to pay more

Q My husband has been ill and is receiving disability payments under his company's insurance plan. I thought disability insurance benefits were not taxable, but now I'm told they are. Which is right?

A The Internal Revenue Service makes a distinction between disability insurance purchased by an individual and that purchased by an employer. If your husband had bought his own insurance and paid his own premiums, the benefits would not be taxable. As it is, since his premiums were paid by his employer, the benefits are taxed as income.

because they don't want to encourage malingerers. But you won't need your full gross salary, in any case, because you won't be paying taxes or the costs of going to work.

■ You can keep premiums down by accepting longer waiting periods before benefits begin. Benefits can start from the first day of disability or they can start six months or a year later. (Some policies have different waiting periods for accident and for illness.) The longer you choose to wait, the lower your premium. Again, self-insurance for relatively small amounts pays off. (If you established the financial plan detailed in Chapter 2, you should have three to six months' income in liquid savings, ready to be tapped in just such an emergency. So you shouldn't need immediate-pay disability benefits.)

■ Premiums vary according to age, income, and policy provisions. In an example provided by the Principal Financial Group, a policy with a 90 day elimination period, paying benefits to age 65, would cost approximately 1 percent of annual gross salary if the policy were purchased at age 25, 2 percent at age 35, 3 percent at age 45, and 4.5 percent at age 55. Many companies have the same premiums for men and for women; where single-sex pricing is used, women pay more.

■ You can choose a policy in which the benefits will be paid for as little as one year or as long as to age 65 (or even longer, if you're still working full time). Again, logically enough, the shorter the benefit period the lower the premium. While saving money *is* important, however, so is having adequate coverage. A longer term of benefits may be worth buying.

■ Your policy should cover both accident and illness. Some policies pay only for accidents.

■ Different policies are renewable under different conditions. The most desirable (although the most expensive and the hardest to find) is non-cancellable, a policy that is guaranteed renewable at a fixed premium rate until a specified age such as 65. Guaranteed renewable policies cannot be canceled, but the company can raise the premium rates for an entire class of policyholders. Optionally renewable insurance (the option is the insurance company's, not yours) is least desirable; the company can't arbitrarily cancel your policy alone, but it can, under this provision, cancel or refuse to renew an entire group of contracts.

■ The kind of work you do affects both your coverage and your premium. If you change jobs, be sure to notify your insurance carrier right away.

■ Some companies are adding long-term care riders to disability income policies. If you don't have a separate long-term care policy, this may be an option to consider—although it could lock you into continuing a disability income policy when it is no longer needed.

Worksheet 19.3: A Disability Policy Checklist

How is disability defined?
- ■ Inability to perform your own job?   _____
- ■ Inability to perform any job?   _____

Does the policy cover:
- ■ Accident?   _____
- ■ Illness?   _____

Are benefits available:
- ■ For total disability?   _____
- ■ For partial disability?   _____
  - ■ Only after total disability?   _____
  - ■ Without a prior period of total disability?   _____

The maximum benefit will replace what
percentage of income?   _____

How long must I be disabled before
premiums are waived?   _____

Is there an option to buy additional coverage, without
evidence of insurability, at a later date?   _____

Does the policy offer an inflation adjustment feature? If so:
- ■ What is the rate of increase?   _____
- ■ How often is it applied?   _____
- ■ For how long?   _____

What does the policy cost?   _____
- ■ With an inflation feature?   _____
- ■ Without an inflation feature?   _____

SPECIAL SITUATIONS

Are you a homemaker? Have you thought it would be a good idea to carry disability income insurance, in case you are disabled and help must be hired to care for small children? Have you ever tried to buy such insurance? Have you found an insurance company that would sell it to you?

Or are you, perhaps, a free lance, running a business out of your home? Have you, as a self-employed businessperson, tried to secure disability income protection? While self-employed men can secure disability income protection without too much difficulty, self-employed women often find it extremely difficult to do so.

The problem is what insurers call a "track record." They don't want to insure you against loss of earnings unless those earnings (and their loss, if you are ill and unable to work) can be independently documented.

The housewife, with no income to verify, has the most difficulty securing coverage, although some companies (the Lutheran Brotherhood, for example) will write disability income policies for homemakers. The self-employed woman may have an income but she has no employer to confirm that she is indeed on sick leave and unable to work. If you are in this position, and unable to find a company to write individual insurance, try to find and join a professional association in your field which sponsors such insurance for its members. Such association insurance, if it meets your needs, may cost less than individual insurance.

Keeping Costs Down

Good health insurance is expensive, and this is one area in which it doesn't pay to cut corners. But you can save some money if you:

■ Self-insure as much as you can afford, by taking a policy with a sizable deductible. If you have no group insurance, you're probably best off paying basic expenses yourself (you shouldn't need reimbursement for every doctor visit) and buying as much major medical coverage as you can afford. Remember, it's the costs of catastrophic illness that can wipe you out.

■ Don't overinsure. The Federal Trade Commission has estimated that over three million Americans have purchased extra health insurance coverage that they can't use and don't need. The only beneficiary of overinsurance is the insurance company that pockets the premiums. With group insurance, as a general rule, you can't collect twice for the same illness even if you have two policies; with individual insurance you may be able to collect, but what's the point? If you make an actual profit on an illness, in fact, that profit is taxable.

■ Take the appropriate tax deductions. Premiums you pay for medical-care policies (but not for hospital indemnity or disability income policies) are tax-deductible if, along with all your other deductible medical expenses (see Chapter 20), they exceed 7.5 percent of your adjusted gross income.

Note: If you are self-employed, you may be able to deduct a portion of your health insurance premiums. Consult a tax adviser because this portion of tax law is frequently changed.

Dos and Don'ts of Health Insurance

■ Compare policies carefully before you buy. Ask three or four companies to suggest a policy best suited for your age, income, and family situation. Then compare both benefits and costs. Remember: There are no standard forms, and health insurance policies differ greatly. Know what your policy does cover, whether you have group or individual insurance, and be sure to file claims promptly when appropriate.

■ Be sure, before you buy, that your policy cannot be canceled or the premiums raised unless the action applies to all policyholders in your class or in your state. Otherwise, you may find yourself out in the cold after an expensive illness.

■ Think about buying your life and health insurance from the same salesperson, if you have an agent in whom you have confidence. With more at stake, the agent is likely to be a strong advocate in your behalf.

■ Tell the whole truth on any application for insurance. Preexisting conditions will usually be covered after a waiting period. If a condition is very serious, you may have to accept a policy with no coverage for that particular ailment (although you should shop around). If you lie about a preexisting condition, however, the company may refuse a claim or even cancel your coverage.

■ Buy from a company licensed to do business in your state. Then disputes, if any, may be referred to your state insurance department.

■ Buy from a company that is solvent and likely to remain in business. Check ratings by A. M. Best Co., Standard & Poor's, and Moody's at your local library.

■ Don't replace a policy simply because it appears to be out-of-date. Instead, ask your company to upgrade the policy or buy supplementary coverage. If you do buy a new policy, keep your old one in effect at least until all waiting periods (for coverage of preexisting conditions) are exhausted.

■ Don't forget other coverage you may have. Automobile insurance policies frequently include medical benefits. Life insurance policies may include disability income riders or double indemnity provisions.

KEY POINTS

- Health insurance reform may, if enacted, provide all Americans with a package of basic benefits.

- Right now, health insurance comes in a variety of forms. Most important: Major medical or comprehensive to cover the big expenses, plus disability income insurance to replace income lost due to long-term illness or injury. Medicare supplement ("Medigap") policies can help older people fill the gaps in Medicare coverage. Long-term care insurance is growing in popularity as a way to meet the costs of long-term custodial care in a nursing home or at home.

- Health maintenance organizations (HMOs) can be an alternative to traditional fee-for-service insurance. HMOs typically cover preventive care as well as treatment, and require little or no paperwork. They may, however, limit your choice of doctors and hospitals.

- If your insurer or HMO requires second surgical opinions and pre-admission authorization for hospital stays, be sure you comply or you can forfeit coverage.

- Most people are insured through group policies. Individual alternatives include extending group coverage when you leave a job, joining an HMO, or taking a policy through a Blue Cross-Blue Shield group or a commercial insurer. For the hard-to-insure, about half the states now have risk pools where coverage may be obtained albeit at a higher price.

- Before buying an individual disability income policy, be sure you understand what coverage may be available to you through your job, through Social Security, through Veterans Affairs or union benefits, and so on. In buying an individual disability income policy, keep costs down by electing a longer waiting period before benefits begin but be sure to keep benefits in force until age 65.

Looking
Ahead

CHAPTER 20

Tax Planning

Taxes play a major part in financial planning. Many thought for a brief moment that the highly touted Tax Reform Act of 1986 would actually "reform" and simplify tax structure. It hasn't worked that way. And it isn't likely to, as long as "the tax bill to end all tax bills" is just one of a long series of complex and confusing changes in the tax code. Tax rates have already begun to inch up again (not surprising, with the size of the federal deficit). Changes in the rules (phasing out both personal exemptions and itemized deductions at specified income levels) mean that some higher-income taxpayers pay sizable hidden taxes. Add to this equation the "indirect" taxes we all pay (including both excise taxes and ever-increasing amounts for Social Security) and the desperate revenue needs of state governments, and you see a formidable tax burden. Under President Clinton's proposals (being considered by Congress at this writing; see p. 568), the burden will only get worse.

According to the Tax Foundation, an independent research organization based in Washington, DC, annual tax increases over the last decade averaged 6.4 percent. If that doesn't sound like much, contrast the figure with a 2.5 percent annual growth in personal income and a 3.9 percent annual average growth in the Consumer Price Index. The combination of higher taxes and ongoing inflation (even though the inflation rate is moderate compared to the recent past) has made the typical family poorer each year from 1989 through 1992 (see Tables 20.1 and 20.2).

In hard dollars and cents, this means that a two-earner family earning $53,984 with two dependent children in 1992 paid out a total of $21,445 in taxes—or just under 40 percent of income. That's more than the average American family pays for food, clothing, and housing combined. Federal income taxes may be down from a high of 17 percent of family budgets in

Table 20.1: Family Income After Taxes and Inflation[1], 1980-1992

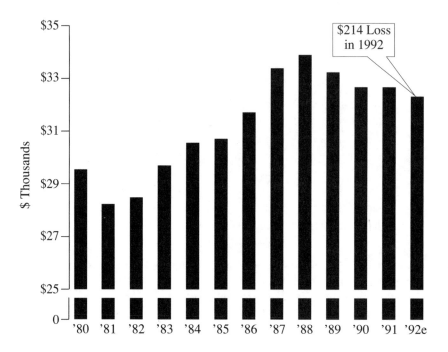

Source: Tax Foundation.

Note: [1]Income after federal taxes and inflation computed in 1992 dollars.

1981 to 12 percent today—but, says the Tax Foundation, this relief has been overwhelmed by the rising toll of Social Security taxes, federal excise taxes, and state and local taxes.

In any case, although many lower-income Americans were removed from the federal income tax rolls by the 1986 measure, one look at the tax law and at the tax forms that must now be filled out will convince most taxpayers that change is not necessarily simplification and that lower tax rates do not necessarily result in lower tax bills. As Table 20.4 indicates, the per capita federal tax burden has moved inexorably upward for the last decade.

Financial decisions should not be governed by tax considerations, but you will want to keep taxes in mind as you plan your finances.

Your Tax Bracket

Income tax rates have gone up and down since the federal income tax began in 1913. Although they have come down in recent years, with so-called

Table 20.2: Net Annual Gain or Loss in Family After-Tax Real Income, 1982-1992

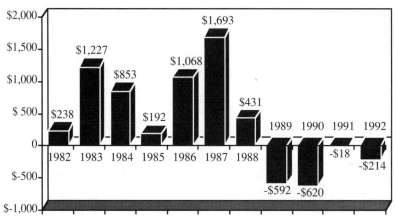

Source: Tax Foundation.

Table 20.3: The Typical American Family's 1992 Budget[1]

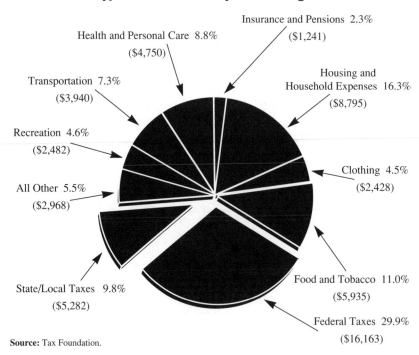

Source: Tax Foundation.

Note: [1]This example uses a two-earner family earning $53,984 per year with two dependent children.

Table 20.4: Per Capita Total Federal Tax Burden, Fiscal Years 1983-1993

Source: Tax Foundation.

tax "reduction" and "simplification," Americans are actually paying more in taxes than is apparent on the surface.

In 1993 (pending adoption of the Clinton proposals) there are three federal income tax brackets: 15, 28, and 31 percent. But it's not that simple. If your adjusted gross income exceeds $100,000 you are subject to a limitation on itemized deductions (see p. 573). Then there's a phaseout of personal exemptions (see p. 581), and a toughened alternative minimum tax (see p. 593). And that's just on the federal level. Nearly half of the 50 states were wrestling with record deficits in 1992, according to the Tax Foundation, and tackling those deficits with across-the-board tax increases.

Planning tip: If you're thinking about a move, think taxes. With combined state and local taxes (income, property, sales, etc.) consuming almost 10 percent of the average family's budget, where you settle can make a big difference in how much money you have left after taxes.

MARGINAL TAX RATES

The marginal rate is the rate of taxation on the top dollar you earn. Suppose you and your spouse, filing a joint return, declare taxable income of $46,000 for 1993 on an earned gross income of $54,000. Your tax is $5,535 plus 28 percent of the amount over $36,900, for a total of $8,083. You can have a joint taxable income of up to $89,150 before that percentage goes to 31 percent. So all the dollars that you earn between $36,900 and $89,150 will be taxed at the marginal rate of 28 percent. This is what you mean when you say that you're in a 28 percent tax bracket. The marginal rate will be higher under the Clinton tax measure, and higher-income taxpayers will pay considerably more (see Table 20.5).

Table 20.5: The Impact of Higher Tax Rates

Contrasting tax liabilities under current tax law and under the Clinton proposals. All four taxpayers are families of four, married filing jointly, with one working spouse. All income is from wages. Taxpayer A uses the standard deduction; Taxpayers B, C, and D itemize their deductions, claiming the average itemized deductions for their respective income ranges.

Taxpayer	Taxable Income	Tax Under Current Law	Tax Under Proposed Law[1]	Percentage Increase
A	$ 25,000	$ 3,750	$ 3,750	0
B	50,000	9,203	9,203	0
C	150,000	39,029	39,529	1.3%
D	300,000	85,529	95,329[2]	11.5%

Source: Ernst & Young, *Financial Planning Reporter.*

Notes: [1] The calculations do not reflect increased Medicare tax on Taxpayers C and D. [2] Includes the 10% surtax on taxable income over $250,000.

An Added Income

John Black is an assistant professor of English at a university in the Northeast, and was the sole wage earner for the family while the children were young. In 1992 his income was $43,000. Then, in 1993, his wife Nancy obtained a part-time job earning $15,000. John, meanwhile, received a $2,000 raise. The Blacks had an additional $17,000 in income ... and wound up the year having to borrow over $2,000 to pay income tax. What happened?

John's withholding assumed a maximum tax rate of 28 percent, while Nancy's withholding was based on a maximum of 15 percent. When they filed a joint tax return, however, Nancy's income added to John's created a joint income taxed at the 31 percent marginal rate.

If Nancy and John had adjusted the amount of tax withheld from their paychecks to reflect the change in bracket, they would have been okay. Or they could have saved the money during the year to meet the tax bill. Instead they wound up in debt. Fewer people are affected by this kind of "bracket creep" since the reduction in the number of tax brackets, but it can still happen. Don't let it happen to you. If your income jumps, for any reason, think of taxes before you spend.

EFFECTIVE TAX RATES

You don't, fortunately, pay your marginal rate on everything you earn. It's easy, and often heartening, to figure out your effective tax rate. Simply take the actual income taxes you pay, in dollars, and divide the figure by the total of your gross income for the year. Using the same example used to illustrate marginal tax rates above, taxes of $8,083 on a gross income of $54,000 equal an effective tax rate of just under 15 percent.

There are, of course, a lot of variables in this equation. The actual number of exemptions and deductions and credits you can claim, and whether or not you itemize deductions at all, will affect your taxable income and hence your tax. Where you live also makes a significant difference. Federal taxes may be the same, and may account for the bulk of your tax outlay, but local taxes, which vary enormously, also make a difference. Residents of New York City, with one of the heaviest tax burdens in the nation, pay both state and city income taxes as well as federal. Residents of Texas, at the other extreme, pay no state income tax at all.

The Clinton Tax Proposals

Before	After
3 tax brackets: 15%, 28%, 31%	4 tax brackets: 15%, 28%, 31%, 36%
Up to 50% of Social Security benefits subject to tax when total income exceeds $32,000 for married couples and $25,000 for singles	Up to 85% of Social Security benefits subject to tax when total income exceeds these limits
Medicare tax is 1.45% up to wages of $135,000	No ceiling; all wages subject to Medicare tax of 1.45%
Alternative minimum tax 24%, with exemptions for joint filers with taxable income up to $40,000, single filers up to $30,000, and married filing separately up to $20,000	Alternative minimum tax: 16% up to $176,000; 28% on excess. Exemptions increased to $45,000, $33,750, and $22,500
Maximum estate and gift tax rate is 50% for transfers over $2.5 million	Maximum estate and gift tax rate is 55% for transfers over $2.5 million

If you live where you face a state income tax and possibly a local income tax as well, you should calculate your overall tax bracket. For example, suppose your federal tax bracket is 31 percent. You have a state income tax of 15 percent. Your combined tax rate is 46 percent, reduced by the federal tax ben-

---

Taxes on Domestic Workers

One of the hottest issues of early 1993 was "Nannygate," the flap about appointees for attorney general who had neglected to pay taxes for domestic workers. In the wake of this brouhaha, Congress is examining the issue and may raise the income threshold at which Social Security taxes are due.

Unless and until action is actually taken, however, these are the rules:

■ Employees hired after November 7, 1986, must be legally eligible for employment in the United States; you are required to verify and maintain records showing this legal eligibility.

■ If you pay a domestic worker cash wages of $50 or more during a calendar quarter, then Social Security and Medicare taxes are due. You may deduct the employee's share from her wages, or pay both halves yourself. (In mid-1993 discussion centered on raising this threshold from $50 a quarter to $1,750 a year, or about the amount by which inflation has raised the $50-a-quarter income level set in 1950.)

■ You must file Form 942, "Employer's Quarterly Tax Return for Household Employees" each quarter, and Form W-2 each year. (If a change is adopted, you may be able to pay Social Security obligations on household help each April 15, as part of your own annual income tax return.)

■ Federal unemployment tax is due for any domestic employee paid $1,000 or more during any calendar quarter.

■ Wages paid to a domestic employee are subject to income tax but you do not have to withhold tax unless you and the employee agree that you will do so.

For more information, "What You Ought To Know About Hiring a Domestic" is available for $5 from Commerce Clearing House, 4025 West Peterson Ave., Chicago, IL 60646; (800) 248-3248.

efit you receive from the deduction of the state taxes on your federal return. This reduction in your tax rate (31 percent of 15 percent, or 4.65 percent) gives you an actual combined tax bracket of 35.65 percent.

Don't forget to consider the impact of taxes other than income taxes: sales taxes, excise taxes, property taxes, and so on. From gasoline to telephone service, a great many products and services, important in our daily lives, carry higher price tags because of hidden taxes.

Note: Social Security and Medicare taxes are called "contributions" by Uncle Sam, but they aren't voluntary and they do add to your tax burden. In 1993, you paid 6.2 percent of wages up to $57,600 toward Social Security and another 1.45 percent of wages up to $135,000 toward Medicare. Double the percentages if you are self-employed.

Both the applicable percentage and the wage base rise regularly, and the impact can be significant. In 1990, when the wage base for the Medicare tax was $125,000, an employee earning this much or more in wages would have paid combined FICA (Federal Insurance Contributions Act) taxes of $3,924; in 1991, at the same wage base, the combined tax became $5,123. Since the self-employed paid both the employee and the employer share, self-employment income of $125,000 or more meant a contribution of $10,246 in 1991, up from $7,848 in 1990. With President Clinton's proposal to impose the Medicare tax on *all* wages, without a ceiling, high-income people will pay considerably more.

Taxes (including state and local income taxes, sales taxes, and property taxes as well as federal income and Social Security taxes) may well be the single largest item in your budget. Take the time to figure out both your marginal tax rate and your effective tax rate. The first will help you decide how best to put your dollars to work (a high marginal rate may make tax-sheltering worthwhile). The second will tell you how much of your own income you actually have to work with after paying taxes.

Q My husband and I are in the midst of divorce proceedings. Rather than pay separate alimony and child support, he wants to make a single monthly payment for both. He claims it will be simpler. Should I accept this?

A No. Alimony is subject to income tax, but child support is not. If they are lumped together, you will have to pay tax on the entire amount. (Your husband, conversely, may claim alimony, but not child support, as a deduction on his tax return—a reason he may want to pay the full sum in alimony alone.)

Taxable Income

The key to your tax bracket is your net or taxable income. Reducing the net is the way to reduce both your bracket and the amount of tax you pay. The Internal Revenue Service (IRS) makes a clear distinction between taxable and nontaxable income, and in at least some instances you can control the category into which your income falls.

Note: Tax law is extremely complex. It also changes regularly. This chapter highlights some of the information, accurate as of this writing, that you can use in your overall financial planning. For specific advice, consult a competent tax adviser.

GROSS INCOME

Your gross income consists of every item of income, from any source, unless it's specifically excluded in the tax law (see below). Gross income includes wages, salary, tips, business receipts, interest and dividends, rents, royalties, annuities, pensions, etc. The IRS is quite literal in its definition of source: If you make $200 at a garage sale (after related expenses and the cost of the goods sold), you are supposed to report it as taxable income. If you belong to a barter club and swap your skill at upholstering for someone else's skill at dentistry (or for "credits" which you can exchange for goods or services at a later date), you are supposed to report the fair market value as part of your gross income.

To compute taxable income, gross income is reduced by exclusions and by deductions, and the resulting tax liability is reduced by credits. **Exclusions** are items not subject to tax; many need not even be listed on your tax return. **Deductions** reduce the amount of taxable income; the actual saving from a deduction depends on your tax bracket. **Credits** are a direct reduction of the tax owed; a dollar credit is a dollar saved.

Exclusions

Some "income" is excluded from gross income right from the start, although some previously customary exclusions have now been dropped from the list. Since passage of the 1986 tax act, for example, all unemployment compensation is taxable as income. So are all dividends, and most awards and prizes. Still, you do not have to count:

■ Accident and health insurance reimbursement, with some exceptions. If you deduct medical expenses in one tax year and receive reimbursement from an insurance company in the next tax year, the reimbursement is includable in gross income in the tax year it is received, up to the amount of the deduction previously taken. Disability insurance (income replacement) benefits are not taxable if you have paid the premiums; they are taxable if your employer has paid the premiums on your behalf.

■ Employer-paid accident and health insurance premiums, and premiums for up to $50,000 of group term life insurance (although there are recurrent proposals to tax as income some or all of employer-paid health insurance premiums).

■ Worker's compensation and similar benefits.

■ Child-support payments from an ex-spouse.

■ The gain on the sale of your home, if you reinvest the proceeds in another home within two years, or a gain of up to $125,000 if you are at least 55 years old and have used the home as your principal residence for at least three of the previous five years. See Chapter 13 for details.

■ Cash rebates on the purchase of a new car or other item (the rebate simply reduces the price you pay; it is not income). Note, however, that some states are levying sales tax on the total purchase price of a car, including a rebate or trade-in (see chapter 15).

■ Proceeds of damage awards, if you win a lawsuit for slander, libel, or personal injury. But interest earned on the money from the time of the award until you actually receive it is taxable, and damages for lost wages or lost profits are entirely taxable.

■ Life insurance proceeds paid to you as a beneficiary. If the proceeds are received in installments, with interest added, however, you may owe some tax on the amount by which the proceeds are greater than they would have been at the insured's date of death.

■ Gifts and inheritances are not taxable as income although they may, as described in Chapter 21, be subject to gift or inheritance tax. Also, if property you receive through gift or inheritance later earns interest, that interest is taxable income.

Q I won $25,000 in a sweepstakes and got a check for the full amount. What do I do about taxes?

A Sweepstake and lottery winnings are taxable and you must declare your winnings as ordinary income when you file your federal income tax return. Should you be lucky enough to win again in the future, you can reduce the taxes due by (1) keeping receipts for all lottery tickets you buy in the course of a year, if you buy them regularly, and deducting the cost of losing tickets, and (2) buying tickets jointly, so that income and taxes are split among several people. Meanwhile, if the winnings will increase the tax you owe this year by a substantial sum, you may have to file a declaration of estimated tax and make quarterly payments. Consult a tax adviser.

■ Most Social Security retirement benefits although up to 50 percent (85 percent under the Clinton proposals) may be subject to tax if total income exceeds specified limits.

■ Interest on most tax-exempt bonds issued by state and local agencies, although the interest on some municipal bonds is subject to the alternative minimum tax (see p. 593). Note: Interest on U.S. Treasury issues is not taxable on state income tax returns.

■ Scholarships and grants, if you are a degree candidate and the payment is made for your education and training. If you must work as a teaching or research assistant in exchange for your grant, the amount is still not taxable as long as the money goes toward tuition and as long as all degree candidates are required to perform similar services. (If you are not a degree candidate, certain limitations apply.)

Adjusted Gross Income

This is a phrase that crops up regularly in tax jargon. It refers to your entire ("gross") income minus specific adjustments. Examples of adjustments include contributions to Individual Retirement Accounts (IRAs) or Keogh plans for those who are eligible, interest lost on time deposits because of early withdrawal, alimony payments, and some disability income payments. (Job-related moving expenses and unreimbursed business expenses, formerly adjustments to gross income, are now treated as itemized deductions.)

The term is a technical one. You'll arrive at it, without necessarily understanding just why certain deductions crop up here and others at a later point in the tax form, simply by following the step-by-step instructions on the form itself.

Other deductions are subtracted from adjusted gross income to arrive at taxable income. Be sure to claim all allowable deductions and you'll shelter some of your income from taxes.

DEDUCTIONS

Itemizing deductions is still a good way for many taxpayers to reduce the tax that is due. Bear in mind, though, that under current federal law taxpayers with adjusted gross income exceeding $100,000 are subject to a limitation on otherwise allowable itemized deductions. That limitation reduces allowable itemized deductions (other than medical expenses, casualty and theft losses, and investment interest expense) by 3 percent of the amount by which adjusted gross income exceeds $100,000. If you are in this category, be sure to consult a tax adviser.

Here are details on some specific deductions:

Individual Retirement Accounts

You do not have to itemize deductions to claim a deduction for contributions to an IRA. The $2,000 a year that may be contributed to an Individual Retirement Account ($4,000 if you and your spouse both hold paying jobs,

$2,250 if only one of you works outside the home) comes right off the top of your gross income—if you are eligible for the deduction (see p. 688). It therefore lowers your taxes.

If, for instance, you are in a 28 percent tax bracket, putting $2,000 into an IRA saves you $560 in taxes. If you don't invest in your own retirement, you won't have the whole $2,000 to invest in something else; you'll only have $1,440. The same deductibility holds for Keogh plans, which are for the self-employed. (**Note:** Depending on your income, you may be entitled to a partial deduction for your IRA contribution.)

Income tax on the interest earned by your IRA and Keogh funds is deferred until you withdraw the money, when, presumably, you will be retired and in a lower tax bracket. IRAs and Keogh plans are, therefore, a superlative tax shelter for middle-income Americans who qualify. (For more on both IRAs and Keogh plans, see Chapter 23).

Moving Expenses

If you moved because you changed jobs, and the new place of work is at least 35 miles farther from your old home than your previous job location, you may deduct some related expenses (subject to certain limitations): house-hunting trips, travel to your new home, temporary living expenses at the new location, moving household goods, and so on. You must file an itemized return in order to claim this deduction, but the deduction is not subject to the 2 percent rule that applies to many miscellaneous deductions (see p. 580).

Here are the requirements:

■ You must be employed full time for at least 39 weeks during the year immediately following the move. If you're self-employed, you must work full time for at least 39 weeks during the first 12 months *and* a total of at least 78 weeks of the two years following the move.

Q My employer has transferred me to another office and is paying my moving expenses. My neighbor says the company must pay the movers directly rather than reimburse me, or I will have to pay tax on the money. Is she right?

A Not exactly. Whether your employer pays the movers directly or reimburses you, the money should be reported as income on your W-2 for the year and you will owe taxes on it. However, if you meet the requirements and if you itemize deductions on your federal income tax return, you may be able to deduct all or most of your moving costs. To do so, complete Form 3903 and attach it to your return.

■ The moving expenses must generally be incurred within a year after you begin your new job.

■ Expenses must be reasonable.

Reasonable deductible expenses include:

■ The costs of moving your household goods and personal effects, including the costs of moving those items from a place other than your old residence if it's no more than the cost of a move from your former home (this might be a good time to clear those wedding presents out of your mother's basement).

■ Travel expenses, including meals and lodging, for yourself and your family (even if you don't travel together), while en route from your old residence to your new one.

■ The costs of pre-move house-hunting trips, after obtaining work in the new location, for you or a member of your family.

■ The costs of occupying temporary quarters (meals and lodging alone) at the new location for a period of up to 30 consecutive days (this deduction is eliminated in the Clinton tax proposal).

■ The costs of selling or acquiring a home. Such fees as real estate commissions (when you sell), escrow fees, attorney's fees, title costs, and the like may be used either to reduce the gain from selling your old home or to add to the basis of your new home. It may be preferable to deduct them as moving expenses, but you'll have to make a decision. You can't do both. (The choice will be eliminated if the Clinton tax proposals are adopted; the costs of selling and buying a home will not be deductible as moving expenses.)

The deduction for house-hunting trips, temporary lodging, and selling and buying a residence is currently limited to $3,000 overall, of which no more than $1,500 may be for house-hunting trips and temporary quarters. But the

---

Q I took a new job 40 miles from where I was living, then bought a new house that is more convenient for commuting but is actually 45 miles from the job location. Can I deduct my moving expenses?

A Yes, but only if you can convince the IRS that there was a good reason for moving farther from your new job. An acceptable reason might be that you would have had to drive 40 miles through congested areas to get to your new job from your old house; the move enabled you to take a train that saves considerable commuting time.

expenses of actually moving household goods and traveling to your new home are fully deductible at this writing with no dollar limitation. Note, though, that a bill pending in Congress would limit the deduction for all moving costs to a total of $5,000 and subject these costs to the 2 percent limitation for miscellaneous deductions (see p. 580).

Charitable Contributions

Only taxpayers who itemize deductions may deduct charitable contributions, and then only to qualifying organizations. Political organizations or lobbying groups, for example, do not qualify.

It's easy to track donations made by check. But you'll also want to keep records of cash contributions (pocket change on the street, several dollars at your door) and on donations of merchandise (canned goods to a food bank, used clothes to a charity's thrift shop, a used car or computer to a school).

Note: You must secure an independent appraisal (not one from the organization receiving the donation) to document the fair market value of donated property worth more than $5,000.

Don't forget out-of-pocket expenses in connection with volunteer activities. If you do volunteer work for a qualified charitable organization, without pay, you may deduct as charitable contributions the direct cost of doing the work: telephone calls, postage, uniforms. You may also deduct travel at either 12 cents a mile or the actual costs of gas and oil; either way you may deduct tolls and parking fees as well.

Q After I was laid off from my job, I went into business as a consultant. I work from home, and I planned to take a deduction for a home office, but a colleague said that I can't. Can she be right?

A Unfortunately, the IRS recently narrowed the definition of an allowable home office. To be your principal place of business, your home office must not only be your sole office, it must also be the place where you spend most of your time. If you are working many hours in your clients' offices (or, as in the specific case the IRS ruled on, if you are a physician working in a hospital but without an office there), you may be out of luck. But don't give up the idea without talking to a knowledgeable tax adviser.

Note: Many tax advisers consider any home office deduction, no matter how legitimate, a "red flag" to the IRS. Rather than trigger an audit, they suggest, skip the deduction. If your claim is valid, however, and if you have the records to document your claim, the home office deduction is permitted by law.

You can also benefit by donating appreciated property. Instead of donating $1,000 in cash, for instance, you might donate securities currently worth $1,000 for which you originally paid $500. In doing so, you may claim a deduction for the current fair market value of $1,000 while avoiding the tax you would pay on the appreciated value of the stock if you sold it. Note, however, that donations of appreciated property generally have to be used in computing the alternative minimum tax.

Medical Expenses

The costs of medical and dental treatment, including a wide range of services, are deductible if you file an itemized return and if they are not reimbursed by insurance, to the extent that they exceed 7.5 percent of adjusted gross income. Drugs are no longer categorized separately; instead, prescription drugs and insulin may be lumped with other medical expenses in seeking the 7.5 percent threshold while over-the-counter medication other than insulin isn't counted at all. Travel expenses for medical care are deductible, either at nine cents a mile or actual out-of-pocket cost. Health insurance premiums are not deductible unless, together with other medical expenditures, they bring you over the 7.5 percent limit (note, though, that the self-employed could until mid-1992 deduct 25 percent of health insurance premiums; the provision expired but is expected to be extended retroactively). Premiums for life insurance policies, disability income policies, and hospital indemnity (cash payment) policies are not deductible at all.

There are frequently differences of opinion between the IRS and individual taxpayers with respect to claims for medical deductions. Sometimes the IRS wins; sometimes, believe it or not, the taxpayer wins. One woman's doctor prescribed a special high-protein diet to alleviate symptoms of hypoglycemia. She claimed a tax deduction for the extra costs of the special diet. The IRS disallowed the deduction, on the basis that the food was simply a substitute for food she would otherwise consume. The tax court, however, disagreed. She was allowed to take the deduction.

Suggestion: Always take a deduction you believe to be legitimate, but be prepared to argue your case.

Q My daughter is gradually going blind from an incurable illness. I know that her medical costs are tax-deductible. But what about all the special equipment she needs?

A You may take a deduction for the cost of equipment related to her condition: special lenses, a special typewriter, a tape recorder, and so on. For specific information, consult IRS Publication No. 907.

Interest

Millions of Americans deduct the interest payable on home mortgage loans (another superlative tax shelter), but other forms of interest used to be fully deductible as well: interest on personal or business loans, interest on installment loans and bank credit cards, prepayment penalties and finance charges, and interest paid on federal income tax balances due. No more. Deductible interest now falls into two main categories:

1) Mortgage interest on first and second homes is still fully deductible, up to the original purchase price of the house if purchased before October 13, 1987 and up to mortgages of $1,000,000 taken after October 13, 1987. Interest on up to $100,000 in home equity loans (see p. 204) is also deductible.

2) A deduction may be taken for interest on loans used to finance investments, but the deduction is generally limited to the amount of investment income. If investment interest exceeds investment income, the excess may be carried forward to offset investment income in future years.

Note: Don't borrow money for a tax-exempt investment, expecting to deduct the interest on the loan while sheltering the interest you receive. You can't have it both ways.

Taxes

If you itemize deductions on your federal income tax return, you may deduct other taxes that you pay during the year: state and local income taxes, real property taxes, and personal property taxes. You may not deduct sales taxes, Social Security or Railroad Retirement taxes withheld from your pay, federal gift and estate taxes, or state inheritance or gift taxes.

Q My bank loaned me $3,000 toward the purchase of a $10,000 certificate of deposit (CD). The interest on the CD, of course, is taxable. But how do I handle the interest I pay on the loan? Do I just report the difference between the two as income?

A No. You may have made a package deal with the bank, but the components are separate transactions as far as the IRS is concerned. You must report the total interest you receive on the $10,000 CD. You may also deduct some of the interest you pay on the $3,000 loan (up to the amount of interest income from the CD plus your other dividend and interest income), but only if you file an itemized return.

Note: State and local income taxes, while deductible, can count in the calculation of whether the alternative minimum tax is due (see p. 593).

Casualty and Theft Losses

Casualty losses stem from damage to property from sudden and unexpected events. Theft losses arise from the unlawful taking of property. In both cases, the 1982 Tax Act made a drastic change: Formerly, uninsured losses exceeding $100 could be deducted on your federal income tax return. If a storm did $500 worth of damage to uninsured property, or if an uninsured ring worth $500 was stolen, you could have deducted $400 on your federal return. If the same property was insured for $200, you would have had a $200 deduction. No more. The $100 that is not deductible remains intact. But what *is* deductible is now limited to losses that exceed 10 percent of your adjusted gross income. If your adjusted gross income is $30,000, your loss would have to exceed $3,000 (plus the $100 floor or $3,100) before you can claim a deduction. It now becomes more important than ever before to carry adequate insurance on your home, your automobile, and your valuable personal property.

The IRS has claimed that amounts that *could* be reimbursed by insurance are not deductible, even if you don't collect. The tax court has ruled, however, that a taxpayer can choose not to file a claim with the insurance company—you might not think it's worth higher rates or the possibility of cancellation—and still deduct the loss on an itemized return. (The case was not decided unanimously, however, and there may be further challenges.)

If you do qualify for a theft deduction—if, for example, a burglar made off with all your jewelry—you can't claim more than you paid for the property, no matter what its current value. (If you insure some items, such as gold jewelry, up to appreciated values, you may even wind up with a taxable gain from the insurance reimbursement. But you can skip all or part of the taxes on the gain by using the insurance proceeds to replace the stolen item within two years.)

You must document your loss, with purchase receipts, appraisals, photos, and/or police reports. Since casualty and theft losses are carefully scrutinized by the IRS, it's a good idea to attach copies of documents directly to your tax return. Don't wait to be challenged. And be sure to keep the originals of all documents submitted with your tax return.

Educational Expenses

You may deduct the costs of going to school, both tuition and transportation costs, if (1) the education is required by your employer or by the law in order to keep your job, or (2) the education maintains or improves skills used in your present work. You may *not* deduct expenses for education that is required of you in order to meet the minimum requirements of your present job, or for education that qualifies you for a new occupation.

Miscellaneous Deductions

There are other deductions available to taxpayers who itemize, from adoption expenses to union dues to fees for tax preparation and advice. Under current law, however, expenses in this category are deductible only to the extent that they, as a group, exceed 2 percent of adjusted gross income. Consult IRS Publication No. 17, "Your Federal Income Tax," for a complete list.

Table 20.6: Average Itemized Deductions on Federal Income Tax Forms in 1990

Adjusted gross income	Medical	Taxes	Gifts	Interest
$ 25-30,000	3,306	2,069	1,129	4,662
30-40,000	3,317	2,477	1,213	5,011
40-50,000	3,621	3,015	1,315	5,667
50-75,000	4,002	4,049	1,665	6,595
75-100,000	6,003	5,888	2,112	8,847
100-200,000	12,087	9,359	3,442	13,324
200-500,000	26,295	20,075	7,367	20,831

Source: Research Institute of America.

TAX CREDITS

A credit is a dollar-for-dollar write-off against taxes due and is therefore more valuable than a deduction. Certain tax credits can be claimed whether or not you file the long form.

Q What are the rules on allowable deductions at different income levels? Are there specific amounts I'm allowed to claim?

A You may claim only what you actually spend. But you may find some guidelines in the statistical averages in Table 20.6, compiled by the Research Institute of America from IRS figures. If your claims are higher, you increase your chances of an audit, so be sure that you have adequate documentation. If your deductions are much smaller, you may have overlooked some things you should claim. Remember, these are just averages and you are entitled to all the legitimate deductions that you can document—no more and no less.

Child and Dependent Care Credit

You have a five-year-old who can't be left alone, yet you need to work. Or you have a disabled spouse or parent. If you must pay someone to care for a child under age 13 or for a dependent adult (a spouse or parent who is physically or mentally incapacitated) so that you can work or look for work, you may claim a tax credit. The credit is on a sliding scale, ranging from $720 for one dependent at an adjusted gross income of $10,000 to $480 at an income of $28,000 or more. The amount is doubled for two or more dependents.

Note: Although the credit may be claimed by taxpayers looking for work, it can't be claimed unless you have earned income during the year. If you pay a sitter and start looking for a first job in November but don't start receiving a paycheck until January, you can't claim the credit for the year in which you've looked but not earned.

Excess Social Security

If you hold two jobs during the year, either both at once or consecutively, you might have too much withheld in Social Security taxes. If so, you may claim the excess as a credit on your tax return. But if you worked for just one employer, and too much Social Security tax was withheld, you may not claim a tax credit. Your employer will have to make the adjustment.

Exemptions

The number of exemptions you claim affects the amount of tax you pay. Each personal exemption is worth $2,350 for 1993, and is adjusted each year for inflation.

But the personal exemption for high-income taxpayers phases out gradually for joint filers with adjusted gross incomes (AGIs) over $162,700 in 1993 and for single taxpayers with AGIs exceeding $108,450. If you exceed

Q My job keeps me away from home from eight to six. The public school my 7-year-old would normally attend has classes only from nine to three. A good private school nearby has before-school and after-school programs specifically for the children of working mothers. If I send him there, can I take a tax credit for the tuition?

A You can't claim a credit for the tuition, but if the school will itemize its bills, you can claim a credit for the special programs before and after regular school hours.

these income limits, each $2,350 personal exemption is reduced by 2 percent for each $2,500 (or fraction thereof) that your adjusted gross income exceeds the threshold amount. In effect, the phase-out raises your tax rate by a little over one-half of 1 percent for each personal exemption you claim.

Note: A new baby is occasion for congratulations. It's also occasion to apply for a Social Security number—now required for any child over the age of one who is claimed as a dependent.

You may claim exemptions for dependents who meet all five of the following tests:

1) You must provide more than half of the dependent's total support during the calendar year.

2) You may not take an exemption for a dependent if that person has gross income of more than a specified amount for the year ($2,350 for 1993, rising with inflation), unless the dependent is your child and is either under 19 at the end of the year or a full-time student for at least five (not necessarily consecutive) months of the year.

Note: Children who can be claimed as dependents on their parents' tax returns may not claim a personal exemption on their own returns as well.

3) Unrelated people may be dependents if they are members of your household for the entire taxable year; certain relatives may be dependents no matter where they live, if they meet the other tests.

4) Your dependents must generally be citizens or residents of the United States.

Q We provided room, board, and spending money for a Swedish high school student from January through mid-June while she attended our local high school. May we claim her as a dependent on our income tax?

A You can't claim her as a dependent, but you may deduct up to $50 of your costs per month as a charitable contribution. IRS rules state that the student, foreign or American, must be both a member of your household (but not a relative or dependent) and a full-time student in the twelfth or lower grade (college exchange students don't qualify). You must have a written agreement with the sponsoring organization, and the purpose of the visit must be to provide educational opportunities for the student. Then itemize your deduction with the description "foreign exchange student living in my home (dates) under an agreement with (organization)." Don't attach the agreement to your tax form, but do keep it with your tax records.

5) You may not claim as a dependent anyone who files a joint return with someone else, unless the only reason for filing a return is to claim a refund of tax withheld. For example: You support your daughter and her husband while they attend college. They owe no taxes but file a return to receive a refund of taxes withheld on her summer job. You may claim them both as dependents, as long as the other tests are met.

WHO IS A DEPENDENT?

It's easy to list the rules, but it's not always quite as easy to interpret them. Here are some special situations in which the above rules apply:

Children

■ A baby born on December 31 counts as an exemption for the entire year, as does a child adopted at any time during the year. A foster child may be claimed if he or she lived in your household for the entire year.

■ College students, on the road between dependence and independence, sometimes create special problems. While age does not count, as long as the child is a full-time student, the other tests still apply. The trickiest of these, for many parents, is the issue of providing at least half of the student's support. Here are two things you should know: Scholarships do not count in calculating support; and the value of lodging you supply your children when they are home on vacation does count toward support. If children have independent income which would edge just over the half-support boundary, have them bank the excess. As long as the money is not actually spent on the student's support, it won't count against your claim of a dependent. Be sure to calculate your youngsters' earnings *and* the income from any assets you've put in their names to reduce taxes. If children earn

Q My daughter is staunchly independent and wants to pay for as much of her own college expenses as she can. This year she's put up $4,300, from summer and year-round part-time jobs. We've contributed $3,500 to her college costs. Is there any way we can still claim the exemption?

A Yes. If you figure in the "fair rental value" of her room and board while she is at home, you'll probably find that you still provide more than half her support. You may also figure in any major purchase, such as a car, which you make for her.

enough to go over the halfway mark, have them save some or you'll lose the exemption.

Divorce and Child Custody

There are special rules to determine which divorced parent gets to claim the exemption for a dependent child. Both *custody* and *support* come into play.

The parent who has custody usually gets to claim the exemption, whether or not that parent actually provides more than half the child's support. But there are three exceptions:

1) If a pre-1985 divorce decree or other written agreement allows your ex-partner to claim the exemption, and if that parent actually contributes $600 a year to each child's support, then your former spouse may claim the exemption.
2) The parents can shift the exemption to the noncustodial parent by filing Form 8332 with the noncustodial parent's return each year.
3) The parents can negotiate a multiple support agreement that allows the child to be claimed by the noncustodial parent.

Suggestion: Think about tax exemptions, as well as about actual levels of support, when you draw up a divorce agreement.

Parents

If you get together with others to support a dependent (for example, if you and your sisters pitch in to support your father), one of you may claim him as a dependent as long as the others sign an agreement specifying that they will not do so for that tax year. You may take turns in subsequent years, if you choose to do so, as long as anyone making the claim contributes at least 10 percent of the support.

Medicare payments do not count as support. You may claim an elderly parent as a dependent even if Medicare payments add up to much more than half the support for the year.

Income that is excludable from the dependent's gross income, such as Social Security benefits, is not counted toward the $2,350 gross income permitted for 1993 (again, this is an amount that rises each year). If that income is actually used for support of the dependent, however, it counts in determining whether you have furnished over one-half of the dependent's support. If your parent has over $2,350 of gross income (for 1993), and therefore cannot be claimed as a dependent, you may still be able to deduct his or her medical expenses, as long as you contribute more than half the support for the year.

Live-Togethers

Internal Revenue Service rulings don't pay any attention to whether a relationship is legal. But state laws do. If you live together, without benefit of matrimony, in a state that frowns upon such behavior, you can expect to have an exemption you claim for your partner disallowed.

Rules of the Tax Game

As in any game, skilled players come out ahead. You can become skilled by learning the rules.

WHO MUST FILE

You are required to file a federal income tax return each year, even if you owe no tax, if you meet IRS specifications. The rules apply whether you are a citizen (living in the United States or abroad) or a noncitizen with resident status.

Wage-Earners

Filing requirements change each year. Just to give you an idea, however, for 1993:

■ If you are single you must file a return if you had $6,050 or more in income. If you are single and over 65 the income requirement changes to $6,950.

■ If you are married and file jointly, you must file a return for 1993 if your combined gross income is $10,900. The requirement is $11,800 if one spouse is 65 or older, and $12,500 if both of you are 65 or more.

Q My parents maintain their own household, with help from me. They manage on $9,000 a year, of which I contribute $3,000. Is there some way I can claim the exemption?

A The IRS will assume that your $3,000 in annual support is divided between your parents and that you are therefore not entitled to a dependency exemption, unless you specify, in writing, that your financial contribution goes to just one parent. Since they live on $4,500 apiece, your $3,000 is clearly more than half the annual support for one parent, and you should be able to claim the exemption. It will help, however, if you can make direct payments for support items such as clothing and medical bills; ask your parent to have the bills sent directly to you, then pay by check and keep both bills and checks as documentation.

Remember, however, that you cannot generally claim a dependency exemption for anyone who files a joint return with someone else. By filing separately, your parents may end up with a greater additional tax liability than your savings from claiming a single extra exemption.

■ For unmarried heads of household, the under-65 threshold is $7,800; for the over-65, it is $8,700.

Even without taxable income, earned or unearned, you should file a return if you are entitled to a tax refund.

The Self-Employed

If you are self-employed, no matter what your age or marital status, you must file a return if you had net earnings from your trade or profession of $400 or more for the year. This rule applies even if your self-employment is part-time and/or temporary.

If you are self-employed, you must also pay the self-employment equivalent of the Social Security tax withheld from an employee's wages. In 1993 the self-employment tax applied toward Social Security retirement benefits was 12.4 percent on the first $57,600 of earnings from self-employment; an additional 2.9 percent for Medicare was levied on net self-employment earnings of up to $135,000. If you also held a paid job, the amount subject to self-employment tax is reduced by any salary on which your employer was liable for Social Security taxes.

If income taxes are not withheld from your income you must file estimated tax returns and pay your taxes quarterly. See p. 594.

Note: If you work for yourself, don't forget possible tax deductions: for an office at home, for inventory storage space, depreciation of equipment, and so on (see pp. 368-370).

Q I don't want to work full time while our children are small, but I am teaching piano at home and earning $88 a week. I am keeping accurate records to report at tax time but should I be setting aside some of this money each week toward taxes?

A If you'll earn more than $500 a year in income not subject to withholding, call your local IRS office and ask for Form 1040-ES. Fill out the accompanying worksheet, and see how much you owe. If you owe more than $500 you must make estimated tax payments on the 15th of April, June, September, and January. You may start at any time during the year, if you see that payments will be due, and you may change your payments if your income changes. The IRS won't remind you when payment is due, so mark your calendar. For more information, see p. 594; also ask the local IRS office for Publication No. 505, "Tax Withholding and Estimated Tax."

Survivors

If you are a surviving spouse, executor, administrator, or legal representative of someone who died during the last tax year, and if that someone had any taxable income, then you must file a federal tax return on that person's behalf. Any taxes due will be paid out of the estate.

Filing Status

Are you married? single? separated? divorced? widowed? Your social status (as legally defined by the state in which you live) determines your filing status with the IRS. Within the broad categories, however, you have some choice and some decisions to make. Here are the categories:

Married Taxpayers

You are considered married for tax purposes if you are married and living together as husband and wife, if you are living together in a common law marriage recognized by your state, married and living apart but not legally separated or divorced, or separated under an interlocutory (not yet final) divorce decree.

If you are married and living with your spouse, you may file a joint return or you may file separate returns. The joint return is usually preferable, because the tax rate is lower, but you might figure your tax both ways to see which is better for you. If one of you has a lower income and higher deductions than the other—particularly if those deductions, like the deduction for medical expenses, require meeting an income threshold—you might be better off filing separately. But there are also advantages to filing jointly, and you should consult a tax adviser before making your decision.

You may also file a joint return if your spouse died during the tax year. You may continue this preferential status for two more years if you have at least one dependent child and if you do not remarry. If you remarry during the

Q I got married on December 27. Do I still need to file jointly for federal income tax, or can we file separately? What are the rules affecting marriage so close to the new year?

A Your filing status for tax purposes is your status on the last day of the tax year. If you are married and living together as husband and wife on December 31, then you are considered married for the entire year. But this does not mean that you must file a joint return. A husband and wife may also file separate returns. If you both had income, you should figure your tax both ways to see which way gives you the lower tax.

tax year in which your spouse dies, and file a joint return with your new spouse, then you must file a return for your deceased spouse as "married, filing separately."

Head of Household

This is the appropriate status for most single parents, people who are unmarried but maintain a home for dependent children or other relatives. The tax rates for heads of households are lower than the rates for single taxpayers or for married people filing separate returns; they are higher than the rates for married people filing jointly.

You can claim head-of-household status if you have paid more than half the cost of maintaining a home for the entire year for any of the following:

- Your unmarried child (including adopted, foster, or stepchildren) or grandchild. This child must have lived with you for the entire year but does not need to be your dependent. For example: You maintain a home for yourself and your unmarried son, age 26; he is not your dependent but you do qualify for head-of-household status.
- Your married child or grandchild who has lived with you and who does qualify as your dependent.
- Your mother or father, who does qualify as your dependent, whether or not the parent has lived with you.
- Any other relative who does qualify as a dependent, if that person has lived with you.

Single Taxpayers

You file as a single taxpayer if on the last day of the tax year (the calendar year, for most taxpayers) you are unmarried or legally divorced or separated in accordance with the laws of your state.

Q I've heard that it can cost a lot more in taxes to be married, and that this is a "marriage penalty." Is this something the government did on purpose? What exactly does it mean?

A It probably wasn't done deliberately, but the net result of congressional efforts to equalize tax liabilities for married and single taxpayers was to make them inequitable in a different way. The traditional one-breadwinner family benefits from today's federal income tax structure, but today's far more prevalent two-income couples lose out. The real losers are two-income couples with relatively high earnings, who lose even more as tax rates go up.

WHAT FORM TO USE

To itemize or not to itemize, that is the question. There are now three possible tax forms, with other variations under development, but you can itemize deductions only on the long form, 1040. Many taxpayers, put off by the complexity of the long form, file a short form instead. Even though they may be legally allowed to do so, they may be shortchanging themselves in the process. Many deductions and credits are available to you only if you file the long form. Don't just take the form the IRS sends you in the mail, therefore; it will send you a short form if that's what you filed last year. Instead, analyze your situation each year and decide which method of filing will do you the most good.

You may use form 1040EZ, the simplest form of them all, if you meet *all* of the following requirements:

- You are single.
- Your taxable income is under $50,000 and comes solely from wages, salaries, tips, taxable scholarship and fellowship grants, and interest of $400 or less.
- You have no dividend income.
- You claim no deductions and no exemptions for being over age 65 or blind.

You are allowed to use the short form, 1040A, if all of your income is from wages, salaries, taxable IRA distributions or Social Security, interest, dividends, and/or unemployment compensation, and your taxable income is under $50,000.

You may not use the short form if any of the following apply:

- You received income from sources other than those listed above, including alimony, self-employment income, or gain from the sale of a home.
- You can be claimed as a dependent on your parents' return and you had interest, dividends, or other unearned income of $1,000 or more.
- You want to apply any part of a tax refund to next year's tax.
- Your financial circumstances are at all complex; see IRS Publication No. 17.

You must use the long form 1040 if your taxable income is $50,000 or more. And you should use it if either of the following apply:

- You can save money by itemizing deductions. Look closely at uninsured medical expenses, interest and taxes on your home, charitable contributions, and uninsured casualty losses.
- You are entitled to adjustments or credits that would reduce your tax, including a disability pension, moving expenses, alimony, the residential energy credit, child care credit, and so on.

The 1040 rarely stands alone. There are special accompanying forms for itemized deductions (Schedule A), declaring interest and dividends (Schedule B), capital gains and losses (Schedule D), and so on.

The Standard Deduction

The standard deduction is the part of your income that is not subject to tax. It is used by taxpayers who do not itemize deductions on Schedule A of Form 1040. The choice is yours, but you'll benefit from the standard deduction (and find filing a lot easier) if your standard deduction is more than the total of your allowable itemized deductions.

Note: Before 1987 what was then called the "zero bracket amount" was built into the rate tables; itemized deductions had to be reduced by the amount for your filing category. Today the standard deduction is subtracted from income before calculating taxes and before itemized deductions, if appropriate, are claimed. Many taxpayers, however, may now find that they are better off not itemizing.

The specific amount changes each year, and depends on your filing status; it is also higher if you or your spouse is over age 65 or blind:

■ If you are married, filing jointly, or a qualifying widow or widower, your standard deduction in 1993 is $6,200.

■ If you are married, filing separately, your standard deduction is $3,100 in 1993.

■ If you are single, your standard deduction for 1993 is $3,700.

■ For heads of household, the standard deduction for 1993 is $5,450.

Q My 10-year-old earned $1,980 last year on the investments in his college custodial account. Does he have to file a tax return?

A Yes, but you have a choice. His income can be reported on his own separate return or included on your return. There's less paperwork if you report his income along with yours, on the same form, but before you do so be sure to determine two things: Will his income push you over the line into a higher state tax bracket? Will it make your income high enough so that you must forgo a medical, casualty loss, or miscellaneous deduction? If the answer to both questions is "no," you may find it easier to file a single form.

But the issue is complicated, and you may want to seek professional help.

WITHHOLDING

Some taxpayers deliberately overpay taxes throughout the year in order to claim a refund at tax time. They do so as a form of forced savings. In fact, since Uncle Sam pays no interest on taxes withheld from your pay, this is a very poor way to save, unless you are absolutely incapable of doing so any other way.

Other taxpayers deliberately underpay taxes so that they can use their money before the IRS stakes its claim. This is okay, if you'll actually have the money on hand when taxes are due *and* if you don't underpay by very much. If you miscalculate, interest and penalties may eat up any investment profit you might otherwise have.

The amount that is withheld from your pay each payday is determined by the W-4 form you file with your employer. This form lists the number of "allowances" you claim. The more you claim, the greater your take-home pay. Your allowances include your dependents. But don't stop there. The IRS also permits extra withholding allowances to reflect anticipated deductions and credits. You may claim an allowance for, among other things, retirement savings via an IRA and for some job-related moving expenses.

Note: If your actual tax liability is greater—because, for example, you have income from interest and dividends—you may not wish to claim the full number of withholding allowances to which you are entitled.

It's up to you, within certain limits, to determine how many withholding allowances you claim. If you want to increase withholding because, for

Q We have always dreamed of retiring overseas, in some warm climate. What are the tax ramifications if we actually do so?

A It depends on just where you retire. If you choose a "treaty" country, one with which the United States has a tax treaty (Italy, Greece, and Great Britain fall into this category), you can probably avoid dual taxation. In a nontreaty country, however (a category which includes Bermuda and the Bahamas), you may be in deep tax trouble. The United States taxes the income of its citizens, without regard to where that income is earned or where the citizens live. If you retire to a treaty country, you'll pay the higher of the taxes levied by the two countries. In a nontreaty country, you could wind up paying both. You could also wind up paying taxes on your Social Security benefits, which are at least partially nontaxable here. Giving up your citizenship, by the way, won't help. Be sure to consult a competent tax adviser, one familiar with overseas taxation, before you pull up stakes.

instance, you expect sizable investment income, you may do so. To have the maximum amount withheld, enter 0 for the total number of allowances you claim. And if you are married, check the box that says "Married, but withhold at higher Single rates." If you want to reduce withholding so that your taxes will come out even, you may claim as many as ten allowances without challenge by the IRS. You may claim more, but be sure you're entitled to them.

If you won't earn enough this year to owe any federal income tax (and you didn't pay tax last year either) you may escape withholding for income taxes (but not for Social Security) by filling in "Exempt" on the W-4 form. Then you won't have to wait for a tax refund to get your money.

Tax is also due on some pensions, on annuities, and on some forms of sick pay. If you don't have tax withheld, you will have to make quarterly payments of estimated tax (see p. 594).

If You Under-Withhold

Think twice before you "borrow" money from Uncle Sam by under-withholding. If you don't end the year having paid within 10 percent of the tax you'll actually owe (except under special circumstances), you may owe penalties as well as interest.

The interest rate is adjusted quarterly. In 1982 the IRS interest rate was 20 percent; in late 1992, it stood at 7 percent. At any level, however, interest due the IRS is now compounded daily.

Penalties are another matter. *Money* magazine reported in mid-1992 that, despite a 1989 law banning excessive penalties, tax penalty collections rose 38 percent between 1989 and 1992. Many penalty notices are in error, generated by a mindless computer, so don't assume that you can't contest a penalty notice. It helps, of course, if you have documentation. Acceptable

Q When my husband died suddenly a few years ago, I was so distraught that I never filed a federal income tax return for that year. After that I was afraid to file. I'd like to set the record straight now. What should I do?

A Contact the IRS (call toll-free, 800-829-1040) and tell them you want to file returns due for prior years. If you come forward voluntarily and explain that you didn't file initially because of your husband's death, there is a good chance that penalties will be waived. You will have to pay interest on any back taxes you owe. However, if paying all at once is a burden, you may be eligible for an installment agreement where you pay back taxes over time. And there's always a possibility that you'll be entitled to a refund.

excuses for late payment, backed by proof, may include serious illness or death in your family, a fire that destroyed your records, erroneous advice (in writing) from an IRS employee.

THE ALTERNATIVE MINIMUM TAX

You can use tax breaks to reduce your tax liability, but only up to a certain point, because of what's called an alternative minimum tax. This tax, which has been considerably toughened under recent law, means that taxpayers using so-called tax preferences (such as interest income from some "tax-free" municipal bonds and paper losses from limited partnerships) must calculate their tax liability under both regular tax rules and under the alternative minimum tax (which adds in otherwise exempt amounts of income). The higher of the two amounts must then be paid.

Note: Shifting income and deductions from one year to another can reduce your exposure to the alternative minimum tax. This is a complicated area, however, and it's best to consult a tax adviser.

EXTENSIONS

If you can't get your federal income tax return in on time, you may secure an automatic four-month extension by filing Form 4868. But the extension of filing time beyond April 15 is not permission to postpone paying taxes. Along with Form 4868 you must send a check for the tax you think you will owe when you complete your return. When the final figures are in, you'll owe interest on any unpaid amount from April 15 until the date you file. If your estimate is low by more than 10 percent, you'll face penalties as well.

An extension until August 15 is automatic, so long as you file the proper form. If you need more time, extensions until October 15 may be secured by filing Form 2688, along with a detailed explanation of the circumstances forcing the delay.

If your state has an income tax, find out the rules for extensions. Some states extend the due date for the state return along with a federal extension; others require a separate application.

AMENDMENTS

If you file the short form and later realize that itemizing would have cost you less, or if you file the long form but overlook a deduction, you may file an amended return on Form 1040X. Do so within three years of the time the original return was filed, submit a separate form for each year for which you claim a refund, and be sure to spell out your reasons and attach adequate documentation for your claim.

If you file an amended return, it does not necessarily mean that an audit of your original return is more likely. If any of your deductions are questionable, however, you might think twice about filing an amended return.

ESTIMATED TAXES

If you do not pay your federal income taxes through withholding or do not have enough withheld, you may have to pay an estimated tax on a quarterly basis. Such a tax might be based on income from pensions (if tax is not withheld), alimony, self-employment, annuities, interest, dividends, rent, capital gains, and so on.

You must pay an estimated tax if you will owe at least $500 in tax on income not subject to withholding. There are also certain income limitations, outlined in IRS Publication No. 505. You may pay the entire estimated tax for the year at once, or you may pay in quarterly installments. Payment dates are the 15th (or the following Monday if the 15th falls on a weekend) of April, June, September, and January. You can amend your estimate, as necessary, during the year.

However you make the payments, your total for the year must equal at least 90 percent of the tax you owe, or you will be subject to a penalty. Generally, you can avoid the penalty if you pay at least as much tax as you paid the previous year, but it's a good idea to figure your estimated tax as closely as possible—especially since new toughened rules are now in effect. You may not base your current year payments on the prior year, using the "safe harbor" of paying at least as much tax as you paid for the year before, if you meet all of these conditions:

1) Your current year adjusted gross income is greater than $75,000,

2) Your current year adjusted gross income exceeds the previous year's income by at least $40,000 (proceeds from the sale of your principal residence are an exception to this rule), and

3) You paid or should have paid estimated tax in any of the last three years.

Q The IRS claims I made a mathematical error on my return and keeps on billing me for additional taxes. I say my return was correct, but my protests have no effect—the bills keep coming. What can I do?

A Call the "taxpayer service information" number (it's usually toll-free) listed in your local telephone directory under U.S. Government, Internal Revenue Service. Ask for the problem resolution officer. These officers (there's one in each IRS district office) won't handle tax questions or problems, but they will hack through red tape and solve administrative or procedural problems such as yours. And they try to respond within five working days.

These new rules, designed to raise enough money to pay for an extension of unemployment benefits, are making life very difficult for many taxpayers. You'll feel the pinch, for example, if you are self-employed and earn most of your income in the early part of the year. Or suppose you're an investor who sells securities for a sizable capital gain early in the year only to incur sizable offsetting losses later in the year. In either case, you'll have to pay the estimated tax in the quarter in which it's due; then, if you're entitled to a refund, you can't collect it until after you file your return the following year.

Self-employed people usually realize that estimated tax is due. Retirees may not. But the same rules apply to taxable income from any source, whatever your age or occupation. Failure to file can result in penalties as well as interest.

AUDITS AND APPEALS

There is a word calculated to strike terror in a taxpayer's heart: audit. An understanding of the process, however, may help you to cope.

Whose Return Is Checked?

The process begins with the selection of returns for audit. Here are some of the items that might flag your return for attention:

- Arithmetic errors. Every return is screened for accuracy. If an error is found, you'll receive either a refund or a bill for additional taxes due. But you'll also bring your return to IRS attention. Check and double-check your arithmetic before you mail your return.
- Mismatched numbers. The IRS matching program, comparing the numbers on your tax return with the numbers on information returns such as the W-2 from wages and 1099s from interest and dividends, is very thorough. You can avoid trouble here by being very careful in your reports. If you have a brokerage account filing one 1099 for all your dividends, don't list separate amounts on your return. Or, if you've borrowed money from a bank to buy a certificate of deposit from the same bank, don't subtract the interest you've paid on the loan from the interest paid to you on the CD; include the full reported amount of interest paid to you on your tax return, as shown on the 1099, and then deduct the interest you've paid (assuming that you itemize your deductions).
- Omissions. Put down an incomplete Social Security number, don't attach all your W-2 forms, forget to sign your return ... and you'll invite scrutiny of the entire tax return.
- High income. While the odds against audit are very high for all taxpayers, you are definitely more likely to be audited if your adjusted gross income is over $100,000. Only about 1 percent of all returns are audited, but the figure is over 5 percent for those in the $100,000-plus category. (You might also secure unwelcome attention, on the other

hand, by filing an itemized return, complete with wide-ranging deductions and credits, and an adjusted gross income of $10,000 or less.)

■ Excessive deductions. If you claim deductions above and beyond the average for your income bracket (see Table 20.6 on p. 580), your return may draw attention. Moral: claim all the deductions to which you are entitled, but have adequate documentation, and attach documentation to your return. Two areas in which to be particularly careful: casualty losses and unreimbursed business expenses for travel and entertainment.

Types of Audits

An IRS audit may be simple or detailed. It may take place through the mail, on the government's home ground, or on yours.

■ A **correspondence audit** may be used when one or two relatively simple items are questioned and the necessary backup evidence may be submitted by mail. When you send such evidence, however, send copies; don't ever send the originals.

■ **Audits in an IRS office** are more usual. Here you will be asked to bring records relating to particular questions. Bring those records, but don't bring anything else. You don't want the audit to go any farther afield or to open up new areas for questioning. You may ask that the meeting be rescheduled if the original date is not convenient. You may bring your accountant or attorney along, if you like, or send him or her in your place; it may be a good idea to do so if this professional prepared your return.

■ A **field audit** is conducted at your home or place of business. It may also be conducted at your accountant's office. Either way, this audit is likely to delve into more details of your financial affairs.

Audit Advice

■ Don't relax just because you received a refund. Your return may still be audited.

■ The IRS is not responsible for advice it gives. You may fill out your return following information received directly from an IRS employee, and you may still be challenged. In the last resort only the tax law applies. (But try to get IRS advice in writing, to buttress any protest you make against fines or penalties.)

■ Court rulings may not even be applicable. IRS Publication No. 556, "Examination of Returns, Appeal Rights, and Claims for Refund," contains this illuminating language: "In some instances, the official position taken by the Internal Revenue Service may differ from certain court decisions. Although the Service will follow Supreme Court decisions, it is not required to follow decisions of any lower court for cases other than those involving the particular taxpayer and issue involved in that lower court. The Service can lose an issue in a lower court and still continue to apply its interpretation of the law to other cases involving similar issues."

■ The outcome of an IRS audit may affect your state income tax liability, and vice versa. If an audit results in changes in tax liability, on any level, you may want to file an amended return. The IRS exchanges information with state tax agencies.

■ Don't panic. Unless you're guilty of fraud (as in any deliberate underreporting of income) the worst outcome of an audit is additional tax due, with interest and, possibly, financial penalties. But you aren't likely to go to jail.

■ If you are called for an audit, be sure that you are thoroughly prepared. Have all the necessary records with you. And see if you can find any additional deductions that you failed to claim but might be entitled to. Example: You forgot, when you filled out your income tax return one year, that the diamond fell out of your engagement ring while you were on a canoe trip and was never recovered. So you never claimed a casualty loss. If your return for that year is audited, and if you meet the requirements for a casualty loss, you can bring up the lost stone.

The Taxpayer Compliance Measurement Program

Some tax returns are selected for audit because the IRS is tracking particular problems, such as tax shelters. Some are flagged because computer or human analysis reveals the likelihood of change. Others are selected simply at random, under the Taxpayer Compliance Measurement Program. TCMP, as it is called, is a statistical measuring instrument for the IRS. It helps to establish taxpayer profiles, and is undoubtedly a very useful tool for the IRS. What it is for the taxpayer, however, is something else. That's because, in the process of establishing this statistical profile, the IRS challenges an entire tax return. That means that the taxpayer must provide documentation for *everything.* Are you married? Where's your marriage certificate? Do you have children? Where are their birth certificates? And so on, and on.

Some taxpayers have challenged the necessity to participate in TCMP. They've all lost.

How to Appeal

An audit does not always result in additional tax liability. You may even emerge with a refund due. But what if the IRS auditor does disallow some deductions? What if he or she asserts that you do owe more money? And what if you disagree?

Simply put, these are your options:

■ The first step, if the audit takes place in an IRS office, is an immediate meeting with a supervisor. You may be able to resolve your difference of opinion right then and there.

■ You can also ask for an appeals conference, which will be scheduled at a convenient time and place. Most differences, says the IRS, are resolved at this level.

■ The next step is going to court. If your case is small, too small to hire an attorney but big enough to fight, you can go to the United States Tax Court's Small Tax Case Division. It has a $10,000 limit on disputes it will hear. It also offers the taxpayer two advantages: Disputes are settled with a minimum of formality and expense, and you do not have to pay the taxes at issue until the court has ruled. The regular Tax Court hears cases without regard to a financial ceiling.

■ You may, alternatively, appeal your case to either the United States Court of Claims or a United States District Court. Here the rules are slightly different: You must first pay the taxes, then file a claim for a refund, and then, either after the refund is rejected or you have waited at least six months and your claim has not been acted upon, file your suit. If you lose, you may appeal to the next-highest court. You may also, at any stage of the appeals process, reach a settlement with the IRS.

While you appeal, remember that interest due the IRS (or due from the IRS) is compounded daily. (The only exception: The penalty due for underpayment of estimated tax will not be compounded.) If the rate (which changes quarterly) is 8 percent, tax and interest due will double in about nine years. It can take several years for an issue to wend its way through tax court, and so if you lose you could owe half again as much.

You'll probably, therefore, think twice before fighting the IRS through the courts ... which is exactly what the IRS wants.

Prevention Starts with Record-keeping

The best defense, the saying goes, is an offense. And the best defense for you, as a taxpayer, is scrupulous record-keeping. Adequate records will help you when you file your returns and, if necessary, when you face an audit.

What Records Should Be Kept?

Every piece of paper relating to a taxable or tax-deductible item should be kept for the period of time during which that tax return may be scrutinized. State laws vary, but the IRS has three years from the filing deadline in which to audit your federal return. A return for 1993, with a filing deadline of April 15, 1994, may be the target of an audit until April 1997. If you fail to report 25 percent of your income, however, the IRS has six years in which to mount a challenge. And if you fail to file at all or file a fraudulent return, there is no time limit.

Once three years are past, assuming you've been honest, you can get rid of most of those scraps of paper cluttering your closets. But don't discard them all. Be sure to keep:

- Copies of your back tax returns. You may decide to file an amended return. And they're a useful source of reference in any case.

- Any records relating to items taxable over a long period of time. You should keep records of stock transactions from the time a stock is purchased until three years after it is sold. And you should keep records of improvements made to your home, which will reduce the amount subject to capital gains tax when the home is sold.

Suggestion: Instead of simply filing all your canceled checks by month and year, as most of us do, why not try this trick used by financial pros: Separate your returned checks, after you balance your statement, according to purpose. File all the home improvement checks in one file, the medical expense checks in another, securities transactions in yet a third. Then, at the end of three years, you can toss the irrelevant items and keep your tax-related items all together.

Professional Help

Have you thrown up your hands at the complexity of the tax forms? Have you decided that you need help? If so, you're not alone. Almost half of all taxpayers hire someone to prepare their tax returns for them.

If you plan to use the short form, and to forgo itemizing, chances are that you can do it yourself. But if you plan to use the long form, and if you have large deductions, you may want help. It's a good idea to seek professional help, in any case, in an eventful year: you've moved, gotten married or divorced, or received an inheritance. A good tax preparer can alert you to tax savings you might otherwise miss.

SOURCES OF HELP

Some help is free:

- For all taxpayers: The IRS offers a variety of free publications. Publication No. 17, "Your Federal Income Tax," is a basic guide issued each year; it is supplemented by a large number of detailed guides, some of which are listed below, that apply to specific questions. The IRS will answer telephone inquiries but you can't count on the accuracy of its advice or, as noted above, rely on it if you're challenged in an audit.

■ For taxpayers over age 60: Free tax help is available via volunteer programs, including those run by the American Association of Retired Persons. For information, write to Tax-Aide, AARP, 601 E St., N.W., Washington, DC 20049.

Some Useful IRS Publications

A complete list of IRS publications can be found in Publication No. 17, "Your Federal Income Tax." Here are some examples of publications you may find helpful (order any of these booklets by calling, toll-free, 800-829-3676):

502: Medical and Dental Expenses
503: Child and Dependent Care Expenses
504: Divorced or Separated Individuals
505: Tax Withholding and Estimated Tax
521: Moving Expenses
523: Selling Your Home
525: Taxable and Nontaxable Income
529: Miscellaneous Deductions
530: Tax Information for First-Time Homeowners
547: Nonbusiness Disasters, Casualties, and Thefts
550: Investment Income and Expenses
552: Recordkeeping for Individuals
554: Tax Information for Older Americans
910: Guide to Free Tax Services

If your return is complicated, however—if you've invested in a tax shelter or had business income or taken an aged parent as a dependent—you'll probably want the help of a paid preparer. That help comes in a variety of skill levels and with a range of costs:

■ Commercial preparers range from the storefront tax offices that spring up like dandelions each spring (and close long before the dandelions in your lawn have died) to professional services that are likely to be there when you need them (should your return, for instance, be audited). At all of these agencies, however, the heaviest burden of work comes in the couple of short months before the Ides of April. That means that extra help is put on, help that may or may not be well trained.

■ Enrolled agents are certified by the IRS after having worked at least five years as an IRS auditor or after passing a government exam. Enrolled agents are authorized to represent you before the IRS; if you are audited, in other words, you can have an enrolled agent who has prepared your return either accompany you or speak for you. A referral service is available through the National Association of Enrolled Agents; call toll-free (800) 424-4339.

■ Public accountants have been trained in accounting, but cannot represent you before the IRS.

■ Certified public accountants (CPAs) have passed a professional qualifying exam, and are authorized to represent you before the IRS. CPAs, moreover, are qualified to provide year-round tax counsel. CPAs will also cost more than most other tax preparers, but if your financial affairs are at all complex, you'll probably find the cost worthwhile. (And remember: The cost of tax advice is tax-deductible if, along with other miscellaneous deductions, it exceeds 2 percent of adjusted gross income. Just be sure to keep your receipts.)

■ Attorneys have passed a bar exam but may or may not have special tax training. Like CPAs, and with comparable fees, tax attorneys are authorized to represent you before the IRS.

What to Ask

Before you settle on any individual tax adviser, however, there are a number of questions you should ask:

■ What is the adviser's training or experience in preparing tax returns? In offering tax advice?

■ Does the adviser take responsibility for accuracy? Does he or she have someone else double-check returns? If so, are they reviewed for arithmetic errors only or for possible errors in interpretation of the tax law as well?

■ Approximately how much will preparing your tax return cost? How is that fee determined?

■ Where can the adviser be found later in the year?

■ Can the adviser represent you if the IRS audits your return? At what charge?

What to Avoid

Stay away from a tax preparer who:

■ Advertises misleadingly low rates. The preparer will either stick to the short form—a form you can prepare for yourself—or will charge you for "extras" that should have been included.

■ Claims, proudly, that no client is ever audited. Many areas of the tax code are subject to interpretation; a good tax adviser will know when to claim deductions that might be challenged—and how to fight a challenge.

■ Guarantees a refund, before completing your return.

■ Suggests that a refund check be mailed to the preparer rather than to you.

■ Suggests that you underreport income, claim nonexistent deductions, or do anything else that hints of fraud.

■ Asks you to sign a blank return or one made out in pencil.

■ Refuses to sign his own name to your tax form. Paid preparers are required by law to sign your return, include address and identifying number, and provide you with copies.

IT'S STILL UP TO YOU

Even if you hire someone to prepare your tax returns, you still have work to do. You have to gather all your tax records, and put them in order for your tax preparer. Failure to do so will cost more time during your tax session ... and time is money. See your tax adviser early; don't wait till April (or even March), when the tax forms are piling up. If you pay a CPA for tax counsel, be sure to have a session before the end of each year to discuss sheltering income and timing deductions and otherwise minimizing taxes that will be due. If you wait till after January 1 to think about taxes, it's too late to do anything constructive for the prior year.

And remember, even if you hire someone to prepare your tax returns, you're not off the IRS hook. You are still personally liable for any additional tax, interest, or penalty. Make sure you know what's going on your tax return, and review the return before you sign it.

 KEY POINTS

■ Determine your tax bracket and effective tax rate.

■ Take full advantage of all exclusions, exemptions, deductions, and credits to which you are entitled.

■ Maintain adequate documentation.

■ Try to do a five-year projection so that you'll anticipate your income and your income tax, and be able to allocate funds for investment.

■ Review your projections regularly and adjust them as necessary.

■ Make tax planning part of your year-round and lifetime financial planning.

CHAPTER 21

Estate Planning

■ When Ted Watson died, he left property worth $150,000 but no will. So the state, by law, stepped in and dictated the distribution of the $150,000. His wife received $50,000, his married son in medical school got $50,000, and his 14-year-old daughter got the remaining $50,000, to be administered for her by a court-appointed guardian. In some states the proportional shares would have been different. But in no state would the distribution have been just as Ted would have wanted. The only way to be sure of that was to write a will.

■ Sharon Curtis, at 27, has given no thought to wills or estates. If she did think about it, she would assume that the man she lives with would keep items she purchased for their home, the stereo and so on, while she might want her younger sister to have her jewelry. If Sharon is hit by a car, however, this is not what would happen. Her live-in lover would receive nothing ... unless her family felt inclined to be generous. Her sister couldn't count on anything either. Just as in any case where someone dies without a will, the state would step in and dictate distribution, usually to the closest blood relatives. In Sharon's case this would be her parents. (Where there are no relatives—a live-in partner does not count—all her belongings would become the property of the state.)

What about you? How much property do you have? (Review your net worth calculations in Chapter 2.) What will happen to that property after you're gone, those assets you've worked so hard to acquire?

Estate planning is not a task reserved for either the elderly or the affluent. Anyone, at any age, who has property to leave has the right to decide how to leave it. Anyone with property, at any age, also has the right to try to minimize taxes on that property. These are the two functions of estate planning.

Leaving Your Property

Your estate consists of everything you own at the time of your death: house, savings accounts, insurance policies, stocks and bonds, pension and profit-sharing benefits, assets of all kinds. Some of this property, such as insurance and pension proceeds, will pass directly to a named beneficiary (if you named one and if he or she survives you). Some of it, such as your home or bank accounts, may belong to a person named as joint owner. There is only one way to be sure that the rest is distributed in accordance with your wishes: Write a will. Whether you are single or married, male or female, age 25 or age 65, if you have any property at all you should have a will.

WHY WRITE A WILL?

Without a will, distribution of your property will be determined by state law. Your parents may get assets your spouse could use. Your minor children, more to the point, may receive funds that their surviving parent needs to raise them. Those funds will be placed under control of the law, if you leave no will, with a court-appointed guardian to watch over them; your estate will pay the guardian's fees. The children will receive the funds when they reach legal age; you might prefer them to be older and more mature.

Only with a will can you distribute hard-earned assets as you think best. Only with a will can you leave everything (including property that is not jointly owned with your spouse) to your spouse, knowing that he or she will care for your children. Only with a will can you spread the distribution of those assets over a period of years, should you choose to do so. Only with a will can you leave property to a favorite charity, a favorite friend or the niece who cared for you in your last illness; only with a will can you disinherit a close but disliked relative. Only with a will can you leave more money to a child who needs special help and less money to another. Only with a will can you make provisions to aid an aged parent, or arrange to let a beloved aunt live rent-free in your house until her death, or skip a generation to help your grandchildren.

Only with a will can you:

- Distribute your property exactly as you wish it to be distributed,
- Select the person who will follow your instructions in making the distribution,
- Eliminate the necessity of a court-appointed—and expensive—administrator,
- Be sure that your beneficiaries will receive the property without unnecessary delay, and
- Minimize taxes and other expenses in the settlement of your estate.

WRITING A WILL

A will may be simple or it may be complex, but it must follow legal forms. In fact, although you are never required by law to use a lawyer to draft your will, you may cause your beneficiaries unnecessary grief and cost them more money if you try to bypass the cost of a lawyer and then leave an improperly drawn will. If you want to prepare your own will, be sure that you understand your state's requirements and follow them to the letter. A good overall guide can be found in *The Complete Will Kit* by Jens C. Appel III and F. Bruce Gentry (Wiley, 1990).

THINGS YOU SHOULD KNOW

- Anyone over legal age may write a will.
- Once written, a will must be signed in the presence of witnesses. Most states require two witnesses; some require three. Keep track of the witnesses, if you can, as they may be called to verify your will after your death.
- A beneficiary under the will should not be a witness, or the legacy may be declared invalid.
- Think carefully before you distribute your assets. A bequest of $10,000 to a favorite relative or cause may be 10 percent of your estate at the time you write the will. What happens if your estate becomes much larger before you die? What happens if it becomes

Q I've written out exactly what I want done with my property after my death, because I don't see why I should have to bother with a lawyer. Now someone tells me this kind of will isn't legal. Is that true?

A It depends on where you live. Some states do recognize handwritten (technically called holographic) wills. Even if yours does, you have to be careful to follow its rules. Find out what those rules are. They may specify that the will be literally handwritten (no typing) or that there be no witnesses (which would put the will in another category) or that they are only valid if written under certain circumstances (such as a sailor at sea). If you break the rules, whatever they are, the will will be invalid. Be very specific, too. Example: Don't leave "the contents of my house" to a favorite nephew and then leave a valuable coin collection in the house ... not unless you want the nephew to have the collection too. All in all, it's advisable to consult a lawyer. A simple will is not expensive, and you will be sure that your wishes will be followed.

much smaller? It may be better to phrase such bequests in terms of percentages instead of dollar amounts. Think through exactly how much you want to leave, and discuss with a competent attorney the best way to phrase the will.

■ Although you may leave as little or as much as you wish to people of your choice, you are restricted in one way: The law does not generally permit you to totally disinherit a spouse (or, in some places, a child). If you are married at the time of your death, in fact, the law in your state may require that you leave a designated minimum to your spouse; that minimum may be what he or she would be entitled to receive if you died without a will. (But a spouse left out of a will does not receive this statutory share automatically; a suit may have to be filed.)

■ If you secure a divorce, you may want to change your will immediately, to remove your ex-partner from any share of your assets. But you may not be able to do so until the divorce is final and you are no longer legally married in the eyes of the law (except, in some instances, if your separation agreement specifies that you may do so or if your spouse has abandoned you). What you can do, in the meantime, if you've earlier willed substantial assets to your spouse and are now in the midst of divorce, is reduce his or her bequest to the minimum amount required by state law. (And, without delay, remove your soon-to-be-ex-spouse as beneficiary of life insurance or retirement plans.) Then, when the decree is final, redo the will.

■ If you are remarrying, you may want to sign an antenuptial (before marriage, sometimes called a premarital) or postnuptial (after marriage) agreement with your spouse, to protect any children you each may have. With such an agreement, you can legally agree that neither of you will make any claim on the other's estate. You can also revoke

Q Why is one dollar sometimes left to a person in a will?

A Some people believe that leaving one dollar to someone you want to disinherit—as a clear indication that leaving nothing more was intentional—stops that person from contesting the will. Not so. A will can be contested by anyone with the legal right to do so. On the other hand, in most states you aren't required to leave money to anyone other than your spouse. You can simply leave the person out of your will or, if you prefer, say "I leave nothing to my son, John, for reasons best known to me." Talk to your lawyer if you fear someone may contest your will.

the agreement later, as long as you both agree to do so ... if, for instance, the marriage works out well and lasts for a long time.

- If you want to disinherit your closest relatives, don't just leave them out of your will or they may mount a successful challenge. Explain in the will that your omission is deliberate. But do so nicely; nastiness may lead to a lawsuit. It is not necessary, as you may have heard, to leave them a token amount, such as one dollar; if you do, in fact, it might be taken as an insult and lead to trouble.

- A husband and wife should each have a will. A wife who does not work outside the home and who is totally dependent on her husband may think a will is unnecessary. She would be wrong. If her husband dies and leaves everything to her, what happens when she dies? What happens if she dies almost immediately, before she has an opportunity to write her own will? The state will step in and make the distribution, regardless of either partner's wishes.

- Your will should specify what happens if a beneficiary dies before you do, or simultaneously, and should name secondary beneficiaries. Otherwise, this might happen (and has): A childless husband and wife are killed in the same accident but she outlives him by an hour. All of his property, inherited by her during that hour, is then distributed in accordance with state law to her relatives. His get nothing.

- The wills of a husband and wife should be separate wills. A joint will, unless it is very carefully drafted, may be treated as a legally binding contract which will lock the surviving partner into a distribution of assets that may no longer be desirable as circumstances change.

Q When I made a new will recently, my lawyer said that he should keep both wills, the old and the new, in his files. I always thought an old will should be destroyed once a new one was written. Why would he want to do this?

A In most instances, old wills are destroyed once they're superseded by new ones, to avoid any confusion. However, if you cut someone out of your will who is entitled to inherit under the laws of intestacy, which spell out who gets what in your state should you die without a will, or if you're leaving less to a particular person than he or she would be entitled to under those laws, your lawyer may be wise to keep both wills (so long as the old one is clearly marked with the date on which it was replaced by a new will). Anyone trying to contest your will would have a harder time of it if, for example, it could be shown that he or she was deliberately left out of both wills.

■ Write your will so that it will reflect your wishes if you die today. When your wishes change, redo your will. Major changes require a new will; minor changes can be taken care of with a **codicil,** or rider. But don't, ever, amend an existing will by writing on it; the addition won't hold up in court and could cost many thousands of dollars in unnecessary legal fees.

■ Review your will regularly, especially if you marry, become a parent, retire, move to another state, divorce, remarry, or do anything that could affect the distribution of your estate and the validity of your existing will. Review your will when any important financial or personal event occurs.

■ Involve your spouse in the planning of your will. Don't present him or her with a *fait accompli.* Estate planning is part of your overall financial planning and is a process that should be a family affair. Remember: You are not the one who will have to live with what your will provides.

■ Sign only the original of your will and keep that original in a safe place (but not your safe deposit box; see below), where it can be easily located by your survivors. You might leave it in your lawyer's files, with an unsigned copy at home for reference. If you name a bank as an executor, the bank will usually keep it for you without charge. Or, in some states, if you have nowhere else to put it, you may leave it (for a small fee) with the local probate or surrogate's court. Just be sure to retrieve it if you decide to make any changes or to make a new will. And be sure to tell someone where it is.

■ A safe deposit box is generally not a good place to keep a will because many states require the sealing of a box upon the death of its owner, until the tax authorities can inspect the contents. Even if the box can be opened under court order to search for a will, the process is time-consuming and unnecessarily troublesome for the survivors. One solution: his and hers safe deposit boxes, each containing individually owned assets and the other's will.

■ You can put funeral directions and requests for organ donations in your will but they may not be read in time. A better way to leave such instructions is in a letter of intent left with your will (reinforced, perhaps, by your spoken instructions ahead of time and an organ donation form such as the one often found on drivers' licenses). This letter can also contain specific bequests—the antique chest to son Mark, the pearl necklace to daughter Anne—which might clutter up your will. It can be combined with your personal record, described on pp. 612-615, but it's important to be aware that in many states such a letter is not legally binding but is more an informal expression of your wishes to your family.

Note: Even with a letter of intent, you'll want to mention disposition of your personal property in your will. Just be careful with your wording.

Attorney Ralph Engel, an estate planning specialist in New York, suggests saying something to this effect: "I leave my personal property to be divided among my three children as they agree" or "I leave my personal property to be divided among my three children in substantially equal shares." Do *not* say you are leaving tangible assets "equally." If you do, in a worst case scenario, your children might agree on who takes the piano and who takes the jewelry—but the Internal Revenue Service (IRS) might say that the one who got the furniture bought two-thirds of the furniture from his sisters and paid for it with his one-third of the other items. The likely result: your children wind up hating each other, and you as well.

Picking an Executor

When you write your will you must name an executor to see that its provisions are carried out. The executor may be almost any adult you choose (except that a few states require that an executor be a resident of the state or a close relative), so you may name a relative, a friend, a professional adviser, a bank, or some combination thereof. Before you decide, look at what your executor must do:

- Deal with your personal effects
- Prepare a complete inventory of all your assets—real estate, securities, cash, bank accounts, and so on
- Collect any money owed you in the form of salary, pension, profit-sharing, veterans benefits, Social Security, outstanding loans, etc.
- Pay off any valid debts you owe to others and challenge questionable claims
- See that life insurance companies are notified of your death
- Arrange for your family's immediate living expenses

Q I put all my affairs in order, including updating my will, before I retired. Now I'm thinking about getting away from cold weather and moving to the Southwest. Will I have to redo my will? Or will it remain valid?

A Different states have different requirements with respect to wills, and so, in general, it's a good idea to review your will when you move. Although a will properly made in another state will be valid, it may not conform to the law of your new state and hence may cost more in the long run. Be very careful about moving your legal residence, especially if you retain any property in another state, or both your old state and your new one may collect death taxes when you die.

- Liquidate assets as necessary and invest others wisely to provide income during the time that the estate is being administered
- Prepare and file, as they become due, all income tax, estate tax, and inheritance tax returns
- Distribute your estate to the people named in your will
- Make an accounting of all receipts and payments to the probate court and to the beneficiaries

The naming of an executor is clearly not a casual task. It's important to choose someone who has both the competence and the time to do the job well, and who is willing to do it. Just inventorying assets and filing the necessary legal documents requires dedication and may take considerable time. But the executor must do more. He or she (a female is called an executrix) must exercise considerable judgment if your estate is to reach your beneficiaries in anything approaching its proper size. Just when assets are sold can make a considerable difference in their value; just when taxes are paid can affect how much is paid. An executor can, of course, secure professional assistance in making these decisions, but professional assistance costs money, and the money comes out of the estate. The executor should, therefore, be someone with financial know-how as well as someone you can trust to carry out your wishes. A spouse may be your first choice, but that spouse may do better with professional backup; if your estate is at all sizable or complicated (if, for instance, you own a family business), you might name a professional such as an attorney or a bank as co-executor.

In naming an executor, remember:

- Executors are paid from the estate, with fees in many states set by law. In New York State, as an example, an executor's commission is 5 percent on the first $100,000 of gross value in the estate, with a sliding scale down to 2 percent on anything over $5,000,000. A single executor on a $300,000 estate would thus receive $13,000.

Note: In some localities, all executors are paid a single amount, to be divided among them. In others, each executor gets a full commission. In some states, banks get a slightly higher commission than individual executors, and some banks may set minimum fees. A spouse, relative, or friend may waive the fee.

- Never name someone who has not expressed willingness to serve. If your named executor declines the post, the court may have to appoint someone.
- You should name an alternate executor, in case the first is either unwilling or unavailable when the time comes.
- Review your choice periodically—especially if you've chosen someone as old or older than yourself.
- Many banks have trust departments that specialize in the administration of estates. But they may be structured to serve large estates best.

Before you name a bank as executor of your will, have a talk with a trust officer or with your attorney and make sure that the bank is willing to handle your estate and will give it the attention it deserves. (But don't underestimate the size of your estate either; inflation has probably made you worth more than you think.)

■ Under the best of circumstances an estate takes some time to settle. Creditors must be allowed an opportunity to come forward and file any claims. Assets may need to be sold to pay debts, taxes, and expenses. All of this takes time. A simple estate may take six months to a year to settle. If your affairs are at all complicated, or federal estate taxes are payable, a delay of two to three years is not at all unusual. Federal estate taxes are not due until nine months after death; the IRS may not finish processing the return for another nine to twelve months, or even more. However, the delay does not mean that your beneficiaries will be temporarily destitute. Periodic distributions may almost always be made from the estate during settlement.

PERSONAL AFFAIRS RECORD

You can make life easier for your executor, whether relative or outsider, by leaving a complete record of your personal affairs. (You'll also make it easier on yourself, while you're living, if your affairs are organized. And you'll save money when you visit a lawyer to have your will drafted if you present a tidy package of information.)

Take some time, now, to create this personal record. (It will take some time; it's a big job, but an important one.) Then update it on a regular basis.

Q When I wrote my will, several years ago, I named my son as the executor. He has since moved out of state and tells me he can't be my executor. Is he right?

A Your state may permit out-of-state executors (most do, some do not, some do if the executor is a close relative), but even if it's legal you could be putting a real burden on your son. An executor has major responsibilities, many of which must be performed where you last lived. Your son may or may not be able to take the time from his family and business to travel to your state to attend to these matters. Even if he is willing, the costs of his travel may be charged against your estate. Instead of naming your son alone, why not name co-executors; your son plus a local attorney or bank? Then your local executor can do most of the work, but your son can still say yea or nay to any decision.

And tell someone—your spouse, a grown child, your executor—where the record is. (Be sure, too, that someone knows your favorite hiding places for valuables. In one recent instance, the base of an old lamp contained $30,000 worth of jewelry; the lamp was about to be tossed out when someone remembered.) Preparing the record *with* your spouse, or reviewing it with him or her, is an ideal way to be sure that you are both fully informed about your financial affairs.

The personal record (use the following worksheet as a guide) should include both the facts about your finances and information about the location of all your important papers. Keep a copy in your desk drawer and another copy clipped to the copy of your will.

Worksheet 21.1: Personal Inventory

1. **Social Security** Number:
   Husband:_____   Wife:_____

2. **Life Insurance** (if more than one policy, list information for each):

   Policy number   Company   Face value   Beneficiary
   _____   _____ _____ _____

   _____   _____ _____ _____

   Name, address, and telephone number of agent:
   _____
   _____

3. **Savings Account** (if more than one, list for each):
   Name and address of financial institution:
   _____
   _____

   Account number:_____
   If joint account, name of other person: _____
   Relationship: _____
   Location of passbook or statements:_____

4. **Checking Account** (if more than one, list for each):
   Name and address of financial institution:
   _____
   _____

   Account number:_____
   If joint account, name of other person: _____
   Relationship: _____
   Location of canceled checks: _____

5. **Time Deposits and Certificates of Deposit:**
    Name of institutions where purchased: _____
    Number(s) and maturity date(s): _____
    Location of documents: _____

6. **U.S. Government Bonds:**
    List of serial numbers and denominations: _____
    Location of bonds: _____
    Names of any co-owners: _____

7. **Securities:**
    Name, address, and telephone number of broker:

    _____

    _____

    Location of securities: _____
    List of stocks and/or bonds

Company	Number of shares	Certificate number	Maturity (bonds)
_____	_____	_____	_____
_____	_____	_____	_____

    List of mutual funds

Company	Number of shares	Account number
_____	_____	_____
_____	_____	_____

8. **Safe Deposit Box:**
    In whose name? _____
    Location: _____
    Location of key: _____
    List of contents: _____

    _____

9. **Pension and Profit-sharing Plan:**
    Company and account number: _____
    Name and address of employer: _____

    _____

    Beneficiary: _____

10. **Keogh Plan and/or Individual Retirement Account:**
    Where? (bank? mutual fund?): _____
    Account number: _____
    Beneficiary: _____

11. **Automobile** (if more than one, list for each):
    Make, type, and year: _____
    Location of ownership papers: _____

Insurance company: _____

Policy number: _____

12. Real Estate (if more than one property, list for each):

Location of property: _____

Title owned by: _____

Location of deed: _____

Mortgage held by: _____

Amount of mortgage: _____

Location of mortgage document: _____

Location of tax receipts: _____

Insurance company: _____

Number of policy and its location: _____

13. Personal Property (jewelry, furs, collections):

Description: _____

_____

Location: _____

_____

14. Health Insurance (include major medical and disability):

Company	Type of policy	Policy number	Location of policy
_____	_____	_____	_____
_____	_____	_____	_____

15. Tax Records:

Name, address, and telephone number of accountant:

_____

_____

Location of tax records: _____

16. Credit Cards (list for each):

Company	Account number	Name on card	Location of card
_____	_____	_____	_____
_____	_____	_____	_____

17. Major Creditors (list for each):

Name, address, and telephone number:

_____

_____

Location of notes, contracts, or receipts: _____

18. Will:

Location of original: _____

Location of copy: _____

Name, address, and telephone number of attorney:

_____

_____

19. **Personal Information** (particularly important if your executor won't have
    this information):
    Parents' names and addresses: _____

    _____

    _____

    Siblings' names and addresses: _____
    Descendants' names, addresses, and date of birth: _____

    _____

    _____

    _____

    _____

    Name of former spouse, if any: _____
    Address: _____
    Date of divorce: _____
    Location of divorce decree: _____
    Date and place of death if deceased: _____

    Name and address of financial planner, if any: _____

    _____

    _____

    _____

This form is a rough guide to your own personal record; you may have
more, or less, information to note. Your attorney or financial adviser may also
have a form you can work with. Either way, be sure to add a page indicating
the location of other valuable documents (if they are not already listed in your
safe deposit box inventory): marriage and birth certificates, school transcripts,
military records, citizenship papers, adoption papers, divorce decrees and
alimony agreements, important warranties and receipts, and so on. Be specific:
Are the papers in a box in the attic? In the upper-left-hand drawer of your
desk? Include proof of membership in any fraternal, professional, veterans or
union organization that entitles the estate to any benefits—and leave instructions to your survivors to claim those benefits. Include information about a
cemetery plot you own, if any, and funeral preferences. Be sure, too, to include
a list of any outstanding debts—money you owe and money owed to you—to
help forestall any false claims against your estate. And attach a list of people
who should be notified of your death.

NAMING A GUARDIAN
It's hard to believe, but fights have been waged over who will care for
young children after their parents' death. Sometimes the fights are between
relatives who want the children; sometimes they're between relatives who

don't. Either way, don't let this happen to your kids. Put your heads together and decide who is best suited to raise your children if you aren't here to do it yourself. Name a successor guardian, just in case something happens to the first.

Note: If you are divorced and have custody of your children, their other biological parent would have the right to raise the children after your death (subject to court approval), regardless of guardianship provisions you've made in your will. This is true even if you've been living in a close supportive relationship, married or not, with someone who treats your children as his or her own—*unless* your new partner has actually adopted the children.

An essential part of a will, if you have one or more minor children, is a guardian to care for them if you (and your spouse, if you are married) both die. That guardian should be chosen with care. A close relative may be your first thought, but similarity of child-raising beliefs may be more important than family ties. Grandparents, who may otherwise be ideal, may not have the energy to cope with youngsters. So, before you decide:

■ Think about what's most important to you in raising your children. Try to select a guardian (and a successor guardian) who would raise your children the way you would, in terms of ethical values, religious beliefs, proper behavior, and so on. Name just one person as guardian, even if that person is part of a couple; you never know what will happen to any marriage.

Q My father became mentally confused a couple of years before he died and his formerly meticulous financial records are a mess. I'm handling his estate and wonder how to track down financial assets such as bank accounts and mutual fund records.

A Start by going through several years of tax records; you can get copies from the IRS if your father or his accountant didn't keep copies. Tax returns would indicate the source of interest or dividend payments, and you can then write to the payor to trace the account. If your father lost track of assets more than four or five years ago, depending on where he lived, the assets may have been turned over to the state's unclaimed property office. You can generally get them back, although you may not receive any interest after the date the state took over, by contacting the appropriate office with your father's name, Social Security number, and address(es). For more information, send a self-addressed stamped envelope to the National Association of Unclaimed Property Administrators, P.O. Box 942850, Sacramento, CA 94250.

■ If your children are old enough (past the earliest school years), discuss the matter with them. It won't alarm them to have a matter-of-fact discussion about people they'd like to live with. And listen to what they have to say: There may be factors important to your children that won't occur to you. It may be particularly important, for instance, especially for a teenager, to stay in the same school and community.

■ Before you make a definite decision, talk to the people you'd like to name. How do they feel about it? Are they willing to accept the responsibility?

Never name a guardian who is reluctant about assuming the responsibility. It's hard enough to raise your own children, harder to raise someone else's, and your children could be the real losers

■ If you've found warm, loving people to serve as guardians for your children, but have some qualms about their financial savvy, you don't have to give them the entire burden. You can name a separate guardian to manage the money and property left to the children. That guardian could be instructed to confer with the other guardian about the distribution of funds on the children's behalf. (A separate guardian of the property may also be desirable if your ex-spouse would wind up raising the kids.)

Note: In many states, a guardian of the property has no authority to do anything without first getting court approval—prompting one attorney to say that "working with a guardianship of property is like giving a bequest to your

---

Q My brother and I are in high school now. What happens to us if our parents die without a will? What happens to our house and our car, our parents' savings, and our education? There's nothing wrong with our parents, but we got to talking with them and they said they don't have a will. If anything should happen to them, what happens to us?

A The only way for your parents (and you, by talking it over with them) to have a say in what happens to you and to their property is by writing a will. If they die without a will, the state will distribute the property according to its laws. Most of it would probably go to you and your brother, but because you are not yet of legal age, a guardian would have to be appointed to care for you and handle the money. The court would decide who that guardian is, and it might or might not be someone you or your parents would choose. Urge your parents to write a will, without delay.

lawyer." It may be preferable to leave assets in trust for the benefit of minor children, with the trustee authorized to consult with the guardian and distribute funds as necessary. Talk to your attorney.

■ If you don't write a will, or don't name a guardian, a court will decide who will care for your children. The judge may ask the children their preference, but isn't obliged to do so. The court will also appoint a caretaker of the children's inheritance, whether or not you would have thought the guardian capable of handling the funds. There will be fees to be paid to the court-appointed guardian and caretaker, fees which will come out of your estate.

Probate

Probate is the legal process of "proving" a will is valid. If you leave a will, your designated executor takes care of the legal formalities, often with the help of an attorney. If you do not leave a will, the probate court (sometimes called surrogate's court) will appoint an administrator to do the job; that administrator will probably select an attorney to help.

Probate has become a swearword in some quarters, largely because of administrative delays and because of the sometimes substantial fees paid (out of the estate) to attorneys, appraisers, and others. Probate procedures differ from state to state, but probate itself is not the problem; abuse of the system is more often a problem. One way in which you can reduce abuse, and reduce excessive fees, is by picking the right attorney and the right executor and making clear to them how you want your affairs handled.

A Uniform Probate Code (UPC), which has been adopted in full in some states and, in modified form, in others, is simplifying the probate process. Under UPC an estate can be distributed without court supervision unless someone actually contests the will. Where UPC has been adopted, too, probate procedures are more apt to reflect the way we live today. For example, in a provision designed to assist older people contemplating remarriage: Under the new code, both a surviving spouse's independent means and the length of the marriage are taken into account in determining inheritance; only in marriages lasting at least 15 years is a spouse guaranteed half of the couple's total assets. Under prior laws, it took a pre- or post-nuptial agreement to waive automatic inheritance by a spouse and protect children from a first marriage.

Should You Avoid Probate?

Avoiding probate, meanwhile, or attempting to avoid it, may leave your beneficiaries in worse shape. This is because the only real way to avoid probate, at present, in virtually every state, is to eliminate any need for a will. The way to avoid the need for a will, if you have any assets at all, is to pass those assets on through means other than a will. A description of some of these means—lifetime gifts, joint ownership, and trusts—is given later in this chapter. Others include "in trust for" bank accounts, "payable on death" arrangements, beneficiary designations on retirement plans and insurance policies.

The point to remember, however, is that every action has a consequence. If you distribute all your assets directly, outside of a will, your estate may not have enough cash on hand to pay final expenses. If you don't write a will, you forgo the opportunity to choose your own guardian for minor children. If you avoid probate, and the costs of probate, you may subject your estate to unnecessary taxes, you may complicate its legal distribution, and you may lose control of your assets during your lifetime. Weigh all these consequences before you decide to take elaborate measures to avoid probate. Try to determine how much, if anything, you'll save by avoiding probate; in many states, the savings are nominal and avoiding probate may cost more in some cases than going through probate.

Q My husband and I have worked very hard to acquire all that we have: a house, two cars, and personal belongings. We are still young: I am 27 and my husband is 34. We have a 2-year-old daughter. We are concerned about what would happen if one of us died. Is there any way to avoid taxes, lawyer's fees, or probate court fees if one of us should die? Why is it important to have a will if everything ends up in probate court anyway?

A Taking your questions one at a time: Inheritance and estate taxes are based on the amount of property you leave, and have absolutely nothing to do with whether or not that property goes through probate. A properly drawn will may well save on estate taxes. Legal fees may be at least as high or higher if you do not leave a will, because the court will appoint an administrator to distribute assets. Estates run by administrators often are required to pay a hefty annual premium for an insurance policy called a surety bond, an expense totally eliminated by most wills and an expense that can considerably exceed the cost of almost any will.

Now, to the heart of your question: Estates go through probate court whether or not there is a will, but if you have a will you can distribute your property the way you prefer and can name the executor. More important, only by writing a will can you name a guardian for your 2-year-old daughter. Write a will, just as soon as you can, and don't worry about probate.

Note: One of the big problems is that people confuse **probate** with **estate administration.** Probate itself, the process of proving the will, takes little time or money if there is no contest about the will. Estate administration, the chore of actually managing and then distributing the estate, takes just as long under a living trust (today's popular choice for avoiding probate) as it does under a will.

Some property does pass directly to your beneficiaries without going through probate. Jointly owned property is one example. U.S. Savings Bonds, when there is a co-owner or surviving beneficiary, is another. Life insurance, under some circumstances, is a third. Insurance proceeds, if there is a designated individual named as beneficiary, pass directly to that beneficiary without having to go through probate. If your beneficiary is your estate, however, the proceeds are included in your estate for probate purposes and distribution may be delayed. Either way, all of your property—including jointly owned property, U.S. Savings Bonds, and insurance—is included in your gross estate for the purpose of calculating estate taxes that may be due (see below). **Avoiding probate does not mean avoiding estate or inheritance taxes.**

The only way to keep property out of your taxable estate is not to own it. In the case of insurance on your own life the policy has to be owned outright by another person or by a trust, with the premiums paid by that person or trust. If you retain any control (such as the right to borrow against the policy or to change the beneficiary), the proceeds remain in your taxable estate.

Estate Taxes

The right to transfer property from one person to another has been taxed for hundreds of years. In fact, in long-ago England (the source of much American law), all property reverted to the king upon death; the estate tax was the price one's heirs paid to get it back.

Before 1977, in this country, there were two different federal transfer tax structures: one for property transferred by gift during life and the other (at a higher rate) for property transferred at death. Since 1976, however, we have had a unified federal gift and estate tax, with property transferred at death considered your final gift.

The Economic Recovery Tax Act of 1981 made major changes in the federal estate tax laws, changes that have now eliminated federal estate taxes from 90 percent of all estates (it was 95 percent, but inflation increased the value of many estates, pushing them once again into taxable categories). Most people no longer have to worry about federal estate taxes. But you should nonetheless be familiar with the law, in case it applies to you (or to your parents) now or in the future. Remember: insurance and retirement plan death benefits make many of us worth more (at least as the tax laws see it) dead than alive.

Here are the highlights of the federal estate tax law:

Taxable Estates and Tax Rates

■ No federal estate tax return need be filed (under current law) for most estates under $600,000. This figure refers to your gross estate. Your taxable estate is less; it is arrived at after subtracting funeral expenses, outstanding debts (including unpaid income taxes), executor's and attorney's fees, and other allowable deductions. An estate could, therefore, total far more than $600,000 and still be exempt from tax. These amounts are also "unified." That means that they incorporate both your estate and certain gifts made during your lifetime. If you give $50,000 to your mother now, much of that gift will in effect be added to your gross estate when you die to determine whether estate taxes are due. (For more on gift taxes, see below.)

■ The maximum federal tax bracket on estates and gifts is currently 55 percent (it is scheduled to drop to 50 percent in 1993, but the consensus in Washington is that, as a Clinton revenue-raiser, the higher rate will be retained). For very large estates, however, complex tax adjustments make the actual tax rate even higher. Additional estate, inheritance and gift taxes may also be owed to your state (see p. 625).

Leaving Assets to Your Spouse

Any amount of money may be given or left to your spouse, without gift or estate tax liability (unless your spouse is not a U.S. citizen, in which case the $600,000 limit applies). This unlimited marital deduction means that you can simply leave everything to your spouse (assuming he or she is a U.S. citi-

---

Q Since my husband's retirement, we have spent six months of each year in Vermont and six months on the Costa del Sol in Spain. We drew up our will while we were still living year-round in the States. Do we need to change it now?

A You might. For one thing, people you've named as executors or trustees in this country might not be allowed to serve abroad. For another, the age of legal majority might be different and there might be some difficulty with bequests to children or grandchildren. And, not least, your estate may wind up paying double estate taxes, especially if you own real property in both countries. One possible solution: separate wills for the assets in each country. Before you do anything, however, show the will prepared in the United States to an attorney familiar with the law in Spain.

Table 21.1: Charting the Estate Tax Burden

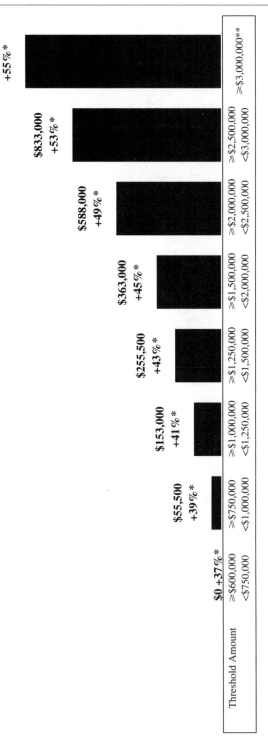

	$0 +37%*	$55,500 +39%*	$153,000 +41%*	$255,500 +43%*	$363,000 +45%*	$588,000 +49%*	$833,000 +53%*	$1,098,000 +55%*
Threshold Amount	≥$600,000 <$750,000	≥$750,000 <$1,000,000	≥$1,000,000 <$1,250,000	≥$1,250,000 <$1,500,000	≥$1,500,000 <$2,000,000	≥$2,000,000 <$2,500,000	≥$2,500,000 <$3,000,000	≥$3,000,000**

Source: Coopers & Lybrand, *Strategies for Your Personal Finances.*

Notes: *Unified estate-gift tax credit exempts first $600,000 from tax. For amounts over $600,000, tax is the figure given plus the percentage of the taxable estate exceeding the threshold amount applicable to you. For example, if your taxable estate is $800,000, your tax would be $55,500 plus 39 percent of $50,000 ($19,500) for a total of $75,000.

** The benefits of the graduated rates and the unified credit are phased out for transfers over $10 million. This produces an effective marginal rate of 60 percent for taxable transfers between $10 million and $21,040,000.

zen), if you wish to do so, without complicated and extensive legal maneuvers to minimize taxes.

Note: Wills should always be reviewed periodically. This is particularly important if you wrote a will referring to the "maximum marital deduction" before September 11, 1981; unless you revise your will, it will be assumed to refer to the old law under which the maximum marital deduction was no more than the larger of half the estate or $250,000.

■ Estate tax may be due later when the *surviving* spouse dies, if your estate and your spouse's total more than the exempt amount. You may want to minimize those taxes through trusts and other techniques described later in this chapter. But taxes are not the only consideration. Your spouse could, for instance, receive your estate and then pass the estate tax-free by remarrying and leaving the entire estate to a second spouse. Your spouse would be doing Uncle Sam out of taxes this way, but might also be doing your children out of their rightful inheritance. If your estate is more than the exempt amount of $600,000, or if you have remarried (which creates enormous estate tax complications), or if your spouse is not a U.S. citizen, consult a knowledgeable attorney for advice. Whatever the size of your estate, however, think about what you want your family to have. Don't get caught up in the arithmetic of tax saving to the exclusion of family considerations.

■ An estate may now be left, tax-free, for a surviving spouse without giving that spouse control over what happens to the assets when he or she dies. In the past, control had to be transferred along with assets. Now a husband might set up a trust to leave his wife income for life, while passing on the principal of the trust, on her death, to his children. This method of planning via trusts (for more detail, see p. 630) has become extremely popular.

■ Where property is jointly owned by husband and wife (and both are U.S. citizens) it will be assumed, for estate tax purposes, that each owns half the property. (For more on joint ownership, see pp. 627-629).

■ If your spouse is *not* a U.S. citizen, the estate tax law has unusual complexities. If your estate is large enough so that it would be taxable if you had no spouse, contact an expert attorney right away and discuss the situation.

The Gift Tax

Just as an estate tax is paid by the estate, a gift tax is paid, when due, by the giver. Here's what you need to know:

■ You may make unlimited outright gifts of up to $10,000 per recipient per calendar year without incurring any gift tax. A married couple may, if they wish, pool their tax-free opportunities and give up to $20,000 per gift each year tax-free, even if the funds come from only one of the partners (if you do it this way, even though no gift tax is due, you may have to file a gift tax return; talk to your tax adviser). Such gifts are a way of reducing your taxable estate. But, again, there are other considerations: Don't give assets away during your lifetime if you may need those assets.

■ In addition to the annual gifts discussed above, unlimited gifts may be made for medical purposes or to pay school tuition, without gift tax, if such payments are made directly to a medical or educational institution for education, training, or care of a specified individual. A grandparent might be able to help a grandchild through medical school, without gift tax liability. Or a niece might be able to pay for long-term care for an elderly aunt. (But don't confuse gift and income taxes. You can pay tuition for a grandchild or a nephew free of gift taxes, but you may not take an income tax deduction for doing so.)

■ Gifts made within three years of death were assumed, under pre-1981 law, to be made in contemplation of death; they were, therefore, included in the estate for estate tax purposes. No more. With certain exceptions (such as life insurance policies), most gifts, no matter when they are made, will no longer be included in the taxable estate.

Note: Any gift tax you pay on gifts made within three years of your death is added to the value of your taxable estate. But it may still save taxes in the long run to give money away before death; if your estate is sizable enough for large gifts to make a difference, consult a knowledgeable attorney.

■ It usually does the recipient more good, in terms of his or her income tax, to receive appreciated assets via your estate. That's because the cost basis for measuring capital gains of inherited assets is fixed at the time of death, while the cost basis of assets you give is fixed (usually) at what you paid. For example: You leave your daughter securities that you bought at $35 a share and that are valued at your death at $50 a share. Your daughter sells the securities for $60 a share. Because they were inherited she pays tax only on the difference between $50 (the "stepped-up basis" at the time of death) and $60. If you had made her a gift of the securities during your lifetime, the tax would be based on the difference between your purchase price of $35 and the selling price of $60.

Generation-Skipping Taxes

Your children have more than enough money to live comfortably, so you want to help their children instead. Good for you. But the federal government and some states impose a separate—and hefty—tax on gifts and bequests to grandchildren, great-grandchildren and, in fact, anyone who is appreciably younger than the giver. Annual per-person tax-free gifts of $10,000 are usually okay but, if you are considering larger gifts or bequests (a total of more than $1,000,000 to members of another generation), consult an expert attorney first.

STATE TAXES

Uncle Sam isn't the only one who wants a piece of the pie. Most states also levy their own death taxes, which don't necessarily conform to federal rules. Some states don't tax gifts. Some states continue to limit the annual gift tax exclusion to $3,000 long after the federal limit was raised to $10,000. Some states do not have a full marital deduction, so that a surviving spouse could wind up owing state taxes on the value of jointly owned property, including the family home. And, to add insult to injury, some state death taxes kick in at a much lower level than the federal tax. In Massachusetts, for example, estates above $200,000 (not the federal $600,000) are subject to tax. *Ri 2007: 600.000 #1,M10*

Note: State lawmakers are beginning to wise up. Recognizing that high death taxes are leading affluent residents to move out of state, thereby depriving the states of income and other taxes, many are considering revising the rules. In recent years, a number of states have eliminated the state surcharges on the federal death tax that resulted in effectively higher taxes.

But almost half the states, at the end of 1992, still levy either estate or inheritance taxes.

An **estate tax** is a tax on the right to dispose of property; it is assessed against the entire estate (after allowable deductions have been calculated) and typically paid out of the assets of the estate before distribution. The federal estate tax is uniform throughout the country. State estate taxes differ, but a credit is allowed against the federal estate tax for state estate taxes actually paid. Several states, however, have tax rates that exceed that credit.

An **inheritance tax** is a tax on the right to receive property and is paid by the recipient after distribution of the estate. Some states have inheritance taxes that are applied differently to different beneficiaries. The closer the relationship, the greater the amount of inheritance exempt from tax and the

---

Q We made our wills about ten years ago. Since then our lawyer has died. Do we have to write new wills?

A Your original wills are still valid—*if* you have or can obtain the signed originals. If the lawyer had kept the signed originals, and if you cannot retrieve them from his office, you will need to draw up new wills. But a will should always be reviewed every few years, in any case. And the significant tax-law revisions of the last few years would make it wise for you to review your wills now even if they are still valid.

smaller the tax assessed. A surviving spouse, as a rule, has the greatest exemption and the lowest tax.

Suggestion: If you are planning to move after retirement, you might take a look at state estate and inheritance taxes before you make a decision. They vary considerably. (Also, before you move, look at how the states tax out-of-state pension income; see Chapter 23 for more information.)

Reducing Your Taxable Estate

There are several popular ways to reduce a taxable estate. They are worth a look, even though the new tax laws remove most estates from tax considerations.

LIFETIME GIFTS

If you give assets away during your lifetime, up to the annual exclusion of $10,000 per gift per person ($20,000 for a married couple), they will generally not be included in your estate when you die. Assets that may be given include cash, securities, real estate, life insurance ... virtually anything at all (although there are special rules regarding life insurance; see below).

You might give your adult children an outright gift of cash and remove that cash from your estate. You can give assets that may increase in value (such as securities or real estate) and eliminate further appreciation of the asset from your taxable estate (note, however, that removing appreciated assets from your estate may cost your children more in capital gains taxes; see p. 624).

But I can't emphasize one point strongly enough: Don't look at taxes to the exclusion of everything else. Don't give away property you may need or wish to control. Plan your finances over your anticipated lifetime and let your heirs, unless you have money to spare, worry about taxes that may become due after you are gone.

LIFE INSURANCE

Life insurance agents often urge the purchase of life insurance (among other reasons) to provide cash to pay final expenses, including estate taxes. Today, with most estates free of estate taxes (including the small family businesses that formerly carried large life insurance policies to ensure the continuation of the business), taxes are no longer the motivating force in the purchase of most life insurance.

But there are still many reasons to buy life insurance (for more on life insurance, see Chapter 18):

■ If you have not yet built assets to the level where your family will be supported in your absence, life insurance provides an "instant estate."

■ If you have assets, but not liquid assets, and you know that there may be substantial final expenses in the form of uninsured medical and hospital bills, funeral costs, income and estate taxes, and the like, life insurance can take care of these bills, so that your survivors need not cash in other assets on a "forced sale" basis.

If you still need life insurance after retirement (see Chapter 23), you should be aware that:

■ If you own a life insurance policy on your own life, the proceeds will be included in your estate and therefore subject to possible estate tax (unless your spouse is your beneficiary and is a U.S. citizen). If you don't own the policy, and have relinquished ownership at least three years before your death, the proceeds will be free of estate tax.

■ You can remove life insurance from your taxable estate by giving up ownership of the policy, transferring it to either an irrevocable trust or an individual; if the latter, an adult child is often a good choice. Trusts are most appropriate for people with large complicated estates. But trusts can be expensive; you have to pay an attorney and name a trustee. And once your life insurance is in trust, you can't tap the cash value if you need some money.

Instead of setting up a trust, you might simply give your life insurance policy to your beneficiary, thereby removing the face value of the policy from your estate. If the policy is term insurance, a whole life policy that has been fully borrowed against, or a brand-new whole life policy, it may have little current value and no gift tax will be due. You can then give your beneficiary an annual gift of cash with which to pay the premiums on the policy, and as long as the gift is less than $10,000, no gift tax will be due. To be sure you do it right, consult a competent adviser.

■ Second-to-die life insurance policies (see p. 500) are a way to provide cash to pay final expenses, including estate taxes, upon the death of a surviving spouse.

JOINT OWNERSHIP

If you are married, you and your spouse may own everything jointly and assume that you don't need a will. If you are single, you may have put your assets in joint ownership with a sibling or a nephew or niece and assume that you don't need a will. Joint ownership has been called "the poor man's will" because assets that are jointly held do pass directly to the joint owner without passing through probate. But unless your estate is modest indeed, joint ownership may be a very poor substitute for a will. Here's why:

■ If you own property jointly, with right of survivorship or as a tenant by the entirety (see p. 278), you have nothing further to say about its future ownership. You may not leave the property (or your share of it) to anyone else in your will. (Joint ownership as tenants in common, without survivorship rights, does allow you to dispose of your share, but this is a form of ownership more often used by business partners than by marriage partners.)

■ Neither owner has exclusive control of jointly owned property. If one owner is away on business or incapacitated by a stroke or simply stubborn, the other owner may be unable to dispose of securities or real estate that is jointly owned. If you and your spouse should divorce, your jointly owned property will be frozen until negotiations are complete—unless you both, as joint owners, agree to the sale.

■ Jointly held bank accounts may be different, however, depending on state law. In some states either owner has the right to take all the money out of the account. This can be convenient. It also means that one may clean out the account without any warning to the other. In other states the one who cleaned out the account would owe half to the other.

■ Jointly held assets pass directly to the surviving owner, but directly does not mean immediately. Joint bank accounts may be temporarily blocked (and outstanding checks stopped) until state tax authorities have reviewed the situation and appropriate documents are filed. This is a good argument for separate bank accounts holding at least enough cash for a surviving spouse to live on for a couple of months.

■ When you place assets in joint ownership with someone other than your spouse, you may incur a gift tax liability. If you place your son's name on your 100 shares of AT&T stock, you may be doing so simply to ensure his ownership of the stock when you die. As far as the Internal Revenue Service is concerned, however, if the total of your gifts to your son that year (including the stock) exceeds $10,000, you've made a taxable gift in your lifetime. (And the gift tax is paid by the person who makes the gift.)

■ Jointly held property may be seized for the debts of either owner. Witness the elderly widow who puts all her savings accounts in joint ownership with her daughter, so that the daughter can pay her mother's bills. But the daughter becomes overextended and declares bankruptcy, or is the party at fault in an automobile accident. Before the mother realizes what is happening, the joint bank account (never mind that it's the mother's money) has been seized to pay the daughter's debts. If you're worried about paying your bills, whether because you are elderly or simply traveling a great deal, give a power of attorney instead of joint ownership. A power of attorney may be as limited (to write checks) or as broad (to handle all your affairs) as you like, and you may revoke it at any time. Or establish a living trust, as described on pp. 630-633.

Joint Ownership in Estate Planning

The biggest problem with joint ownership in the past—the presumption that everything in a joint account was put there by the first to die (unless the survivor could prove otherwise) and was therefore includable in his or her gross estate—no longer applies when joint ownership is between spouses and both are U.S. citizens. (**Note:** Special rules apply in community property states; see Chapter 1.) Husband and wife can now own assets jointly, even if one spouse earns no income, and each will be assumed to own half. There is no gift or estate tax problem. This modernization of the law does not, however, remove all complications.

For example: You and your spouse jointly own a house (your primary residence) for which you paid $36,000 some years ago. The house is now worth $150,000. One of you dies, and the other wants to sell the house. If the house were wholly owned by the first partner to die, it would pass free of estate taxes to the surviving partner as part of the unlimited marital deduction. In addition, the "cost" of the house for income (capital gains) tax purposes would be the full value of the house at the time of the first partner's death, or $150,000. (This is the "stepped up" basis—the initial cost of the property, stepped up to its value at the time of death—a provision in tax law that reduces capital gains tax when inherited property which has increased in value is sold.) If the house is jointly owned by you and your spouse (and you are both U.S. citizens), however, only half of the value is included in the estate. Thus one-half of the current value ($75,000), plus half the original cost ($18,000), would be the new "cost" for the surviving spouse. If he or she then sells the house for $150,000, $57,000 would be taxable gain (unless the survivor is over age 55 or defers the tax by buying another house to use as a principal residence). If he or she keeps the house, instead, the value of the entire house would be taxable in his or her estate, raising the cost basis for the children who then receive it to the value in that estate.

Some attorneys suggest, therefore, that it's a good idea to have appreciating assets, such as a house, in the name of the spouse most likely to die first. This advice assumes that you can figure out which one that is.

Whatever you do about your primary residence, however, any out-of-state property might better be jointly owned to reduce death-related expenses. If you live in New Jersey and own a vacation cottage in Massachusetts, both states will insist on probating your will. If you own the property jointly, it will pass to your joint owner without the need for probate (but death taxes may still be collected by both states).

Note: The change in the tax law with respect to joint ownership applies *only* to spouses and *only* if both spouses are U.S. citizens. If you own property jointly with anyone else, relative or friend or investment partner, the entire value of the property will be assumed to belong to the first to die and will be included in his or her gross estate for estate tax purposes. It will be so assumed for the second to die as well and, if there is a third owner, for the third. Unless it can be proved to the satisfaction of the Internal Revenue Service that the money to buy the property came from separate funds (no easy task; keeping good records will help), the property may be subject to estate tax two, three, or more times, as many times as there are joint owners.

Trusts in Estate Planning

A trust, despite its forbidding sound, is simply a three-party agreement in which the owner of property (the grantor) transfers legal title to that property to someone else (the trustee) for the benefit of one or more third parties (the beneficiaries).

A **testamentary** trust takes effect at the death of the testator (this is what the grantor is called when a trust is created at death). An **inter vivos** (living) trust takes effect as soon as it is established and may or may not continue after death. Living trusts, furthermore, may be **revocable,** meaning subject to change during the grantor's lifetime, or **irrevocable,** not subject to change.

When you create a revocable trust, you retain control; because you retain control the assets in the trust are included in your estate for estate tax purposes and are subject to estate tax if tax is due. Contrary to popular belief (and contrary to the advice given in a great many "seminars" by people trying to sell their services), revocable living trusts produce absolutely no tax savings of any kind; in some circumstances living trusts can actually increase gift and estate taxes. Whether or not a living trust will save you money at all depends on the costs of probate in your state; living trusts have been very popular in California, for example, where probate costs are high. The assets held in a revocable living trust will go directly to your beneficiaries when you die, however, (unless the trust instrument provides otherwise) without probate and its delays. Don't create a trust, however, unless you're old enough to be reasonably sure that your financial situation and your life won't change significantly; living trusts are generally most appropriate for older people with substantial property.

With an irrevocable trust, if you part with all right to receive benefits from and control the assets, you may gain the tax advantage of removing the assets from your estate but you also lose control of your assets. Don't create an irrevocable trust unless you are wealthy enough so that (1) estate taxes will be an issue, and (2) you'll have enough other property in your control to ensure continuation of your life-style.

SOME USES OF TRUSTS

That said, trusts are not just for the wealthy. You might want to set up a trust for any one of a number of reasons:

■ To manage your own assets, either because you are too busy during your working life to pay proper attention, you face a serious illness, or you have retired and don't want to worry about financial matters.
  Via a living trust, revocable when you wish, you can name a trustee to handle investments and manage your funds. You can direct the trustee to consult with you on major decisions, or you can give the trustee full power to act. This trust will not save any income or estate taxes, but that is not your goal.

■ To manage assets left in your will to children or grandchildren, until the age at which you would like them to receive the property. (If you die without a will and without making such provisions, a guardian will be named by the courts and the children will receive the funds as soon as they reach legal age, which in many states is 18.)

■ To provide income to your surviving spouse (or children), and then pass your estate on to your children (or grandchildren). These **credit shelter** or **bypass** trusts are frequently used to shelter estates of up to $1.2 million from estate taxes. They work like this: Each partner as an individual owns half the assets (this is important). Each leaves $600,000 in trust and the rest outright to the surviving spouse. When the surviving spouse dies, the $600,000 in trust plus up to $600,000 in other assets passes to beneficiaries free of estate tax.

■ To avoid multiple probates, if you own real estate in more than one state.

■ To deal with a possible will contest.

■ To avoid probate delays, in some states, if one or more of your heirs is legally incapacitated or you have no close relatives.

■ To keep life insurance proceeds out of your (and your spouse's) estate to save estate taxes.

Q We have two children, ages 12 and 15, and are writing simple wills in which we leave everything to each other and then, when the survivor dies, to the children. But we don't want to just give each child half of whatever we leave (it won't be that much) because we can't tell at this point how much money each child will need to finish an education. We can't tell if one will have special medical needs. Is there some way we can leave our assets intact, for the benefit of both children, with a manager able to make decisions in the best interests of the children?

A Yes. You can leave all or part of your estate in what is called a "sprinkling" or "spray" or "discretionary" trust, with a named trustee empowered to distribute the assets between the children as they are needed, equally or unequally. That trustee may be the guardian named to actually care personally for the children. Or it may be a separate individual or institution, in which case you might require consultation with the guardian. You can also determine the age or ages at which you want the children to receive any money left in the trust. If remaining amounts will be sizable, you might want to stagger the distribution: so much when the younger child reaches age 25, so much at age 30, and so on. That decision will depend on the maturity of your children and the amount of money you expect to leave.

■ To provide for persons who are now or may become incapacitated and still permit them to qualify for Medicaid.
■ To bypass probate, by disposing of assets outside your will.

ADVANTAGES OF A LIVING TRUST

Testamentary trusts permit you to determine what happens to your property after your death. Living trusts have additional advantages:

Avoidance of Probate

Living trusts permit your estate to skip probate proceedings with respect to the assets in the trust, thereby saving both time and fees. But this is so only with respect to assets actually owned by the trust. The saving is lost if the assets are in your name and pass to the trust under your will. In many instances, in fact, the savings will be nominal or even nonexistent.

Some advisers recommend that an entire estate be kept out of probate via the mechanism of living trusts. But this represents an unreasoning fear of probate, and can complicate affairs for you and for your survivors. For you, it means transferring ownership of all your assets, including your home and your car, to the trust; this may sometimes result in being unable to refinance your mortgage or insure your car, if lenders or insurers don't want to deal with trusts. For your survivors, it may mean coming face to face with this question: What if you come into money upon your death that you have not foreseen? It could happen if, as one example, your death is caused by an automobile accident and a settlement is made to your estate. Create a living trust, if you like, but also leave a will for the remainder of your property.

Note: Removing property from probate does *not* mean removing it from your taxable estate. The only way to do that is to divest yourself permanently of control and enjoyment of your assets during your lifetime, via an irrevocable trust. Few people want or can afford to do this.

Professional Management

A living trust can provide professional management of your assets while you are living. If you should become ill or incapacitated—a special consideration for the elderly—your trustee can continue to take care of all your financial affairs, pay your bills, and so on.

You can establish a living trust for this purpose while you are hale and hearty, and do away with concerns about handling your affairs in the event of disability. A living trust, controlled by you while you are willing and able to do so, is an alternative to a power of attorney (which, unless you are careful to draw up a **durable power of attorney,** automatically ends with incapacity) or guardianship (also called conservatorship or incompetence, which can go beyond financial management to remove all independence from an elderly person's life).

Note: If your state permits durable powers of attorney, the kind which remain in effect despite incapacity, such a power of attorney may provide equivalent benefits at considerably lower cost.

Coordination of Assets

A trust can be designed to coordinate all your assets, so that securities, life insurance, pension and profit-sharing benefits, real estate, etc., can be transferred to your trust when you die and administered in one central place for the benefit of your heirs. A properly drawn will can accomplish this too.

Privacy

A trust agreement, unlike a will, is a private matter. A will becomes public when it is submitted to the court for probate. If you have a trust in effect when you die, no one needs to know what you've left or to whom (although in some states and under some circumstances, a trust may have to be filed in court and thus made public). Unless you're a celebrity or very affluent, however, privacy probably isn't an issue.

MARITAL TRUSTS

Trusts can be tailored to meet almost any need. But that need should be evaluated as a family affair, or lingering resentment can be the result. A marital trust, for example, can be set up (either as a living trust or as a testamentary trust under a will) to administer an estate and distribute income to a surviving spouse. The purpose might be reduction of estate taxes. It might be protection of the survivor's interests. And it might be the distribution of assets in a situation, such as remarriage, in which you want to control who gets your assets after you and your spouse both die.

With the full marital exemption, under which all assets pass to a surviving spouse without federal estate tax, concern about taxes is no longer a reason to establish a trust for the surviving spouse. But the full amount inherited tax-free by the surviving spouse will be subject to estate tax when the second spouse dies. And that spouse (unless he or she remarries, leaves the assets to the new spouse and thus becomes entitled to another full marital exemption) will be entitled (in 1993) to a maximum exemption of $600,000. If you own sufficient property (a net worth of over $600,000) so that estate taxes will be a consideration for your surviving spouse, the use of trusts to hold what is exempt from estate tax at your death (up to a maximum of $600,000) might be appropriate to avoid tax at the second death. You should talk to an attorney who specializes in estate planning.

Note: Don't get the impression that a trust is all or nothing. You may put any proportion of your assets into one or more trusts, and do as you like with the remainder.

When both partners come to a late-life remarriage with sizable assets, each might execute a trust with income to the surviving spouse and the principal (once the surviving spouse has died) to the trustmaker's children. (Provision may be made for the principal to be invaded for the surviving spouse in case of need.) Both sets of children will be protected. And the trust of the first to die will qualify for the marital deduction. If you are in this situation, you may also want to draw up a premarital agreement (see p. 606).

NAMING A TRUSTEE

A trustee, like an executor, may be an individual or an institution. However, an executor has an essentially limited responsibility, ending when the estate has been distributed to the beneficiaries, while a trustee has an ongoing responsibility. The trustee must administer the assets in the trust for the duration of the trust, making wise investment decisions. Trust fees are generally regulated by state law, and are generally a percentage of the assets in the trust.

Should You Use a Bank as Trustee?

Banks frequently advertise their trust services, and those services are extensive (although they may be most effective with, and actually limited to, larger estates). A bank can offer:

- Stability. The institution will endure, where an individual might not.
- Professional administration. With computerized systems, banks can offer documentation and follow-up on an impressive scale.
- Interdepartmental efforts on your behalf. An investment officer may make investment decisions, a tax officer handle tax planning and the trust's tax returns, while a custodial department handles day-to-day management of your account, and a trust officer deals with the trust's beneficiaries.

Q When my wife and I divorced, I agreed to name her and our son as irrevocable beneficiaries of my life insurance. I also want to leave my son the rest of my property. But I've been a major source of support for my mother, now almost 70, and I want to be sure that she's taken care of if I die first. What's the best way to handle this?

A You might leave your property (other than the life insurance, which is covered by your agreement with your ex-wife) in a trust, with the income paid to your mother during her lifetime and the principal then going to your son at her death. You can word it so that your son must be at least a certain age before coming into the money. Then if your mother dies before he is old enough (in your estimation) to handle the funds, the trust would continue to be administered on his behalf. You can also include wording so that your son becomes the trust's sole beneficiary if your mother dies before you do, or even skip the trust in such an event. If you wish, you can provide that the trust is for the benefit of both your mother and your son as long as both are living. Clarify your own goals, then talk to a competent attorney.

■ The ability to say "no" when the answer should be "no" and an individual may be reluctant to stand up to the beneficiary. (On the other hand, a bank officer may be more rigid and less inclined to be flexible.)

A bank, on the other hand, is not personalized. The trust officer you talk to now may not be the one who later administers your estate. The trust officer, known to you or not, may simply not appreciate the life-style your family enjoys and may not give them all the money you would want them to have. If you're going to use a bank as trustee, be sure to put your specific wishes in writing, in the trust and its accompanying documents. Better yet, name co-trustees, such as your spouse or a friend (for the personal touch) and a bank (to do the work). And, if you select a bank, be sure it offers comprehensive trust services.

Understand, too, if an institution is your sole trustee, that unless a trust document contains authorization to do so, there will be no way a beneficiary can change the trustee—even if fees go up and performance is incompetent. There are three ways around this: Name a relative or friend as co-trustee with an institution, with the power to change the hired trustee. Name a trusted individual as sole trustee, and that person can hire a bank to provide service to the trust. Or name an institution but give your heirs a limited right to choose a new trustee from among a selected list of acceptable institutions (get good advice on this choice; the IRS may challenge the trust).

How Much Cash Will Be Available for Final Expenses?

Whatever your net worth, your survivors will need cash on hand to wrap things up. Give them a hand, now, by using the following worksheet to estimate what will be needed and what will be available:

Worksheet 21.2: Estate Planning

Estate settlement costs		Cash on hand	
Medical/hospital bills		Checking accounts	
Funeral costs		Savings accounts	
Federal estate tax		Certificates of deposit	
State death taxes		Money market funds	
Administration costs		Insurance proceeds	
Other outstanding liabilities		Pension or profit-sharing proceeds	
TOTAL		Money owed you	
		Other assets quickly convertible to cash	
		TOTAL	

Will there be enough?

Remember: After a death, assets may be tied up for weeks or months. Be sure each spouse has enough cash or cash equivalents in his or her own name to run the household for at least a few months.

Estate Planning Is a Family Affair

Don't think about the future by yourself; estate planning is not a do-it-alone proposition.

If You are Married

If you are married, estate planning is both a joint and an individual endeavor. You *each* need a will. You each need a net worth statement. You each need to be able to put your hands, quickly, on liquid assets. You each need to understand your (and your spouse's) financial affairs. Don't assume, whatever your age, that either one of you will necessarily die first. You simply can't tell. Make your calculations, and your preparations, to cover any eventuality.

The widow who knows absolutely nothing about financial affairs (and it's most often, but not always, a widow) may be a figure of fun in comic strips, but the joke turns bitter all too soon in real life. There is enough to cope with at the time of death, without starting from the beginning in financial management.

Couples always divide family responsibilities. Someone balances the checkbook just as someone (not necessarily the same someone) handles the investments. Someone makes the trip to the safe deposit box and keeps track of valuable papers, while someone fills out the tax forms. Someone, for that matter, knows whom to call to repair the furnace and someone knows how the household appliances work. Share this information. Don't wait until one of you must face the unfamiliar alone.

Then, after you've told each other all you know about your financial affairs, swap jobs for practice. Each of you take on the other's financial responsibilities for a couple of months: balance the checkbook, pay the mortgage, enter a running tally of dividends received, and so on. You may find it takes longer to get the job done—but it's better to have the learning period now, by choice, and with your spouse around to answer questions, than later, by necessity.

Discuss, together, what you will do about:

- Writing a will. Decide how you want to distribute your property and make wills, one for each of you, saying so. Do it without delay.
- Choosing an executor. It should be a person and/or an institution in whom you both have confidence.
- Naming a guardian. It's even more important that you agree on this person, and that you consult your minor children (if they are old enough) before naming anyone.
- Establishing testamentary or living trusts, if appropriate, and naming a trustee.

Worksheet 21.3: Estate Planning

Question	Answer

1. Has a will been prepared or reviewed by an estate planning expert within the last three years for:

    a. Your Spouse?   Yes _____ No _____

    b. You?   Yes _____ No _____

2. Do you know the name and telephone number of the attorney, accountant, or other personal financial adviser you would contact for assistance upon learning of your spouse's death?   Yes _____ No _____

3. Are you comfortable with the following individuals who would have responsibilities affecting your assets following the death of your spouse:

    a. Executor?   Yes _____ No _____

    b. Attorney?   Yes _____ No _____

    c. Trustee?   Yes _____ No _____

    d. Accountant?   Yes _____ No _____

    e. Investment Adviser?   Yes _____ No _____

    f. Personal Financial Adviser?   Yes _____ No _____

4. Do you understand generally how assets and income would flow following your spouse's death under:

    a. Your spouse's will and trust agreements?   Yes _____ No _____

    b. Insurance plans and policies?   Yes _____ No _____

    c. Retirement and benefit plans?   Yes _____ No _____

5. Do you know the approximate annual cost of continuing your current life-style following your spouse's death?   Yes _____ No _____

6. Do you know approximately how long you could afford to continue your current life-style following your spouse's death?   Yes _____ No _____

7. Do you know whether the following documents exist, and if so, where they are located:

    a. Your spouse's will?   Yes _____ No _____

    b. Your spouse's military discharge papers (if any)?   Yes _____ No _____

    c. Instructions regarding funeral and burial arrangements for your spouse?   Yes _____ No _____

    d. Your spouse's birth certificate?   Yes _____ No _____

    e. Your and your spouse's marriage certificate?   Yes _____ No _____

    f. Property agreements and divorce decrees if you or your spouse has been divorced?   Yes _____ No _____

    g. Trust agreements naming your spouse as a beneficiary? Yes _____ No _____

    h. Trust agreements naming you and/or your children as beneficiaries?   Yes _____ No _____

    i. Life insurance policies on your spouse's life?   Yes _____ No _____

j. Beneficiary designations for employment-related
benefits provided to your spouse?   Yes _____   No _____

k. Tax returns filed by you and your spouse
for the last three years?   Yes _____   No _____

l. The most recent gift tax return (if any)
filed by your spouse?   Yes _____   No _____

m. Communications from tax authorities regarding
pending audits or challenges of your spouse's previously
filed tax returns?   Yes _____   No _____

n. Notes and other evidence of debts owed
by your spouse?   Yes _____   No _____

o. Notes and other evidence of amounts
owed to your spouse?   Yes _____   No _____

p. Deeds, leases, options, bonds, stock certificates,
and other evidence of assets owned by your spouse?   Yes _____   No _____

q. Partnership agreements for all closely held companies
in which your spouse owns an interest?   Yes _____   No _____

r. Shareholder agreements for all closely held companies
in which your spouse owns an interest?   Yes _____   No _____

s. A listing of credit cards in your spouse's name? Yes _____   No _____

t. A listing of bank, savings and loan, brokerage,
and other cash accounts in your spouse's name?   Yes _____   No _____

u. A listing of all clubs and associations in
which your spouse maintains memberships?   Yes _____   No _____

v. A listing of safe deposit boxes in your spouse's name? Yes _____   No _____

8. Do you know who you should contact at your spouse's employer to obtain assistance
upon learning of your spouse's death?   Yes _____   No _____

Source: Arthur Andersen & Co.

If You are a Single Older Adult

You may also want to share your plans with someone close, a relative or friend, as well as talking to your attorney and/or accountant. If you are a widow or widower with grown children, you should tell them (roughly, not necessarily in detail) about your affairs. Don't let them put you off by telling you that you will live forever. You won't. Tell them:

■ Where your will is located and why you've made any specific provisions therein
■ Where your personal affairs record is located
■ Whom to contact: your lawyer and accountant and stockbroker, as well as far-flung relatives and friends

Do your estate planning as part of your lifetime financial plan—the plan that includes maximizing your assets while you're alive and distributing them when you're gone. Make your arrangements now, whatever your age, as if you might die tomorrow. Then review your plans, and change them as necessary, as you move along through life.

 ## KEY POINTS

- Write a will. This is the only way to be sure that your assets will be distributed as you would like them to be.

- A personal affairs record and a letter of instructions, supplementing your will, will make your executor's task much easier.

- Probate is the legal process of validating a will. You can bypass probate by distributing your assets outside of a will: through joint ownership, a trust, or outright gifts while you are alive. Doing so with all your assets, however, may leave you without adequate funds while you are alive, or complicate your life unnecessarily; it may also deprive your estate of the funds needed to pay final bills. Remember that bypassing probate via a revocable living trust does not reduce or eliminate estate taxes.

- Federal estate tax returns must be filed when estates exceed designated amounts. You may, however, leave any amount to your spouse (or inherit any amount from a spouse) without federal estate taxes being due (unless the surviving spouse is not a U.S. citizen). Taxes will then be due, if the estate is large enough, on the death of the surviving spouse.

- If your affairs are at all complicated, or your assets at all extensive, don't be a do-it-yourself estate planner. Get the professional help of a competent attorney.

CHAPTER 22

Planning for the Later Years

■ Jonathan got the call at work: His 79-year-old mother had broken her hip. Jonathan flew to Boston, expecting to take a few days to put everything in order, then return to his normal routine. Six months later, his mother was back in her own home... but Jonathan's days continued to be fragmented by telephone calls with doctors, insurance companies, and care-givers, and his work was suffering.

■ Jane's mother-in-law from her first marriage is physically frail, at 88, but mentally alert. Jane's father is physically well even as he suffers a gradually devastating loss of mental abilities from Alzheimer's disease. And Jane's father-in-law, from her current marriage, was recently widowed and needs help to continue living on his own. Jane feels responsible for all three people; her husband and children are feeling her absence as she tends to the older generation's needs after long hours at work.

One in eight Americans is currently over the age of 65. By the year 2030, one in five will be over 65. The fastest growing segment of the elderly population consists of men and women (mostly women) over the age of 85; there were twice as many people in this age group in 1990 as in 1960. Viewed from another vantage point, fully 40 percent of people in their late fifties have at least one living parent, compared with only 25 percent as recently as the early 1970s. You stand a good chance of having elderly parents ... and a very good chance of reaching 85 yourself.

It can be wonderful to have a four-generation family. But, almost inevitably, aging takes its toll. While many octogenarians are physically and mentally well and fully able to manage their own affairs, fully half of those over the age of 85 require assistance with daily living due to chronic illness or disability.

That need for assistance takes both an emotional and a financial toll, a toll made worse when you are caring for both children and parents. In a 1992 study called "The Financial Impact of Multiple Financial Responsibilities on Midlife and Older People" by the American Association of Retired Persons (AARP), each household in the sample was assisting an average of over four family members, young and old, to an average tune of almost $20,000 a year. Much of this outlay probably went toward educational costs for children, but many care-givers of the elderly report out-of-pocket expense plus lost opportunities as the demands of care-giving force them to pass up chances for promotion, reduce working hours, liquidate assets, and take on debt.

Yet we as a nation are just beginning to come to grips with the pressing need for eldercare services, a need made more urgent by the mobility that may put adult children hundreds or thousands of miles from their parents, by a rate of divorce that splinters families along with family responsibilities (sometimes adding to the burden as we care for members of an extended and even an ex-family), and by the fact that most women, traditional care-givers, now work outside the home.

Whatever your current age, you are likely to be affected—sooner or later—by the need for eldercare. Perhaps you are a young adult, witnessing your parents coping (emotionally and financially) with the onset of dependency in their parents. You may yourself be a member of the sandwich generation, squeezed in the triple crunch of paying for college, saving for your own retirement, and helping your parents. Or you may be retired, with every intention of remaining independent but with an underlying fear of the physical or financial problems that may lie ahead.

Wherever you are in the life cycle right now, here's an outline of what you need to know (more resources are listed in the bibliography) about health, housing, and finances in the later years.

Health Planning

Health insurance, advance directives, and geriatric screening all fall under the heading of health planning for an aging population.

LONG-TERM CARE AND HEALTH INSURANCE

The kind of health care most needed by elderly Americans is not covered by most health insurance policies. Our health insurance system, although likely to see drastic change within the next year or two, is currently designed to meet acute medical needs—the kind of need that responds to doctors and surgery and hospitals. But the kind of care most elderly people need is long-term custodial care involving home health aides, social workers, and housekeeping assistance. Since neither Medicare nor private health insurance covers these services to any extent, most of the money for these services comes out of the family's pocket.

Medicare pays in full for 20 days of nursing home care, and in part for another 80 days—but only when the care is medically necessary skilled nursing care in a Medicare-approved skilled nursing facility following a hospital stay. Some Medicare supplement ("Medigap") policies plug some of these gaps, by paying the copayment when the insured is in a nursing home longer than 20 days. But neither Medicare nor Medigap cover the long-term custodial care that many older people need. (See Chapter 19 for more information on Medicare and Medigap coverage.)

The only insurance product currently on the market that addresses the need is long-term care coverage, also described in detail in Chapter 19. Long-term care policies, issued individually or on a group basis, typically provide a specified number of dollars per day for nursing home or at-home care. But long-term care policies are prohibitively expensive for most older people. And the younger, midlife adults who can afford to buy the insurance may see good reasons for not doing so. Among those reasons:

- Unless a policy's benefits are pegged to rising costs, they will be meaningless in two or three decades when they are likely to be needed. Inflation riders add significantly to the cost of coverage.

- Premiums may rise sharply in later years because (a) insurers have little experience in this relatively new field and may find their costs increasing, and (b) they have the right, as is typically not the case with other forms of insurance, to raise rates in the future.

- This same dearth of experience has led to considerable instability in the field. *Consumer Reports* surveyed insurers writing long-term coverage in 1988 and again in 1991; fully one-third of the companies reported on in 1988 were no longer selling long-term care policies by 1991.

- Everyone expects the federal government to come up with a health plan which will include long-term care. Meanwhile, some state governments have started to step in. New York State now has a plan, modeled after a similar effort in Connecticut, under which residents can buy a private insurance policy covering the cost of modest nursing home care for three years. After three years, should the individual continue to need nursing home care, Medicaid (the federal-state program for low-income people) will pay the bill; the individual's income will be tapped to help pay for care, but family assets will be left intact. Other states are expected to follow suit.

Insurance covering long-term care may be appealing to people with assets to protect. If you are interested, be sure to read the information on pp. 533-535 on what to look for in a policy.

The Uninsured

Without insurance, the enormous costs of long-term care must be borne by the family. In 1990 one year in a nursing home cost about $30,000 on average; nursing homes in some high-cost urban areas can go as high as $100,000 a year. At-home cost can also come to a tidy sum. The occasional housekeeper or home health aide may earn from $6 to $15 an hour, depending on where you live, but skilled care costs more, and the round-the-clock care that a seriously ill or demented person needs can cost many thousands of dollars a year. It's not unusual, according to James Firman, president of United Seniors Health Cooperative, for long-term home care to cost $30,000 or more a year.

It can help to plan ahead but, unfortunately, many of us just don't want to face the possibility of needing help. If you are concerned about your parents, try to talk to them about their finances; try to ascertain, without prying, if they may need financial help in the future. If you are the senior generation, talk to your children about your own situation so that, together, you can build for the future. More information on financial planning for eldercare starts on p. 652.

ADVANCE DIRECTIVES

Insurance is only one form of security for the future. You should also consider preparing (or having your parents prepare) advance directives about the kind of medical care you do or don't want. In fact, although you can't be required to prepare an advance directive, federal law does insist that Medicare recipients be asked whether they have done so when they enter a hospital or other health-related facility.

There are two forms of advance directives, living wills and durable powers of attorney for health care. You may want both (see below).

Living Wills

A living will describes the type of health care you want or don't want if you become terminally ill and can't make decisions for yourself about life-sustaining treatment. It's a way to convey your attitude, philosophy, and values to your family and doctors, just in case you are unable to do so when the need arises. It generally takes two physicians—your own and another—to determine that you have a terminal condition, are no longer able to make decisions about whether or not you want life-sustaining treatment (medication to reduce pain will still be given), and whether it's time to invoke the living will.

Your living will should be in writing, signed, dated, and witnessed by two adults; neither family members nor your physician should act as a witness. Once you've made a living will, be sure both your family and your doctor know that you have done so, and know where it is. You may even want to leave a copy in your doctor's office, to be kept with your medical records.

Durable Powers of Attorney for Health Care

This document, also called a health care proxy, is better in certain ways than a living will because it is more flexible. Instead of listing specific treatments you do and do not want, with a durable power of attorney for health care you designate someone (a proxy) to make medical decisions if you are unable to do so. (A durable power of attorney for financial matters, as described on p. 654, cannot be applied for health-related decisions; you need a specific document for this purpose.)

A health care proxy must be in writing, signed and dated, and witnessed (in many states) by at least one adult. Again, family and doctors should know that you've executed such a document and where it can be found.

You may want to execute both a living will and a durable power of attorney. Different states have different rules about which will be accepted; for additional information about both documents, and which state accepts which, a booklet called "Making Health Care Decisions: Your Right To Decide" is available for $5; call Commerce Clearing House, 800-248-3248, to place your order.

GERIATRIC ASSESSMENT

Our bodies change as we age. The clear-cut symptoms of appendicitis in a young adult may be confusingly different in her grandmother. Poor nutrition may produce symptoms that appear to be senility. Medication itself, because it has a different impact on an older body, may cause confusion. Doctors who deal with a younger patient population may not be as familiar with these facts; older adults can often benefit from the care of physicians specially trained to meet their needs. There are more geriatricians these days, as medical schools see where the next population bulge (and patient population) will be, but you may still have to seek one out in or near your community.

If an older member of your family is exhibiting physical or mental symptoms that are not responding to care by his or her regular physician, you may also want to consider a special geriatric assessment or evaluation. Your local or state Office on Aging can probably refer you to a center providing these comprehensive evaluations, typically involving a geriatrician and a social worker. Between them, they can asses physical and mental health and make appropriate recommendations.

Housing

Older adults can make the same housing decisions, described in Chapter 9, as younger adults. But older adults, particularly the very old, may be faced with some additional choices as well. In general, failing abilities may necessitate some housing adjustments.

Initially, the adjustments are easy. Simply increasing lighting, being sure rugs won't skid, installing lever handles instead of knobs on doors, turning down the temperature on the hot water heater, and putting in a telephone with large buttons and easy-to-read numbers can make a big difference in the older person's ability to live independently.

As time passes, more adjustments may become necessary. As people reach the mid-eighties they are increasingly likely to have difficulty with personal care and with home management. Personal care, in the jargon of social workers, involves specific activities of daily living (ADLs): walking (this is where most people have difficulty), bathing, going outside the house, getting in and out of a bed or a chair (called "transferring"), dressing, getting to and using the toilet, and eating (the least difficult). Home management (instrumental activities of daily living, or IADLs) means the ability to do heavy housework (again, where most people have difficulty; see Table 22.1), shop, do light housework, prepare meals, manage money, and use the telephone.

The difference that comes with age is dramatic. In one study, 17 percent of 65- to 74-year-olds and 49 percent of those 85 or over had some difficulties with personal care; 21 percent of the 65-to 74-year-old group and 55 percent of the over-85 group had some limitations when it came to home management. There are some interesting gender differences in these statistics. Women, on average, live longer than men. But women are more often plagued with the chronic illnesses and disabilities that make personal care and home management difficult. According to a 1992 Census Bureau report, "Elderly women are likely to have long-term chronic disabling diseases, while men tend to develop relatively short-term fatal diseases."

If you plan ahead, and if you secure help when needed, it's possible to compensate for many of these limitations within the familiar walls of a home you know and love. There may come a time, however, when you (or your parents) will be more comfortable in a new environment.

Table 22.1: People Over Age 65 With Limitations Affecting Housing

Problems with personal care:

Eating:	2%
Using the toilet:	4%
Dressing:	6%
Transferring (getting out of a bed or a chair):	8%
Getting outside:	10%
Bathing:	10%
Walking:	19%

Problems with home management:

Using the telephone:	5%
Managing money:	5%
Preparing meals:	7%
Doing light housework:	7%
Shopping:	11%
Doing heavy housework:	24%

Source: National Center for Health Statistics; Public Policy Institute of the American Association of Retired Persons.

STAYING PUT

You may well prefer to remain in your own home, but find upkeep and maintenance increasingly onerous as the years go by. Before you decide you must move (or that it's essential to move your parents out of their familiar surroundings), consider the following:

■ Homemaking services may be available at little or no cost through a local volunteer or agency program. If not, perhaps a local college student could be offered a room in exchange for light housekeeping or a responsible high school student might appreciate an after-school job doing shopping and meal preparation.

■ Chore services in many communities offer volunteer labor (you pay for materials) to help elderly residents with household maintenance and repairs—fixing a leaky faucet, repairing a broken window, and other minor but necessary chores.

■ Some towns and counties, and some utilities, offer low-interest or no-interest loans for home repair. In some cases, these loans do not have to be repaid until the home is sold.

■ Meals on Wheels and similar programs provide one or two hot meals a day for elderly people in most communities around the United States, generally at very low cost. Again, the local Office on Aging can provide the information you need.

■ Transportation services, in the form of a regular bus route or a pick-up-on-request service, can help people who no longer drive and would otherwise be housebound.

■ Telephone reassurance programs, also staffed by volunteers, can call shut-ins to be sure they are okay and call a back-up number if they are not.

Q Property taxes have skyrocketed in the town where my retired mother lives. Is there anything she can do to reduce her tax burden—other than sell her house?

A Many municipalities offer reduced property taxes to senior citizens; be sure your mother is paying no more than she must. Also, in many areas, your mother may be able to borrow money to pay her property taxes under a program run by the local or state government. These programs typically provide that she does not have to repay the money until she moves or sells her home; if she dies, her estate would pay the bill. Contact the tax assessor in your mother's town to determine if this or other special breaks exist for senior citizens.

■ Part-time aides, although you may have to pay the tab yourself, can help with meals and shopping, laundry and housekeeping, making it possible to stay in your own home.

The Office on Aging in your state, county, or city can provide information about programs of this kind.

Adult or Retirement Communities

These age-segregated communities are often the first retirement move for those who want maintenance-free living and organized social activities. They may be a good move for the active "young-old" but they may be less desirable for the frail elderly. Some of the potential drawbacks:

■ Enclaves that are billed as "secure" because they are isolated in a rural area may be too isolated when you are no longer able to drive or when sophisticated medical care is needed.

■ A community may start out, when it is newly built, with a population of active sixty-somethings. As everyone ages in place, you may find yourself surrounded by large numbers of people in their eighties and nineties. Even when you are eighty-something yourself, you may prefer the stimulation of mixing with younger people—and you may be happier without the constant background noise of ambulance sirens.

That said, there's no reason why your first retirement move has to be your last ... and no reason why you shouldn't enjoy an adult community for a decade or two. Just go into it with your eyes open.

Assisted Living

Most people prefer to remain in their own homes just as long as possible and, with the help of some of the community services outlined above, many elderly do live independently. But, for some, there comes a time when a move is necessary. That move may be to a nursing home. But it may not need to be, if there is an assisted living facility nearby. This relatively new concept, intended for people who need more help than they can get at home but who are not ill enough to need a nursing home, takes several forms:

Board and Care Homes

These congregate living facilities are rental arrangements where you may have your own room or apartment but receive housekeeping, meals, and some personal care services. These homes are state-licensed, but vary widely in the services they offer and in the quality of care. Some are little more than warehouses for the old, some have abused their residents, while others offer family-style living in a pleasant communal setting combined with personal privacy and the ability to come and go as you please. Never commit to a move—to a board and care home or any other kind of facility—without a thorough investigation.

Senior Residences

Another form of congregate living, senior residences offer (with some variation from place to place) private apartments plus communal meals (usually either one or two a day), housekeeping services, social activities, and (often) an on-premises nurse. As the American Association of Retired Persons puts it in a valuable booklet called "Your Home, Your Choice" (see bibliography), "Congregate housing is an updated version of the old resort hotel that served meals in a central dining room and provided housekeeping services."

These senior residences are a lot less expensive than nursing homes, because they need not provide round-the-clock medical care. And they are usually a lot more pleasant and home-like as places to live.

But there are financial considerations: Ask exactly what the monthly fee covers. Is there a flat rate that covers everything? Or do you pay only for the services you actually use? Also, be aware that potential profits from an aging population have lured commercial developers to assisted living developments, with mixed results; while hotel chains like Hyatt and Marriott run some successful senior residences, other developers have failed. If the residence operates on a straight rental basis, you won't suffer financially from a business failure although you will face the disruption of an involuntary move. If you've put up a large entrance fee, however, you could suffer a great deal. Always have the residence's financial status reviewed by a financial adviser before you make a major move.

Continuing Care Communities

These arrangements, sometimes called life care communities, are a variation on the senior residence theme. Here people live in independent apartments. But the community also has an on-premises nursing home (some have intermediate care facilities as well) so that a resident who becomes ill or too frail to live independently can remain in the same community. Best of all, a well spouse can continue living independently while being close enough for daily visits.

Many continuing care communities are sponsored by religious groups. The Quakers, forerunners in this field, run several well-regarded communities in Pennsylvania; waiting lists can extend for a decade. In fact, because there are nowhere near enough continuing care communities to meet the demand, waiting lists at the best communities often run for years. If you are now in your sixties or seventies and living independently but think you might be interested later on, it could be a good idea to do some research now and put your name on the list of the community you choose. You can always turn down an apartment if you're not ready when it's offered, and remain in line for the next vacancy. Whatever you do, don't wait until the last moment. The best communities are likely to be fully occupied, if you wait, and your physical condition could then preclude admission; every community requires that entrants be able to live on their own.

But here, even more, it's vitally important to check into a community's financial standing. Since many communities require entrance fees of $100,000 or more (typically paid from the equity in a home sold to make the move), as well as sizable monthly fees, be extra-careful about scrutinizing the track record of the operating company. Some have gone out of business, leaving residents in the lurch.

You should also be aware that monthly fees can rise steeply, and that some communities charge extra for services (such as meals) that others include. And be sure you understand the arrangement for nursing care; some communities guarantee nursing home care at no additional cost (these generally have higher nonrefundable entrance fees to cover anticipated costs), while others give a preferential rate to residents but charge for the care, and some do nothing for residents except offer them a bed *if* one is available.

Some additional questions to ask:

■ Is the entrance fee refundable? Under what circumstances? (Note that refundable entrance fees are generally higher.)

■ How much have monthly fees risen over the last few years? What happens if a resident can't pay a scheduled increase? (A tax-exempt facility can't evict people who run out of money, but you should check the contract carefully on this point.)

Q My 67-year-old father, who needs special therapy after an auto accident, must be moved from a hospital to a nursing home. The nursing home is asking for a $2,000 deposit. Won't Medicare pay his bills?

A Yes. It is against the law for a nursing home to require an advance deposit from a Medicare patient in this situation: If your father is admitted to a certified skilled nursing facility for medically directed treatment or rehabilitation following three days in a hospital, Medicare will pay the entire tab for the first 20 days. From the 21st to the 100th day, Medicare pays all but a specified sum, rising each year; in 1993, your father's out-of-pocket cost would be $84.50 a day. Note, though, that each day of nursing home care must meet Medicare's guidelines for medical necessity; very few patients meet these guidelines for the full benefit period of 100 days. Moreover, Medigap policies seldom cover nursing home care; the only policies that do are those specifically intended for long-term care (see pp. 533-535).

■ What services are included in the monthly fees? Is local transportation included? Laundry? Tray service, if you can't take meals in the dining room?

■ Exactly what health and medical coverage is included in the regular fees? Will you be required to carry a Medicare supplement policy and long-term care coverage of your own?

■ What is the community's policy about transferring residents from independent living to the nursing facility? Who makes the decision? How are the fees adjusted if a single person is involved? What if one-half of a couple needs nursing care while the other continues to live independently?

Nursing Homes

Best suited for those requiring health and personal care beyond the capabilities of either home care or the other assisted living arrangements described above, nursing homes provide round-the-clock supervision under a physician's direction. A nursing home is never the first choice on anyone's housing agenda—both because they are expensive (a year in an average nursing home runs $30,000; in some expensive urban areas, a year can be more than three times that sum) and because they are impersonal places to live. Despite their negative image, however, a carefully chosen nursing home can be a comfortable place to live if it becomes necessary to do so.

What to Ask in Evaluating a Nursing Home:

■ What is the ratio of staff to patients, at night as well as during the day?

■ Is a physician on 24-hour call? What happens if a patient becomes ill?

■ What arrangements are made for dental, vision, and podiatry care?

■ Is there a social director? What social and recreational activities are offered on a regular basis?

■ Is there a residents' council that meets regularly with administrators?

■ Are visitors welcome? What about children?

■ Can residents bring personal possessions? Have any say about roommates?

■ How varied is the menu? Are snacks available between meals?

Nursing homes that are licensed as skilled nursing facilities offer skilled nursing care. Medicare will pay for a portion of treatment in a skilled nursing facility if you are admitted following hospitalization because you need medical care. Intermediate care facilities are more appropriate for people who don't need intensive care but who do need assistance with personal care. Medicare does not pay for intermediate nursing facilities.

Selecting a nursing home is a difficult task, compounded by the fact that most people do it under the stress of needing an immediate placement. Discharge planning staff at the hospital can be very helpful in the selection (if the patient is moving to a nursing home from a hospital), but you will have to do some research yourself. In addition to visiting several facilities, and determining that the home and its residents are clean and well-cared-for and that the atmosphere is supportive, find out:

- Exactly what is included in the fees. Despite annual charges of $30,000 or more, you can expect to pay extra for medical care, prescription medication, and special therapy.
- Whether the facility is approved by Medicare and Medicaid (see below for more information on Medicaid). You may qualify for coverage by one of these programs, but only if the facility is appropriately certified.

Medicaid Planning

Right now, patients and their families pay more than half of the enormous tab for long-term care; private insurance covers about 1 percent, Medicare covers 5 percent, and Medicaid (the federal-state program for those below specified income limits) pays 38 percent.

Although Medicaid is designed specifically for the poor, many middle-class people have qualified. Some do so by actually spending all of their money on nursing home bills; unfortunately, this technique often leaves a healthy spouse impoverished as well. Others do so by sophisticated strategies involving the transfer of assets to other family members or into irrevocable trusts. Opinion is divided on the ethics of doing this, but many middle-class people see little choice when the alternative is abandoning a spouse to poverty or using up a lifetime's worth of hard-earned money in paying for nursing home care.

Be sure you understand the difference: **Medicare** is a federal program and the rules are the same everywhere. **Medicaid** is run by the states, although federal money is involved, and the rules differ dramatically from place to place. In general, though, there is more protection for the well spouse than there used to be. Under recent federal rules, the healthy spouse must be allowed income of $900 to $1,700 a month and assets ranging from $14,000 to $70,000. The exact amount depends on the state in which you live.

If you have assets but want to qualify for Medicaid, or want your parents to do so, you should consult an attorney who specializes in the relatively new field of elder law. The National Academy of Elder Law Attorneys (655 North Alvernon Way, Suite 108, Tucson, AZ 85711) can provide information, and your local Office on Aging may be able to provide a referral. Don't do anything without expert advice. But here are some things to consider (and see the bibliography at the end of this book for some helpful reading matter):

- Some advisers recommend retaining enough assets to pay for two or three years of nursing home care. This accomplishes two purposes. First, there is a waiting period of up to 30 months after assets have been transferred before those assets are exempt under Medicaid rules. Second, some good nursing homes don't take Medicaid patients; they will take private patients who later become eligible for Medicaid.
- The family home is exempt, even after the Medicaid recipient's death, so long as a spouse, minor child, or disabled child still lives there. After that, however, Medicaid may claim a share in the value of the home as reimbursement. Some advisers suggest getting around this by deeding a home to an adult child while you are still in good health, but retaining the legal right to continue living there.
- Transferring assets at least two and a half years before you need a nursing home may ensure that Medicaid will pay for the nursing home. But transferring assets also has a significant drawback: You are giving up control of your assets and, if you transfer ownership to your children, must henceforth rely on the good will of those children. Again, get expert legal and financial advice before you do anything.

Financial Planning

I've been urging you to get a handle on your finances, whatever your age, throughout this book. But if you (or your parents) are retired, with limited income, at an age when more and more help may be needed, it's particularly important to review current resources and think about ways to make money stretch.

BOOSTING INCOME

While most people are inclined to become more conservative in their investing as they age, some assets should continue to be deployed for growth at almost any age (see Chapter 23). At the same time, income investments should be reviewed periodically and tailored to current interest rates. Older people who had been relying on certificates of deposit for current income, for example, suffered seriously reduced incomes when interest rates dropped sharply in the early 1990s. For some, a solution might entail laddering Treasury obligations (see p.162). Conversely, when interest rates were high, too many older people stuck to familiar savings accounts when they could have earned considerably more, safely, in a money market mutual fund.

If you (or your parents) need money to meet living expenses, consider these tactics:

- An existing whole life or universal life insurance policy might be borrowed against or, if there is no one depending on the proceeds, the policy might be surrendered; either way, the money can then be invested to yield current income.
- Equity conversion, as described in Chapter 11, can free up money locked into a paid-up residence; another way to tap equity is to sell the house and move to less-expensive quarters.
- Or an adult child might buy the parents' home, assuming both the mortgage liability and the tax benefits, while renting the home back to the parents. Instead of collecting rent, the purchaser might give the parents a life estate in the property, entitling them to remain living there throughout their lifetime. Consult an attorney before doing this or any of the other strategies briefly described here.
- Gifts to your parents, if you can afford to make them, are free of gift tax (at this writing) up to $10,000 per person per year.
- Loans to your parents, if you prefer to keep things businesslike, can be repaid from their estate.

TALKING THINGS THROUGH

Many aging adults see no need to share financial information with adult children; many adult children feel uncomfortable asking. But a realistic grasp of financial realities, by both generations, can go a long way toward assuring a financially comfortable old age. And, while money doesn't buy happiness, it certainly makes it possible to pay for services that can make you happier.

So sit down with your parents (or with your adult children), before a problem arises, and discuss where the older people would like to live, whether resources are adequate, what might be done to augment resources or to provide the help they need. Be sure estate plans have been made and wills have been drawn, and that advance directives (see p. 643) are also in place.

Specific questions to ask:

- Can you comfortably meet your expenses? What are your sources of income?
- Where would you like to live? Have you thought about where you might like to live if your first choice (such as staying put) is no longer working out?

■ Do you have health insurance to supplement Medicare?

■ Where do you keep your important documents? Where is your bank? Who are your financial advisers? Have you made a will?

■ Who will handle your affairs if you are unable to do so? Do you have a durable power of attorney?

■ Have you named a health care proxy? Made a living will?

DAY-TO-DAY HELP

There may come a time when you must help your elderly parents manage their money ... or when a relative must help you manage yours. Some concrete suggestions can minimize the burden:

■ Have Social Security and pension checks directly deposited into a bank account.

■ Arrange direct payment from the bank account for regular bills: utilities, mortgage, etc.

■ Consider a joint checking account, so that you can pay your parent's bills. A lot of people do this, but you should be aware that there are some drawbacks. For one thing, if either of you get into financial trouble, creditors can take the money held in joint name. For another, you will own the money when your parent dies, but this may not appear equitable to your siblings. One solution: Have the older person state in bank documents and in letters to the other siblings that this is a joint account for convenience only without the right of survivorship.

■ Sign up for a third-party notification arrangement, so that utilities are not cut off if a payment is missed, and/or try to arrange to have copies of health insurance premium notices, utility bills, and so on, sent directly to a responsible person.

■ Set up a brokerage account, with a trusted broker, and place securities in safekeeping. When an older person has multiple holdings, with multiple dividend checks or dividend reinvestment statements as well as annual tax documents, the paper flow can seem endless; this step will reduce the paper (you'll get a single consolidated 1099 for income tax reporting on all the investments, for example) and greatly simplify everyone's life.

■ Arrange to have a durable power of attorney signed, so that a trusted person can sign checks, pay bills, and take care of financial affairs. Be sure the power of attorney is durable; this means that it remains in effect if you become incapacitated. If you are reluctant to sign over authority over your affairs while you are perfectly competent, you can sign a "springing" durable power, one that will become effective when your doctor (or two doctors, if you prefer) attest that you can no longer manage your own affairs.

Note: Some banks and brokerage firms insist on their own power of attorney forms, and you may want to sign these as well as a general power.

It's important to name the person you'll want to handle your affairs, in advance, to forestall the need for guardianship or conservatorship proceedings. If you become incapacitated without having made prior arrangements, your family will have to go to court to get the right to handle your affairs. This is expensive; it's also unpleasant for everyone involved.

TAX IMPLICATIONS

If you are helping an elderly parent, there are tax strategies that may help to ease the financial burden (consult a tax adviser for details and interpretations):

Your Parent as Your Dependent

First, if your parent's taxable income is under a specified amount ($2,350 in 1993, adjusted annually for inflation) and if you contribute more than half of your parent's living expenses, you may claim your parent as a dependent on your federal income tax return.

You may be able to deduct medical expenses you pay for your parent, even if her income exceeds the specified amount, if you contributed more than half of her support. The medical deduction, however, is limited to the amount by which all your medical expenses (including the money spent for your parent) exceed 7.5 percent of your adjusted gross income.

Multiple Support Agreements

If you and your siblings share in financially supporting your parent, so that no one of you contributes more than half the amount spent on support, you

---

Q My husband's name is on a lot of our investments, but we've always done everything jointly. Now his memory is slipping, and I'm afraid he won't be able to manage much longer. Can't I simply go on handling the investments if he becomes unable to do so?

A No, not unless you jointly own the assets. If your husband owns them alone, you can't do anything unless he has given you a durable power of attorney. Even if both names are on your house, you may find it difficult to refinance or sell the house if your husband isn't able to sign as a co-owner. Try to have him sign a durable power of attorney naming you as his agent. And you should sign one as well, naming a trusted person (probably not your husband if, as you say, his memory is slipping) to act for you should it become necessary.

may enter into a multiple support agreement under which one of you, with the agreement of the others, claims the exemption. You can alternate years, if you wish, or decide from year to year who gets the exemption.

The rules are that the exemption may be claimed by any one of you who actually contributes more than 10 percent of the total support, so long as all of you together pay more than 50 percent of the total support. If you claim the exemption, you must attach Form 2120, "Multiple Support Declaration," to your federal income tax return. The form must be signed by each person who contributes more than 10 percent.

Note: If you are involved in a multiple support agreement, you can deduct medical expenses paid for your parent only if you actually pay the expenses and you are not reimbursed by anyone else. Suggestion: Divide the nonmedical support among you but let one person, preferably the one who will gain the most from the deduction, pay the medical expenses; this may mean that the child with a lower income pays the medical expenses in order to meet the 7.5 percent threshold.

Dependent Care Credit

The same tax break that helps working parents defray some of the cost of child care can help if you are caring for a parent. If your parent lives with you, is disabled (physically or mentally incapable of caring for himself), and you must hire someone to care for him while you go to work, you may claim a credit of $480 to $720; the exact amount depends on how much you spend for the care

---

Q Are we allowed to claim my elderly mother as a dependent on our income tax return? We pay most, but not all, of her living expenses.

A You may claim your mother as a dependent if both of these requirements are met:

1) Her taxable income (not her total income), which may include a portion of her Social Security benefits, must be under $2,350 for 1993, and

2) You must contribute more than half of the amount that is actually spent on her support. Savings and amounts spent on nonsupport items (such as life insurance premiums) don't count. If her taxable income is $8,000 and she puts $2,000 in the bank, for example, you must then contribute $6,001 in order to exceed the $6,000 that she is spending to support herself.

and on your income. You may also be able to claim the credit if your parent lives with you, but spends several hours a day in an adult day care center.

A credit is a dollar-for-dollar reduction of taxes, and can be taken even if you do not itemize deductions. You must pay more than half his support, but your parent does not have to meet the income limitation that makes him eligible as your dependent.

Note: You may be better off with a dependent care spending account, if your employer offers one (over 40 percent of major employers do), instead of the dependent care credit (you may use one or the other, not both). Many of these plans permit you to pay with pretax dollars as much as $5,000 of the amount you spend for the care of a parent who lives with you.

EMPLOYER DEPENDENT CARE PROGRAMS

Even before the Family and Medical Leave Act was passed in 1993, many large companies offered some form of eldercare program. According to Hewitt Associates, a benefits consulting firm, almost 90 percent of these programs took the form of dependent care spending accounts (see above). About 30 percent of the surveyed companies offered resource and referral programs. Relatively few companies offer long-term care insurance; when they do, the employee pays the entire tab (although typically at somewhat lower group rates) and can often include parents under the policy.

If you are thrust into the role of a care-giver for an elderly parent, contact your employee benefits office to see if any help is available.

LONG-DISTANCE CARE-GIVING

Being responsible for an elderly relative is difficult enough if you live nearby. If you live hundreds or thousands of miles away, as is very likely in our mobile society, care-giving can become a nightmare. One place to turn if you live in New York and your mother lives in Florida, or if you are on one

---

Q I'm separated and had been filing income tax returns as a single, until my father moved in with me and gave me head of household status. This was a real break, letting me save money on taxes. But now he needs more care than I can give him and will have to move to a residence. If I continue to pay for his support, can I still file as a head of household?

A Yes. So long as your father qualifies as your dependent, and so long as you pay more than half of his support (the multiple support rules don't apply in this instance), you may continue to file as a head of household.

coast and your parents on another, is the fairly new profession of geriatric care managers.

Geriatric care managers, often trained as social workers or nurses, can assess need, coordinate services, and monitor care. They can be helpful for nearby care-givers, in determining the options and helping to make decisions. But they really play a role in long-distance care-giving. The service isn't cheap; you might pay several hundred dollars for an initial evaluation, then from $60 to $125 an hour for ongoing monitoring. The costs are not covered by insurance, but it may be worth the cost of an initial evaluation to receive recommendations on how to best help an ailing parent.

Be careful, however; this is a new, unregulated field and you need to check references very carefully. For a referral, contact the National Association of Private Geriatric Care Managers, 655 North Alvernon, Suite 108, Tucson, AZ 85711.

Before you turn to a private care manager, in any case, call your state or county Office on Aging to see if a nonprofit agency can provide similar service. If so, fees will generally be on a sliding scale related to income.

These Offices on Aging, by the way, provide invaluable service. Mandated by Congress, they exist all over the country and can refer you to local transportation and nutrition services, adult day care centers, and specific services of all kinds.

KEY POINTS

- With an aging population—the fastest growing segment of our population consists of those over age 85—almost all of us will give and/or receive eldercare.

- Long-term care is not covered by Medicare or by private health insurance; long-term care policies are available but have some drawbacks.

- Advance directives in the form of a living will or a health care proxy can speak for you when you can no longer speak for yourself.

- Housing adjustments may include modifying a present home or moving to an assisted living facility.

- A durable power of attorney should be in place, in advance of need, so that a trusted person is on hand to help with finances should help become necessary.

- Tax benefits may reduce some of the financial burden of care-giving.

- Your state or county Office on Aging is an invaluable resource for information and referral.

CHAPTER 23

Retirement Planning

■ John is 36, preoccupied with his career. On the personal front, his biggest financial goal is buying a house. The last thing on his mind is retirement.

■ Jean is 49. Finished paying college tuition for one child, she has two more children to go. With six more years of college bills, she can't think about saving toward retirement. Yet she's always wanted to retire early and to travel—and she'll be 55 when the last child graduates.

■ At 62, Howard plans to keep working into his seventies. That gives him a good ten years to set the stage for retirement ... if he stays healthy, and is able to work as long as he plans.

For most of us, it never seems to be the "right time" to think about retirement. We're too busy living in the present, making ends meet, and saving for short-term goals. Sometimes, too, we're fearful of retirement, thinking of it as a time when life begins to go downhill. Yet planning for retirement is essential if retirement is to be a positive experience, the experience it ought to be. Planning for retirement is just the culmination of lifelong financial planning, the time when it all comes together.

Planning for retirement is also a lot easier if you start early. Put aside $1,000 a year for 15 years at 8 percent, starting in your twenties, and you'll have more than twice as much money at retirement—if you never save another penny—than your twin brother who skipped those 15 years and then saved $1,000 a year for the next 30 years (see Table 23.1).

This chapter will dispel some of the myths surrounding retirement, help you to assess how much money you'll need in retirement, and show you how to reach that goal. It will also treat retirement as a starting point, not a conclusion, and describe ways to keep making your money grow and get the most out of life after you've received that pat on the back from your employer.

Table 23.1: Start Early, Come Out Ahead

| | Employee 1 Saves 15 Years Until Age 35 | | Employee 2 Saves 30 Years From Age 35 to 65 | |
Age	Annual Savings	Year End Value	Annual Savings	Year End Value
21	$1,000.00	$1,080.00	$0.00	$0.00
22	$1,000.00	$2,246.40	$0.00	$0.00
23	$1,000.00	$3,506.11	$0.00	$0.00
24	$1,000.00	$4,866.60	$0.00	$0.00
25	$1,000.00	$6,335.93	$0.00	$0.00
26	$1,000.00	$7,922.80	$0.00	$0.00
27	$1,000.00	$9,636.63	$0.00	$0.00
28	$1,000.00	$11,487.56	$0.00	$0.00
29	$1,000.00	$13,486.56	$0.00	$0.00
30	$1,000.00	$15,645.49	$0.00	$0.00
31	$1,000.00	$17,977.13	$0.00	$0.00
32	$1,000.00	$20,495.30	$0.00	$0.00
33	$1,000.00	$23,214.92	$0.00	$0.00
34	$1,000.00	$26,152.11	$0.00	$0.00
35	$1,000.00	$29,354.28	$0.00	$0.00
36	$0.00	$31,670.22	$1,000.00	$1,080.00
37	$0.00	$34,203.84	$1,000.00	$2,246.40
38	$0.00	$36,940.15	$1,000.00	$3,506.11
39	$0.00	$39,895.36	$1,000.00	$4,866.60
40	$0.00	$43,086.99	$1,000.00	$6,335.93
41	$0.00	$46,533.95	$1,000.00	$7,922.80
42	$0.00	$50,256.66	$1,000.00	$9,636.63
43	$0.00	$54,277.20	$1,000.00	$11,487.56
44	$0.00	$58,619.37	$1,000.00	$13,486.56
45	$0.00	$63,308.92	$1,000.00	$15,645.49
46	$0.00	$68,373.63	$1,000.00	$17,977.13
47	$0.00	$73,843.53	$1,000.00	$20,495.30
48	$0.00	$79,751.01	$1,000.00	$23,214.92
49	$0.00	$86,131.09	$1,000.00	$26,152.11
50	$0.00	$93,021.58	$1,000.00	$29,324.28
51	$0.00	$100,463.30	$1,000.00	$32,750.23
52	$0.00	$108,500.37	$1,000.00	$36,450.24
53	$0.00	$117,180.39	$1,000.00	$40,446.26
54	$0.00	$126,554.83	$1,000.00	$44,761.96
55	$0.00	$136,679.21	$1,000.00	$49,422.92
56	$0.00	$147,613.55	$1,000.00	$54,456.76
57	$0.00	$159,422.63	$1,000.00	$59,893.30
58	$0.00	$172,176.44	$1,000.00	$65,764.76
59	$0.00	$185,950.56	$1,000.00	$72,105.94
60	$0.00	$200,826.60	$1,000.00	$78,954.42
61	$0.00	$216,892.73	$1,000.00	$86,350.77
62	$0.00	$234,244.15	$1,000.00	$94,338.83
63	$0.00	$252,983.68	$1,000.00	$102,965.94
64	$0.00	$273,222.38	$1,000.00	$112,283.21
65	$0.00	$295,080.17	$1,000.00	$122,345.87

Although Employee 1 saves only 15 years, he has a larger account balance at age 65 than Employee 2 who saves for 30 years because of the effect of compounding at 8 percent interest over 30 years.

Source: © Booke & Company, Consultants/Actuaries®.

The Later Years Are Good Years

Here are some facts about the retirement years:

■ A man of 65 can expect to live over 15 more years, a woman 19 (see Table 23.2). These are averages, of course, and some people will live considerably longer. Plan your retirement with as much thought as you've given to planning your career. It may last almost as long.

■ "Senior citizens," men and women over 65, are not all alike. Far from it. There is as much individual variation among the over-65 as among any generational grouping. Broadly speaking, however, the "young old," those from 65 to 75 or 80, are often energetic, healthy, and thoroughly involved in life. The "old old," those over 75 or 80, are more likely to be slowing down, although not all do. There's no reason to anticipate illness and disability just because you reach a particular birthday. At least 70 percent of the elderly, according to one study, rate their health as good or excellent. No more than 5 percent of the elderly are in hospitals or nursing homes at any time. Most live in the community, most are independent.

■ Women live longer than men. For every 100 women age 65 and over, there are only 68 men. For every 100 women age 75 and over, there are only 56 men. Most elderly men, not surprisingly, are married; many elderly women are not. But women are better survivors, adjusting to widowhood. Men, if they don't remarry after a wife dies, frequently succumb themselves within a few short years.

■ With longer life expectancy (see Table 23.3), three- and even four-generation families are increasingly common. The result: You may be helping to support elderly parents while meeting your own retirement needs; with later marriages, and remarriages, you may be putting children through college at the same time. Planning ahead is more important than ever.

■ The well-being of the retired depends in large part on the source of their retirement income. Social Security benefits and some pensions are indexed to the cost of living, so that income increases over time. Investments may also yield proportionately more when interest rates are high. Fixed benefits, of course, lose much of their purchasing power with the passing years.

■ One of the most significant trends among the older population over the last two decades has been a marked improvement in financial standing. The median incomes of older men and women have grown at a faster pace than the median incomes of men and women in the general population, rising from $9,250 in 1980 to $17,612 in 1990. Nonetheless, personal income is often cut by a third to a half after retirement. Some work-related expenditures are eliminated, but more is spent on travel by the well-off "young-old," more on health care by the "old-old."

Table 23.2: Expectation of Life at Various Ages in the United States, 1988-1991

Age	1988			1989			1990[1]			1991[2]		
	Male	Female	Total	Male	Female	Total	Male	Female	Total	Male	Female	Total
0	71.5	78.3	74.9	71.8	78.6	75.3	72.0	78.8	75.4	72.0	78.8	75.4
15	57.6	64.3	61.0	57.9	64.6	61.3	58.1	64.7	61.5	58.0	64.7	61.4
25	48.4	54.6	51.6	48.7	54.9	51.9	48.9	55.1	52.1	48.8	55.0	52.0
35	39.3	45.0	42.2	39.6	45.3	42.5	39.8	45.4	42.7	39.7	45.4	42.6
45	30.3	35.5	33.0	30.7	35.8	33.4	30.9	36.0	33.6	30.8	36.0	33.5
55	22.0	26.6	24.4	22.3	26.9	24.7	22.5	27.0	24.9	22.4	27.0	24.9
65	14.9	18.6	16.9	15.2	18.8	17.2	15.3	19.0	17.3	15.2	19.0	17.3
75	9.1	11.7	10.7	9.4	11.9	10.9	9.4	12.1	11.0	9.3	12.0	10.9
85	5.1	6.3	6.0	5.3	6.6	6.2	5.4	6.7	6.3	5.2	6.5	6.1

Source: National Center for Health Statistics, U.S. Department of Health and Human Services, and Metropolitan Life Insurance Company.

Notes: Some dates are revised. [1] Provisional. [2] Estimated.

Table 23.3: Expectation of Life at Birth in the U.S., 1900-1991 (Years)

Year	White			All Other			Total		
	Male	Female	Total	Male	Female	Total	Male	Female	Total
1900	46.6	48.7	47.6	32.5	33.5	33.0	46.3	48.3	47.3
1910	48.6	52.0	50.3	33.8	37.5	35.6	48.4	51.8	50.0
1920	54.4	55.6	54.9	45.5	45.2	45.3	53.6	54.6	54.1
1930	59.7	63.5	61.4	47.3	49.2	48.1	58.1	61.6	59.7
1940	62.1	66.6	64.2	51.5	54.9	53.1	60.8	65.2	62.9
1950	66.5	72.2	69.1	59.1	62.9	60.8	65.6	71.1	68.2
1960	67.4	74.1	70.6	61.1	66.3	63.6	66.6	73.1	69.7
1965	67.6	74.7	71.0	61.1	67.4	64.1	66.8	73.7	70.2
1970	68.0	75.6	71.7	61.3	69.4	65.3	67.1	74.8	70.9
1971	68.3	75.8	72.0	61.6	69.8	65.6	67.4	75.0	71.1
1972	68.3	75.9	72.0	61.5	70.1	65.7	67.4	75.1	71.2
1973	68.5	76.1	72.2	62.0	70.3	66.1	67.6	75.3	71.4
1974	69.0	76.7	72.8	62.9	71.3	67.1	68.2	75.9	72.0
1975	69.5	77.3	73.4	63.7	72.4	68.0	68.8	76.6	72.6
1976	69.9	77.5	73.6	64.2	72.7	68.4	69.1	76.8	72.9
1977	70.2	77.9	74.0	64.7	73.2	68.9	69.5	77.2	73.3
1978	70.4	78.0	74.1	65.0	73.5	69.3	69.6	77.3	73.5
1979	70.8	78.4	74.6	65.4	74.1	69.8	70.0	77.8	73.9
1980	70.7	78.1	74.4	65.3	73.6	69.5	70.0	77.4	73.7
1981	71.1	78.4	74.8	66.1	74.4	70.3	70.4	77.8	74.2
1982	71.5	78.7	75.1	66.8	75.0	71.0	70.9	78.1	74.5
1983	71.7	78.7	75.2	67.2	74.9	71.1	71.0	78.1	74.6
1984	71.8	78.7	75.3	67.4	75.0	71.3	71.2	78.2	74.7
1985	71.9	78.7	75.3	67.2	75.0	71.2	71.2	78.2	74.7
1986	72.0	78.8	75.4	67.2	75.1	71.2	71.3	78.3	74.8
1987	72.2	78.9	75.6	67.3	75.2	71.3	71.5	78.4	75.0
1988	72.3	78.9	75.6	67.1	75.1	71.2	71.5	78.3	74.9
1989	72.7	79.2	76.0	67.1	75.2	71.7	71.8	78.6	75.3
1990[1]	72.6	79.3	76.0	68.4	76.3	72.4	72.0	78.8	75.4
1991[2]	N.A.	N.A.	N.A.	N.A.	N.A.	N.A.	72.0	78.8	75.4

Source: National Center for Health Statistics, U.S. Department of Health and Human Services, and Metropolitan Life Insurance Company.

Notes: [1]Provisional. [2]Estimated. N.A. means not available.

Since you can't know exactly what expenditures you will face, but you *can* expect to live a good many years in retirement, it's essential to plan ahead.

Your Retirement Budget

Whether you are 40 or 50 or 60, you owe it to yourself to fit retirement planning in among your other financial goals. As you make investments, buy insurance, and manage your cash, look ahead to the days when the fruits of your efforts will be a comfortable retirement. The keystones of that comfortable retirement are Social Security, an employer pension (if you have one), an Individual Retirement Account (IRA) or Keogh plan (if you are eligible), and your own investments. Supplemental income may be derived, when the time comes, by taking on another job or by tapping the equity in your home.

Before evaluating any of these sources of income, however, it's important to figure out just how much you'll need. This is easier to do if you're closer to retirement, but it's important to rough out a retirement budget even if retirement is still 20 years in the future. Then you can evaluate your sources of income and see what you must do to fill any gaps.

Table 23.4: How the Income Gap Grows

The following example, based on inflation at 5 percent, shows how the income gap can grow year by year:

	Pension	Social Security	Income from Savings	Gap
Income at retirement:	$36,100	$31,179	$17,481	0
Five years later:	36,100	39,909	17,481	15,003
Ten years later:	36,100	50,822	17,481	33,756
Fifteen years later:	36,100	64,852	17,481	57,868

Source: Ernst and Young.

HOW MUCH MONEY WILL YOU NEED?

For most people, a livable postretirement income amounts to at least two-thirds of preretirement income; three-quarters provides a more comfortable margin. How much you will actually need depends on how much you're used to having and on your postretirement life-style. Remember, though, that you're aiming at a moving target: First, your income will grow between now and the time you retire, so you'll be talking about three-quarters of a larger number. Second, achieving three-quarters of your preretirement income works only for the first postretirement year. After that, you'll need more each year just to keep up with a rising cost of living (see Table 23.4). And you'll have to provide most of that additional income from your own resources because, while Social Security is (at least for now) indexed to the cost of living, most pensions are not.

Worksheet 23.1: Adjusting Retirement Calculations for Inflation

	Step 1: Current expenses	Step 2: Estimated Annual retirement expenses
Food	_____	_____
Housing	_____	_____
Transportation	_____	_____
Clothing	_____	_____
Medical	_____	_____
Savings and investments	_____	_____
Life insurance	_____	_____
Other	_____	_____
TOTAL	_____	_____

Step 3: Projection for inflation

Multiply the total from Step 2 by the appropriate inflation factor from Table 23.5 on p. 666. For example, if you are ten years from retirement, and assume an inflation factor of 5 percent, you'll use inflation factor 1.6 to learn how much you'll actually need that first retirement year. After that, project for five years into retirement and make any other projections you think are necessary.

| Your first retirement year: _____ | Five years after retirement: _____ | Further projections: _____ |

Source: U.S. Department of Agriculture.

PREPARING A BUDGET

Your own retirement budget starts with your current budget. Look at the budget worksheets in Chapter 2, and write down your current expenditures in every category. Then, and this is the hard part, project those expenditures to postretirement. There are three considerations:

Actual dollars and cents. You'll spend less after retirement on work-related expenses: clothing, lunches out, transportation. You may spend less on taxes, too, since some of your income (including at least part of your Social Security) should be tax-free and the rest (pending possible changes under the Clinton Administration) may be taxed at a lower rate. Property taxes may come down, if your community has an exemption or discount for older residents. Health care may cost more (unless you can manage to continue good health insurance into retirement—or unless, by the time you retire, we have good workable health coverage for all). Your life-style, more or less costly, will be at least partly up to you.

Inflation. Although the rate of inflation has slowed, the decreasing value of the dollar must be a consideration to anyone planning to live on a fixed income. Even when inflation is at a relatively modest 4 percent a year, your spending power is cut approximately in half after 17 years. Retire today with an annual income of $50,000 and, after 17 years of inflation at 4 percent, you will need $97,500 to achieve the same purchasing power. You can work inflation into your retirement calculations by using Worksheet 23.1 and Table 23.5.

When you plan to retire. Retire at 65 and you may have 20 or 25 years in retirement. Retire at 55, and you may have to finance 30 years or more. Be sure you can do so, before you cut the ties that bind. Unfortunately, with corporations scaling down and offering early retirement as a way of trimming their work force, you may not have as much choice as you would like. But do the calculations carefully; even when an early retirement offer is sweetened, it rarely makes up for the retirement income you could have had if you had worked longer.

Table 23.5: Inflation Factor

Percentage Rate of Inflation

Years to Retirement	4%	5%	6%	7%	8%	9%	10%	11%
5	1.2	1.3	1.3	1.4	1.5	1.5	1.6	1.7
8	1.4	1.5	1.6	1.7	1.8	2.0	2.1	2.3
10	1.5	1.6	1.8	2.0	2.2	2.4	2.6	2.8
12	1.6	1.8	2.0	2.3	2.5	2.8	3.1	3.5
15	1.8	2.1	2.4	2.8	3.2	3.6	4.2	4.8
18	2.0	2.4	2.8	3.4	4.0	4.7	5.6	6.5
20	2.2	2.6	3.2	3.9	4.7	5.6	6.7	8.1
25	2.7	3.4	4.3	5.4	6.8	8.6	10.0	13.6

Source: U.S. Department of Agriculture.

You can meet your retirement needs, and resist the impact of inflation, by planning ahead now, while you are at the height of your earning power. Your plans should include preparing a retirement budget and revising it periodically as you move closer to retirement, understanding Social Security and any pension benefits to which you may be entitled, opening and maintaining a high-yielding Individual Retirement Account, making and modifying investments to make the most of your assets both before and after retirement, and managing cash and credit well.

Table 23.6: Annual Investment Required to Save $200,000 Over Varying Time Periods, in an Investment Earning 9 Percent

Investment Period	Annual Contribution	Total Contribution	Total Earnings	Total Saved
30 years	$1,346	$40,380	$159,620	$200,000
25 years	2,166	54,150	145,850	200,000
20 years	3,587	71,750	128,260	200,000
15 years	6,249	93,735	106,265	200,000
10 years	12,077	120,770	79,230	200,000

Source: T.Rowe Price *Retirement Planning Workbook.*

Social Security

Since 1935 the Social Security system has been the foundation on which retirement plans can be made. But it is only a foundation. Social Security was never intended to ensure a financially secure retirement by itself. Nor was it ever an actual insurance program, with your contributions set aside for your future use. Despite some shakiness in recent years, however, the system still does exactly what it was intended to do: It provides a base on which you can build additional retirement security. And it does so as originally planned, via transfer taxes on the current working population to fund the benefits of current retirees.

The crunch you've heard so much about, when there won't be enough current workers to fund retirement benefits, is currently expected about the year 2015. That's when the "baby boomers" will begin to retire—and the sheer size of that population bulge will have a significant impact on Social Security. But there's a long time between now and then, and current plans to trim the deficit may affect Social Security benefits long before the baby boomers do. For now, this is what you need to know.

SOCIAL SECURITY BENEFITS

The Social Security tax that you pay during your working years is matched by an equal amount paid by your employer. These taxes provide four distinct benefits:

Retirement benefits, which you can elect to receive at any time after age 62, are based on the number of years (actually calendar quarters) that you've worked and the amount that you've earned. Your spouse and, in some cases, your children may also be eligible for benefits based on your earnings record.

Survivors' benefits are a form of life insurance, providing payments to your spouse and dependent children (up to a specified age) after your death.

Disability insurance, described in Chapter 19, ensures you a monthly income if you are unable to work because of an illness or other disability. Disability benefits are important to every worker long before retirement age.

Medicare, also described in Chapter 19, provides both hospital insurance and voluntary medical insurance for men and women over age 65 (as well as benefits for some disabled younger people).

How to Estimate Your Retirement Benefit

Within this system based on length of working life and the amount you've earned over the years, benefits vary enormously. A 65-year-old worker retiring in 1993 could receive a maximum monthly benefit of $1,128. But the average retired worker in 1993 actually received $819 a month. There are additional variations, depending on whether a worker retires later, has a spouse receiving benefits, and so on.

How much you'll get from Social Security depends, in large part, on how much you earn. Lower-paid workers have a higher "replacement ratio" than higher-paid workers. If you earn the maximum currently subject to Social Security tax, you can expect to receive about 27 percent of your preretirement income from Social Security retirement benefits. If you earn an "average" income, your ratio will be 41 percent. And if you're at the bottom of the wage ladder, you'll probably get about 54 percent of what you earn. Social Security, remember, was never designed to allow you to live in the style to which you are currently accustomed—not without help from other resources. Social Security benefits are not taxable, however (unless your total income is above

Q I'm working two jobs to make ends meet, and both employers withhold Social Security tax from my paycheck. Are they supposed to?

A Yes. You owe Social Security taxes on the full "wage base" earned (the actual amount changes each year), from one or more jobs. Each employer is required to withhold the tax up to the mandated limit, without regard to whether you are working at another job as well. If too much is withheld for the year, you can apply the excess against your federal income tax. If some is still left over, you can request a refund.

$25,000 as an individual or $32,000 as a married couple), which increases their actual value to you.

It's a complicated system, but it's a lot easier than it used to be to determine how much you will actually receive in monthly retirement benefits—even if you are still some distance from retirement. Simply call Social Security (toll-free, 800-772-1213) and ask for form SSA 7004, Request for Personal Earnings and Benefit Estimate Statement. Mail in the completed form and, within a few weeks, you'll get a statement showing your annual earnings (on which Social Security tax has been credited) and a personalized estimate of the benefits you'll receive. Compare the earnings report with your own records (from year-end W-2 forms or, if you're self-employed, tax returns) and report any discrepancy to the Social Security Administration. It's wise to do this at least every three years, because Social Security warns that it becomes much harder to correct any errors after three years have gone by. (Nonetheless, it was some 12 years after the fact when I was able to correct a Social Security error on my own earnings record: According to Social Security, I had no earnings whatsoever in 1977; my tax return showed otherwise and they made the change.)

WHEN TO RETIRE

Although federal law prohibits mandatory retirement (in most fields), Social Security retirement benefits are still based on a "normal" retirement age of 65. You will have to decide, based on a number of factors—personal as well as financial—just when you want to retire.

You have three options under Social Security:

■ Retire between 62 and 65 on a reduced benefit
■ Retire at 65 on a full benefit (but see p. 676 for an upcoming change in the "normal" retirement age)

Q I kept my maiden name for business purposes, but file a Schedule C to report business income with our joint income tax form. Am I going to run into any trouble as far as having Social Security benefits properly credited?

A You might. Federal income tax forms now contain lines for first and last names of both spouses, but until a few years ago the Internal Revenue Service reported self-employment (Social Security) taxes paid with joint returns under the husband's last name alone. As a result, some self-employed women were not properly credited. If your business is more than a few years old, so that you might fall into this category, it's particularly important for you to check your Social Security earnings record and correct any errors.

■ Continue working and get a bonus for each year of work past your 65th birthday up to age 70

Whenever you retire, apply for retirement benefits a few months before you want them to start. This will allow time for all the necessary paperwork. You'll need your Social Security number, proof of age, and evidence of recent earnings (W-2 forms from the last two years or, if you're self-employed, copies of your last two tax returns).

Important: Social Security benefits are not automatic. You must apply for them. You must also apply for Medicare before you retire. (And, if you'll need insurance to supplement Medicare, be sure to act promptly; if you apply within six months of Medicare eligibility, you must be accepted without regard to preexisting conditions. For details on Medicare and on Medicare supplement insurance, see Chapter 19.)

If You Retire Early

If you retire at age 62 your basic Social Security benefit will be reduced by 20 percent; the reduction is smaller for each year closer to age 65. The reduction is permanent. You will never receive as much as you would have if you had retired later. But your monthly check may change, in one of three ways:

■ You'll receive your share of general increases, such as cost-of-living increases, in Social Security benefits.

Q I want to retire at 63 but know that I will have to take a reduced Social Security benefit. Would I be better off waiting until 65?

A Not necessarily. People who retire at 62 (the earliest permissible retirement age under the current Social Security system) must accept a benefit that is 80 percent of the amount they would have received at age 65 (based, of course, on the earnings record to that date; working longer could raise the basic benefit). At 63, your benefit is 86.6 percent of your full age-65 benefit. If you wait to 64, you'll get 93.3 percent. What few people realize, according to tax publishers Prentice-Hall, is that these are generous levels. Most people who begin to collect at 62 will collect so much before age 65 that it would take 12 years of the higher "full-65" benefits to make up for what they were paid in the three years from ages 62 to 65. So make your retirement decision not just on the amount of Social Security you'll receive, but on the overall basis of what's best for you.

■ If you become eligible for disability benefits after you retire but before age 65, you will probably receive a larger check. So be sure to notify your local Social Security office if you become disabled after taking early retirement but before reaching age 65.

■ You can increase your monthly check by returning to work either before you turn 65 (your benefits will go up because you've received fewer early benefits) or after 65 (if your income raises the lifetime earnings average on which your Social Security payments are based). Example: Betsy retired at age 62, receiving $280 a month or 80 percent of her basic benefit of $350. She returned to work for one full year, at age 65, and when she retired again, her monthly benefit was $309.

If You Retire at 65

You'll receive more in your monthly retirement checks if you retire at 65 (or at whatever "normal" retirement age is then the rule) than if you retire early. Not only will your benefit be the full benefit, rather than a reduced proportion thereof, but you may increase your benefit by earning more in your last years at work and dropping from the calculations earlier less-well-paid years.

If You Continue Working Past "Normal" Retirement

If you continue working past 65, you will receive a larger basic Social Security benefit. You'll also receive a "delayed retirement credit" which increases your benefits by 3 percent for each year between ages 65 and 70 in which you receive no benefits because you are at work.

Q I was married for 16 years and then divorced. I have not remarried but my ex-husband has. Will his new wife get all his Social Security? Or am I still entitled to any benefits?

A Divorced wives are eligible for Social Security on their former husbands' earnings records as long as they were married for at least 10 years (until 1979, it was 20 years) and have not remarried. You will therefore receive exactly what you would if you were still married: the spouse's benefit of 50 percent of your ex-husband's retirement benefit. His new wife will be entitled to the same amount. Neither of you affects the benefit received by the other. (And either or both of you may choose to receive benefits based on your own individual earnings record if it will provide a higher benefit.) You may start collecting on your ex-husband's wage record when he is age 62 and eligible to receive benefits; you need not wait until he has actually retired.

There are "earnings limitations," changing each year, which limit the amount you may earn while still receiving Social Security benefits. Those limitations end at age 70 and you may then earn as much as you can without forgoing any benefits.

FAMILY BENEFITS

You are not the only one to receive monthly Social Security checks based on your income over the years. Some of your dependents are also eligible for benefits.

If you are receiving retirement or disability benefits, monthly payments may also be made to your:

- Unmarried children under 18 (or under 19 if full-time high school students)
- Unmarried children over 18 who become severely disabled before age 22 and who continue to be disabled
- Wife or husband 62 or over
- Wife or husband under 62 if she or he is caring for a child under 16 or a disabled child who is getting a benefit based on your earnings

After your death, monthly payments may be made to:

- Unmarried children under 18 (or under 19 if full-time high school students)
- Unmarried children over 18 but who become severely disabled before age 22
- Widow or widower 60 or older

Q My 14-year-old son lives with me and my second husband. His father, my former husband, has retired and is receiving monthly Social Security payments. Is my son eligible for benefits as well?

A Yes. In a situation like yours, where a minor child lives with mother and stepfather, the child may be entitled to Social Security benefits (for retirement or disability) from three insured adults: mother, stepfather, and natural father. Get in touch with your local Social Security office and arrange for benefits for your son. However, your son is entitled to only one benefit. He won't be allowed to collect on his father's record, on yours, and on his stepfather's all at once.

- Widow, widower, or surviving former spouse who is caring for your under-16 or disabled child if the child is receiving a benefit based on your earnings
- Widow or widower 50 or older who becomes disabled within seven years after your death or within seven years after the end of benefits paid as a child's caretaker
- Dependent parents age 62 or older

Checks can also go to a former spouse, married to the worker for ten or more years, at 62 for a divorced spouse, at 60 for a surviving divorced spouse, and at 50 for a disabled surviving divorced spouse. Under certain conditions children may be eligible for Social Security benefits based on a grandparent's earnings.

WOMEN AND SOCIAL SECURITY

When Jerry retired at age 65 in 1993, after earning $40,000 in 1992, his last year of work, he received $1,064 in monthly retirement benefits. His wife, who had been a homemaker for most of their marriage, received the spouse's 50 percent, adding $532 to the couple's monthly income for a combined family total of $1,596. Jerry's neighbors retired at the same time. But Ed and Betty each earned $20,000 for a total of $40,000. Each received a monthly Social Security check of $749, for a total of $1,498. The same yearly family income, the same monthly contributions over the years, and $98 less every month from Social Security.

As the Social Security Administration points out, of course, Betty had some benefits that Jerry's wife never had. Because she was covered by Social Security in her own right:

- She was covered by disability insurance while working
- Her children would have received survivor's benefits if she had died while they were young
- She had a choice about when to retire. While the homemaker cannot collect Social Security benefits until her husband retires, the working wife can elect to retire at age 62 and collect a reduced benefit on her own earnings record.

But the Social Security system was designed in the 1930s, and it still, to a surprising extent, reflects the social patterns of the 1930s: lifelong marriages in which women were homemakers, dependent on the economic support of men. It may have made sense in 1935 for retirement benefits to be based on one earner's income, with dependent spouses entitled to a proportionate share of those benefits. It doesn't seem to make as much sense today, with the majority of women working outside the home, increasing numbers of self-supporting women, and a changing view of marriage as an economic partnership.

In fact, the proportion of women age 62 or older who are receiving benefits based only on a husband's earnings declined from 57 percent in 1960 to

40 percent in 1990. At the same time, the proportion of women entitled to benefits on the basis of both their own earnings record and that of their husbands has increased from 5 percent in 1960 to 23 percent in 1990. Nonetheless, many women are still forced into an unfortunate choice.

Table 23.7: What a Difference a Wage-Earner Makes: Average Annual Lifetime Earnings and 1992 Monthly Social Security Retirement Benefits

	Cleavers	Bunkers	Keatons	Seavers
Earnings				
Husband	$24,000	$16,000	$12,000	$24,000
Wife	0	8,000	12,000	8,000
Family Total	$24,000	$24,000	$24,000	$32,000
Benefits				
Husband	$ 957	$ 712	$ 591	$ 957
Wife	478[1]	468	591	478
Family Total	$1,435	$1,180	$1,182	$1,435
Survivor Benefits				
Amount	$ 957	$ 712	$ 591[2]	$ 957
As % of Couples Benefit	67%	60%	50%	67%

Source: Subcommittee on Retirement Income and Employment of the Select Committee on Aging, House of Representatives.

Notes: [1]Spousal benefit for a nonearning spouse; all others are worker's benefits. [2]Spouse continues to collect on her own benefit; survivor benefit does not apply.

There have been some changes. Gender distinctions within Social Security law have been eliminated. Benefits are now applicable without regard to sex. The "widow's" benefit is now a "survivor's" benefit. But inequities remain:

■ A married woman worker is entitled to a retirement benefit based on her own earnings or to a benefit of up to 50 percent of her husband's benefit, whichever is greater. She cannot receive both. This means that the protection she earns as a worker may duplicate, rather than add to, the protection she already has as a spouse. All the Social Security contributions she makes over the years may yield no return, since she can receive just as much protection in many cases without making contributions at all.

■ Some two-income couples, like Betty and Ed, receive less in benefits than a one-income couple with a comparable income. The system is still geared to man-as-breadwinner, woman-as-homemaker (see Table 23.7).

■ Widowed homemakers under age 60 cannot receive benefits unless they are either at least age 50 and disabled or are caring for children. As a result, many widows have no Social Security protection during the period when they may face difficulty entering or reentering the labor force.

■ Married women workers, in general, get substantially lower benefits than men both because women frequently spend time out of the paid labor force while they care for family members (first children and, later, elderly parents) and because women, on the average, earn less than men. (The Social Security Administration counts 35 years of earned income in determining Social Security benefits; if a woman is out of the work force for some of those years, she has zero earnings added in to her lifetime total. Bills have been introduced and reintroduced into Congress to reduce the number of years that are counted but, in 1993, we are still awaiting action.)

■ Homemakers may be without disability protection just when they need it most because benefits are not provided for disabled homemakers or their children if the woman has not worked in recent years.

What You Should Do

A major overhaul of the system has been proposed to amend these inequities. Until such an overhaul takes place—and it's likely to be sidetracked by the entire system's pressing need for financial support (see below)—you have to do what you can to protect yourself. Here are a few things you should do:

■ Be sure to keep Social Security records up-to-date when you change your name. Whether you are currently in the paid labor force or not, it's important to have the correct name on Social Security records. Otherwise, earnings may not be properly credited and you may have difficulty when you apply for benefits.

■ If you've earned your own Social Security credits you'll have to decide whether you'll receive a larger benefit based on your own record or on your husband's. But you'll also have other options. Suppose your husband continues to work past age 65, and earns too much to collect retirement benefits. Or suppose he's younger than you are. You can go ahead and retire on your own record. Then, when he does retire, you can elect to receive the spousal benefits if they would be higher. Or, regardless of your husband's age, you can take reduced benefits on your own wage record before age 65. If you do, however, your payment will always be reduced—even if you take reduced benefits on your own record and then take wife's benefits when your husband retires.

■ Try to retain eligibility for Social Security survivors' and disability benefits, even while you're a young mother at home with children. You may be able to keep previous work credits up to date with relatively little effort. In 1993 it took only $590 in earnings for the entire year to entitle a worker to a quarter of work credit; $400 of net income from self-employment did the same. So if you're tied down at home, any kind of part-time work that produces this much income can help to retain your eligibility for survivors' and disability benefits, as long as you maintain careful records and file the necessary tax returns.

PROBLEMS AND SOLUTIONS

Recently, the Social Security system has been in difficulty as a result of both demographic and economic factors.

On the demographic side, increasing numbers of retirees must have their benefits funded by a decreasing pool of workers. When Social Security began, in 1935, 15 workers paid retirement benefits for each retiree. In the 1980s the ratio reached 3.3 to one. By 2030 or so, when the mass of the "baby boom" generation of the 1950s will have retired, the ratio may be as low as two to one. If this happens, and if no other changes are made, the level of taxes will be intolerable.

On the economic side, the system's outgo has outdistanced income. With benefits indexed to prices while taxes are indexed to wages, and with prices rising faster than wages, benefits are outpacing the ability of taxation to keep up. But Congress has taken action, and may yet take further steps. Among the measures which will affect your retirement planning:

■ "Normal" retirement age will be raised to age 67. The change will take place gradually and only workers born after 1938 will be affected. The "delayed retirement credits" discussed earlier, currently at 3 percent, will gradually be raised to 8 percent by the year 2008 in order to encourage retirement at a later age. With longer life spans and increased good health in the later years this change, although controversial, makes a good deal of sense.

■ Steeper payroll taxes on working folk are designed to increase revenues. The employee share of the Social Security payroll tax currently stands at 7.65 percent of wages. This covers both Social Security and Medicare. In 1993, you pay 6.2 percent for Social Security (and your employer pays an equivalent amount) on wages of up to $57,600; you pay 1.45 percent for Medicare (and so does your employer) on wages of up to $135,000. These numbers go up each year (and the Clinton Administration is talking about dropping any wage ceiling on the Medicare contribution). The self-employed pay the combined employee-employer rate, for a 1993 total of 15.3 percent.

■ Since 1984, up to half of Social Security retirement benefits (formerly completely tax-free) is subject to income tax if your adjusted gross income, including nontaxable income such as interest on municipal bonds, exceeds $25,000 for an individual and $32,000 for a married couple filing jointly. At the outset only a small proportion of Social Security recipients were subject to tax under this provision. But these threshold figures are fixed, not indexed to inflation; normal growth in income over the years pushes more and more retirees over the limit. Furthermore, as the federal government struggles under the weight of the deficit, a greater proportion of benefits may become subject to tax.

Pension Plans

In 1930 only 15 percent of Americans working in private industry were covered by pension plans. By 1991, according to the Employee Benefit Research Institute, over 55 percent of civilian employers (private and government) offered some form of pension coverage; about 43 percent of all workers participated in pension plans other than Social Security. Pensions have become a fact of American life, part of the benefit package many employees have come to expect.

But significant changes are taking place today, and all is not rosy on the pension scene. There are frequent tales of woe:

■ Al has followed an ever-upward career track, one that has required a considerable amount of job mobility—out of school and into a two-year management training program, then eight years at another company, followed by two more moves. Now, at 43, he's suddenly realized that he has no pension; he's moved, from a retirement planning standpoint, too much.

■ Harold had every reason to expect a comfortable pension, after working for the same company for 33 years. But the company was absorbed by another company and the old pension plan was eliminated. Harold was told he would have to work for another ten years to qualify for a pension, and a smaller pension at that.

■ Veronica's husband had long assured her that she would be protected by his pension plan if he died first. Joe did die, just 13 days before his 55th birthday ... and that's when Veronica found that the option to elect widow's benefits was presented to employees only when they had reached age 55. Despite Joe's 30 years of employment with the same company, Veronica received nothing.

If you're covered by a pension or profit-sharing plan, it's vitally important to understand its provisions long before you're actually ready to retire. In order to plan your financial future, you have to figure out today what you can expect to receive tomorrow.

UNDERSTANDING YOUR PENSION PLAN

There are a number of important things to find out about your pension coverage:

What Type of Plan Is It?

There are two basic types of pension plan: defined benefit and defined contribution.

Defined Benefit Plans

These traditional pension plans spell out what your pension will be in dollars and cents or specify the formula which will be used to determine benefits. The company must then make whatever contributions are necessary to fund the designated benefits. You are, in other words, guaranteed a benefit.

If you are covered by a defined benefit plan, you need to find out how your pension benefits are calculated. Are they based on your salary? your years of employment? a combination? How old must you be to collect? What if you want to retire early? What happens if you die before you retire? Your company or union personnel or benefits office can provide the answers to these questions.

The pension formula may reflect wages in every year of employment, or only those in the last few years before retirement. You'll probably come out ahead with the last-few-years formula, simply because you're likely to be earning more in those later years (unless you change jobs frequently; see Table 23.9, p. 683). The benefit may provide a fixed amount, or it may contain cost-of-living escalators; the latter, of course, is preferable from your point of view. Benefits may start at a fixed retirement age or at one of several optional retirement dates; benefits will vary with the option selected.

Some pension plans are designed to be "integrated" with Social Security, with benefit formulas designed—together with Social Security—to replace a specified percentage of preretirement income. When Social Security benefits go up, pension benefits under such plans often go down. Until recently, lower-paid workers sometimes lost their entire pension this way. Now a new law says that, no matter how much Social Security a retiree receives, he or she must also receive at least one-half of the pension earned on the job after 1988.

If you are covered by a defined benefit pension plan, you have some rights spelled out in the law:

■ The right to information. You are supposed to receive annual statements indicating whether or not you are entitled to a pension and how much that pension would be, at retirement age, if you stopped working now. In addition, as retirement nears, you should receive a detailed statement setting forth the exact dollar amount of your full lifetime pension, your pension reduced to provide a survivor's benefit, and the amount of any survivor's benefit.

■ The right to protection. Although you can lose out if your company goes out of business or discontinues its plan, you'll have some protection if you were covered under the typical defined benefit plan. The Pension Benefit Guaranty Corporation (PBGC), a federal agency, provides insurance—although there are persistent rumors, in 1993, that it may not be able to cope with a rising tide of business bankruptcies and plan terminations. Even if it can cope, PBGC coverage is incomplete. Some plans, such as those run by church programs or local governments, may be exempt from PBGC coverage. And amounts paid to employees under covered plans are limited; in 1993 the maximum guaranty is $2,437.50 a month ($29,250 a year) to a beneficiary of a terminated plan, regardless of how much more you would have been entitled to receive under the plan itself.

Defined Contribution Plans

These newer plans work the other way around, with either the contributions or the formula for determining them fixed and your future benefits based on the investment return received on the contributions. The pension is not guaranteed and, if investment returns are poor, so is the pension.

Defined contribution plans such as profit-sharing and 401(k) plans are becoming more widespread as employers shift the retirement burden to employees. Between May 1983 and May 1988, the number of workers covered by 401(k) plans rose from 7.1 million to 27.5 million, or from 7.1 percent of all workers to 24.2 percent. These numbers are undoubtedly higher by now,

Q My husband never wanted me to take a job outside the home. He always said I'd be protected under his pension plan. Now, after 28 years of marriage, we're being divorced. Do I have any of that protection?

A You very well might, but only if you take steps to claim your rights. Since 1984, federal law has specifically recognized that a pension may be considered marital property and, therefore, that it may be divided at divorce. Tell your lawyer to include your husband's pension in negotiations and, depending on the property settlement you reach, you may claim part of the pension or its equivalent value in other property.

but statistics always lag behind real life; this data was published by the Employee Benefit Research Institute in 1993.

Defined contribution plans have some advantages: Your employer may match part of your contribution, increasing your yield. A 50 percent match, where your employer puts in 50 cents for every dollar you contribute, is equivalent to an immediate risk-free return of 50 percent. Money in the plan compounds on a tax-deferred basis, also increasing your return. And, if you really need the money, you do have access to it—either by withdrawal (hardship must usually be demonstrated) or, at many companies, by borrowing against it. If you tap your 401(k) for a loan, you must generally repay the loan within five years (except that loans for the purchase of a home may, at the employer's option, run longer); meanwhile the interest you pay goes into your retirement account.

But defined contribution plans also have some disadvantages: They are not guaranteed by the PBGC. Assets in such plans must be segregated from company assets but, if a company goes bankrupt, employees can be caught in the middle. Even when plans stay healthy, you must make the investment decisions that can make or break your retirement.

Under new rules starting January 1, 1994, employers wanting to be relieved of fiduciary responsibility for plan investments (shifting the burden to employees) must offer at least three diversified investment options, allow at

Q I'll be changing jobs soon and will be entitled to a lump-sum distribution from my company's profit-sharing plan. Can I take some of the money in cash and put the rest in my new employer's pension plan?

A Yes. But a law effective at the beginning of 1993 greatly complicates the tax treatment of retirement plan distributions. Even though you still have 60 days to transfer funds and avoid tax penalties, the new law says that your current employer must withhold 20 percent of any retirement money distributed directly to you—both the amount you plan to take in cash and the portion you plan to roll into another plan. Although you can get back the tax on the amount you roll into the other plan, you won't get it back until after you file your federal income tax return for the year; meanwhile, you'll be out the 20 percent.

To avoid the withholding tax, along with any penalties that may apply, have your employer transfer the distribution directly into either your new employer's plan or an IRA. Talk to a tax adviser. And try to make your decision before you leave your current job.

least quarterly switches between investments, and provide adequate disclosure of the options. Prior to this rule, more than three-quarters of plans offered a choice between company stock and a portfolio of guaranteed investment contracts (see below); given this limited choice, employees were hard put to ensure retirement income. Far more employers should now be offering a diversified stock fund as another alternative.

To make the most of your 401(k):

- Contribute as much as you can, up to the legal limit each year, to take advantage of the tax-deferred buildup. Many pension experts are concerned that younger employees, with many demands on their income, are not making contributions and will wind up in a poverty-stricken old age.
- Diversify your investments within the plan. Even when employers offer adequate choice, most employees are far too conservative. In 1991, only 16 percent of employee 401(k) assets was invested in equities—even though, over time, the return on equities has far outdistanced the return on other investments. When you do go into equities, don't stick to your company stock; letting your current income and your future retirement income ride on the fortunes of a single company is far too risky. And don't be taken in by the implicit promise in Guaranteed Investment Certificates. The "guarantee" in GICs, as they are known, is only as good as the issuing insurance company; even if the insurer makes good, GICs are fixed-income investments, bound to lose the race with inflation. See Table 23.8.

Table 23.8: Investing 401(K) Money "Safely" Can Cost a Lot in the Long Run

With annual contributions of $600 to a 401(k) at 6% or 8% return, here's how the difference adds up over time:

	At 8% interest	At 6% interest	Percent increase in total savings
5 years	$ 3,520	$ 3,382	4%
10 years	8,692	7,908	10%
20 years	27,457	22,071	24%
30 years	67,970	47,435	43%

Source: Booke & Company.

- Pay attention to your investment. Study and keep the annual statement you get from your company showing the beginning value of your account, your contributions, and any employer contributions during the year, as well as net return on investments and the ending value of the account.

■ Keep an eye on the health of your company. If it looks as if it's heading for bankruptcy or a takeover and you have the option of a lump-sum withdrawal under your plan, you may want to consider taking the money and rolling it over into an IRA (see the rules, below) rather than running the risk that your money will disappear or become temporarily inaccessible.

Pension Plan Rules

Whatever type of pension coverage you have, here are some things you should know:

What Are the Eligibility Requirements?

How old do you have to be, and how long do you have to work for your present employer, in order to qualify for pension benefits? Don't assume that you are covered just because you work for a company with a pension plan. There may be specific requirements for coverage.

In general, employees must be enrolled after attaining age 21 or one year's employment, whichever is later—except that plans with immediate vesting (see below) may require three years of employment. Part-time employees, those working fewer than 1,000 hours a year, may be excluded from coverage.

When Do Your Pension Benefits Become Vested?

At what point do you retain the right to some or all of your pension benefits whether or not you keep working for the same employer, are laid off, or are fired?

Q My employer is offering a "salary reduction" plan as a way of saving for retirement. Should I participate?

A A salary reduction plan can be a very good thing, if you can afford to defer receipt of some of your salary. It works like this: A percentage of your salary is set aside as an investment in your future; your employer may match all or part of your contribution. The amount you contribute is not included in your gross income, so you do not pay any income tax on it. You also don't pay Social Security tax on this amount. In addition, investment earnings accumulate without being taxed. Then, if you take the money in a lump sum at retirement, it qualifies for special income tax treatment allowing you to pay taxes on the lump sum as if it were received over a five-year period. Money withdrawn from an IRA at retirement, by contrast, is taxed as regular income.

Before 1974 workers had no protection against the wholesale termination of a plan or against the loss of individual benefits during, for example, an extended layoff. Today, if a company has a pension plan (no legislation requires that your employer offer a pension plan in the first place), it must meet one of two minimum vesting standards:

- 100 percent vesting after five years on the job (this is a fairly recent improvement; it used to be ten years—and still is under multi-employer union plans). If you leave your job before you've put in five years, you get nothing (except a return of your own contributions, if any).
- 20 percent vesting after three years of service, plus 20 percent for each year thereafter, with benefits 100 percent vested after seven years of service.

Vesting ensures pension coverage to people who change jobs frequently; if you're such an employee, however, bear in mind that the pension you receive will probably be smaller than if you had stayed on at one company. Job-hoppers fare better under defined contribution plans, according to a study by Hewitt Associates, a benefit consulting firm in Lincolnshire, Illinois, because they can take their own contributions with them; they do far worse under traditional defined benefit formulas favoring continuous employment with the same company. This is not to say that you should stay put. But, before you change jobs, evaluate future pension benefits as well as current income and other perks (see Table 23.9).

Table 23.9: The Impact of Job-hopping on Pension Benefits

Both employees have a starting salary of $20,000; salary increases match the rate of inflation, assumed to be 6 percent. Pension benefits are based on 1 percent per year of service multiplied by final salary.

	Years of Service	Pension Percentage		Final Salary	Annual Pension
Employee A					
First job	10	10%	x	$ 35,817 =	$ 3,582
Second job	10	10%	x	64,143 =	6,414
Third job	10	10%	x	114,870 =	11,487
Fourth job	10	10%	x	205,714 =	20,571
				Total pension =	$42,054
Employee B					
First job	40	40%	x	$205,714 =	$82,286
				Total pension =	$82,286

Source: Federal Reserve Bank of Boston.

Are Your Pension Benefits Portable?

Social Security is completely portable; it stays with you wherever you work. By and large, with the exception of some employees covered by union-sponsored pension plans, most private pensions are not portable. If you change jobs, you can and usually do lose the right to accumulated pension benefits.

But you do, under federal legislation, retain a vested right to certain pension benefits after specified periods. Those benefits aren't strictly portable; they don't go with you to your next job and create a cumulative pension. But they are yours, and tax law provides some relief on vested benefits. For example: If you change jobs and if you would otherwise have to pay income tax on a lump-sum payment of the vested pension benefits, you may defer those taxes by immediately investing the lump sum in an Individual Retirement Account or by depositing money in the pension plan at your new company.

Note: Reinvesting pension benefits in another tax-qualified plan does more than save taxes; it keeps your retirement money working toward your retirement. While a few thousand dollars may seem like a windfall better spent on a new car than saved toward a far-distant retirement, that money (after compounding in a tax-sheltered plan for many years) could make a significant difference to your retirement life-style.

What Are the Payment Options?

Does your pension plan protect your dependents? or you alone? Will you automatically receive monthly payments? Or may you elect a single lump-sum payout if you decide to do so?

PROTECTION FOR DEPENDENTS

A pension may be paid in the form of a **life annuity,** with monthly payments made for the lifetime of the retired worker. A pension may also be paid

Q I stopped working in 1974, after 12 years with one company, to become a full-time homemaker. I've heard that there's a law that says I'm entitled to some retirement benefits. Is that true?

A I'm afraid not. If you had still been working for your company on January 1, 1976, when the Employee Retirement Income Security Act of 1974 took effect, and if your employer had a pension plan, your earlier years of service would have counted toward a pension. As it is, you've almost certainly lost pension credit for the years you worked. Even if you were to go back to that company now, such a lengthy break in service would almost certainly force you to start over again (in terms of pension credits) as a new employee.

as a **joint and survivor annuity,** with monthly payments made for life to the worker and, at the worker's death, continuing (usually in a reduced amount) for the life of the designated survivor. The worker's benefit may be reduced in order to provide the continuing benefit to the survivor. Where a man might receive $600 a month under a life annuity option, as an example (specific figures will vary), he might receive $540 a month under the joint and survivor form, with the guarantee that his wife (if she survives him) will continue to receive $270 a month for the rest of her life.

Pension plans offering annuity payments must offer a joint and survivor option, under which a continuing pension benefit of at least 50 percent of the worker's benefit is paid to the survivor when the retired worker dies; this option, furthermore, goes into effect automatically for married employees unless both the employee and the spouse reject it in writing prior to retirement.

If a plan offers early-retirement pension benefits, it must also offer a **preretirement survivor annuity** under which benefits are paid to a surviving spouse even if an employee dies before normal retirement age. These preretirement benefits are payable to all vested employees. Under this option, the monthly benefits to be received at normal retirement age may be reduced.

LUMP-SUM VS. MONTHLY PAYMENTS

When Dora K. retired last year, at age 65, she was earning just over $20,000 a year. She now receives about $6,000 a year in Social Security retirement benefits and another $6,000 a year in monthly checks from her company's pension plan.

Anita M. also retired last year. With the same years on the job and about the same preretirement income, her Social Security benefits are about the same. So is her pension—or it would be, if she took it in monthly installments. But

Q I want my son to be my beneficiary under my company pension plan. But I've been told that my husband (we're separated, but not divorced) will get my benefits after my death unless he agrees, in writing, to let them go. What can I do?

A One of the unfortunate by-products of laws intended to benefit dependent spouses (usually women), is that both men and women lose some control over their own pensions. If you don't know where your husband is, and can convince your pension plan administrator that you've tried unsuccessfully to find him, you may be allowed to name your son instead. If you can find him, try to get his consent to a waiver; otherwise, he will retain his interest in your pension and will receive the survivor's benefit after your death.

Anita's employer offered her a choice. Instead of $500 a month in pension benefits, or $6,000 a year, she elected to take $50,000 in a lump-sum distribution.

You may be offered a lump-sum payment at the time of retirement instead of monthly payments for life. Which should you take?

There are advantages and disadvantages to each approach (although the lump sum generally makes more sense for highly paid employees). Here's what you should consider:

■ What rate of return would you have to earn on your lump sum to give you the monthly payments you would otherwise receive from the pension? Do you have confidence that your investment skills would provide this rate of return, even if interest rates decline?

■ A lump-sum distribution is equivalent to your expected lifetime pension, reduced by the amount of interest the company could otherwise expect to earn on the money. What is your company's "discount rate"? You are more likely to come out ahead if the rate is less than current investment yields.

■ How long do you expect to live? And will you need your pension to live on? With monthly payments, your income is guaranteed for life no matter how long you live. With a lump-sum payout, you run the risk of losing it all on a bad investment or simply outliving your income. Unless you have other sources of retirement income, therefore, you might be better off with regular monthly payments.

■ Does your company make cost-of-living adjustments to pensions? If it does, bear in mind that a lump-sum payment, once taken, is finished; there will be no adjustments. Monthly payments, on the other hand, may be increased to help you cope with rising prices.

■ Think about the tax implications. Pensions are taxable, but lump-sum distributions are eligible for one-time-only special tax treatment, so that the money you receive in one year can be taxed as if it were averaged over a five-year period (when the lump-sum distribution is under $70,000, up to $10,000 may be totally tax-free).

Note: If you were born on or before December 31, 1935, you may be able to make a choice between five-year averaging and ten-year averaging for tax purposes. The longer period is better for most people, but you may want to consult a tax adviser before making your decision.

Or all taxes may be deferred until you reach age 70½ if you put the lump-sum payment, within 60 days, into an Individual Retirement Account. This latter option is generally preferable, especially for younger workers taking a lump-sum distribution because of a job change, but heed this note of caution: If you expect to take another job, do not roll the lump sum distribution into an existing IRA. Putting it into a new "rollover IRA" keeps your options open so that you can later move the money into a new employer's retirement plan.

■ Think about your family. If you take a lump-sum distribution, your survivors will have the money if you die shortly after retirement. If you take a regular pension, you have to elect a joint and survivor option (with its, usually, lower benefits) to ensure income for your survivor.

TAXATION OF PENSION BENEFITS

Monthly pension payments, with the exception of the amounts you contributed, are taxable as received, as ordinary income. Taxes are automatically withheld from most pension checks unless you file a form requesting exemption.

You do not retire from paying income taxes just because you retire from work. If you do not have taxes withheld from pension payments or if you have taxable income from other sources, and if you will owe income taxes at the end of the year, then you must make quarterly payments of the tax that will be due. For more information, see IRS Publication No. 575, "Tax Information on Pension and Annuity Income."

Q A life insurance agent suggested that my husband take a monthly pension ending at his death instead of a smaller pension that would continue through both his lifetime and mine. He says my husband can provide income for me, and "maximize his pension," by using the extra pension money to buy life insurance. Is this a good idea?

A Not unless your husband receives enough extra money (net of income taxes) to do two things: Provide extra income for you both during his lifetime and buy a guaranteed insurance policy that provides you with an income after his death equivalent to what you'd receive with a survivorship pension.

Even then, if you don't have survivorship pension benefits, you might lose out on postretirement medical benefits if your husband dies first. You could lose everything if you were to be divorced and he stopped paying insurance premiums. Another important consideration: If interest rates decline and if the rate within the insurance policy is not guaranteed, the insurance may not provide as much income as projected; pension payments are guaranteed. Many employers make it more attractive to elect a survivorship pension. Don't give yours up unless you are sure that you'll have adequate income from other sources.

Note: You also may not escape state income tax on your pension (or, for that matter, on withdrawals from an Individual Retirement Account) simply by moving out of state. A number of states take the position that pensions based on money earned in that state are taxable by that state. Some—California, in particular, has earned a reputation for being aggressive—are tracking down pension recipients in other states and assessing back taxes, interest, and penalties.

Uncle Sam also doesn't want you to collect too much. If your combined annual income from all your tax-deferred retirement accounts (pension, IRA, 401(k), or profit-sharing plan) exceeds $150,000, you will owe a 15 percent tax on the so-called excess. Most people are better off letting money in tax-deferred retirement accounts grow until it must be tapped, at age 70½. If you are fortunate enough to fall into the excess distribution tax trap (and anyone making $75,000 or more before retirement should be concerned), you may want to start withdrawing some of your IRA earlier. You may also want to think twice before taking a sizable withdrawal from a 401(k) plan or IRA in order, for example, to buy a retirement home; doing so could bump you into an excess distribution category for the year.

Other Retirement Income

In addition to Social Security and on-the-job pension benefits, you can fund some of your own retirement income through an Individual Retirement Account (or a Keogh plan if you're self-employed), an annuity, and your own investments. IRA and Keogh plans are "qualified" retirement plans, as defined by the Internal Revenue Service, with superior tax benefits. But the amounts that may be contributed to them are limited by law. Annuities, which also provide some tax advantages, may offer you a way to save additional money toward retirement. Your personal investments can fill in any remaining gaps.

INDIVIDUAL RETIREMENT ACCOUNTS (IRAs)

Individual Retirement Accounts were authorized by Congress in 1974, to encourage employees who were not covered by any pension plan to save toward their own retirement. Covered employees could not participate. Then, from 1981 through 1986, any wage-earner, regardless of other pension coverage, could open an IRA.

In 1987 the rules changed again. Although some policymakers believe it wise to boost the U.S. savings rate by increasing the number of people who can make deductible contributions to IRAs, and a further change in the law is definitely possible, at this writing only workers without other pension coverage or with incomes below $25,000 as an individual or $40,000 as a married couple may take the full IRA deduction of $2,000 a year. A partial deduction is allowed for single individuals earning between $25,000 and $35,000 a year and for married couples earning between $40,000 and $50,000 a year.

Contributions made to an IRA, if you meet the requirements outlined above, are tax-deductible. If you put $2,000 into an IRA and are in the 28 percent tax bracket, you save $560 in taxes; thus the net annual cost of the IRA is actually $1,440. If you don't qualify for a full or partial IRA deduction, however, you are still permitted to make annual contributions to an IRA; the contribution will not be deductible but interest earned on the IRA will accumulate on a tax-deferred basis until it is withdrawn. It's arguable whether nondeductible IRAs are a good thing; see p. 690.

Earned income for IRA purposes includes salaries and wages, professional fees, commissions, tips, bonuses, alimony, self-employment income, even income to a retired partner from work-in-process or accounts receivable as of retirement date. Earned income does not include rents, interest, or dividends, or income earned from sources outside the United States.

Two-income couples may set aside a total of $4,000 each year in two separate accounts, as long as each has at least $2,000 in earned income. (If you work part-time, and earn $2,000, you may contribute your entire income to an IRA.) One-income couples may establish a "spousal" IRA, with an annual maximum contribution of $2,250; this account may be divided as you wish, as long as no more than $2,000 is allocated to either spouse.

Disadvantages to an IRA

Although Individual Retirement Accounts can be an excellent way to save for retirement, all is not rosy. If you dip into your IRA before you reach age 59½ (unless you're totally disabled, or annuitize payments over at least five years; see p. 696), you will lose the tax deferment on the amount withdrawn, which will then be taxed as ordinary income, and you will pay a penalty tax of 10 percent. You also must start withdrawing your money by the time you are 70½, whether or not you are still working.

Q I'm a homemaker, with no outside income. My husband has established a spousal IRA, with contributions in my name, but now we're divorcing. What happens to my retirement benefits from that IRA?

A Your retirement benefits are still your retirement benefits. In addition, your husband's IRA (like a pension) is marital property subject to distribution in divorce. If it is transferred to you, it won't be taxable even if you're under age 59½. Once it is transferred, however, all IRA rules apply.

Should you open a deductible IRA? Yes. Even with these restrictions, an IRA is one of the best tax-sheltered investments that a middle-income person can have. It should, without question, be included in your plans for retirement.

Should you open an IRA if you can't afford $2,000 a year? Yes, assuming that you qualify for the deduction. You'll have more money for retirement if you can save more money now, while you're working. And you'll have more if you can put the maximum allowed by law into the tax-deferred vehicle of an IRA. But you'll still come out ahead even if you make smaller contributions.

Should you open an IRA if you're still in your twenties? Yes, assuming that it's deductible. You may think retirement is too far away. You may think you'll need the money and be unable to get it. But you'll have a lot more money when you do retire if you start it compounding early. And if you leave the money on deposit even a few years before you have to touch it (assuming that you may need to do so), you'll still come out ahead.

Should you open an IRA if you're now close to retirement age? Yes, again assuming that you qualify for the tax deduction. While you will end up with a lot more money if you start earlier, it still makes sense to start an IRA at 50 or 55 or even 65. If you are now age 55 and you put away $2,000 a year until you are 70 years old, your total investment will amount to $30,000. At 9 percent interest, however, you'll have $64,007 waiting for you at the end of the 15 years. At age 60 your ten years of investing will add up to $20,000, and you'll have $33,120 at age 70. And if you start at age 65, with just five years to go, the $10,000 you invest will grow to $13,047. Remember, too, that even when you begin to make your withdrawals, the remainder of your account continues to earn interest and to grow.

Should you open a nondeductible IRA? Maybe, if you find it a valuable form of forced savings for retirement. But be prepared for massive paper-

Q Together, my spouse and I earn $55,000. Only one of us is covered by a pension plan at work. Can the other open a deductible IRA?

A Sorry, no. Joint filers, whether they have one or two pension plans between them, are forbidden from opening an IRA for the noncovered spouse and making deductible contributions. Since this provision is patently discriminatory—far fewer women than men are covered by pension plans, and women are most often left in poverty after divorce or widowhood—you might want to write to your congressional representatives and senators and urge a change.

Retirement Planning

work headaches. If you make a nondeductible contribution you must file Form 8606 with your yearly tax return, and hold on to that form for years; you'll need it when you reach retirement age and start making withdrawals from the IRA so that you can calculate the tax due on the withdrawals. What's more, the IRS insists that all your Individual Retirement Accounts, deductible and non-deductible, are lumped together for tax purposes and treated as a single account; taxes are figured on proportionate amounts. So you can't deplete your tax-deductible account first, then the other. If the math is beyond you or just too much trouble, do your retirement savings elsewhere. You may even come out ahead, especially with a shorter time frame; a nondeductible IRA works best over a long time period. See Table 23.10.

Table 23.10: How an Annual $2,000 Investment Grows in Various Accounts

The Personal Financial Planning group within the accounting firm of Price Waterhouse shows what could happen if you invest $2,000 a year in a nondeductible IRA, a taxable certificate of deposit (CD), and a non-taxable municipal bond fund; the table assumes a 31 percent tax rate.

Years to Retirement	Nondeductible IRA at 8%	CD at 8%	Municipal Bond Fund at 6%
5	$11,196	$11,167	$11,274
10	26,190	25,775	26,360
15	46,770	44,885	46,550
20	75,550	69,885	73,570
25	116,385	102,590	109,730
30	174,930	145,375	158,115
35	259,497	201,347	222,870

Source: The Price Waterhouse Retirement Planning Adviser.

Where to Invest Your IRA Funds

There are a bewildering array of choices available for IRA investment. Before you decide on any specific investment, look at several factors:

■ How much risk can you afford to take? If you have other retirement income, from a company pension and/or other investments, you may choose to put your IRA funds into a risky but potentially profitable investment. If your IRA will make up the bulk of your retirement income, it's best to be conservative.

■ How much risk can you tolerate? Whether or not you can afford risk doesn't have anything to do with whether you can sleep comfortably at night. Make your IRA investment, as you make all investments, in accordance with both your pocketbook and your temperament.

■ How old are you? If you have many years before retirement, you can look to capital appreciation. If you're very close to retirement age, however, capital preservation may be more important.

■ Do you want to manage your investments yourself? Are you willing to pay fees and commissions for the privilege?

With all this in mind, and remembering that you can divide your IRA contributions among more than one account, look at these possibilities:

Financial institutions (banks, thrifts, and credit unions) offer time deposits of varying lengths, with either fixed or variable interest rates. When interest rates are high (and if you think they're unlikely to go much higher) you might consider locking in your return by using one of the longer-term accounts. When interest rates are low, as they have been recently, you may do better elsewhere. If you do like the insured security of a financial institution, shop around. Rates and compounding intervals vary. To compare actual yields: Narrow your choices, then ask each institution to tell you (in dollars and cents) exactly how much you will earn in one year on $1,000.

The advantages of using a financial institution are convenience (there's a bank or thrift on almost every corner; your credit union, if you have one, is probably at your place of work), low cost (there are few, if any, fees), and security (accounts of up to $100,000 are insured by an agency of the federal government).

Note: If you maintain it in the same institution to compound for 30 or more years, your IRA could grow to considerably more than the insured $100,000. If insurance is important to you, think about opening later accounts in different institutions.

There are disadvantages as well. Rates may not be as high as interest rates elsewhere. And if you need your money or want to switch it to another account after putting it into a time deposit, you'll face loss of interest and other penalties. Be very careful, in fact, before signing any time deposit form. With some institutions, you may not be allowed to withdraw your funds early even if you're willing to pay the penalty.

Mutual funds are the choice of increasing numbers of investors. With a mutual fund, opened through a brokerage firm or by mail, you can invest your IRA dollars in just about anything: stocks, bonds, Treasury issues, even (via a money market mutual fund) money itself. With a "family" of funds, in fact (see p. 136), you can switch your IRA funds, without penalty and often without cost, to meet your own changing needs and the changing investment climate. When you have many years to retirement, a growth fund can help your retirement money keep pace with rising costs. As you get closer to retirement, a portion of your IRA can be shifted to income funds to conserve principal.

Advantages: If you choose a "no-load" fund, one without an upfront commission to a salesperson, all of your contribution will go directly to building your own retirement income. Maintenance fees are typically low. Disadvantages: Yields will vary with the market. And mutual funds are generally not insured, although you can, if you're worried, select an income fund that invests solely in U.S. government obligations. (Remember, though, that there's more than one kind of risk. If you're still some years from retirement, you may face greater risk in an income fund where you'll almost certainly lose purchasing power to inflation, than in a stock fund where market prices may fluctuate.)

Insurance companies are attracting a share of the IRA market with new annuity products, with rates of return pegged to current interest rates. Advantages are relatively low fees, safety, and relatively high rates of return. Disadvantages are that the high rate of return is not guaranteed (rates may fall as low as 3 or 4 percent), and surrender charges are usually imposed if you terminate your account before a specified time. Moreover, the earnings in an annuity are already tax-deferred. Why put them into a tax shelter such as an IRA? If you want an annuity to augment your retirement income (see pp. 699-701), buy one separately.

Self-directed accounts allow you to manage your own investments. You can buy and sell stocks or bonds; you can invest in real estate or in oil wells or in equipment leasing. But you will pay both a start-up fee and an annual maintenance fee for a self-directed account at a brokerage house, plus brokerage commissions every time you buy or sell. Compare both costs and service carefully; discount brokerage firms, for example, typically charge lower fees and commissions than full-service brokerage firms; in return, you make your own decisions without advice or recommendations.

Advantage: potentially significant gains from capital appreciation (although capital gains within an IRA are treated as ordinary income, and cap-

Q I opened an Individual Retirement Account early this year with $2,000 and now I need the money. I know I can't take it out yet, but can I borrow on it?

A No, not without penalties. Any portion of your IRA used as security for a loan will be treated—and taxed—as current income. In addition, if you are under 59½ and not disabled, you'll have to pay a 10 percent penalty just as you would for early withdrawal. The penalties are not too bad when compared with the tax-deferred interest earned in an IRA over a period of several years. In your case, since your IRA is so new, you will lose out. See if you can find a less costly source of funds before you borrow against your IRA. Or use the IRA, without penalty, by returning the money within 60 days.

ital losses cannot be deducted against other gains). Disadvantages: potential loss of capital, no guarantees and no insurance, relatively high fees.

IRA Strategies

Whether you choose professional management or your own self-directed account, there are ways to make the most of an IRA investment. Here are some hints:

- You may open as many IRAs as you like, as long as your total contribution for any calendar year does not exceed the maximum then set by law. This means that you may open different types of accounts to achieve different investment objectives. You might put part of your annual contribution into an insured deposit in a financial institution, for instance, and part into a growth-oriented mutual fund. (However, if you are no longer contributing to an IRA and have several similar IRA accounts at different institutions, you may want to consider consolidating them to make record-keeping easier.)

- You may borrow to invest in an Individual Retirement Account, and it may be worthwhile to do so (if you are eligible for the IRA deduction) and reap the tax advantages. Just be sure to do some careful arithmetic first, comparing borrowing costs and your tax-sheltered return.

- Don't forget that administrative fees connected with opening an IRA are tax-deductible if you pay them by separate check and if you itemize your deductions on your federal return.

- Stay out of tax-free investments. While you are permitted to put your IRA contributions into municipal bonds or annuities, it does not make sense to do so. As the Internal Revenue Service has noted, income from an IRA is taxable upon withdrawal and you would actually be turning a tax-free investment into a taxable one.

- Look at specialized investments. Zero-coupon corporate bonds, for example (described on p. 157), are particularly suitable for retirement plans and not for ordinary investing. Why? Because you receive no interest but are taxed, outside an IRA, as if you do.

- You may switch your money from one IRA to another as many times as you like, as long as you don't actually take possession of the funds. This provision makes it possible to modify your investments in tune with a changing investment climate.

- You may also actually get your hands on your money, and use it for any purpose you like, as long as you do so no more than once a year and as long as you keep the money in your possession no more than 60 days. This makes it possible to use your IRA funds, without penalty, on a short-term basis.

- If you're locked into a certificate of deposit, want to make a change but don't want to take the penalty for early withdrawal, you have another option: Withdraw the accumulated interest—there's generally no penalty as long as you don't invade the principal—and use it to open the other account.

■ If you're in your fifties when you open your IRA, compare institutional regulations carefully. There are no federal tax penalties for withdrawing your IRA money after age 59½, but some financial institutions have their own penalties for withdrawing funds before a stated maturity date. Banks are permitted to waive penalties if you're over 59½, but they are not required to do so. Find out your bank's policy before you commit your funds.

■ If your employer offers an IRA through payroll deduction, consider the pros and cons before you enroll. On the plus side is sheer convenience. There is also an element of forced saving, which you may appreciate if you would otherwise find it difficult to put money aside for retirement. On the other hand, you'll save far more if you can manage to put $2,000 into your IRA at the beginning of each year. While it's better to contribute monthly to an IRA than not at all, it's better still to get tax-sheltered money working early.

Q My mother died recently and left her IRA account equally to her three children. Can all three of us roll over our shares of the IRA so that we can keep it going for our own retirement?

A No. None of you can. Only a surviving spouse can roll over an inherited IRA and keep it going; other beneficiaries must follow different (and complicated) rules.

If your mother had started to receive payments from the IRA and was over age 70½, the balance in the IRA account must be distributed at least as rapidly as if she had lived. This means at most spreading payments over your mother's life expectancy. The IRS has life expectancy tables.

If your mother had started withdrawing money from her IRA but was not yet 70½, the IRA contract may spell out the method of distribution or allow you to choose between these two options: You may take the entire amount out of the account by the fifth anniversary of her death. Or, if the three of you are actually named beneficiaries on the IRA account (rather than receiving the IRA as part of your mother's estate), you may withdraw the money over the life expectancy of the oldest beneficiary.

■ Upon your death, the money in your Individual Retirement Account goes to your named beneficiary. The money may be taken in a lump sum, or withdrawn over a period of no more than 60 months, unless you're past age 70½ and have already started to receive periodic distributions which your beneficiary may then continue. The money is included in your estate for estate tax purposes, and the beneficiary will have to pay ordinary income tax on the money as received. Or, if the beneficiary is your spouse, he or she can roll over the IRA into his or her own IRA, prolonging the tax-free compounding. The annual ceiling on contributions does not apply in this instance. It also does not apply if you transfer your own accumulated pension benefits into an IRA.

When You Retire

You may start withdrawing money from your IRA, without penalty, at any time after age 59½. Under special rules, you may also start withdrawing money earlier, so long as you withdraw it in the form of an annuity, with equal payments made at least once a year for your anticipated lifetime. Once you start these early annuitized withdrawals, you must continue to receive them for at least five years and at least until you reach age 59½. Otherwise, early withdrawal penalties will be assessed.

At the other end of the IRS boundary lines, you may leave your IRA untouched until age 70½, when you must start to withdraw. This is when you must make a choice: Take the money in a lump sum? Or withdraw it in installments, over a period of years?

Deductible IRA withdrawals, remember, are taxed as ordinary income when they are received. (Nondeductible contributions will be merged with any deductible IRA you have and a proportionate share will be taxable; you can't take one, and then the other.) Don't take a lump sum, therefore, unless you really need the cash.

If you elect to receive the money in installments, you will have to comply with IRS tables on life expectancy; otherwise you'll face a significant penalty. The institution where you have your funds can provide you with the tables you'll need. You can base your IRA withdrawals on your own life expectancy or on joint life expectancy for you and your beneficiary. And you may recalculate your withdrawals each year, so that you won't outlive your IRA.

Note: Naming a child or grandchild as your beneficiary, if you have significant amounts in your IRA, can extend the distribution period. But be sure to consult a tax adviser before doing so, because special rules apply.

Your IRA account can continue to grow even while you make withdrawals. If you start your account at age 40, depositing $2,000 a year for 25 years, you'll have put in $50,000 of your own money. At age 65, after compounding at 9 percent, the account is worth $184,648 ... an amount which gives an annual retirement income for 15 years of $21,016. This is much more than $184,648 divided by 15, which would be $12,310. The reason: continued compounding of the balance left in the account. Table 23.11 indicates how much you can withdraw each year, starting at age 65, if you recalculate your life expectancy each year.

Table 23.11: IRA Withdrawal Program

If you retire at age 65 with $250,000 in an IRA earning 9 percent, annual withdrawals based on recalculating life expectancy each year would look like this:

Age	Life Expectancy	Amount Withdrawn	Year-End Balance
65	20.0 years	$12,500	$261,000
66	19.2	13,591	271,840
67	18.4	14,774	282,566
68	17.6	16,055	293,018
69	16.8	17,442	303,063
70	16.0	18,941	312,551
75	12.5	27,429	347,598
80	9.5	36,864	346,200
85	6.9	44,508	291,407
90	5.0	42,343	189,237

Source: T.Rowe Price, *Retirees Financial Guide.*

Note: The account balance increases over the first 12 years because annual earnings exceed annual withdrawals during this period.

KEOGH PLANS

Keogh plans have major advantages for the self-employed. Contributions, up to $30,000 a year, are deductible. Earnings, like those in an Individual Retirement Account, grow on a tax-deferred basis; accumulations are not subject to income tax until they are withdrawn. Again, as in an IRA, there are withdrawal penalties before age 59½ (unless you die or become disabled), and money must start to be withdrawn by age 70½.

Things You Should Know

■ Contributions to a Keogh must be made from earned income; "unearned" income, such as stock dividends, may not be the basis of a contribution.

■ If you have any employees, you must include in your Keogh plan those who work for you full time, are at least age 21, and have been with the company for at least one year.

■ Most Keogh plans are "defined contribution" plans, either "money-purchase" or "profit-sharing." You may contribute up to 25 percent of your net income to a money-purchase plan (and must then contribute the designated amount each year) or up to 15 percent to a profit-sharing plan (but can reduce or skip these contributions if business isn't good). Or you may have a combined or "paired" plan. Whatever your choice, under new rules net earnings must be reduced by your contribution before the contribution is made, and by the self-employment (Social Security) tax, effectively reducing the percentage of your income you may contribute (although the maximum remains at $30,000).

■ Another type of Keogh is the "defined benefit" plan under which you establish a benefit goal for yourself and make contributions accordingly; you may be able to contribute a larger percentage of income to a defined benefit plan, but you may also have to make contributions each and every year. Defined benefit plans are more expensive to establish and maintain (an actuary must calculate the annual contribution), and are most appropriate for self-employed individuals who are over age 50 and who are earning sizable sums.

■ You are allowed to contribute to a Keogh as long as you have income from self-employment, even after age 70½. You'll have to withdraw some money at that point, but you can make contributions as well. (An IRA, on the other hand, forbids contributions after age 70½.)

■ If you take a salaried job after setting up a Keogh on the basis of being self-employed, you can no longer make contributions (unless, of course, you continue to have some self-employment income). But you can leave your plan in place, accumulating earned interest, until

Q I'm in business as a writer, preparing advertising brochures and company reports as well as an occasional magazine article. I never know just how much my income will be. How can I make a contribution to my Keogh plan before the year is over?

A You don't have to. As long as your plan is opened before the end of the year, you can make your contribution up to the time you file your income tax return for that year—April 15 or, if you get an automatic extension, August 15. You'll build your retirement funds faster, however, if you start your money compounding earlier in the year. Why don't you do this: Make a basic contribution early in the year, figured on the minimum you expect to earn; then add to it as you get a clear picture of your income toward the end of the year, with a final contribution once the year is done. Just be careful not to contribute too much, or you'll face penalties.

you are ready for retirement. You should leave it at least until age 59½ or you will have to pay the penalties.

■ You may open a Keogh plan in any of the vehicles described in the section on Individual Retirement Accounts. You may also switch your plan from one vehicle to another, as long as the institutions transfer the money directly and it does not pass through your hands.

■ When you reach age 70½, you must decide whether to take the money in a lump sum or in installments. If the lump-sum option is selected, five-year income averaging may be used as long as you've had your plan in effect for five years; if you take the money in installments, regular tax rates apply. This may make it worthwhile to take a lump-sum distribution from your Keogh plan earlier, at age 59½, because then you can continue making contributions and building your retirement fund while you continue to be self-employed.

ANNUITIES

Simply put, an annuity provides a guaranteed lifetime income. You can outlive the proceeds of your investments. You can't outlive an annuity.

You can buy an annuity to provide extra retirement income over and above your Individual Retirement Account, pension, Social Security, and investments. You can also buy an annuity with the proceeds of an IRA or of a company pension plan. You can buy an annuity with as little as $1,000, but annuities make more sense as supplemental retirement income for people who can invest considerably more. If you come into a sizable amount of money, through an inheritance or selling a business or some other windfall, you might consider purchasing an annuity as part (not all) of your preretirement portfolio.

How Annuities Work

■ An annuity may be **immediate,** in which case it starts as soon as you pay the premium, or **deferred,** starting at a designated later date.

■ The premium may be a single lump-sum payment, either cash out of your pocket or a rollover from an IRA or pension plan, or it may be paid in periodic installments. Installment annuities are always deferred annuities, but it is single-premium deferred annuities that have received the most attention in recent years.

■ Earned interest accumulates tax-free throughout the deferral period. Payments are taxed, as you receive them, to the extent that they exceed your contribution.

■ The annuity itself may be **fixed** providing a fixed income for life, or **variable,** with payouts above a guaranteed minimum level depending on investment return. The variable annuity may offer you a choice of investment vehicles (see pp. 164-168 for more on variable annuities as an investment).

■ Payout may be in one of several forms. **Straight life** provides payments to you for your lifetime. A **refund** annuity pays somewhat less than straight life because it provides for payment of at least the amount paid in premiums, regardless of when the annuitant dies; any refund will be made to the beneficiary in a lump sum or in installments. A **joint and survivor** annuity provides payments for as long as either you or your designated survivor lives. And a **certain period** annuity makes payments for life, with a guaranteed minimum number of years.

A few years ago, annuities were paying attractive rates of return. But in the early 1990s interest rates on fixed annuities, like interest rates on other fixed investments, hit new lows. As an example, however: Larry, age 50, buys a single-premium deferred annuity with a maturity date timed for retirement at 65. Assuming that the $25,000 accumulates at 5.5 percent for the next 15 years, Larry could choose:

■ a lump-sum distribution of $55,812,

■ an annuity of $428 a month for life,

■ a ten-year certain annuity of $408 a month,

■ a refund annuity of $403 a month,

■ a joint and survivor annuity, with the full amount continuing to his named beneficiary, of $360 a month.

(These figures, provided by the American Council of Life Insurance, are based on Larry and his wife reaching age 65 together; precise benefits from any annuity are always based on the specific age of the annuitant.)

Note: Interest rates on fixed annuities are typically fixed for an initial period of about three years, then adjusted annually. The rate may go up, which is just fine. Or it may go down, which is not. If it falls below a specified level, the insurance company may offer you the option of withdrawing your money; withdrawal won't do much good, however, if all interest rates are low at the time and you can't do any better elsewhere.

Should You Buy An Annuity?

The rate of return on annuities is often pegged to market rates. Formerly formidable front-end fees have been reduced or eliminated by many companies—although there may be penalties, instead, for withdrawal before a specified time.

An annuity can be viewed as an investment. But it is designed to provide guaranteed income during retirement. The 1982 tax law reinforced this long-term view of annuities by providing that early withdrawals (before age 59½) are both fully taxable and subject to tax penalty.

Think about buying an annuity, therefore, only if:

■ You have a few thousand dollars to put aside as supplementary retirement income, and you'll leave the money in place until you do retire.

■ You are in a tax bracket where you will benefit from the tax-free accumulation of funds.

■ You want to be sure that you can't outlive your income.

Compare Annuities Before You Buy

Fixed annuities are sold with many different features. Here's what to find out before you buy:

■ What is the current interest rate, how often does it change, and by what index does it change? Will a currently high interest rate be in effect for five years? or just for the next few months?

■ What is the minimum interest rate guaranteed in the contract? This rate may be as low as 3.5 or 4 percent.

■ Is there a "bailout option" that permits you to cash in the annuity, without withdrawal penalties (there may be tax penalties), if the interest rate drops below a specified figure? That figure is usually below the current market rate but well above the guaranteed contract minimum.

■ What penalties are there for early liquidation? Regardless of bailout privileges, there may be graduated penalties over a period of years. You might, for example, be penalized by 7 percent of the principal withdrawn during the first year, 6 percent in the second year, and so on, until the penalty disappears. You might, with other companies, face a constant never-ending penalty of 6 to 7 percent.

■ Are there front-end load (sales) charges? And, if so, how much will they reduce the amount of money that is going to work for you? Many companies have dropped front-end charges, but some still have them. Be sure to ask.

■ Are annual administrative fees levied at a flat rate (typically $25 to $40) or at a percentage of the principal amount? Find out before you buy.

■ How much of the cash value can you take as a loan? How long must the annuity be in force before any loan can be made? And what is the rate of interest you will be charged? (Remember: IRS rules treat a loan against an annuity as a withdrawal; you may be subject to both tax and penalty.)

■ What will you get for your money? The rates of payout vary considerably from company to company. Ask what rate is current ... and what rate is guaranteed.

Note: Some companies are introducing variable annuities that are variable during both the accumulation phase and the payout phase. Before buying such an annuity to provide retirement income, be sure you understand that the income may vary and how it may vary.

YOUR OWN INVESTMENTS

You may or may not be able to count on a pension. Slightly more than half of all employers offer any kind of pension plan, an average inflated by the fact that most government-sector workers are included. Private-sector workers do not fare as well. Many small companies, particularly in service industries, do not provide pensions at all. And some very large corporations, facing financial difficulties, are backing out of prior pension promises.

The only way to be sure that you will have enough income in retirement, therefore, is to build a personal investment portfolio to supplement pensions, Social Security, and tax-deferred savings through IRAs, Keogh plans, and annuities. Furthermore, the only way to be sure that you will have enough income in retirement, keeping pace with inflation, is to invest for growth both *before* and *after* you retire. Discard the old-fashioned notion that all investments must be converted from growth to income as you reach 65; following this track is likely to leave you in the poorhouse by the time you reach your eighties.

Instead, try this approach:

■ Keep at least 50 percent to 60 percent of your investments in common stock in the years prior to retirement, gradually shifting to 30 percent to 40 percent by the time you reach your seventies, with the balance in investments yielding income. Investing for growth can mean an important difference in your retirement nest egg. At $2,000 a year for 30 years, according to the benefits consulting firm of Booke & Company, fixed-income returns of 6 percent would build to $158,000; an investment in equities yielding an average of 8 percent would build to $226,000—a difference of $68,000 that could make a big difference in retirement life-style. Even at smaller annual contributions, the difference can be significant.

■ Continue to diversify your investments. Before retirement, include a small portion in aggressive growth stock or stock funds; after retirement, stick to balanced growth, growth and income, or index funds. Both before and after, include both large-company and small-company stock funds, as well as a small percentage in international stock funds. (You'll find additional asset allocation suggestions in Chapter 5.)

■ Reinvest dividends, if you can, at least until you retire, to increase your total return.

■ Be prepared to invade principal if necessary. Otherwise, you may have to be more aggressive than you'd like to generate the additional income you'll need. In the words of Coral Gables, Florida financial planner Harold Evensky, "Do you want to keep your capital intact and short pork bellies?" These are the years you've been saving for; don't shortchange your golden years by holding on to money you can and should spend.

Just do your calculations carefully. Look at your life expectancy, double it to be on the safe side, and consult Table 23.12 to get an idea of how much money you can withdraw and for how long on a regular basis to supplement your other income from other sources.

Table 23.12: Monthly Withdrawals Possible for a Given Number of Years from an Account of Given Size Yielding 10 Percent

Number of years	Beginning Balance			
	$25,000	$50,000	$75,000	$100,000
10	$330	$661	$991	$1,322
15	269	537	806	1,075
20	241	483	724	965
25	227	454	682	909
Unlimited (interest only each month)	208	417	625	833

Source: Savings & Community Bankers of America.

OTHER SOURCES OF RETIREMENT INCOME

You can also increase your postretirement income by reducing spending, taking a second job, and making productive use of property you already own. Here's how:

Reduce Spending

This suggestion may appear all too obvious. But cutting back on spending well before you retire does two things: It permits you to adjust, both financially and psychologically, to a reduced budget, and it frees money, while you're still working, for investments that will augment your retirement income.

Your preretirement budget estimates are designed to pave the way for an easy retirement. But estimates may well have to be changed in the clear daylight of actual retirement. One way to come as close as possible in your preliminary estimates is to practice. That's right: Practice being retired. Use weekends and vacation time to rehearse your retirement life-style. Here's what the Hendersons did on one two-week vacation: Instead of taking the opportunity to stay at a resort hotel, they rented a cottage. There, they lived within their planned retirement budget. They ate out, but occasionally instead of every day, and at lunch, when menu prices are often lower, rather than at dinner. They went to the movies, but they also sought free and low-priced entertainment: a musical production at the local high school, a flea market, beachcombing, and long strolls along the water. They found, in fact, that they restricted themselves too much; the budget allowed room for some extras.

When you're within a few years of your planned retirement, start phasing down all your living expenses to fit within your projected retirement income. Keep track, if you haven't done so earlier, of all your "optional" spending, the money you may spend on impulse or not-really-necessary purchases of everything from candy bars to garden equipment and clothing. Once you keep track of such expenditures, you can begin to see what really gives you pleasure and what does not. Would you rather, if you must make a choice, buy workshop equipment or build a vacation fund?

As you reduce your spending, do so slowly, until you reach a level that you think will be comfortable after retirement. If you can't pinpoint your postretirement income, then work toward a level of two-thirds to three-quarters of preretirement spending. But do so slowly. The whole point of this exercise is that a gradual cutback won't hurt; a drastic postretirement change in life-style can hurt a great deal.

Take a Second Job

Another job can bring in additional income. Just be sure, if you take a second job before retirement, that it's not costing you more in travel costs and extra income taxes than it is producing. Many people find it preferable to move into a second job after retirement, when taxable income is down. Don't sell yourself short. You can look within your own field for a postretirement job. You can also look beyond it, to something you've enjoyed as an avocation throughout your working life. An avid gardener, for instance, might find employment in a nursery, with a landscape gardener, or as a teacher of hobbyists.

Note: You can earn several thousand dollars a year without affecting your Social Security payments. In 1993, Social Security recipients under age 65 lose $1 of benefits for every $2 of earnings above $7,680; those between 65 and 69 lose $1 of benefits for every $3 in earnings exceeding $10,560. The numbers go up each year.

Look to Income-producing Property You May Own

If you have a country cottage, for example, and use it just part of a year, think about renting it out in other months. Your summer hideaway may make good September-to-June rental housing for nearby college students. Or if you're not using your trailer or recreational vehicle on a regular basis, think about renting it out to add to your spending money.

Be resourceful as you plan your retirement and you'll develop other income-producing ideas of your own.

Pulling It All Together

You've spent a lifetime earning, spending, and investing your money. Once you retire you may or may not continue to earn. But you will continue to spend, and you should, if at all possible, continue to invest. Here are some of the additional areas you should consider:

INSURANCE

You've probably carried life insurance over the years to protect your family. Once your children are grown and your other assets are sizable, you may not feel life insurance is necessary. Remember, though, that your pension will either come to an end at your death or, if you've elected the joint and survivor option, be sharply reduced. Your own Social Security will also stop and your surviving spouse will receive a curtailed benefit. You may, therefore, want to keep enough life insurance in force to provide a cushion for your spouse. But don't keep excess amounts. And review the possibility of reducing coverage or converting to paid-up protection; you may save substantial amounts in premiums.

If you keep any life insurance in force, be sure that the application of dividends, the beneficiary designation, and the settlement options are all in line with your current wishes. See Chapter 18 for more information.

Health insurance is another story. Some companies are eliminating promised postretirement health benefits. Others are curtailing such benefits or increasing the cost to retirees. Medicare doesn't cover everything. And Medicare supplements ("Medigap") can still leave you with sizable out-of-pocket expenses. Neither Medicare nor Medicare supplements cover long-term care; separate policies are sold for this purpose. Try to protect yourself and your family before you retire, to the extent you can. And keep informed; sizable changes are probably coming in health insurance, for people of all ages. You'll find more information in Chapter 19.

CREDIT

If you've somehow reached retirement age without establishing a credit rating, do so at once, before you retire. Credit can be very handy to have, and it may be very difficult to establish once you no longer have a regular income.

If you're a woman who has had credit only in tandem with her husband, take steps, right now, to establish your own credit identity. All you have to do is write to credit issuers and request that the record of payment on the cards you hold jointly be reported in both your names. The Equal Credit Opportunity Act then ensures that you will have a credit identity, but it won't happen unless you first make the request.

Remember: Credit discrimination because of age is illegal, but some of the conditions that go along with age, such as reduced income, may make it difficult to secure credit for the first time.

HOUSING

■ Elinor and Hal sold their upstate New York home when Hal retired, and moved to an adult community on Florida's gulf coast. The climate was warm, the people friendly, the community pleasant. But the pull of family and of old friends was too strong. Within a year they made the expensive move back to New York.

■ The Martins looked forward to retirement and the opportunity to move to the community where their only daughter lived. They did move, and within six months, their daughter's husband changed jobs and moved his family to another state. The Martins could not afford to move again. They had to stay where they were and, somehow, make new friends and put down new roots.

■ Mary and George, unlike the others, have no wanderlust. They'd like nothing better than to stay right where they are ... except that the house is too large and hard to maintain. They may, after a while, have to think about moving.

There are a lot of reasons for pulling up stakes in retirement, and a lot of reasons for staying put. If you're thinking about moving, be sure to consider every side of the question:

■ Your old house may be big and expensive to heat. But your mortgage may be paid up. Will you save any money by moving to a smaller house? By taking on a mortgage?

■ Remember that moving itself costs money. The movers themselves are only the initial cost. You must also consider closing costs and

Q We are thinking about moving to a warmer climate after we retire. How can we get a full picture of the cost of living in a new location?

A One big element in the cost of living anywhere is taxes. Before you move, contact the tax authorities in the state or states you're considering and ask about:

■ Personal income taxes, both state and local, and whether pension and Social Security benefits are considered taxable income. A few states don't have income taxes, but this isn't necessarily a big plus; other taxes may hit you hard in the pocketbook.

■ Sales tax, both state and local, and what it covers. In many states, there is no sales tax applied to food or to prescription drugs.

■ Residential property tax, and whether there are special programs to reduce these taxes for the elderly.

■ Personal property tax, if any, which might be levied on a car, furniture, and other items.

■ Estate or inheritance taxes, if any, in addition to federal taxes.

landscaping if you buy, appliances and furniture and window hangings even if you don't. Some of your furniture may fit; a lot of it simply won't.

- Consider *all* the alternatives: a private house, a rental apartment, a cooperative apartment, a condominium, a mobile home. All have their good points, and their not-so-good. You have to decide what's best for you.
- Retirement or "adult" communities deserve a word to themselves. You may be attracted to a peaceful enclave, where maintenance is provided, where a pool of potential friends of your generation awaits. Just be sure, before you make such a move, that you (1) appreciate age stratification, (2) like the planned social activities that often go along with community living (and that you pick a community with the level of activity you prefer), and (3) that the finances will work out as planned (review the developer's credentials, and talk to residents before you make a decision).
- Most retirees remain independent, but moving in with children may be an option that presents itself in later years. Again, think carefully before you do. Sort out the emotional implications: Will you be able to refrain from interfering in their lives? and they in yours? Will you each have privacy? And be sure to spell out the financial considerations: Will you contribute to the running of the household? Will you, in fact, help your children to buy their home? If you do, perhaps by providing the down payment while they take care of monthly payments, what will happen if they run into financial difficulty? Will you have to bail them out? What happens if a job change necessitates a move? Try to anticipate every eventuality, and set the ground rules, before you move in. And try, as hard as it may be, to be objective about money with your children; it's the only way house-sharing can work.
- If you do want to remain in your own home, but finances are a problem, consider the possibilities outlined earlier in this book: You may be able to tap the equity in your house via a home equity loan; you may want to find someone to share the house, and its costs, with you; you may find a reverse annuity mortgage or equity sharing with an outside investor your best solution. Talk to your lawyer, your accountant, your banker, a real estate broker, and local community agencies before you decide you can no longer afford to remain in a home you love.
- If you decide to move, look at all the variables: the cost of living, the presence or absence of state and local income taxes, the level of property taxes, and the range of state estate and inheritance taxes. Find out about any tax breaks to which you may be entitled, and include them in the equation as well. And don't forget housing and medical costs, which may be much higher in some parts of the country than others.
- If you decide to move, after considering all the facts, try to keep your options open. Retain ownership and rent out your current home, if

you can, while you move to the new community. Then, if the move doesn't work out for any reason at all, you'll have an open door to return. Don't be in a hurry to buy in your new community, for the same reason; flexibility is important, until you're sure the move is right for you.

Suggestion: Before you do anything, try swapping homes with someone in the community you're considering. A stay of a few months, even a few weeks, will tell you a lot more about a community than a brief stay in a hotel, and it won't be nearly as expensive. You can arrange a swap through several agencies devoted to that purpose; one well-known agency is the Vacation Exchange Club, P.O. Box 650, Key West, FL 33041; (800) 638-3841.

 KEY POINTS

- Project your retirement budget by first figuring out how much money you will need and then figuring out how much you will have. Don't forget to include an inflation factor in your estimates, and to redo your estimates at regular intervals as you get closer to retirement.

- File Form SSA 7004 with the Social Security Administration every three to four years to be sure that your Social Security contributions are accurately recorded and to get an estimate of the benefits you will receive. Make an actual application for benefits several months before you plan to retire.

- Ask your company personnel office for details of your company pension plan. Be sure you understand when you will be vested and entitled to benefits under the plan. Find out what the payment options are and select the one most appropriate for you; discuss your decision with your spouse.

- Open an Individual Retirement Account, if you're eligible for the deduction, and set aside tax-sheltered money for your own retirement. If you're self-employed, use a Keogh plan instead.

- Make the maximum contribution to a 401(k) plan, if your employer sponsors one, to take advantage of the tax benefits and any employer matching of contributions.

- Think about purchasing an annuity if you believe that it fits into your retirement income objectives. Compare provisions carefully, however, before you buy.

- Continue investing, for growth as well as income, both before and after retirement.

■ Augment your retirement income by reducing spending and investing the surplus, by considering a second job, and by making the most of all the assets you have.

■ Review your investments, insurance, credit rating, and housing situation. Now is the time to pull all the strands of your lifetime financial plan together. Now is the time to make the most of all that you have.

CHAPTER 24

Inflation, Recession, and You

Our spending habits are shaped by our financial know-how, by individual temperament, and by our stage of life; they are also shaped by the economic climate in which we live.

You don't have to be an economist to recognize the economic turbulence of recent years. After the post-World War II decades of economic well-being, inflation began to soar. By the end of the 1970s, Americans had almost become accustomed to double-digit inflation. Savings dropped as prices rose, which led to some forecasts of doom (because savings provide investment money for a society's capital growth), but as long as individual incomes rose more or less in tandem with inflation, ordinary people did not seem too upset.

In fact, however, real family income rose rapidly until 1970, then leveled off and, in the last year or so, declined just slightly. The median family income (half of all families have income above the median and half below), adjusted for inflation, was $36,841 in 1990 and $35,939 in 1991. Meanwhile, prices continued to rise. According to the Commerce Department, 1991 was the first time in 11 years that growth in per-capita income failed to keep pace with rising prices. Progress, for most people, came to a halt. Many families have been able to maintain their standard of living only because they now rely on two incomes instead of one. Those same two incomes, however, often mean a larger tax bite as well as higher child care and going-to-work expenses and hence more running in place to stand still.

The recession of the last couple of years hasn't helped. Although recovery is supposed to be underway, as I write, employers are still "downsizing" and the structure of the work force is undergoing drastic and, some fear, permanent change. We now have a work force in which:

■ More and more workers are temporary or "contingent" workers, called on only when needed, with no job security and no benefits. Exact figures aren't available but Labor Secretary Robert B. Reich suggested in the spring of 1993 that at least 30 percent of the total work force was composed of contingent workers; among new jobs, far more appear to be temporary or part time. As a result, new high school and college graduates often can't find permanent jobs (for those with thousands of dollars in student loans—see Chapter 17—not being able to find a job has devastating long-range implications). Professionals with temporary jobs call themselves consultants. And workers who have loyally given 15 or 20 or 25 years to one employer are finding both jobs and benefits eliminated.

■ Official statistics understate the jobless rate, in several ways: by disregarding those who are so discouraged that they no longer seek work, by discounting those who file for unemployment benefits directly with the federal government under its supplemental benefits program rather than with the state, and by listing as full-time workers those who may in fact hold two or three part-time jobs in an effort to make ends meet.

■ Wages have stagnated or even fallen, by one estimate, for four out of five American households. Recent reports indicate that high school graduates now earn over 26 percent less in entry-level jobs than high school graduates did in 1979. And there has been a sharp increase in the last decade, according to a 1992 Census Bureau report, in the number of full-time workers earning less than the official poverty wage for a family of four of $12,195 a year or $6.10 an hour.

■ Fewer jobs are available in manufacturing and more in the service sector. In 1950 about 39 percent of private-sector jobs were in manufacturing, and almost 14 percent in services; by 1989, under 22 percent were in manufacturing and just under 30 percent in services. The difference: Manufacturing jobs have traditionally been governed by collective bargaining agreements and provided superior health and retirement benefits; service sector positions are lower-paying and frequently provide no benefits at all. This trend, along with others (such as the shift from promised defined benefit pension plans to self-determining defined contribution plans described in Chapter 23) make it absolutely essential that you design your own portable benefit package, one that will move with you from job to job and stay with you if you have no job.

Inflation

The good news, perhaps, is that inflation is down significantly from its double-digit levels of the late 1970s. The Consumer Price Index (see below), which stood at 6.1 percent in 1982 (in itself an enormous improvement over the previous couple of years) has hovered around 4 percent for most of the last decade. This is not **deflation,** which economists describe as a dropping of prices. Instead it's **disinflation,** defined as a period in which prices rise but not nearly as quickly as they had been rising.

Some prices have actually come down. According to *Consumer Reports,* which calculated prices of consumer goods in terms of how long it took to earn them, the average American had to work a shorter period of time in 1992 than in 1962 to pay for film, ground beef, milk, long-distance telephone calls, and most major appliances. But we had to work a lot longer to pay for big-ticket items including health care, higher education, and a house.

Falling prices may sound good, in theory, but they have a down side as well. When home prices keep falling, to take just one example, would-be buyers wait to see if they will fall still further. If people don't buy, anxious sellers lower their prices still more. The resulting game of cat-and-mouse keeps local economies at a standstill; houses don't change hands, owners can't move, and people are reluctant to spend.

Lower inflation, and lower interest rates, are good for some people but bad for others. Lower interest rates are positive for prospective homeowners. They can also benefit homeowners who don't want to move but who can refinance at a lower rate, freeing cash for other purchases. Lower interest rates, in other words, benefit debtors (except when you must pay much more for money you borrow than you can earn on money you save; in July 1993, a 30-year fixed-rate mortgage could be had for 7.47 percent, while credit card issuers continued to charge an average of over 18 percent in interest). But lower interest rates can harm investors. Municipal bond yields in the spring of 1993 plunged to 5.6 percent, a low last seen a full 20 years earlier. Mortgage-backed securities, volatile at best, become even more volatile when homeowners refinance their mortgages to secure lower rates. Certificates of deposit (CDs) are at their lowest rate in many years, a particularly troublesome fact for older Americans, on fixed incomes, relying on interest income from CDs.

The Consumer Price Index

How do we judge the cost of living, beyond the repeated onslaught of the supermarket? The most commonly accepted—as well as frequently criticized—measure is the Consumer Price Index (CPI).

The CPI, as defined by the U.S. Department of Labor Bureau of Labor Statistics, is a statistical measure of change, over time, in the prices of goods and services in major expenditure categories—such as food, housing, apparel, transportation, and health and recreation—typically purchased by most consumers. Essentially it measures the purchasing power of consumers' dollars by comparing what a sample "market basket" of goods and services costs today with what the same sample market basket cost at an earlier date.

The CPI thus is an index of changes in prices and a measure of inflation. It is *not,* as the Bureau of Labor Statistics points out, an index of the cost of living.

The CPI is not a valid measure of the cost of living, even though it's often taken to be, because:

- It looks only at the retail prices of specific goods and services; it does not look at taxes, which take more and more of everyone's income and account for an increasing share of the actual cost of living.
- It does not attempt to report changes in style of living, or shifting consumer spending patterns. If you start to eat more chicken when beef becomes expensive, the CPI continues to report changes in the price of beef. If you eat out more often at fast-food restaurants, or buy more convenience foods to eat at home, the CPI may take several years to reflect this fact.
- It does not reflect noncash consumption, such as on-the-job fringe benefits or government services which can add to your standard of living.

Nonetheless, by charting the course of prices over a period of time, the CPI does provide a useful measure of inflation. It also has other uses, attached to it over the years.

The Uses of the CPI

The primary use of the CPI is, as noted, as an index of changing prices. It is also used:

- As an economic indicator. Thus it measures the success or failure of government policies.
- To negotiate wage increases, particularly wages based on collective bargaining contracts.
- To adjust federal benefits, including Social Security, military and civil service pensions, and food stamps.
- To establish the official estimate of the poverty threshold. This estimate is the basis of eligibility for many health and welfare programs.
- To guide many private-sector agreements. Rental, royalty, and child support agreements now often include escalator clauses based on the Consumer Price Index.
- To index income tax brackets and set personal exemption amounts for federal income tax purposes.

Table 24.1, based on the CPI, provides a rough estimate of the impact of price increases over time. For example, reading down the first column, it took $1.47 to buy the same goods and services in 1992 that $1 bought in 1982. You can use the same table to calculate how much your income needed to increase in order to keep up; if you earned $25,000 in 1982, for example, you would have needed 1.47 times that much in 1992, or $36,750, to have the same purchasing power.

Table 24.1: Consumer Price Index Comparisons, 1982-1992

	1982	1983	1984	1985	1986	1987	1988	1989	1990	1991	1992
1982	1.00										
1983	1.03	1.00									
1984	1.08	1.04	1.00								
1985	1.12	1.08	1.04	1.00							
1986	1.14	1.10	1.05	1.02	1.00						
1987	1.18	1.14	1.09	1.06	1.04	1.00					
1988	1.23	1.19	1.14	1.10	1.08	1.04	1.00				
1989	1.28	1.24	1.19	1.15	1.13	1.09	1.05	1.00			
1990	1.35	1.31	1.26	1.21	1.19	1.15	1.10	1.05	1.00		
1991	1.41	1.37	1.31	1.27	1.24	1.20	1.15	1.10	1.04	1.00	
1992	1.47	1.42	1.37	1.32	1.29	1.25	1.20	1.14	1.09	1.04	1.00

Source: Credit Union National Association.

Your Personal Inflation Index

■ A 25-year-old secretary, making $19,000 a year, lives alone in a Manhattan apartment, has no car, keeps a tight budget, and finds that food and rent account for about two-thirds of her total expenditures.

■ A two-income family, in their early forties, with one child in college, live in a private home in a New York suburb. He's a manager. She's a reporter. Each needs a car. Combined income: $61,000.

Which life-style suffered more from inflation? If you guessed Manhattan, you're wrong.

The cost of owning a home, the expense involved in running two cars and, most important, the cost of keeping a child in college made the suburbanites far more subject to inflation than the secretary.

The Consumer Price Index may indicate an annual average rate of inflation for the nation as a whole. As these examples demonstrate, however, the national average may not apply to you. Your own personal cost of living may be higher, or lower, than the national average. It depends on where you live and on what you buy. You can keep your personal CPI below the national average if you walk to work, buy a used car instead of a new one, live in a moderate climate, and have a larger proportion of your overall expenses devoted to fixed expenses and/or to categories relatively untouched by inflation. (Staying healthy—or having adequate health insurance—may be the most important thing you can do; see Table 24.2.) Your cost of living is, to at least some extent, up to you.

Table 24.2: Components of the CPI

Year	Food	Clothing	Housing	Trans-portation	Health Care	Enter-tainment
1978	9.7	3.6	8.7	4.6	8.4	5.3
1979	10.7	7.1	12.3	14.3	9.2	6.7
1980	8.5	6.3	15.7	17.9	11.0	9.0
1981	7.8	4.8	11.5	12.2	10.7	7.8
1982	4.1	2.6	7.2	4.1	11.6	6.6
1983	2.1	2.5	2.7	2.4	8.8	4.3
1984	3.8	1.9	4.1	4.4	6.2	3.7
1985	2.3	2.8	4.0	2.6	6.3	4.0
1986	3.2	0.9	3.0	-3.9	7.5	3.4
1987	4.1	4.4	3.0	3.0	6.6	3.3
1988	4.1	4.3	3.8	3.8	6.5	4.3
1989	5.8	2.8	3.8	3.8	7.7	5.2
1990	5.8	4.6	4.5	4.5	9.0	4.7
1991	3.6	3.7	4.0	4.0	8.7	4.5
1992	1.6	1.4	2.6	3.0	6.6	2.8
15-year averages	**5.11**	**3.57**	**5.99**	**5.27**	**8.31**	**5.03**

Source: Bureau of Labor Statistics; American Society of CLU & ChFC.

THE ECONOMY AND YOU

What does it all mean? What does it matter to you, personally, if we are having an inflation, a deflation, a disinflation, a recession, or, heaven forbid, a depression? (A recession has been defined, flippantly, as when your neighbor is out of work, a depression as when you yourself are out of work. A depression involves more of the population for a longer period of time than a recession. Unemployment figures are higher, people are hungrier....) The meaning comes through in both psychological and practical terms.

The Psychology of Inflation

We grew so accustomed to rapid inflation during the 1970s and early 1980s that we expected it to continue. Inflation, in short, became a fact of life.

Even when *statistics* indicated a sharp decline in rising prices, *people* believed that prices were rising just as rapidly as ever.

We also tend to act on our beliefs. If we think that prices are still rising rapidly while the dollar is losing its value, then we'll think in terms of going into debt to pay off the debt with cheaper dollars. If we're convinced that home ownership is the best buffer against inflation, then we'll do almost anything to buy a house. Such actions may be dangerous, if we look more closely at what is actually happening.

The Practical Effect of Disinflation

Inflation has been "Public Enemy Number One" for so long that it's hard to realize that we've actually grown accustomed to living with it. But we have. In the last 15 years we've changed our patterns of both saving and spending to suit inflationary times. When times change, we have to adjust, or we have a problem.

Here's what can happen:

- You took on a big mortgage in the perfectly reasonable expectation, after years of merit plus cost-of-living raises, that your income would continue to grow. Now your income is not growing as fast as you expected (it may not be growing at all even if you're still doing well at the same job you've held for years, because hard-hit companies are reducing raises, freezing salaries, sometimes cutting wages as well), but those mortgage payments won't go away.

- You've felt rich in the last few years, secure in the knowledge that the house you bought for $28,000 in 1961 could be sold for $275,000. That was a bundle of money that could be tapped by taking a home equity loan, or by selling the house and moving up to something bigger and better. Or perhaps you planned to use the house as your retirement nest egg, selling it when the time came, moving to something smaller, and using the extra cash to generate income. But times have changed. The value of real estate has fallen faster than just about anything else. You can probably still get a home equity loan, but it might be for less than you think. Should you want (or need) to sell, you might not easily find a buyer even if you are ready to sell at a lower price. A great many "house-rich" Americans are no longer as rich as they thought they were.

- You invested in real estate, in fine art, in gold, in rare coins, in the type of hard-asset collectible that is very attractive when inflation rates are high. When inflation starts to slow, the value of these investments levels off or even declines. If you joined the bandwagon late, when prices were near their peak, you may have lost sizable sums.

- You sold a home and took back a mortgage, expecting to get all your cash via a balloon payment in three to five years. Now the buyer has lost his job, can't refinance, and you have to either extend the loan or foreclose on the house. Neither option will do wonders for your pocketbook.

■ You closed your savings account, after several years of hearing the "experts" tell you that money market mutual funds would pay far more interest on your savings, and put your money in a money market mutual fund. Now you let your money sit there, just as it did in the savings account. Don't. Interest rates on savings accounts may be down, in the low-interest environment of the early 1990s, but interest rates on money market funds are just as low. Unless you need the money liquid, as your safety cushion, invest some of it for a higher return (see Chapter 6).

■ You're on Social Security and you've gotten used to double-digit cost-of-living increases in your monthly check. Not any more, not with disinflation. The increase that took effect in January 1993 was just 3 percent—and the same increase is projected, at this writing, for 1994. You also have relied on healthy returns from your certificates of deposit. Today that return has dwindled.

None of this is meant to indicate that inflation is good and disinflation is bad. Inflation has caused a great deal of grief to the nation's economy as well as to individuals. But it does give the advantage to borrowers rather than to lenders. Anyone with large debts—the young, growing, and overextended family is a good example—can benefit from inflation because those debts are paid off with less valuable dollars. Anyone holding fixed assets—such as senior citizens living on accumulated capital—suffers when inflation makes those assets worth less and less.

Those who benefit from inflation often suffer from disinflation, as borrowers are now at a disadvantage. Lenders, however, are not necessarily better off. The homeowner who can't manage to pay his high mortgage payments is no help to the bank that is relying on his payments to keep itself solvent. It's possible that with disinflation everyone loses—but the real losers are people who fail to adapt to a changing world.

Concerns for the 21st Century

As we move through the 1990s, we will come face to face with a number of issues rooted in a changing economy as well as changing demographics:

■ With economic recovery uncertain and interest rates at their lowest level in decades, we must rethink our entire approach to saving money and planning for the future.

■ With real estate values continuing to drop in many parts of the country, we must reconsider our long-held belief that home ownership is always best. We must also recognize that stagnating wages make it harder for today's young adults to buy a first home, and leads them to

question whether they can ever reach the standard of living enjoyed
by their parents.

■ With most women in the work force—the only way single mothers
can support their children and families can keep their heads above
water—we need adequate affordable day care. And, with most
women already in the work force, it will take creative thinking to augment family income.

■ With more people retiring earlier and living longer, we must save and
invest in order to have adequate income for 30 or more years in retirement.

■ With an aging population, we also have to come to terms with the
need for eldercare.

■ With fewer secure jobs, and hence fewer on-the-job benefits, we will
have to invest for our own retirement and provide our own insurance.
Even if the federal government succeeds in its effort to provide some
sort of universal health care, we may well need to fill in the gaps with
private insurance.

But all is not doom and gloom. For one thing, we have learned some
lessons from what is now seen as the excesses of the 1980s. We are paying down
debt, and incurring less. Outstanding installment debt, mostly credit card debt
and car loans, has fallen in each of the last two years. We are also spending less,
overall (which helps our personal pocketbooks while restraining the economic
recovery that is built on consumer confidence). Household net worth is up,
partly because the stock market remained up and partly because of the growth in
pension funds. We have provided more financial security for the older generation, although partly at the expense of the youngest Americans. And we are
expecting a major intergenerational transfer of wealth in the coming years, as an
older generation which benefitted from the post-World War II run-up in housing
values and a generally robust economy passes its accumulated assets to the
younger generation. The United States still has the highest standard of living in
the world, and more opportunity for individuals to get ahead.

What we need is a relatively stable (not stagnant) economy. What we also
need, as individuals, is the ability to adjust to a changing economy in terms of
our personal money management. We have to pay attention to the world around
us, even as we are preoccupied with earning a living and doing the most with
our money. We also have to be aware that life events, both predictable and
unexpected, can mean drastic change in the money we bring in and the money
we spend.

As I said at the outset, money management is not a one-time affair. The
time to buy a house, the kind of investments we make, the amount of credit we
use, the places we keep our money... all are affected, or should be, by our own
stage of life and by the contemporary economic climate. Keep your eyes open,
develop a financial plan, adjust your patterns of spending and saving and
investing as necessary, and you'll come out ahead.

Suggested Reading

Life Cycle Planning

Bird, Caroline. *The Two-Paycheck Marriage,* Rawson, Wade, 1979.

Estess, Patricia Schiff. *Remarriage and Your Money: Once Again, For Richer or Poorer,* Little, Brown, 1992.

Hochschild, Arlie. *The Second Shift,* Viking Penguin, 1989.

Koff, Gail J., Esquire. *The Jacoby and Meyers Guide to Divorce,* Henry Holt, 1993.

Leonard, Frances. *Money and the Mature Woman,* Addison-Wesley, 1993.

Leonard, Frances. *Women and Money,* Addison-Wesley, 1991.

Trunzo, Candace E. *Financial Planning for the Two-Career Family,* Houghton Mifflin, 1990.

Weinstein, Grace W. *Children and Money: A Parents' Guide,* NAL/Plume, 1985; Signet, 1987.

Weinstein, Grace W. *Men, Women and Money: New Roles, New Rules,* NAL Books 1986; Signet 1988.

Weitzman, Lenore J. *The Divorce Revolution,* Free Press, 1985.

Weitzman, Lenore J. *The Marriage Contract: A Guide to Living With Lovers and Spouses,* Free Press, 1981.

Woodhouse, Violet, and Victoria Felton-Collins. *Divorce and Money: Everything You Need to Know About Dividing Property,* Nolo Press, 1993. Nolo Press publishes a series of self-help law books, most updated regularly; in your bookstore, or call (800)992-6656.

Budgets

Blankinship, John T., Jr., and Charles E. Foster II. *The Six Cups: How to Manage Your Money,* Kendall/Hunt, 1992. Order by calling (800)228-0810.

"Facts About Financial Planners," American Association of Retired Persons. Available through AARP Fulfillment,

601 E Street, N.W., Washington, DC 20049.

Mason, Jerald W. *The Easy Family Budget,* Houghton Mifflin, 1990.

"Tips on Financial Planners," Better Business Bureau Pub. No. 24-225, Council of Better Business Bureaus, 4299 Wilson Blvd., Arlington, VA 22203

Cash Management

Davidson, Jeff, and the editors of Consumer Reports Books. *Your Bank— How to Get Better Service,* Consumer Reports Books, 1992.

Heller, Warren G. *Is Your Money Safe: How to Protect Your Savings in the Current Banking Crisis,* Berkley Books, 1990. Heller is research director of Veribanc, Inc., a bank rating agency.

"How to Get Safety From Your Financial Institution," Weiss Research, Inc., 1992. What to ask banks, brokerage firms, and insurance companies. Available by sending $2 to Weiss Research, 2200 North Florida Mango Rd., West Palm Beach, FL 33409 or, to bill to a credit card, call (800)289-9222.

Investing

Fredman, Albert J., and George Cole Scott. *Investing in Closed-End Funds: Finding Value and Building Wealth,* New York Institute of Finance, 1991.

Gould, Carole. *The New York Times Guide to Mutual Funds,* Times Books, 1992.

The Handbook For No-Load Fund Investors, published annually by The

No-Load Fund Investor, Inc., P.O. Box 318, Irvington-on-Hudson, NY 10533.

"How to Read a Financial Report," MLPF&S, Marketing Services, 800 Scudders Mill Rd., Plainsboro, NJ 08540.

Investors Rights Manual, New York Institute of Finance, 1989.

Kinder, Peter, Steven Lydenberg, and Amy Domini. *The Social Investment Almanac,* Henry Holt, 1992.

Krefetz, Gerald. *The Basics of Bonds,* Dearborn Financial Publishing, 1992.

Krefetz, Gerald. *The Basics of Stocks,* Dearborn Financial Publishing, 1992.

Lynch, Peter. *Beating the Street,* Simon & Schuster, 1993.

Lynch, Peter. *One up on Wall Street,* Simon & Schuster, 1989. The former manager of the Fidelity Magellan Fund tells "how to use what you already know to make money in the market."

Mercer Discount Brokerage Directory, issued annually by Mercer Inc., 379 West Broadway, Suite 400, New York, NY 10012; call (800)582-9854, in New York State, (212)334-6212.

Miller, Alan J. *Socially Responsible Investing: How to Invest With Your Conscience,* New York Institute of Finance, 1991.

Ochsner, Neal. *How to Make Basic Investment Decisions,* Houghton Mifflin, 1990.

O'Higgins, Michael, with John Downes. *Beating the Dow,* Harper Collins, 1991.

Rosenberg, Jerry. *Dictionary of Investing,* Wiley, 1993.

Silverstein, Michael. *The Environmental Factor,* Dearborn Financial Publishing, 1990.

Slatter, John. *Safe Investing: How to Make Money Without Losing Your Shirt,* New York Institute of Finance, 1991.

Williamson, Gordon K. *All About Annuities,* Wiley, 1993.

Credit

Detweiler, Gerri. *The Ultimate Credit Handbook,* Plume, 1993. Detweiler is director of BankCard Holders of America.

Elias, Stephen, Albin Renauer, and Robin Leonard. *How to File for Bankruptcy,* Nolo Press, 1993.

Feinberg, Andrew. *Downsize Your Debt,* Penguin, 1993.

Leonard, Robin. *Money Troubles: Legal Strategies to Cope With Your Debts,* Nolo Press, 1993.

Thomsett, Michael C. *How to Get out of Debt,* Dow Jones-Irwin, 1990.

Warner, Ralph. *Everybody's Guide to Small Claims Court,* Nolo Press, 1991.

Weiss, Martin. *How to Borrow Money and Use Credit,* Houghton Mifflin, 1990.

"Your Legal Guide to Consumer Credit" (Product Code #235-0010). Available for $2.50 from Order Fulfillment, American Bar Association, 750 North Lake Shore Dr., Chicago, IL 60611.

Housing

Bell, W. Frazier. *How to Get the Best Home Loan,* Wiley, 1992.

Block, Julian. *The Homeowner's Tax Guide,* Runzheimer, 1991.

Changing Times magazine staff. *Kiplinger's Buying and Selling a Home,* Kiplinger Books, 1990.

Dorfman, John R., and the editors of Consumer Reports Books. *The Mortgage Book,* Consumer Reports Books, 1992.

Irwin, Robert. *Mingles: A Home-Buying Guide for Unmarried Couples,* McGraw Hill, 1984.

Janik, Carolyn, and Ruth Rejnis. *All America's Real Estate Book,* Viking, 1985.

Jones, Peter. *How to Buy Your First Home,* Houghton Mifflin, 1990.

Kennedy, David W. *The Condominium and Cooperative Apartment Buyer's and Seller's Guide,* 2d ed., Wiley, 1987.

Kibbey, H. L. *First Home Buying Guide,* Panoply Press, 1991.

Madorma, James. *The Home Buyer's Inspection Guide,* Betterway Publications, 1990.

Philbin, Tom. *How to Hire a Home Improvement Contractor Without Getting Chiseled,* St. Martin's Press, 1991.

Scholen, Ken. *Retirement Income on the House: Cashing in on Your Home With a "Reverse Mortgage,"* National Center for Home Equity Conversion (Apple Valley, MN), 1992. Order by calling (800)247-6553.

Shenkman, Martin M. *The Total Real Estate Tax Planner,* Wiley, 1988.

Thomsett, Michael C. *Save $ on Your Home Mortgage: Mortgage Acceleration Techniques,* Wiley, 1989.

Volgenau, Coleman, Jr. *Money-Saving Guide to Managing Your Home Remodeling,* Wiley, 1992.

"Your Home, Your Choice" (D12143), American Association of Retired Persons. Available through AARP Fulfillment, 601 E Street, N.W., Washington, DC 20049.

Life and Health Insurance

Applegarth, Virginia. *How to Protect Your Family With Insurance,* Houghton Mifflin, 1990.

Evensky, Harold, and Deena Katz. *Planning for Long-Term Health Care,* Houghton Mifflin, 1992.

Hunt, James H. *Taking the Bite out of Insurance: How to Save Money on Life Insurance,* National Insurance Consumer Organization, 1991; updated periodically. Available for $13.95 from NICO, 121 North Payne St., Alexandria, VA 22314.

Korn, Donald Jay. *Your Money or Your Life: How to Save Thousands on Your Health-Care Insurance,* Collier Books, 1992.

Lesko, Matthew. *What to Do When You Can't Afford Health Care: An "A to Z" Source Book for the Entire Family,* Information USA, 1993.

O'Donnell, Jeff. *Insurance Smart,* Wiley, 1991.

Booklets available free from the Health Insurance Association of America, 1025 Connecticut Ave., N.W., Washington, DC 20036-3998.

"The Consumer's Guide to Health Insurance" (C103)

"The Consumer's Guide to Disability Insurance" (C104)

"The Consumer's Guide to Long-term Care Insurance" (C101)

"The Consumer's Guide to Medicare Supplement Insurance" (C102)

Automobile

Boerger, James A. *The AAA Car Buyer's Handbook!,* Consumer's Automotive Resources Ltd., 1989.

Gillis, Jack. *The Car Book,* Harper-Collins, 1993; updated annually.

College

Blum, Laurie. *Free Money for College,* Facts on File, 1992.

The College Cost Book, published annually by the College Entrance Examination Board.

Kirby, Debra M. *Fund Your Way Through College,* Visible Ink Press, 1992.

Leider, Robert, and Anna Leider. *Don't Miss Out,* part of a helpful series of booklets published annually by Octameron Press, P.O. Box 2748, Alexandria, VA 22301.

T.Rowe Price College Planning Kit. To order, call (800)638-5660.

Tax Planning

Block, Julian. *Julian Block's Year-Round Tax Strategies for the $40,000-Plus Household,* Prima, 1992.

Daily, Frederick W. *Stand up to the IRS,*

Nolo Press, 1992.

The Ernst and Young Tax Guide, published annually by Wiley. A comprehensive guide to the annual chore of filling out income tax returns.

The Ernst and Young Tax-Saving Strategies Guide, published annually by Wiley. A succinct guide to personal financial planning and year-round tax planning.

J. K. Lasser's Your Income Tax, published annually by Prentice-Hall.

The Price Waterhouse Personal Tax Adviser, Pocket Books, 1992; updated annually.

Estate Planning

Belin, David W. *Leaving Money Wisely,* Scribner's, 1990.

Clifford, Denis. *Make Your Own Living Trust,* Nolo Press, 1993.

Clifford, Denis. *Plan Your Estate With a Living Trust: Wills, Probate Avoidance and Taxes,* Nolo Press, 1992.

Koff, Gail J., Esquire. *The Jacoby and Meyers Guide to Wills and Estates,* Henry Holt, 1993.

Magee, David S. *Everything Your Heirs Need to Know: Your Assets, Family History and Final Wishes,* Dearborn Financial Publishing, 1991.

Plotnick, Charles K., LL.B., Stephan R. Leimberg, J.D., and the editors of Consumer Reports Books. *How to Settle an Estate,* Consumer Report Books, 1991.

Shenkman, Martin M. *The Complete Book of Trusts,* Wiley, 1993.

Shenkman, Martin M. *The Estate Plan-*

ning Guide, Wiley, 1991.

Tillman, Fred, and Susan G. Parker. *Your Will and Estate Planning,* Houghton Mifflin, 1990.

Series of booklets available for $5 each from Commerce Clearing House, 4025 West Peterson Ave., Chicago, IL 60646; (800)248-3248.

"What Every Executor Ought to Know"

"What to Do When Your Spouse Dies"

"What You Ought To Know About Living Trusts"

Planning for the Later Years

Clifford, Denis, and Mary Randolph. *Who Will Handle Your Finances If You Can't?,* Nolo Press, 1992.

"Making Health Care Decisions: Your Right to Decide." Available for $5 through Commerce Clearing House, 4025 West Peterson Ave., Chicago, IL 60646; (800)248-3248.

Matthews, Joseph. *Beat the Nursing Home Trap,* Nolo Press, 1993.

Shelley, Florence D. *When Your Parents Grow Old,* Harper & Row, 1988.

Strauss, Peter J., Robert Wolf, and Dana Shilling. "What Every Caregiver Ought to Know," Commerce Clearing House, 1992. Available for $5 through Commerce Clearing House, 4025 West Peterson Ave., Chicago, IL 60646; (800)248-3248.

Werner, Anne, and James Firman. *Home Care for Older People: A Consumer's Guide.* Available for $12 from United Seniors Health Cooperative, 1331 H St., N.W., Suite 500, Washington, DC 20005.

Booklets available free from the American Association of Retired Persons. Write AARP Fulfillment, 601 E St. N.W., Washington, DC 20049.

"Miles Away and Still Caring: A Guide For Long-Distance Caregivers" (D12895)

"A Handbook About Care in the Home" (D955)

Retirement Planning

Dickinson, Peter A. *Retirement Edens Outside the Sunbelt,* AARP Books, 1987. This book is out of print, but you may want to check your library.

Dickinson, Peter A. *Sunbelt Retirement,* Regnery-Gateway, 1992.

Dickinson, Peter A. *Travel and Retirement Edens Abroad,* AARP Books, 1987. This book is out of print, but you may want to check your library.

Dickman, Barry, Trudy Lieberman, and the editors of Consumer Reports Books. *How to Plan for a Secure Retirement,* Consumer Reports Books, 1992.

Ernst and Young/Kiplinger Guide to Retirement Security (booklet plus video), Conrad and Associates, 1989; call (800)342-0443.

"A Guide to Understanding Your Pension Plan," American Association of Retired Persons. Available free through AARP Fulfillment, 601 E St., N.W., Washington, DC 2049.

Jenks, Jim, and Brian Zevnik. *Planning for a Financially Secure Retirement,* Houghton Mifflin, 1990.

Matthews, Joseph L. *Social Security, Medicare and Pensions: The Sourcebook for Older Americans,* Nolo Press, 1990.

The Price Waterhouse Retirement Planning Adviser, Pocket Books, 1992; updated annually.

"Protecting Your Pension Money." Available for $7.95 from the Pension Rights Center, Suite 704, 918 16th St., N.W., Washington, DC 20006

T.Rowe Price *Retirement Planning Kit* and *Retirees Financial Guide,* Available free by calling T.Rowe Price, (800)541-0295; retirement planning software costs $15 and may be ordered by calling (800)541-4041.

Index

Italicized page numbers denote figures and worksheets; *t* denotes tables.